THE ORGANIC CONSTITUENTS OF HIGHER PLANTS

Their Chemistry and Interrelationships

Fourth Edition

by

Trevor Robinson

Department of Biochemistry

University of Massachusetts

Amherst, Mass.

Published by:

Cordus Press

P.O. Box 587

North Amherst, Mass. 01059

PREFACE

Chemistry is becoming more and more an essential tool for biological investigations. Yet, although the biologist to be effective in many areas of study needs a strong knowledge of chemistry, the kinds of things he needs to know are not necessarily the same things which a chemist needs to know. In many ways the biologist's knowledge of chemistry must be more comprehensive than the chemist's since he is usually unable to choose the compounds with which he must work. They are presented to him in a bewildering variety. On the other hand, the lifeblood of chemical investigations into natural products is made up of degradations, proof of structure and synthesis; none of these is usually of much concern to the biologist. What the biologist wants to know is, "What sort of compound is this which I have found to be involved in such and such a process; from what precursors is it made, and what happens to it later?" The exact structure of a compound down to the location of every double bond and the precise spatial configuration and conformation of the atoms are problems which ultimately must be faced, but by a chemist rather than a biologist. Because of this difference between chemical and biological outlook, the wealth of literature and courses on the chemistry of natural products seldom give the biologist satisfying answers to his questions, or else delivers these answers with effort and in the midst of much extraneous information. There are multvolume and multiauthor works which direct their discussions of the chemistry of natural products toward biologists, but despite their enormous coverage and depth, even if the individual could afford to have them all at his fingertips, he would find large gaps and unevenness in the information which they provide. Certain classes of compounds are not adequately described, others are well-treated per se but not contrasted with other types of compounds which they resemble or which are found in nature along with them. Sometimes detailed and elaborate methods of characterization are given which are essential for laboratories engaged in an intensive investigation of a certain type of compound but which merely frustrate an individual who just wants to know if he has a compound of that type. It is for these various reasons, and others, that this book was conceived.

It may appear that undue prominence is given here to some relatively unimportant classes of compounds. This has been intentional, and it is an important justification for the book. A reader who desires general information about carbohydrates or amino acids can turn to many excellent sources; but should he want to know something about naturally-occurring lignans or acetylenes, he can at present find no discussion at a level of complexity suitable for the interested non-specialist.

It should be evident that this is a book of chemistry rather than biochemistry. Although the metabolic interrelationships of compounds are summarized, I have avoided the temptation to discuss the enzymology of these processes or their place in the total picture of plant physiology. Nevertheless, a brief summary of metabolic pathways should be helpful in orientation, and, if one compound has been found, may point the way to finding others that may be associated with it. I have assumed that the reader is familiar with elementary organic and biological chemistry. Many simple concepts which are well covered in general textbooks of these subjects are therefore omitted, assumed, or briefly referred to.

While this book has been directed primarily toward botanists and pharmaceutical chemists, perhaps by glancing through it organic chemists with an intensive knowledge of one area or another will be brought to see an immense number of untouched problems which await their notice. Certain classes of natural products have received much attention from many chemists; others may be the private province of a single laboratory or even completely ignored.

In the five years that have passed since the 3rd edition, many new compounds have been discovered, but very few new types of compounds. The greatest advances have been in analytical methods and in the understanding of metabolic pathways. Since I rely on original literature rather than reveiws, the book as a whole can be regarded as a selective review reflecting my judgment of what is useful and important. Despite selectivity the number of literature citations has risen from about 1600 to over 2200. About half of the total are new to this edition. By reducing the size of several figures I have been able to add much new information with a very small increase in the number of pages.

Many people have offered useful suggestions and other kinds of help in the preparation of this book. I look forward to producing new editions as long as there is need for them, and I welcome any advice that will lead to improvements. Finally, I thank my wife without whose help these pages could not have been produced.

Trevor Robinson

Amherst, Mass.
January 1980

CONTENTS

SONG OF A MODERN BIOLOGIST

I am the very model of a modern-day life scientist.
I've information that would floor a chemist or cosmogonist
With Fourier analysis I study crystal lattices
And many cheerful facts concerning sets and all their matrices.
I've gone beyond the calculus to fields and probability.
I can program a computer with extravagant facility.
In short, in matters physical I stagger any physicist.
I am the very model of a modern-day life scientist.
I know fiscal requirements of all the granting agencies
From AEC to ONR, and private in emergencies.
I'm very well acquainted too with nomenclature chemical.
I understand mRNA, both innate and inimical.
I know a compound's mysteries from NMR to triplet state,
Or ESR to indicate just how electrons resonate.
I quote the classic articles of Watson, Crick and van der Waals.
In chelates and transition states I detail all the orbitals.
I can tell undoubted ribosomes from oxysomes or quantasomes;
I even know the character of artifactual microsomes.
I can apply statistics to the helix of an isozyme,
And measure its kinetics or chromatogram elution time.
I can induce or derepress a Jacobean operon
And tell you every detail of a cistron or a replicon.
In short, in matters dear to every chemist or a physicist.
I am the very model of a modern-day life scientist.
In fact, when I know what is meant by ganglion and vacuole,
When I can tell at sight a platyhelminth from a petiole,
When in affairs like field trips and habits I'm more knowledgy,
And when I know precisely what is meant by ichthyology,
When I can tell a living thing outside of a homogenate,
When I know more of wildlife than a halfwit or a neonate,
In short when I've a smattering of regular *biology*,
You'll say I have transcended instrumental methodology.
For my knowledge of real creatures, though I'm plucky and adventury,
Is only just aware of the last decade of this century;
But still, in matters dear to every chemist or a physicist
I am the very model of a modern-day life scientist.

Trevor Robinson
BioScience February 1966

Chapter 1
INTRODUCTION

This chapter is intended to provide an orientation in the field of plant chemistry, the general nature of compounds encountered, methods of dealing with them, and the ways that they are biochemically interrelated. With one or two exceptions the other chapters are all organized into the following sections:

1. A general view of the compounds included, their chemical and physical properties, occurrence and function in plants.
2. Methods used for isolating the compounds from plant material.
3. Qualitative analytical methods useful for characterising the compounds.
4. A brief synopsis of present knowledge regarding the biochemical pathways by which the compounds are synthesized and broken down.
5. Pertinent literature. Rather than an exhaustive review, a few key articles have usually been selected. These will lead to others.

In the present, introductory chapter, the topics listed above will be discussed in more general terms with indications as to what may be expected in the specific chapter.

LITERATURE

The literature on plant chemistry extends across several special fields, each with a slightly different point of view. Five chief points of view may be summarized as follows:

BOTANICAL - the occurrence and functions of the compounds in plants
BIOCHEMICAL - the chemical reactions (usually enzymatic) which the compounds undergo in plants
CHEMICAL - the chemical properties and non-enzymatic reactions of the compounds
PHARMACEUTICAL - plant constituents useful in medicine, their isolation and identification
FOOD SCIENCE - the constituents of food plants important for nutrition and flavor

The following list is an attempt to summarize some of the more advanced literature which is pertinent to investigations in the chemistry of plant constituents. The leading journal for papers in plant biochemistry is Phytochemistry.

Botany, advanced texts, reviews:
    Ruhland, W., Handbuch der Pflanzenphysiologie 18 Vols., Springer
                Verlag, Berlin, 1958-1967.
    Pirson, A. & Zimmermann, M. H., Encyclopedia of Plant Physiology,
                Springer-Verlag, N. Y., 1975-present.
    Annual Review of Plant Physiology, Annual Reviews, Inc., Palo Alto,
                California, Vol. 1 1950-present.
    Steward, F. C., Plant Physiology, A Treatise 6 Vols., in 11 parts,
                Academic Press, N. Y., 1969-1972.
    The Botanical Review

Biochemistry, advanced texts, reviews:
    Bonner, J. & Varner, J. E., eds., Plant Biochemistry 3rd ed. Academic
                Press, N. Y., 1976.
    Goodwin, T. W., ed., Chemistry and Biochemistry of Plant Pigments,
                2nd ed. Academic Press, N. Y. 1976.
    Goodwin, T. W. & Mercer, E. I., Introduction to Plant Biochemistry,
                Pergamon Press, Oxford, 1972.
    Kindl, H. & Wöber, G., Biochemie der Pflanzen, Springer-Verlag,
                Berlin, 1974.
    Northcote, D. H., ed., Plant Biochemistry, 2 Vols., Univ. Park Press,
                Baltimore, 1974, 1977.
    Annual Review of Biochemistry, Annual Reviews Inc., Palo Alto,
                California, yearly, 1 1932-present.
    Progress in Phytochemistry, Vols. 1-3, Wiley, N. Y., Vols. 4-5,
                Pergamon, Oxford, 1968-1978.

Chemistry, advanced texts, reviews:
    Devon, T. K. & Scott, A. I., Handbook of Naturally Occurring Compounds,
                3 Vols., Academic Press, N. Y., 1972- .
    Geissman, T. A. & Crout, D. H. G., Organic Chemistry of Secondary
                Plant Metabolism, Freeman-Cooper, San Francisco, 1969.
    Harborne, J. B., Phytochemical Methods, Chapman & Hall, London, 1973.
    Ikan, R., Natural Products, A Laboratory Guide, Academic Press, N. Y.,
                1969.
    Miller, L. P., ed., Phytochemistry, 3 Vols., Van Nostrand-Reinhold,
                N. Y., 1973.
    Paech, K. & Tracey, M. V., Moderne Methoden der Pflanzenanalyse,
                7 Vols., Springer-Verlag, Berlin, 1956-1964.
    Zechmeister, L. et al., eds., Fortschritte der Chemie Organischer Natur-
                stoffe, Springer Verlag, Vienna, Vol. 1 1938-present.
    Chemical Reviews, American Chemical Society.
    Quarterly Reviews
    Record of Chemical Progress
    Annual Reports on the Progress of Chemistry
    A Key to Pharmaceutical and Medicinal Chemistry Literature, American
                Chemical Society, Washington, D. C., 1956.
    Bibliography of Chemical Reviews, American Chemical Society, Washington,
                D. C., 1960- .
    Mellon, M. G., Chemical Publications: Their Nature and Use, 4th ed.,
                McGraw-Hill, N. Y., 1965.

Pharmacy, advanced texts, reviews:

Trease, G. E. & Evans, W. C., Pharmacognosy, 10th ed., Bailliere Tindall, London, 1972.

Tyler, V. E., Jr., Brady, L. R., & Robbers, J. E., Pharmocognosy, 7th ed., Lea & Febiger, Philadelphia, 1976.

Food Science:

Aurand, L. W. & Woods, A. E., Food Chemistry, AVI Publishing, Westport. Conn., 1973.

Berk, Z., Braverman's Introduction to the Biochemistry of Foods, 2nd ed., Elsevier, N. Y., 1976.

Butler, G. W. & Bailey, R. W., eds., Chemistry and Biochemistry of Herbage, Vol. 1, Academic Press, N. Y., 1974.

Hulme, A. C., ed., The Biochemistry of Fruits and Their Products, 2 Vols., Academic Press, N. Y., 1970.

In the chapters which follow frequent reference is made to the treatises of Miller and of Paech and Tracey. In the bibliographies they are cited merely by giving the editors' names.

PROPERTIES, OCCURRENCE, AND FUNCTION

For the compounds discussed usually only a few salient properties are described under this heading in order to give a general picture. More specific properties are more conveniently described in the section "Characterization." Within any group of compounds several specific compounds are selected for structural representation. The most familiar or important compounds of a group are almost always included; beyond this there is no attempt at an exhaustive survey of plant products. Rather, structures have been chosen to illustrate the range of possibilities within a group. In order to make this gamut clear, rare compounds at the extreme ends of it have sometimes been depicted to the exclusion of more common derivatives which lie well within the range of variation. Knowing what the extreme cases are, the reader can presumably interpolate other structures which probably occur in nature. For example, if two natural benzene derivatives are indicated differing in that one has only a single phenolic hydroxyl group while the other has three methoxyl groups, it may be assumed that other compounds probably exist with intermediate structures. Reference to the organic chemical literature, or such books as that of W. Karrer, will then confirm or deny the validity of such interpolation.

As with structures chosen, examples of the natural occurrence of plant products are illustrative rather than exhaustive. In general, coverage has been restricted to the higher plants (botanically the Embryophyta) but occasional references to algae and fungi have been made when it seemed pertinent to do so. Where a plant is named as the source of a compound, it is almost never true that it is the only plant which has this constituent---- though it will usually be the one richest in it. Almost every natural product is found in more than one species although there is often a taxonomic pattern restricting a compound or a class of compounds to a certain genus, family, or order. In other cases such restriction is statistical rather than absolute or quantitative rather than qualitative. Usually no indication is given here as to the part of a plant richest in a constituent or the stage of maturity

at which the highest concentration may be found, although these variables
are of crucial importance to anyone wishing to isolate a compound. Several
references are valuable for listing the occurrence of compounds in particular
plants or listing plants containing a particular compound. To some extent
Paech and Tracey provides this information, but the following sources are
specifically intended for this purpose:

    Hegnauer, R., <u>Chemotaxonomie der Pflanzen</u>, 6 Vols., Birkhauser, Basel,
        1962-1973.
    Karrer, W., <u>Konstitution und Vorkommen der Organischen Pflanzenstoffe</u>,
        Birkhauser, Basel, 1958, Ergänzungsband 1961.
    Schermerhorn, J. W. & Quimby, M. W., <u>The Lynn Index</u>, Massachusetts
        College of Pharmacy, Boston, Mass. (later volumes under
        the senior authorship of N. R. Farnsworth and published
        by the College of Pharmacy, University of Illinois),
        8 Vols., 1957-1974.

Only very brief indications are given as to the functions of compounds
in plants or their pharmacological properties. These two extremely interesting
areas fall just beyond the scope of the present book, but they are worthy
of mention since it is because of such properties that workers in botany or
pharmacy are led to seek information on the chemistry of plant constituents.
There are a number of papers that discuss possible functions of secondary
plant products (1-5).

ISOLATION

Procedures for isolating substances from plants are nearly as varied as
the substances themselves, but I have tried to indicate methods which are
generally useful for a group of compounds rather than methods which have
been used for specific members of the group. Often particular compounds
continue to be isolated by tried and true methods rather than by adopting
recent methods of more general utility. Thus, while the recommended way to
purify an unknown alkaloid might well be chromatography on a cation exchange
resin, it would be unusual to purify strychnine in this way.

In preparing plant materials for isolation of individual compounds the
most important precaution is the avoidance of artifacts. If living tissue
is processed too slowly, enzymatic action may cause profound changes in certain
constituents. Oxidation and hydrolysis are the most common degradative processes; and if constituents are sought which are subject to them, care must
be taken to avoid such effects. On the other hand, if tissues are heated
to prevent enzymatic action, certain heat-labile substances may undergo change.
Even drying in a rotary evaporator at relatively low temperatures can result
in condensation reactions between sugars and amino compounds (6). Probably
the safest general method for all eventualities is immersion in liquid
nitrogen followed by freeze-drying, and extraction of dried material with
solvents which do not permit degradative changes to occur (7). A somewhat
more convenient method using dry ice has also been described (8). Such
drastic measures are seldom necessary, however, and a consideration of the
properties of the substances to be isolated will usually point the way to
simpler yet adequate procedures for preparing the plant material. General
methods for preparing extracts are reviewed by Pirie (9). Special preparative methods using column chromatography, countercurrent distribution,
electrophoresis, etc. are well-reviewed in two books (10, 11). Gel filtration
methods which separate molecules according to size are applicable over a

wide range of molecular weight (12). New methods are regularly reported in the journal <u>Separation</u> <u>Science</u>, and there is a bibliography of papers on separations by column chromatography (13).

Cheronis (14) has proposed a general fractionation procedure applicable to any aqueous plant tissue extract. The broad outlines of this procedure are indicated by the following diagram. Further separation of the different fractions can be achieved by appropriate methods of column chromatography.

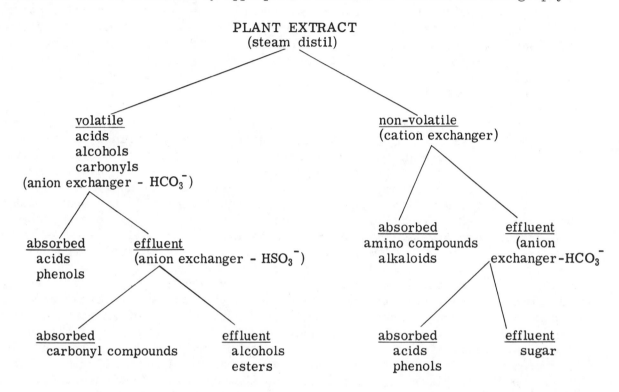

Obviously many types of compounds present in plants are not shown in this scheme, but everything must fall (even though incompletely) into one fraction or another, so that as a preliminary separation the method has much to offer. Another, similar, general procedure has been developed for 0.05-100 mg. samples of leaf, bark, or wood (15). Further fractionation must take into account the properties of the desired compounds. As with any fractionation scheme, it can be applied most intelligently if some qualitative information is available regarding the constituents of the original mixture. The following discussion of "Characterization" is intended to suggest means for obtaining such information.

CHARACTERIZATION

Under characterization are included methods for identifying a pure compound and also methods for determining what types of compounds are present in a crude mixture. Many times characterization procedures necessarily include the separation of somewhat purified compounds from mixtures, so that characterization cannot be strictly distinguished from the isolation methods described in the previous section. Complete characterization of a mixture requires quantitative analysis of the constituents in addition to knowledge of what they are. However, because of the space that would be required, all quantitative determinations have been excluded from this book. In most cases qualitative determinations performed with care permit some rough

quantitative conclusions to be drawn, so that major and minor components of
a mixture can be distinguished from one another. The work of Paech and Tracey
describes quantitative procedures for a large number of plant constituents.
Recent developments in biochemical analysis are reviewed annually in Analytical
Chemistry.

Over the years many simple color tests and spot reactions have been
developed to indicate the presence of particular compounds or classes of
compounds. Some of these tests have proven themselves to be consistently
specific and sensitive. Others, unfortunately, have resulted in false conclusions which still persist in the literature. The most useful spot tests
and color reactions have been described, with their limitations, in the
appropriate chapters. A complete coverage of such methods may be found in
the works of Feigl (16).

Chromatographic methods are now the preferred way of characterizing
compounds or mixtures. By column chromatography, as mentioned under "Isolation," mixtures are separated into fractions which may then be characterized
by their physical and chemical properties. The quantities involved may be
large enough to permit several tests to be performed on each fraction, and
it is these tests rather than the chromatographic separation itself which
are most important for characterization. In chromatography on paper sheets
the quantities of material involved are usually much smaller (e.g. 1-100
micrograms), only a few tests may be applied to the separated compounds, and
the way that they migrate in various solvent systems offers important information for characterizing them. In thin layer chromatography, adsorbants
are spread on glass strips, then used much in the same way as paper sheets.
Separations are much faster than on paper, however, and often better resolution is attained. Gas chromatography permits fine separation of minute
amounts of material and rapid determination of the number of components in a
mixture. Tentative identification of compounds can be made by comparison of
their retention times on the column with the times of known materials. Final
identification must, however, depend on isolation of a fraction and its
characterization by other techniques. The most recently developed type of
chromatography for analytical separations is high pressure liquid chromatography in narrow bore columns.

There are several comprehensive books dealing with all aspects of
chromatography (17, 18). Paper chromatography is dealt with in (19, 20), thin
layer chromatography in (21, 22), gas chromatography in (23), and high performance liquid chromatography in (24-26). In addition to these books there
are several regular bibliographic listings of chromatographic techniques in
Analytical Chemistry, The Journal of Chromatography, Chromatographic Reviews,
Advances in Chromatography, and the Journal of Chromatographic Science. For
thin layer chromatography abstracts of papers are published regularly (27, 28).
The special application of chromatography to higher plants is considered in (29-
31). A few other references are selected for special mention:

the problem of reproducibility   (32)

identification of substances by paper and thin layer
    chromatography   (33)

instrumentation for thin layer chromatography   (34)

In the chapters which follow I have selected solvent mixtures and
detection reagents which seem generally applicable to a class of compounds.
Reference to the above books will usually reveal several other procedures
that may be used once some indication is available regarding the nature of
the compounds to be characterized. The R$_f$ value is a physical constant for
each compound and is defined as the distance from the starting point to which
the compound has migrated divided by the distance the solvent has migrated.
R$_f$ values vary with temperature, direction of paper grain, and amount of
material applied. They, therefore, cannot be relied upon without question
for identification. Known compounds should be run for comparison alongside
of unknowns. In addition to specific detection reagents useful to indicate
various types of compounds on paper or thin layer chromatograms, there are
a few general reagents which detect almost any organic compound. Alkaline
silver nitrate is a common one of these, and its use is described in detail
by Smith (17). Other such general reagents are iodine vapor, alkaline potassium
permanganate solution, ozone, and ammonium sulfate (41).

Electrophoretic methods of analysis are widely used for the separation
of charged compounds such as proteins and amino acids. In addition, it may
be possible to separate compounds which are normally uncharged by forming
suitable derivatives of them, for instance the borate complexes of carbohydrates. Recent developments in electrophoresis are reviewed annually in
Analytical Chemistry. Application to plant extracts is described in (30).

One of the most important and widely used techniques for characterization
of organic compounds is the measurement of absorption spectra by the use
of photoelectric spectrophotometers. The light absorption spectrum of a
molecule is one of its most distinctive properties, and excellent instruments
are available which permit determination of this spectrum with very small
quantities of material. In addition the material is not destroyed by
making such measurements, and may be used later for other tests. Often
in recent years the combination of chromatography with spectrophotometry
has made possible the complete fractionation of a very small quantity of some
natural mixtures and the unequivocal identification of each component.

Three types of absorption spectra are commonly distinguished, infrared,
visible, and ultraviolet. Absorption of radiation in the infrared region
depends on the vibration and rotation of atoms in the molecule. Rotational
spectra have been little studied, and for practical purposes the infrared
spectra which are normally measured are entirely due to vibration. Different
atomic groups can vibrate only at specific frequencies and absorb radiation
of just these frequencies. These absorption bands appear in the region of
wavelengths from 2-100 microns, but most instruments cover this range only
up to about 25. From about 2-8 the absorption bands observed are highly
characteristic of certain atomic groups and therefore give good indications
of what functional groups are present. For example, hydroxyl groups absorb

at about 2.8µ, carbonyl groups at 5.8µ, nitrile groups at 4.4µ, etc.
The region above 8µ is referred to as the "fingerprint region" since it is
unique for the molecule as a whole rather than for specific groups. Frequently the positions of infrared absorption bands are expressed as wave-
numbers rather than wavelengths. The wavenumber is the reciprocal of the
wavelength expressed in centimeters (1cm. = 10,000µ). The identity of the
infrared spectrum of a pure, unknown compound with that of a known sample
may be taken (with rare exceptions) as proof that the two compounds are
identical. Recent improvements in technique permit determination of spectra
from only a few micrograms of compound which may be available from chromatographic separation (36-38). Raman spectroscopy yields information similar
to infrared spectroscopy, and its application to natural products research
is described in (42).

Ultraviolet and visible absorption spectra depend not on the vibration
of atoms in a molecule but on the fact that certain loosely-held electrons
may be raised to higher energy levels by absorbing radiation of specific
wavelengths. For this reason ultraviolet and visible spectra may be lumped
together as electronic spectra. There is no theoretical difference between
them. Since loosely-held electrons are required for absorption to occur, molecules with unsaturated bonds are the ones which absorb in this region.
However, specific absorption bands do not indicate specific functional
groups as in infrared spectra, rather they are more characteristic of the
molecule as a whole. They may often permit decisions to be made as to
the class of compounds involved (e.g. an anthocyanin vs. a naphthoquinone)
but give little indication as to details of structure. The common commercial
instruments permit spectral measurements to be made over the ranges 200-
400 nm (ultraviolet) and 400-750 nm (visible). Observations in the near
infrared (750-2000 nm) can be made but are seldom useful. While electronic
spectra are not as important as infrared for identification or structural
determination of a molecule, they have other important advantages----usually
smaller amounts of material are required; it is easier to determine the
quantity of a substance which is present; and many solvents are available
which do not absorb in the ultraviolet - visible regions.

There is no space here for a more thorough description of spectrophotometric theory and procedures. General discussions of spectra may be found
in the article of Glover (43) and several books (44-46). Infrared spectroscopy is the subject of several excellent books (47, 48), and Scott (49) has
discussed the ultraviolet spectra of natural products. Comprehensive
catalogs of spectral data are also available (50-58).

With the advent of commercial instruments the application of nuclear
magnetic resonance spectra to the characterization of natural products has
greatly increased. Nuclear magnetic resonance (NMR) spectra are dependent
on the absorption of radio frequency signals on exposure of certain atomic
nuclei to a radio frequency field and a strong magnetic field. Of the so-
called magnetic nuclei which respond in this way the ones of interest in
natural products research are hydrogen and ^{13}C. Instrumentation for work
with the latter isotope is expensive and not widely available, so discussion
here will be limited to the former and the technique referred to as proton
resonance spectroscopy. Spectra are plotted as signal strength vs. magnetic
field strength. Although only the hydrogen nuclei of a molecule are responsible for the spectrum, a variety of peaks is obtained depending on the
environments of the different hydrogen nuclei. Thus, indirectly, functional
groups may be detected since, for example, the hydrogen of a hydroxyl
group will show a peak different from the hydrogen of an aldehyde group.

The technique is especially valuable for indicating molecular configuration and is often the best, if not the only, method available for this purpose. Additional information may be found in a review article (59) and two books (45, 60).

The use of mass spectrometry in characterization of organic compounds has increased greatly in the last few years in spite of the expense and complexity of the instrumentation. The difficulty of interpreting the mass spectra of large organic molecules is also a serious limitation at present, but it seems likely that availablility of instruments and of computers to carry out the interpretation will make this technique more and more accessible to the casual user. The combination of mass spectrometry with gas chromatography is potentially the most convenient way of separating pure compounds from a few milligrams of a complex mixture and of ascertaining the concentration and total structure of each within an hour or so. Computer programs for retrieval of mass spectral data are available and can be used throughout the world to search the file of spectra at a large central library (61). An average search to identify an unknown spectrum with one in the file can be completed in 5-15 minutes. General discussion of the application of mass spectroscopy to natural product research can be found in several articles and books (45, 62-64). The powerful technique of coupling gas chromatography and mass spectroscopy is described in (65-67), and specialized applications will be referred to many times in the following chapters.

Optical rotatory dispersion and circular dichroism measurements are valuable in certain cases of structure determination but probably not of great general usefulness to the reader of this book. They are described in (68, 69).

A comprehensive treatise on all instrumental methods for determining organic structures is available (70).

METABOLIC PATHWAYS

Although metabolism as such is outside the central scope of the book, division into chapters has been made on the basis of metabolic pathways. The brief sections on metabolism are therefore intended to demonstrate the unity which a knowledge of biosynthesis can bring to the diversity of natural products. Organization on this basis is novel and has placed together compounds which are traditionally discussed separately. For example, terpenoids (which are usually included with "essential oils") and steroids are covered in the same chapter since their biosynthesis proceeds along almost identical pathways. For some natural products the pathways of biosynthesis remain unknown, but by analogy it is often possible to arrive at reasonable hypotheses. For instance, the stimulating ideas of Birch have introduced a unity into Chapter 6 which is very attractive.

Presentation of many metabolic pathways of higher plants may be found in (71-75). Annual reviews of the literature dealing with biosynthetic pathways of several plant constituents are published by the Chemical Society (76, 77). Indexes to biochemical reviews are also useful in locating information on specific areas of metabolism (78). An abbreviated overall scheme of the metabolic pathways assumed in this book is shown in Fig. 1-1. The numbers in parentheses indicate the chapter in which the various classes of compounds are discussed. More detailed schemes are presented in each chapter.

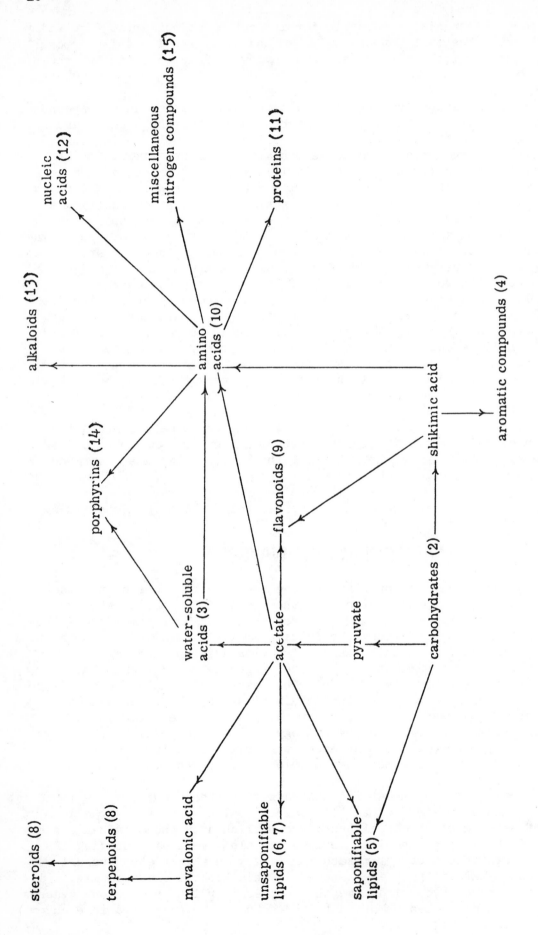

FIGURE 1-1: GENERAL METABOLIC PATHWAYS

BIBLIOGRAPHY

1. Fraenkel, G. S. (1959) Science 129 1466-1470
2. Weinberg, E. D. (1971) Persp. Biol. Med. 14 565-577.
3. Seigler, D. and Price, P. W. (1976) Amer. Naturalist 110 101-105
4. Swain, T. (1977) Ann. Rev. Plant Physiol. 28 479-501.
5. Rosenthal, G. A. and Janzen, D. H. eds. (1979) Herbivores: Their Interaction with Secondary Plant Metabolites, Academic Press, N. Y.
6. Dawson, R. and Mopper, K. (1978) Anal. Biochem. 84 186-190.
7. Schrauwen, J. A. M. and Linskens, H. F. (1974) Acta Bot. Neerland. 23 42-47
8. Bieleski, R. L. (1964) Anal. Biochem. 9 431-442.
9. Pirie, N. W. in Paech and Tracey 1 26-55.
10. Karger, B. L., Snyder, L. R., and Horvath, C., eds. (1973) Introduction to Separation Science Wiley, N. Y.
11. Morris, C. J. O. R. and Morris, P. (1976) Separation Methods in Biochemistry, Wiley, N. Y.
12. Determann, H. (1969) Gel Chromatography, 2nd ed., Springer-Verlag, N. Y.
13. Anon. (1973) J. Chromatog. Suppl. 3.
14. Cheronis, N. D. (1956) Trans N. Y. Acad. Sci. 18 516-521.
15. Dickson, R. E. (1979) Physiol. Plantarum 45 480-488.
16. Feigl, F. (1966) Spot Tests in Organic Analysis, 7th ed., Elsevier, Amsterdam.
17. Smith, I. (1969) Chromatographic and Electrophoretic Techniques, 3rd ed., 2 vols., Wiley-Interscience, N. Y.
18. Mikeš, O., ed. (1979) Laboratory Handbook of Chromatographic and Allied Methods, Wiley, N.Y.
19. Hais, I. M. and Macek, K. (1964) Paper Chromatography, Academic Press, N. Y.
20. Zweig, G., Sherma, J. and Whitaker, J. R. (1971) Paper Chromatography and Electrophoresis, 2 vols., Academic Press, N. Y.
21. Stahl, E. (1969) Thin Layer Chromatography, A Laboratory Handbook, Springer-Verlag, Berlin.
22. Niederwieser, A. and Pataki, G. (1970-1972) Progress in Thin Layer Chromatography and Related Methods, Ann Arbor Science Publishers, Ann Arbor, Michigan.
23. Grob, R. L., ed. (1977) Modern Practice of Gas Chromatography, Wiley, N. Y.
24. Snyder, L. R. and Kirkland, J. J. (1979) Introduction to Modern Liquid Chromatography, 2nd ed., Wiley, N. Y.
25. Kingston, D. G. I. (1979) Lloydia 42 237-260.
26. Pryde, A. and Gilbert, M. T. (1979) Applications of High Performance Liquid Chromatography, Chapman and Hall, London, Wiley, N. Y.
27. Scott, R. M. (1972) TLC Abstracts 1968-1971, Ann Arbor Science Publishers, Ann Arbor, Mich.
28. Scott, R. M. and Lundeen, M. (1973) TLC Abstracts 1971-1973, Ann Arbor Science Publishers, Ann Arbor, Mich.
29. Linskens, H. F. (1955) Papier Chromatographie in der Botanik, Springer-Verlag, Berlin.
30. Cook, A. R. and Bieleski, R. L. (1969) Anal. Biochem. 28 428-435.
31. Tyihák, E. and Held, G. (1971) Prog. Thin Layer Chromatog. 2 183-234.
32. Macek, K., ed. (1968) J. Chromatog. 33 No. 1, 2 (pp. 1-409).
33. Hais, I. M., Lederer, M., and Macek, K., eds. (1970) J. Chromatog. 48 1-339.
34. Hurtubise, R. J., Lott, P. F. and Dias, J. R. (1973) J. Chromatog. Sci. 11 476-491.
35. Amos, R. and Perry, S. G. (1973) J. Chromatog. 83 245-254.
36. Krivis, A. F. and Forist, A. A. (1961) Microchem. J. 5 553-558.
37. deKlein, W. J. (1969) Anal. Chem. 41 667-668.
38. Stahl, E. and Schild, W. (1970) J. Chromatog. 53 387-389.
39. Kaiser, R. (1967) Chimia 21 235-246.
40. Pierce, A. (1971) Silylation of Organic Compounds, Pierce Chemical Co., Rockford, Ill.
41. Walker, B. L. (1971) J. Chromatog. 56 320-323.
42. Freeman, S. K. (1973) J. Agric. Food Chem. 21 521-525.
43. Glover, J., in Paech and Tracey 1 149-244.
44. Oster, G. and Pollister, A. W. (1955) Physical Techniques in Biological Research, 1, Optical Techniques, Academic Press, N. Y.
45. Creswell, C. J., Runquist, O. A., and Campbell, M. M. (1972) Spectral Analysis of Organic Compounds, 2nd ed., Burgess Publishing Co., Milwaukee.
46. Silverstein, R. M., Bassler, C. G., and Morrill, T. C. (1974) Spectrometric Identification of Organic Compounds, Wiley, N.Y.
47. Bellamy, L. J. (1959) The Infra-Red Spectra of Complex Molecules, John Wiley, N. Y.
48. Parker, F. S. (1971) Applications of Infrared Spectra in Biochemistry, Biology, and Medicine, Plenum, N. Y.

49. Scott, A. I. (1964) Interpretation of Ultraviolet Spectra of Natural Products, Pergamon Press, N. Y.
50. Yamaguchi, K. (1970) Spectral Data of Natural Products, 1, Elsevier, N. Y.
51. Pouchert, C. J. (1971) The Aldrich Library of Infrared Spectra, Aldrich Chemical Co., Milwaukee.
52. Kamlet, M. J., ed. (1960) Organic Electronic Spectral Data, 1, Interscience Publishers, N.Y.
53. Ungnade, H. E., ed. (1960) Organic Electronic Spectral Data, 2, Interscience Publishers, N. Y.
54. Wheeler, O. H. and Kaplan, L. A., ed. (1966) Organic Electronic Spectral Data, 3, Interscience Publishers, N. Y.
55. Phillips, J. P. and Nachod, F. C. (1963) Organic Electronic Spectral Data 4, Interscience Publishers, N. Y.
56. Sadtler, P. (1960-date) Infrared Spectra, S. P. Sadtler + Son, Philadelphia
57. Sadtler, P. (1960-date) Ultra-Violet Spectra, S. P. Sadtler + Son, Philadelphia
58. ----UV Atlas of Organic Compounds, 5 Vols., Plenum Press, N. Y.(1966-date).
59. Seelig, J. (1973) Experientia 24 509-516.
60. Casy, A. F. (1971) PMR Spectroscopy in Medicinal and Biological Chemistry, Academic Press, N. Y.
61. Heller, S. R. (1972) Anal. Chem. 44 1951-1961.
62. Foltz, R. L. (1972) Lloydia 35 344-353.
63. Ligon, W. V., Jr. (1979) Science 205 151-159.
64. Waller, G. R., ed. (1972) Biochemical Applications of Mass Spectroscopy, Wiley-Interscience, N. Y. (2nd ed. expected 1980).
65. ten Noever de Brauw, M. C. (1979) J. Chromatog. 165 207-233.
66. Ryhage, R. (1973) Quart. Rev. Biophys. 6 311-335.
67. McFadden, W. H. (1973) Techniques of Combined Gas Chromatography/ Mass Spectrometry, Wiley-Interscience, N. Y.
68. Wong, K.-P. (1974) J. Chem. Educ. 51 A573-A578.
69. Crabbé, P. (1972) ORD and CD in Chemistry and Biochemistry, Academic Press, N. Y.
70. Nachod, F. C., ed. (1955-1973) Determination of Organic Structures by Physical Methods, 5 Vols., Academic Press, N. Y.
71. Milborrow, B. V., ed. (1973) Biosynthesis and Its Control in Plants, Academic Press, N. Y.
72. Luckner, M. (1972) Secondary Metabolism in Plants and Animals, Academic Press, N. Y.
73. Mann, J. (1978) Secondary Metabolism, Oxford U. Press, Oxford.
74. Grisebach, H. (1973) Pure Appl. Chem. 34 487-513.
75. Luckner, M., Nover, L., and Böhm, H. (1977) Secondary Metabolism and Cell Differentiation, Springer-Verlag, Berlin.
76. Bu'Lock, J. D., ed. (1976) A Specialist Periodical Report on Biosynthesis, Vol. 4 Chemical Society, London.
77. Bu'Lock, J. D., ed. (1977) A Specialist Periodical Report on Biosynthesis, Vol. 5 Chemical Society, London.
78. Arnstein, R. E., Harvey, M., & Arnstein, H. R. V. (1979) FEBS Letters 103 Suppl. 1-84.

Chapter 2
CARBOHYDRATES

The universal distribution and physiological importance of carbohydrates have entitled them to rather full treatment in general texts of organic and biochemistry. Therefore, many elementary aspects of their chemistry can be passed over lightly in a work such as the present one. As early products of photosynthesis, carbohydrates are key compounds in the biochemistry of green plants. Ultimately, all other constituents can be derived from them. Aside from this role as precursors, the different varieties of carbohydrates themselves serve several quite different functions. Starch and the simple sugars are generally involved with the storage and utilization of the energy required for the processes of growth, ion transport, water uptake, etc. As cellulose and the hemicelluloses, carbohydrates contribute to structural strength and binding cells together. Other less common derivatives -- glycosides, ethers, esters, gums -- have less clear roles and are frequently assigned a protective function in wound healing or as being toxic to parasites. Linkage with a carbohydrate moiety may improve solubility characteristics of non-polar compounds.

As the different classes of carbohydrates are discussed, it must be noted that nomenclature described with reference to one class is frequently directly transferable to another class (e.g. prefixes such as *arabo*, *threo* defined for the monosaccharides may be applied just as well to the sugar acids or alcohols.) Comprehensive rules of carbohydrate nomenclature are given in reference (1).

MONOSACCHARIDES

The monosaccharides or simple sugars are fundamentally polyhydroxy aldehydes or ketones, although glycolaldehyde with only one hydroxyl group can be included. They are colorless, optically active, water-soluble compounds. The vast majority have straight carbon chains.

When the structures are written vertically with the carbonyl group nearest the top of the chain, the configuration around the lowest asymmetric carbon atom determines whether the sugar belongs to the D or L series. Sugars of both series occur naturally although L-arabinose is the only common L-sugar (as a component of many polysaccharides and free in the heartwood of conifers). Structures of the D-family of sugars are given in Figure 2-2. The open-chain aldehyde formulas are shown for convenience although it is well-known that sugars normally exist as cyclic hemiacetals where such a structure is possible. The hexoses are more frequently found with a six-membered pyranose ring, but may in some cases have the five-membered furanose ring. Pentoses are also found with either a furanose or pyranose ring. This type of structural representation is

given for some common sugars in Figure 2-3. It will be noted that free
hydroxyl groups written to the right in the straight chain formula are
written below the plane of the ring. The designations α and β describe
the position of the new free hydroxyl group generated by ring closure,
the α form having this hydroxyl group below the plane of the ring for D-sugars.
The pair of isomers differing only in the configuration around this carbon
are called "anomers." If asymmetric carbons are present in the "tail"
portion extending from the ring their configurations are represented by
the straight chain convention (cf. glucofuranose).

```
Sugars
      Monosaccharides (aldoses and ketoses)
            Trioses
            Tetroses
            Pentoses
            Hexoses etc.
      Oligosaccharides
            Disaccharides
            Trisaccharides etc.

Sugar derivatives
      Alcohols
      Acids
      Esters
      Glycosides
Polysaccharides (glycans)
      Hexosans
            Glucans
            Fructans
            Galactans
            Mannans
            Glucomannans
            Galactomannans
      Pentosans
            Xylans
            Arabans
      Glycouronans (polyuronides)
            Glucouronans
            Galactouronans
```

FIGURE 2-1: OUTLINE OF THE CARBOHYDRATES

The names of the common aldehyde sugars have been used to derive
prefixes descriptive of hydroxylation patterns in less common carbohydrates.
For example, sedoheptulose may be named as D-altro-heptulose to indicate:

a. It belongs to the D-series (i.e. the highest numbered asymmetric
    carbon is written to the right in the open chain structure).
b. It has four asymmetric hydroxylated carbons with the same con-
    figuration as the four in altrose.
c. It has seven carbons.
d. It is a keto sugar.

This prefix system is not likely to supplant the common names of
already known sugars, but it is useful in naming new or little known sugars
or their derivatives. The ending "-ulose" is used to designate keto sugars.

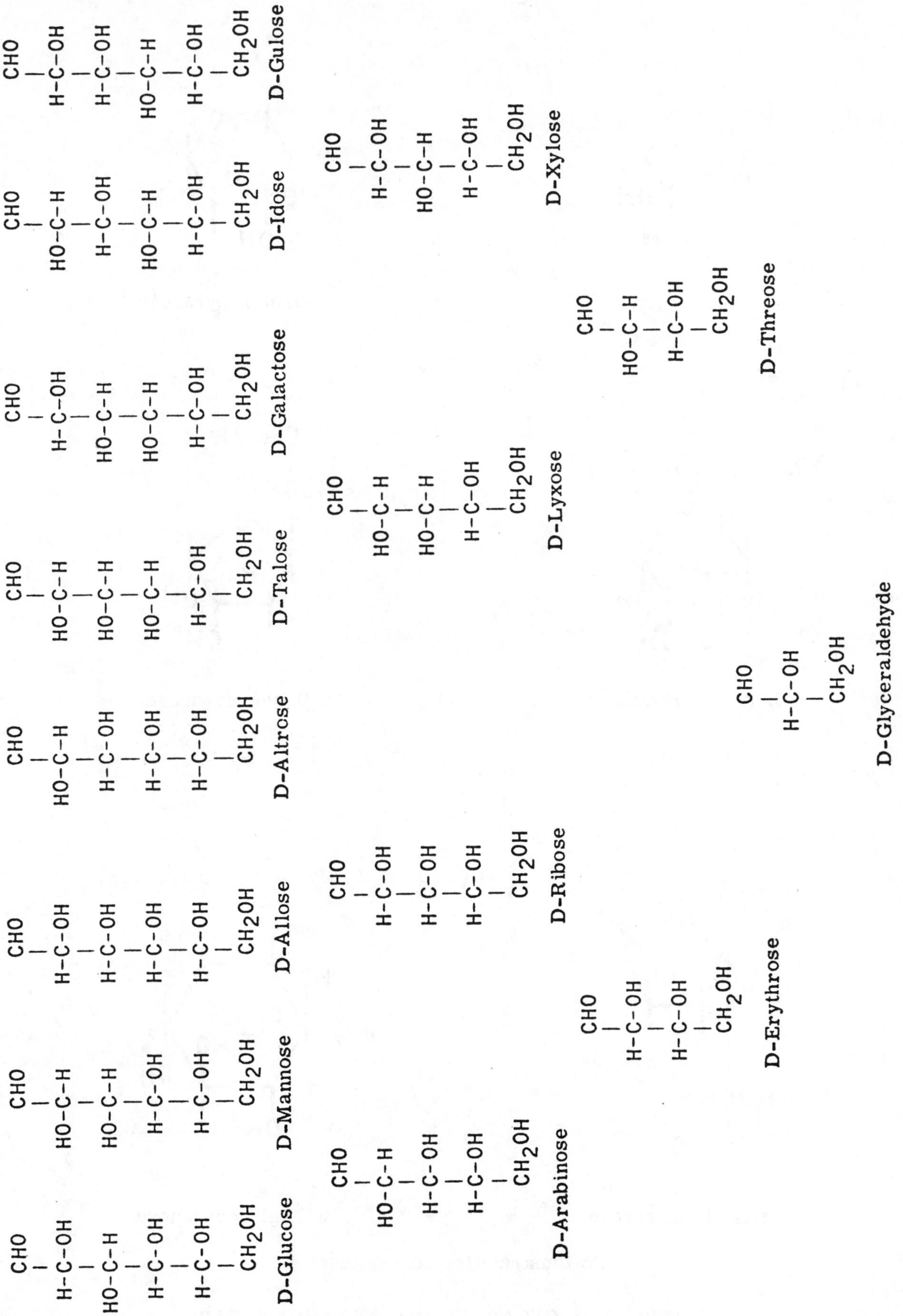

CHO
H-C-OH
HO-C-H
H-C-OH
H-C-OH
CH₂OH
D-Glucose

CHO
HO-C-H
HO-C-H
H-C-OH
H-C-OH
CH₂OH
D-Mannose

CHO
HO-C-H
H-C-OH
H-C-OH
CH₂OH
D-Arabinose

CHO
H-C-OH
H-C-OH
H-C-OH
H-C-OH
CH₂OH
D-Allose

CHO
HO-C-H
H-C-OH
H-C-OH
H-C-OH
CH₂OH
D-Altrose

CHO
H-C-OH
H-C-OH
H-C-OH
CH₂OH
D-Ribose

CHO
H-C-OH
H-C-OH
CH₂OH
D-Erythrose

CHO
HO-C-H
HO-C-H
H-C-OH
H-C-OH
CH₂OH
D-Talose

CHO
HO-C-H
HO-C-H
H-C-OH
CH₂OH
D-Lyxose

CHO
H-C-OH
HO-C-H
HO-C-H
H-C-OH
CH₂OH
D-Galactose

CHO
H-C-OH
HO-C-H
H-C-OH
CH₂OH
D-Xylose

CHO
HO-C-H
H-C-OH
HO-C-H
H-C-OH
CH₂OH
D-Idose

CHO
H-C-OH
H-C-OH
HO-C-H
H-C-OH
CH₂OH
D-Gulose

CHO
HO-C-H
H-C-OH
CH₂OH
D-Threose

CHO
H-C-OH
CH₂OH
D-Glyceraldehyde

FIGURE 2-2: STRUCTURES OF THE D-ALDOSES

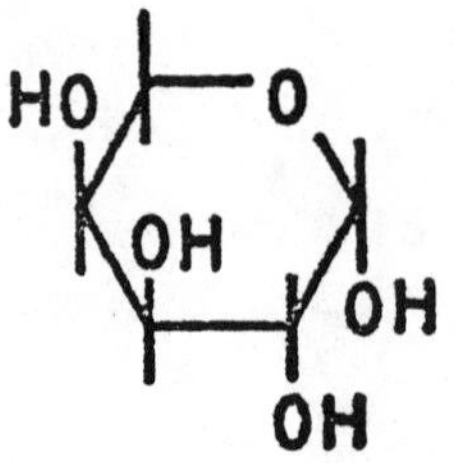

β-L-arabinopyranose 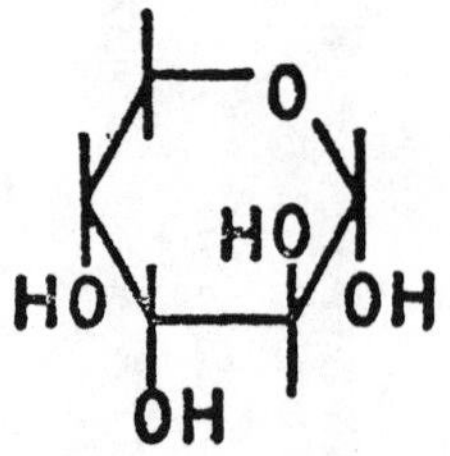   α-D-arabinopyranose

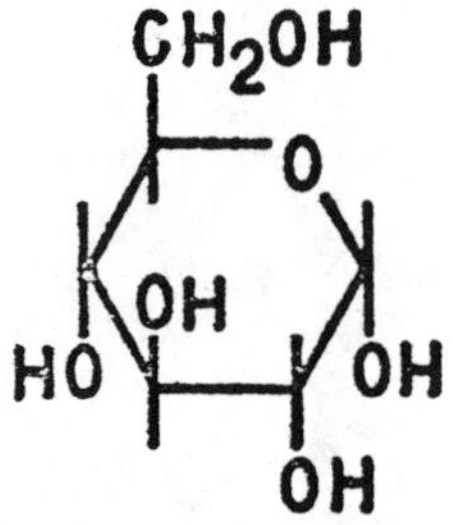

α-D-glucopyranose 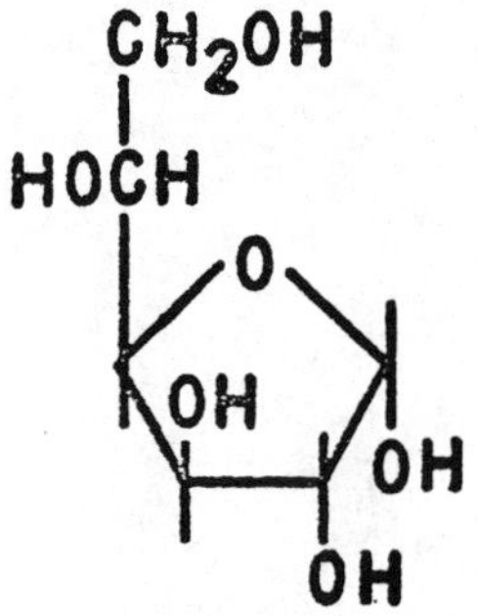   α-D-glucofuranose

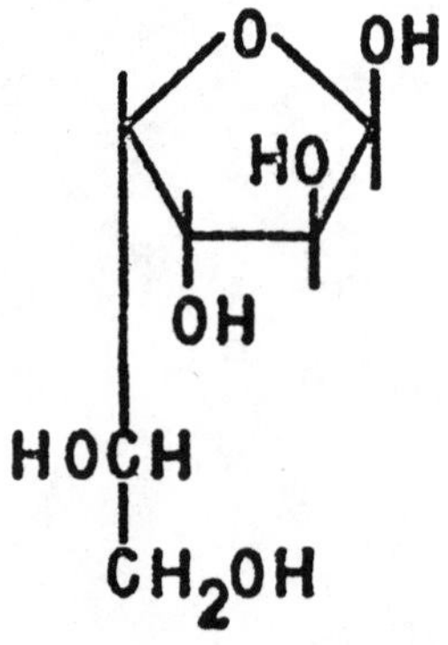

α-L-glucofuranose 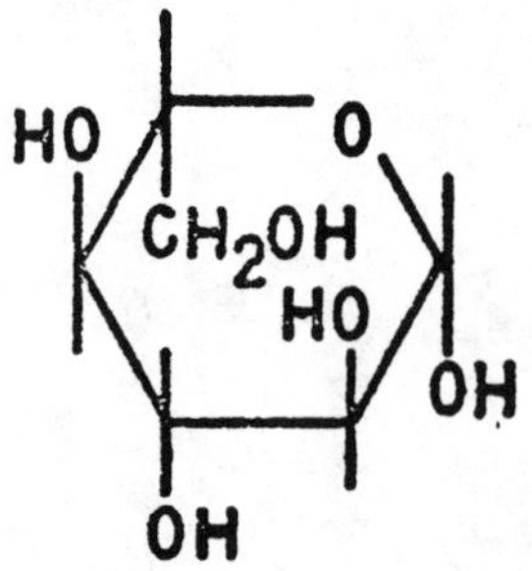   β-L-glucopyranose

(to illustrate the conventions)

FIGURE 2-3: CYCLIC FORMS OF SOME SUGARS

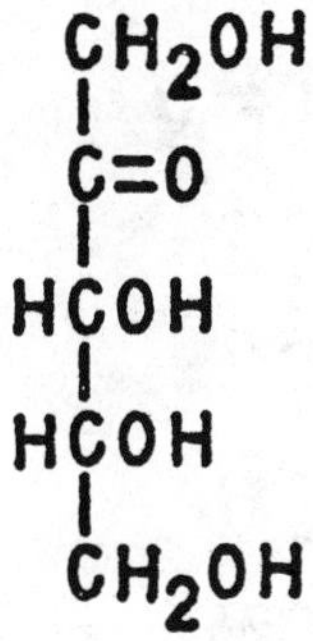
CH2OH
C=O
HCOH
HCOH
CH2OH

D-ribulose
(D-*erythro*-pentulose)

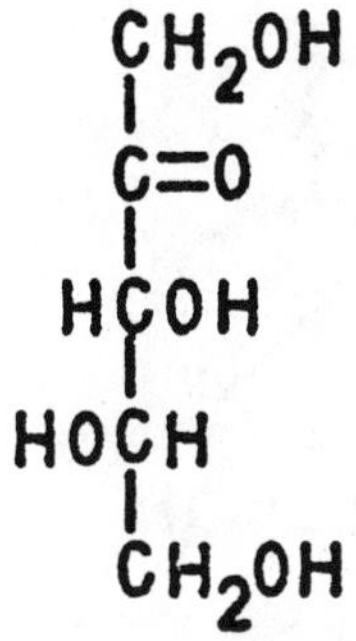
CH2OH
C=O
HCOH
HOCH
CH2OH

L-xylulose
(L-*threo*-pentulose)

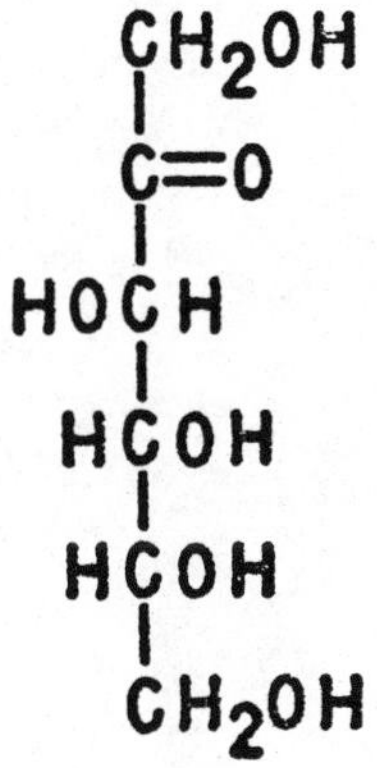
CH2OH
C=O
HOCH
HCOH
HCOH
CH2OH

keto-D-fructose

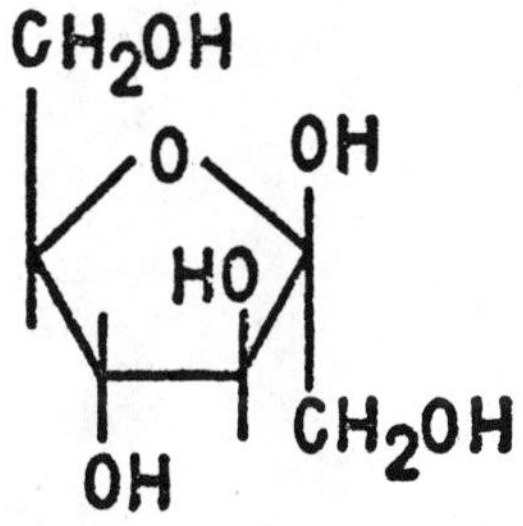
CH2OH
O
OH
HO
CH2OH
OH

β-D-fructofuranose

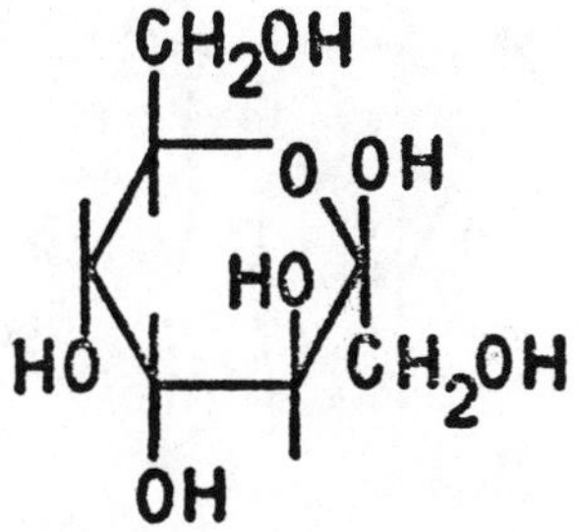
CH2OH
O
OH
HO
HO
CH2OH
OH

sedoheptulose

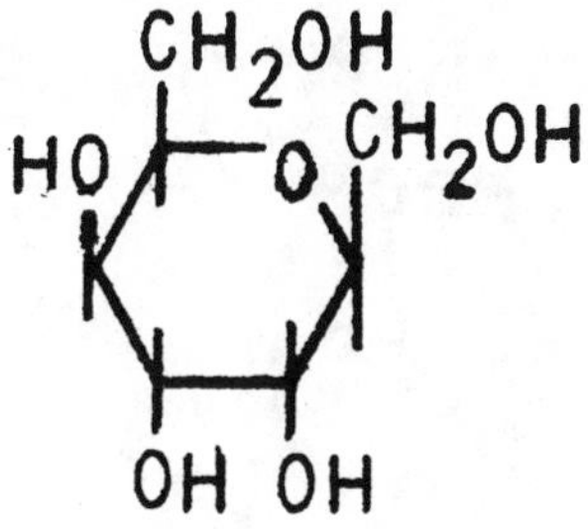
CH2OH
HO
O
CH2OH
OH OH

α-D- *manno*-heptulose

FIGURE 2-4: SOME KETOSES

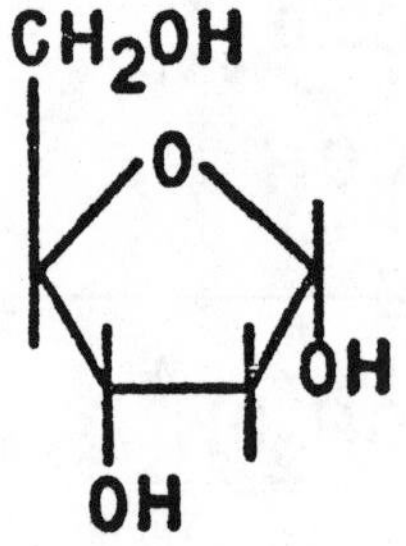

2-deoxy-D-*erythro*-pentofuranose

(2-deoxy-D-ribose)

aldehydo-L-rhamnose

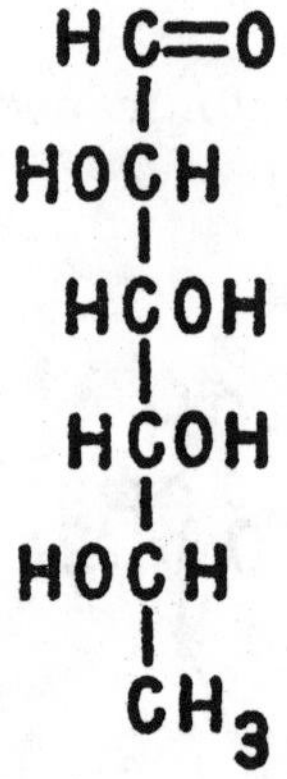

aldehydo-L-fucose

(6-deoxy-L-galactose)

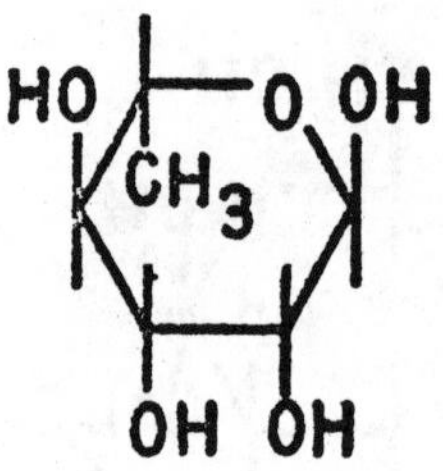

α-L-rhamnopyranose

FIGURE 2-5: SOME DEOXY SUGARS

(Although not all keto sugars are named in accordance with this rule.)
Structures of some of the keto sugars are given in Figure 2-4.

Some of the most widespread sugars contain non-hydroxylated carbons
and are named as deoxy sugars. Some illustrations are given in Figure 2-5.

A few of the monosaccharides are found free in plant saps. Glucose
is almost universally found in this way as are sedoheptulose and D-*manno*-
heptulose. Free fructose is found in many fruits, rhamnose in poison ivy
(*Rhus radicans*), and D-*glycero*-D-*manno*-octulose in avocados (*Persea
americana*). Many more of the monosaccharides do not occur as free sugars
but are very common as esters, polymers, glycosides and other derivatives
to be discussed below.

Some monosaccharides have branched carbon chains. For instance,
hamamelose is found as an ester in the tannin of witch hazel (*Hamamelis
virginiana*) Apiose, first found as the glycoside, apiin, of parsley (*Petroselinum hortense*) is now known to be widely distributed as a part of cell
wall polysaccharides (2).

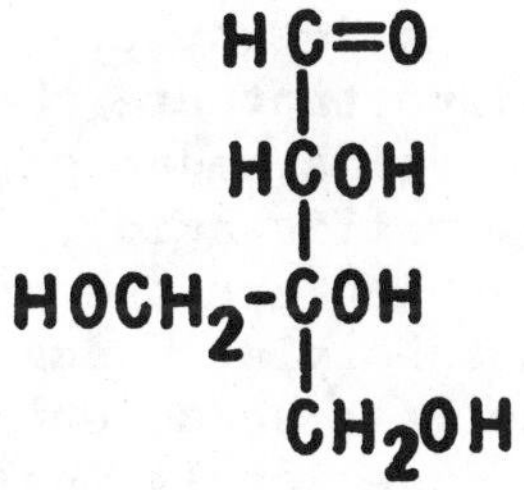

$$
\begin{array}{c}
HC=O \\
| \\
HCOH \\
| \\
HOCH_2-COH \\
| \\
CH_2OH
\end{array}
\qquad\qquad
\begin{array}{c}
HC=O \\
| \\
HOCH_2-COH \\
| \\
HCOH \\
| \\
HCOH \\
| \\
CH_2OH
\end{array}
$$

apiose 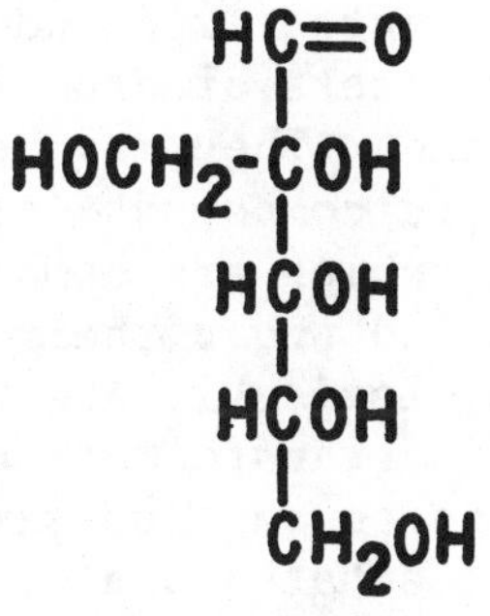   hamamelose

GLYCOSIDES AND OTHER ETHERS

As hydroxyl compounds the carbohydrates are capable of forming ethers
with other alcohols. Most important of these are the glycosides, which
have the ether group linked to the anomeric carbon atom. Ethers involving
the other carbon atoms are important as synthetic compounds and for studies
of carbohydrate structure, but they are rare in nature. 3-O-methyl-D-
galactose is found in the hydrolysis products of slippery elm (*Ulmus fulva*)
mucilage. It and other O-methyl sugars also occur as units in polysaccharides
of many deciduous tree leaves (3).

The glycosides are distinguished from other ethers by their ease of
hydrolysis. Short boiling in dilute acid is usually sufficient to hydrolyze
the sugar moiety from the aglycone. Glycosides may be named by designating
the attached alkyl group first and replacing the "-ose" ending of the
sugar with "-oside" as in α-methyl-D-glucoside. Many common glycosides
are best known by trivial names which do not indicate their structures
(e.g. "arbutin" is hydroquinone β-D-glucoside). Nearly all natural glycosides have the β configuration. Both chemically and physiologically
the natural glycosides are distinguished more by their aglycone portions
than by their glycosyl portions; and they are accordingly treated in this
book -- for instance, under terpenoids, flavonoids, etc. Glycosidic bonds
are also found, of course, in the oligosaccharides and polysaccharides.

Glucose is the sugar most frequently found in glycosides. However, other common sugars are not found as often as one would expect. Some rare sugars are peculiar to specific glycosides. In particular the cardiac glycosides regularly contain deoxy sugars that are not encountered in any other place. Rhamnose is a deoxy sugar that occurs widely in glycosides but not in other forms.

Nucleosides may be thought of as glycosides where the aglycone is an amine rather than an alcohol. They share some of the properties of the other glycosides and are sometimes referred to as N-glycosides in contrast to the O-glycosides. Peculiar and toxic azoxy-glycosides are found in cycad roots (4).

Thioglycosides have a thiol rather than an alcohol as the aglycone. These are discussed under their aglycones in Chapter 15.

ESTERS

As alcohols the carbohydrates are capable of forming esters with acids. Many have been synthesized and are important derivatives in characterizing sugars. A few esters of aromatic acids also occur naturally and are evidently widespread. They may be important intermediates in the transformations of aromatic compounds (cf. Chapter 4). More important are the hydrolyzable tannins which are complex esters of phenolic acids and sugars. They are discussed under their acid components (e.g. gallic acid). Most important physiologically are the phosphate esters, which are the prime intermediates in transformations of the sugars. Phosphorylated sugar moieties also go to make up several coenzymes and nucleic acid derivatives (q.v.). The phosphates are strong acids which are conveniently isolated as their slightly soluble barium salts. Their stability in water varies with the location of the phosphate group. The glycosyl phosphates (phosphorylated at the anomeric carbon, as glucose-1-phosphate) are notably more easily hydrolyzed than compounds phosphorylated in other positions. Phosphate adjacent to the carbonyl function is also more readily hydrolyzed than phosphate farther removed. Thus in fructose-1, 6-bisphosphate the 1 phosphate is hydrolyzed more than ten times faster than the 6-phosphate. Triose phosphates are peculiarly unstable in alkali, and their determination may be based on this characteristic.

There has been some indication of the natural occurrence of sugar sulfates. It is likely that many of these are intermediates in a degradation pathway analogous to glycolysis but starting with sulfoquinovose rather than glucose (5). Sulfoquinovose is a component of chloroplast lipids (cf. Chap. 5). Sulfates of certain polysaccharides are widespread in nature but apparently not found in higher plants.

ALCOHOLS (Glycitols)

Reduction of the carbonyl group of a sugar yields a polyhydroxy alcohol. A few of these are well-known natural products. Except for lack of the reducing function, they generally resemble the sugars in their properties. It must be noted that reduction of the anomeric carbon changes the possibilities for isomerism, so that the same sugar-alcohol may be derived from several different sugars, as sorbitol from glucose, gulose, or fructose.

Glycerol is undoubtedly the best-known sugar alcohol. Glucosides of glycerol occur in the Easter lily (6), and aromatic esters in several plant tissues (7, 8) but the major role of glycerol is as a building block of lipids (cf. Chap. 5). The higher sugar-alcohols are given the ending -itol. The four carbon erythritol occurs in algae, lichens, and grasses. Ribitol is found free in *Adonis vernalis* but more importantly as a part of the ubiquitous riboflavin molecule. The six and seven carbon sugar-alcohols are the most common representatives of this class. Mannitol and sorbitol are found in many plants, the former in exudates, the latter especially in fruits but also in leaves. Only two natural heptitols are known. An octitol has been reported in avocado (9).

The carbocyclic inositols (C_6 cyclitols) although not derived from sugars by simple reduction, are conveniently treated here since they are quite similar in chemical properties. The particular isomer *myo*-inositol (formerly called meso-inositol) occurs widely in plants both free and as phytic acid, an anhydride of its hexaphosphate. Phytin is a calcium magnesium salt of phytic acid. Inositol-based lipids are also widespread (Chap. 5), as are various methyl ethers of the inositols. A few examples are given in Fig. 2-6. Among less common derivatives are galactinol (1-0-α-D-galactosyl-*myo*-inositol) of sugar beet, esters with aromatic acids (10), esters with indole-3-acetic acid (Chap. 15), and a triprenyl derivative (11). Free *myo*-inositol is an essential growth factor for certain plant tissue cultures (12) but its exact metabolic role is unclear. Phytic acid is an inhibitor of α-amylase (13). Several reviews are available on the chemistry, natural occurrence, and metabolism of cyclitols (14, 15).

SUGAR ACIDS

Oxidation of one or both of the terminal carbon atoms of a sugar molecule to a carboxyl group yields a sugar acid. Oxidation of the aldehyde group forms an aldonic acid. If the other terminal carbon is oxidized, the product is a uronic acid. The simplest of these would be glyoxylic and glycolic acids but since they are important in organic acid metabolism rather than carbohydrate metabolism, they are treated in Chapter 3. D-glyceric acid is chiefly important as its phosphate esters, which are inter-mediates in carbohydrate breakdown and in photosynthesis. The tartaric acids may be thought of as erythrose derivatives with both terminal carbons oxidized to carboxyl groups. The six-carbon sugar acids occur in small amounts, chiefly as intermediates in the degradation of hexoses to form pentoses and as building blocks and degradation products of pectin, gums, and mucilages. All are water soluble and frequently exist as lactones so that their acidic properties are not apparent on titration in the cold. The uronic acids are easily decarboxylated by boiling with acid. This leads to errors when polysaccharides containing them are broken down by acidic hydrolysis. Structures of the important sugar acids appear in Figure 2-9.

The most important free sugar acid, L-ascorbic acid, is not only a vitamin for man but may play a role in the metabolism of plants. One established function is as a coenzyme for some thioglucosidases (16). It has been suggested to have a more general function in the control of protein synthesis and mitosis (17, 18). It is a strong reducing agent and may be readily distinguished by this property, although the four-carbon enediol, dihydroxy-fumaric acid occurs in nature to a limited extent and has similar properties. Ascorbic acid owes its acidic nature to the two enolic hydrogens

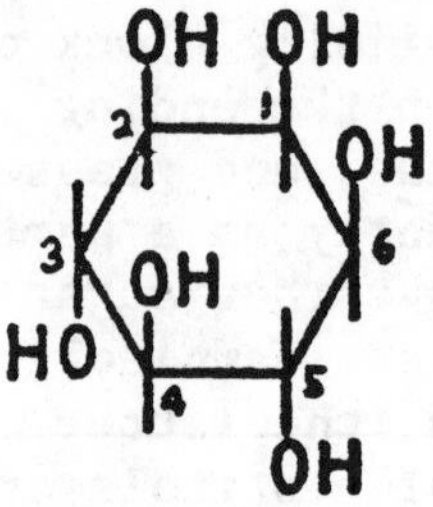

myo-inositol

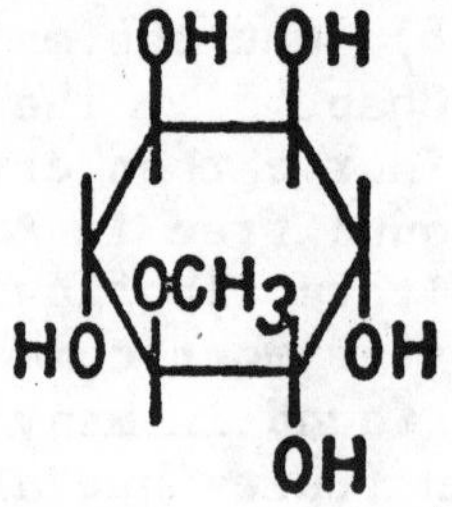

pinitol

(5-O-methyl-D-inositol)

(in many conifers and some
other plants)

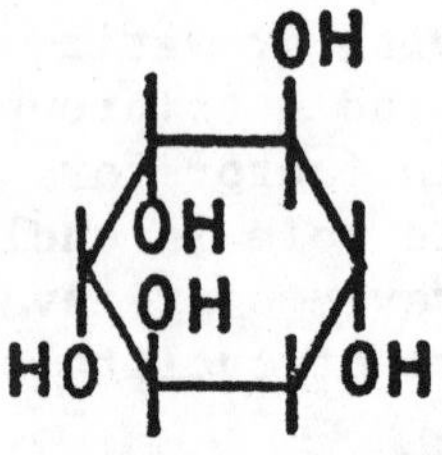

(+)-quercitol

(D-1-deoxy-muco-inositol)

(in acorn and other places)

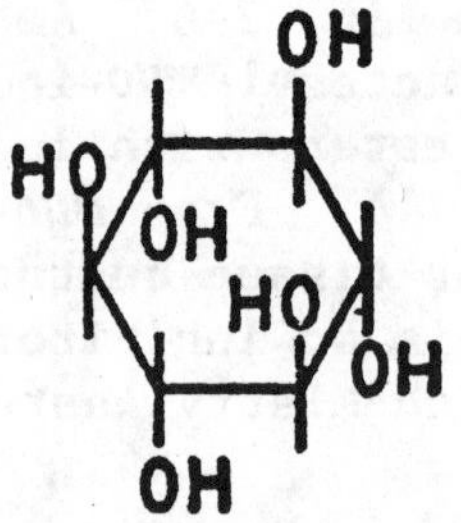

scyllo-inositol

(in dogwood, palms, acorns)

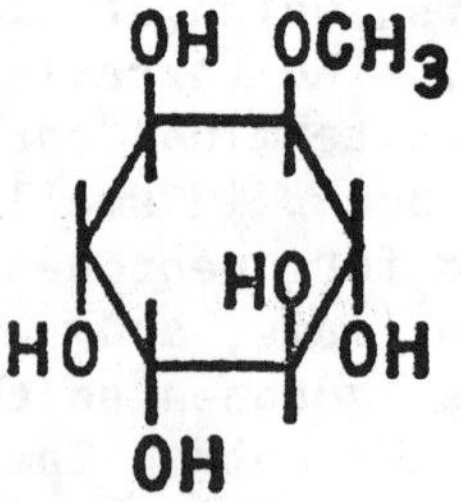

quebrachitol

(1-O-methyl-L-inositol)

(in many plants)

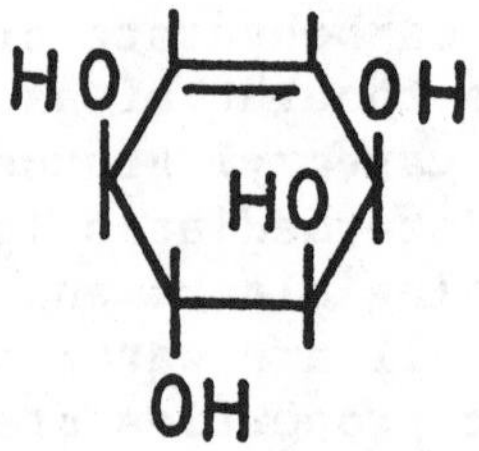

L-leucanthemitol

(widespread)

FIGURE 2-6: SOME INOSITOL DERIVATIVES

since it has a lactone ring rather than a free carboxyl group. Ascorbic acid occurs in certain plant extracts as an indole derivative, ascorbigen, which is an artifact of preparation (cf. Chapter 15). A symposium publication (19) contains many papers on all aspects of ascorbic acid.

OLIGOSACCHARIDES

The oligosaccharides are polymers formed by the linking together of several monosaccharide units through glycosidic bonds. Although oligosaccharides are arbitrarily limited to molecules containing less than ten monosaccharide units, the commonest have only 2, 3, or 4 units; and hexose units are by far the most frequent. One awkward case is the water-soluble glucan (polyglucoside) of barley roots which contains 7-11 units and may, therefore be classed as either an oligosaccharide or a polysaccharide (20).

The raffinose and planteose families of oligosaccharides are both widespread in higher plants, the former probably more than the latter (21). Both can be regarded as made by the addition of α-galactosyl units to sucrose. In the raffinose family this addition occurs at C-6 of the glucose moiety and in the planteose family at C-6 of the fructose moiety.

Aldobiouronic acids are oligosaccharides containing uronic acid units. They are found as hydrolysis products of certain gums, mucilages, and polysaccharides (q.v.) but apparently do not occur as natural plant constituents.

The oligosaccharides are water-soluble, optically active compounds, distinguished most readily from the monosaccharides by their hydrolysis to the monomers. They may be reducing or non-reducing, depending on whether or not all the potential carbonyl groups are tied up in glycosidic linkages. Oligosaccharides also occur as components of glycosides. For example, rutinose is a part of the flavonoid compounds rutin and hesperidin but apparently does not occur in the free state. Other rare oligosaccharides are components of steroid and triterpene glycosides. Some fructosyl sucroses (trisaccharides) which occur in monocots may be intermediates in fructan biosynthesis (see below).

Structures and occurrence of some of the natural oligosaccharides are given in Table 2-1.

POLYSACCHARIDES GENERALLY

Polysaccharides or glycans are arbitrarily defined as polymers of monosaccharides (and their derivatives) containing 10 or more units. However, most natural polysaccharides contain many more than 10 units and may have several thousand. Despite the vast number of polysaccharides that would be possible, the known representatives account for only a few of the structural possibilities. Where a polysaccharide is composed of more than one monosaccharide, the units fall into an orderly sequence; and only certain ones of the available hydroxyl groups are utilized in forming the glycosidic bonds. Generally, the structural polysaccharides are straight-chain compounds, while reserve food polysaccharides tend to be branched. Branched molecules are more easily dispersed in water to form hydrophilic

TABLE 2-1.   STRUCTURES AND OCCURRENCE OF SOME OLIGOSACCHARIDES

Gentiobiose: 6-O-β-D-glucopyranosyl-D-glucose (various glycosides)

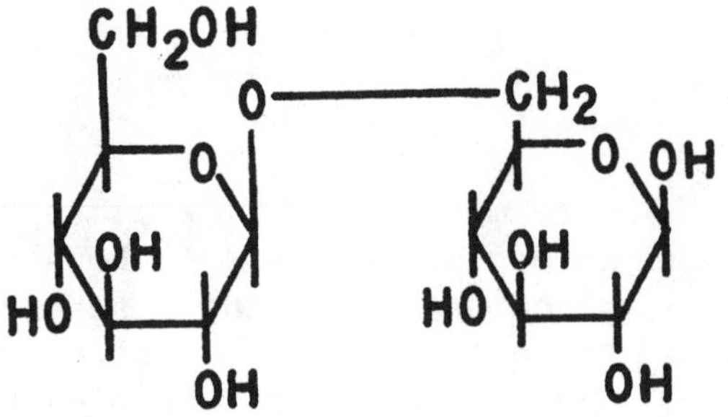

Melibiose: 6-O-α-D-galactopyranosyl-D-glucose (*Fraxinus* spp.)

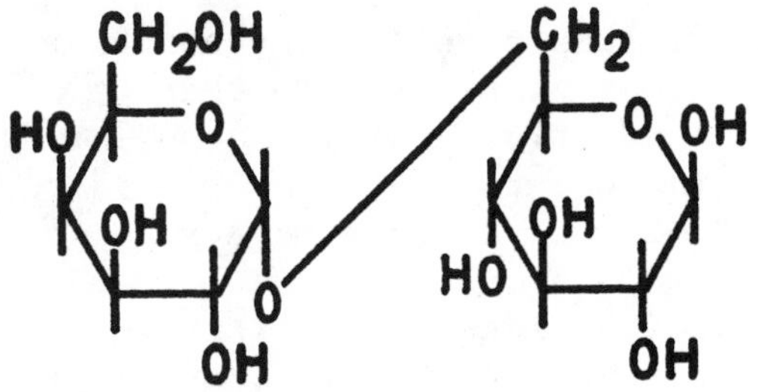

Sucrose: α-D-glucopyranosyl-β-D-fructofuranoside (throughout the plant kingdom)

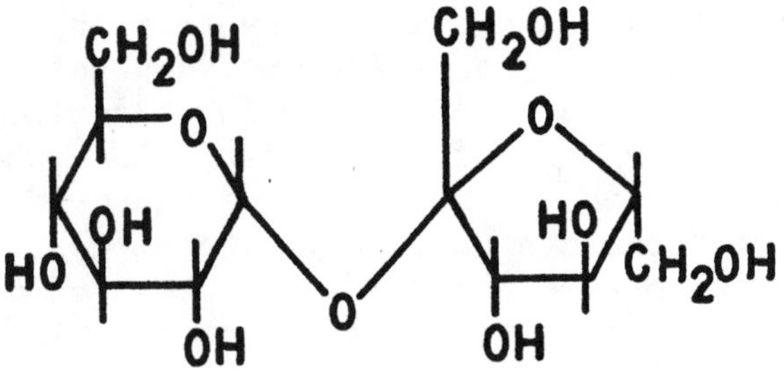

Trehalose: α-D-glucopyranosyl-α-D-glucopyranoside (*Selaginella lepidophylla*)

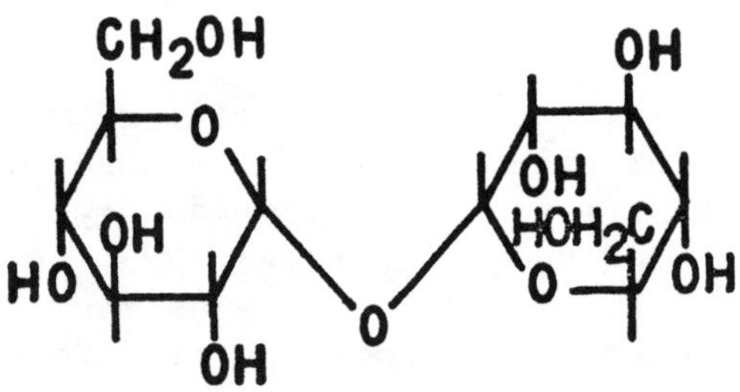

Sophorose: 2-O-β-D-glucopyranosyl-β-glucopyranose (various glycosides)

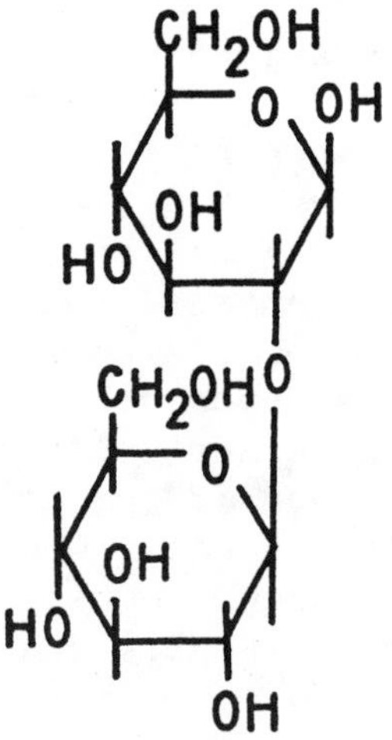

Table 2-1. Continued

Primoverose: 6-O-β-D-xylosyl-
      D-glucose (various glycosides)

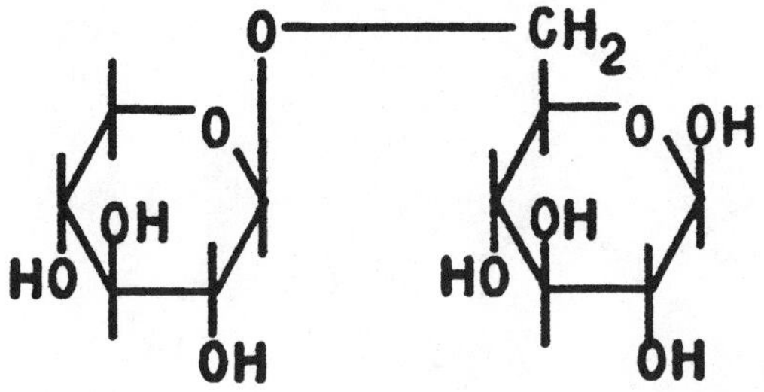

Rutinose: 6-O-λ-L-rhammosyl-D
      glucose (glycosides)

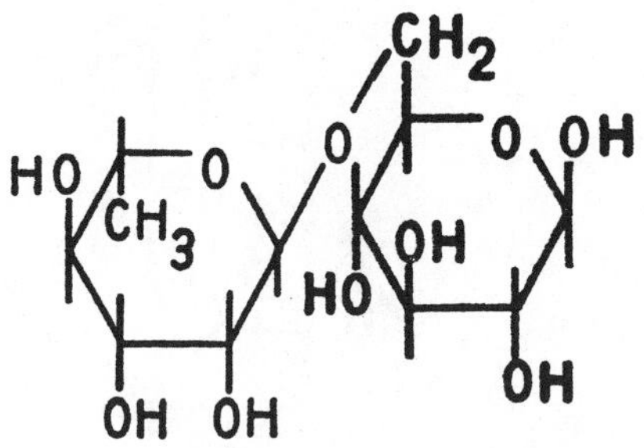

Gentianose: O-β-D-glucopyranosyl (1→6)-O-α-D-glucopyranosyl-(1→2)-β-D-
      fructofuranoside. (rhizomes of *Gentiana* spp.).

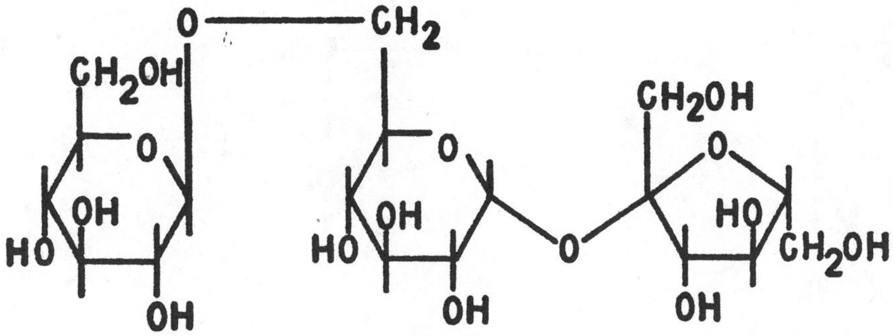

Melezitose: O-α-D-glucopyranosyl-(1→3)-O-β-D-fructofuranosyl-(2→1)-α-D-
      glucopyranoside. (exudates of many trees)

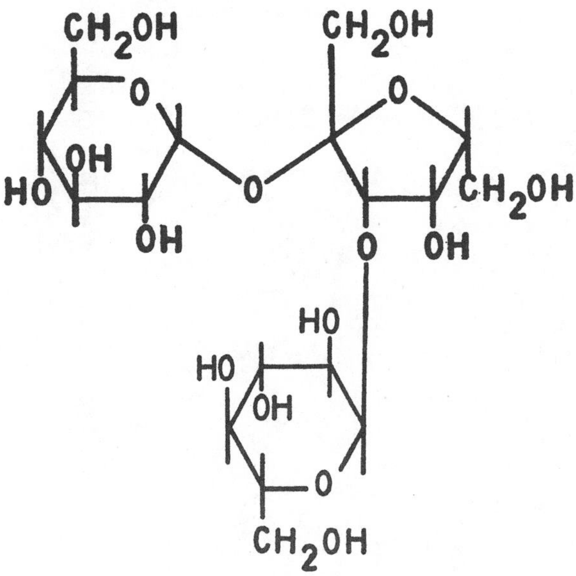

Table 2-1. Continued

Raffinose: O-α-D-galactopyranosyl-(1→6)-O-α-D-glucopyranosyl-(1→2)-β-D-fructofuranoside (throughout the plant kingdom)

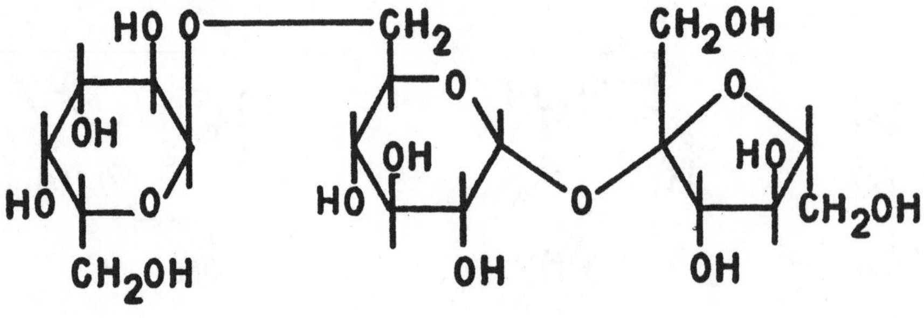

Stachyose: O-α-D-galactopyranosyl-(1→6)-O-α-D-galactopyranosyl-(1→6)-O-α-D-glucopyranosyl-(1→2)-β-D-fructofuranoside. (widely distributed)

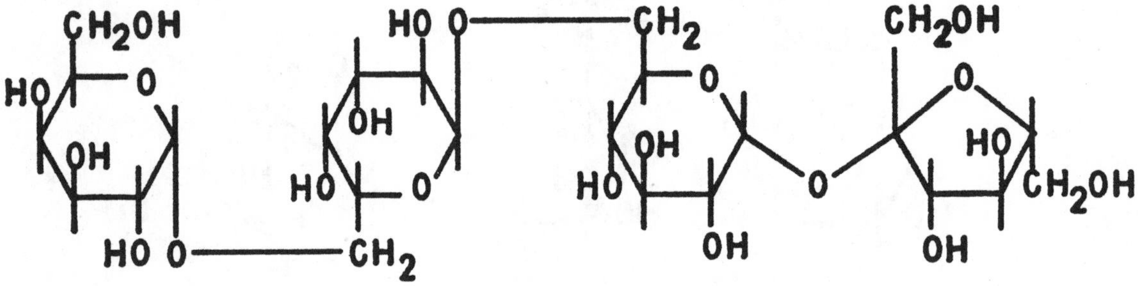

Verbascose: O-α-D-galactopyranosyl-(1→6)-O-α-D-galactopyranosyl-(1→6)-O-α-D-galactopyranosyl-(1→6)-O-α-D-glucopyranosyl-(1→2)-β-D-fructofuranoside. (roots of *Verbascum thapsus*)

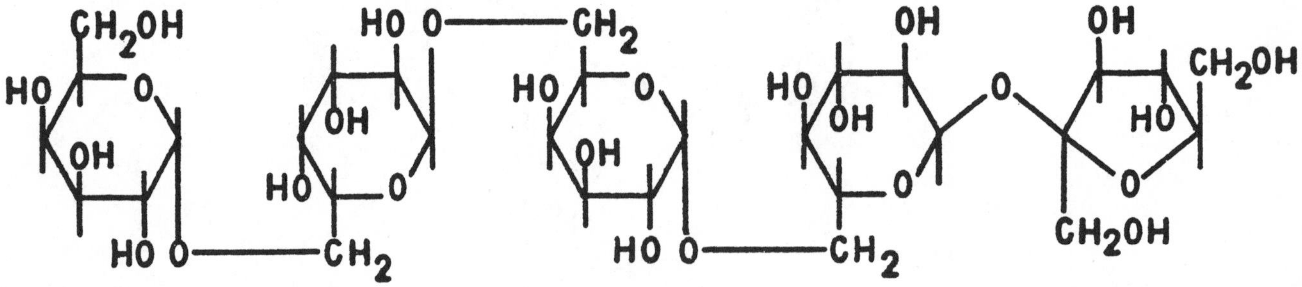

colloid systems that may be very viscous. The straight-chain polysaccharides, on the other hand, are slightly soluble or insoluble. Polysaccharides are usually obtained as amorphous rather than crystalline solids, although a degree of crystal order may be detected by x-ray diffraction methods. Some of the different classes of polysaccharides will be discussed separately. Ideally, a classification should be based on structure, but this is possible only to a limited extent with present knowledge.

STRUCTURAL POLYSACCHARIDES

Cellulose is one of the main constituents of plant cell walls, in particular the secondary cell walls which are most important for structural strength. Cellulose is a linear polymer of D-glucose units with β-(1→4) linkages. In cotton cellulose there are about three thousand glucose units comprising a molecule that is about 16,000A long and 4x8A in cross-section. In the cell wall cellulose molecules are grouped together parallel to each other to form micelles with a diameter of about 60A. In the micelles certain regions show a crystalline structure where the cellulose molecules are arranged in an orderly way; other areas show a random arrangement. The micelles are in turn arranged into microfibrils (diameter 200-250A) and these into fibrils, visible in the ordinary microscope. Hydrolysis of cellulose by acid or enzymes yields first cellodextrins containing 30 or fewer glucose units, then cellobiose and finally glucose. The intermediates between glucose and cellulose do not occur naturally. In pea epicotyls cellulose molecules were found with from 500-8,000 glucose units, the larger the older the plant (22). A cell-wall glucan from corn coleoptiles has both (1→4) and (1→3) linkages (23). A polymer called "amyloid" is made of (1→4)-β-D-glucosyl units with galactosyl-xylosyl residues attached (1→6) at regular intervals (24).

The hemicelluloses were originally named because they were found associated with cellulose in cell walls and thought to be intermediates in its formation. They comprise the polysaccharide material extractable from cell walls by 17.5% sodium hydroxide, but wherever possible it is advisable to avoid the term "hemicellulose" and refer to the components of this group in terms of their specific structures (e.g. "xylans", "mannans" etc.).

The most abundant polysaccharide cell wall materials after cellulose are the xylans. There are several different types, occurring in almost all higher plants. They seem to occur especially in association with lignin. In non-lignified tissues pectic substances become more prominent. The basic unit of xylan structure is D-xylose; but, depending on the plant source they may be branched or unbranched and may or may not contain additional units such as L-arabinose or D-glucuronic acid. Corn cob xylan contains about 200 sugar units as a straight chain with β-(1→4) links. On the contrary wheat straw xylan has only about 40 D-xylose units but in addition five L-arabinose units and three D-glucuronic acid units. The "acidic hemicelluloses" are those with a relatively large proportion of glucuronic acid units connected to the backbones. They are readily soluble in dilute (4%) sodium hydroxide. However, there is no sharp dividing line between neutral and acidic hemicelluloses, so that extraction with increasing concentrations of alkali may yield a series of fractions with gradually increasing content of uronic acid. Hydrolysis of hemicelluloses which contain glucuronic acid produces along with the monosaccharides some aldobiouronic acid, a disaccharide in which the glycosyl group is a uronic

acid. These appear in the hydrolysate because the glycosidic bond is
peculiarly resistant to hydrolysis when it is formed from a uronic acid.

The pectic substances of plants are found in primary cell walls and
intercellular cement. They are a mixture (and to some extent a chemical
combination) of an araban, a galactan, and the methyl ester of a galacturonan.
The araban is a low molecular weight branched chain of α (1→5) and α (1→3)
L-arabinofuranose units, at least some of which are attached to the free
positions of galactans (25). The galactan is a straight chain of about 120
β-(1→4) D-galactopyranose units. Most of the properties of pectin, however,
and the name itself are referrable to the galactouran component which has
about 200 (1→4)-α-D-galactopyranosyluronic acid units. Pectin actually
occurs in plants as insoluble protopectin which contains bound calcium
and phosphate and has a much larger molecular weight (1000 or more units).
With senescence or acid treatment of the plant tissue water-soluble pectin
is obtained by hydrolysis of some of the glycosidic bonds. Alkaline hydrolysis
of pectin removes the methyl ester leaving pectic acid. The so-called
pectinic acids are intermediate hydrolysis products with some carboxyl and
some ester groups. The calcium and magnesium salts of pectic acid are the
important cementing substances of the middle lamella.

In addition to the arabinogalactans of pectic substances other arabinogalactans with a branched galactan backbone are at least as widespread
and found in mnay different tissues. In these the galactan chain is linked
1→3 and 1→6. Arabinose units can be interspersed in the backbone or as
substituents on the branches. The best-known of these arabinogalactans is
extracted from the wood of Western larch (*Larix occidentalis*)which may
contain up to 18% of it. Not only does the arabinose content of these
polysaccharides vary with the source, but some of them also contain small
amounts (up to 5%) of covalently bound protein. The latter are called
proteoglycans, and the two parts are joined by glycosyl bonds to serine or
hydroxyproline units (25). Although it is usually assumed that the galactose
units in these polymers have the D-configuration, some L-galactose may also
be present (26).

Polymeric derivatives of glucosamine and galactosamine have been found
in higher plants. Some are soluble in 80% acetone and may be classed with
lipids, but others are insoluble in this solvent and are probably glycoproteins (i.e. proteins with oligosaccharide prosthetic groups). (27, and
Chap. 11). Free glucosamine and UDP-N-acetylglucosamine occur in plants
(28, 29). Earlier reports of the occurrence of sialic acid are now in
doubt (30, 31).

The composition of plant cell walls is taking on new importance with
the realization that changes in cell wall components are a condition of
growth. A percentage analysis of cell wall components for *Acer pseudoplatanus*
cells in culture is as follows (32).

cellulose	23
xyloglucan	21
rhamnogalacturonan	16
araban	10
protein	10
tetra-arabinosides (attached to hydroxyproline or serine)	9

         4- linked galactan   8
         3,6- linked arabinogalactan   2

Less complete data are available for the cell wall composition of several
other plants (33, 34).

FOOD RESERVE POLYSACCHARIDES

     Starch, like cellulose, is composed only of D-glucose units, but
joined by α rather than β glycosidic linkages. Starch is normally a mixture of two types of polysaccharide, amylose and amylopectin. The former
is a straight chain molecule of about 300 units joined 1→4. The latter
contains a thousand or more units of which a majority are also 1→4 but
with about 4% 1→6 linkages so that there is on an average about one branch
for every 25 glucose residues. In most starches there is about 25% amylose
to 75% amylopectin; but the ratio may be reversed in some varieties. In
some starches (e.g. potato) the amylopectin is partially esterified with
phosphates at C-6 positions. Some starches contain a third polysaccharide
which is a short chain-length amylopectin having 13-16 residues (35).
Starch is found widely in the plant kingdom where it serves as food storage
material. However, some higher plants do not contain starch and use other
carbohydrates as food reserves. A high molecular weight, highly branched
glucan essentially identical to oyster glycogen has been reported from the
tree *Cecropia peltata* (36).

     Fructans (polymeric fructosides) take the place of starch in a wide
variety of plants and supplement starch as food reserves in others. The
best known of these is inulin which contains about 25-28 2→1-linked β-fructo-
furanoside units per molecule and is soluble in hot but not cold water.
It occurs especially in the Compositae. Other shorter chain fructans are
also known, especially in the grasses and lilies (37,38). In contrast to
inulin these contain only about 10 units, are linked 2→6 and are soluble
in cold water. Many of the fructans, including inulin, seem to contain
glucose, probably as terminal groups. Some fructans are linear, while
others are highly branched.

     Mannans are also distributed in groups as widely separated as grasses
and conifers. At least in some cases they serve as reserve carbohydrate
but may be structural material in other cases. Some plant mucilages also
contain mannans. The mannans of palm seeds have been most studied. They
contain about seventy-five mannose residues linked with β-(1→4) bonds.
Mannans may be rather widespread in the cell walls of ferns (39).

     Galactomannans, polysaccharides containing both D-galactose and D-
mannose serve as a food reserve in many legume endosperms and seeds of
palm and coffee trees. The carob bean *(Ceratonia siliqua)*, in particular,
is a commercial source of these galactomannans which are used as thickeners.
They have a linear chain of β-(1→4)-mannopyranoside units with galactopyranose
units linked α-(1→6) as side chains. Because of their physical properties
and occurrence in seeds the galactomannans have sometimes been classed
with the mucilages. If a distinction is to be made, it must be in terms
of function -- i.e., the galactomannans seem to be mostly food reserves,
while the mucilages are more concerned with binding water.

     An interesting polysaccharide has been reported in the fruit of the
chicle plant *(Achras sapota)* by Venkataramen and Reithel (40). It is

apparently composed of glucose and galactose since as the fruit ripens,
lactose appears as a breakdown product. This accounts for one of the rare
appearances of lactose in the plant kingdom.

PLANT GUMS AND MUCILAGES

Both of these constituents are polymers containing more than one type
of monosaccharide, but uronic acids are generally present. Traditionally,
mucilages have been defined as normal plant constituents; and since they
occur in xerophytes, seeds, and young buds, they may be concerned with
imbibition and holding of water. Gums, on the other hand, are produced
in response to injury and are found as exudates on various trees, sometimes
associated with triterpenoid compounds as gum-resins.

Gums and mucilages are all either soluble in water or strongly hydrophilic. Solutions are levorotatory. They frequently occur with some of
the glucuronic acid groups as sodium, potassium, or calcium salts, but
enough free carboxyl groups usually remain to produce a slightly acidic
reaction. The monosaccharide components of some plant gums and mucilages
are listed in Table 2-2. It must be noted that hydrolysis normally results
in the appearance of aldobiouronic acids which are cleaved to the monosaccharides only under more drastic treatment. Occasionally, hydroxyl groups
may be methylated or acetylated. Plant gums always contain small amounts
of nitrogen (0.08-5.6%, probably as protein but perhaps some with
glucosamine as well (41).

TABLE 2-2. SUGAR COMPONENTS OF SOME PLANT GUMS AND MUCILAGES

GUMS

Name	Source	Hydrolysis Products
Gum arabic	*Acacia* spp.	D-galactose, L-arabinose, L-rhammose, D-glucuronic acid
Mesquite gum	*Prosopis* spp.	L-arabinose, D-galactose, 4-O-methyl-D-glucuronic acid
Cherry gum	*Prunus* spp.	L-arabinose, D-xylose, D-mannose, D-galactose, D-glucuronic acid

MUCILAGES

Name	Source	Hydrolysis Products
Flaxseed Mucilage	*Linum* spp.	D-xylose, L-galactose, L-rhamnose, D-galacturonic acid
Blond Psyllium Mucilage	*Plantago* spp.	D-xylose, L-arabinose, L-rhamnose, D-galacturonic acid
Slippery elm Mucilage	*Ulmus fulva*	D-galactose, 3-O-methyl-D-galactose, L-rhamnose, D-galacturonic acid

ISOLATION

Many of the carbohydrates are soluble in water. Prolonged extraction of defatted material with neutral boiling water will leave undissolved the cell-wall polysaccharides, as well as non-carbohydrate materials. Lignin can be removed from the insoluble cell-wall material by treatment with chlorine dioxide (42). Extraction with cold alkali now removes hemicelluloses leaving a residue of cellulose. The strength of alkali can be varied if selective extraction of hemicelluloses is desired. 24% KOH (or 17.5% NaOH) is commonly used and leaves a residue known as "α-cellulose," which may, however, contain as much as 40% other polysaccharides such as xylans, mannans, etc., depending on the source. It is therefore apparent that alkaline extraction does not quantitatively remove all hemicelluloses. Further purification of the cellulose involves solution in 85% phosphoric acid and precipitation of cellulose by adding three volumes of distilled water (43). Cellulose so obtained has suffered considerable degradation (e.g. to a chain length of about 160 glucose units as compared to several thousand in native cellulose). Unfortunately, purification is necessarily attended by degradation, and pure, native cellulose can only be obtained from a plant source like cotton which is almost pure cellulose already.

Returning to the alkaline solution of hemicelluloses, this may be fractionated making it acidic (pH ca. 4.5) whereupon the hemicelluloses of high molecular weight precipitate. Linear xylans can be precipitated by the addition of iodine to a solution of hemicelluloses (44). Hemicelluloses remaining in solution can be precipitated by adding acetone, alcohol, etc. to the remaining solution. Other techniques for fractionation of hemicellulose mixtures are chromatography on ion exchange cellulose or Sephadex and specific metal ion precipitations (45, 46). A separation by affinity chromatography has been found useful for branched chain compounds (47).

The hot water extract contains low molecular weight compounds in free solution as well as colloidal suspensions of the hydrophilic polysaccharides (and non-carbohydrate material such as organic acids and amino acids). If fructans are known to be present, a cold water extract may be preferred since some of them are readily hydrolyzed. Pectic substances are usually extracted using dilute acid (pH 2.5) or ammonium oxalate solution (0.5%). Depending on the source, the polysaccharides in the water extract might be gums, mucilages, starch, fructans, pectic substances, galactomannans, etc. There is no need of general methods to separate any one of these from all the others since in a given material only two or three types at most will be present, and methods chosen will depend on previous characterization. Generally all of them can be precipitated by adding ethanol to reach a concentration of 80%. (0.5% ammonium sulfate may aid the ethanol precipitation.) However, some of the shorter chain fructans are soluble in this concentration of ethanol. Amylose is separated from amylopectin by adding compounds such as butanol, thymol, or nitrobenzene to a hot starch suspension. Amylose is precipitated as an insoluble complex which can be decomposed by ethanol to recover the amylose.

Low molecular weight carbohydrates may be obtained from the 80% ethanol supernatant prepared as described above; or if only these carbohydrates are of interest, they may be extracted immediately from plant material using ethanol or 2-propanol sufficient to give a concentration of 80% when diluted by whatever water is present. Some components (e.g. diphosphates) are strongly bound to tissue and must be extracted with 20% ethanol or other solvents. Ionic substances (salts, amino acids, organic acids) are best removed by ion exchange resins although strongly basic or acidic resins may have some effect on the sugars. Sugar acids and phosphates will be removed by anion exchange resins but may be separated from noncarbohydrate components either by appropriate fraction cutting (48), or, in the case of phosphates, by precipitation with barium hydroxide and conversion to sodium salts. In order to avoid enzymatic hydrolysis of phosphate esters during extraction of plant material, a procedure involving rapid freezing and inactivation of phosphatases has been developed (49).

Special methods may be available for purification of the remaining neutral sugars. If one is in large excess, simple concentration of the solution may allow it to crystallize. If the desired component is not metabolized by yeast, impurities can frequently be removed by yeast fermentation.

The most general method for purification of the neutral sugars and derivatives is column chromatography using such adsorbents as charcoal, cellulose powder, starch, and Florex, with rather polar developing solvents such as lower alcohols and mixtures of them with water. On addition of borate, polyhydroxy compounds form anionic borate complexes which may be separated on a column of anion exchange resin using borate buffers as eluants (50). After elution, cations are removed from the fraction with a cation exchange resin and borate removed as volatile methyl borate by repeated distillation with methanol. Bisulfite addition compounds can also be used as ionizing derivatives of aldehyde sugars (51). Sugar mixtures can also be separated according to molecular size or partition coefficients using ion exchange resins (51, 52) or gel filtration media (53).

A generalized outline of the procedures described above is shown below.

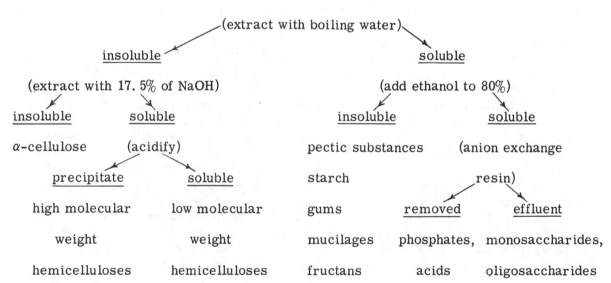

RAW MATERIAL

(extract with boiling water)

insoluble   soluble

(extract with 17.5% of NaOH)   (add ethanol to 80%)

insoluble   soluble   insoluble   soluble

α-cellulose   (acidify)   pectic substances   (anion exchange

                precipitate   soluble   starch   resin)

high molecular   low molecular   gums   removed   effluent

weight   weight   mucilages   phosphates,   monosaccharides,

hemicelluloses   hemicelluloses   fructans   acids   oligosaccharides

Obviously each plant is a special case, and this outline cannot be followed rigidly, but it may be a useful guide. Another method of successive extractions dissolves monosaccharides first and polysaccharides last (54). Consultation of the literature will fill in experimental details for known plants and carbohydrates, but no cut-and-dried procedure can substitute for an understanding of the principles involved or for constant checking of each step in the isolation by characterization of the product obtained.

CHARACTERIZATION

Aside from the standard methods of organic chemistry, innumerable color tests have been developed for the different classes of carbohydrates. A general reaction given by all carbohydrates is the formation of a color when heated with sulfuric acid and a phenol such as resorcinol, anthrone, a-naphthol, thymol, etc. Cellulose is distinguished by its lack of solubility in all but the strongest acids and alkalies, but ready solubility in cuprammonium hydroxide (Schweizer's reagent). Starch gives the well-known blue color with iodine due to its amylose component. Amylopectin gives a red-purple color with iodine. Pentoses and polysaccharides containing them give a red violet color with phloroglucinol in hydrochloric acid. Uronic acids also give a positive test; but they may be distinguished by not giving the Bial reaction (a blue color on heating with orcinol and $FeCl_3$ in hydrochloric acid). Ketoses are detected by heating with hydrochloric acid and resorcinol when they give a red color (Seliwanoff test). A blue-green color with diazouracil (Raybin reaction) is given by sucrose and other oligosaccharides containing a sucrose moiety such as raffinose and stachyose (55). Fructose and fructans give a red color on heating with urea in concentrated hydrochloric acid (56). The presence of uronic acids and their polymers can be detected by the evolution of carbon dioxide on heating with 12% hydrochloric acid. Other tests for certain classes of carbohydrates depend on their non-specific reducing power as in the reaction with Fehlings solution, Benedict's solution, ammoniacal silver nitrate, alkaline dinitrosalicyclic acid, etc. Ascorbic acid is distinguished by its especially strong reducing action as shown by reduction of the dye 2,6-dichlorophenolindophenol, or of silver nitrate in *acidic* solution.

With pure compounds measurement of optical rotation is useful in identification. This method can be applied even to polysaccharides that give cloudy aqueous solutions by adding calcium chloride to cause clarification.

The characterization of polysaccharides may be divided into two problems -- (a) identification of the monosaccharide components, and (b) the structural arrangement and number of monomers comprising the polymer molecule. Only the first of these two problems is considered to be within the scope of this book although some idea of the proportions of different monomers in a polysaccharide may be gained by relatively simple methods. Conditions for acidic hydrolysis of polysaccharides vary widely. Cellulose requires strong acids and/or high temperatures, whereas fructans are readily hydrolyzed by very dilute acid on short boiling. Whatever conditions are used, a mixture of monosaccharides is obtained, and the problem is resolved to one of identifying them. The method of choice is unquestionably chromatography.

The literature on paper chromatography of carbohydrates is extensive.

It is well reviewed in several of the general reference books on carbohydrates as well as in general books on chromatography. The commonest
solvents have been water-saturated phenol or mixtures of two, three and
four-carbon alcohols with water. Addition of acid to the solvent is not
usually as necessary with the sugars as with ionizing substances; but it
does help prevent background color with some sprays, and is helpful in
improving separation of the acidic sugar phosphates and glucuronic acid.
More and more, thin layer methods are replacing paper sheets because of
the advantages in speed and compactness of spots. Layers of cellulose
powder and solvents similar to those used with sheets seem to be used
most frequently, but several variations have also been recommended (57-60).
The same detection reagents are useful for paper sheets or thin layers.
Many of these are described in elementary laboratory manuals. Some references
to special reagents are:

for acids, lactones, esters	(61)
for ascorbic acid	(62)
for phosphates	(63,64)
for cyclitols	(65)
for distinguishing 1→4 from 1→6 linkages	(66)

Recently, high performance liquid chromatography has been used effectively for analysis of carbohydrate mixtures. Both low molecular weight
sugars and polysaccharides can be separated by appropriate choices of medium
(67-69).

Gas chromatographic analysis demands the extra step of preparing volatile
derivatives such as acetates or trimethylsilyl ethers. In spite of this
drawback there are advantages to this method, one of the greatest being that
coupling of the gas chromatograph to a mass spectrometer allows for the
determination of structure (70). Many applications to plant extracts have
been described (71-73).

METABOLIC PATHWAYS

Reviews and advanced textbooks summarize well the interrelationships
of carbohydrates in higher plants and are the primary sources of information
for the accompanying diagrams. The glycolytic and pentose phosphate
cycles are so well-known as to need little clarification here. Although
both cycles are widespread in plants, their relative importance probably
varies from plant to plant, organ to organ, and time to time. The complex
control mechanisms that apply to these pathways are at the heart of an
understanding of plant metabolism. Much work has been done to identify
the control point enzymes, the ways that circumstances influence them,
and the ways that their activities determine morphological events (74-80).
In Figures 2-7 and 2-8 the two schemes are shown separately but with names of
compounds common to each boxed to indicate points of interconnection.
Activation of starch synthesis by light is partially mediated by the concentrations of ATP and 3-phosphoglyceric acid, which are positive modulators of
ADP-glucose pyrophosphorylase (81).

A third group of pathways which has taken on importance in recent
years is shown in Figure 2-9 which indicates the key importance of sugar
nucleotides as the gateway to many important syntheses. Sugar-1-phosphates

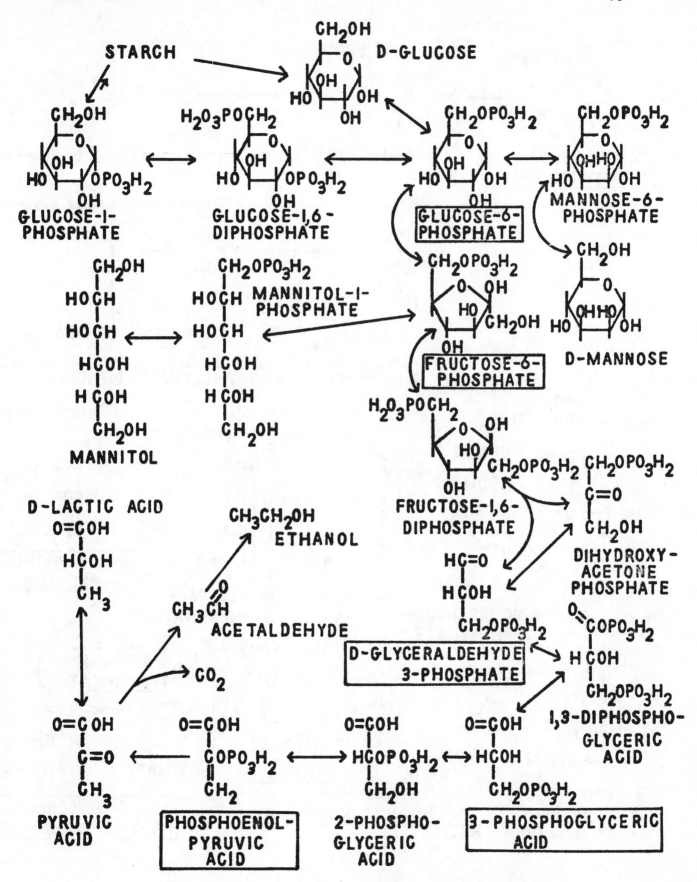

FIGURE 2-7: GLYCOLYTIC AND RELATED PATHWAYS

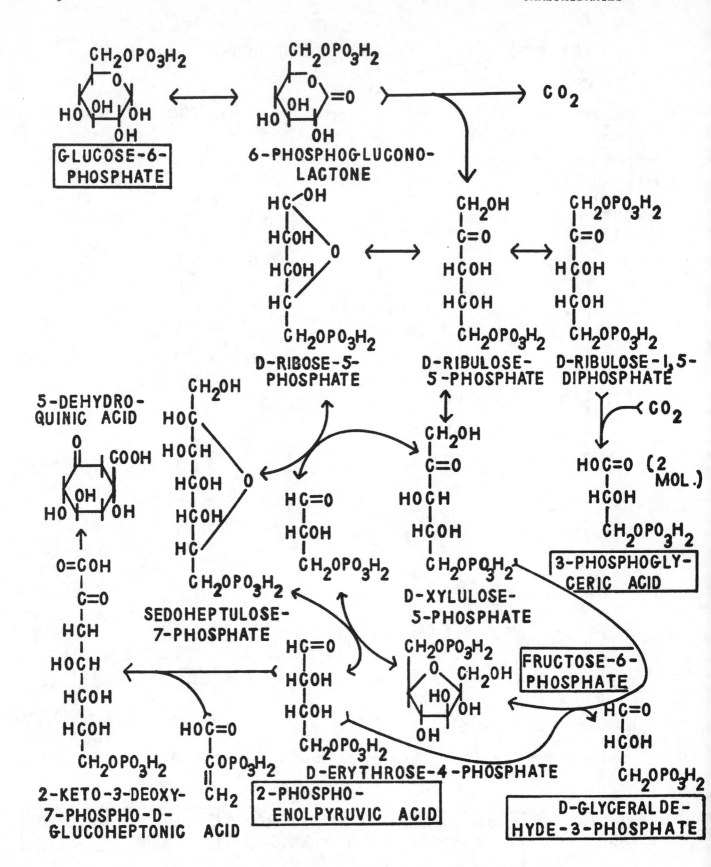

FIGURE 2-8: PENTOSE PHOSPHATE CYCLE AND PHOTOSYNTHETIC
CARBON DIOXIDE FIXATION

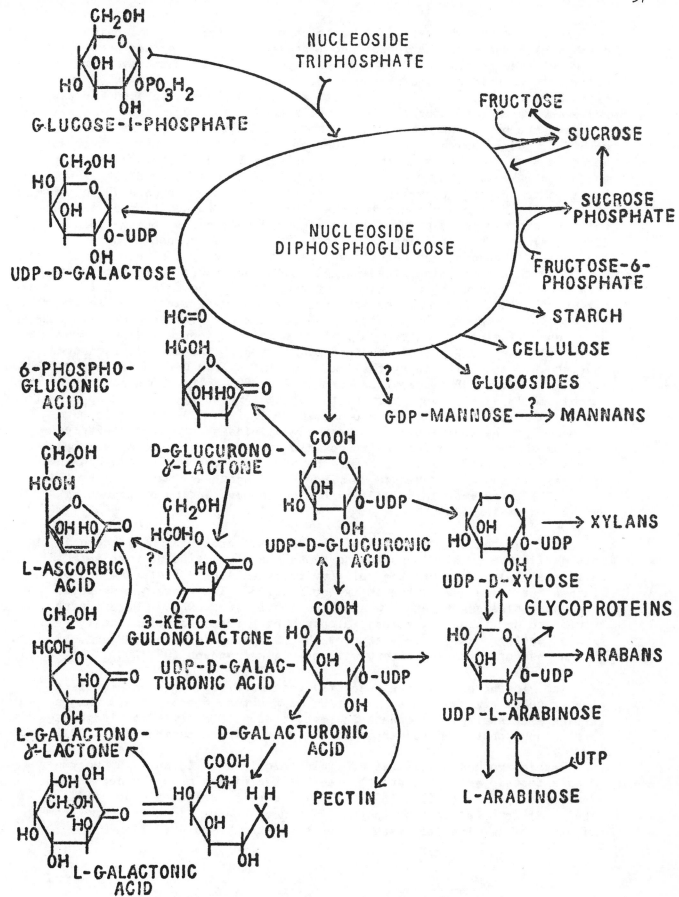

FIGURE 2-9: SUGAR NUCLEOTIDE PATHWAYS

may enter this pathway by direct reaction with a suitable nucleoside triphosphate and modification of the monosaccharide moiety may occur before it is released or combines. The first studies of these pathways gave prominence to uridinediphospho sugar derivatives. Since then sugar nucleotides based on all five of the nucleic acid bases have been found in plants, and each presumably functions in a specific pathway. Only some of these pathways are now clear. Sucrose synthesis utilizes UDP-glucose reacting with fructose-6-phosphate to form sucrose phosphate that is subsequently acted on by a phosphatase. The enzyme originally named sucrose synthetase, which can make sucrose in one step from UDP-glucose plus fructose, is now believed to function normally in the reverse direction to make UDP-glucose or other nucleoside diphosphoglucoses (82, 83). The addition of galactosyl units to sucrose to make umbelliferose uses UDP-galactose as the galactosyl donor (84), but the addition of galactosyl units to sucrose leading to raffinose, stachyose, and verbascose does not occur by a direct reaction of sucrose with a nucleoside diphosphogalactose; but there is an intermediate formation of galactinol and subsequent transfer of the galactosyl unit to the oligosaccharide. Thus myo-inositol acts as a transferring coenzyme for this process (85). The synthesis of amylose can use UDP-glucose or ADP-glucose as a donor of glucosyl units (86). It may be that younger tissues preferentially use UDPG and older tissues ADPG (87). Various plant tissues have shown the ability to synthesize mannolipids from GDP-mannose and glucosaminolipids from UDP-N-acetylglucosamine (88, 89). The lipid portion of the mannolipid is a polyprenyl similar to dolichol phosphate, but it appears to be something different in the glucosaminolipid (90, 91). There is more evidence for the functioning of these glycolipids as precursors of glycoproteins than there is for their possible role as precursors of simple polysaccharides (88, 92). Although the role of phosphorylase in starch synthesis is now considered to be minor, some synthesis may occur by this route (93). Amylopectin is made by the subsequent action of branching enzymes on amylose (94).

Although the configuration of the glucosyl group in UDP-glucose is α, this derivative is also used in the synthesis of β-glucans such as cellulose (95). However, the relative importance of UDP-glucose and GDP-glucose for cellulose synthesis is not settled. Incorporating systems from young tissues prefer GDPG and from old tissues UDPG. The products formed are not identical either, although both resemble cellulose (96-98). Similar systems make β (1→3) glucans (95, 97), and if also provided with GDP-mannose or a mannan primer, will make glucomannans (99, 100).

The biosynthesis of the N-acetylglucosamine units present in plant glycoproteins begins with an amination of fructose-6-phosphate. The resulting glucosamine-6-phosphate is acetylated with acetyl CoA, isomerized to the 1-phosphate and converted to UDP-N-acetylglucosamine (101, 102).

Pectin synthesis utilizes UDP-galacturonic acid to build up polymers of galacturonic acid that are then methylated with a methyl group from S-adenosylmethionine (103). Polymers of glucuronic acid are made similarly (104). It is possible that in some instances the uronic acids come from oxidation of myo-inositol rather than the pathway shown in Figure 2-9 (105, 106).

Sugar phosphates or nucleotides are not used in the biosynthesis of fructans. Rather, through the action of two or more fructosyl transferases fructose units are removed from sucrose molecules and added one at a time to the fructose end of another sucrose molecule (107). This process accounts for the appearance of glucose as a terminal unit in fructans.

In the biosynthesis of other compounds containing glycosyl units the usual donors are nucleoside diphospho sugars. However, the occasional participation of other donors is possible (108, 109), and in the formation of C-glycosides sugar-1-phosphates may react directly with anionic carbon atoms (110).

There appear to be two separate pathways for the formation of L-ascorbic acid from D-glucose in plants (111). By one pathway the aldehyde group carbon becomes the carboxyl carbon of ascorbic acid; by the other the glucose chain is "inverted" so that C-6 of glucose becomes C-1 of ascorbic acid. The first pathway probably goes from 6-phosphogluconate with inversion of configuration at C-5. The second pathway goes by way of galactose, D-galacturonic acid and L-galactono-ɣ-lactone. It seems likely that the first pathway is quantitatively more important, while the second represents a "salvage route" by which breakdown products of polysaccharides may be utilized. The questioned pathway shown from 3-keto-L-gulonic acid occurs in mammals and perhaps to a small extent in plants (111).

The branched-chain sugar apiose derives the branch hydroxymethyl group from C-3 of D-glucuronic acid and the actual rearrangement is of UDP-glucuronic acid to UDP-apiose (112). Hamamelose is probably derived from rearrangement of a hexose phosphate (113). The deoxy sugars have been little investigated, but rhamnose is evidently made by a direct reduction of glucose without any scission or rearrangement of the C6 chain (114). Inositols and related cyclic compounds are also made from the intact glucose molecule with C-1 of glucose becoming C-6 of myo-inositol. In detail, a cycloaldolase converts D-glucose-6-phosphate to myo-inositol-1-phosphate (115). Most other cycliclitol derivatives come from further transformations rather than different cyclizations (116-118), but there are apparent exceptions (119, 120). The breakdown of inositols probably goes via the uronic acid derivatives mentioned above and thence via UDP-xylose and the pentose phosphate pathway (121). The metabolism and significance of other sugar alcohols in plants is reviewed in (9).

An important branch from the pentose phosphate pathway is the condensation of phosphoenolpyruvic acid with erythrose-4-phosphate to yield a C_7 precursor of most naturally occurring aromatic compounds. Enzymes catalyzing the two steps of this pathway that are shown in Fig. 2-8 have been described from higher plants (122, 123). Later steps are described in Chap. 4.

GENERAL REFERENCES

Advances in Carbohydrate Chemistry, Vol. 1, 1945 to present (after Vol. 23, Advances in Carbohydrate Chemistry and Biochemistry).
Aspinall, G. O. (1970) Polysaccharides, Pergamon Press, Oxford.
Brimacombe, J. S., ed. (1977) Carbohydrate Chemistry 9, Chemical Society, London.
Devon, T. K. & Scott, A. I. (1972) Handbook of Naturally Occurring Compounds, 1, Acetogenins, Shikimates, and Carbohydrates, Academic Press, N. Y.
Isbell, H. S. (1973) Carbohydrates, American Chemical Society, Washington, D. C.

Loewus, F. (1971) Carbohydrate Interconversions, Ann. Rev. Plant Physiol. 22 337-364.

Pigman, W. & Horton, D., eds. (1970) The Carbohydrates, 2nd ed., Academic Press, N. Y.

Pridham, J. B., ed., (1974) Plant Carbohydrate Biochemistry, Academic Press, N. Y.

Whistler, R. L. & Paschall, E. F. (1965) Starch, Academic Press, N. Y.

Whistler, R. L. & Wolfrom, M. L. (1962-1963) Methods in Carbohydrate Chemistry, Vols. 1-2, Academic Press, N. Y.

Whistler, R. L. & BeMiller, J. N. eds. (1963-1965) Methods in Carbohydrate Chemistry, Vols. 3-5, Academic Press, N. Y.

Wilkie, K. C. B. (1979) "The Hemicelluloses of Grasses and Cereals," Adv. Carbohyd. Chem. 36 215-264.

Many articles in Miller 1

Many articles in Paech & Tracey 2

BIBLIOGRAPHY

1. Anon. (1971) Biochim. Biophys. Acta 244 223-302.
2. Watson, R. R. and Orenstein, N. S. (1975) Adv. Carbohyd. Chem. 31 135-184.
3. Bacon, J. S. D. and Cheshire, M. V. (1971) Biochem. J. 124 555-562.
4. Weiss, U. (1964) Fed. Proc. 23 1357-1360.
5. Lee, R. F. and Benson, A. A. (1972) Biochim. Biophys. Acta 261 35-37.
6. Kaneda, M., Mizutani, K., Takahashi, Y., Kurono, G. and Nishikawa, Y. (1974) Tetra Letts. 3937-3940.
7. Asakawa, Y., Takemoto, T., Wollenweber, E. and Aratani, T. (1977) Phytochemistry 16 1791-1795.
8. Cooper, R., Gottlieb, H. E. and Lavie, D. (1978) Phytochemistry 17 1673-1675.
9. Stacey, B. E. (1974) in J. B. Pridham, ed. Plant Carbohydrate Biochemistry, Academic Press, N. Y., pp. 47-59.
10. Dittrich, P. and Danböck, T. (1977) Plant Physiol. 59 279-281.
11. Fazldeen, H., Hegarty, M. P. and Lahey, F. N. (1978) Phytochemistry 17 1609-1612.
12. Verma, D. C. and Dougall, D. K. (1979) Ann. Botany 43 259-269.
13. Sharma, C. B., Goel, M. and Irshad, M. (1978) Phytochemistry 17 201-204.
14. Loewus, F. (1971) Ann. Rev. Plant Physiol. 22 337-364.
15. Posternak, T. (1965) The Cyclitols, Holden-Day, San Francisco.
16. Ohtsuru, M. and Hata, T. (1979) Biochim. Biophys. Acta 567 384-391.
17. Arrigoni, O., Arrigoni-Lino, R. and Calabrese, G. (1977) FEBS Letters 82 135-138.
18. Mathew, T., Dave, I. C. and Gaur, B. K. (1978) Z. Pflanzenphysiol. 86 23-29.
19. King, C. G. and Burns, J. J., eds., (1975) "Second Conference on Vitamin C", Ann. N.Y. Acad. Sci. 258.
20. Hassid, W. Z. (1939) J. Am. Chem. Soc. 61 1223-1225.
21. Amuti, K. S. and Pollard, C. J. (1977) Phytochemistry 16 529-532.
22. Spencer, F. S. and Maclachlan, G. A. (1972) Plant Physiol. 49 58-63.
23. Kivilaan, A., Bandurski, R. S., and Schulze, A. (1971) Plant Physiol. 48 389-393.
24. Kooiman, P. (1967) Phytochemistry 6 1665-1673.
25. Clarke, A. E., Anderson, R. L. and Stone, B. A. (1979) Phytochemistry 18 521-540.
26. Roberts, R. M. and Harrer, E. (1973) Phytochemistry 12 2679-2682.
27. Racusen, D. and Foote, M. (1974) Can. J. Botany 52 2111-2113.
28. Solms, J. and Hassid, W. Z. (1957) J. Biol. Chem. 228 357-364.
29. Roberts, R. M. (1970) Plant Physiol. 45 263-267.
30. Hayashi, H., Nikaido, Y. and Hirano, S. (1977) Agric. Biol. Chem. 41 215-216.
31. Cherry, J. M., Buckhout, T. J. and Morré, D. J. (1978) Experientia 34 1433-1434.
32. Talmadge, K. W., Keegstra, K., Bauer, W. D. and Albersheim, P. (1973) Plant Physiol. 51 158-173.
33. Ring, S. G. and Selmendran, R. R. (1978) Phytochemistry 17 745-752.
34. Labavitch, J. M. and Ray, P. M. (1978) Phytochemistry 17 933-937.
35. Manners, D. J. (1962) Adv. Carbohyd. Chem. 17 371-430.
36. Rickson, F. R. (1971) Science 173 344-347.
37. Pollock, C. J., Hall, M. A. and Roberts, D. P. (1979) J. Chromatog. 171 411-415.
38. Darbyshire, B. and Henry, R. J. (1978) New Phytol. 81 29-34.
39. Bailey, R. W. and Pain, V. (1971) Phytochemistry 10 1065-1073.
40. Venkataraman, R. and Reithel, F. J. (1958) Arch. Biochem. Biophys. 75 443-452.
41. Anderson, D. M. W., Hendrie, A., and Munro, A. C. (1972) Phytochemistry 11 733-736.
42. Wise, L. E., Murphy, M. and D'Addieco, A. A. (1946) Paper Trade J. 122 No. 2, 35-43.
43. Hirst, E. L., Isherwood, F. A., Jermyn, M. A. and Jones, J. K. N. (1949) J. Chem. Soc. 1949 Suppl. 182-184.

44. Blake, J. D. and Richards, G. H. (1971) Carbohydrate Res. 17 253-268.
45. Reid, J. S. G. and Wilkie, K. C. B. (1969) Phytochemistry 8 2045-2051.
46. ibid. 2053-2058, 2059-2065.
47. Kennedy, J. F. and Rosevear, A. (1973) J. Chem. Soc. Perkin I 2041-2046.
48. Hofer, H. W. (1974) Anal. Biochem. 61 54-61.
49. Isherwood, F. A. and Barrett, F. C. (1967) Biochem. J. 104 922-933.
50. Lambert, A. T. V. and Dirkx, M. H. (1978) Carbohydr. Res. 62 197-202.
51. Jandera, P. and Churáček, J. (1974) J. Chromatog. 98 55-104.
52. Päärt, E. and Samuelson, O. (1973) J. Chromatog. 85 93-100.
53. John, M. and Dellweg, H. (1973) Separ. Purif. Methods 2 231-257.
54. Aspinall, G. O. and Fanshawe, R. S. (1961) J. Chem. Soc. 1961 4215-4225.
55. Raybin, H. W. (1937) J. Am. Chem. Soc. 59 1402-1403.
56. Quillet, M. (1956) Compt. Rend. 242 2475-2478.
57. Hansen, S. A. (1975) J. Chromatog. 107 224-226.
58. Ghebrezzabher, M., Rufini, S., Monaldi, B. and Lato, M. (1976) J. Chromatog. 127 133-162.
59. Walkley, J. W. and Tillman, J. (1977) J. Chromatog. 132 172-174.
60. Papin, J.-P. and Udiman, M. (1979) J. Chromatog. 170 490-494.
61. Abdel-Akher, M. and Smith, F. (1951) J. Am. Chem. Soc. 73 5859-5860.
62. Milletti, M. (1959) Ann. Chim. 49 224-232.
63. Mann, A. F., Hucklesby, D. P. and Hewitt, E. J. (1979) Anal. Biochem. 96 6.
64. Steinitz, K. (1961) Anal. Biochem. 2 497-501.
65. Kindl, H. and Hoffmann-Ostenhof, O. (1966) Phytochemistry 5 1091-1102.
66. Schwimmer, S. and Bevenue, A. (1956) Science 123 543-544.
67. Wheals, B. B. and White, P.C. (1979) J. Chromatog. 176 421-426.
68. Linden, J. C. and Lawhead, C. L. (1975) J. Chromatog. 105 125-133.
69. Aitzetmüller, K. (1978) J. Chromatog. 156 354-358.
70. Zinbo, M. and Sherman, W. R. (1970) J. Am. Chem. Soc. 92 2105-2114.
71. Phillips, D. V. and Smith, A. E. (1973) Anal. Biochem. 54 95-101.
72. Harvey, D. J. and Horning, M. G. (1973) J. Chromatog. 76 51-62.
73. Petersson, G. (1974) Carbohyd. Res. 33 47-61.
74. Turner, J. F. and Turner, D. H. (1975) Ann. Rev. Plant Physiol. 26 159-186.
75. Davies, D. D. (1979) Ann. Rev. Plant Physiol. 30 131-158.
76. Scharrenberger, C., Tetour, M. and Herbert, M. (1975) Plant Physiol. 56 836-840.
77. Salminen, S. O. and Young, R. E. (1975) Plant Physiol. 55 45-50.
78. Anderson, L. E. and Duggan, J. X. (1976) Plant Physiol. 58 135-139.
79. Kovacs, M. I. P. and Simpson, G. M. (1976) Phytochemistry 15 455-458.
80. Ruffner, H. P. and Hawker, J. S. (1977) Phytochemistry 16 1171-1175.
81. Kaiser, W. M. and Bassham, J.A. (1979) Plant Physiol. 63 105-108, 109-113.
82. Rollit, J. and Maclachlan, G. A. (1974) Phytochemistry 13 367-374.
83. Delmer, D. P. (1972) Plant Physiol. 50 469-472.
84. Hopf, H. and Kandler, O. (1974) Plant Physiol. 54 13-14.
85. Lehle, L. and Tanner, W. (1973) Biochem. J. 38 103-110.
86. Ozbun, J. L. and 5 others (1973) Plant Physiol. 51 1-5.
87. Baxter, E. D. and Duffus, C. M. (1971) Phytochemistry 10 2641-2644.
88. Elbein, A. D. (1979) Ann. Rev. Plant Physiol. 30 239-272.
89. Marriott, K. M. and Tanner, W. (1979) Plant Physiol. 64 445-449.
90. Ericson, M. C., Gafford, J. T. and Elbein, A. D. (1978) Plant Physiol. 61 274-277.
91. Smith, M. M., Axelos, M. and Péaud-Lenoël, C. (1976) Biochimie 58 1195-1211.
92. Davies, H. M. and Delmer, D. P. (1979) Planta 146 513-520.
93. de Fekete, M. A. R. and Vieweg, G. H. (1974) in J. B. Pridham, ed. Plant Carbohydrate Biochemistry, Academic Press, N. Y. pp. 127-144.
94. Hassid, W. Z. (1969) Science 165 137-144.
95. Villemez, C. L. (1974) in J. B. Pridham, ed., Plant Carbohydrate Biochemistry, Academic Press, N. Y. pp. 183-189.
96. Delmer, D. P., Beasley, C. A. and Ordin, L. (1974) Plant Physiol. 53 149-153.
97. Tsai, C. M. and Hassid, W. Z. (1973) Plant Physiol. 51 998-1001.
98. Flowers, H. M., Batra, K. K., Kemp, J. and Hassid, W. Z. (1969) J. Biol. Chem. 244 4969-4974.
99. Elbein, A. D. (1969) J. Biol. Chem. 244 1608-1616.
100. Villemez, C. L. and Heller, J. S. (1970) Nature 227 80-81.
101. Roberts, R. M. (1970) Plant Physiol. 45 263-267.
102. Vessal, M. and Hassid, W. Z. (1972) Plant Physiol. 49 977-981.

103. Kauss, H. (1974) in J. B. Pridham, ed., Plant Carbohydrate Biochemistry, Academic Press, N. Y., pp. 191-205.
104. Kauss, H. (1969) Phytochemistry 8 985-988.
105. Asamizu, T. and Nishi, A. (1979) Planta 146 49-54.
106. Maiti, I. B. and Loewus, F. A. (1978) Plant Physiol. 62 280-283.
107. Bhatia, I. S. and Nandra, K. S. (1979) Phytochemistry 18 923-927.
108. Linden, J. C., Tanner, W. and Kandler, O. (1974) Plant Physiol. 54 752-757.
109. Tandecarz, J., Lavintman, N. and Cardini, C. E. (1975) Biochim. Biophys. Acta 399 345-355.
110. Bhatia, V. K. and Seshadri, T. R. (1967) Current Sci. 36 111-115.
111. Loewus, F. A., Wagner, G. and Yang, J. C. (1975) Ann. N. Y. Acad. Sci. 258 7-23.
112. Mendicino, J. and Abou-Issa, H. (1974) Biochim. Biophys. Acta 364 159-172.
113. Gilck, H. and Beck, E. (1974) Z. Pflanzenphysiol. 72 395-409.
114. Andrews, P., Hough, L. and Picken, J. M. (1965) Biochem. J. 97 27-31.
115. Ogunyemi, E. O., Pittner, F. and Hoffmann-Ostenhof, O. (1978) Z. Physiol. Chem. 359 613-616.
116. Ruis, H. and Hoffmann-Ostenhof, O. (1969) Europ. J. Biochem. 7 442-448.
117. Hofmann, H. and Hoffmann-Ostenhof, O. (1969) Monatsh. 100 231-235.
118. Schilling, N., Dittrich, P. and Kandler, O. (1972) Phytochemistry 11 1401-1404.
119. Kindl, H. and Hoffmann-Ostenhof, O. (1967) Phytochemistry 6 77-83.
120. Kindl, H., Scholda, R. and Hoffmann-Ostenhof, O. (1967) Phytochemistry 6 237-244.
121. Maiti, I. B. and Loewus, F. A. (1978) Planta 142 55-60.
122. Huisman, O. C. and Kosuge, T. (1974) J. Biol. Chem. 249 6842-6848.
123. Saijo, R. and Kosuge, T. (1978) Phytochemistry 17 223-225.

Chapter 3
WATER-SOLUBLE ORGANIC ACIDS

The occurrence of a variety of free acids in plants has been well-known for many years. Some plant organs accumulate rather large quantities of specific acids which are primarily concentrated in the vacuolar sap. As a result of such accumulation the pH of this sap may fall to values as low as 2 or 3. Many of the common plant acids are those which participate in the familiar citric acid cycle of metabolism; and since this cycle is believed to be of fundamental importance in the biochemistry of almost all organisms, acids participating in it must occur to some extent in all plants. However, the mere operation of this cycle does not entail any accumulation of acids. Moreover, the reactions of the citric acid cycle take place in the mitochondria, whereas acids which accumulate do so in the vacuole. Therefore, while this cycle may provide the reaction pathways for synthesis of several common plant acids, it does not explain how a particular plant organ often accumulates just one acid from the cycle in the vacuoles of its cells. That there is such a selectivity is evident from a consideration of the major acids in some common fruits -- e.g. citric acid in lemons (*Citrus limonica*), isocitric in blackberries (*Rubus* spp.) and malic in apples (*Malus* spp.)

Besides the plant acids involved in the citric acid cycle, several other water-soluble acids are of very common occurrence in plants. Some of these may be grouped as lower members of the fatty acid series (cf. Chapter 5); some are intermediates in the pathway leading from carbohydrates to aromatic compounds (cf. Chapter 4); some are, in fact, carbohydrates (cf. Chapter 2); some are isoprenoid derivatives (Chapter 8); and, finally, some are formed by peculiar or unknown metabolic pathways. Table 3-1 lists some of the non-citric cycle acids with examples of plants where they are found in relatively high concentrations.

The table on page 44 is by no means complete. The bibliography of Buch listed under general references has about 30 water-soluble, aliphatic plant acids not including sugar acids or lower fatty acids. While most of these acids occur free or as salts, a few (chiefly the lower fatty acids) are often found as esters in essential oils (cf. Chapter 8). Hydroxy acids such as malic and tartaric also occur as depsides with aromatic acids (1).

The common plant acids are colorless substances which are usually soluble, not only in water, but also in organic solvents such as ethanol and ether. They are insoluble in the very non-polar solvents like benzene or petroleum ether. Many of the plant acids are optically active, and normally only one of the enantiomorphs is naturally occurring. Compared with the mineral acids they are only weakly acidic. Their sodium and potassium

TABLE 3-1. SOME NATURALLY OCCURRING ORGANIC ACIDS

Acid	Source	Acid	Source
HCOOH formic	stinging nettle hairs (*Urtica urens*)	COOH | COOH oxalic	*Oxalis* spp. (3)
CH$_3$COOH acetic	esterified in fruit essential oils	COOH | CH$_2$ | COOH malonic	many Leguminosae
CH$_3$CH$_2$CH$_2$COOH butyric	esterified in fruit essential oils		
CH$_3$ \\ CHCH$_2$COOH / CH$_3$ isovaleric	*Valeriana* spp.	 shikimic	widespread (2)
COOH | HCOH | HOCH | COOH L-(+)-tartaric	*Vitis* spp.	 quinic	high in woody dicots (2)
COOH | HCOH | CH$_3$ D-(-) lactic	widespread in roots, germinating seeds	 chelidonic	widespread (4)
CH$_2$OH | COOH glycolic	widespread	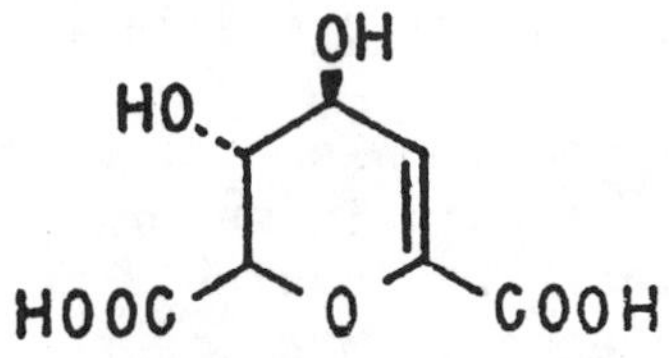 daucic	carrot (5)

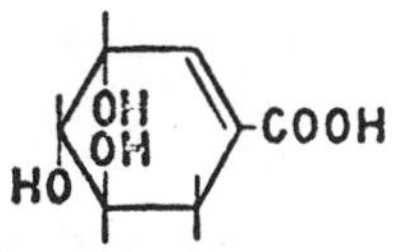

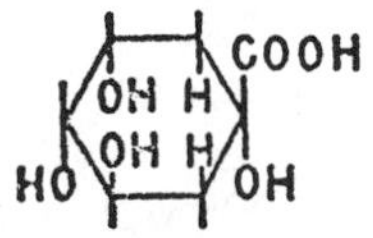

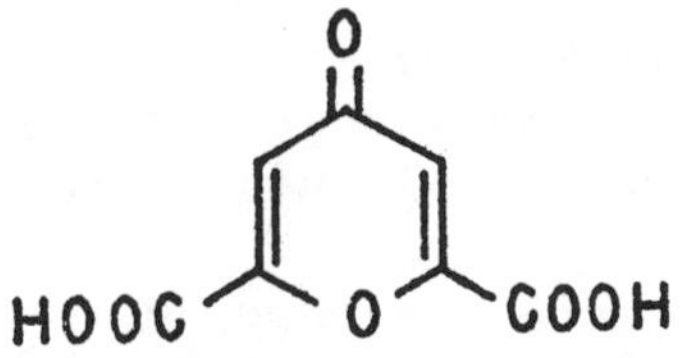

salts are water soluble, but calcium and barium salts are usually insoluble or only slightly soluble in water. Crystals of calcium oxalate appear as raphides in the cytoplasm of many plant cells.

The function of plant acids in respiratory cycles is well-known; but aside from this role in energy metabolism, several other functions have been suggested for them, particularly for those which accumulate or are excreted and apparently are not involved in active metabolism. They are often considered as waste products which are not further utilized. However, they may accumulate at one stage and disappear at a later stage -- as malic acid in green apples. Malic acid acts as a specific attracting agent for spermatozoids of some mosses and ferns and is presumably secreted by the archegonia or egg cells (6). Citric acid is a specific growth factor for callus cultures of *Citrus sinensis* (7). Those acids which occur in the vacuole as salts may participate in establishing a proper acid-base balance. Acids which form iron chelates may aid in the vascular transport of this cation (8). More and more malonyl derivatives are being discovered in higher plants, and it may be that malonylation is a general process for modifying the activity or permeability of other constituents such as flavonoids (see Chap. 9), D-amino acids (see Chap. 10), and growth regulators (see Chap. 15).

LACTONES

Hydroxy acids may exist as lactones or inner esters if the hydroxyl group is situated so that the lactone has a 5 or 6-membered ring. Of the common plant acids isocitric is often found in the lactone form:

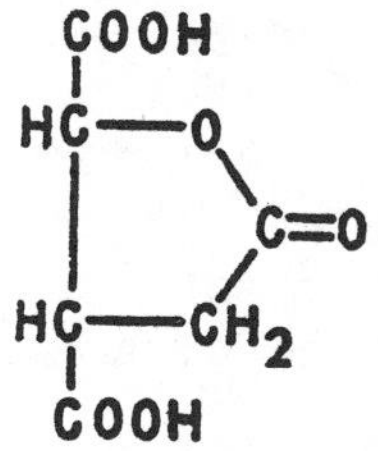

$$
\begin{array}{c}
\text{COOH} \\
| \\
\text{HC}\!-\!\text{O} \\
|\qquad\quad \text{C}\!=\!\text{O} \\
\text{HC}\!-\!\text{CH}_2 \\
| \\
\text{COOH}
\end{array}
$$

Lactone-forming acids are particularly common in succulent plants (9). A few unusual hydroxy acids are never found in the free carboxyl form, and only the lactones are known. Among these lactones are several compounds of interest in physiology since they are often very powerful irritants of skin and mucous membranes and some are fungicidal. Structures and occurrence of some simple lactones are shown below. Those with hydroxyl groups may exist naturally as glycosides. Other lactones will be found described in other chapters along with related compounds (e.g., terpenoids, fatty acids, etc.). Unsaturated lactones of higher plants are reviewed in (10).

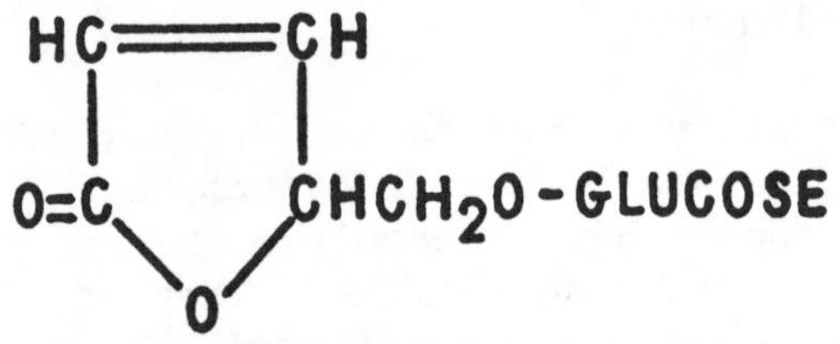

HC$=$CH
O$=$C   CHCH$_2$O$-$GLUCOSE
          O

ranunculin *(Ranunculus bulbosus)*

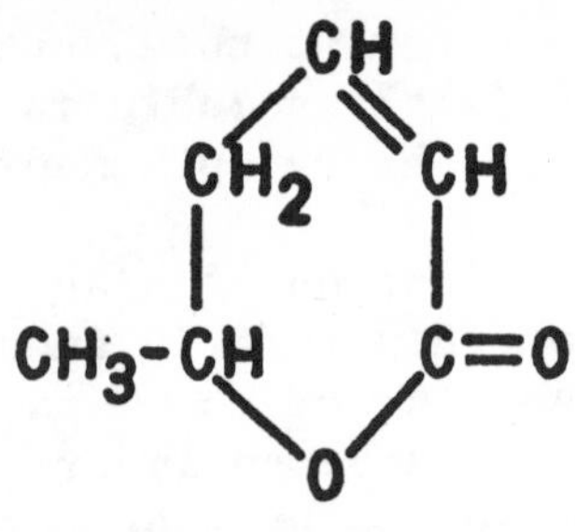

CH
CH$_2$ CH
CH$_3$$-$CH   C$=$O
          O

parasorbic acid *(Sorbus aucuparia)*

Lactones may be recognized by their titration behavior. Unlike the free acids, they do not neutralize sodium hydroxide rapidly in the cold, but do so on heating or with long standing. On reacidifying, the lactone usually reforms.

ISOLATION

In the standard procedure for isolating low molecular weight acids, the plant material is made strongly acidic (pH 1.0) with sulfuric acid and then extracted thoroughly (sometimes for several days) with peroxide-free ether. The ether extract contains the free acids which may be purified further. This procedure is most conveniently applied to dry material, but the difficulties of drying plant material safely may overcome the simplicity of the extraction procedure. Drying with heat removes volatile acids, destroys keto acids, causes ester formation, etc. Freeze drying is doubtless the best method since it precludes any chemical change, but volatile acids or esters may be lost. If the plant material is neutralized before drying, all acids will be present as non-volatile salts. Interfering lipids and esters may also be removed by a preliminary extraction of the neutralized material with ether.

Rather than ether extraction, the plant acids may be concentrated by the use of anion exchange resins. When an aqueous plant extract is passed through a column of weakly basic anion exchange resin in the hydroxide form, anions are absorbed. After washing the column, free acids may be eluted with 0.1 N HCl. If several fractions of eluate are taken, some separation of the acids can be achieved. If strongly basic anion exchange resin is used in the hydroxide form, there is danger that sugars in the plant extracts will be decomposed to form such acids as lactic and glycolic. Weakly basic resins avoid this difficulty but have a lower exchange capacity.

After preparation of a concentrated extract containing the total organic acids by one of the methods described above, separation of the individual components may be undertaken. If the acid mixture has been obtained by ether extraction, it must be transferred from ether to water by shaking with sodium hydroxide solution. Sodium sulfate may be removed by adjusting the aqueous solution to pH 1 H$_2$SO$_4$, adding two volumes of ethanol, and allowing to stand in the cold overnight. The solution of organic acids is then separated by filtration from precipitated sodium

sulfate. The lower fatty acids up to caproic (C_6) are volatile with
steam and may be prepared by a steam distillation. Caprylic (C_8) and
capric (C_{10}) acids are slightly volatile with steam but require long
periods of distillation for complete removal. Separation of the different
volatile fatty acids can be achieved by gas chromatography of the mixture or partition chromatography on silica gel using as solvents butanol
in chloroform for C_1-C_4 acids and methanol in isooctane for the C_5-C_{10}
acids. Fractional distillation is inefficient for the separation of acids
differing by only two carbon atoms and useful only when dealing with rather
large quantities of material.

Separation of the remaining non-volatile acids from each other has
often been carried out by converting the free acids to methyl esters and
fractionally distilling. It is, however, difficult to achieve complete
separations this way unless large amounts are involved. Another method
of separation relies on the different solubilities of lead, barium, and
calcium salts in water and in alcohol; but, again, this method is suitable
only if it is known that a limited number of acids is present so that the
strategy can be based on knowledge of the solubilities concerned. Special
methods for separating individual acids by such procedures will be found
in the general references. In particular, oxalic acid may be separated
from all others by the great insolubility of its calcium salt in water.
The keto acids may be removed from an aqueous solution by adding 2,4-
dinitrophenylhydrazine to precipitate them as hydrazones. The 2,4-dini-
trophenylhydrazones may be extracted with ether and further purified by
crystallization or subjected to a chromatographic separation. Column
chromatography of dinitrophenylhydrazones may be carried out on diatomaceous
earth ("Celite") with ethanol in ethyl ether as the solvent or on cellulose
powder with n-amyl alcohol saturated with ammonia as the solvent. The
instability of many keto acids makes it desirable to separate them as
derivatives rather than as the free acids.

The best generally applicable procedure for separating and isolating
the plant acids from a mixture is column chromatography either using ion
exchange methods or partition chromatography. Resins have more capacity
per gram than the partition absorbents; but the latter have the advantage
that an indicator may be incorporated to follow the passage of acid bands
through the column, and they apparently permit somewhat cleaner separations
than ion exchange resin columns do. Ion exchange separations may be carried out on strongly basic resins in the hydroxide form if sugars have been
removed by a preliminary purification step. No general procedure can be
recommended since preparation of the column and the method of elution will
vary with the acids to be separated. 0.1 N hydrochloric acid is often
used as an eluant, fractions collected arbitrarily, and analyzed for acids
by paper chromatography or specific color reactions. Appropriate fractions
can then be pooled and concentrated to obtain the pure acids. Several
hundred milligrams of mixed acids can be separated using only about 10 g.
of resin. Monocarboxylic acids come through first, followed by di - and
tricarboxylic compounds. Further discussion of ion exchange procedures
and their application to plant extracts can be found in references (11-13).

Separations by partition chromatography have used as support for the
aqueous stationary phase such substances as silica gel, Celite, or cellulose
powder. It is desirable either to suppress the ionization of the acids
by mixing some dilute mineral acid into the absorbant or to insure complete

ionization of the acids by mixing some ammonium hydroxide with the absorbant. In the latter case, an indicator such as bromcresol green can also be admixed and changes color where acidic bands are present. As the mobile phase, mixtures of 1-butanol and chloroform (saturated with the stationary phase) are most commonly used. The proportion of these two solvents is varied according to the polarities of the acids to be separated, and it is often recommended to increase gradually the ratio of butanol/chloroform as the development proceeds. In some cases the use of ethyl ether as a mobile phase separates pairs of acids that can not be resolved by butanol-chloroform. Some pairs of acids tenaciously resist separation. About 100 mg. of mixed acids can be separated on a 25 g. column of silica gel. General books on chromatographic methods offer much useful information regarding these techniques. See also the paper of Freeman (14).

Paper sheet chromatography (see below) can also be used to purify rather large amounts (up to 100 mg.) of acids if streaks of the acid mixture are applied to thick sheets of prewashed filter paper.

CHARACTERIZATION

Before attempting to identify the organic acids in a plant tissue or crude extract it is ordinarily desirable to make a preliminary separation of the acids from other plant constituents using one of the methods described in the previous section. Certain color tests and precipitation reactions may be used to indicate the presence of certain acids. Since each one of these represents a special case, the general references should be consulted for their application. General methods for analysis of mixtures of acids use paper chromatography, thin layer chromatography, or gas chromatography. The latter two techniques seem to be supplanting paper chromatography because of their better resolution and sensitivity, but most of the detection methods devised for paper sheets should be directly transferrable to TLC plates. In either thin layer or paper sheet chromatography the acids must be converted into a single ionic form to prevent streaking. They can be run as the free acids using highly acidic solvents or as ammonium salts by using solvents which contain ammonium hydroxide. The latter procedure must be used for the volatile acids. If a large amount of oxalic acid is present, it tends to smear and obscure other acids. It may be removed by a preliminary precipitation with calcium or by chromatography on acidic silica gel. Application of an acid mixture to the paper should carry about 10-100 µg of each acid unless very thick filter papers are used. One of the best general-purpose acidic solvents is the upper phase of an equilibrated mixture of 1-butanol/90% formic acid/water, 10:3:10, with the lower phase placed in the chamber. A common basic solvent mixture is 1-propanol/conc. ammonium hydroxide, 7:3 or 3:2. Two dimensional chromatograms are generally run using a basic solvent in the first direction and an acidic solvent in the second, but innumerable combinations are possible. Extensive paper chromatographic data are given in references (12, 15, 16). Thin layer procedures generally use cellulose powder or silica gel layers and solvents like the ones used with paper sheets (12-14, 17, 18). The most generally used detection reagents are acid-base indicators such as bromcresol green or bromthymol blue. Background color may be adjusted by exposing the paper sheet to ammonia vapor to make the best distinction of acidic areas. Spots indicated by this method usually fade rapidly. Another general detection procedure has been developed by Burness and King (19). In this method the chromatograms are developed in a solvent containing ethylamine. When the paper is dried, ethylamine remains as a salt where acids are present, and may be indicated with ninhydrin. Exposure of the paper to pyridine vapor and short-wave ultraviolet light shows up acids as white spots against a dark background (20). Special detection reagents are also available for different acids or classes of acids. Those that chelate iron can be revealed by an iron thiocyanate reaction (21). Keto acids can be first reacted with 2, 4-dinitrophenylhydrazine and the dinitrophenylhydrazones chromatographed (22). This procedure is better than chromatographing the free keto acids, which are subject to decomposition, although reagents have been developed to detect free keto acids on chromatograms. The dinitrophenylhydrazones can be eluted from the paper and identified by their absorption spectra in sodium hydroxide solution as well as by their R_F values. Other specific reagents will be found described in the general references.

If the apparatus and suitable standards are available, gas chromatographic analysis is extremely convenient for the organic acids. Nonvolatile acids must first be converted to trimethylsilyl derivatives (12, 23) For additional information gas chromatography can be coupled to mass spectroscopy (24). High performance liquid chromatography has also been used for these compounds (25).

METABOLIC PATHWAYS

A review of organic acid metabolism in plants has been presented by Beevers *et al.* (26).

As stated in the beginning of this chapter, most of the plant acids are either in or closely related to the citric acid cycle. Several other major pathways may be discussed in terms of their relationship to the citric acid cycle·

1. The so-called glyoxylate cycle was first found in several microorganisms. Its occurrence in higher plants has since been amply demonstrated, chiefly in germinating oil seeds where it functions in the conversion of fatty acids to carbohydrates. There is, however, some evidence that these reactions also occur in other places (27, 28). The glyoxylate cycle provides a by-pass between isocitrate and malate, a route for the synthesis of glyoxylate (and possibly oxalate), and a point of entry for acetate. The fact that acetate derived from breakdown of lipids can enter the glyoxylate by-pass and lead to a net synthesis of pyruvate provides a pathway for the synthesis of carbohydrate from fat since pyruvate can enter the glycolytic pathways leading back to starch. Pyruvic decarboxylation which forms acetate plus carbon dioxide is an irreversible reaction.

2. The fixation of carbon dioxide into organic acids is a very widespread process. The formation of C_4 acids in the light is a crucial part of photosynthetic CO_2 fixation in certain plants called "C_4 plants" that are noted for their high efficiency in photosynthesis. Tropical grasses such as sugar cane are the most

studied members of this group, but other plants also belong to it.
Phosphoenolpyruvic acid is the immediate acceptor of carbon
dioxide, and the immediate product is oxalacetic acid. The further
cyclic pathways are complex and still under active investigation.
They lead to release of carbon dioxide that is refixed by
ribulose bisphosphate carboxylase and regeneration of the phosphoenolpyruvic acid. Many reviews are available on this subject
(29, 30). The dark fixation of carbon dioxide into organic
acids is also important especially in the succulent xerophytes
where CO_2 is fixed into acids at night and then recycled to
carbohydrates during the day. Carboxylation of phosphoenolpyruvic acid is the key reaction here also, and the resulting
oxalacetic acid is then quickly reduced to malic acid which
accumulates (31-33).

3. Some acids seem structurally related to components of the citric
    acid cycle but the pathways connecting them have not been demon-
    strated. They have been so indicated in the accompanying figure
    by question marks beside the arrows.

4. The two-carbon acids glycolic and oxalic seem obviously related
    to glyoxylic acid by reduction and oxidation respectively, and
    could, therefore, be represented on a branch from the glyoxylate
    cycle. There is experimental evidence for such a relationship
    functioning in both directions (34, 35). In addition glycolic
    acid appears as an early product of photosynthetic carbon dioxide
    fixation, from the functioning of ribulose bisphosphate carboxylase
    as an oxygenase, so that the ribulose bisphosphate rather then
    accepting CO_2 is decomposed to phosphoglycolic acid and 3-
    phosphoglyceric acid. Glycolic acid then results from action of a
    phosphatase on the phosphoglycolic acid (36, 37). Successive
    oxidations of glycolic acid yield glyoxylic acid, oxalic acid
    (38, 39), formic acid (40), and carbon dioxide (41). In spinach
    the major precursor of oxalate is not glyoxylate but oxalacetate (42).
    An alternative route also leading to CO_2 from glycolate involves
    transamination of glyoxylate to glycine and then two molecules
    of glycine going to one molecule of serine plus a molecule of
    CO_2 (43). Serine produced from this pathway may be an important
    precursor of pyruvate and acetyl-CoA in some tissues (44).
    Condensation of glyoxylic acid with oxalacetic acid yields
    α-keto-γ-hydroxy-glutaric acid, a constituent of *Oxalis* spp. (45).

5. Malonic acid can be made by oxidation of propionic acid or de-
    carboxylation of oxalacetic acid, but the major pathway is pro-
    bably carboxylation of acetyl-CoA (46).

6. Chelidonic acid is probably derived from a condensation of C_3
    and C_4 units related to phosphoenolpyruvic acid and erythrose-
    4-phosphate (47).

7. Parasorbic acid is probably derived from the acetate-malonate
    pathway rather than from a hexose (48). Its immediate precursor
    is a glucoside (49).

8. In geranium tartaric acid is made by cleavage of ascorbic acid
    (or a closely related compound) between C-2 and C-3 giving oxalic

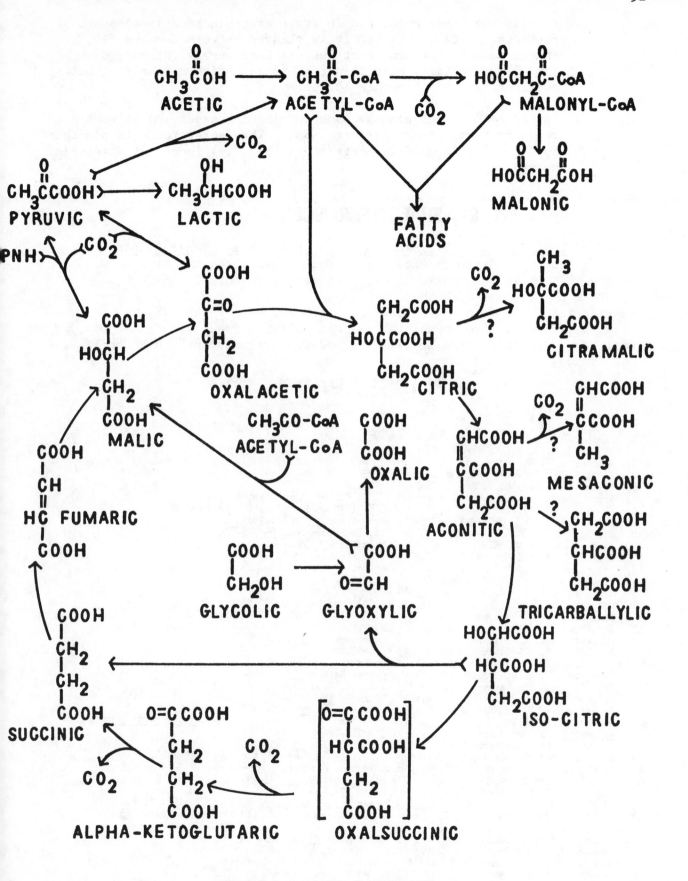

FIGURE 3-1: ACID PATHWAYS

acid as the other product. In grape ascorbic acid is also the precursor of tartaric; but it is cleaved between C-4 and C-5, and gives a C_2 fragment that has not been surely identified (50, 51). Tartaric acid is not a highly active metabolite, but some turnover of it occurs (52).

9. Lactic acid is produced by some germinating seeds and in some roots by reduction of pyruvate (53). The isomer found in plants is D-(-)-lactic acid in contrast to the L-(+) isomer of anaerobic muscle.

GENERAL REFERENCES

Buch, M. L. (1960) A Bibliography of Organic Acids in Higher Plants, Agricultural Handbook #164, U. S. Dept. Agric., Washingtin, D. C.
Ranson, S. L., "Non-Volatile Mono-, Di-, and Tricarboxylic Acids," in Paech & Tracey 2 539-582.
Scarisbrick, R., "Volatile Acids," in Paech & Tracey 2 444-477.
Wang, D., "Nonvolatile Organic Acids," in Miller 3 74-111.
Wolf, J., "Nichtfluchtige Mono-, Di-, und Tricarbonsauren," in Paech & Tracey 2 478-538.

BIBLIOGRAPHY

1. Yoshihara, T. and Sakamura, S. (1977) Agric. Biol. Chem. 41 2427-2429.
2. Yoshida, S., Tazaki, K. and Minamikawa, T. (1975) Phytochemistry 14 195-197.
3. Zindler-Frank, E. (1976) Z. Pflanzenphysiol. 80 1-13.
4. Atkinson, M. R. and Eckermann, G. (1965) Austral. J. Biol. Sci. 18 437-439.
5. Barton, D. H. R., Brown, B. D., Ridley, D. D., Widdowson, D. A., Keys, A. J. and Leaver, C. J. (1975) J. Chem. Soc. Perkin I 2069-2076.
6. Brokaw, C. J. (1958) J. Exptl. Biol. 35 192-196.
7. Erner, Y., Reuveni, O. and Goldschmidt, E. E. (1975) Plant Physiol. 56 279-282.
8. Clark, R. B., Tiffin, L. O. and Brown, J. C. (1973) Plant Physiol. 52 147-150.
9. Kringstad, R. and Nordal, A. (1975) Phytochemistry 14 1868-1870.
10. Schmid, H. (1957) Coll. Intern. Centre Nat. Recherche Sci. 64 303-316.
11. Jandera, P. and Churáček, J. (1973) J. Chromatog. 86 351-421.
12. Stumpf, D. K. and Burris, R. H. (1979) Anal. Biochem. 95 311-315.
13. Tokumitsu, Y. and Ui, M. (1974) Anal. Biochem. 59 110-121.
14. Freeman, G. G. (1967) J. Chromatog. 28 338-343.
15. Howe, J. R. (1960) J. Chromatog. 3 389-405.
16. Jorysch, D., Sarris, P. and Marcus, S. (1962) Food Technol. 16 No. 3 90-93.
17. Beaudoin, A. R., Moorjani, S. and Lemonde, A. (1973) Can. J. Chem. 51 318-320.
18. Hansen, S. A. (1976) J. Chromatog. 124 123-126.
19. Burness, A. T. H. and King, H. K. (1958) Biochem. J. 68 32P.
20. Bachur, N. R. (1965) Anal. Biochem. 13 463-468.
21. Firmin, J. L. and Gray, D. O. (1974) J. Chromatog. 94 294-297.
22. Isherwood, F. A. and Cruickshank, D. M. (1954) Nature 173 121-122.
23. Boland, R. L. and Garner, G. B. (1973) J. Agric. Food Chem. 21 661-665.
24. Schramm, R. W. (1979) Biochem. Physiol. Pflanzen 174 398-403.
25. Turkelson, V. T. and Richards, M. (1978) Anal. Chem. 50 1420-1423.
26. Beevers, H., Stiller, M. L. and Butt, V. S. (1966) in Steward, F. C. ed. Plant Physiology a Treatise, Academic Press, N. Y., Vol. IVB 119-262.
27. Newman, J. C. and Briggs, D. E. (1976) Phytochemistry 15 1453-1458.
28. Hunt, L., Skvarla, J. J., and Fletcher, J. S. (1978) Plant Physiol. 61 1010-1013.
29. Hatch, M. D. and Kagawa, T. (1974) Arch. Biochem. Biophys. 160 346-349.
30. Ray, T. B. and Black, C. C., Jr. (1977) Plant Physiol. 60 193-196.
31. Osmund, C. B. (1978) Ann. Rev. Plant Physiol. 29 379-414.
32. Kluge, M. and Ting, I. P. (1978) Crassulacean Acid Metabolism, Springer-Verlag, N. Y.
33. Spalding, M. H., Schmitt, M. R., Ku, S. B. and Edwards, G. E. (1979) Plant Physiol. 63 738-743.
34. Sinha, S. K. and Cossins, E. A. (1965) Biochem. J. 96 254-261.
35. Tanner, W. H. and Beevers, H. (1965) Plant Physiol. 40 971-976.
36. Andrews, T. J., Lorimer, G. H. and Tolbert, N. E. (1973) Biochemistry 12 11-18.
37. Jensen, R. G. and Bahr, J. T. (1977) Ann. Rev. Plant Physiol. 28 379-400.
38. Seal, S. N. and Sen, S. P. (1970) Plant and Cell Physiol. 11 119-128.
39. Chang, C.-C. and Beevers, H. (1968) Plant Physiol. 43 1821-1828.

40. Giovanelli, J. (1966) Biochim. Biophys. Acta 118 124-143.
41. Zelitch, I. (1972) Plant Physiol. 50 109-113.
42. Glidewell, S. M., Raven, J. A. (1979) Plant Physiol. 63 Suppl. 614.
43. Kisaki, T. and Tolbert, N. E. (1970) Plant and Cell Physiol. 11 247-258.
44. Hill, H. M., Shah, S. P. J. and Roberts, L. J. (1970) Phytochemistry 9 749-755.
45. Morton, R. K. and Wells, J. R. E. (1964) Nature 201 477-479.
46. Cavalié, G. and Cailliau-Commanay, L. (1971) Compt. Rend. 272 3275-3278.
47. Malcolm, M. J. and Gear, J. R. (1971) Can. J. Biochem. 49 412-416.
48. Crombie, L. and Firth, P. A. (1968) J. Chem. Soc. (C) 2852-2856.
49. Pyysalo, H. and Kuusi, T. (1974) J. Food Sci. 39 636-638.
50. Ruffner, H. and Rast, D. (1974) Z. Pflanzenphysiol. 73 45-55.
51. Williams, M., Saito, K. and Loewus, F. A. (1979) Phytochemistry 18 953-956.
52. Takimoto, K., Saito, K. and Kasai, Z. (1977) Phytochemistry 16 1641-1645.
53. Davies, D. D., Grego, S. and Kenworthy, P. (1974) Planta 118 297-310.

Chapter 4
AROMATIC COMPOUNDS

The chemical concept of aromaticity, of course, has nothing to do with aroma. For present purposes it will be sufficient to define aromatic compounds as those whose structural formulas contain at least one benzene ring. A great variety of plant constituents may be classed as aromatic compounds, and several groups of these are included in other chapters. The unity within the present chapter comes from the presumption that all compounds included are biosynthetically derived via 5-dehydroquinic acid. Flavonoids and aromatic amino acids are also derived from 5-dehydroquinic acid but are more conveniently discussed in Chapters 9 and 10 respectively. Aromatic compounds, such as anthraquinones and chromones, which are probably derived from acetate, are covered in Chapter 6; terpenoid aromatic compounds are in Chapter 8, and aromatic amines in Chapter 15.

SIMPLE PHENOLS AND AROMATIC ACIDS

The simple phenols are colorless solids when pure, but usually oxidize and become dark on exposure to air. Water solubility increases with the number of hydroxyl groups present, but solubility in polar organic solvents is generally high. Phenols which are only slightly soluble in water are readily soluble in dilute, aqueous solutions of sodium hydroxide; but under basic conditions their rate of oxidation is increased considerably, so that any prolonged treatment with strong alkali should be avoided.

There are a few naturally occurring aromatic acids which have carboxyl as their only functional group. However, most natural aromatic acids also have phenolic groups and thus share properties with other phenols. Water insoluble phenolic acids can be distinguished from other water insoluble phenols by the fact that they may be dissolved in sodium bicarbonate solution whereas the less acidic phenols require more alkaline solvents. Many natural phenolic compounds have at least one hydroxyl group combined as an ether, ester or glycoside rather than free. Ethers or esters are less soluble in water than the parent phenols while the glycosides are more water-soluble. One reviewer of this area suggests that free phenols are mostly in woody tissues whereas phenols in other sites are glycosylated (1).

The natural aromatic compounds are usually characterized by having at least one aliphatic side chain attached to the aromatic ring. The variety of possible side chains combined with the structural variations already mentioned creates a bewildering array of substances in this class. In certain cases the complexity of the aliphatic side chain makes the aromatic portion of the molecule appear to be an almost incidental structural feature. Table 4-1 depicts a few simple aromatic compounds found in plants, but it is impossible in so little space to more than hint at the variety found in nature.

Several simple aromatic compounds are of physiological or economic interest. Vanillin, methyl salicylate, and piperonal are responsible for the odors of vanilla, wintergreen (*Gaultheria Procumbens*), and heliotrope respectively.

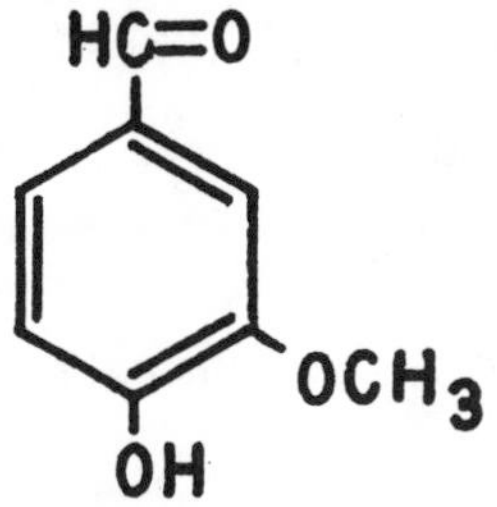

Vanillin 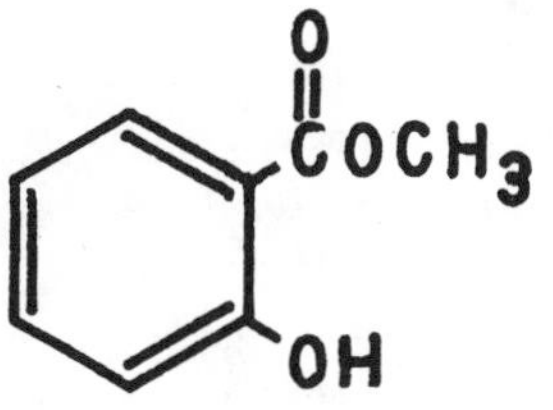   Methyl Salicylate 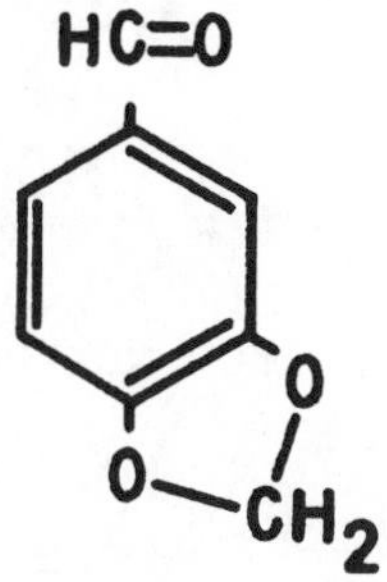   Piperonal

The physiological activities of plant phenolic compounds are many and diverse. There are at least suspicions that some may have functional importance in the internal physiology of the plants that make them, whereas others may be important in ecological relationships. Still others show physiological effects on animals, which may be quite fortuitous. In the first category there have been several suggestions for a role of simple phenols in photosynthetic electron transport (2, 3) and in the regulation of the activities of such enzymes as indole-3-acetic acid oxidase (4, 5), glucose-6-phosphate dehydrogenase (6), and peroxidase (7). As more general phenomena there are phenolic inhibitors of seed germination (8, 9), of membrane transport processes (10, 11), and several types of hormone-induced growth (8, 12-14). Phenols that absorb ultraviolet light may have a role in guiding pollinating insects to flowers that contain them (15). Some plants appear to gain resistance to fungal attack as a result of their phenol content, but others show no such correlation (16, 17). Some phenolic constituents are repellent or toxic to herbivores (18, 19) while others affect rodent reproduction (20). The powerful irritant activity of poison ivy, poison sumac and other members of the Anacardiaceae is well-known and results from the presence of ortho-diphenols with long, unsaturated side-chains (21). Similar, but less powerful, irritants are found in fruits of *Ginkgo biloba* (22, 23) and in ginger root (24). Still less toxic alkyl meta-diphenols are found in several cereal grains, especially rye (25). Finally, in contrast to such irritant compounds, kavain and related constituents of kava-kava root (*Piper methysticum*) are responsible for the sedative and intoxicating action of this plant.

BENZOQUINONES

Benzoquinones are common fungal pigments but rarely encountered in higher plants in noticeably high concentrations. Hydroxy- and methoxy-benzoquinones are found in a few higher plants and are of some economic importance. 2-methoxybenzoquinone appears as a pink coloration in whole wheat flour after long-standing as the result of hydrolysis and oxidation

TABLE 4-1. SOME SIMPLE AROMATIC COMPOUNDS,
STRUCTURES AND OCCURRENCE

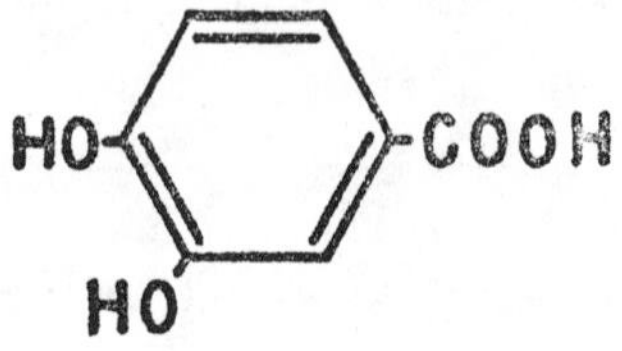

protocatechuic acid (*Allium* spp.)

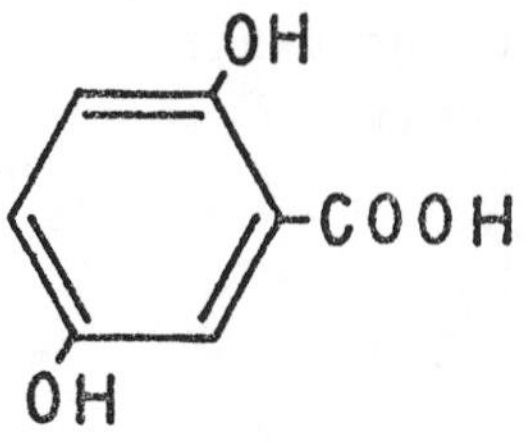

gentisic acid (*Theobroma cacao*)

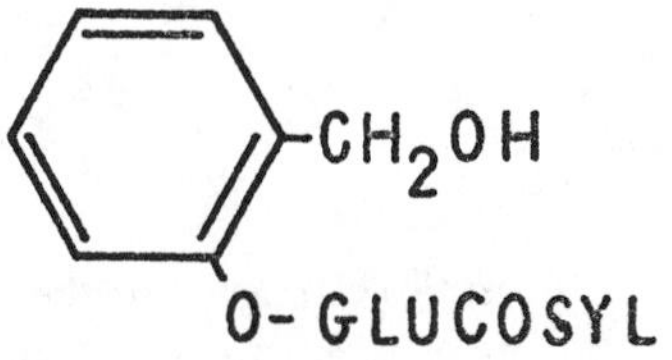

salicin (bark of *Salix* spp.)

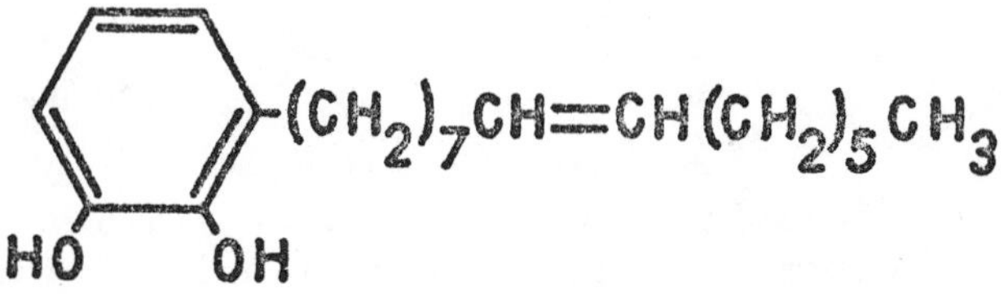

urushiol (*Rhus* spp.)

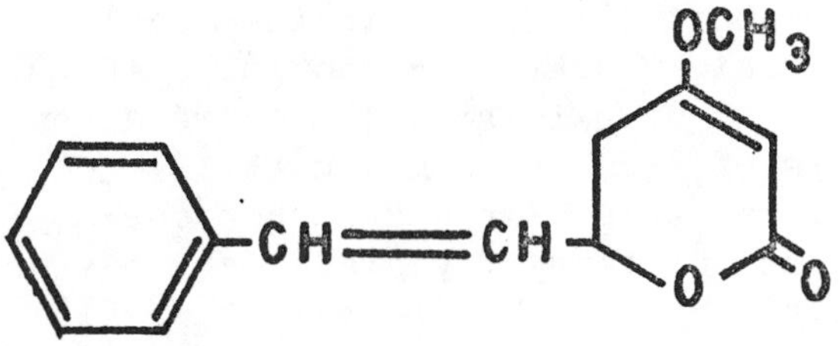

kavain (*Piper methysticum*)

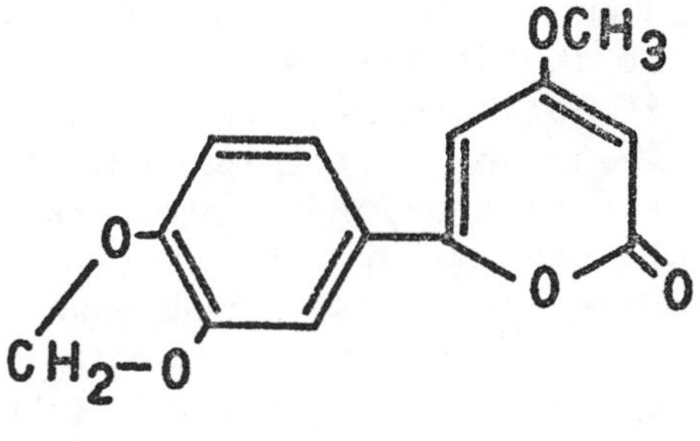

4-methoxyparacotoin (*Aniba duckei*)

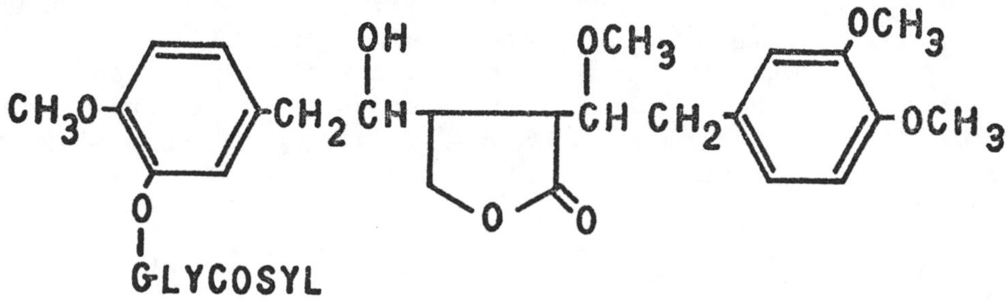

tracheloside (*Trachelospermum asiaticum*)

of a glucoside present in wheat germ. A contact allergen present in several
woods is 2, 6- dimethoxy-1, 4- benzoquinone (26). The dried fruit of
Embelia ribes is used in India for treatment of tapeworm and skin diseases.
Its active ingredient, embelin is a dihydroxyquinone. Other alkylhydroxy-
quinones similar to embelin are found in a few other plants which have
been used for many years as vermifuges.

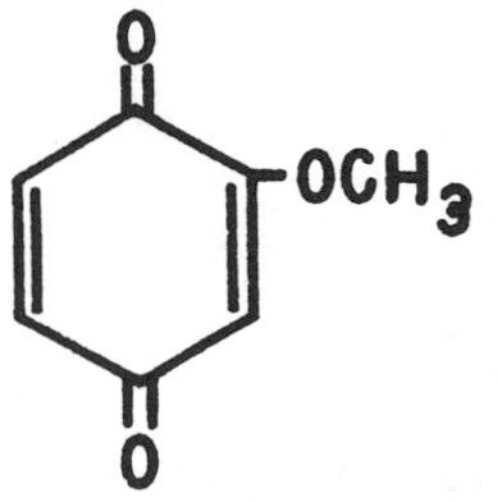

2-Methoxybenzoquinone 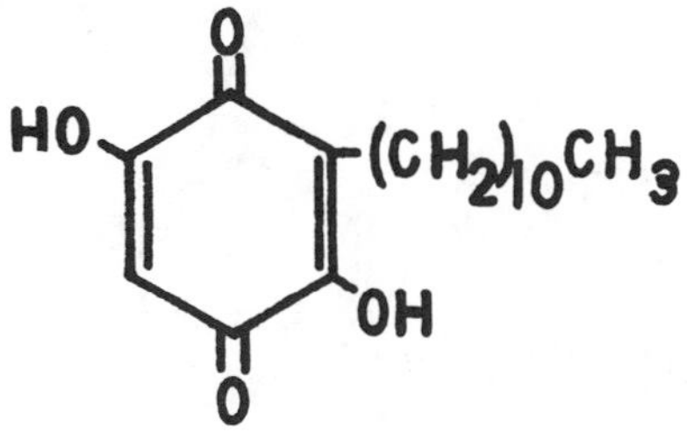   Embelin

These hydroxybenzoquinones are orange, crystalline solids which are
readily reduced by sodium dithionite to colorless hydroquinones. Alkaline
solutions are blue-purple in color. Naturally occurring quinones are
extensively reviewed by Thomson (27).

The plastoquinones of chloroplasts are functionally important benzoquinone derivatives, believed to serve as redox carriers in photosynthesis
(28). They have isoprenoid side-chains of varying length. Among the
plastoquinones, PQ-A (or PQ-9) is best-known and usually found at the
highest concentration, but there are at least 12 others in two groups--
the C-type having an allylic hydroxyl and the B-type having this hydroxyl
esterified with palmitic acid. There may also be a Z-type having two
hydroxyl groups, one of them esterified (29). In some leaves there is
more C-type than PQ-A. All have the same ultraviolet absorption spectrum
(30).

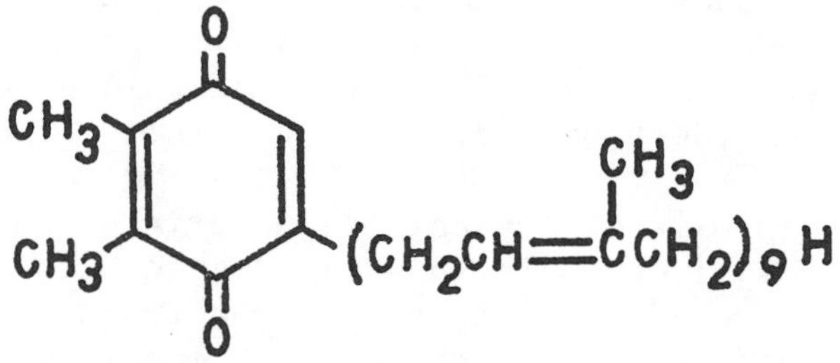

plastoquinone - 9

The ubiquinones of mitochondria closely resemble in structure the
plastoquinones, and there are several members differing in the number of
isoprenoid residues in the side-chain. They presumably act as hydrogen
carriers of the respiratory chain, but their precise role is still unclear
(31, 32).

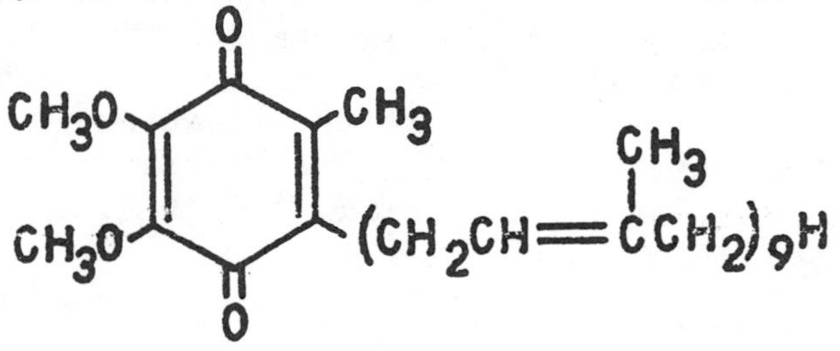

ubiquinone - 9

The tocopherols, or various forms of vitamin E, are important anti-oxidants found in seed oils (e.g. wheat germ). The predominant member of this group is α-tocopherol; others differ from it by having fewer   methyl groups. While their relationship to the ubiquinones and plastoquinones is not immediately obvious, they could be derived from an ubiquinone-type structure by reduction and ring closure.

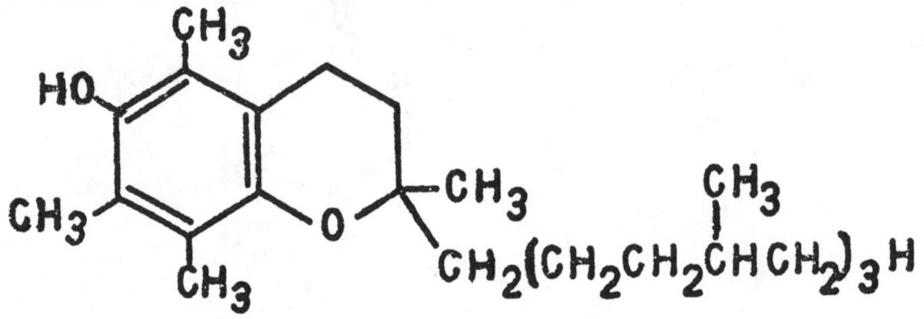

α-tocopherol

The various tocopherols are apparently interconvertible in the plant and may possibly act as growth or differentiation regulators or in photo-synthetic electron transport (33-35). In general α-tocopherol seems to occur in plastids and the others in the cytosol (36).

NAPHTHOQUINONES

A large number of naphthoquinones are found in nature as yellow-red plant pigments. Vitamin K_1 and related K vitamins are functionally the most important of the naphthoquinones. Like the ubiquinones they have isoprenoid side-chains; and also like the ubiquinones they are thought to play some role in electron transport (36). Previous controversy about the occurrence of vitamin K_1 in chloroplasts has been resolved, and it is definitely present (37). The structures of vitamin K_1 and of some other naturally occurring naphthoquinones are given in Table 4-2 along with their natural occurrence. Dimeric derivatives of naphthoquinone are found in *Diospyros* spp. where they are responsible for antihelminthic properties of the fruit and the dark color of the wood (38, 39).

All of these quinones are oils or crystalline materials ranging in color from yellow to red and easily soluble in such organic solvents as benzene. Some of them are toxic and anti-microbial; plants containing them have been used as drugs and poisons since prehistoric times (e.g. chima-philin, plumbagin, eleutherin). Others have been equally important as dyestuffs. Lawsone is the chief ingredient of henna; lapachol is extracted from various woods and used for dying cotton; alkannin is the coloring matter obtained by alkaline treatment of the root of *Alkanna tinctoria* (dyer's bugloss). At least a few of these compounds do not exist as such in plants, but are formed during the extraction process. Thus the native form of alkannin is an ester of angelic acid with the hydroxyl group of the side-chain; juglone is formed by hydrolysis and oxidation of 1-hydro-juglone-4-β-D glucoside. Plumbagin is formed by hydrolysis and oxidation of dianellin, a yellow naphthol glycoside of *Dianella laevis*.

PHENYLPROPANE COMPOUNDS IN GENERAL

A large number of natural aromatic compounds may be described as

TABLE 4-2. SOME NATURALLY-OCCURRING NAPHTHOQUINONES

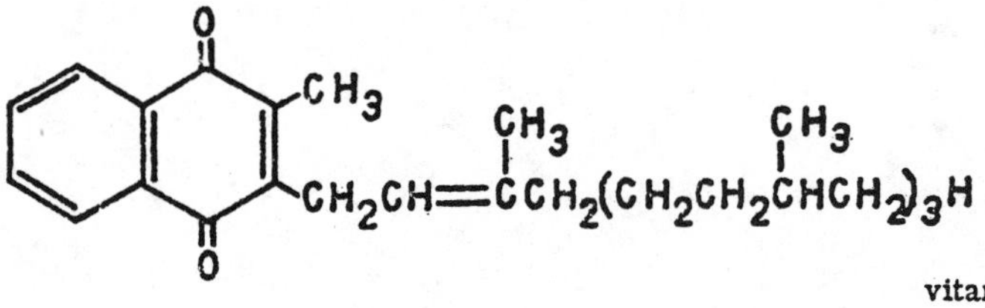

vitamin K_1 (widespread)

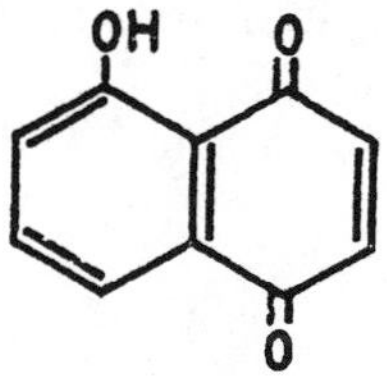

juglone *(Juglans regia)*

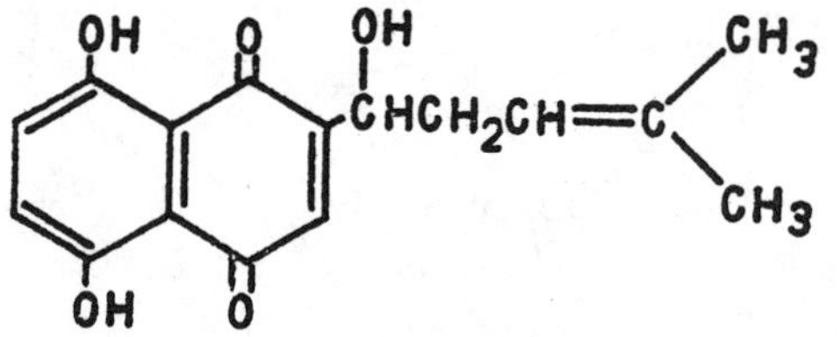

alkannin *(Alkanna tinctoria* and other *Boraginaceae)*

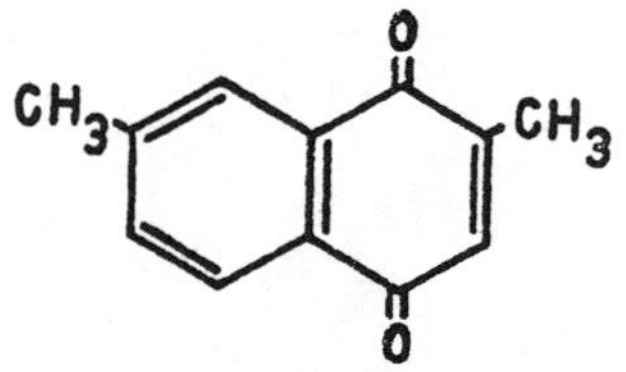

chimaphilin (Several species of the *Ericaceae)*

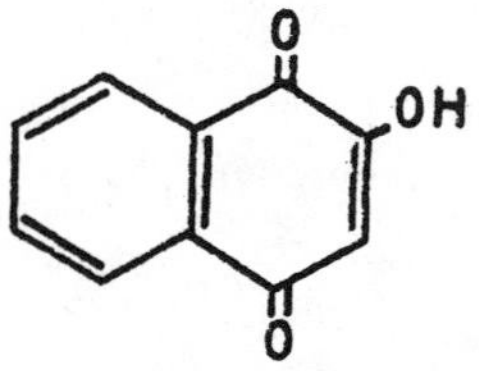

lawsone *(Lawsonia alba)*

Table 4-2. Continued

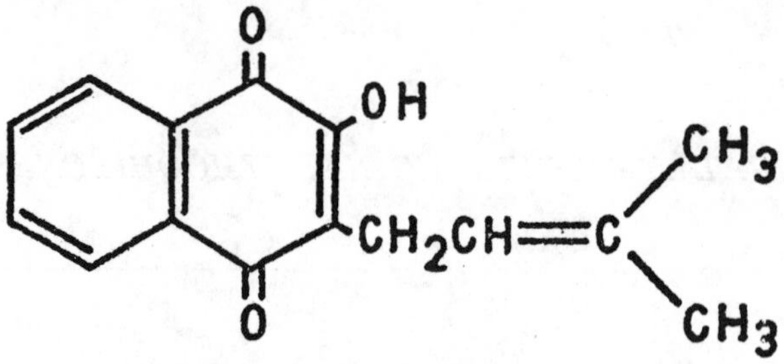

lapachol (*Tecoma* spp.)

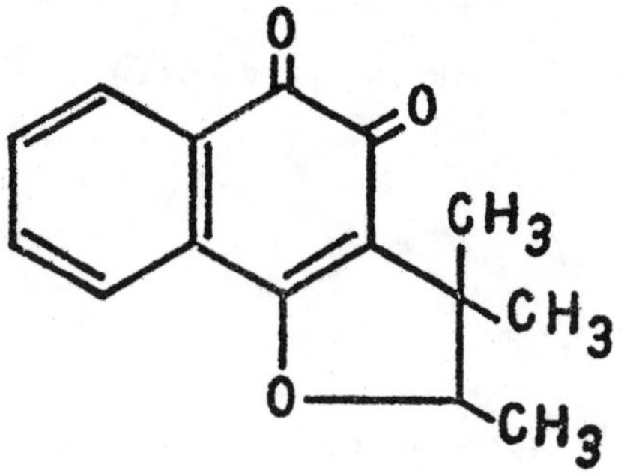

dunnione *(Streptocarpus dunni)*

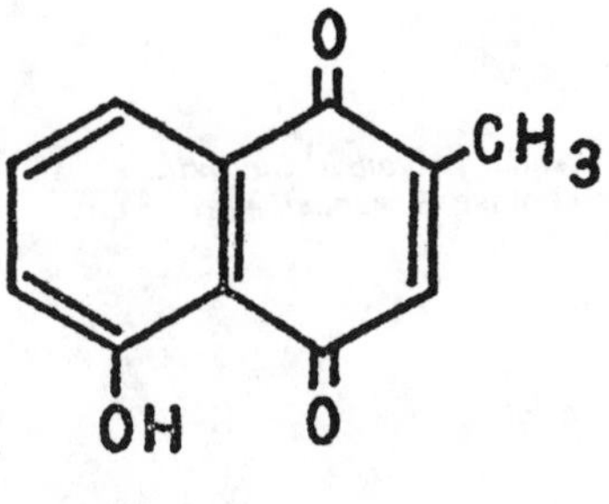

plumbagin
(*Plumbago* and *Drosera* spp.)

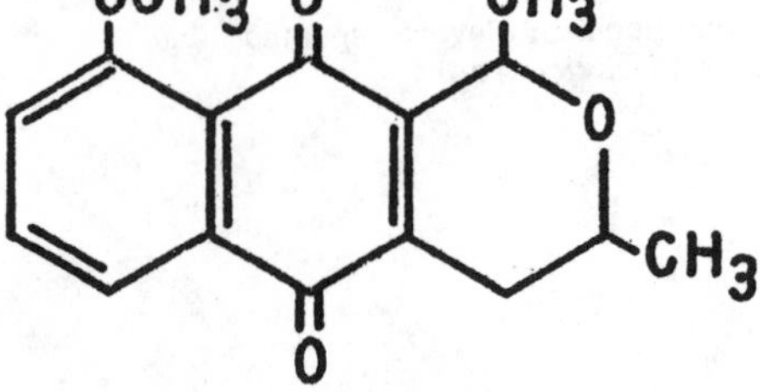

eleutherin *(Eleutherine bulbosa)*

phenylpropane derivatives since they have a benzene ring attached to C-1
of a three carbon chain:

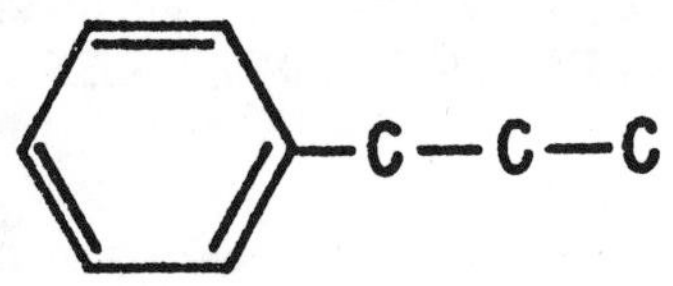

A few other compounds are found which have a phenyl group attached to the
middle carbon of the C_3 chain. Some of these may be formed by rearrangement
of 1-phenylpropane compounds, whereas others seem to be more closely
related to the monoterpenoids. Examples of these two types of 2-phenyl-
propane derivatives are, respectively, tropic acid and thymoquinone:

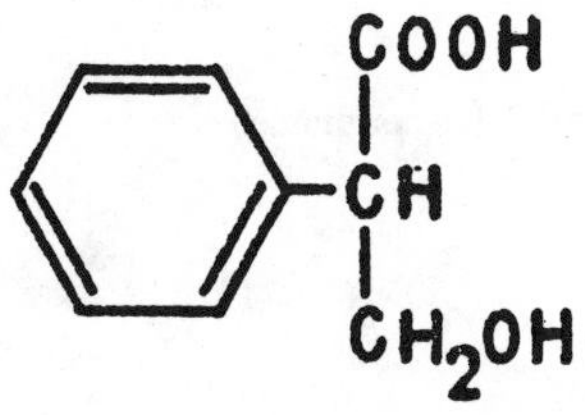

Tropic Acid 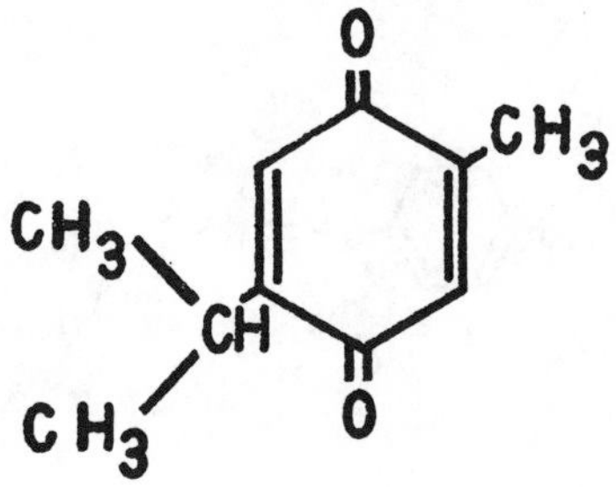   Thymoquinone

Other 1-phenyl propane derivatives will be discussed in more detail in
following sections of this chapter. The flavonoids (Chapter 9) also contain a phenylpropane group joined to a phloroglucinol group.

OPEN-CHAIN PHENYLPROPANE DERIVATIVES

     Some open-chain phenylpropane derivatives are among the best-known
and most widespread natural aromatic compounds. Most of them may be
described as hydroxylated cinnamic acid derivatives:

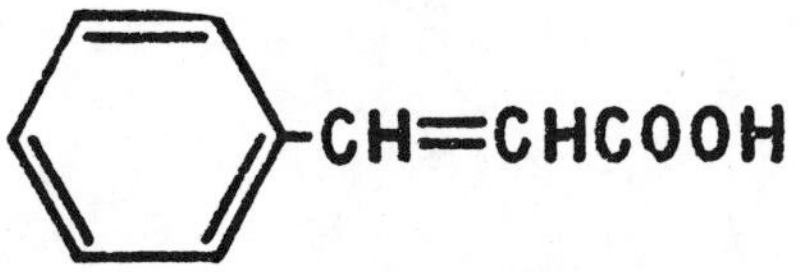

Cinnamic Acid

They usually have the trans configuration, but exposure to ultraviolet
light can cause isomerization to cis (40). The variations on this basic
structure are distinguished by different patterns of ring hydroxylation or
methoxylation and modification of the carboxyl group by esterification or
reduction to an aldehyde or alcohol. There are also other open-chain
phenylpropanes which cannot conveniently be described at all as derivatives of
cinnamic acid. Table 4-3 illustrates some of the various compounds of
this class.

TABLE 4-3.   SOME OPEN CHAIN PHENYLPROPANE DERIVATIVES, STRUCTURES AND OCCURRENCE

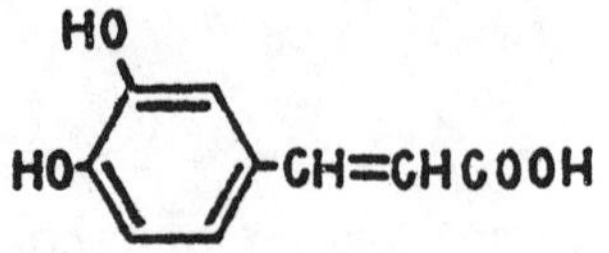

caffeic acid (widespread)

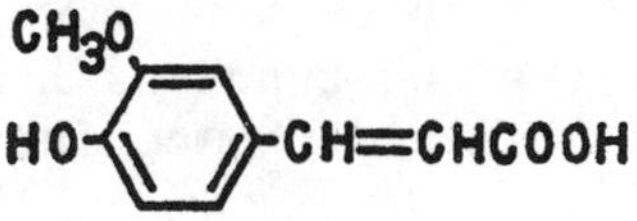

ferulic acid (widespread)

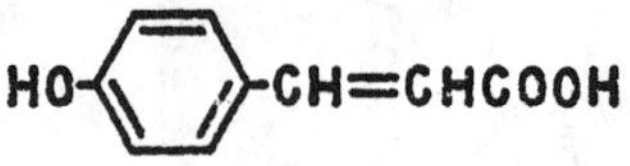

p-coumaric acid (widespread)

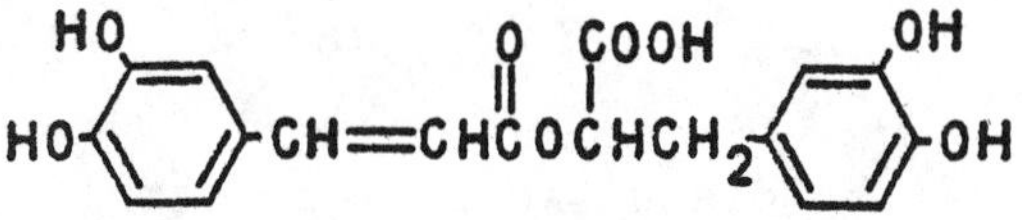

rosmarinic acid
(*Rosmarinus officinalis*)

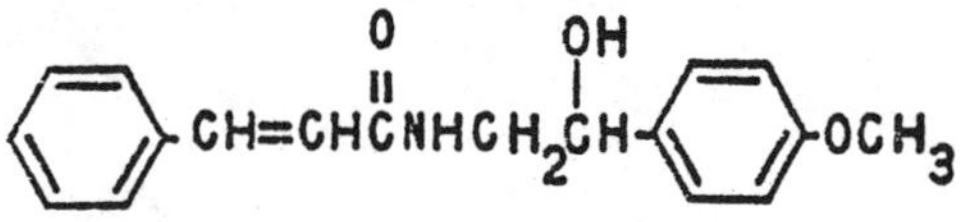

aegelin (*Aegle marmelus*)

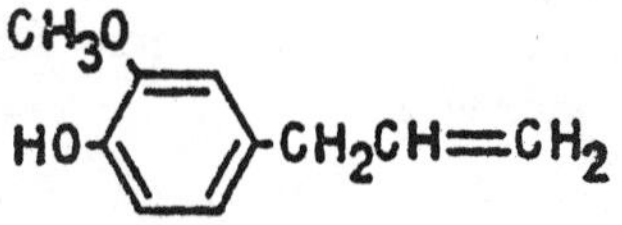

eugenol (*Eugenia aromatica*)

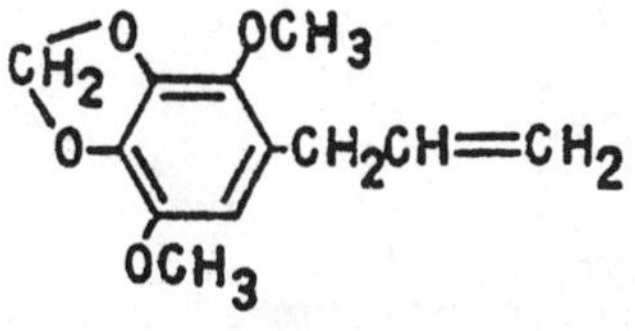

apiol (*Petroselinum crispum*)

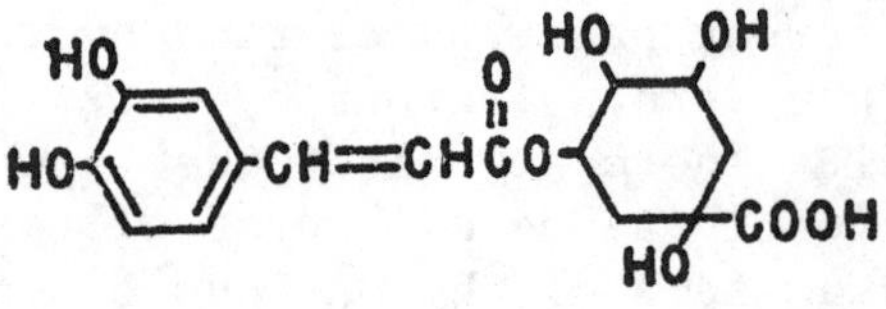

chlorogenic acid (widespread)

Caffeic acid is one of the most widespread of all plant phenolic compounds (41), followed closely by ferulic and p-coumaric acids. Caffeic acid, however, frequently occurs as esters rather than the free acid. The best-known caffeic acid ester is chlorogenic acid (Table 4-3), but there exists a whole series of isomeric compounds in which the esterification is at other hydroxyl groups of the quinic acid moiety, and some in which two molecules of caffeic acid are esterified with one molecule of quinic acid (42, 43). All of these compounds which are esters formed from two hydroxy acids are known as "depsides". Other examples have caffeic acid esterified with tartaric acid (43, 44) or malic acid (45). Sugar esters of various hydroxycinnamic acids are also widespread in plants (46, 47). Polysaccharides and proteins have also been found acylated with these acids (48-50). *Nicotiana* spp. have putrescine derivatives of them (51, 52), and water ferns have sulfate esters (53). Some of these derivatives could have a role as intermediates in lignin biosynthesis (54) or protein biosynthesis (50).

The simple phenylpropanes are colorless, crystalline solids whose chemical reactivity may be understood by reference to the particular functional groups which are present. Those members having several free phenolic hydroxyls are readily oxidized in the air especially under alkaline conditions. The oxidation products are dark-colored polymers. Green substances are formed by oxidation of caffeic acid esters in the presence of ammonia or amino acids. This formation of a green substance accounts for the name of chlorogenic acid. The more volatile members of this group are very important commercially since they contribute the characteristic flavors and odors to many valuable herbs and spices. Cinnamaldehyde of cinnamon, eugenol of cloves, and apiol of parsley are but three of the best-known examples of phenylpropane flavor compounds.

COUMARINS AND ISOCOUMARINS

The coumarins are lactones of o-hydroxycinnamic acid. This basic nucleus with its ring-numbering is as follows:

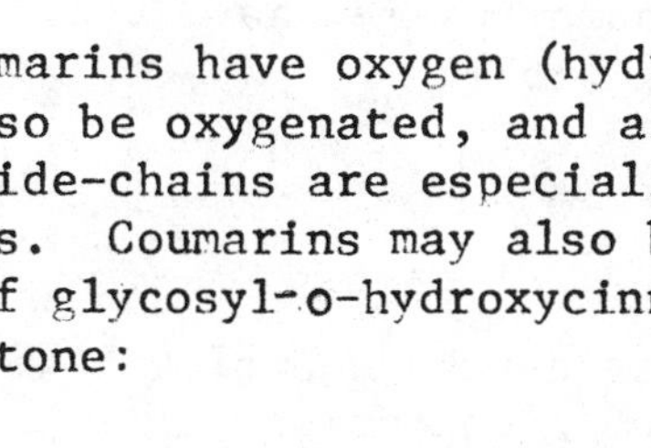

Almost all natural coumarins have oxygen (hydroxyl or alkoxyl) at C-7. Other positions may also be oxygenated, and alkyl side-chains are frequently present. Isoprenoid side-chains are especially common. Some coumarins are found as glycosides. Coumarins may also be artifacts which arise from enzymatic hydrolysis of glycosyl-o-hydroxycinnamic acid and immediate cyclization to the lactone:

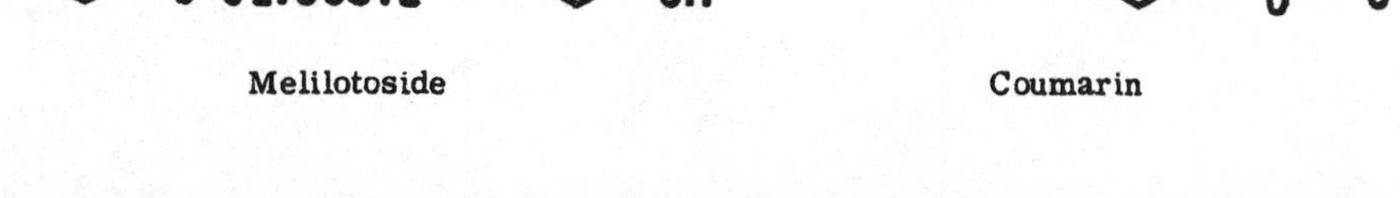

Melilotoside   Coumarin

Ring closure to the lactone occurs only with o-hydroxy-cis-cinnamic acids (coumarinic acids). Ortho-hydroxy-trans-cinnamic acids (coumaric acids) do not form lactones directly. However, isomerization to the cis form can be brought about by treatment with ultraviolet light whereupon immediate ring closure ensues. The lactone ring of coumarins is opened by hydrolysis with warm alkali, but immediately reforms on acidification. Fusion with alkali splits off the alkyl group forming simple phenols (e.g. resorcinol from umbelliferone).

Structures of several natural coumarins are given in Table 4-4. They occur in all parts of plants and are widely distributed in the plant kingdom but especially common in grasses, orchids, citrus fruits, and legumes. Scopoletin is the most common coumarin of higher plants.

Much rarer than the coumarins are isocoumarins or 3,4-benzopyrones. A dihydroisocoumarin, phyllodulcin, is the sweet principle of *Hydrangea macrophylla* (55), while another is responsible for the bitter taste occasionally found in carrots that have been infected with a fungus or treated with ethylene (56). Bergenin from rhizomes of *Bergenia crassifolia* is an unusual isocoumarin which contains a fused ring apparently derived from glucose (57):

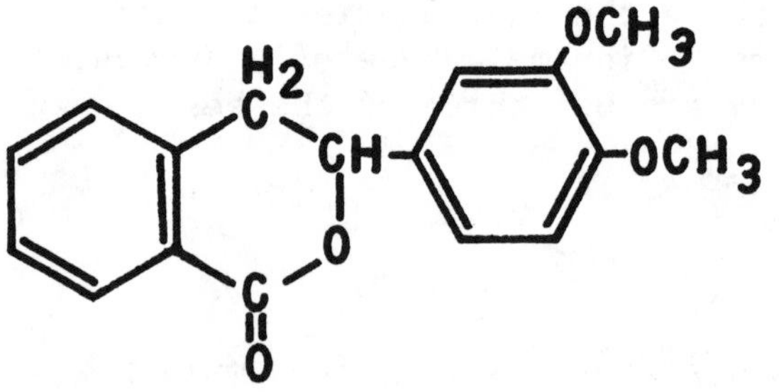

Phyllodulcin

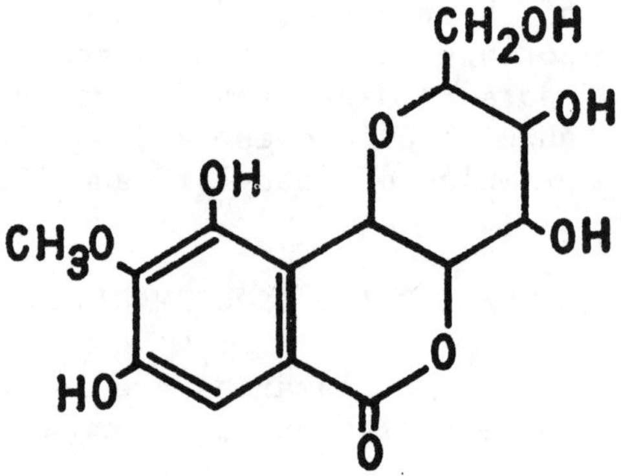

Bergenin

The coumarins have varied physiological effects on both plants and animals. In plants their effects may be exercised by inhibiting or stimulating indole-3-acetic acid oxidase (7, 59), stimulating ethylene production (60), inhibiting cellulose synthesis (61, 62) or increasing membrane permeability (63). Simple coumarins may have toxic effects on microorganisms (64). Mammein is insecticidal (65).

FURANO- AND PYRANOCOUMARINS

Several natural products are known which have a pyran or furan ring fused with the benzene ring of a coumarin:

TABLE 4-4.   SOME NATURALLY OCCURRING COUMARINS

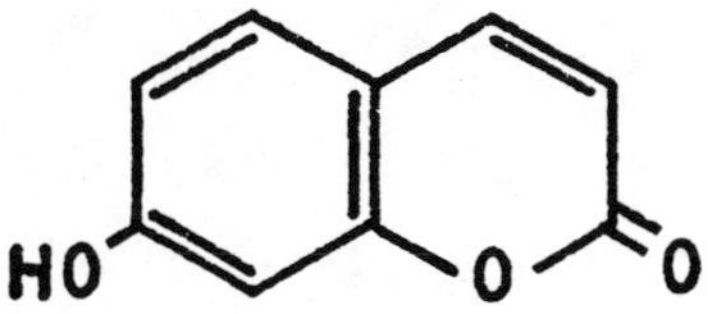

umbelliferone
(resins of *Umbelliferae*)

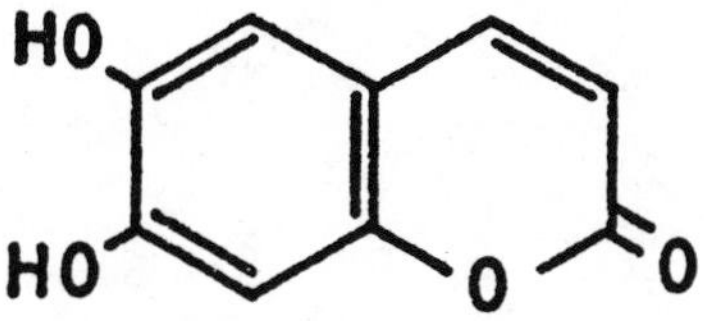

esculetin
(*Aesculus* and *Fraxinus* spp.)

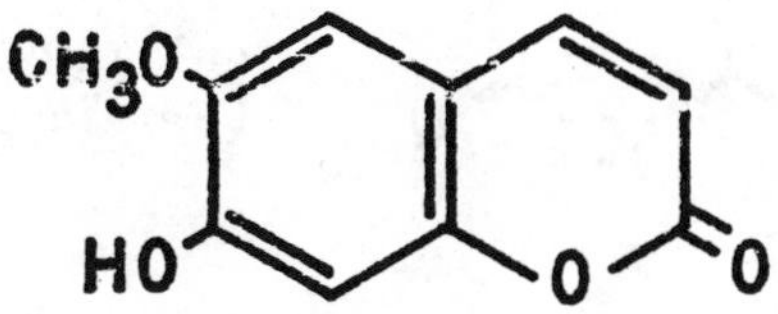

scopoletin
(*Murraya exotica*)

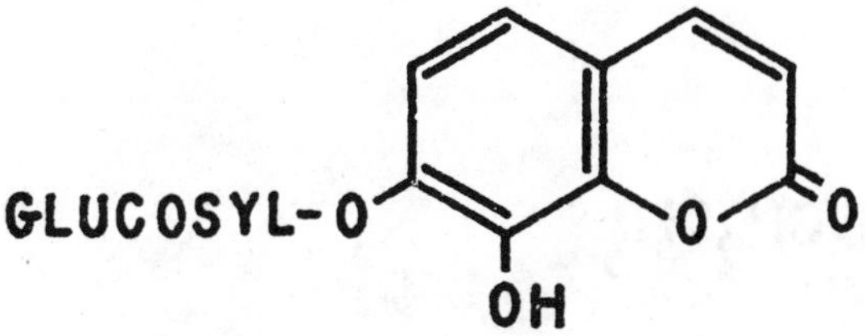

daphnin
(*Fraxinus* spp.)

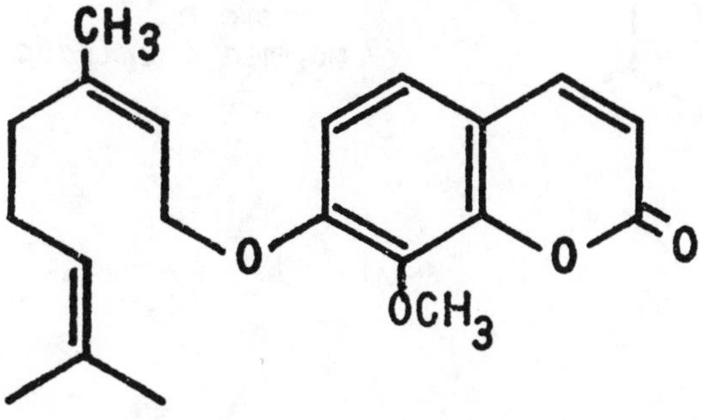

collinin
(*Flindersia collina*)

66

AROMATIC COMPOUNDS

Table 4-4. Continued

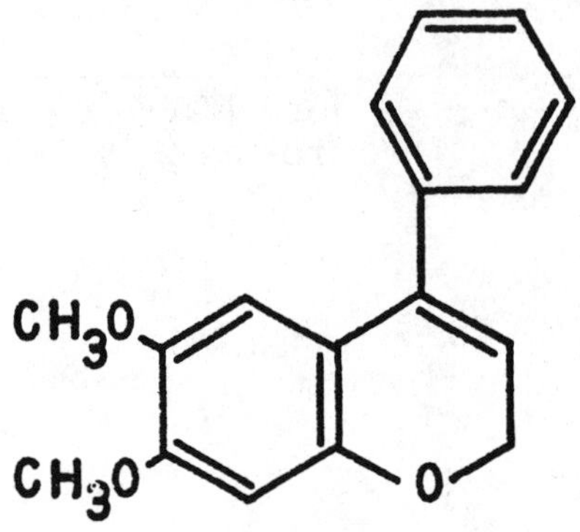

dalbergin methyl ether
(*Dalbergia sissoo*)

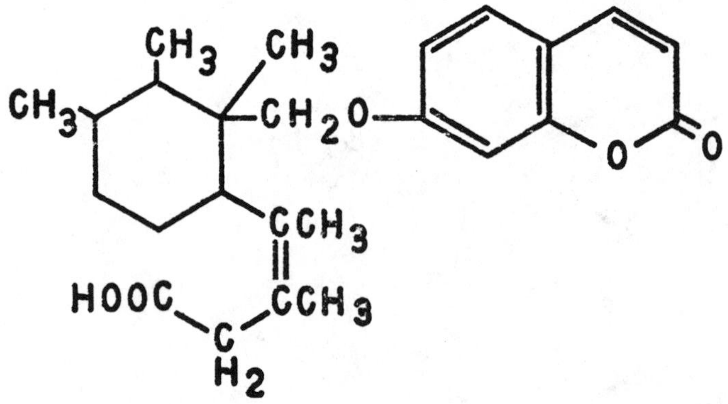

galbanic acid
(*Ferula* spp.)

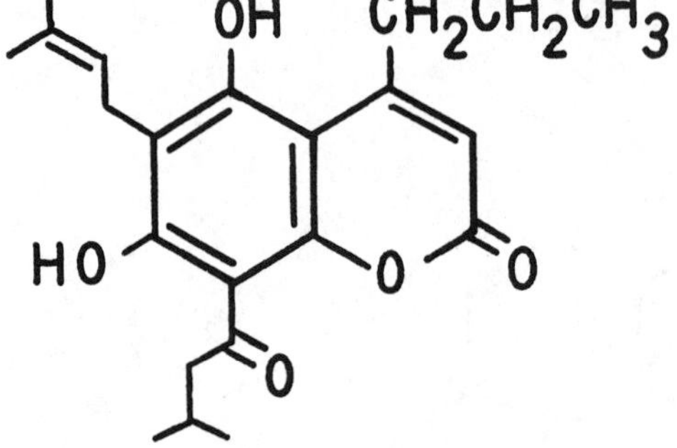

mammein
(*Mammea americana*)

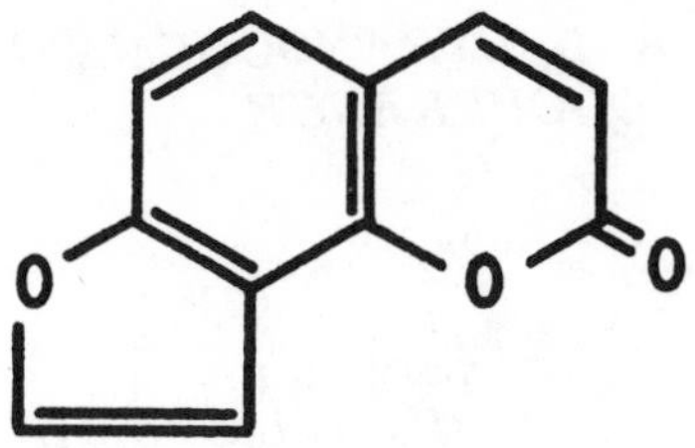

Furanocoumarins 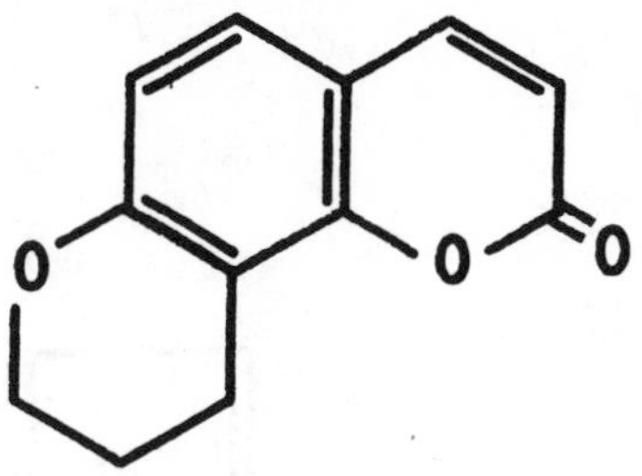   Pyranocoumarins

The ring fusion may also be at positions 6 and 7 of the coumarin nucleus.
These compounds resemble the simple coumarins. Alkaline hydrolysis
under ordinary conditions affects only the lactone ring, but alkaline
fusion or drastic hydrolysis conditions may destroy the two heterocylic
rings to form simple phenols. Structures of some representative compounds
are given in Table 4-5. It will be noted that all pyranocoumarins have an
isoprenoid carbon skeleton in the pyran ring as do some of the furanocoumarins. They are most common in the Rutaceae and Umbelliferae, and their
distribution in the Rutaceae is reviewed in (66). Extraordinary representatives having covalently bound chlorine are present in *Monotropa hypopitys*
(67).

The furanocoumarins are of some economic importance as the active
ingredients of fish poisons used by some primitive peoples. In higher
animals they may show spasmolytic and vasodilating effects. Psoralen
derivatives taken orally have been used to promote suntanning of the skin.
They become linked to DNA on irradiation with ultraviolet light (68).
Some show toxic and repellent effects toward insects (19).

LIGNANS

The lignans may be regarded as formed by the union of two phenylpropanes through their aliphatic side chains. The usual basic structure is:

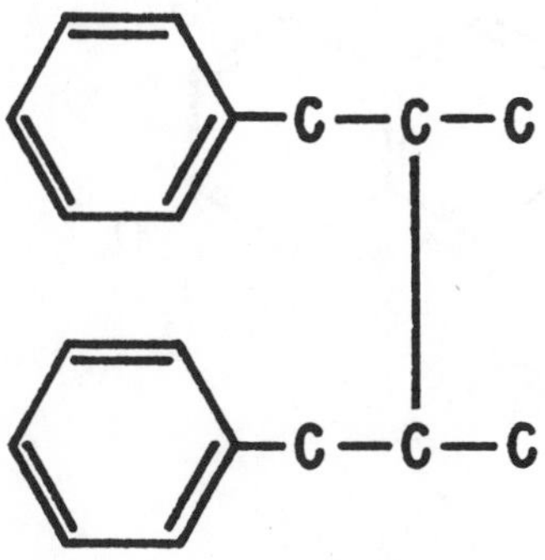

The aromatic rings are always oxygenated. Additional ring closures may
also be present. All of the natural lignans contain one or more asymmetric
carbon atoms and are optically active. Rarely a lignan with the 2-phenyl-
propane structure may be encountered as in pinastric acid from *Lepraria
flava* (69):

TABLE 4-5.   SOME FURANO- AND PYRANOCOUMARINS,
STRUCTURES AND OCCURRENCE

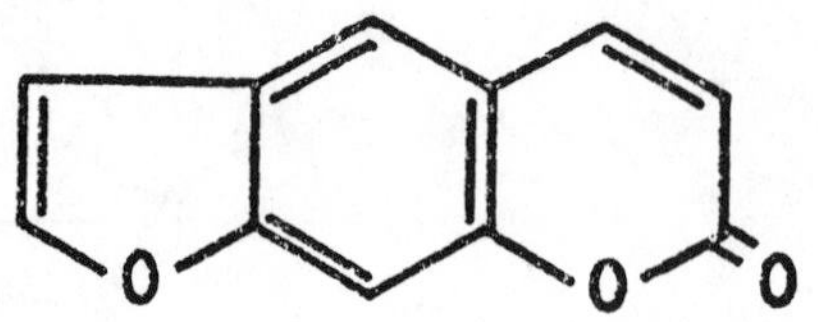

psoralen
(Psoralea corylifolia)

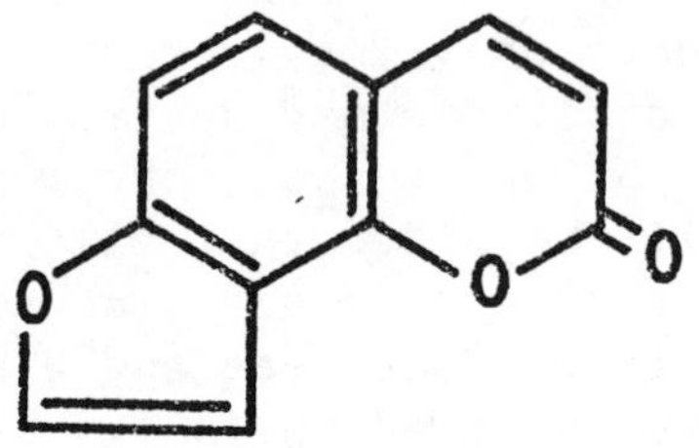

angelicin
(Archangelica officinalis)

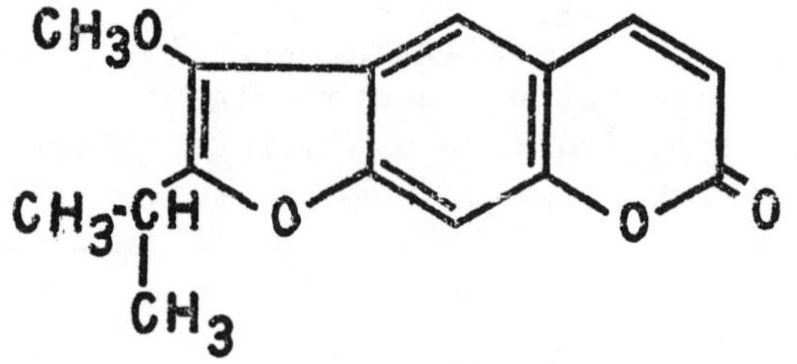

peucedanin
(Peucedanum officinale)

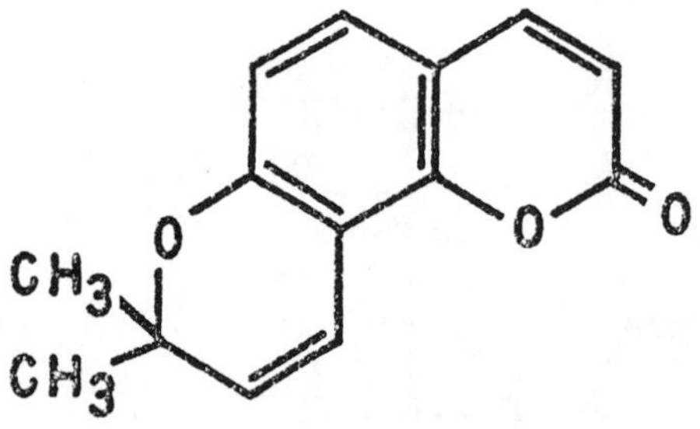

seselin·
(Seseli indicum)

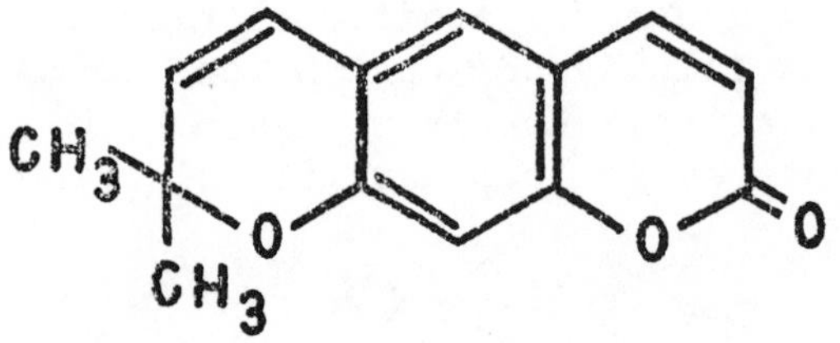

xanthoxyletin
(Xanthoxylum americanum)

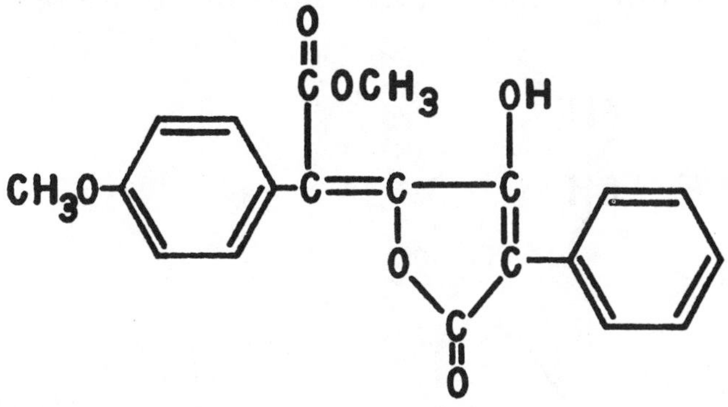

The lignans are colorless, crystalline solids which resemble other simple aromatic compounds in their chemical behavior. They are widespread in the plant kingdom, occurring in heartwood, leaves, resinous exudates, and other plant parts. Occasionally they are found as glycosides. Some apparently related compounds appear to be rearranged lignans. The name "neo-lignan" has been proposed for such products (70). There are also dilignans made of four C_9 units (71).

Examples of some natural lignans are given in Table 4-6. About three dozen are known at present. Some have shown limited commercial success as antioxidants in food. Sesamin has some importance as a synergistic ingredient in pyrethrum insecticides. Lignans are also the active constituents in certain medicinal plants. Podophyllin, a resinous extract of may apple (*Podophyllum peltatum*), has been used as a powerful cathartic. It is a complex mixture. However, its lignan constituent, podophyllotoxin, is of interest for having a cytotoxic action like that of colchicine (72). Podophyllotoxin and other lignans having the partially reduced naphthalene nucleus have shown some promise in treatment of certain types of neoplasms. In plants lignans have been regarded as intermediates in the biosynthesis of lignin (see below under "Metabolic Pathways").

Freudenberg and Weinges (73) have proposed a comprehensive system of nomenclature for the lignans.

LIGNIN

Lignin is the strengthening material which occurs along with cellulose in the cell walls of woody plants. The amount varies from a few percent (herbaceous plants) to about 30% (conifers). Ferns and club mosses apparently contain true lignin, but its occurrence is doubtful in Thallophytes or *Equisetum* spp. Certain giant mosses may have something like lignin, but small species lack it (74). Chemically lignin is a polymer made up of several different kinds of phenylpropane units. All lignins contain units related to coniferyl alcohol. In addition, the lignin of most dicots has sinapyl groups. Primitive dicots contain a smaller proportion of sinapyl units than advanced ones (75). *Lycopodium* lignin resembles that of gymnosperms and *Sclaginella* lignin that of angiosperms (76). The p-hydroxylphenylpropane units found in lignin of grasses are probably present as esterified p-coumaric acid rather than as monomeric units of the polymer (77). Glycosides of the same cinnamyl alcohols also occur widely in plants (e.g. coniferin, syringin) and may be precursors of lignin (78). Lignin itself

TABLE 4-6. SOME LIGNANS, STRUCTURES AND OCCURRENCE

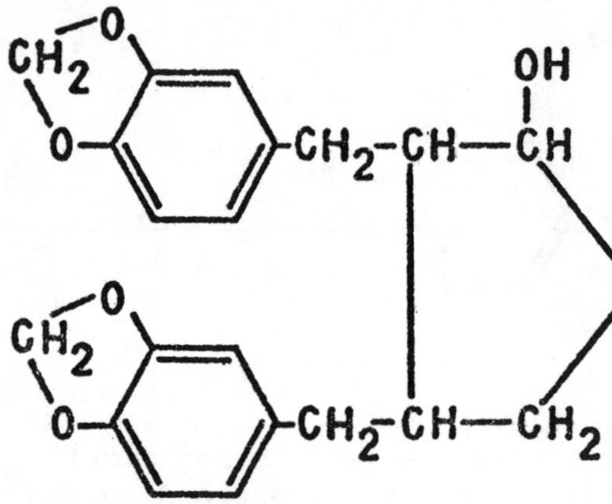

cubebin
(*Piper cubeba*)

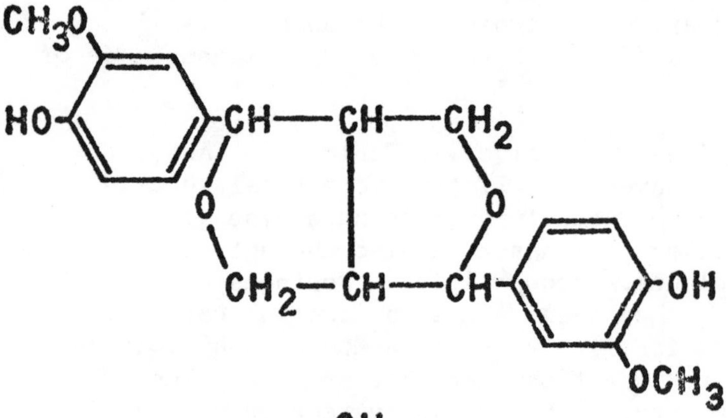

pinoresinol
(*Pinus* and *Picea*
 spp.)

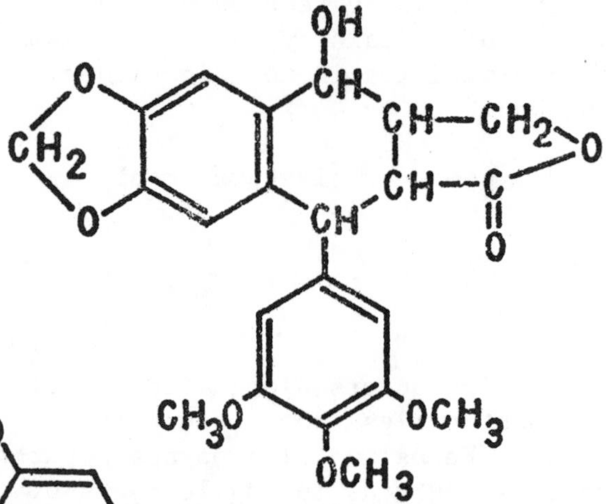

podophyllotoxin
(*Podophyllum* spp.)

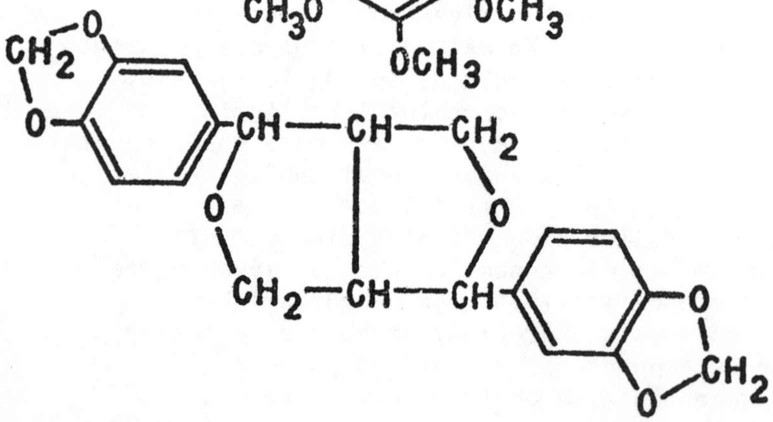

sesamin
(*Sesamum* spp.)

also has some covalent bonds to polysaccharides (79, 80). The great
majority of chemical research on lignin has been carried out using spruce
lignin, and most statements regarding lignin may be interpreted as applying
strictly only to this particular type which is composed almost entirely
of coniferyl alcohol units. Hardwood lignin may be very different (81).

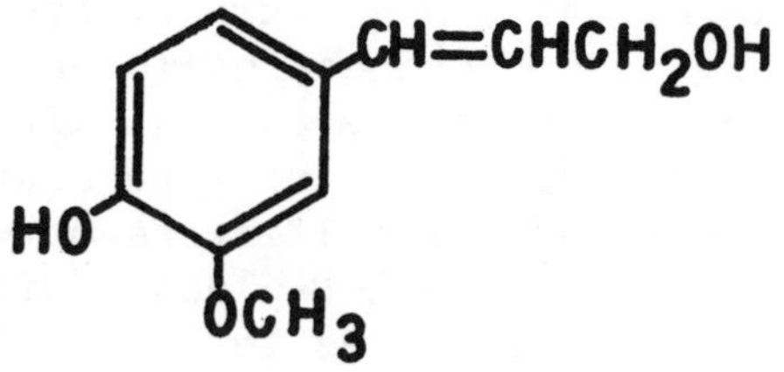

CH=CHCH$_2$OH

HO OCH$_3$

Coniferyl alcohol

CH$_3$O CH=CHCH$_2$OH

HO OCH$_3$

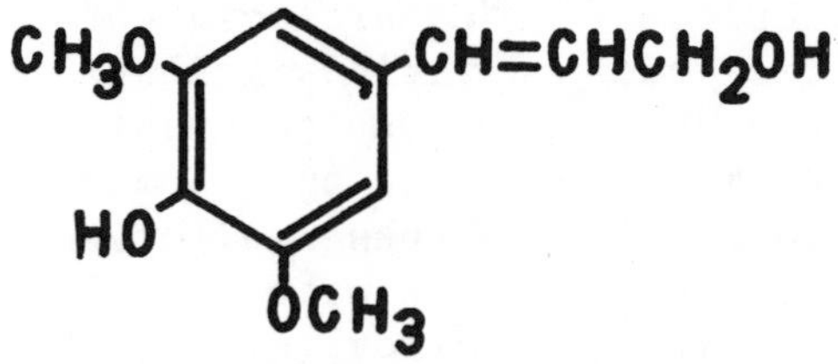

Sinapyl alcohol

Lignin itself as obtained by various isolation procedures (see below)
is a brown, amorphous solid which is insoluble in water and most organic
solvents. Lignin preparations (which may have suffered some degradation
during isolation) have shown molecular weights ranging from 2800 to 6700.
It is probable that there are many types of linkage between the repeating
units of lignin. The dehydrodiisoeugenol structure shown below is at
least a likely possibility for a part of the molecule:

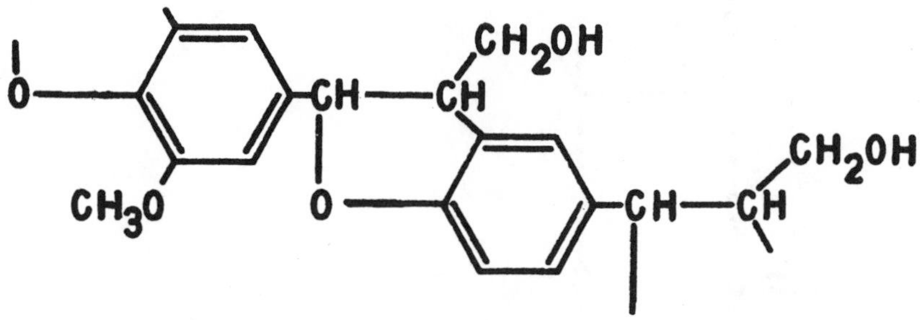

CH$_2$OH

CH CH

CH$_3$O O

CH$_2$OH

CH CH

According to this formulation lignin made up solely of sinapyl units cannot
occur because the methoxyl group at C-5 blocks condensation with the side-
chain of another molecule. More extended representations of lignin structure
may be found in (82) and the general references listed at the end of this
chapter.

HYDROLYZABLE TANNINS

A variety of phenolic plant constituents possess an astringent taste
and the ability to tan leather, but chemically the plant tannins are divided into two groups. Condensed or catechin tannins are discussed in
Chapter 9. The so-called hydrolyzable tannins contain ester linkages
which may be hydrolyzed by boiling with dilute hydrochloric acid. The
alcoholic component of the ester is usually a sugar, but in Tara tannin it
is a quinic acid. Structures of some of the phenolic acids found in tannins are shown in Table 4-7. Gallic acid is probably the one of most common occurrence. Ellagic acid is a secondary product formed on hydrolysis
of some tannins which are actually esters of hexaoxydiphenic acid. It appears as a "bloom" on the surface of leather which has been processed with

ellagitannins. Similarly, chebulic acid can be a secondary product of tannin hydrolysis, formed by lactonization of a carboxyl group which in the
native tannin is esterified with a sugar.

The hydrolyzable tannins are often complex mixtures containing several
different phenolic acids esterified to different positions of the sugar
molecule. The "tannic acid" of commerce is actually a mixture of free
gallic acid and various galloyl esters of glucose. Chinese gallotannin
is probably the most thoroughly investigated hydrolyzable tannin. It is
found in aphid galls on a sumac plant (*Rhus semialata*) native to south-
western Asia. Chinese gallotannin is a mixture of galloyl esters of glucose. The basic structure is 1, 2, 3, 4, 6-pentagalloyl-β-glucose with
3–5 additional galloyl groups attached by depside linkages to form a
chain of 2 or 3 m-galloyl groups (83).

An example of an ellagitannin is chebulagic acid of dividivi, the
dried fruit of *Caesalpinia coriaria*. On hydrolysis this tannin yields glucose, gallic acid, ellagic acid, and chebulic acid. Its structure has been
formulated as:

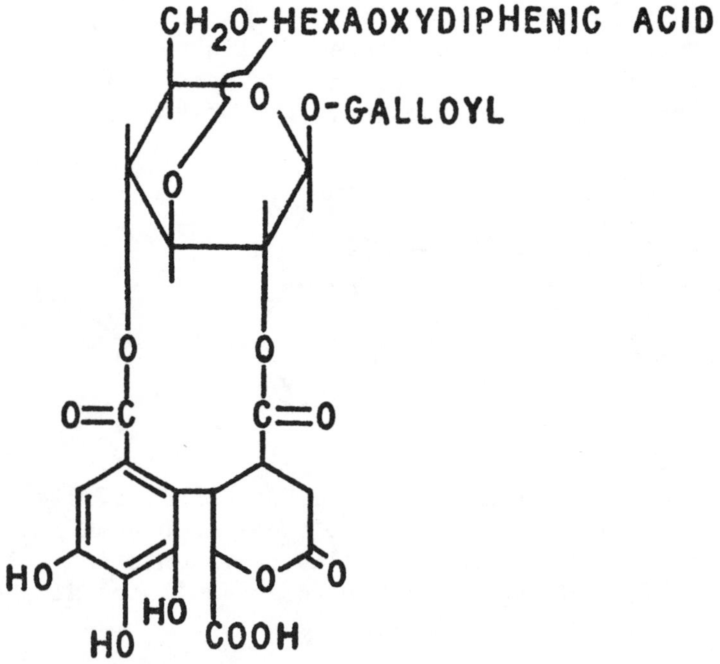

Oak and chestnut tannins may have three gallic acid units joined to
each other by C–C bonds and all esterified with a unit derived from glucose (84).

The hydrolyzable tannins are usually amorphous, hygroscopic, yellow-
brown substances which dissolve in water (especially hot) to form colloidal
rather than true solutions. The purer they are, the less soluble they are
in water and the more readily they may be obtained in a crystalline form.
They are also soluble, at least to some extent, in polar organic solvents,
but not in non-polar organic solvents like benzene or chloroform. From
aqueous solution the tannins may be precipitated by mineral acids or salts.
The ability of tannins to react with and precipitate proteins causes problems in preparation of enzymes or other proteins from some plants (cf. also
Chapter 11). A high tannin content may help to repel herbivores (18).

TABLE 4-7. *ACID COMPONENTS OF HYDROLYZABLE TANNINS*

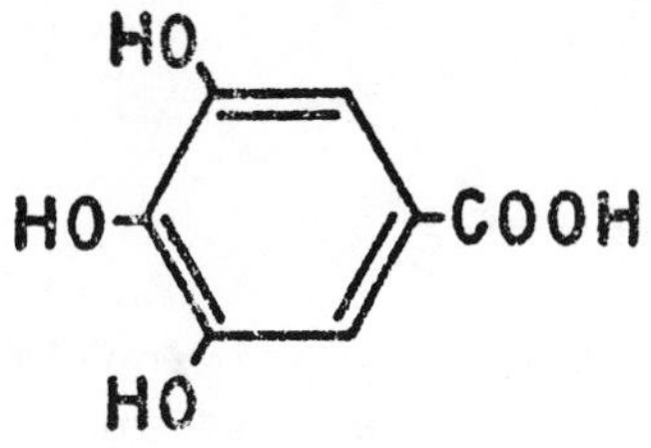

Gallic acid

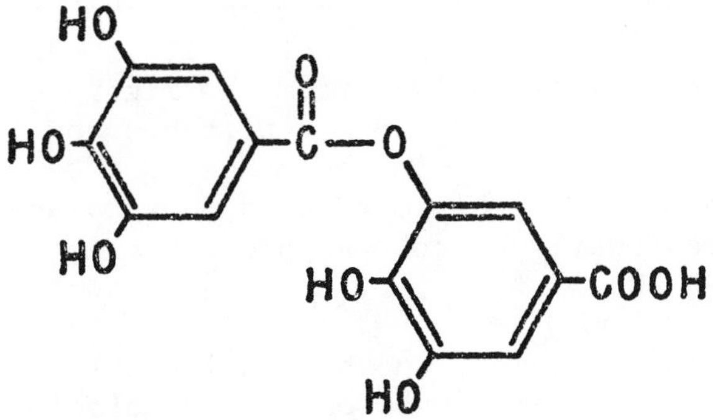

m-digallic acid

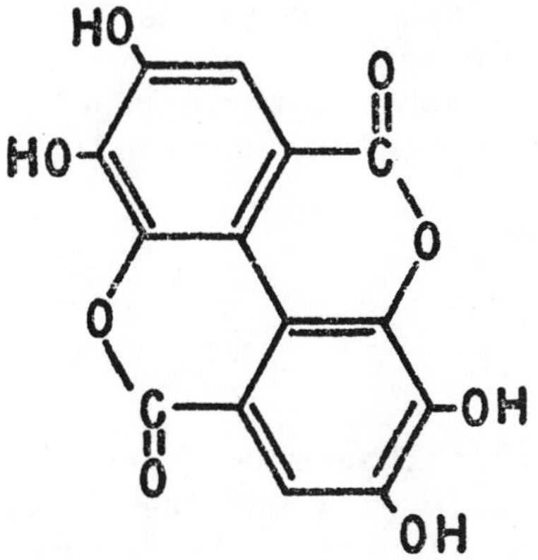

ellagic acid

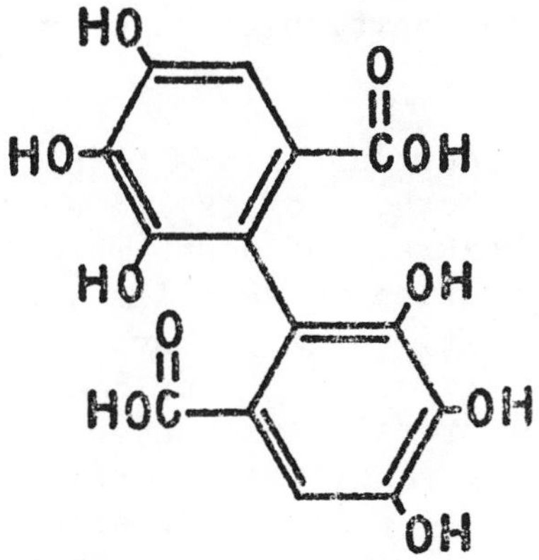

hexaoxydiphenic acid

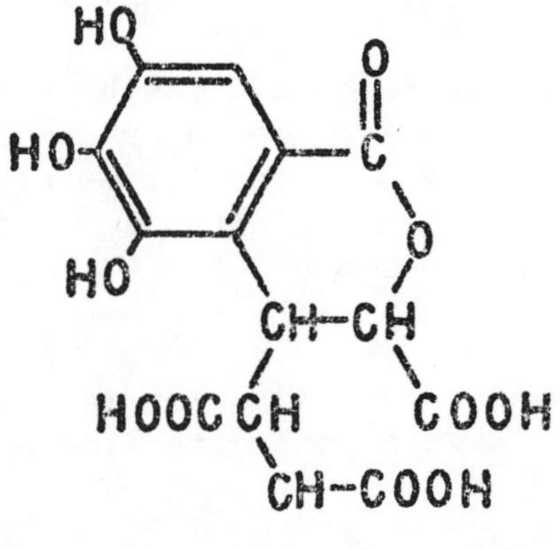

chebulic acid

In addition to articles on tannins in the general references there are reviews by Haslam (85) and Hillis (86).

HUMIC ACID, PLANT MELANINS, ALLAGOCHROME

Humic acid is a very poorly defined entity originally prepared by extracting basic substances from humus with dilute acid and then extracting the residue with dilute ammonium hydroxide. Acidification of the ammoniacal extract precipitates a crude mixture known as humic acid. It is generally believed that the humic acid in soil is derived from the lignin or carbohydrates of decaying plants; but it may also contain nitrogen and inorganic matter. The usual molecular weight is in the range 20,000-50,000. Structurally, it is regarded as having a highly condensed core composed largely of aromatic groups to which easily hydrolyzed protein and carbohydrate units may be attached (87, 88).

So-called "plant melanins" and a pigment known as allagochrome are even less well-defined than humic acid. Although some plant melanins may resemble animal melanins in being derived from indole compounds (Chapter 15), others are polymers of oxidized chlorogenic acid and contain no nitrogen (89). Allagochrome, similarly, is derived from chlorogenic acid. It is a blue-green, water soluble pigment with a molecular weight of 750-1400 found in many plants (90).

ISOLATION

Inasmuch as the compounds described in this chapter vary considerably in their properties, no single isolation procedure will suffice to separate all of them as a group from all other plant constituents. In devising isolation schemes the special properties of the particular category under investigation must be considered.

Many of the simple aromatic compounds occurring in plants have free phenolic hydroxyl groups, carboxyl groups, or both. Carboxylic acids may be extracted from plant material or an ether extract of plant material with 2% sodium bicarbonate solution. When this solution is acidified, the acids often precipitate or may be extracted with ether. After removal of carboxylic acids, phenols may be extracted with 5% sodium hydroxide solution. Like the acids, they may be precipitated or extracted into ether after acidification. Because many phenols are highly sensitive to oxidation under alkaline conditions, it may be advisable to exclude air or add a reducing agent like sodium dithionite during the alkali treatment.

Some of the lower molecular weight aromatic compounds may be purified by distillation or sublimation under atmospheric or reduced pressure. Phenols are usually not steam distillable, but phenol ethers or esters, being less polar than the parent hydroxyl compounds, can often be distilled with steam. Coumarin, for example, is customarily isolated by steam distillation.

Solvent extraction procedures find widespread application in purification of natural aromatic compounds. Common organic solvents like acetone,

ether and benzene are often employed. Multiple partition between water
or buffer solutions and an immiscible organic solvent has been used to
purify compounds with suitable solubility properties. The hydrolyzable
tannins and glycosides may be extracted with hot water or water-ethanol
mixtures. Synthetic resins, both ionic and uncharged, have been found
useful in removing phenolic materials from plant extracts (91, 92).

The naphthoquinones may be extracted from plant tissues with benzene
or other non-polar solvents. The 1, 4-quinones are often steam distillable
and may be removed from many other lipids by this procedure. Another
property which may be used in their separation from other lipids is their
solubility in weakly basic aqueous solutions such as sodium carbonate or
bicarbonate. Treatment with strong base in the presence of air frequently
brings about oxidative decomposition. 1, 2-quinones are not steam distill-
lable, but are soluble in solutions of sodium bisulfite. Final purification may be achieved with chromatography on inactivated alumina or weaker
adsorbents.

In purifying coumarins a crude preparation can be treated with warm
dilute alkali to open the lactone ring and form a water-soluble sodium
coumarinate. Neutral organic impurities may then be extracted with ether.
On acidification of the water solution the coumarin reforms so that the
coumarin with any acidic compounds can be extracted into ether. Acid impurities can then be removed from the ether by shaking with sodium bicarbonate solution.

Lignans may be extracted with acetone or ethanol and are often precipitated as slightly soluble potassium salts by adding concentrated,
aqueous potassium hydroxide to an alcoholic solution. As a variant on this
procedure, Freudenberg and Knof (93) converted lignans to insoluble, crystalline products using potassium acetate in ethanol. After collecting
the crystalline material free lignans could be regenerated by decomposing
with water. Acids or alkalies are to be avoided in preparing lignans, as
they often produce isomerization.

The problem of isolating native lignin has called forth several special and ingenious approaches. Older procedures relied on either removing
cellulose and other polysaccharides with strong sulfuric or hydrochloric
acids, or else dissolving the lignin with alkali. Such harsh procedures
doubtless cause considerable degradation of the native lignin. A more
recent procedure uses 2N sodium hydroxide along with boron trichloride and
thioacetic acid (94). A so-called "native lignin" can be extracted from
sawdust using acetone or alcohol at room temperature. This extraction procedure, however, removes only 1/2 to 3% of the total lignin. The solubility
of lignin can be increased somewhat by grinding the wood flour very fine
in a ball mill. Another technique has been to remove cellulose from wood
by allowing fungi or purified cellulase to act on sawdust. By such treat-
ments 25-30% of the total lignin can be obtained in a soluble form. It
is believed by some workers that any soluble lignin is by definition not
native lignin. Nevertheless, the study of soluble lignins is necessary
for an understanding of the chemical nature of lignin.

Traditional methods for preparation of plant tannins have used extraction with hot water, salting out with sodium chloride, reextraction of the

precipitate into acetone, and removal of lipids from the acetone-extractable
material with ether. By adding sodium chloride in successive small portions some fractional precipitation of a tannin mixture can be achieved.
Lead or zinc acetates (10%) are often used to precipitate tannins which may
be recovered from the precipitate by decomposing it with hydrogen sulfide.
Gelatin also forms a precipitate with aqueous solutions of tannins. Ethanol
can then be used to redissolve tannin from this precipitate. Precipitation
by adding an alcoholic solution of potassium acetate to an alcoholic solution of tannin is often of preparative value in tannin isolation. Tannins
can be precipitated with caffeine and then recovered by continuous extraction of the caffeine into chloroform (95).

Chromatographic procedures have been applied to the purification of
practically all the types of compounds discussed in this chapter. Chromatography on silicic acid has been used to separate such compounds as lignan
glycosides (96) or caffeic and chlorogenic isomers from various plants
(97, 98). Chromatography on alumina using such solvents as ethyl acetate or
ethyl acetate-methanol mixtures has been used for lignans (99) and coumarins
(100). Tannins have been purified on Solka-Floc, developing with 5% acetic
acid (101). Phenolic substances having free carboxyl groups can be separated from less acidic phenols by anion exchange chromatography (102).

CHARACTERIZATION

Because of the large number of different substances included in this
chapter there is a vast number of specific reactions which have been applied to their characterization. Only a few can be mentioned here for
each class of compounds.

A large proportion of the natural aromatic compounds have phenolic
hydroxyl groups and are, therefore, distinguished by the weakly acidic
nature of this group. Thus, they are often only slightly soluble in water
or sodium bicarbonate solution, but readily soluble in dilute aqueous
sodium hydroxide. The aromatic compounds with free carboxylic groups are
(like other organic acids) slightly soluble in water but easily soluble
with effervescence in sodium bicarbonate solution. If all phenolic groups
are combined as esters or ethers, the oxygenated benzene ring may still be
recognized by the formation of colored azo dyes on reaction with diazotized
sulfanilic acid or p-nitroaniline (Pauli reaction). Many phenols also
reduce Fehling's solution or ammoniacal silver nitrate. Production of
color with a 1% ferric chloride solution is also characteristic of many
phenols. Other color reactions will be found in the general references.
Many paper chromatographic studies of phenolic compounds have been made.
Bate-Smith (102) surveyed the leaves of many plants and found that the best
solvent system for separating the phenolic compounds was acetic acid/hydro-
chloric acid/water 30:3:10. Appearance in ultraviolet light and treatment
with several different spray reagents could be used to identify different
classes of compounds. Paper chromatography continues to be used for these
compounds (103) but is being replaced more and more by other methods. Van
Sumere (104) made an extensive survey of plant phenols using thin layer
chromatography on cellulose-silica gel. Other surveys of phenolics have
also relied on thin layer chromatography (105-107) and a combination of

thin layer chromatography and electrophoresis (108). For detection observation in ultraviolet light and diazonium sprays are most commonly used, but there are many recommendations for other reagents offering certain advantages (109-112). Other general surveys of plant phenolics have used gas chromatography of trimethylsilyl derivatives (113, 114).

As in other areas, the analysis of phenolic compounds by high performance liquid chromatography has become prominent recently and offers many advantages over earlier methods. It has been applied not only to the simpler phenolic acids (115-117) but also to prenylquinones (118) and more complex compounds (44, 119).

Particular analyses of caffeic acid and related compounds have been made by paper, gas, and thin layer chromatography (106, 120, 121). During paper chromatography caffeic acid can be converted into the coumarin esculetin if oxygen, ultraviolet light, and traces of metal ions are present (122).

The properties of naphthoquinones used in their isolation may also be put to good use in their characterization. Thus, a steam distillable, yellow-red solid which is soluble in benzene or sodium carbonate solution but insoluble in water is very likely to be a 1, 4-naphthoquinone. Additional indications are given by color reactions and spectra. 1, 4-naphthoquinones give yellow solutions in benzene, changing to red in alkali. 1, 2-quinones are usually red, rather than yellow, when crystalline or dissolved in benzene; in alkali they become blue-violet. If a double bond in a side chain of a 1, 4-quinone is conjugated with bonds in the quinone ring, the color reactions shown are like those of 1, 2-quinones. Other characteristic color reactions are given with concentrated sulfuric acid. Measurement of absorption spectra shows maxima at about 250 nm for 1, 4-quinones and one or more longer wavelength bands depending on what substituents are present. The basic nucleus absorbs at about 330 nm. When oxygen substitution is present there are other maxima toward the red, sometimes nearly to 600 nm, and the 330 maximum may not be apparent. 1, 2-naphthoquinone has the same ultraviolet absorption bands as the 1, 4-quinone, but additional bands at about 400 and 530 nm. As with the 1, 4-quinones, the positions of all bands except the lowest are greatly influenced by oxygen substitution on the rings. Characterization of 1, 4-naphthoquinones is discussed by Sawicki and Elbert (123). If hydroxyl groups are not present at C-2, the naphthoquinones react with o-aminothiophenol to yield red-blue colors. If C-2 hydroxyl groups are present, there is no reaction with this reagent, but a color reaction is given with o-phenylenediamine. Various characteristic reactions of quinones on chromatograms have been described (124). A general review on tocopherols includes analytical information (34).

Most of the common coumarins are strongly fluorescent when exposed to ultraviolet light. Sen and Bagchi (125) determined the absorption spectra of various coumarins and chromones, concluding that these two similar classes may be distinguished from each other on the basis of their spectra. The paper and thin layer chromatography of coumarins and furocoumarins has been studied (126-128). When coumarins are separated by paper chromatography they may be detected by fluorescence or by spraying with Emerson's reagent (0.5% Na_2CO_3, 0.9% of 4-aminoantipyrine, 5.4% $K_3Fe(CN)_6$) (129).

The fluorescent spots may also be cut from the paper, eluted, and absorption spectra of the eluates determined for identification (130). Since coumarins (and other phenols) often occur as glycosides, it may be advisable to submit plant materials to acidic hydrolysis before attempting to detect free coumarins. The proton magnetic resonance spectra for more than one hundred natural coumarins have been listed and analyzed (131).

Furanocoumarins may be identified by the fact that oxidation with hydrogen peroxide in sodium hydroxide produces furan-2, 3-dicarboxylic acid. Since all natural pyranocoumarins have a 2, 2-dimethylpyran structure, they may be identified by the fact that acetone is formed by prolonged alkaline hydrolysis. Alkaline hydrolysis does not affect the furan ring of furanocoumarins. Thin layer chromatography has been used for furanocoumarins (132), but high pressure liquid chromatography has been recommended as superior (133). Mass spectra are tabulated in (134).

There is no simple test to distinguish lignans from other natural phenolic compounds. Lignans have been separated by paper chromatography using as solvents mixtures of formamide with several other organic liquids (93, 134). Detection of the spots can be done using diazotized sulfanilic acid or antimony pentachloride.

The presence of lignin in plant tissues is easily recognized by such simple reactions as the appearance of a bright red color when moistened with a saturated solution of phloroglucinol in concentrated hydrochloric acid. Other cinnamaldehyde derivatives give the same reaction; but they can usually be removed by a preliminary extraction with acetone, which does not dissolve lignin. Lignin containing sinapyl groups may be recognized by the Maulé reaction -- formation of a red color when treated successively with chlorine water and ammonia (135). Gymnosperm lignin, which contains only coniferyl units, gives a brown color in this test. For more complete identification of the units present in lignin oxidation with alkaline nitrobenzene is used to degrade the lignin to benzaldehyde derivatives. Stone and Blundell (136) developed a method using 50 mg. samples of wood placed in stainless steel bombs with nitrobenzene and sodium hydroxide at 160° for 2.5 hours. When reaction was complete, 0.2 ml. of reaction mixture could be spotted directly onto a paper chromatogram and the products detected by spraying with 2, 4-dinitrophenylhydrazine. All lignins form vanillin by this treatment. Dicot lignins show syringylaldehyde as well, and grass lignins usually form p-hydroxybenzaldehyde.

One of the best-known tests for tannins is their precipitation of gelatin. A 0.5% solution of tannin is added to an equal volume of 0.5% gelatin. All tannins show some degree of precipitation, but other phenolic compounds may also give a positive test. The sensitivity of the reaction may be increased by adjusting the pH to about 4 and adding some sodium chloride. Other precipitation reactions with amines or metal ions have often been used to characterize tannins. Like other phenolic compounds the tannins give blue-violet colors with ferric chloride.

Several tests are available to distinguish between the hydrolyzable tannins (gallotannins) and condensed tannins (catechin tannins). Addition of 2 volumes of 10% acetic acid and 1 volume of 10% lead acetate solution to a filtered 0.4% tannin solution forms a precipitate with gallotannins within 5 minutes, but condensed tannins remain in solution. Other special tests can be used to distinguish between different types of hydrolyzable tannins. Several groups of investigators have applied paper chromatography to tannin mixtures. Solvents containing a good proportion of water seem to be most useful. Spots are revealed by exposure to ammonia and examination in ultraviolet light, or by spraying with ferric chloride solution.

METABOLIC PATHWAYS

Biosynthetic pathways of aromatic compounds in plants have been reviewed in (137) and (138). The present discussion is restricted to those aromatic compounds derived from 5-dehydroquinic acid. Other types of aromatic compounds will be found in Chapters 6 and 9. The pathways shown in Figures 4-1 and 4-2 are at least probable for higher plants, and many steps of the shikimic-chorismic pathway have now been studied with purified enzymes from plants with the aim of clarifying regulatory aspects of the scheme (139,140). It is possible that quinic acid is not so closely related to this pathway as the figure suggests (141). The steps leading from carbohydrates to 5-dehydroquinic acid have been shown in Figure 2-8 of Chapter 2. Only a few points will be made here in clarification of the figures:

1. The conversion of 5-dehydroshikimic acid to protocatechuic acid and gallic acid appears reasonable, and there is some experimental evidence to support it (141, 142). However, it is also possible that the various hydroxybenzoic acids arise by degradation of larger molecules (143-145).
2. It is now generally believed that the main pathway for forming cinnamic and p-coumaric acids from phenylalanine and tyrosine respectively does not go through the corresponding keto and hydroxy acids, but occurs by a one-step elimination of ammonia. Deaminases catalyzing these reactions have been extensively studied, and phenylalanine ammonia lyase (PAL) is said to be the most studied enzyme of secondary plant metabolism (146). It is found in all green plants and some lower plants. Tyrosine ammonia lyase (tyrase) activity is often associated with PAL and has never been obtained free of PAL although the reverse is often true (147). Dicots are more likely than monocots to lack tyrase activity. The general acceptance of the importance of PAL still leaves some questions unanswered. It appears that the activity of PAL may not always be rate-limiting in the pathway to phenylpropanoids (148). The availability of phenylalanine and compartmentation effects are perhaps more important (149). There are even some lingering suggestions of alternate pathways (150, 151).
3. Hydroxylation of the aromatic ring evidently must occur at several points in the scheme, but the exact location of these points is not clear. Tracer experiments have established that cinnamic acid fed to plants is readily hydroxylated in several positions (152). Enzymological studies have shown that the initial hydroxylation of cinnamic acid to o-coumaric or p-coumaric acid is catalyzed by a microsomal P 450 system (153, 154). However, the second hydroxylation converting p-coumaric acid to caffeic acid is the result of phenol oxidase action (155, 156). In the biosynthesis of esters of caffeic acid esterification of p-coumaric acid may precede hydroxylation of the p-coumaroyl moiety (157).

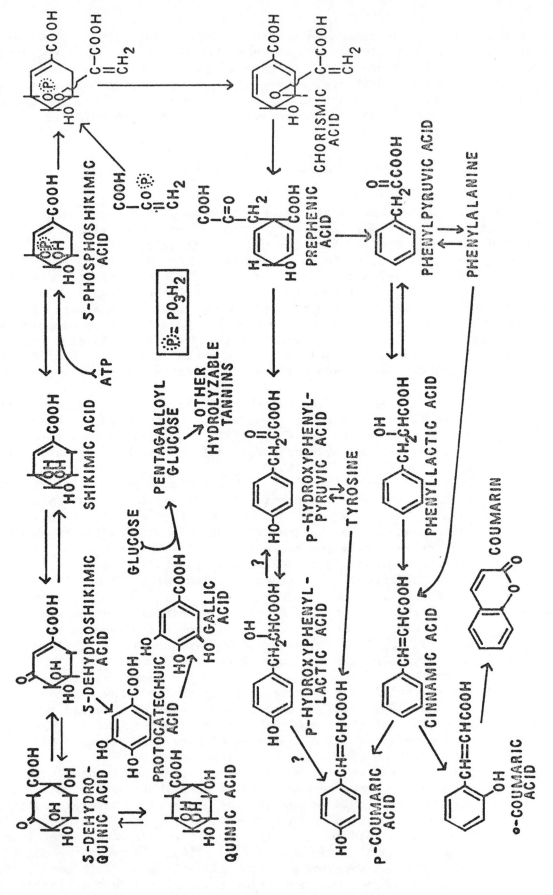

FIGURE 4-1: AROMATIC COMPOUNDS DERIVED FROM 5-DEHYDROQUINIC ACID

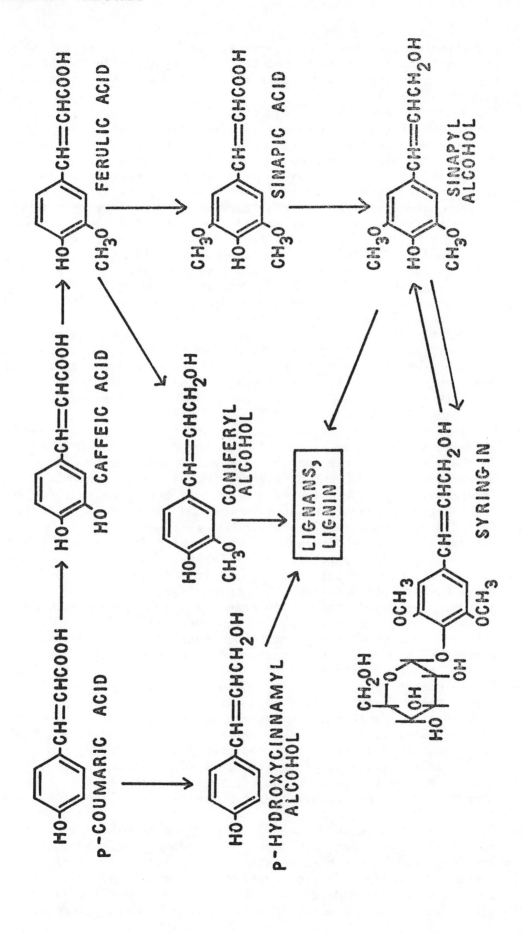

FIGURE 4-2: AROMATIC COMPOUNDS DERIVED FROM p-COUMARIC ACID

4. Formation of coenzyme A derivatives precedes the esterification
    of cinnamic acids or their reduction to the alcohols (157-160).
    Eugenol is derived from ferulic acid, but the mechanism is not
    clear (161, 162).

5. The coumarins are believed to form following hydrolysis of 2-0-
    glucosides of cis-cinnamic acids. 2-hydroxylation of a trans-
    cinnamic acid followed by glucoside formation and isomerization
    would be the preceding steps (163-165). A mechanism for the
    hydroxylation and ring closure has been proposed (166). The
    trans-cis isomerization may be non-enzymatic, catalyzed by light.
    (167). Both linear and angular furanocoumarins have been shown to
    derive their two additional carbon atoms from C-4 and C-5 of
    mevalonic acid. An isoprenyl group is first added to a 7-hydroxy-
    coumarin like umbelliferone followed by ring closure and loss of
    three carbons (168). Psoralen in several plants is a precursor
    of other furanocoumarins (169). Although they are mentioned in
    this chapter, the isocoumarins are actually related metabolically
    to the chromones of Chap. 6. (170).

6. The O-methylation reactions evident in the accompanying schemes
    utilize S-adenosylmethionine as the methyl donor, and some of them
    have been studied in vitro (171-174). It is interesting that the
    requirement of cytokinin for lignification is probably the result
    of activation by cytokinin or a particular methylase needed for
    synthesis of ferulic acid (175).

7. Biosynthesis of the ubiquinones, plastoquinones, and tocopherols
    has been shown in several plants to proceed from shikimic acid.
    To the ubiquinones the pathway is via p-coumaric acid and p-
    hydroxybenzoic acid, but to plastoquinones and tocopherols the
    intermediates are phenylpyruvic and homogentisic acids (34, 176).
    One C-methyl group of the ubiquinones and tocopherols is derived
    from C-3 of tyrosine (177). Pathways to the naphthoquinones
    are extraordinarily diverse. In fact four different ones have
    been discovered, functioning in different plants. Three of them
    start with shikimic acid and gain their additional carbons
    respectively from succinate, 1 isoprenyl group, or 2 isoprenyl
    groups. The fourth pathway is actually a polyacetate pathway in
    which the rings are built in the way outlined in Chap. 6 (178-180).
    Further transformations of naphthoquinones lead to various other
    compounds such as the catalpalactone of Catalpa ovata (181).

8. Several types of evidence (182) indicate that polygalloyl glucose
    is the parent compound of many, if not all, the hydrolyzable tan-
    nins. Thus, it is believed that the ellagitannins are derived
    by oxidative coupling of two molecules of gallic acid which are
    already esterified to glucose, rather than by esterification of
    the sugar with preformed hexaoxydiphenic acid. On the other
    hand, Wenkert (183) has suggested that diphenyl and diphenyl ether
    systems may be formed by carbohydrate-type condensation of hydro-
    aromatic precursors rather than by oxidative coupling of aromatic
    rings.

9. Since the complete structure of lignin remains unknown, the exact
    mechanism of its formation cannot be shown. Freudenberg (184)
    has suggested that the first step is enzymatic removal of a
    phenolic hydrogen atom from coniferyl alcohol to produce a free
    radical which can undergo non-enzymatic rearrangements and reac-
    tions with other molecules leading first to dimers (of which

lignans are one type) and finally to lignin. The removal of
hydrogen is a reaction which is probably catalyzed by peroxidase
of the cell wall (185). Xylem tissue of angiosperms can reduce
ferulic and sinapic acids to their alcohols, but gymnosperm tissue
can reduce only ferulic acid. This difference may account for the
different types of lignin in the two divisions (186). Control
mechanisms in the biosynthesis of lignin are reviewed in (187).

10. The well-known binding of lignin to carbohydrate in cell walls
    may come about by coupling of one of the free radical intermediates
    mentioned above with the hydroxyl group of a carbohydrate to form
    an ether bond (188).

11. C-alkylation is a feature of many of the aromatic compounds con-
    sidered above, and it has been shown that C-methyl groups general-
    ly come from methionine (189-191). Isoprenyl and longer isoprenoid
    chains come from mevalonic acid, but their exact mechanism of ad-
    dition is unknown 168). The C_{12} alkyl side chain of gingerols
    contains 9 carbon atoms derived from acetate. The other 3 carbons
    of the side chain, and the ring, constitute a C_6-C_3 unit (192).
    Similar precursors may be expected for the urushiols.

12. Many of the phenolic compounds found in plants are often referred
    to as "secondary" metabolites and thought to be rather inert
    once formed. In fact, experiments have shown that some of them
    turn over at an appreciable rate and can be completely metabolized
    to carbon dioxide (193, 194). Consequently there may be functional
    significance for those that do accumulate.

GENERAL REFERENCES

Billek, G., ed. (1966) Biosynthesis of Aromatic Compounds, Pergamon Press,
    Oxford.

Freudenberg, K. & Neish, A. C. (1968) Constitution and Biosynthesis of Lignin,
    Springer-Verlag, Berlin.

Harborne, J. B., ed. (1964) Biochemistry of Phenolic Compounds, Academic Press,
    N. Y.

Haslam, E. (1975) The Shikimate Pathway, Butterworth's, London.

Pridham, J. B., ed. (1964) Methods in Polyphenol Chemistry, Pergamon Press,
    Oxford.

Sarkanen, K. V. & Ludwig, C. H., eds. (1971) Lignins, Wiley-Interscience, N. Y.

Schubert, W. J., "Lignin", in Miller 3 132-153.

Swain, T., Harborne, J. B., & Van Sumere, C. F., eds. (1979) Biochemistry of
    Plant Phenolics, Academic Press, N. Y.

Many articles in Paech & Tracey 3.

BIBLIOGRAPHY

1. Hopkinson, S. M. (1969) Quart. Rev. 23 98-124.
2. Siedow, J. N. and San Pietro, A. (1974) Arch. Biochem. Biophys. 164 145-155.
3. Krogmann, D. W. and Stiller, M. L. (1962) Biochem. Biophys. Res. Comms. 7 46-49.
4. Imbert, M. P. and Wilson, L. A. (1972) Phytochemistry 11 2671-2676.
5. Ozawa, T., Nishikiori, T. and Takino, Y. (1977) Agric. Biol. Chem. 41 359-367.
6. Hoover, J. D., Wender, S. H. and Smith, E. C. (1977) Phytochemistry 16 195-197, 199-201.
7. Bolasimha, D., Ram, G. and Tewari, M. N. (1977) Biochem. Physiol. Pflanzen. 171 49-54.
8. Siegel, S. M. (1976) Phytochemistry 15 566-567.
9. Lavie, D., Levy, E. C., Cohen, A., Evenari, M. and Guttermann, Y. (1974) Nature 249 388.
10. Glass, A. D. M. (1975) Phytochemistry 14 2127-2130.
11. Demos, E. K., Woolwine, M., Wilson, R. H. and McMillan, C. (1975) Amer. J. Botany 62 97-102.
12. Corcoran, M. R., Geissman, T. A. and Phinney, B. O. (1972) Plant Physiol. 49 323-330.
13. Russell, D. W. and Galston, A. W. (1969) Plant Physiol. 44 1211-1216.
14. Macháčková, I., Gančeva, K. and Zmrhal, Z. (1975) Phytochemistry 14 1251-1254.
15. Thorp, R. W., Briggs, D. L., Estes, J. R. and Erickson, E. H. (1975) Science 189 476-478.
16. Tripathi, R. D., Srivastava, H. S. and Dixit, S. N. (1977) Experientia 34 51-52.
17. Challice, J. S. and Westwood, M. N. (1972) Phytochemistry 11 37-44.
18. McKey, D., Waterman, P. G., Mbi, C. N., Gartlan, J. S. and Struhsaker, T. T. (1978)
    Science 202 61-64.
19. Berenbaum, M. (1978) Science 201 532-534.
20. Berger, P. J., Sanders, E. H., Gardner, P. D. and Negus, N. C. (1977) Science 195 575-577.
21. Craig, J. C., Waller, C. W., Billets, S. and Elsohly, M. A. (1978) J. Pharm. Sci. 67
    483-485.
22. Morimoto, H., Kawamatsu, Y. and Sugihara, H. (1968) Chem. Pharm. Bull. 16 2282-2286.
23. Byck, J. S. and Dawson, C. R. (1968) Anal. Biochem. 25 123-135.
24. Connell, D. W. and Sutherland, M. D. (1969) Austral. J. Chem. 22 1033-1043.
25. Verdeal, K. and Lorenz, K. (1977) Cereal Chem. 54 475-483.
26. Schmalle, H. and Jarchow, O. (1977) Naturwissenschaften 64 534-535.
27. Thomson, R. H. (1971) Naturally Occurring Quinones, 2nd ed., Academic Press, N. Y.
28. Trebst, A. (1978) Phil. Trans. Royal Soc. B. 284 591-599.
29. Wallwork, J. C. and Pennock, J. F. (1968) Chem. and Indust. 1571-1572.
30. Griffiths, W. T., Wallwork, J. C. and Pennock, J. F. (1966) Nature 211 1037-1039.
31. Threlfall, D. R. and Whistance, G. R. (1970) Phytochem. 9 355-359.
32. Palmer, J. M. (1976) Ann. Rev. Plant Physiol. 27 133-157.
33. Janiszowska, W. and Pennock, J. F. (1976) Vitamins and Hormones 34 77-105.
34. Threlfall, D. R. and Whistance, G. R. (1971) Methods Enzymol. 18C 369-396.
35. Barr, R. and Crane, F. L. (1977) Plant Physiol. 59 433-436.
36. Newton, R. P. and Pennock, J. F. (1971) Phytochemistry 10 2323-2328.
37. Kegel, L. P. and Crane, F. L. (1962) Nature 194 1282.
38. Lillie, T. J., Musgrave, O. C. and Skoyles, D. (1976) J. Chem. Soc. Perkin I 2546.
39. Borsub, L., Thebtaranonth, Y., Ruchirawat, S. and Sadavongvivad, C. (1976) Tetrahedron
    Letters 105-108.
40. Engelsma, G. (1974) Plant Physiol. 54 702-705.
41. Herrmann, K. (1978) Fortschr. Chem. Org. Naturstoffe 35 73-132.
42. Sondheimer, E. (1964) Botan. Rev. 30 667-712.
43. Hanefeld, M. and Herrmann, K. (1976) J. Chromatog. 123 391-395.
44. Ong, B. Y. and Nagel, C. W. (1978) J. Chromatogr. 157 345-355.
45. Scarpati, M. L. and Oriente, G. (1960) Gazz. Chim. Ital. 90 212-219.
46. Krause, J. and Strack, D. (1979) J. Chromatog. 176 465-469.
47. Krause, J. (1978) Z. Pflanzenphysiol. 88 465-470.
48. Hartley, R. D., Jones, E. C. and Wood, T. M. (1976) Phytochemistry 15 305-307.
49. Whitmore, F. W. (1974) Plant Physiol. 53 728-731.
50. von Sumeré, C. F., de Pooter, H., Ali, H. and Degrauw-van Bussel, M. (1973) Phytochemistry
    12 407-411.
51. Martin, C. and Gallet, M. (1973) Compt. Rend. D 276 1433-1435.
52. Buta, J. G. and Izac, R. R. (1972) Phytochemistry 11 1188-1189.
53. Cooper-Driver, G. and Swain, T. (1975) Phytochemistry 14 2506-2507.
54. El-Basyouni, S. Z. and Neish, A. C. (1966) Phytochemistry 5 683-691.
55. Hashimoto, Y., Moriyasu, M., Kanai, Y. and Hirase, M. (1979) J. Chromatog. 171 494-496.
56. Coxon, D. T., Curtis, F., Price, K. R. and Levett, G. (1973) Phytochemistry 12 1881-1885.
57. Kindl, H. (1965) Monatsh. 95 1561-1563.
58. Murray, R. D. H. (1978) Fortschr. Chem. Org. Naturstoffe 35 199-429.
59. Goren, R. and Tomer, E. (1971) Plant Physiol. 47 312-316.
60. Morgan, P. W. and Powell, R. D. (1970) Plant Physiol. 45 553-557.
61. Satoh, S., Matsuda, K. and Tamari, K. (1976) Plant Cell Physiol. 17 1243-1254.
62. Hopp, H. E., Romero, P. A. and Lezica, R. P. (1978) FEBS Letters 86 259-262.
63. Junttila, O. (1976) Physiol. Plantarum 36 374-378.
64. Jurd, L., King, A. D., Jr. and Mihara, K. (1971) Phytochemistry 10 2965-2970.
65. Djerassi, C., Eisenbraun, E. J., Finnegan, R. A. and Gilbert, B. (1960) J. Org. Chem. 25
    2164-2169.
66. Gray, A. I. and Waterman, P. G. (1978) Phytochemistry 17 845-864.
67. Trofast, J. (1978) Phytochemistry 17 1359-1361.
68. Song, P.-S. and Tapley, K. J., Jr. (1979) Photochem. Photobiol. 29 1177-1197.

69. Grover, P. K. and Seshadri, T. R. (1958) Tetrahedron 6 312-314.
70. Gottlieb, O. R. (1978) Fortschr. Chem. Org. Naturstoffe 35 1-72.
71. Ichihara, A., Kanai, S., Nakamura, Y. and Sakamura, S. (1978) Tetrahedron Lett. 3035-3038.
72. **Brewer, C. F., Loike, J. D., Horwitz, S. B., Sternlicht, H., and Gensler, W. J. (1979) J. Med. Chem. 22 215-221.**
73. Freudenberg, K. and Weinges, K. (1961) Tetrahedron 15 115-128.
74. Miksche, G. E. and Yasuda, S. (1978) Phytochemistry 17 503-504.
75. Towers, G. H. N. and Gibbs, R. D. (1953) Nature 172 25-26.
76. White, E. and Towers, G. H. N. (1967) Phytochemistry 6 663-667.
77. Higuchi, T., Ito, Y., Shimada, M. and Kawamura, I. (1967) Phytochemistry 6 1551-1556.
78. Marcinowski, S. and Grisebach, H. (1977) Phytochemistry 16 1665-1667.
79. Davydov, V. D., Veselova, L. N., Potemkina, I. I. and Frolov, Y. M. (1970) Chem. Nat. Compounds 6 257-263.
80. Morrison, I. M. (1974) Phytochemistry 13 1161-1165.
81. Miksche, G. E. and Yasuda, S. (1976) Annalen 1323-1332.
82. Nimz, H. (1974) Angew. Chem. Intern. Ed. 13 313-321.
83. Haworth, R. D. (1961) Proc. Chem. Soc. 1961 401-410.
84. Mayer, W., Kuhlmann, F. and Schilling, G. (1971) Ann. 747 51-59.
85. Haslam, E. (1966) Chemistry of the Vegetable Tannins, Academic Press, N. Y.
86. Hillis, W. E. (1972) Phytochemistry 11 1207-1218.
87. Ogner, G. and Schnitzer, M. (1971) Can. J. Chem. 49 1053-1063.
88. Grant, D. (1977) Nature 270 709-711.
89. Andrews, R. S. and Pridham, J. B. (1967) Phytochemistry 6 13-18.
90. Habermann, H. M. (1972) Botan. Gaz. 134 221-232.
91. Gray, J. C. (1978) Phytochemistry 17 495-497.
92. Jahangir, L. M. and Samuelson, O. (1977) Anal. Chim. Acta. 92 329-335.
93. Freudenberg, K. and Knof, L. (1957) Chem. Ber. 90 2857-2869.
94. Nimz, H. (1969) Chem. Ber. 102 799-810.
95. Wall, M. E., Taylor, H., Ambrosio, L., and Davis, K. (1969) J. Pharm. Sci. 58 839-841.
96. Warthurg, A. V., Angliker, E. and Renz, J. (1957) Helv. Chim. Acta 40 1331-1357.
97. Sondheimer, E. (1958) Arch. Biochem. Biophys. 74 131-138.
98. Hanson, K. R. and Zucker, M. (1963) J. Biol. Chem. 238 1105-1115.
99. Hartwell, J. L. and Detty, W. E. (1950) J. Am. Chem. Soc. 72 246-253.
100. Chatterjee, A. and Choudhury, A. (1955) Naturwissenschaften 42 535-536.
101. King, H. G. C. and White, T. (1961) J. Chem. Soc. 1961 3231-3234.
102. Bate-Smith, E. C. (1956) Sci. Proc. Royal Dublin Soc. 27 165-176.
103. Seoane, E. and Carnicer, A. (1967) Microchem. J. 12 291-306.
104. van Sumere, C. F., Wolf, G., Teuchy, H. and Kint, J. (1965) J. Chromatog. 20 48-60.
105. Jangaard, N. O. (1970) J. Chromatog. 50 148-149.
106. Clifford, M. N. (1974) J. Chromatog. 99 261-266.
107. Dass, H. C. and Weaver, G. M. (1972) J. Chromatog. 67 105-111.
108. May, C. E. and Brown, J. M. A. (1970) J. Chromatog. 53 399-402.
109. Bhatia, I. S., Singh, J. and Bajaj, K. L. (1973) J. Chromatog. 79 351-352.
110. Somarov, B. H., Thakur, M. L. and Grant, W. F. (1973) J. Chromatog. 87 290-293.
111. Bajaj, K. L. and Bhatia, M. S. (1976) J. Chromatog. 117 445-448.
112. Krisnangkura, K. and Gold, M. H. (1979) J. Chromatog. 408-409.
113. Steele, J. W. and Bolan, M. (1972) J. Chromatog. 71 427-434.
114. Casteele, K. V., De Pooter, H., and Van Sumere, C. F. (1976) J. Chromatog. 121 49-63.
115. Wulf, L. W. and Nagel, C. W. (1976) J. Chromatog. 116 271-279.
116. Court, W. A. (1977) J. Chromatog. 130 287-291.
117. Murphy, J. B. and Stutte, C. A. (1978) Anal. Biochem. 86 220-228.
118. Lichtenthaler, H. K. and Prenzel, U. (1977) J. Chromatog. 135 493-498.
119. Okuda, T., Mori, K., Seno, K. and Hatano, T. (1979) J. Chromatog. 171 313-320.
120. Hedin, P. A., Minyard, J. P., Jr. and Thompson, A. C. (1967) J. Chromatog. 30 43-53.
121. Andersen, R. A. and Vaughn, T. H. (1970) J. Chromatog. 52 385-392.
122. Butler, W. L. and Siegelman, H. W. (1959) Nature 183 1813-1814.
123. Sawicki, E. and Elbert, W. C. (1960) Anal. Chim. Acta 23 205-208.
124. Simatupang, M. H. and Hausen, B. M. (1970) J. Chromatog. 52 180-183.
125. Sen, K. and Bagchi, P. (1959) J. Org. Chem. 24 316-319.
126. Grujić-Vasić, J. (1961) Monatsh. 92 236-239.
127. Karlsen, J., Dubbeld, G. and Fischer, F. C. (1974) J. Chromatog. 92 179-181.
128. Lau-Cam, C. A. (1978) J. Chromatogr. 151 391-395.
129. Fujita, M. and Furuya, T. (1958) Chem. Pharm. Bull. 6 511-517.
130. Saxby, M. J. (1964) Anal. Chem. 36 1145-1146.
131. Steck, W. and Mazurek, M. (1972) Lloydia 35 418-439.
132. Karlsen, J., Boomsa, L. E. J. and Svendsen, A. B. (1969) J. Chromatog. 42 550-551.
133. Stermitz, F. R. and Thomas, R. D. (1973) J. Chromatog. 77 431-437.
134. Saiki, Y., Uchida, M., Okegawa, O., and Fukushima, S. (1974) Chem. Pharm. Bull. 22 1227-1232.
135. Towers, G. H. N. and Gibbs, R. D. (1953) Nature 172 25-26.
136. Stone, J. E. and Blundell, M. J. (1951) Anal. Chem. 23 771-774.
137. **Towers, G. H. N. and Wat, C.-K. (1979) Planta Med. 37 97-114.**
138. Weiss, U. and Edwards, J. M. (1979) The Biosynthesis of Aromatic Compounds, Wiley-Interscience, N. Y.

139. Koshiba, T. (1978) Biochim. Biophys. Acta 522 10-18.
140. Bickel, H. and Schultz, G. (1979) Phytochemistry 18 498-499.
141. Tazaki, K., Minamikawa, T. and Yoshida, S. (1974) Plant Cell Physiol. 15 205-211.
142. Dewick, P. M. and Haslam, E. (1969) Biochem. J. 113 539-542.
143. Barz, W., Mohr, F. and Teufel, E. (1974) Phytochemistry 13 1785-1787.
144. Hagel, P. and Kindl, H. (1975) FEBS Letters 59 120-124.
145. French, C. J., Vance, C. P. and Towers, G. H. N. (1976) Phytochemistry 15 564-566.
146. Camm, E. L. and Towers, G. H. N. (1973) Phytochemistry 12 961-973.
147. Gupta, S. and Acton, G. J. (1979) Biochim. Biophys. Acta 570 187-197.
148. Margna, U. (1977) Phytochemistry 16 419-426.
149. Steiner, A. M. (1977) Phytochemistry 16 1703-1704.
150. Hillis, W. E. and Ishikura, N. (1970) Phytochemistry 9 1517-1528.
151. Hasegawa, S. and Maier, V. P. (1970) Phytochemistry 9 2483-2487.
152. Harborne, J. B. and Corner, J. J. (1961) Biochem. J. 81 242-250.
153. Benveniste, I., Salaün, J.-P., and Durst, F. (1978) Phytochemistry 17 359-363.
154. Diesperger, H. and Sandermann, H., Jr. (1978) FEBS Letters 85 333-336.
155. Mayer, A. M. and Harel, E. (1979) Phytochemistry 18 193-215.
156. McIntyre, R. J. and Vaughan, P. F. T. (1975) Biochem. J. 149 447-461.
157. Rhodes, M. J. C. and Wooltorton, L. S. C. (1976) Phytochemistry 15 947-951.
158. Mansell, R. L., Gross, G. G., Stöckigt, J., Franke, H. and Zenk, M. H. (1974) Phytochemistry 13 2427-2435.
159. Lamb, C. J. (1979) Arch. Biochem. Biophys. 192 311-317.
160. Mansell, R. L., Babbel, G. R. and Zenk, M. H. (1976) Phytochemistry 15 1849-1853.
161. Klischies, M., Stöckigt, J. and Zenk, M. H. (1975) Chem. Commun. 879-880.
162. Senanayake, U. M., Wills, R. B. H. and Lee, T. H. (1977) Phytochemistry 16 2032-2033.
163. Brown, S. A. (1979) Planta Med. 36 299-310.
164. Fritig, B., Hirth, L. and Ourisson, G. (1970) Phytochemistry 9 1963-1975.
165. Satô, M. and Hasegawa, M. (1972) Phytochemistry 11 657-662.
166. Satô, M. (1967) Phytochemistry 6 1363-1373.
167. Edwards, K. G. and Stoker, J. R. (1967) Phytochemistry 6 655-661.
168. Grundon, M. F. (1978) Tetrahedron 34 143-161.
169. Brown, S. A. and Sampathkumar, S. (1977) Can. J. Biochem. 55 686-692.
170. Sarkar, S. K. and Phan, C. T. (1975) Physiol. Plant. 33 108-112.
171. Poulton, J., Hahlbrock, K. and Grisebach, H. (1976) Arch. Biochem. Biophys. 176 449-456.
172. Legrand, M., Firtig, B. and Hirth, L. (1976) FEBS Letters 70 131-136.
173. Thompson, H. J., Sharma, S. K. and Brown, S. A. (1978) Arch. Biochem. Biophys. 188 272-281.
174. Tsang, Y.-F. and Ibrahim, R. K. (1979) Phytochemistry 18 1131-1136.
175. Yamada, Y. and Kuboi, T. (1976) Phytochemistry 15 395-396.
176. Löffelhardt, W. and Kindl, H. (1979) FEBS Letters 104 332-334.
177. Whistance, G. R. and Threlfall, D. R. (1968) Biochem. J. 109 577-595.
178. Durand, R. and Zenk, M. H. (1976) Biochem. Physiol. Pflanzen 169 213-217.
179. Müller, W.-U. and Leistner, E. (1978) Phytochemistry 17 1735-1738.
180. Inouye, H., Ueda, S., Inoue, K. and Matsumura, H. (1979) Phytochemistry 18 1301-1308.
181. Inouye, H., Ueda, S., Inoue, K., Shiobara, Y. and Wada, I. (1978) Tetra. Letters 4551-4554.
182. Haworth, R. D. (1961) Proc. Chem. Soc. 1961 401-410.
183. Wenkert, E. (1959) Chem. and Indust. 1959 906-907.
184. Freudenberg, K. (1965) Science 148 595-600.
185. Grisebach, H. (1977) Naturwissenschaften 64 619-625.
186. Nakamura, Y., Fushiki, H. and Higuchi, T. (1974) Phytochemistry 13 1777-1784.
187. Hahlbrock, K. and Grisebach, H. (1979) Ann. Rev. Plant Physiol. 30 105-130.
188. Whitmore, Frank W. (1976) Phytochemistry 15 375-378.
189. Threlfall, D. R., Whistance, G. R., and Goodwin, T. W. (1968) Biochem. J. 106 107-112.
190. Wellburn, A. R. (1970) Phytochemistry 9 743-748.
191. Klischies, M. and Zenk, M. H. (1978) Phytochemistry 17 1281-1284.
192. Denniff, P. and Whiting, D. A. (1976) Chem. Commun. 711-712.
193. Molderez, M., Nagels, L. and Parmentier, F. (1978) Phytochemistry 17 1747-1750.
194. Ellis, B. E. (1974) Lloydia 37 168-184.

Chapter 5
SAPONIFIABLE LIPIDS

The saponifiable lipids are operationally defined as those materials which are insoluble in water but soluble in organic solvents such as ether or chloroform, and which on heating with alkali form water-soluble soaps. The soaps are salts of long-chain fatty acids, so that these fatty acids are a necessary component of any saponifiable lipid. In this chapter a few compounds have been included which do not have long enough fatty acid molecules to form real soaps since their salts in water form true solutions rather than colloidal micelles. With this one exception the above definition will be strictly followed. The saponifiable lipids are classified according to their structures into a few major categories:

> Fatty acids
> Simple lipids (fatty acid esters)
> Phospholipids or phosphatides
> Glycolipids

These categories are broken down into subgroups which will be described in the following sections.

FATTY ACIDS

All aliphatic carboxylic acids may be described as "fatty acids," but the term is usually restricted to the longer chain members of the series, which are practically insoluble in water but soluble in organic solvents. In this chapter the line will be arbitrarily drawn below the C_8 acids and the lower members included in Chapter 3.

The free acids or their salts are of much less frequent occurrence in the plant kingdom than are their esters which make up the other classes of saponifiable lipids. Nevertheless, occasional examples of unesterified acids are found, particularly in waxes. Fatty acids found in nature almost always have an even number of carbon atoms; but all of the straight chain, odd-carbon acids from C_7-C_{25} have been found free or as esters in higher plants. The vast majority of natural fatty acids have an unbranched carbon chain and differ from one another in chain length and degree of unsaturation. Oleic acid is the most widespread natural fatty acid, occurring in practically every natural lipid mixture. Palmitic acid is nearly as ubiquitous, and these two are then followed by the somewhat less common linoleic, palmitoleic, myristic, and stearic acids. In the structures shown in Table 5-1 no attempt is made to indicate *cis-trans* isomerism. Most naturally-occurring structures are *cis*.

Other fatty acids are peculiar to lipids of plants of particular taxonomic groups rather than being widespread in the plant kingdom. They include acids with acetylenic unsaturation, hydroxyl groups, carbocyclic rings, and branched chains. Sometimes the hydroxy acids are found as inner esters or lactones. Examples of some of these more unusual fatty acids are listed in Table 5-2 with their place of occurrence in the plant kingdom. Fern lipids are notable for a high content of C_{20} polyunsaturated acids (1). In animals C_{20} acids are important as precursors for prostaglandins. Most searches for prostaglandins in plants have been negative, but one has apparently been found in onions (2); and bran contains a compound of related structure (3). It is interesting that the so-called "wound hormone" (traumatin) of plants is also produced by oxidation of unsaturated fatty acids. It is 12- oxo-*trans* -10-dodecenoic acid (4). Many free fatty acids have modulating effects on plant enzymes and may act as natural regulators (5, 6).

TABLE 5-1.   SOME COMMON FATTY ACIDS

Name	Structure
Lauric	$CH_3(CH_2)_{10}COOH$
Myristic	$CH_3(CH_2)_{12}COOH$
Palmitic	$CH_3(CH_2)_{14}COOH$
Stearic	$CH_3(CH_2)_{16}COOH$
Arachidic	$CH_3(CH_2)_{18}COOH$
Behenic	$CH_3(CH_2)_{20}COOH$
Lignoceric	$CH_3(CH_2)_{22}COOH$
Palmitoleic	$CH_3(CH_2)_5CH = CH(CH_2)_7COOH$
Oleic	$CH_3(CH_2)_7CH = CH(CH_2)_7COOH$
Petroselinic	$CH_3(CH_2)_{10}CH = CH(CH_2)_4COOH$
Linoleic	$CH_3(CH_2)_4CH = CHCH_2CH = CH(CH_2)_7COOH$
Linolenic	$CH_3CH_2CH = CHCH_2CH = CHCH_2CH = CH(CH_2)_7COOH$
Elaeostearic	$CH_3(CH_2)_3CH = CHCH = CHCH = CH(CH_2)_7COOH$
Arachidonic	$CH_3(CH_2)_4CH = CHCH_2CH = CHCH_2CH = CHCH_2CH = CHCH_2(CH_2)_2COOH$
Erucic	$CH_3(CH_2)_7CH = CH(CH_2)_{11}COOH$

TABLE 5-2. SOME UNUSUAL FATTY ACIDS, STRUCTURES AND OCCURRENCE

Name of Acid	Structure	Occurrence
tariric	$CH_3(CH_2)_{10}C \equiv C(CH_2)_4COOH$	*Picramnia* spp.
ximenynic	$CH_3(CH_2)_5CH = CHC \equiv C(CH_2)_7COOH$	*Ximenia* spp.
sterculic	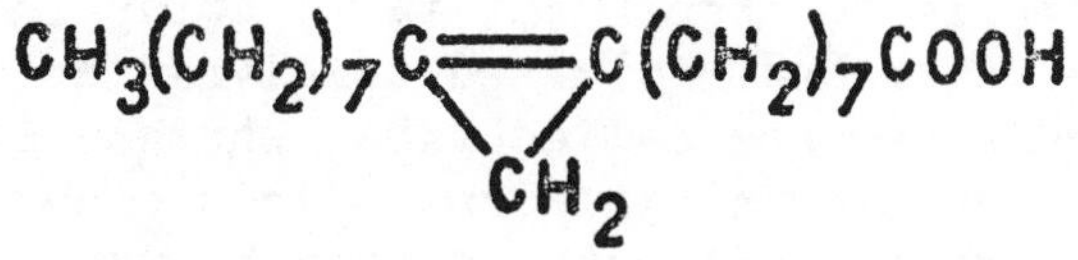 $CH_3(CH_2)_7C = C(CH_2)_7COOH$ with bridging CH_2	*Sterculia* spp.
chaulmoogric	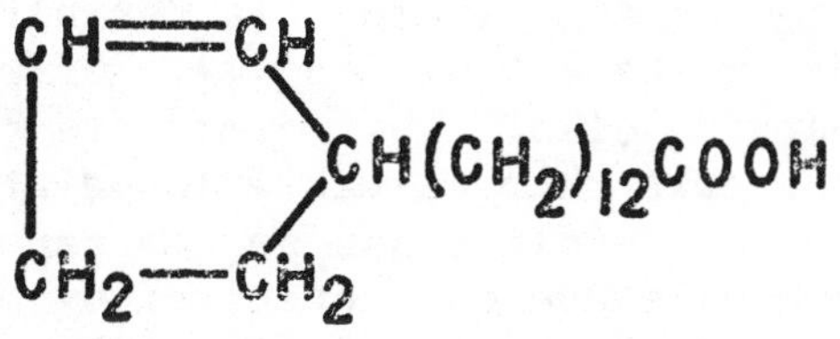 cyclopentene ring–$CH(CH_2)_{12}COOH$	*Flacourtiaceae*
ricinoleic	$CH_3(CH_2)_5CHCH_2CH = CH(CH_2)_7COOH$ with OH	*Ricinus communis*
vernolic	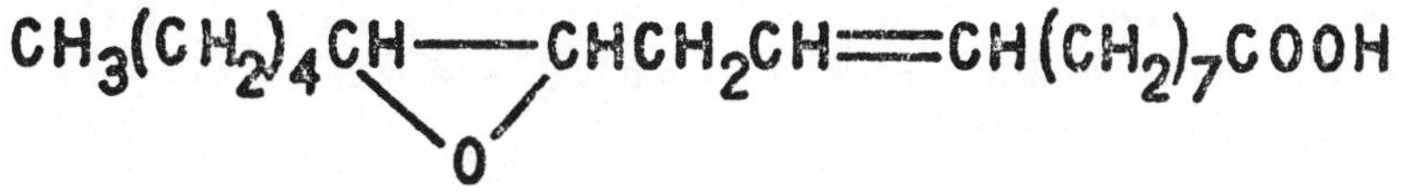 $CH_3(CH_2)_4CH \!-\! CHCH_2CH = CH(CH_2)_7COOH$ (epoxide O)	*Vernonia anthelmintica*
japanic	$HOOC(CH_2)_{19}COOH$	*Rhus* spp.
licanic	$CH_3(CH_2)_3(CH = CH)_3(CH_2)_4\overset{O}{C}CH_2CH_2COOH$	*Licania rigida*

TRIGLYCERIDES

Triglycerides are esters of glycerol with three fatty acid molecules:

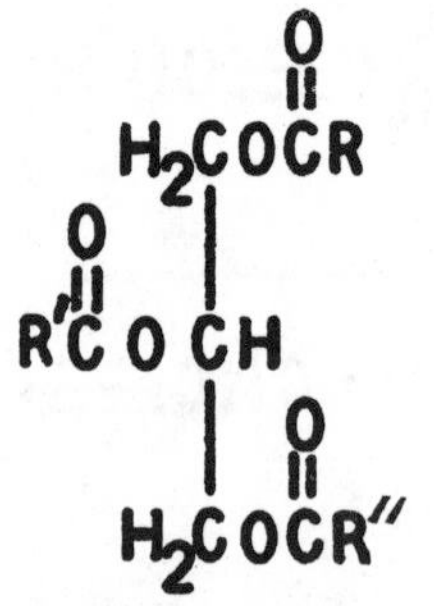

$$
\begin{array}{c}
\overset{\displaystyle O}{\overset{\|}{}} \\[-2pt]
H_2COCR \\
| \\
\overset{\displaystyle O}{\overset{\|}{R'CO}}\; CH \\
| \quad \overset{\displaystyle O}{\overset{\|}{}} \\
H_2COCR''
\end{array}
$$

The normal situation is for the three fatty acids to be different and the molecule therefore described as a "mixed triglyceride." Those which are solid at room temperature are called fats, whereas liquid triglycerides are called oils. Most natural fats and oils are not single compounds but mixtures of triglycerides, although one may be predominant. Chemically, fats contain a larger proportion of saturated fatty acids, and oils have more of the unsaturated acids. There is a definite preference for unsaturated fatty acids at the 2-position (7). Oils are further subdivided into drying and non-drying oils. The former are oxidized in the air to form tough films which make them valuable in paints and varnishes. The latter, while they may be oxidized and become rancid, remain liquids. Chemically, the drying oils are characterized by having a high proportion of polyunsaturated acids such as linolenic. The edible oils are characterized rather by having acids such as oleic and palmitoleic. The oxidation of unsaturated fatty acids begins with the attack of oxygen on an allylic carbon atom, leading to formation of a hydroperoxide:

$$
-CH_2CH = CH - \xrightarrow{\;\;O_2\;\;} \underset{\displaystyle OOH}{-\,CHCH = CH -}
$$

The hydroperoxide then undergoes secondary reactions to produce epoxides, glycols, and split products such as aldehydes and shorter chain carboxylic acids. It is these secondary products which are responsible for the rancid taste of oxidized fats and oils.

In plants fats and oils constitute important food storage materials, but they constitute a negligible fraction of the total lipids in such actively metabolizing organs as leaves. Low-lipid storage organs like potatoes and carrots can have triglycerides as a major fraction of their total lipids (8, 9). The breakdown of triglycerides yields more energy per gram than that of any other storage material, and their insolubility in water avoids the osmotic problems associated with maintaining a high concentration of water soluble material in cells. The majority of energy yielded by fat breakdown is probably produced by conversion of the fat to acetyl-CoA and oxidation of this through the glyoxylate and citric acid cycles (Chapter 3).

Table 5-3 gives the fatty acid composition of some common fats and oils. Extensive surveys by Hilditch (cf. general references) and others have indicated a close relation between plant families and their seed glycerides when fatty acid components are tabulated quantitatively and compared to botanical classification.

TABLE 5-3. FATTY ACID COMPOSITION OF SOME VEGETABLE FATS AND OILS
Figures are approximate percentage by weight.

olive oil . . . .   saturated acids 12, oleic 80, linoleic 8

coconut oil. . . . .   capric 12, lauric 45, myristic 17, palmitic 8

cacao butter . . . .   palmitic 24, stearic 35, oleic 38

peanut oil . . . .   palmitic 9, oleic 59, linoleic 21

castor oil . . . .   linoleic 5, ricinoleic 92

rape seed oil. . . . .   oleic 17, linoleic 18, linolenic 1, erucic 49

cottonseed oil . . . .   palmitic 20, oleic 30, linoleic 45

soy bean oil . . . .   saturated acids 19, oleic 22, linoleic 49,
linolenic 10

corn oil . . . .   saturated acids 15, oleic 24, linoleic 61

linseed oil . . . .   saturated acids 18, oleic 15, linoleic 15,
linolenic 52

OTHER FATTY ACID ESTERS

Besides the triglycerides, other simple esters of long-chain fatty
acids are commonly found in plants. Whereas the triglycerides usually
function as food storage components, the other fatty acid esters seem to
be more concerned in protective coatings on leaves, fruits, stems, etc.
They are chemical constituents of the substances known botanically as wax,
cutin, cork, etc., although each of these substances contains other types
of compounds as well (cf. Chaps. 6, 8). Rarely, seeds are found which
contain high-molecular weight esters used as food reserves (10), and some
triglycerides resemble waxes in being found as coatings on fruit. Plant
waxes are reviewed in (11, 12).

The most familiar ester components of plant waxes contain long-chain
alcohols combined with the fatty acids. The acids found in such waxes
are generally longer chain compounds than the acids of triglycerides.
The C_{24} - C_{36} acids are most common. The alcohols have the same range of
chain-lengths, and both the alcohols and acids are usually saturated.
Unsaturated alcohols are more common than unsaturated acids. Secondary
alcohols and dihydroxy alcohols are also found occasionally. Small amounts
of unesterified fatty acids and alcohols may be found in plant waxes. As
examples of some esters found in common plant waxes, carnauba wax contains
75% myricyl cerotate; snow brush wax, 80% of a mixture of ceryl palmitate
and ceryl stearate.

Other variants on the long-chain ester structure are found in certain
plant waxes which have hydroxy acids (13). When these are present, esters
may form between the carboxyl group and the hydroxyl group of the same
acid or with the hydroxyl group of another acid. In the first case lactones are formed. An example is aparajitin from the leaf wax of *Clitoria*
ternatea, which is also interesting for its branched chain structure:

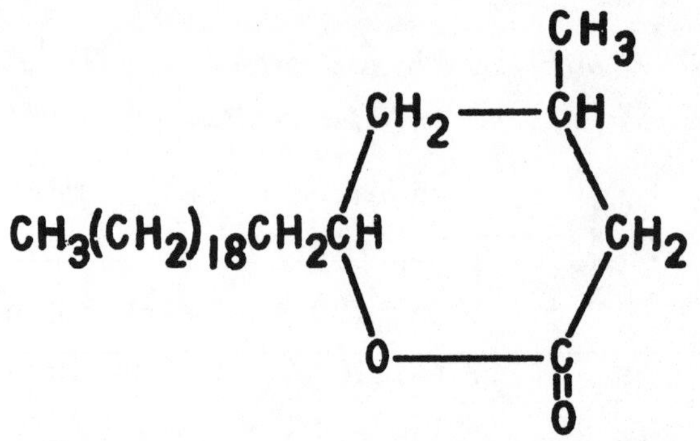

Macrocyclic lactones with a musk-like odor are exaltolide from *Angelica* roots and ambrettolide from seeds of *Hibiscus abelmoschus*.

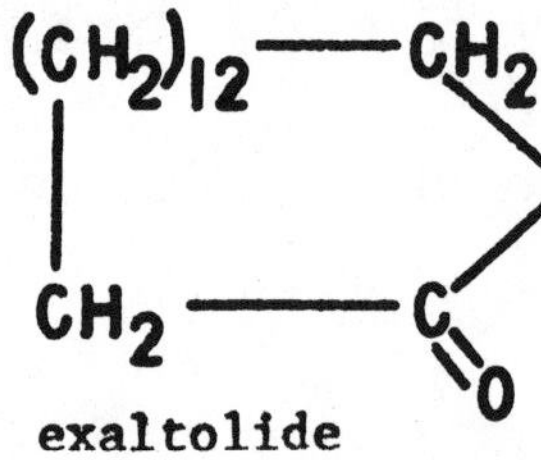

exaltolide 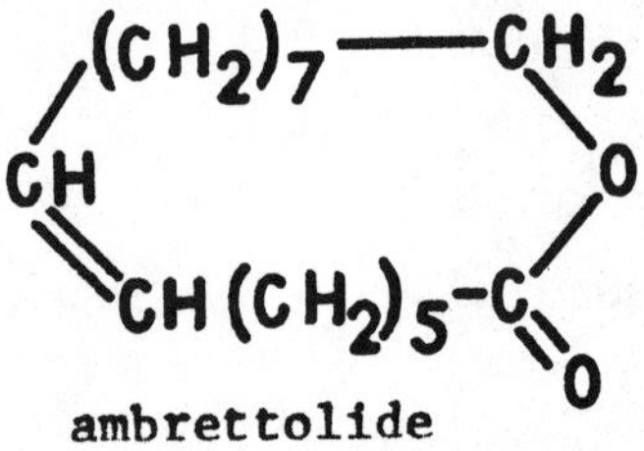   ambrettolide

Waxes containing polymeric esters formed by the linking of several hydroxy acids to each other are especially prominent in the waxy coatings of conifer needles. The two most common acids found in such waxes are sabinic and juniperic:

$$HOCH_2(CH_2)_{14}COOH \qquad\qquad HOCH_2(CH_2)_{10}COOH$$

The polymers may be linear or cyclic. The general term used for this type of wax constituent is "etholide" or "estolide".

TABLE 5-4.   *SOME LONG CHAIN SATURATED ACIDS AND ALCOHOLS FOUND FREE OR ESTERIFIED IN PLANT WAXES*

Number of Carbons	Acid	Alcohol
24	lignoceric	lignoceryl (n-tetrocosanol)
26	cerotic	ceryl (n-hexacosanol)
28	montanic	octacosyl (n-octacosanol)
30	melissic	n-myricyl (n-triacontanol)
32	lacceroic	n-lacceryl (n-dotriacontanol)
34	n-tetratriacontanoic	tetratriacontyl (n-tetratriacontanol)

The lipid constituents of cork and cuticle are known respectively as suberin and cutin. Although cutin is characteristic of aerial parts and suberin of underground parts, both may be found in the stem -- cutin in epidermis and suberin in endodermis (14). Cutin is tightly bound to other constituents within the cuticle layer and is, therefore, distinguished from easily removed outer deposits of wax. Although the exact chemical nature of cutin and suberin remains unclear, what evidence there is indicates that it is reasonable to group them with the polymeric esters. Hydrolysis of suberin yields a little glycerol but large amounts of dicarboxylic acids (15). Cutin is more resistant than suberin to attack by enzymes or chemical reagents. It does not yield any glycerol on hydrolysis but is characterized by large amounts of hydroxy, epoxy, and keto acids of chain length C_{14}-C_{22} (16, 17). The C_{16} acids predominate in apple leaves and C_{18} acids in apple fruits (18). Some *vic*-dihydroxy compounds may be artifacts produced by hydrolysis of epoxides. Both cutin and suberin have some unsaturated acids (19).

$$\overset{\text{OH}}{HO(CH_2)_6\overset{|}{CH}(CH_2)_9COOH}$$ 10,16-dihydroxypalmitic acid

$$HOOC(CH_2)_7\overset{O}{\overset{/\backslash}{CH-CH}}(CH_2)_7COOH$$ 9,10-epoxyoctadecan-1,18-dioic acid

$$HO(CH_2)_8\overset{\text{OH}}{\overset{|}{CH}}\overset{\text{OH}}{\overset{|}{CH}}(CH_2)_7COOH$$ phloionolic acid (*threo*-9,10,18-tri-hydroxyoctadecanoic acid)

$$HOOC(CH_2)_7\overset{\text{OH}}{\overset{|}{CH}}\overset{\text{OH}}{\overset{|}{CH}}(CH_2)_7COOH$$ phloionic acid

It seems likely that cutin and suberin are complex polymeric esters similar to the etholides but possibly having additional ester linkages to other constituents of cuticle or cork such as lignin, cellulose, tannins, or phenolic acids (20). The acids with more than one hydroxy group may form cross-linked polymers. The complexity of these compounds is pointed up by the finding of 41 component fragments in the cutin of cranberries (21). Reviews on plant cuticles and cutin are (22) and (23).

Sporopollenine, the chief constituent of the outer layer (exine) of pollen grains is a complex material, but an important part of it (55-65%) is derived from cross-linked hydroxy acid esters (24). It is, therefore, related structurally to cutin and suberin.

A group of relatively low molecular weight esters of acetylenic acids is characteristic of the family Compositae. Long-chain acetylenic C_{18} acids have already been mentioned as occurring in some triglycerides. The Compositae compounds are methyl esters of C_{10} acids. Two of the most widespread compounds in the family are the following:

$$CH_3CH = CH - C \equiv C - C \equiv C - CH = CH \overset{O}{\overset{\parallel}{C}}OCH_3$$

matricaria ester

$$CH_3CH_2CH_2C \equiv C - C \equiv C - CH = CH \overset{O}{\overset{\parallel}{C}}OCH_3$$

lachnophyllum ester

The composites also contain acetylenic alcohols and hydrocarbons which will be described in Chapter 6. Phytoalexins (e.g. wyerone) made by some legumes are derivatives of C_{14} acetylenic acids (25).

Esters of long-chain acids with short-chain alcohols are less familiar in plants than other fatty acid esters but are interesting for their enhancement of auxin effects (26). Other rare ester lipids have ethan- propan- or butandiols as the alcohol components (27). Glucosyl esters of $C_{16}-C_{20}$ fatty acids are widespread in seeds (28). Seed lipids of a few plants have cyanogenic compounds in which fatty acids are esterified with a C_5 hydroxy or dihydroxynitrile (29, 30). Poisonous substances from roots of several Convolvulaceae have $C_{10}-C_{16}$ hydroxy acids esterified with each other and also glycosylated (31).

PHOSPHOLIPIDS OR PHOSPHATIDES

Several different types of phosphorus-containing lipids are found in plants. They reach their highest concentration in seeds (up to 2% of dry weight). All are esters of phosphoric acid and long chain fatty acids. The simplest phospholipids are the phosphatidic acids which have fatty acid groups and phosphoric acid esterified with glycerol:

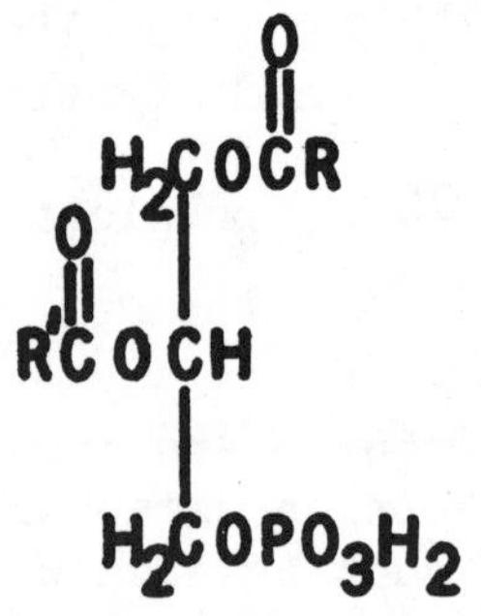

$$
\begin{array}{c}
\quad\quad\quad\quad O \\
\quad\quad\quad\quad \parallel \\
H_2COCR \\
O \\
\parallel \\
R'C\,O\,CH \\
\\
H_2COPO_3H_2
\end{array}
$$

Reports of the occurrences of phosphatidic acids in plants must be inter- preted with caution since active hydrolytic enzymes are often present which would break down other phosphatides to phosphatidic acids when the tissue is disintegrated. The phosphatidic acids are oily liquids soluble in the usual fat solvents. Since they contain a large proportion of un- saturated fatty acids, they are readily oxidized in the air forming hard products which are insoluble in organic solvents. The barium and calcium salts are insoluble in water and alcohol but soluble in ether.

The best-known of all the plant phospholipids are phosphatidylcholine (lecithin) and phosphatidylethanolamine. Phosphatidylserine is a well- known phospholipid that occurs at low concentration in plants. These com- pounds include the phosphatidic acid structure, but in addition, contain a nitrogenous compound linked as an ester with the phosphate.

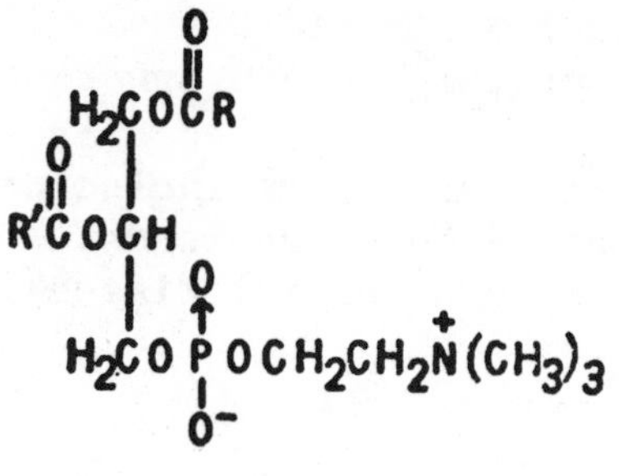

phosphatidylcholine (lecithin) 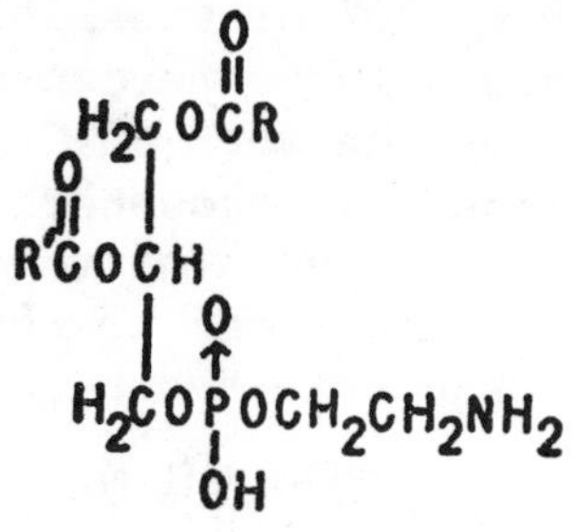   phosphatidylethanolamine 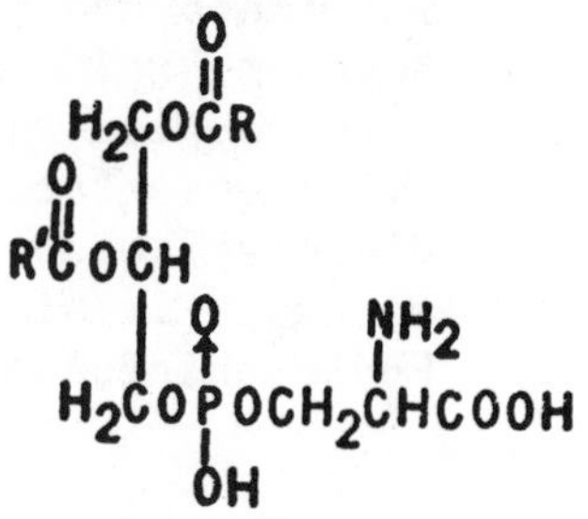   phosphatidylserine

The fatty acid at C-2 in these phospholipids is practically always unsaturated, and the other one may be (32). Different fatty acid compositions are found in different tissues and different organelles of the same plant (32, 33). In the same tissue the fatty acid compositions are not the same when different classes are compared to each other (34, 35). The phosphoglycerides are colorless, waxy solids which rapidly oxidize and darken on exposure to light and air. They are soluble in the usual fat solvents with certain exceptions which have been used in separating them from each other. Both substances are hygroscopic but form emulsions rather than true solutions in water. They may be precipitated from these solutions by adding acetone.

Other types of phospholipid have been found in plants, but much less is known about them. N-acylphosphatidylethanolamines occur widely in plant seeds, especially at early developmental stages (36, 37). Phosphatidyl glycerol and diphosphatidyl glycerol have been found in algae and higher plants, especially in chloroplasts and mitochondria (38, 39). The otherwise rare acid Δ^3-hexadecenoic is a major component of plastid phosphatidyl glycerol (40). Phosphatidyl inositols are also widespread

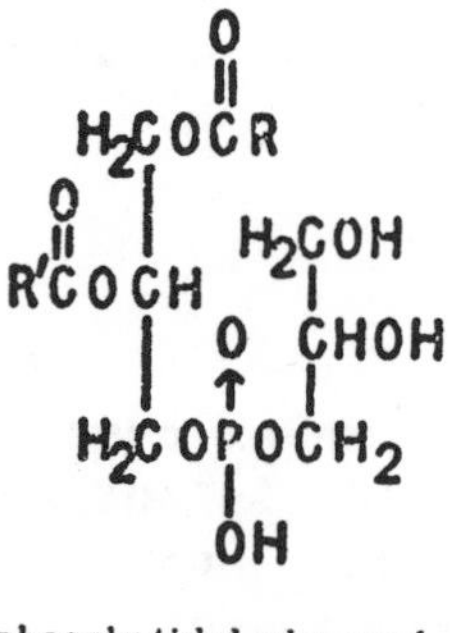

phosphatidyl glycerol

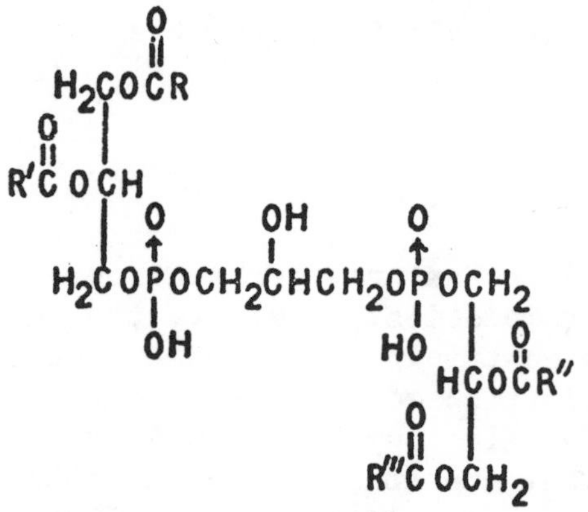

diphosphatidyl glycerol

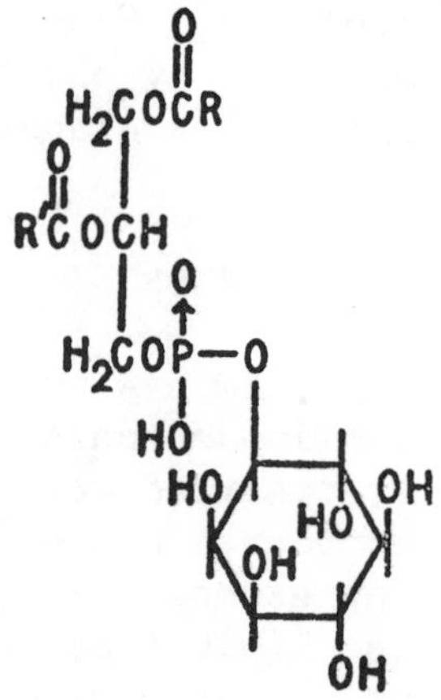

phosphatidyl inositol

in plants and may make up to 20% of the lipids of photosynthetic tissues (41).
Soybean lipids also contain a large percentage of inositol but are apparently
more complex as indicated by the work of Carter et al., (42) who found on
hydrolysis fatty acids, inositol, phosphoric acid, several sugars including
glucosamine and a uronic acid, and a nitrogen base named "phytosphingosine"
since it is similar but not identical to the sphingosine of animal tissues.
Phytosphingosine has the structure shown below:

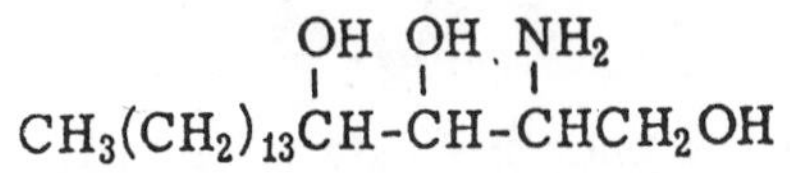

$$\overset{\overset{\displaystyle OH}{|}\,\overset{\displaystyle OH}{|}\,\overset{\displaystyle NH_2}{|}}{CH_3(CH_2)_{13}CH\text{-}CH\text{-}CHCH_2OH}$$

The sphingolipid molecule has an overall structure as follows:

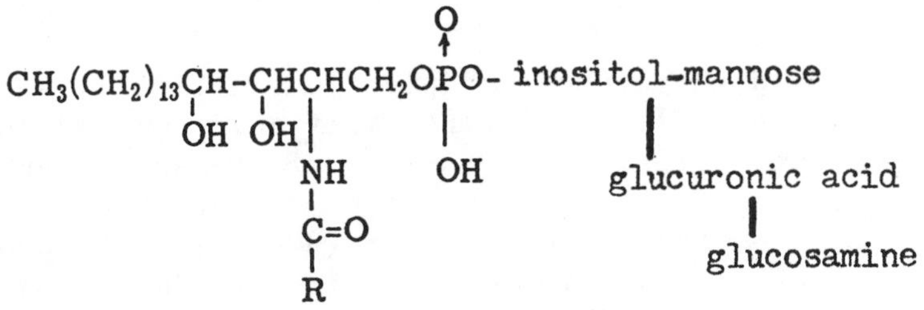

$$CH_3(CH_2)_{13}CH\text{-}\underset{\underset{\underset{\underset{R}{|}}{\overset{\displaystyle C=O}{|}}}{\overset{\displaystyle NH}{|}}}{CH}CHCH_2\overset{\overset{\displaystyle O}{\uparrow}}{O P O}\text{-}\underset{\overset{\displaystyle |}{OH}}{inositol}\text{-}mannose$$

with OH OH on the CH-CH positions; a branch reading: glucuronic acid — glucosamine.

The N-acylsphingosine portion is named "ceramide". Such structures are
found in leaves as well as seeds (43-45). The lipositols and sphingolipids
resemble the other phospholipids in many of their properties except for
somewhat different solubilities.

The phospholipids are probably most important in cells because of
their involvement in membrane structures and as bridges or binding agents
between polar and non-polar cell constituents (46). This latter function
is illustrated by the difficulty found in purifying many plant phospholipids since they are often tightly bound in complexes with carbohydrate
and/or protein. The precise structure of such complexes is unknown.
Proteolipids are defined as lipid-protein complexes with solubility properties like the lipids, whereas lipoproteins have solubility like the
proteins. From time to time it is suggested that phospholipids being
anionic may play a dynamic role in cation transport as well as a structural
role in membranes (47).

GLYCOLIPIDS

As has been noted in the previous section, some of the complex phospholipids contain sugar moieties. However, the term "glycolipid" is normally reserved for lipids containing sugar units but not phosphorus. Such
compounds are widely distributed in plants, especially in green leaves.
For example in alfalfa galactosyl compounds are the major component of
the lipid fraction. They are concentrated in chloroplasts and may comprise over 50% of the membrane lipids (38). They are much lower or non-
existent in mitochondrial lipids (39, 48, 49). The general structure of a
monogalactosyl diglyceride is shown below. Higher homologues have as many
as 5 galactose residues linked (1→6) to each other. The fatty acids are
usually highly unsaturated with linolenic acid predominating (33, 40, 48),
but a hexadecatrienoic acid also present (50). As with other glycerides
the unsaturated acids are almost entirely at C-2 (50). Possible involvement of galactolipids in membrane ion transport has been discussed (51, 52).

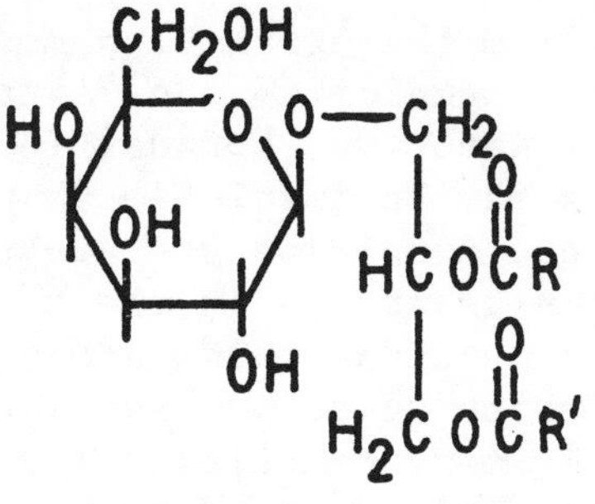

$$CH_2OH$$

monogalactosyl diglyceride

A sulfolipid related to 6-deoxyglucose (quinovose) is the major anionic lipid in chloroplasts of many plants (53) but also occurs in mitochondria (48). Its structure is:

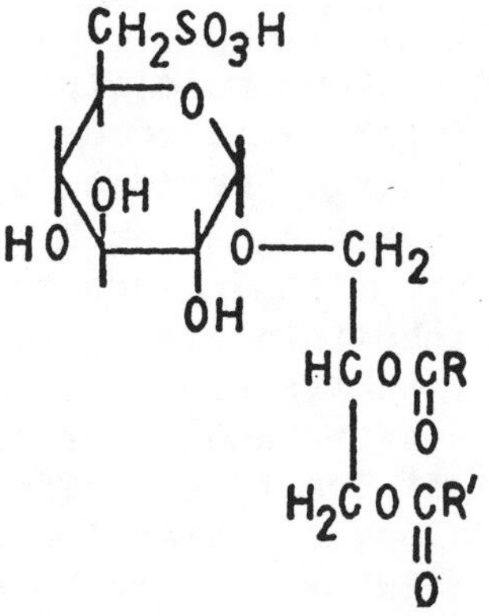

$$CH_2SO_3H$$

Palmitic is the predominant fatty acid and is preferentially at C-2 with stearic acid commonly at C-1 (54). Plants that grow in early spring have been found to contain sulfolipid with an unusual amount of C_{25} cyclopropane acid (55).

Glycolipids that yield neither glycerol nor phosphorus on hydrolysis are less well known and generally make up less than 1% of the total lipid of a plant. They resemble animal cerebrosides but probably no pure compounds have yet been studied. Hydrolysis of the mixtures gives various derivatives of sphingosine and phytosphingosine; fatty acids of C_{20}-C_{26}, most of them 2-hydroxy; and several types of carbohydrate units (56-59).

ISOLATION

Isolation of the different categories of lipids has relied heavily on differences in their solubilities. As with many other plant products, the first precaution to be observed is inactivation of degradative or transferring enzymes with heat before disintegration of the plant tissue. This precaution is especially necessary for the phospholipids (60, 61). A second precaution which must be taken when isolating highly unsaturated lipids is to exclude oxygen and strong light.

The total lipid may be extracted from tissue with mixtures of methanol-chloroform, ethanol-chloroform, or ethanol-ether. Boiling solvents have often been used, but homogenization at room temperature offers less chance for degradation to occur. If only non-polar and unbound lipids are desired, the alcohol may be omitted from the extracting medium or solvents like benzene, petroleum ether, etc. employed. For extraction of seed lipids the recommended solvent is water-saturated butanol (60, 62). Lipid-protein or lipid-carbohydrate complexes may be insoluble in non-polar solvents. In the presence of alcohols these complexes are broken, so that the lipid extracted gives no indication as to how it may have been complexed in situ. On the other hand, proteo-or peptido-lipids are known which are soluble in lipid solvents but release amino acids on hydrolysis (cf. Chap. 11). In the presence of phospholipids many non-lipids are extracted into lipid solvents. They can be effectively removed by mixing a 2:1 chloroform-methanol extract with 0.2 its volume of water. After centrifuging or long standing to separate the layers, non-lipid material is found in the upper, aqueous layer (63). Proteolipids form a fluffy layer at the interface and can be separated from other constituents (64).

By addition of acetone to a lipid extract prepared as described above phospholipids (with small amounts of sterolins and some waxes) are largely precipitated. Triglycerides, other esters, sterols, terpenes, etc. remain in solution. However, if much triglyceride is present, it will carry some phospholipid with it into the acetone-soluble fraction. Fractionation of the phospholipid precipitate will depend to some extent on what types of components are present. A differential extraction method using acetone containing ethanolamine has been devised to separate the three major classes (65). If inositol lipids are desired, the other phospholipids can be removed by prolonged extraction with cold, glacial acetic acid and partition between glacial acetic and benzene. Inositol lipid goes into the benzene phase. After evaporation of the benzene, sterolins (if present) may be removed by extraction with 2:1 ethanol-chloroform mixture leaving relatively pure inositol lipid (66). Another method for fractionation of the phospholipids depends on precipitating lecithin as a cadmium salt from alcoholic solution. The cadmium salt is subjected to further purification steps and finally the lecithin recovered by dissolving the salt in chloroform and shaking this solution with an equal volume of 30% methanol. Pure lecithin dissolves in the chloroform layer, and the cadmium chloride goes into the aqueous methanol. After removal of lecithin the remaining phospholipids may be fractionated by dissolving in chloroform and adding ethanol stepwise. Inositol lipids precipitate first, followed by phosphatidyl-serine, and finally phosphatidylethanolamine. A procedure using counter-current distribution and chromatography on DEAE cellulose and silicic acid has been devised for efficient separation of the different classes of complex lipids from leaves (67).

Going back to the solution of lipids remaining after removal of phospholipids, separation of these constituents in their original form is very difficult. Free fatty acids may be removed by extraction with sodium carbonate solution, long-chain hydrocarbons and alcohols as urea complexes (Chap. 6) and sterols as digitonides or tomatinides (Chap. 8). The lower terpenes and other volatile compounds may be removed by distillation (or steam distillation); higher terpenoid acids will be extracted with free fatty acids into sodium carbonate solution. The long-chain fatty acids may then be separated as urea complexes from the higher terpenoid acids (68). Glycolipids are not precipitated by acetone but can be separated from everything except triglycerides by partitioning the mixture of acetone-soluble components between methanol and heptane. Glycolipids (including sterolins) and triglycerides go into the methanol layer. Further separation depends on chromatography (69).

A mixture containing chiefly triglycerides and/or ester waxes may be separated into its ester components only by tedious and unsatisfactory procedures. Of most general application are fractional distillation at very low pressures or fractional crystallization from acetone at very low temperatures. The more usual procedure is to submit the esters to saponification and then identify the constituent acids and alcohols. This, of course, gives no information as to how they were originally combined. Triglycerides are saponified by refluxing for 1-2 hours with about five times their weight of 6% potassium hydroxide in 95% ethanol. The long-chain ester waxes require more drastic conditions for complete hydrolysis -- e.g. refluxing for 12 hours a solution of wax in benzene plus an equal volume of 10% KOH in alcohol. This difference in ease of hydrolysis makes it possible to remove some triglycerides from an ester wax by saponification without too much loss of the wax. The chief danger to be noted in saponification is that prolonged heating may cause isomeric changes in the double bond positions of polyunsaturated acids. It is sometimes recommended that lecithin be hydrolyzed by standing with N potassium hydroxide for 16 hours at 37° C.

After hydrolysis long-chain alcohols resulting from saponification of ester waxes may be removed (along with any unsaponified material) by extraction with benzene, etc. The remaining mixture is then acidified and fatty acids extracted with ether.

Mixtures of long chain fatty acids either naturally occurring or derived by saponification can be separated by various crystallization and distillation procedures. A common method is to dissolve the fatty acids in acetone and cool to -60° to -70° C. Polyunsaturated acids remain in solution while others crystallize out. Redissolving the precipitate and recrystallizing at -30° to -40° C. leaves most of the mono-unsaturated acids in solution. A final recrystallization from ether at -30° deposits most of the saturated acids. The separations are not perfect, but by repetition and combination with other methods, a satisfactory fractionation can usually be achieved according to degree of unsaturation. Another type of separation depends on the fact that lead salts of the saturated acids are insoluble in ether or alcohol, whereas, those of the unsaturated acids are soluble. Further fractionation may be achieved by distillation of methyl esters of the acids under reduced pressure (0.1-5.0 mm. of mercury).

Chromatographic purification offers many advantages over solvent fractionation methods for the lipids, although some preliminary solvent fractionation of a complex mixture may be necessary. Several reviews are available covering lipids in general (70), phospholipids (71), and plant waxes (72). Silicic acid chromatography is particularly useful for anionic lipids since less polar lipids move rapidly through the column. Thus phospholipids may be readily separated from other lipids, and then further subdivided among themselves. A typical procedure would be to slurry the silica gel with chloroform-methanol 2:1, add the lipid solution in chloroform, and start development with pure chloroform. As non-polar lipids move through the column, the concentration of methanol in the developing solvent is gradually increased. Finally the most polar substances are eluted with pure methanol. Carroll (73) has suggested that Florisil offers many advantages over silicic acid as an adsorbent for lipid chromatography. Separations are similar but more convenient. Ion exchange chromatography on DEAE cellulose or ECTEOLA cellulose has been valuable

in isolation of phospholipids and sulfolipid and in separating sulfolipid from phospholipid (74, 75).

The elution peaks can often be recognized by measuring absorption at
300 nm. This absorption is given by oxidation products of the unsaturated
fatty acids when careful exclusion of oxygen is not practiced. Another
way of identifying lipid-containing eluate fractions is to spot a small
amount on a ferrotype plate. When the volatile solvent evaporates, small
amounts of lipid are easily visible (76).

Although the above procedures have been written as though a given
lipid mixture might contain every possible constituent, the situation in
nature is seldom quite so discouraging. In many cases one lipid, or at
least one type of lipid, will be predominant; and the problem is only to
remove small amounts of a few other constituents. For instance, cuticle
waxes may rise to the surface as a film if fruits, leaves, etc. are merely
immersed for a few minutes in boiling water. Such a preparation would
contain no phospholipids and probably only traces of triglycerides.

Procedures have not been given for preparation of the rarer types of
lipids which have been mentioned. Since at the present state of our knowledge each one is a special case, the original papers on them should be
consulted. Although suberin and cutin are hardly rare in the plant kingdom, they are practically defined by the arbitrary and involved methods
by which they have been prepared, and small variations in experimental
details might yield quite different products. For preparation of suberin,
cutin, sporopollenine, etc. references (18, 22, 24, 77) may be consulted.

CHARACTERIZATION

Many common methods used for characterization of saponifiable lipids
are well described in elementary texts of organic chemistry and biochemistry. They include such determinations as iodine number, saponification
value, etc. and depend for their interpretation on a knowledge of what
type of lipid is being dealt with.

The most convenient source of up to date information on lipid analytical methods is the monthly bibliography in The Journal of Lipid Research.
General methods for fatty acid esters   are described in (78).

Several color tests are available to indicate what types of lipids
may be present in a mixture. Phospholipids are indicated by color reactions for phosphorus such as may be given by adding ammonium molybdate
solution and concentrated sulfuric acid to an ethereal solution. Glycolipids are indicated by positive tests for carbohydrate such as the
Molisch reaction. For identification of other components, the simplest
procedure is probably saponification of the lipid mixture, followed by
separation of the non-saponifiable material. The latter may be tested
for the presence of sterols, long-chain alcohols, hydrocarbons, etc. by
methods described in the appropriate chapters. The presence of soap in
the aqueous layer is obvious on shaking and indicates the presence of
long-chain fatty acids. After acidification of the saponification mixture and removal of the fatty acids, glycerol may be detected by evaporating

to a small volume. If triglycerides or other glycerol derivatives were
present in the original lipid, the odor of acrolein will be apparent on
heating this concentrated solution strongly with sodium bisulfate. Sphingosine is released from sphingolipids only by a combination of basic and acid
hydrolysis, but acidic hydrolysis alone produces a free amino group which
may be detected by its color reaction with ninhydrin. The other types of
nitrogenous compounds released on hydrolysis of phospholipids may be
detected by methods described in Chapter 15. Ester waxes may be distinguished from triglycerides by the fact that after saponification long-
chain alcohols appear in the benzene-soluble fraction and may be identified
by methods described in Chapter 6. If the individual fatty acids are separated and identified, the appearance of acids containing more than 30
carbon atoms is also evidence for the presence of ester waxes.

A good general review of lipid chromatography is (70). Characterization by means of paper chromatography has not been of much value when
applied to the triglycerides as such. Early separations used paper impregnated with silicic acid or mineral oil but these techniques have now
been superseded by thin layer chromatography. A preliminary group separation by liquid column chromatography has been recommended to precede a
high resolution thin layer separation (79), but group separations can also
be achieved on silica gel thin layer plates by using double development
(80, 81) or complex solvent mixtures (82). After a group separation other
procedures permit separations within the various classes such as fatty
acids (83), polar lipids (84, 85), phospholipids (86), neutral lipids (87),
etc. (88). Incorporation of urea or thiourea into the adsorbent makes
possible separations dependent on degree of branching since branched
chains form clathrates with thiourea and straight chains with urea (89).
Incorporation of silver nitrate into the adsorbent retards compounds according to the degree of unsaturation of the fatty acid chain (90). Detection of compounds can use general methods or reagents specific for
different lipid classes. All types of lipids are revealed with protoporphyrin in hydrochloric acid (91), malachite green (92), rhodamine B-dichloro-
fluorescein (93), Rhodamine 6G (71), or Sudan black (94). Phospholipids
can be detected with a molybdate reagent (95).

Gas chromatography is useful for analysis of fatty acids (96), usually
after conversion to methyl or benzyl esters (97-99). Triglyceride mixtures can also be separated (100). Phospholipids and sphingolipids are
converted to trimethylsilyl derivatives (101). Mass spectroscopy has also
been coupled with gas chromatography for analysis of these compounds (97,
100, 101).

As in other areas, high performance liquid chromatography is recently
being applied to the analysis of lipids (102). A long and useful review
containing applications to plants is given in (103). Most lipid peaks can
be detected in column effluent by measuring absorption at 206 nm (104).

Spectral measurements have a special place in the characterization of
saponifiable lipids. Compounds with conjugated unsaturations are the only
lipids to show absorption peaks in the ultra-violet range from 210-400 nm.
The only common fatty acid with conjugated double bonds is elaeostearic;
and fats containing it or other conjugated trienes show absorption at
about 270 nm. Conjugated dienes absorb at about 230 nm, tetraenes at 310
nm, and pentaenes at 330 nm. Conjugated systems containing acetylenic
bonds give about the same wavelength maxima as systems of ethylenic bonds,
but they may be recognized by other spectral differences such as intensity

and side bands. The ultra-violet spectrophotometry of fatty acids has been
reviewed by Pitt and Morton (105). Ultra-violet spectrophotometry may also
be applied to non-conjugated unsaturated compounds by first heating them
45 minutes at 180° C. in the presence of 7.5% potassium hydroxide in
glycerol or ethylene glycol. This treatment isomerizes 1, 4 unsaturated
systems to conjugated 1, 3 systems which then show the absorption spectra
described above. By observing the spectrum before and after isomerization
both conjugated and non-conjugated constituents may be identified. This
procedure can also be used for quantitative estimation by weighing the
sample of fat and measuring extinction coefficients at the appropriate
wavelengths for the different unsaturated acids. Allen _et al_. have presented infrared spectra of many complex lipids (67). Infrared spectra
can be used to distinguish between the different classes of nitrogenous
phospholipids (106).

METABOLIC PATHWAYS

The metabolic pathways for synthesis of the saponifiable lipids may
be divided by considering the biosynthesis of the products formed on hydrolysis and then the assembly of these portions to make the complete
lipid. Except for the fatty acids, biosynthesis of other lipid components
is covered in other chapters. A general review of fatty acid biosynthesis
is given in (107).

In addition to the pathways shown in the diagram only a few points
will be stressed here.

1. The acetyl CoA needed for fatty acid biosynthesis in cytoplasm
   is derived from citrate that is released from mitochondria and
   then cleaved by the action of ATP-citrate lyase (108, 109).
   Systems that can synthesize long-chain acids from acetyl CoA
   are present both in plastid membranes and the cytoplasm. Systems
   that can elongate palmitic acid to its higher homologues are
   present also in the plastid stroma and in mitochondria (110-112).
   Elongation systems are obviously important in the synthesis of
   long-chain ester waxes (113, 114).
2. A multifunctional enzyme system is functional in the biosynthesis
   of fatty acids; but in higher plants fractionation of this complex has been achieved; and a small protein, the acyl carrier
   protein (ACP), has been isolated that actually binds the acyl
   groups. Coenzyme A functions in feeding acetate and malonate to
   the system but does not carry intermediates.
3. The pathways for biosynthesis of unsaturated fatty acids in
   plants are still not entirely clarified. Four distinct routes
   have been proposed:
   a. Exogenous, free saturated acids cannot be desaturated. They
      can be converted to CoA derivatives, but the initial desatura-
      tion only occurs with ACP derivatives, and transferases may
      be lacking for the transfer of long-chain acyl groups from
      CoA to ACP. Stearoyl-ACP can be desaturated to oleyl-ACP (115,
      116).
   b. A microsomal system is known that can convert oleyl-CoA to
      linoleyl-CoA. Oleyl-ACP is not a substrate. Oxygen and

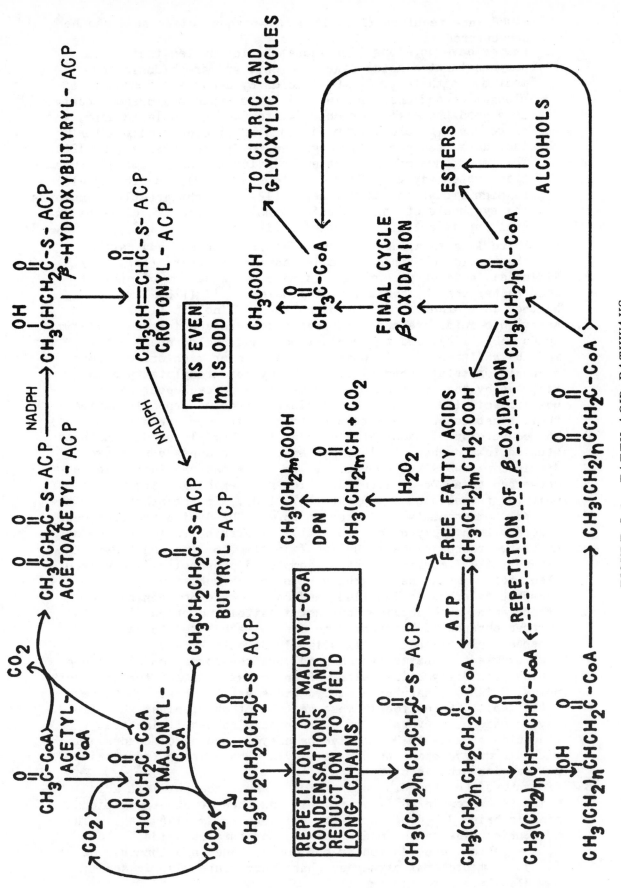

FIGURE 5-1. FATTY ACID PATHWAYS

$NADPH_2$ are required (117, 118). Exogenous oleic acid can be desaturated (119).

c. Leaves have an elongation—desaturation system that makes polyunsaturated acids like linolenic and arachidonic from medium length (e.g. C_{10}-C_{12}) acids by a concerted process of elongation and desaturation. By this process exogenous acetate is a good precursor for only C-1 to C-9 of linolenic acid, and exogenous C_{18} acids are precursors of linolenic only after they have been partially degraded to C_{12} precursors (120-122). The importance of this system relative to the direct desaturation system may vary from leaf to leaf (123), and it may also be significant in other tissues (124). Light greatly stimulates the synthesis of chloroplastic linolenic acid, which is essential for galactolipid synthesis (125

d. There is some evidence that an oleyl group already part of phosphatidylcholine can be desaturated further (127, 127).

4. Ricinoleic acid of castorbeans is made by oxidation of oleic acid rather than by hydration of linoleic acid (128, 129). Neither is ricinoleic acid a precursor of linoleic (130).

5. Acetylenic acids are made by further dehydrogenation of ethylenic acids (131, 132), and the cyclopropane and cyclopropene acids made by addition of a C_1 unit from formate or methionine across a double or triple bond (133, 134). Cyclopentenyl fatty acids are made by the addition of acetate units to cyclopentene carboxylic acid (135). Branched chain fatty acids probably derive their substituent groups from the methyl group of methionine (136).

6. The conversion of phosphatidic acids to other glycerides has been studied in a number of plant systems, and it appears that two distinct pathways are operative. In one a phosphatidic acid is converted to a CDP-diglyceride which next exchanges its CMP unit for the alcohol component (137, 138). In the other route the alcohol component is activated to form a CDP-derivative that next reacts with a diglyceride (139-141). The relative importance of these two routes probably shifts from time to time and tissue to tissue (142). Modifications of completed phospholipids can occur also for example the decarboxylation of phosphatidylserine to phosphatidylethanolamine (143) and an exchange between serine, ethanolamine, and choline (but not inositol) moieties (143, 144). Whether phosphatidylethanolamine can be methylated to make phosphatidylcholine is still slightly doubtful (143).

7. A chloroplastic enzyme system catalyzes the formation of galactolipids from diglycerides with UDP-galactose donating the galactosyl units. Highly unsaturated diglycerides are the best substrates (145, 146). The sulfoquinovose portion of chloroplast sulfolipid may be made by conversion of cysteic acid to 3-sulfolactate, reduction of this to 3-sulfolactoaldehyde, and aldol condensation with dihydroxyacetone phosphate (147). There is no information on the biosynthesis of sphingolipids.

8. Biosynthesis of the C_{16} cutin acids starts from palmitic acid which is hydroxylated first at C-16 and then at other positions, finally being dehydrogenated to make keto acids (148, 149). The C_{18} cutin acids can be made from Δ^9 unsaturated acids by 18-hydroxylation, epoxidation at the double bond, and then hydration (150). A microsomal oxygenase that hydroxylates lauric acid may also have a role here (151).

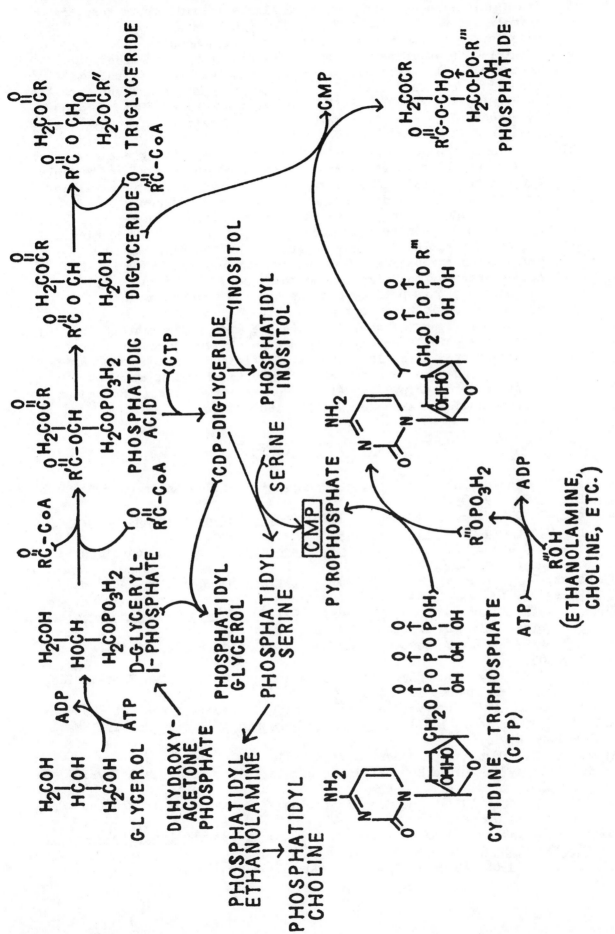

FIGURE 5-2. TRIGLYCERIDE AND PHOSPHATIDE PATHWAYS

9. The β-oxidation of fatty acids in plants is similar to that of animals except that in tissues with glyoxysomes they are a major site for the process rather than mitochondria (152). Carnitine is a carrier of acyl units across the mitochondrial membrane (153). Beta oxidation of ricinoleic acid is unusually slow and stops at C_{10} or C_{12}; the remaining steps are unclear (154). In germinating fatty seeds the acetyl CoA derived from β-oxidation is converted to carbohydrate by way of the glyoxylate cycle (see Chap. 3).

10. The α-oxidation of long chain fatty acids is a major pathway in several higher plant tissues (for example leaves, seeds, and freshly cut potato tubers). The first step in this process is catalyzed by a microsomal mixed function oxidase that produces a D- 2-hydroperoxide. This intermediate is partially reduced to a 2-hydroxy acid and partially decarboxylated to an aldehyde plus CO_2 and water. Either dehydrogenation of the aldehyde or oxidative decarboxylation of the hydroxy acid leads to a fatty acid shorter by one carbon atom than the starting fatty acid (155). In addition, this pathway can explain the occurrence of α-hydroxy acids in plant ceramides (156).

11. Lipoxidase (lipoxygenase) is an enzyme widely distributed in plants (especially seeds), which has no obvious function. From an unsaturated acid like linoleic it first forms a hydroperoxide that then goes on to a number of products of which some could be related to cutin acids (157), some to traumatin (158), and some to prostaglandin-like products (159, 160).

GENERAL REFERENCES

Fedili, E. & Jacini, G. (1971) "Lipid Composition of Vegetable Oils," Adv. Lipid. Res. 9 335-382.

Galliard, T. & Mercer, E. I., eds. (1975) Recent Advances in the Chemistry and Biochemistry of Plant Lipids, Academic Press, N. Y.

Gurr, M. I. & James, A. T. (1976) Lipid Biochemistry: An Introduction, Halsted Press, N. Y.

Hitchcock, C. & Nichols, B. W. (1971) Plant Lipid Biochemistry, Academic Press, N. Y.

Johnson, A. R. & Davenport, J. B., eds. (1971) Biochemistry and Methodology of Lipids, Wiley-Interscience, N. Y.

Kates, M. (1970) "Plant Phospholipids and Glycolipids," Adv. Lipid Res. 8 225-265.

Kunau, W. H. (1976) "Chemistry and Biochemistry of Unsaturated Fatty Acids," Angew. Chem. Intern. Ed. 15 61-74.

Litchfield, C. (1972) Analysis of Triglycerides, Academic Press, N. Y.

Marinetti, G. V., ed. (1967) Lipid Chromatographic Analysis, 2 Vols., Marcel Dekker, N. Y.

Martin, J. T., "Cutins and Suberins," in Miller 3 154-161.

Mazliak, P. (1973) "Lipid Metabolism in Plants," Ann. Rev. Plant Physiol. 24 287-310.

Smith, C. R., Jr. (1971) "Occurrence of Unusual Fatty Acids in Plants," Prog. Chem. Fats Other Lipids 11 137-177.

Tevini, M. & Lichtenthaler, H. K., eds. (1977) Lipids and Lipid Polymers in Higher Plants, Springer-Verlag, N. Y.

Wolff, I. A. (1966) "Seed Lipids," Science 154 1140-1149.

BIBLIOGRAPHY

1. Jamieson, G. R. and Reid, E. H. (1975) Phytochemistry $\underline{14}$ 2229-2232.
2. Attrep, K., Attrep, M., Jr., Bellman, W. P., Lee, J. B. and Brazelton, W., Jr. (1979) Am. Chem. Soc. Mtg. Abstr. April, Biol. Chem. Sect. 70.
3. Albro, P. W. and Fishbein, L. (1971) Phytochemistry $\underline{10}$ 631-636.
4. Zimmerman, D. C. and Coudron, C. A. (1979) Plant Physiol. $\underline{63}$ 536-541.
5. Mattoo, A. K. and Modi, V. V. (1975) Biochim. Biophys. Acta $\underline{397}$ 318-330.
6. Groenewald, E. G. and Visser, J. H. (1978) Z. Pflanzenphysiol. $\underline{88}$ 423-429.
7. Weber, E. J., De La Roche, I. A. and Alexander, D. E. (1971) Lipids $\underline{6}$ 525-530.
8. Galliard, T. (1968) Phytochemistry $\underline{7}$ 1907-1914.
9. Soimajärvi, J. and Linko, R. R. (1973) Acta Chem. Scand. $\underline{27}$ 1053-1055.
10. Moreau, R. A. and Huang, A. H. C. (1977) Plant Physiol. $\underline{60}$ 329-333.
11. Kolattukudy, P. E. (1970) Lipids $\underline{5}$ 259-275.
12. Caldicott, A. P. and Eglinton, G. in Miller, L. P., ed., Phytochemistry $\underline{3}$, Van Nostrand-Reinhold, N. Y., 1973, 162-194.
13. Downing, D. T. (1961) Revs. Pure Appl. Chem. $\underline{11}$ 196-211.
14. Espelie, K. E. and Kolattukudy, P. E. (1979) Plant Physiol. $\underline{63}$ 433-435.
15. Kolattukudy, P. E. and Agrawal, V. P. (1974) Lipids $\underline{9}$ 682-691.
16. Hunneman, D. H. and Eglinton, G. (1972) Phytochemistry $\underline{11}$ 1989-2001.
17. Deas, A. H. B., Baker, E. A. and Holloway, P. J. (1974) Phytochemistry $\underline{13}$ 1901-1905.
18. Holloway, P. J. (1974) Phytochemistry $\underline{13}$ 2201-2207.
19. Kolattukudy, P. E. and Dean, B. B. (1974) Plant Physiol. $\underline{54}$ 116-121.
20. Riley, R. G. and Kolattukudy, P. E. (1975) Plant Physiol. $\underline{56}$ 650-654.
21. Croteau, R. and Fagerson, I. S. (1972) Phytochemistry $\underline{11}$ 353-363.
22. Mazliak, P. (1968) Progress in Phytochemistry $\underline{1}$ 49-111.
23. Holloway, P. J. (1977) Biochem. Soc. Trans. $\underline{5}$ 1263-1266.
24. Brooks, J., Grant, P. R., Muir, M., van Gijzel, P. and Shaw, G. eds., Sporopollenin, Academic Press, N. Y. 1971.
25. Hargreaves, J. A., Mansfield, J. W., Coxon, D. T. and Price, K. R. (1976) Phytochemistry $\underline{15}$ 1119-1121.
26. Iwata, T. and Stowe, B. B. (1973) Plant Physiol. $\underline{51}$ 691-701.
27. Bergelson, L. D. (1973) Fette-Seifen-Anstrichs. $\underline{75}$ 89-96.
28. Chandra, G. R., Mandava, N. and Warthen, J. D. (1978) Plant Physiol. $\underline{61}$ Suppl. 96.
29. Mikolajczak, K. L., Smith, C. R., Jr. and Tjarks, L. W. (1970) Lipids $\underline{5}$ 812-817
30. Seigler, D. (1974) Phytochemistry $\underline{13}$ 841-843.
31. Khanna, S. N. and Gupta, P. C. (1967) Phytochemistry $\underline{6}$ 735-739.
32. Devor, K. A. and Mudd, J. B. (1971) J. Lipid Res. $\underline{12}$ 396-402.
33. Hawke, J. C., Rumsby, M. G. and Leech, R. M. (1974) Plant Physiol. $\underline{53}$ 555-561.
34. Kondoh, H. and Kawabe, S. (1975) Agric. Biol. Chem. $\underline{39}$ 745-746.
35. Harwood, J. L. (1976) Phytochemistry $\underline{15}$ 1459-1463.
36. Aneja, R., Chadha, J. S. and Knaggs, J. A. (1969) Biochem. Biophys. Res. Commun. $\underline{36}$ 401-406.
37. Wilson, R. F. and Rinne, R. W. (1974) Plant Physiol. $\underline{54}$ 744-747.
38. Mackender, R. O. and Leech, R. M. (1974) Plant Physiol. $\underline{53}$ 496-502.
39. Kalra, S. K. and Brooks, J. L. (1973) Phytochemistry $\underline{12}$ 487-492.
40. Panter, R. A. and Boardman, N. K. (1973) J. Lipid Res. $\underline{14}$ 664-671.
41. Le Page, M., Mumma, R., and Benson, A. A. (1960) J. Am. Chem. Soc. $\underline{82}$ 3712-3715.
42. Carter, H. E., Strobach, D. R. and Hawthorne, J. N. (1969) Biochemistry $\underline{8}$ 383-388.
43. Kaul, K. and Lester, R. L. (1975) Plant Physiol. $\underline{55}$ 120-129.
44. Kameyama, H. and Urakami, C. (1979) J. Am. Oil Chemists Soc. $\underline{56}$ 549-551.
45. Kaul, K. and Lester, R. L. (1975) Plant Physiol. $\underline{55}$ 120-129.
46. Benson, A. A. (1964) Ann. Rev. Plant Physiol. $\underline{15}$ 1-16.
47. Oursel, A., Lamant, A., Salsac, L. and Mazliak, P. (1973) Phytochemistry $\underline{12}$ 1865-1874.
48. Schwertner, H. A. and Biale, J. B. (1973) J. Lipid Res. $\underline{14}$ 235-242.
49. McCarty, R. E., Douce, R., and Benson, A. A. (1973) Biochim. Biophys. Acta, $\underline{316}$ 266-270.
50. Auling, G., Heinz, E., and Tulloch, A. P. (1971) Z. Physiol. Chem. $\underline{352}$ 905-912.

51. Kuiper, P. J. C. (1968) Plant Physiol. 43 1372-1374.
52. Roughan, P. G. (1970) Biochem. J. 117 1-8.
53. Haines, T. H. (1971) Prog. Chem. Fats Other Lipids 11 299-345.
54. Tulloch, A. P., Heinz, E. and Fischer, W. (1973) Z. Physiol. Chem. 354 879-889.
55. Kuiper, P. J. C. and Stuiver, B. (1972) Plant Physiol. 49 307-309.
56. Carter, H. E. and Koob, J. L. (1969) J. Lipid Res. 10 363-369.
57. Miyazawa, T., Ito, S. and Fujino, Y. (1974) Agric. Biol. Chem. (Japan) 38 1387-1391.
58. Ito, S. and Fujino, Y. (1973) Can. J. Biochem. 51 957-961.
59. Fujino, Y., Sakata, S. and Nakano, M. (1974) J. Food Sci. 39 471-473.
60. Fishwick, M. J. and Wright, A. J. (1977) Phytochemistry 16 1507-1510.
61. Roughan, P. G., Slack, C. R., and Holland, R. (1978) Lipids 13 497-503.
62. Colborne, A. J. and Laidman, D. L. (1975) Phytochemistry 14 2639-2645.
63. Folch, J., Lees, M. and Stanley, G. H. S. (1957) J. Biol. Chem. 226 497-509.
64. Zill, L. P. and Harmon, E. A. (1961) Biochim. Biophys. Acta 53 579-581.
65. Aneja, R., Chadha, J. S. and Yoell, R. W. (1971) Fette-Seifen-Anstrichs. 73 643-651.
66. Carter, H. E., Celmer, W. D., Lands, W. E., Mueller, K. L. and Tomizawa, H. H. (1954) J. Biol. Chem. 206 613-623.
67. Allen, C. F., Good, P., Davis, H. F., Chisum, P. and Fowler, S. D. (1966) J. Am. Oil Chemists Soc. 43 223-231.
68. Schlenk, H. (1954) Prog. Chem. Fats Other Lipids 2 243-267.
69. Carter, H. E., Ohno, K., Nojima, S., Tipton, C. L. and Stanacev, N. Z. (1961) J. Lipid Res. 2 215-222.
70. Kuksis, A. (1977) J. Chromatog. 143 1-30.
71. Marinetti, G. V. (1962) J. Lipid Research 3 1-20.
72. Cole, L. J. N. and Brown, J. B. (1960) J. Am. Oil Chemists Soc. 37 359-364.
73. Carroll, K. K. (1961) J. Lipid Res. 2 135-141.
74. Rouser, G., Galli, C. and Lieber, E. (1964) J. Am. Oil Chemists Soc. 41 836-840.
75. Klopfenstein, W. E. and Shigley, J. W. (1966) J. Lipid Res. 7 564-565.
76. Lands, W. E. M. and Dean, C. S. (1962) J. Lipid Research 3 129-130.
77. Holloway, P. J. (1973) Phytochemistry 12 2913-2920.
78. Ackman, R. G. and Metcalfe, L. D., eds., (1975) J. Chromatog. Sci. 13 Nos. 9 and 10.
79. Price, P. B. and Parsons, J. G. (1974) Lipids 9 560-566.
80. French, J. A. and Andersen, D. W. (1973) J. Chromatog. 80 133-136.
81. Hojnacki, J. L. and Smith, S. C. (1974) J. Chromatog. 90 365-367.
82. Kunz, F. (1973) Biochim. Biophys. Acta 296 331-334.
83. Mangold, H. K. and Kammereck, R., Chem. and Ind. 1961 1032-1034.
84. Renkonen, O. (1971) Prog. Thin Layer Chromatog. 2 143-181.
85. Khan, M.-U. and Williams, J. P. (1977) J. Chromatog. 140 179-185.
86. Parsons, J. G. and Price, P. B. (1979) J. Agric. Food Chem. 27 913-915.
87. Schlotzhauer, P. F., Ellington, J. J., and Schepartz, A. I. (1977) Lipids 12 239-241.
88. Roughan, P. G. and Batt, R. D. (1969) Phytochemistry 8 363-369.
89. Bhatnagar, V. M. and Liberti, A. (1966) J. Chromatog. 18 177-178.
90. Holub, B. J. and Kuksis, A. (1971) J. Lipid Res. 12 510-512.
91. Sulya, L. L. and Smith, R. R. (1960) Biochem. Biophys. Research Comms. 2 59-62.
92. Teichman, R. J., Takei, G. H. and Cummins, J. M. (1974) J. Chromatog. 88 425-427.
93. Duden, R. and Fricker (1977) Fette-Seifen-Anstrichsmittel 80 489-491.
94. Cormier, M., Jouan, P., and Girre, L. (1959) Bull. soc. chim. biol. 41 1037-1046.
95. Kundu, S. K., Chakravarty, S., Bhaduri, N. and Saha, H. K. (1977) J. Lipid Res. 18 128-130.
96. Ottenstein, D. M. and Supina, W. R. (1974) J. Chromatog. 91 119-126.
97. Hintze, U., Röper, H. and Gercken, G. (1973) J. Chromatog. 87 481-489.
98. Greeley, R. H. (1974) J. Chromatog. 88 229-233.
99. Suyama, K., Hori, K. and Adachi, S. (1979) J. Chromatog. 174 234-238.
100. Murata, T. and Takahashi, S. (1973) Anal. Chem. 45 1816-1823.
101. Viswanathan, C. V. (1974) J. Chromatog. 98 105-128.
102. Karger, B. L. and Giese, R. W. (1978) Anal. Chem. 50 1048A-1073A.
103. Aitzetmüller, K. (1975) J. Chromatog. 113 231-266.
104. Hax, W. M. A. and von Kessel, W. S. M. G. (1977) J. Chromatog. 142 735-741.
105. Pitt, G. A. J. and Morton, R. A. (1957) Prog. Chem. Fats Other Lipids 4 227-274.
106. Baer, E. (1968) Lipids 3 384-385.
107. Katiyar, S. S. and Porter, J. W. (1977) Life Sciences 20 737-760.
108. Nelson, D. R. and Rinne, R. W. (1977) Plant Cell Physiol. 18 1021-1027.
109. Fritsch, H. and Beevers, H. (1979) Plant Physiol. 63 687-691.
110. Bolton, P. and Harwood, J. L. (1977) Biochem. J. 168 261-269.

111. Vick, B. and Beevers, H. (1978) Plant Physiol. 62 173-178.
112. Vance, W. A. and Stumpf, P. K. (1978) Arch. Biochem. Biophys. 190 210-220.
113. Cassagne, C. and Lessire, R. (1978) Arch. Biochem. Biophys. 191 146-152.
114. Pollard, M. R., McKeon, T., Gupta, L. M. and Stumpf, P. K. (1979) Lipids 14 651-662.
115. Jacobson, B. S., Jaworski, J. G., and Stumpf, P. K. (1974) Plant Physiol. 54 484-486.
116. Stumpf, P. K. and Porra, R. J. (1976) Arch. Biochem. Biophys. 176 63-70.
117. Vijay, I. K. and Stumpf, P. K. (1972) J. Biol. Chem. 247 360-366.
118. Dubacq, J. P., Mazliak, P. and Trémolières, A. (1976) FEBS Letters 66 183-186.
119. Haigh, W. G., Safford, R. and James, A. T. (1969) Biochim. Biophys. Acta 176 647-650.
120. Trémolières, A. and Dubacq, J. P. (1976) Phytochemistry 15 1123-1124.
121. Kannangara, C. G., Jacobson, B. S., and Stumpf, P. K. (1973) Biochem. Biophys. Res. Commun. 52 648-655.
122. Jacobson, B. S., Kannangara, C. G. and Stumpf, P. K. (1973) Biochem. Biophys. Res. Commun. 52 1190-1198.
123. Murphy, D. J. and Stumpf, P. K. (1979) Plant Physiol. 64 428-430.
124. Mazliak, P., Grosbois, M., and Decotte, A. M. (1975) Biochimie 57 943-950.
125. Trémolières, A. (1972) Phytochemistry 11 3453-3460.
126. Slack, C. R., Roughan, P. G. and Browse, J. (1979) Biochem. J. 179 649-656.
127. Stymne, S. and Appelquist, L.-A. (1978) Europ. J. Biochem. 90 223-229.
128. Galliard, T. and Stumpf, P. K. (1966) J. Biol. Chem. 241 5806-5812.
129. Morris, L. J. (1967) Biochem. Biophys. Res. Communs. 29 311-315.
130. James, A. T., Hadaway, H. C. and Webb, J. P. W. (1965) Biochem. J. 95 448-452.
131. Jente, R. and Richter, E. (1976) Phytochemistry 15 1673-1679.
132. Gellerman, J. L., Anderson, W. H., and Schlenk, H. (1977) Biochemistry 16 1258-1262.
133. Hooper, N. K. and Law, J. H. (1965) Biochem. Biophys. Res. Commun. 18 426-429.
134. Smith, G. N. and Bu' Lock, J. D. (1965) Chem. and Ind. 1965 1840-1841.
135. Cramer, U. and Spener, F. (1977) Europ. J. Biochem. 74 495-500.
136. Ghisalberti, E. L., Jeffries, P. R., and Toia, R. F. (1979) Phytochemistry 18 65-69.
137. Moore, T. S., Jr. (1974) Plant Physiol. 54 164-168.
138. Bahl, J., Guillot-Salomon, T. and Douce, R. (1970) Physiol. Vég. 8 55-74.
139. Macher, B. A. and Mudd, J. B. (1974) Plant Physiol. 53 171-175.
140. Harwood, J. L. (1976) Biochem. Soc. Trans. 4 50-52.
141. Montague, M. J. and Ray, P. M. (1977) Plant Physiol. 59 225-230.
142. Moore, T. S., Jr. (1976) Plant Physiol. 57 383-386.
143. Marshall, M. O. and Kates, M. (1974) Can. J. Biochem. 52 469-482.
144. Moore, T.S., Jr. (1975) Plant Physiol. 56 177-180.
145. Williams, J. P., Khan, M., and Leung, S. (1975) J. Lipid Res. 16 61-66.
146. Williams, J. P., Watson, G. R., Khan, M.-U., and Leung, S. (1975) Plant Physiol. 55 1038-1048.
147. Harwood, J. L. (1975) Biochim. Biophys. Acta 398 224-230.
148. Soliday, C. L. and Kolattukudy, P. E. (1977) Plant Physiol. 59 1116-1121.
149. Agrawal, V. P. and Kolattukudy, P. E. (1977) Plant Physiol. 59 667-672.
150. Croteau, R. and Kolattukudy, P. E. (1974) Arch. Biochem. Biophys. 162 458-470, 471-480.
151. Salaün, J.-P., Benveniste, I., Reichhart, D. and Durst, F. (1978) Europ. J. Biochem. 90 155-159.
152. Mazliak, P. (1973) Ann. Rev. Plant Physiol. 24 287-310.
153. McNeil, P. H. and Thomas, D. R. (1976) J. Exper. Botany 27 1163-1180.
154. Donaldson, R. P. (1977) Plant Physiol. 59 1064-1066.
155. Shine, W. E. and Stumpf, P. K. (1974) Arch. Biochem. Biophys. 162 147-157.
156. Jordan, B. R. and Harwood, J. L. (1979) Biochim. Biophys. Acta 523 218-221.
157. Matthew, J. A. and Galliard, T. (1978) Phytochemistry 17 1043-1044.
158. Vick, B. A. and Zimmerman, D. C. (1976) Plant Physiol. 57 780-788.
159. Bild, G. S., Bhat, S. G., Ramadoss, C. S. and Axelrod, B. (1978) J. Biol. Chem. 253 21-23.
160. Vick, B. A. and Zimmermann, D. C. (1979) Plant Physiol. 64 203-205.

Chapter 6
MISCELLANEOUS
UNSAPONIFIABLE LIPIDS

The compounds grouped together in this chapter are very different in most chemical properties, but similar in that they are soluble in lipid solvents rather than in water and not saponified by alkali. The anthroquinones fit the above description, however, they normally occur in plants not free, but as water-soluble glycosides. All of the compounds included appear to be biosynthetically related in being derived by condensation of several molecules of acetate (or, more specifically, malonyl-coenzyme A). Thus they are also closely related to the long chain fatty acids discussed in Chapter 5. Speculation regarding biosynthesis of all such polyacetate compounds may be found in articles by Birch (1, 2). Because of the diversity of properties shown by compounds in this chapter, discussions of isolation, characterization, and biosynthesis are included under each separate section, rather than for the chapter as a whole.

LONG CHAIN HYDROCARBONS,
ALCOHOLS AND KETONES

The most familiar long-chain aliphatic compounds are the fatty acids discussed in Chapter 5, and it is not often realized that they are only one representative of this class of plant constituents. The normal, aliphatic hydrocarbons found in plants usually have an odd number of carbon atoms, and it seems evident that they are derived by loss of carbon dioxide from even-carbon fatty acids:

$$CH_3(CH_2)_nCOOH \rightarrow CH_3(CH_2)_{n-1}CH_3 + CO_2$$

Tracer experiments have supported this pathway (3). The lowest natural member of this group, n-heptane, occurs as a constituent of the turpentine from several species of pine. The turpentines of *Pinus jeffreyi* and *P. sabiniana* are nearly pure n-heptane and contain no terpene hydrocarbons. Higher molecular weight hydrocarbons are often found in plant cuticle and pollen waxes where their chainlength generally falls in the range C_{25}-C_{37}. Commercial candelilla wax from *Euphorbia* spp. contains 50-60% n-hentriacontane ($C_{31}H_{64}$). Cuticle waxes of several common fruits have n-nonacosane ($C_{29}H_{60}$). The unsaponifiable material in olive oil contains hydrocarbons ranging from C_{13}-C_{28}. Horsetails and mosses have saturated and unsaturated hydrocarbons ranging from C_{21} to C_{31} (4-6). Costus oil (*Saussurea lappa*) has aplotaxene (heptadeca-1,8,11,14-tetraene) (7). Acetylenic hydrocarbons are of widespread occurrence in the Compositae. Five of them from coreopsis are C_{13} hydrocarbons (8). One was shown to have the following structure:

$$CH_2 = CH - CH = CH - C \equiv C - C \equiv C - C \equiv C - CH = CHCH_3$$

Similar compounds contain a benzene ring at one end of the aliphatic chain, e.g.:

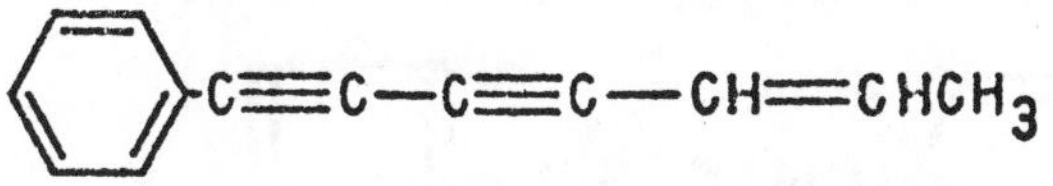

More than 600 polyacetylenic compounds have now been isolated from fungi and higher plants. Bohlmann (9) and Ross (10) have surveyed their occurrence, characterization, and biosynthesis. Several of these highly unsaturated, conjugated compounds show light absorption in the visible region and may therefore be classed as plant pigments which are similar in color and other properties to some carotenoids.

Long chain aliphatic alcohols and ketones are also frequent constituents of plant waxes. The alcohols almost always have an even number of carbons like the fatty acids, whereas the ketones have an odd number like the hydrocarbons Long-chain alcohols which occur in the form of esters are discussed in Chapter 5. The unesterified alcohols are particularly common in the leaf waxes of monocots, but also appear in other types of plant waxes. Unsaturated, long-chain alcohols are uncommon in plants, but a few have been reported. A C_{17} example from avocados is a plant growth inhibitor (11); and a plant growth stimulant originally extracted from alfalfa meal has been identified as triacontanol (12). Sugar cane and some flower waxes are unusual in containing polymeric, long-chain aldehydes (13, 14). Some examples of the occurrence of these compounds are summarized in Table 6-1.

Table 6-1 SOME LONG-CHAIN ALCOHOLS

Compound	Structure	Source
octanol	$CH_2(CH_2)_6CH_2OH$	fruit of *Heracleum gigantum*
dodecanol	$CH_3(CH_2)_{10}CH_2OH$	cuticle wax of *Rhamnus purshiana*
hexacosanol (ceryl alcohol)	$CH_3(CH_2)_{24}CH_2OH$	many cuticle waxes
octacosanol	$CH_3(CH_2)_{26}CH_2OH$	several cuticle waxes
triacontanol (melissyl alcohol)	$CH_3(CH_2)_{28}CH_2OH$	several cuticle and leaf waxes
takakibyl alcohol	$CH_3(CH_2)_{42}CH_2OH$	*Sorghum vulgare*
10-nonacosanol	$CH_3(CH_2)_8CHOH(CH_2)_{18}CH_3$	apple cuticle wax
11-eicosenol	$CH_3(CH_2)_7CH=CH(CH_2)_9CH_2OH$	*Simmondsia chinensis*
15-nonacosanone	$CH_3(CH_2)_{13}CO(CH_2)_{13}CH_3$	*Brassica* spp.

Long-chain acetylenic alcohols and ketones are of interest because of their pronounced pharmacological effects. The first acetylenic compound to be isolated from plants, carlina oxide from *Carlina acaulis* is strongly toxic to animals and also bacteriocidal:

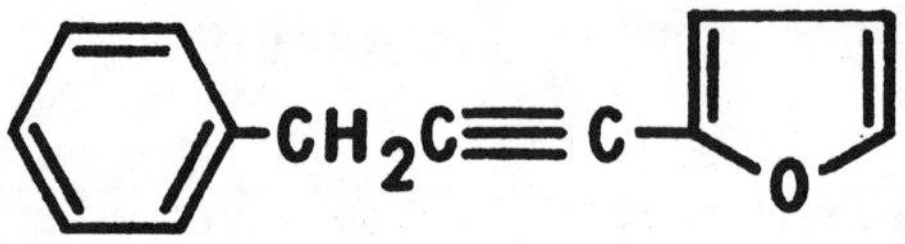

It appears related to an acetylenic alcohol found as an acetate in *Coreopsis*:

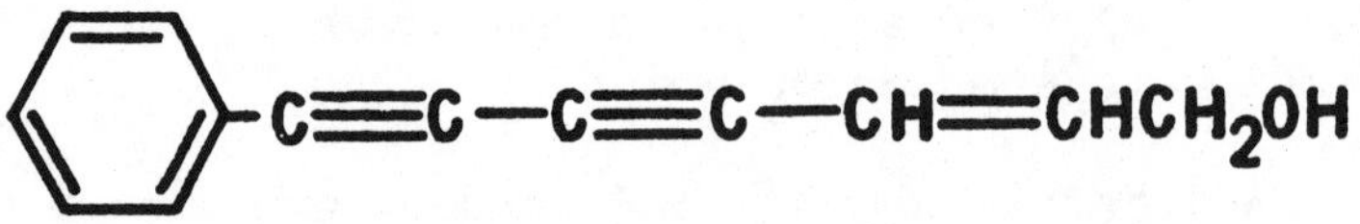

Both of these aromatic compounds could be derived by ring closure from a C_{13} alcohol also found as an acetate in *Carlina acaulis*:

$$CH_2 = CHCH = CH - C \equiv C - C \equiv C - C \equiv CCH = CHCH_2OH$$

A C_{17} acetylenic diol, falcarindiol, occurs in several plants and is interesting for its powerful inhibition of fungal growth (15). The roots of several umbelliferous plants owe their great toxicity to long-chain acetylenic alcohols, of which the following are examples:

$$HOCH_2CH_2CH_2C \equiv C - C \equiv C(CH = CH)_3 \overset{OH}{\underset{|}{C}}HCH_2CH_2CH_3$$

cicutoxin *(Cicuta virosa)*

$$HOCH_2CH = CHC \equiv C - C \equiv CCH = CHCH = CHCH_2CH_2\overset{OH}{\underset{|}{C}}HCH_2CH_2CH_3$$

oenanthotoxin *(Oenanthe crocata)*

The mechanism of toxicity may be the uncoupling of mitochondrial oxidative phosphorylation (16). A few L-rhamnosides of C_{17} acetylene alcohols have been found in roots of the tribe Cynaeae (17).

Long chain acetylenic ketones are also found in several plants and are apparently less toxic than the alcohols. Two examples follow:

$$CH_3C \equiv C - C \equiv C - C \equiv CCH = CH \, CH_2CH_2\overset{O}{\overset{\|}{C}}CH_2CH_3$$

artemisia ketone *(Artemisia vulgaris)*

$$CH_3CH = CH - C \equiv C - C \equiv CCH = CHCH = CHCH_2CH_2 \, \overset{O}{\overset{\|}{C}}CH_2CH_2CH_3$$

oenanthetone *(Oenanthe crocata)*

Unfortunately the name "artemisia ketone" has also been given to a terpenoid from the same plant (cf. Chap. 8).

All these long-chain compounds show physical properties similar to the fatty acids but are less polar and less soluble in the common lipid solvents. The C_{24} alcohol is soluble in benzene and chloroform at room temperature, but the longer chain alcohols and ketones dissolve in these solvents only when hot and then only to a limited degree. The aliphatic hydrocarbons may be dissolved in such solvents as petroleum ether or carbon disulfide.

Isolation of these compounds is usually carried out by solvent extraction, steam distillation, or fractional distillation at low pressures. Heating operations should, however, be avoided in isolation of the highly unsaturated, acetylenic compounds which are often very unstable. The formation of urea adducts is a characteristic property of compounds with long, aliphatic carbon chains and may be used to separate them from other compounds (e.g. sterols) with similar solubility. To some extent this method may also be used for the separation of different classes of aliphatic compounds since they differ in the ease with which the adducts are formed and decompose. Completely saturated hydrocarbons react most readily and form the most stable complexes, whereas, the conjugated acetylenic compounds may show practically no tendency to complex formation. Oxygenated derivatives react less readily than corresponding hydrocarbons. Urea inclusion methods are also discussed in Chapters 5 and 8 where methods are described in more detail and references given. Final purification is effectively carried out by adsorption chromatography on alumina using such solvents as petroleum ether or benzene. Since these compounds are not colored or fluorescent, bands of them on a column may be detected by using alumina impregnated with morin and observing quenching bands in ultraviolet light (18), or fractions may be collected arbitrarily and each one analyzed.

Characterization of these long-chain aliphatic compounds is made difficult by their low reactivity. Even the alcohols and ketones react only slowly with usual hydroxyl and carbonyl reagents. A method which combines identification of the components with a partial separation was developed by Chibnall et al. (19). Ketones may be separated from hydrocarbons by reacting them with hydroxylamine to form oximes, which are more soluble than the hydrocarbons in ether/acetone. In recent years various chromatographic approaches have been most usefully applied to this difficult group of compounds (20).

Kaufmann and Kessen (21) have described a procedure whereby long-chain aliphatic alcohols are converted to urethanes and these chromatographed on paper impregnated with undecane, using acetic acid/acetonitrile 3·2 as the mobile phase. Spots were detected by forming mercury complexes and showing up the mercury with hydrogen sulfide.

Gas chromatography has demonstrated its great usefulness in separating and identifying leaf wax hydrocarbons (18, 22). The hydrocarbons can first be separated as a group from oxygenated compounds by chromatography on alumina (23). Combination of gas chromatography with mass spectrometry has been applied to several leaf paraffins (20, 22, 24). Where the instrumentation is available, this elegant approach is probably the best one. Thin layer chromatography on silica gel developed with n-hexane is also possible, and the spots may be visualized by spraying with Rhodamine 6G (20).

Spectral measurements have limited usefulness for characterization of these compounds. Where conjugated unsaturation is present, it may be

detected by ultraviolet spectra as described in Chapter 5. Infrared
spectroscopy may be used to determine whether hydroxyl or carbonyl groups
are present. X-ray crystallography has been very useful in proving the
structure of certain natural, long-chain alcohols, but discussion of this
specialized technique is beyond the scope of this book.

All of the compounds of this group are derived primarily from long-
chain fatty acids, and in recent years considerable detail has been learned
about the steps (25-27). The compounds with carbon chains longer than
the usual fatty acids are produced by an elongation process. For example,
the 18 carbons of stearic acid become C-11 to C-29 of the n-nonacosane in
broccoli leaf wax. The remaining carbon atoms come from acetate, giving
a C_{30} acid that is decarboxylated to the hydrocarbon then oxidized successively to secondary alcohol and ketone (28). The occasional branched
chains that occur may be built up from a starting unit derived from a
branched-chain amino acid (25). The polyacetylenes, being shorter, have
no elongation step in their biosynthesis but are produced by dehydrogenation of oleic acid, then rearrangements, oxygenations, ring closures, etc.
(29, 30).

PHLOROGLUCINOL DERIVATIVES

Several natural products contain the phloroglucinol nucleus in their
structure.

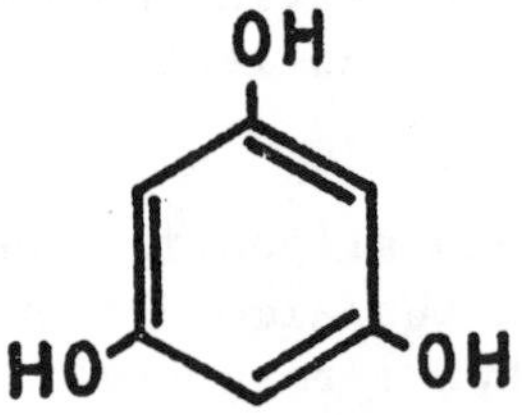

phloroglucinol

The most familiar of such compounds are the flavonoids discussed in Chapter
9. According to the hypothesis of Birch (1, 2) all compounds containing an
aromatic nucleus with *meta* hydroxyl groups may be regarded as derived
from three molecules of acetic acid, and this scheme has been corroborated
using labelled acetate for the phloroglucinol nucleus of the flavonoids.

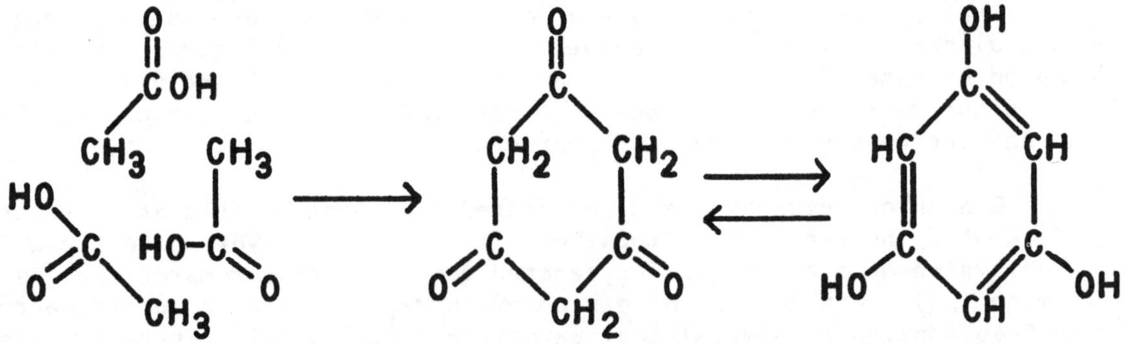

As indicated above phloroglucinol may be represented as a tautomeric
triketone, and many reactions of phloroglucinol derivatives are best understood by reference to this ketone structure.

Old reports of the widespread occurrence of free phloroglucinol in plants have not been confirmed, and most such reports are questionable since the tests used give a positive result for complex phloroglucinol derivatives as well as for the compound itself. The simplest, natural phloroglucinol derivatives are a group of cyclic triketones (phloroglucinol tautomers) which are widespread in ferns of the family Pteridaceae but also found in essential oils of some angiosperms (31, 32). Plants containing such compounds have been used for centuries as antihelmintic drugs, and the compounds have also been shown to possess insecticidal and bacteriocidal activity (33). Desaspidin is an inhibitor of photo-phosphorylation (34). The bitter substances found in hops (*Humulus lupulus*) have isoprenoid side chains attached to the phloroglucinol nucleus, or to a cyclopentatrione ring which can also be regarded as derived from 3 acetate units. The native lupulones and humulones of hops are isomerized and oxidized to complex structures in the production of beer (35, 36). These derivatives are important for flavor, but their value as preservatives is now doubted (36, 37).

Several generalizations can be made regarding these structures:

1. All three hydroxyl groups of the phloroglucinol nucleus are never free. In some cases loss of available hydrogens stabilizes the keto form; frequently one hydroxyl group is methylated.
2. An acyl group is always present at C-2.
3. Extra methyl groups are common, often giving the superficial appearance of a terpenoid structure.

Several compounds that are interesting for their biological effects appear to be structurally related to the phloroglucinols although the aromatic ring does not carry three oxygen atoms or has further modifications -- for example aloenin of *Aloe* spp. (38), grandinol of *Eucalyptus grandis* (39), and tremetone of *Eupatorium* spp. (40).

The simple phloroglucinol derivatives may be extracted from plant tissues using organic solvents such as ether and then further purified by taking advantage of their phenolic properties -- e.g. extraction from organic solvents with sodium hydroxide solution. Purification of hop constituents of this type has been achieved using countercurrent distribution between phosphate buffer and iso-octane (41).

These phloroglucinol derivatives are for the most part colorless, crystalline compounds, although some (e.g. ceroptene) are yellow pigments. Those that have a free phenolic hydroxyl group show typical phenol reactions such as giving a color with ferric chloride. Heating with sodium hydroxide and zinc dust causes reductive removal of the 2-acyl group, and the resulting derivatives give a red color with vanillin-conc. hydrochloric acid. Identification of these derivatives has been an important procedure in structure determination. The infrared and ultraviolet spectra of 2-acyl-cyclohexane-1, 3-diones have been discussed by Chan and Hassall (42). They generally have one absorption maximum in the range 223-233 nm and another at 271-293 nm. Godin (43) has separated crude filicin from male fern (*Aspidium*) into several different phloroglucinol derivatives using paper chromatography in an aqueous solvent containing sodium carbonate and sodium sulfite. Spots were revealed by the diazonium reaction. Phloroglucinol derivatives of *Dryopteris* were separated on buffered filter

TABLE 6-2.   SOME NATURALLY OCCURRING PHLOROGLUCINOL DERIVATIVES

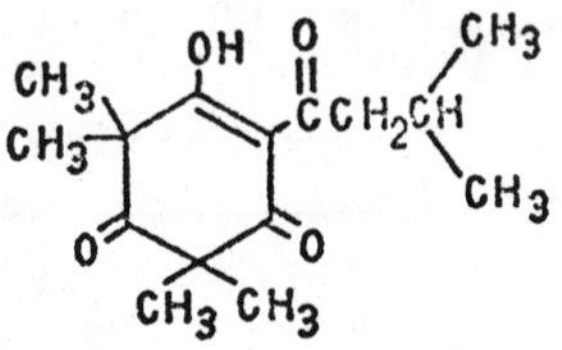

leptospermone (essential oil of *Leptospermum* spp.)

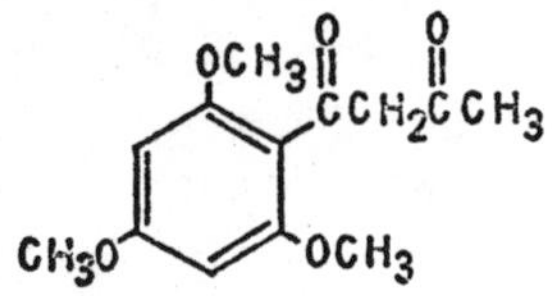

eugenone (essential oil of *Eugenia caryophyllata*)

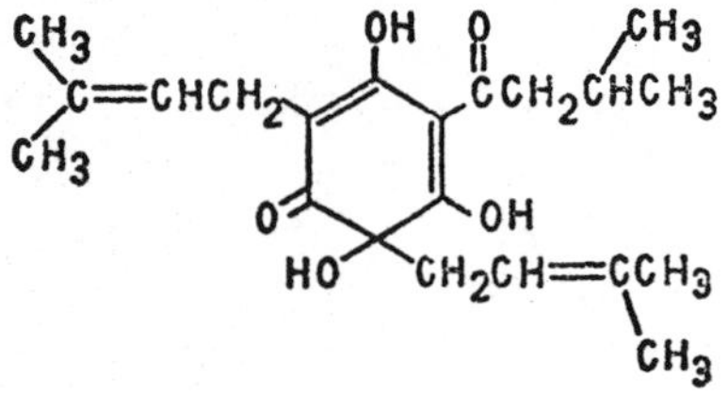

humulone (*Humulus lupulus*)

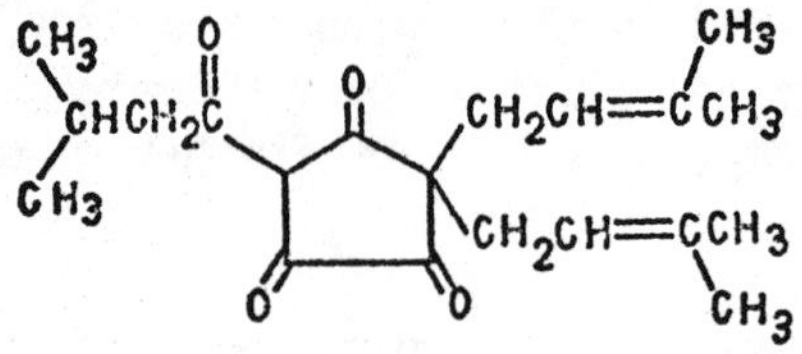

hulupone (*Humulus lupulus*)

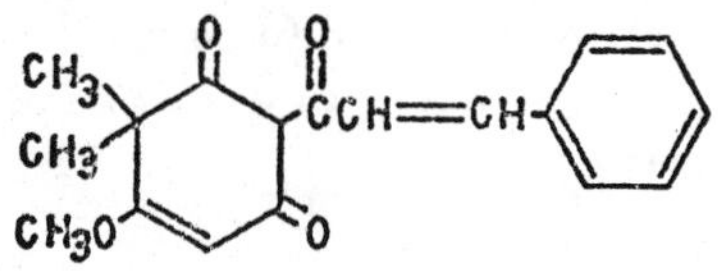

ceroptene (coating on fronds of *Pityrogramma triangularis*)

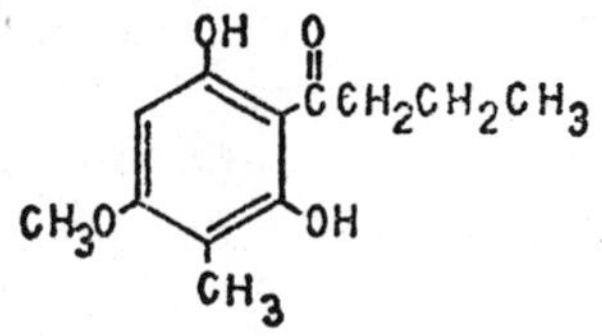

aspidinol (rhizomes of *Aspidium* spp.)

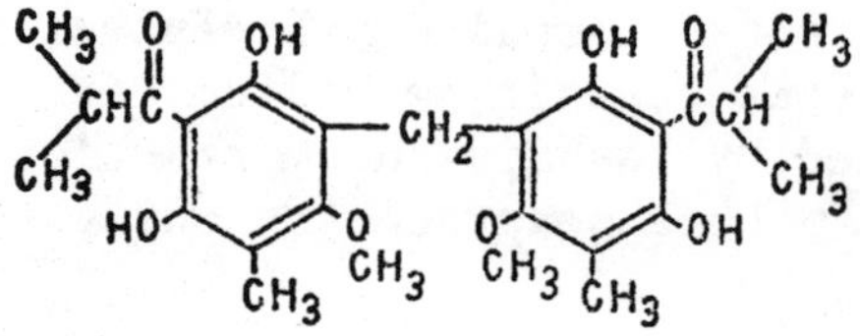

α-kosin (flowers of *Hagenia abyssinica*)

TABLE 6-2.   Continued

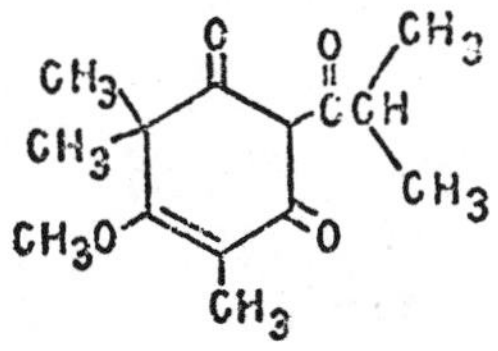

tasmanone (essential oil of
Eucalyptus risdoni)

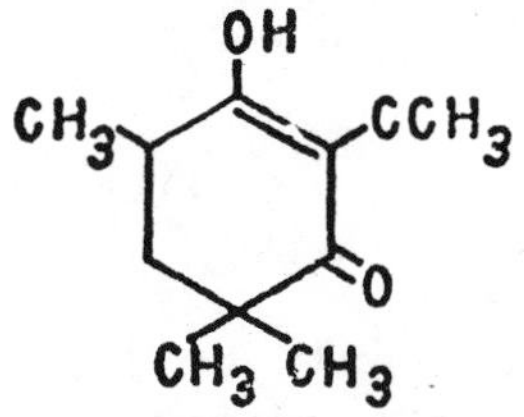

angustione (essential oil of
Backhousia angustifolia)

paper impregnated with formamide and a benzene/chloroform solvent (44).
Gas liquid chromatography, high pressure liquid chromatography, and
mass spectrometry have been applied to analysis of the hop compounds in
beer (35-37). Mass spectra have been published for the fern phloroglucinols
(45).

Studies on biosynthesis have shown the origin of the phloroglucinol
ring from acetate, the branched side chains from leucine or mevalonate, and the
C- and O-methyl groups from methionine (40, 46).

CHROMONES

The chromone nucleus with its numbering system is as follows:

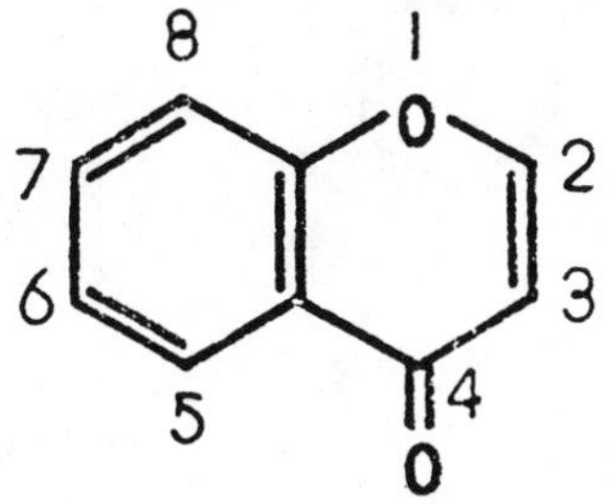

Naturally-occurring chromones generally have a methyl group at C-2 and are oxygenated at C-5 and C-7. Thus despite their overall resemblance to the carbon skeleton of the coumarins (Chapter 4), they may be regarded as derived from the condensation of five molecules of acetic acid. A tracer feeding experiment has supported the role of acetate as a precursor of the chromones of *Ammi visnaga* (47). The coumarins, on the other hand, are probably derived by the shikimic acid pathway, which rarely results in oxygenation at C-5:

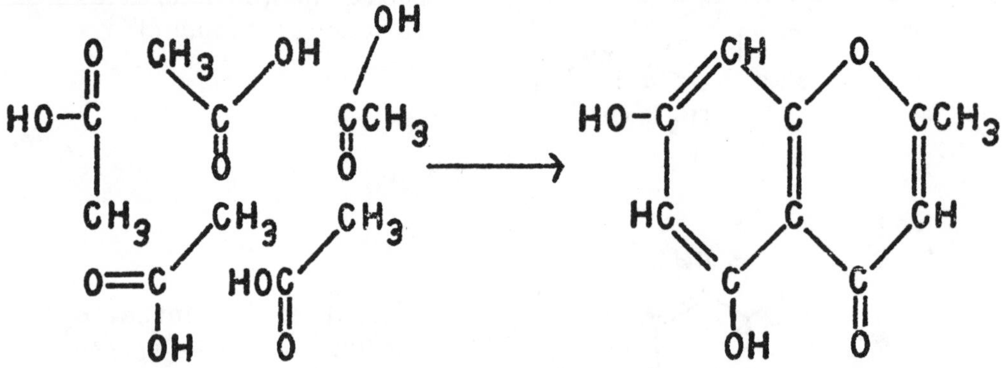

However, it is possible that some chromones could be formed by the addition of an acetate unit to a phenylpropane intermediate (48).

        Analogous to the furanocoumarins are furanochromones with the following basic structure:

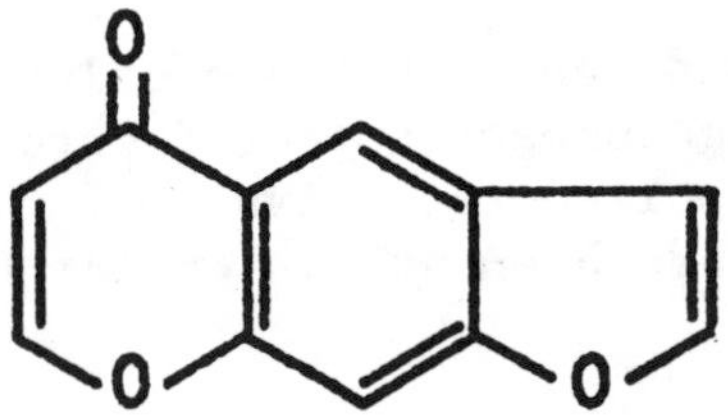

Some structures of a few natural chromones are shown below:

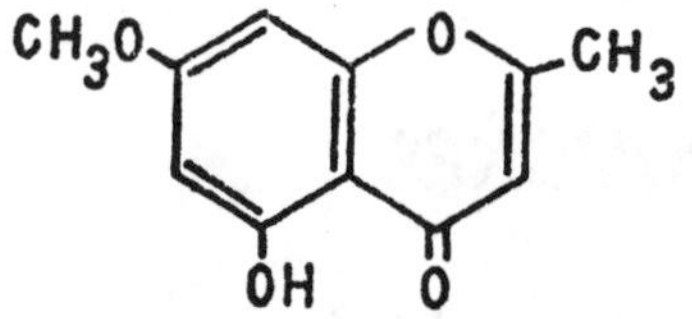

eugenin (*Eugenia caryophyllata*)

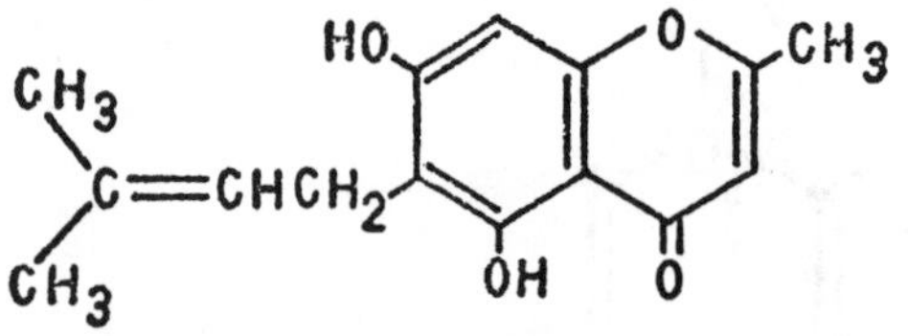

peucenin (*Peucedanum ostruthium*)

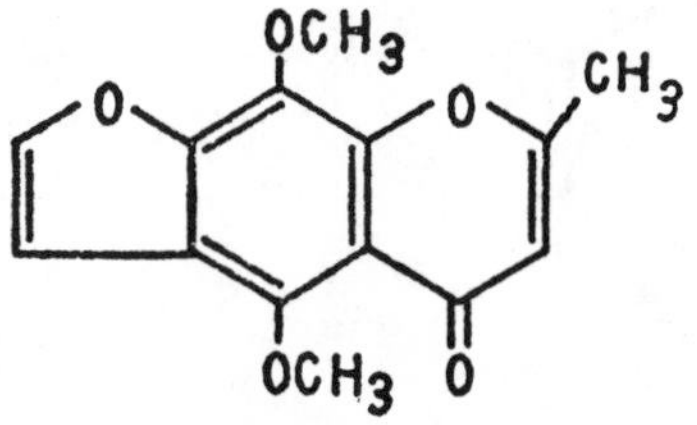

khellin (*Ammi visnaga*)

There is an obvious resemblance of these structures to the 2-acylphloro-glucinols discussed in the previous section of this chapter (e.g., compare eugenone and eugenin). Naturally occurring chromones have been reviewed by Schmid (49) and the furanochromones by Huttrer and Dale (50). Both groups together contain only about a dozen compounds.

The chromones are of interest as the active ingredients of several plants used for centuries in folk medicine. Khellin is valuable as an antispasmodic and for relieving the pain of renal colic, dental caries, angina pectoris, etc. Its primary action may be as a vasodilator.

Chromones are extracted from dried plant material using such solvents as ether, chloroform, or acetone. They may be crystallized directly from these solvents or purified by chromatography on magnesium oxide or neutral, deactivated alumina. Chromones with phenolic hydroxyl groups can be extracted from ether solution with dilute, aqueous sodium hydroxide. Chromone glycosides are extracted by methanol.

Chromones are usually colorless but form yellow-orange oxonium salts in the presence of strong mineral acids. This color reaction is useful for indicating the presence of chromones, but proof of structure rests on degradation and identification of split products. The ultraviolet absorption spectrum of chromones usually shows a main band at about 295 nm with weaker absorption at about 250 nm. Substitution at C-8 or presence of the furan ring may increase the absorption maximum to as much as 340 nm (51). Paper chromatographic separation of chromones can be made using water/2-propanol mixtures as the solvents.

ANTHRAQUINONES

The largest group of natural quinones is made up of anthraquinones. Some of them have been important as dyestuffs and others as purgatives. The plant families richest in this type of compound are the Rubiaceae, Rhamnaceae and Polygonaceae. The fundamental anthraquinone structure is shown below with the ring-numbering system:

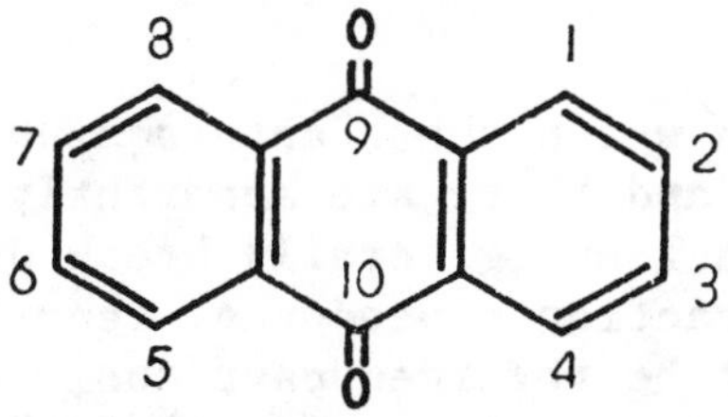

Most anthraquinones from higher plants are hydroxylated at C-1 and C-2, although anthraquinone itself has been reported to occur in various plant tannin extracts (52), and 2-methylanthraquinone is known to be a constituent of teak wood. The hydroxylated anthraquinones probably do not often occur in plants as such but rather as glycosides. Treatment of the plants to obtain the commercially desirable products has the effect of hydrolyzing the glycosides, and in some cases producing additional oxidative changes. Since the free anthraquinones are the products usually dealt with, some typical structures will be considered in Table 6-3 followed by a general discussion of the native glycosides. All of these anthraquinones are

high-melting crystalline compounds soluble in the usual organic solvents.
They are usually red in color, but different ones range from yellow to brown.
They dissolve in aqueous alkali with the formation of red-violet colors.

TABLE 6-3. SOME NATURALLY OCCURRING ANTHRAQUINONES

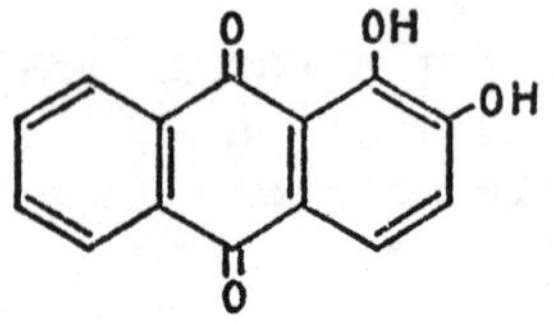

alizarin *(Rubia tinctorum)*

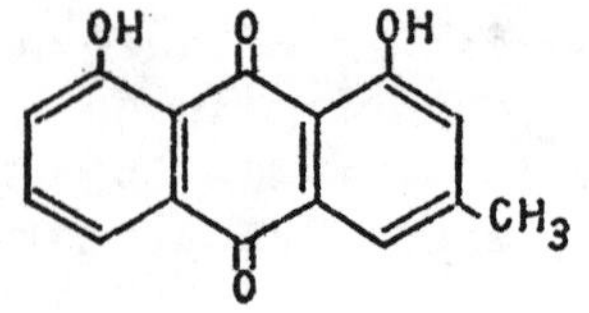

chrysophanol, chrysophanic ac
(Rheum and *Rumex* spp.)

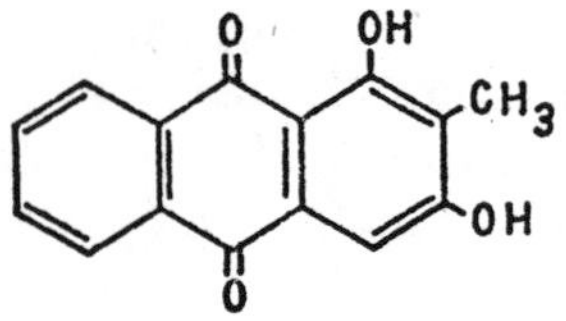

rubiadin
(Rubia and *Galium* spp.)

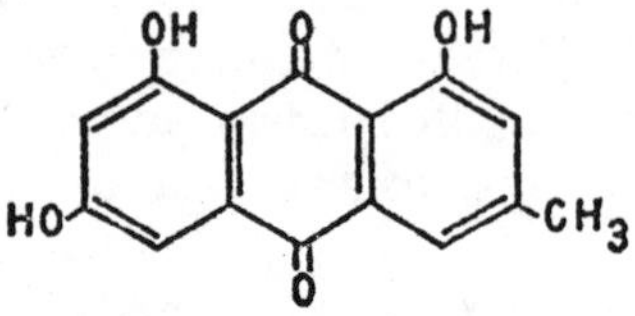

emodin, frangula-emodin
(Rheum and *Rumex* spp.)

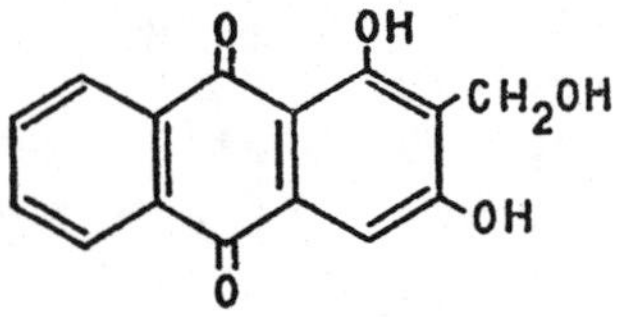

lucidin
(Coprosma spp.)

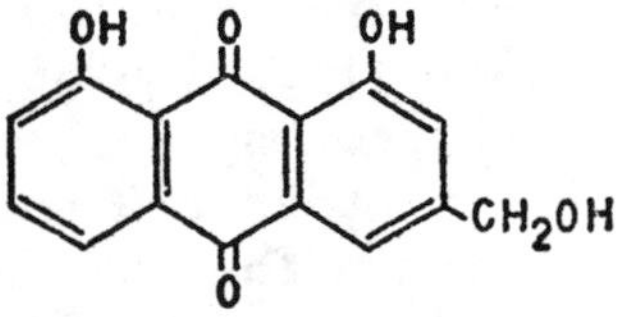

aloe-emodin
(Aloe, Rheum and *Rhamnus* sp

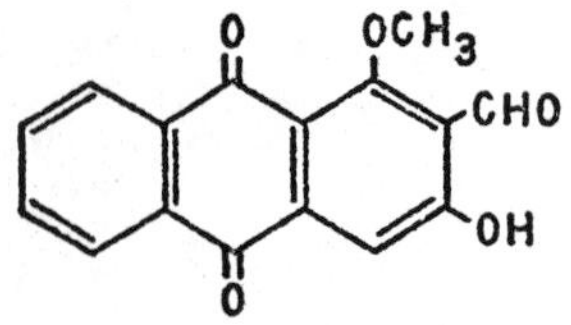

damnacanthal
(Damnacanthus spp.)

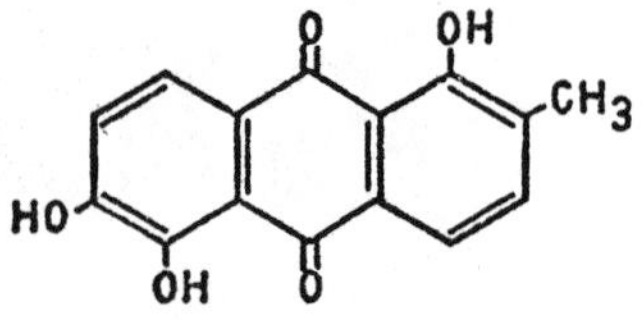

morindone
(Morinda spp.)

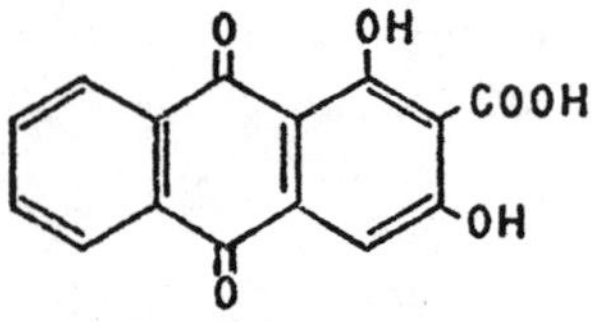

munjistin
(Rubia spp.)

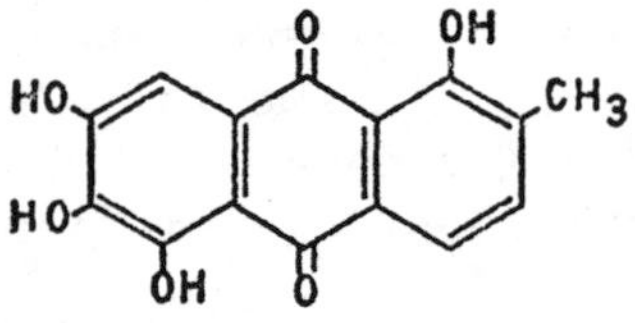

copareolatin *(Coprosma aerola*

The problem of the form in which these anthraquinones actually exist
in plants remains a knotty one, and there are apparently several possibilities. Since the native precursors generally break down readily under
the influence of enzymes or extraction procedures, reports of the appearance of free anthraquinones must be regarded cautiously. However, in some
cases sufficient pains have been taken to assure that the simple compounds
are true natural products. Many of the anthraquinones occur as glycosides
with the sugar residue linked through one of the phenolic hydroxyl groups.
Several different sugars are found in such glycosides. Thus, alizarin
occurs as a 2-primoveroside (ruberythric acid); rubiadin from madder
(*Rubia tinctoria*) as a 3-glucoside and from *Galium* spp. as a 3-primoveroside;
morindone from *Coprosma australis* as a 6-rutinoside and from *Morinda
persicaefolia* as a 6-primoveroside. Sulfate esters of the glycosides
have also been identified (53).

In many cases it appears that the native glycosides have as their aglycones a reduced form of the anthraquinone, known as anthrone. The sugars in these reduced glycosides may be linked as usual through phenolic oxygens in the outside rings or they may be attached at C-9 to the enol form of anthrone, anthranol:

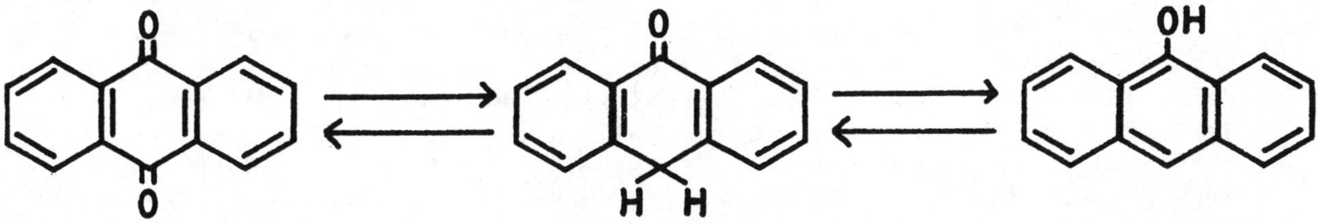

anthraquinone   anthrone   anthranol

Enzymatic (or chemical) hydrolysis of a C-9 glycoside of anthranol is followed by oxidation of the anthrone to an anthraquinone if oxygen is present. If the sugar is linked at some other position, anthranol glycosides may be directly oxidized to anthraquinone glycosides.

Although aloe-emodin occurs in *Rheum* spp. as an ordinary glycoside, in aloes it is found as barbaloin, an unusual compound in which a glucose-like group is linked by a carbon-carbon bond to a partially reduced anthraquinone (anthrone):

barbaloin

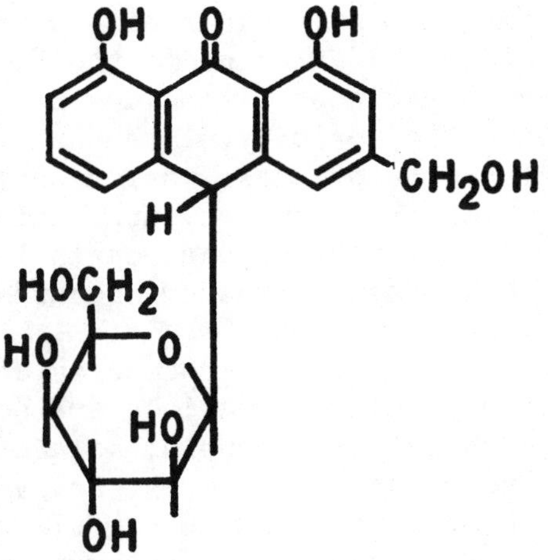

Other compounds apparently similar to barbaloin occur in other species of aloes. Unlike glycosides they are stable toward acid hydrolysis, but may be split with ferric chloride to form aloe-emodin (54).

Still more complex are the sennosides, the active cathartics of senna. These compounds are dianthrones. One of them, sennidin, has the following structure:

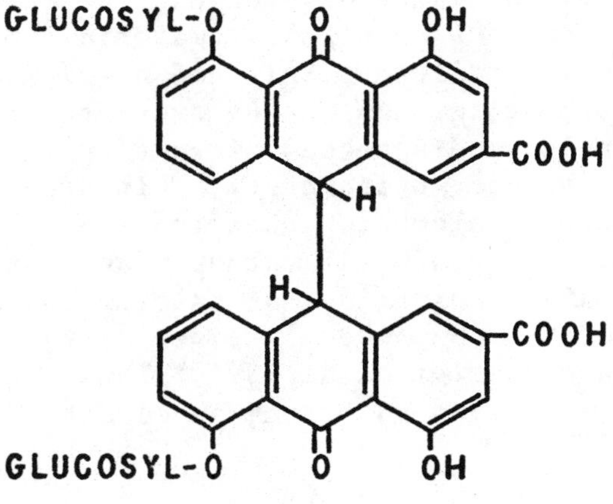

The chemistry of the sennosides has been reviewed by Stoll and Becker (55). It seems at least possible that other anthraquinones are derived from such natural precursors by oxidative splitting. For instance the native glycosides of *Rhamnus frangula* bark (cascara) may be dianthrone glycosides which are oxidized on storage to form aloe-emodin and its glycosides (56).

The foregoing discussion illustrates some of the complexity which may be involved in studying anthraquinone derivatives as they occur naturally in plants. Adding to the problem is that more than one type of derivative may be present, andfrequently the nature of the constituents varies with the age of the plant. For example, in the common rhubarb (*Rheum undulatum*) young leaves contain mostly anthranol glycosides, whereas older leaves have glycosides of anthraquinones.

The physiological activity of several of these anthracene derivatives has made them important cathartics for many hundreds of years. Only recently has it been shown that the pharmacologically important compounds are the 3-alkyl di-or tri-hydroxyanthraquinones (57). The fact that pharmacopeias recommend storage of purgative plants for periods up to one year before use is explained by the necessity for slow hydrolysis of the glycosides. If storage is too long, however, oxidation destroys activity. Anthraquinone glycosides are excessively irritating and are probably responsible for the toxicity of rhubarb leaves (57). Nothing is known regarding any function of these various anthracene derivatives in plants. The ease with which the reaction anthraquinone →anthrone may be brought about in the laboratory has raised the possibility that these compounds may somehow participate in hydrogen-transfer or oxidation-reduction reactions (58).

Isolation procedures depend on whether free aglycones or the various glycosidic derivatives are desired. For the first, extraction of the plant with rather non-polar solvents such as ether or benzene is effective. The sugar derivatives, however, are extracted using water, ethanol, or water-ethanol mixtures. If anthrones or anthranols are to be isolated, care must be taken to avoid their oxidation by oxygen in the air. This oxidation is particularly rapid in alkaline solutions and leads to the formation of dianthrones and polyanthrones as well as to anthraquinones. After extraction a solution of glycosides may be concentrated under reduced pressure to obtain crude crystals. These crude crystals may then be purified by repeated crystallization from acetone-water. The glycosides on heating with acetic acid or dilute (e.g. 5%) alcoholic HCl are readily hydrolyzed within one hour at 70°. After hydrolysis a 1:1 mixture of ethanol-benzene is added and then diluted with 0.5% aqueous HCl. A layer of benzene separates containing the aglycones. The aglycones obtained by hydrolysis or direct extraction of plant materials may be purified by extraction from benzene into dilute alkali and precipitation with acid. (Aglycones with free carboxyl groups can be extracted from benzene using sodium bicarbonate solution and a second extraction with sodium hydroxide used to remove any less acidic substances.) This crude precipitate is crystallized from benzene or alcohol. Purification of the aglycones by column chromatography is successful if rather weak adsorbents are used, for example magnesium oxide, polyamide, or calcium phosphate. Some indication as to the nature of the compounds is given by the way they migrate when chromatographed on magnesium oxide (59). Thus, *ortho*-dihydroxyphenols are not eluted with even as strong an eluant as acetic acid.

For identification of anthraquinone derivatives the Bornträger reaction is routinely used (60). Some of the unknown material is boiled in dilute, aqueous potassium hydroxide for a few minutes. This not only hydrolyzes glycosides but also oxidizes anthrones or anthranols to anthraquinones. The alkaline solution is cooled, acidified, and extracted with benzene. When the benzene phase is separated and shaken with dilute alkali, the benzene loses its yellow color and the alkaline phase becomes red if quinones are present. The test is not specific for anthraquinones; naphthoquinones also give a positive reaction. If partially reduced anthraquinones are present, the original solution does not turn red immediately on making alkaline but turns yellow with greenfluorescence and then gradually becomes red as oxidation occurs. If desired, the oxidation may be hastened by adding a little 3% hydrogen peroxide. The Bornträger reaction can also be made the basis of a quantitative colorimetric determination. Direct spectral observations of a benzene solution may also be made for characterization of anthracene derivatives. Anthraquinones show a broad absorption peak at about 440 nm, whereas, the reduced forms absorb at about 360 nm with no significant absorption at 440. 1, 4-dihydroxy-anthraquinones fluoresce in acetic acid solution. The colors given with alcoholic magnesium acetate solutions are characteristic of different hydroxylation patterns (61). *Meta* hydroxyls give an orange color, *para* a purple color, and *ortho* violet.

Proof that an isolated compound has the anthracene nucleus may be obtained by dry distillation in the presence of zinc dust. This drastic treatment breaks down anthraquinone or anthrone derivatives to anthracene which distills over and may be identified by its melting point (216° C.). Methylated derivatives form 2-methylanthracene (m.p. 245°). These hydrocarbons are easily distinguished from naphthalene (m.p. 80°) which is formed from a naphthoquinone.

High performance liquid chromatography has been applied to separation and detection of anthraquinone glycosides (62). Earlier studies used paper chromatography for both the glycosides and free anthraquinones (63, 64). Spots may be revealed by spraying with 0.5% magnesium acetate in methanol and heating at 90° C for five minutes. Characteristic colors appear, as described above (61).

The biosynthesis of anthracene derivatives by polyacetate condensations would follow a pathway as outlined below:

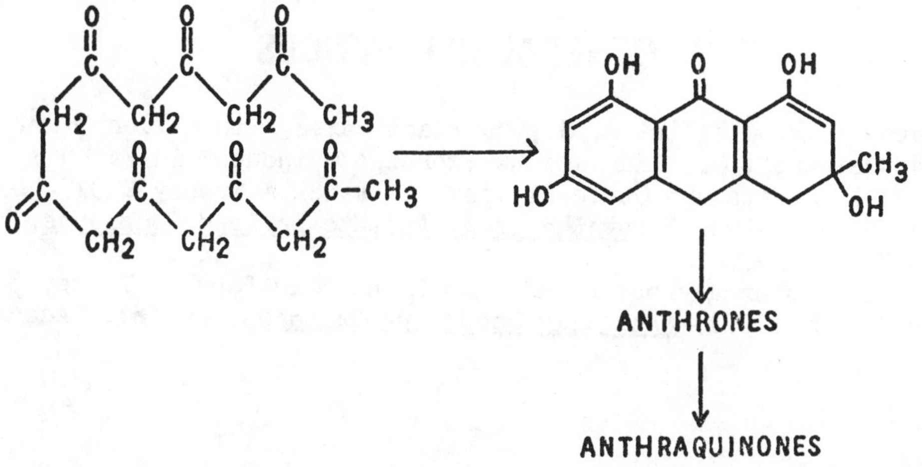

ANTHRONES

ANTHRAQUINONES

Such a scheme accounts perfectly for the structure of emodin, and tracer-feeding experiments have shown that such a pathway can function (65-67). However, other experiments show that some anthraquinones are made, rather, from the addition of an isoprene unit to a naphthoquinone following synthesis of the naphthoquinone by the shikimate pathway (see Chap. 4) (68-70). Some results show the same plant making two different anthraquinones by these two different pathways (67), and there are other cases where the same compound is made by the two different pathways in two different plants (66, 69).

OTHER POLYNUCLEAR QUINONES

Some other condensed, polynuclear quinones have been isolated from higher plants. The best-known is hypericin from leaves of St. John's Wort (*Hypericum perforatum*) :

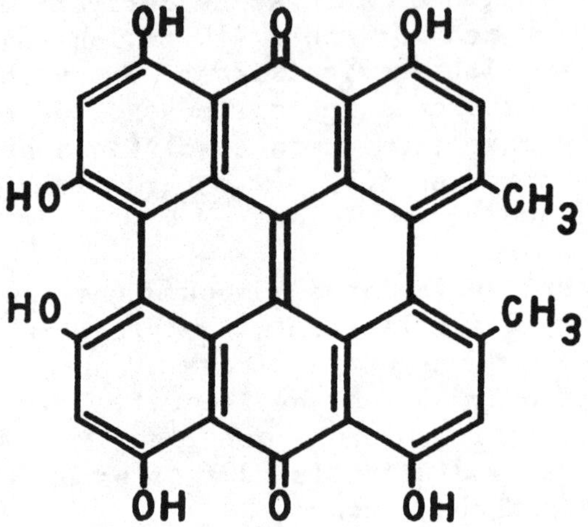

Other species of *Hypericum* contain a pigment of related structure, psudohypericin; and buckwheat(*Fagopyrum* spp.) has a more complex compound of this type, fagopyrin (71, 72). These compounds are of interest because of their effect in concentrating in the skin of animals that eat them and causing photosensitization. There is a paper chromatographic method for analysis of hypericin (73).

It is probable that hypericin is biosynthesized by condensation of two anthrone molecules, and presumed   intermediate compounds have been isolated. Other polynuclear quinones found in plants are probably related to the terpenoids (74, 75).

GENERAL REFERENCES

Caldicott, A. B. & Eglinton, G., "Surface Waxes," in Miller 3 162-194.
Hoffmann-Ostenhof, O., "Eun und Zweikernige Chinone," in Paech & Tracey 3 359-391.
Meara, M. L., "Fats and Other Lipids," in Paech & Tracey 2 317-402.
Packter, N. M. (1973) Biosynthesis of Acetate-Derived Compounds, Wiley-Interscience N. Y.
Schmid, W., "Anthraglykoside und Dianthrone," in Paech & Tracey 3 549-564.
Thomson, R. H. (1971) Naturally Occurring Quinones, 2nd ed., Academic Press, N. Y.

BIBLIOGRAPHY

1. Birch, A. J. (1968) Ann. Rev. Plant Physiol. 19 321-332.
2. Birch, A. J. (1967) Science 156 202-206.
3. Sandermann, W. and Schweers, W. (1960) Chem. Ber. 93 2266-2271.
4. Glet, E. and Gutschmidt, J. (1937) Deut. Apoth. Ztg. 52 265-266 (Chem. Abstr. 31 3206).
5. Karunen, P. (1974) Phytochemistry 13 2209-2213.
6. Haas, K., Buchloh, G., Baydur, B., and Tertinegg, W. (1978) Z. Pflanzenphysiol. 86 389-394.
7. Romanuk, M., Herout, V., and Sorm, F. (1958) Chem. Listy 52 1965-1968 (Chem. Abstr. 53 2383).
8. Sörensen, J. S. and Sörensen, N. A. (1968) Acta Chem. Scand. 12 756-764.
9. Bohlmann, F., Burkhardt, T., and Zdero, C. (1973) Naturally Occurring Acetylenes, Academic Press, N. Y.
10. Ross, R. A. M. (1972) Phytochemistry 11 221-227.
11. Bittner, S., Gazit, S., and Blumenfeld, A. (1971) Phytochemistry 10 1417-1421.
12. Ries, S. K., Wert, V., Sweeley, C. C., and Leavitt, R. A. (1977) Science 195 1339-1341.
13. Lamberton, J. A. and Redcliffe, A. H (1960) Austral. J. Chem. 13 261-268.
14. Mladenova, K., Stoianova-Ivanova, B., and Daskalov, R. M. (1976) Phytochemistry 15 419-420.
15. Kemp, M. S. (1978) Phytochemistry 17 1002.
16. Clark, J. B. (1969) Biochem. Pharmacol. 18 73-83.
17. Bohlmann, F., Rode, K.-M., and Waldau, E. (1967) Chem. Ber. 100 1915-1926.
18. Brockman, H. and Volpers, F. (1947) Chem. Ber. 80 77-82.
19. Chibnall, A. C., Piper, S. H., Pollard, A., Smith, J. A. B., and Williams, E. F. (1931) Biochem. J. 25 2095-2110.
20. Nagy, B., Modzeleski, V., and Murphy, M. T. J. (1965) Phytochemistry 4 945-950.
21. Kaufmann, H. P. and Kessen, G. (1959) Z. Physiol. Chem. 317 43-48.
22. Matsuo, A., Nakayama, M., Goto, H., Hayashi, S., and Nishimoto, S. (1974) Phytochemistry 13 957-959.
23. Eglinton, G. and Hamilton, R. J. (1967) Science 156 1322-1335.
24. Oró, J., Nooner, D. W., and Wikström, S. A. (1965) Science 147 871-873.
25. Kolattukudy, P. E. (1970) Ann. Rev. Plant Physiol. 21 163-192.
26. Cassagne, C. and Lessire, R. (1974) Arch. Biochem. Biophys. 165 274-280.
27. Netting, A. G. and van Wettstein-Knowles, P. (1976) Arch. Biochem. Biophys. 174 613-621.
28. Kolattukudy, P. E., Buckner, J. S., and Liu, T.-Y. J. (1973) Arch. Biochem. Biophys. 156 613-620.
29. Bohlmann, F. and Thefeld, W. (1969) Chem. Ber. 102 1698-1701.
30. Bohlmann, F. and Burkhardt, T. (1969) Chem. Ber. 102 1702-1706.
31. Berti, G. and Bottari, F. (1968) Progress in Phytochemistry 1 589-685.
32. Penttilä, A. and Sundman, J. (1970) J. Pharm. Pharmacol. 22 393-404.
33. Nilsson, M. (1959) Acta Chem. Scand. 13 750-757.
34. Tsujimoto, H. Y., McSwain, B. D., and Arnon, D. I. (1966) Plant Physiol. 41 1376-1380.
35. Verzele, M., Vanluchene, E., and Van Dyck, J. (1973) Anal. Chem. 45 1549-1552.
36. Verzele, M. and de Potter, M. (1978) J. Chromatog. 166 320-326.
37. Tressl, R., Friese, L., Fendesock, F., and Köppler, H. (1978) J. Agric. Food Chem. 26 1426-1430.
38. Hirata, T. and Suga, T. (1978) Bull. Chem. Soc. Japan 51 842-849.
39. Crow, W. D., Osawa, T., Paton, D. M., and Willing, R. R. (1977) Tetrahedron Letters 1073-1074.
40. Lin, T.-J., Ramstad, E., and Heinstein, P. (1974) Phytochemistry 13 1809-1815.
41. Howard, G. A. and Tatchell, A. R. (1954) J. Chem. Soc. 1954 2400-2405.
42. Chan, W. R. and Hassall, C. H. (1955) J. Chem. Soc. 1955 2860-2865.
43. Godin, S. (1958) Experientia 14 208.
44. Penttilä, A. and Sundman, J. (1961) J. Pharm. Pharmacol. 13 531-535.
45. Lounasmaa, M. (1973) Planta Medica 24 148-157.
46. Drawert, F. and Beier, J. (1976) Phytochem. 15 1689-1690. 1691-1692. 1693-1694. 1695-1696.
47. Harrison, P. G., Bailey, B. K., and Steck, W. (1971) Can. J. Biochem. 49 964-970.
48. Pendse, R., Rama Rao, A. V., and Venkataraman, K. (1973) Phytochemistry 12 2033-2034.
49. Schmid, H. (1954) Fortschr. Chem. Org. Naturstoffe 11 124-179.
50. Huttrer, C. P. and Dale, E. (1950) Chem. Revs. 48 543-579.
51. Sen, K. and Bagchi, P. (1959) J. Org. Chem. 24 316-319.
52. Kirby, K. S. and White, T. (1955) Biochem. J. 60 582-590.
53. Harborne, J. B. and Mokhtari, N. (1977) Phytochemistry 16 1314-1315.
54. Hay, J. E. and Haynes, L. J. (1956) J. Chem. Soc. 1956 3141-3147.
55. Stoll, A. and Becker, B. (1950) Fortschr. Chem. Org. Naturstoffe 7 248-269.
56. Hörhammer, L., Wagner, H., and Köhler, O. (1959) Arch. Pharm. 292 591-601.
57. Fairbairn, J. W., ed. (1976) Pharmacology 14 Suppl. 1-105.
58. Fairbairn, J. W. (1964) Lloydia 27 79-87.
59. Briggs, L. H., Nicholls, G. A., and Patterson, R. M. L. (1952) J. Chem. Soc. 1952 1718-1722.
60. Auterhoff, H. and Boehme, K. (1968) Arch. Pharm. 301 793-799.
61. Shibata, S., Takido, M., and Tanaka, O. (1950) J. Am. Chem. Soc. 72 2789-2790.
62. Komolafe, O. O. (1978) J. Chromatog. Sci. 16 496-499.
63. Siesto, A. J. and Bartoli, A. (1957) Farmaco, Ed. prat. 12 517-523. (Chem. Abstr. 52 12323).

64. Betts, T. J., Fairbairn, J. W., and Mital, V. K. (1958) J. Pharm. and Pharmacol. 10 436-441. (Chem. Abstr. 52 20886).
65. Leistner, E. (1971) Phytochemistry 10 3015-3020.
66. Fairbairn, J. W. and Muhtadi, F. J. (1972) Phytochemistry 11 215-219.
67. Leistner, E. (1973) Phytochemistry 12 1669-1674.
68. Burnett, A. R. and Thomson, R. H. (1967) Chem. Commun. 1125-1126.
69. Meynaud, A., Ville, A., and Pacheco, H. (1968) Compt. rend. (D) 266 1783-1786.
70. Stöckigt, J., Srocka, U., and Zenk, M. H. (1973) Phytochemistry 12 2389-2391.
71. Brockmann, H. (1957) Fortschr. Chem. Org. Naturstoffe. 14 141-185.
72. Brockmann, H. and Lackner, H. (1979) Tetra. Letts. 1575-1578.
73. Kučera, M. (1958) Ceskoslov. Farm. 7 436-438 (Chem. Abstr. 53 7507).
74. Edwards, J. M. and Weiss, U. (1970) Phytochemistry 9 1653-1657.
75. Cooke, R. G. and Down, J. G. (1970) Tetra. Letts. 583-584.

Chapter 7
MISCELLANEOUS
VOLATILE COMPOUNDS

A large variety of volatile alcohols, aldehydes, ketones and esters is found in plants, though usually in very small amounts. These compounds, despite their low concentration, are of great aesthetic and commercial interest because of the contribution they make to the flavor and odor of foods, flowers, perfumes, etc. In terms of total amount terpenoids are the most important flavor and odor constituents of plants; but because of their special pathway of biosynthesis, they are treated separately in Chapter 8. The compounds discussed in the present chapter have the same types of functional groups as many of the terpenoids, but their carbon chains show much less branching and are often completely unbranched. As minor constituents of essential oils they add distinctive characteristics to products which are predominantly terpenoid; as flavor and odor constituents of fruits and flowers they may be much more significant. Their role in the plant may lie in their attractiveness to insect pollinators and animal seed-disseminators. The compound 2-hexenal ("leaf aldehyde") is largely responsible for the distinctive odor of crushed leaves. It is also reported to act as an antibiotic, wound hormone, and seed germination stimulant (1).

All of the straight chain alcohols up to C_{10} have been found in plants either free, esterified, or as glycosides (2). A few branched chain and unsaturated alcohols are also known. Aliphatic aldehydes up to C_{12} have been found and ketones up to C_{13}. Unlike the fatty acids, there seems to be no preference for even-carbon chains among these compounds. Branching, if present, is usually confined to a single methyl group near the end of the chain. Secondary alcohols are rather common, but they usually have their hydroxyl groups at C-2, and never farther removed from the end of a chain than C-3. The ketones are almost without exception methyl ketones. The esters usually have lower fatty acids comprising their acyl groups, but sometimes aromatic acids are present. Acids of the citric acid cycle, or closely related acids, are never found in esters. The complexity of natural fruit flavors has been fully revealed only by modern investigations utilizing gas chromatography. Earlier lists suggesting a dozen or so constituents of a fruit essence have been overwhelmed by findings of many dozens of components. Many of these will be terpenoids, but straight-chain compounds will almost always be present in addition. The record at this writing seems to be held by the banana in whose volatile fraction 350 components have been demonstrated and nearly 200 identified (3). Similar but less extensive lists are available for pears (4), peaches (5), grapes (6), citrus fruits (7, 8), strawberries (9), raspberries (10), tomatoes (11), black currants (12), and apples (13). Table 7-1 illustrates structures of a variety of volatile compounds of frequent occurrence. From the wealth of data it can be observed that certain types of compounds are characteristic of particular fruits

-- for example, methyl and ethyl esters of trans-2-cis-4-decadienoic acid in Bartlett pears (4), methyl ketones and secondary alcohols in wild strawberries (9), and cis-3-hexenal in tomatoes (11).

An important volatile compound released by many plants and plant parts is the simple hydrocarbon ethylene. Its role as a stimulant of fruit ripening is widely known, but its mode of action remains obscure (14, 15). Even more surprising than ethylene as a plant emanation, is carbon monoxide which is produced by various seedlings, germinating seeds, and leaves (16, 17).

ISOLATION

The volatile components of fruits and flowers are present in such minute amounts that tremendous quantities of starting material are necessary for the isolation of any workable quantity of product. Because of their volatility these compounds are also difficult to isolate, and they are frequently converted en masse to non-volatile derivatives which can then be fractionated.

Three general methods are available for removing volatile components from plants: distillation, solvent extraction, and aeration. Distillation (or steam distillation) at atmospheric pressure may bring about some decomposition. Distillation under reduced pressure and lower temperatures may permit enzymatic degradations to proceed causing changes in constituents of the tissue. If oxidative reactions are a problem, distillation can be carried out in a nitrogen atmosphere. Solvent extraction methods are usable in special cases especially for the less polar compounds. Some of the lower molecular weight volatile compounds are too soluble in water to be extracted efficiently by organic solvents. In the aeration process only compounds evolved into the air are isolated by passing a stream of air over the plant material for a long period of time and condensing any entrained substances in cooled receivers; or the stream of air may be passed through reagents which react with at least some of the compounds to produce non-volatile derivatives. Methods for preparing fruit essences for gas chromatography are compared in (18) and (19).

A mixture of volatile substances isolated by one of the above procedures may be fractionated by distillation or chromatography. Chromatographic separations can be made on liquid partition columns or by gas chromatography. Alternatively, derivatives of different components of the mixture may be used to separate them. Thus, aldehydes and methyl ketones form water-soluble bisulfite compounds and may be removed from other compounds in organic extracts by passage over a bisulfite column (20). They may also be converted to solid 2, 4-dinitrophenylhydrazones, and remaining volatile compounds removed by distillation. Aldehydes form water-insoluble derivatives with dimedone. Ketones do not react with this reagent. Alcohols can be converted into solid urethanes by reaction with isocyanates or into 3, 5-dinitrobenzoates by reaction with 3, 5-dinitrobenzoyl chloride. Remaining volatile compounds are then removed by distillation. Esters cannot be separated as such by chemical means since derivatives formed represent either the alcohol or the acid portion of the ester rather than the intact compound. After the various types of derivatives have been prepared, they are usually separated by chromatographic

TABLE 7-1. SOME VOLATILE ALCOHOLS AND CARBONYL COMPOUNDS FOUND IN PLANTS

Compound	Occurrence
CH_3OH methanol	widespread, usually as esters
CH_3CH_2OH ethanol	widespread, free or as esters
$\overset{\displaystyle CH_3}{\vert}$ CH_3CHCH_2OH iso-butyl alcohol	fruits, free or as esters
$CH_3CH_2CH = CHCH_2CH_2OH$ *cis*-3-hexenol-1	free in many leaves and flowers
$CH_3(CH_2)_5CHCH_3$ $\vert$ OH 2-octanol	geranium oil (*Pelargonium* spp.)
$CH_3C\overset{\displaystyle O}{\underset{\displaystyle H}{}}$ ethanal, acetaldehyde	many fruits
$CH_3(CH_2)_4C\overset{\displaystyle O}{\underset{\displaystyle H}{}}$ hexanal, caproaldehyde	*Eucalyptus* spp.
$CH_3(CH_2)_{10}C\overset{\displaystyle O}{\underset{\displaystyle H}{}}$ dodecanal, lauraldehyde	citrus fruits
$\overset{\displaystyle O}{\overset{\Vert}{}}$ CH_3CCH_3 acetone	many essential oils
$\overset{\displaystyle O}{\overset{\Vert}{}}$ $CH_3C(CH_2)_5CH_3$ 2-octanone	rue (*Ruta* spp.)
$\overset{\displaystyle O\ \ O}{\overset{\Vert\ \ \Vert}{}}$ $CH_3C\ C\ CH_3$ diacetyl, 2,3-butandione	raspberries (*Rubus idaeus*)

procedures as described below under "Characterization". In a few cases
it is possible to recover the original compounds from purified derivatives,
but there is usually no reason to do this.

CHARACTERIZATION

Identification of isolated volatile alcohols and carbonyl compounds
can be carried out by standard procedures of qualitative organic analysis
if enough material is available, but usually it is not.

There are many common spot tests and color reactions to indicate the
presence of alcohols, aldehydes, ketones, and esters. Detailed information on procedures may be found in any text book of qualitative organic
anaylsis. Primary and secondary alcohols form xanthates by reaction with
carbon disulfide and solid sodium hydroxide. The xanthates treated with
molybdic acid give a violet color which is extractable into chloroform.
Aldehydes and ketones form insoluble red precipitates when treated with
a dilute (0.4%) solution of 2, 4-dinitrophenylhydrazine in dilute sulfuric
acid. Aldehydes give a pink color with Schiff's reagent (reduced rosaniline
hydrochloride), but ketones do not. Esters react on heating with hydroxylamine in hot alkaline solution. When this solution is cooled and made
acidic, the hydroxamic acids which have been formed give a purple color
with ferric chloride solution.

Characterization of a mixture can also be performed by chromatographic
methods. Most useful in this regard is probably gas chromatography since
it has a high resolving power, and the compounds involved are readily
volatile (21). The fractions may be collected separately as they pass
from the column by bubbling into chilled carbon disulfide or by using a
liquid air trap, but the amounts obtainable are minute. They may be identified to some extent by their rates of migration on columns of different
materials, or identification can be made using infrared or mass spectroscopy.

Rather than attempt characterization of the volatile compounds as
such, it is often more convenient to form various derivatives which can be
purified and identified. Some of these derivatives are mentioned under
"Isolation Methods." If derivatives of pure compounds have been prepared,
they may be identified by physical properties such as absorption spectra
or melting points. More often mixtures of derivatives must be fractionated
and the compounds separately identified. Alcohol dinitrobenzoates have
been separated on columns of silicic acid-celite developed with petroleum
ether/ethyl ether mixtures (22). Dinitrobenzoates can also be chromatographed on paper using heptane/methanol as the solvent (23). Partial
identification can be made by R_f value. Dinitrophenylhydrazones of the
aldehydes and ketones can be separated on columns (silicic acid or bento-
nite) using such solvents as hexane, ethyl ether, chloroform, and benzene,
or mixtures of them (24). They can also be analyzed by paper or thin
layer chromatography (25). The absorption spectra of dinitrophenylhydrazones may be used to identify them by comparing spectra with those of
known phenylhydrazones in neutral and alkaline solution (26). An ester
can be hydrolyzed and the alcohols and acid characterized separately by
paper chromatography or other means (cf. Chapter 3). Another procedure is
to form derivatives directly from the ester without previous saponification. For example, by heating with 3, 5-dinitrobenzoyl chloride and

sulfuric acid, a dinitrobenzoate of the alcohol portion may be prepared and characterized. By treating with alkaline hydroxylamine the acid portions can be converted to hydroxamic acids and these chromatographed in butanol/acetic acid/water, 4:1:5 (27). The hydroxamic acid spots are detected by spraying with ferric chloride in water-saturated butanol.

METABOLIC PATHWAYS

Some information is available regarding the biosynthesis of the diverse compounds covered in this chapter. A review (28) of the pathways for banana volatiles concludes that branched chain compounds are derived from leucine and valine; phenolic ethers from phenylalanine; esters, alcohols and ketones from $C_2 - C_{10}$ fatty acids; and unsaturated aldehydes from unsaturated fatty acids. A few of these pathways have been studied using plant homogenates and partially purified enzyme systems, for instance the conversion of amino acids to alcohols and aldehydes in tomato extracts (29, 30). The conversion of acids to esters and alcohols has been observed in apple slices (31) and strawberry fruits (32).

It appears that quite a number of volatile substances are produced in plants by the action of lipoxygenase on C_{18} unsaturated fatty acids followed by further transformations catalyzed by isomerases, reductases, etc. The C_6 alcohols and aldehydes, in particular, arise by this route from 13-hydroperoxides and the C_9 compounds from 9-hydroperoxides (33-35). Alkanes such as ethane and pentane may also be produced (36, 37).

There has been much interest in elucidating the pathway for ethylene formation. The possibility still exists that there are different routes to ethylene, with different systems using different precursors (14). Most workers now favor a pathway from methionine, and the most recent evidence suggests that S-adenosylmethionine and 1-aminocyclopropane-1-carboxylic acid are intermediates in the pathway (38-40). Oxygen is required for the conversion of the latter compound to ethylene, and free-radical steps are presumably involved (38, 39, 41). There is still some suggestion of a pathway from β-alanine to ethylene (42), but earlier proposals starting with fumaric acid or linolenic acid are now discredited. Ethylene is metabolized by plants to ethylene oxide (43), ethylene glycol (44), and carbon dioxide (45).

Carbon monoxide can be either oxidized to carbon dioxide or reduced to formate, depending on the plant (46).

GENERAL REFERENCES

Abeles, F. B. (1973) Ethylene in Plant Biology, Academic Press, N. Y.
Forss, D. A. (1972) "Odor and Flavor Compounds from Lipids," Prog. Chem. Fats Other Lipids 13 177-258.
Guenther, E. (1948-1952) The Essential Oils, 6 Vols., Van Nostrand, N. Y.
Masada, Y. (1976) Analysis of Essential Oils by Gas Chromatography and Mass Spectrometry, Wiley-Interscience, N. Y.
Meigh, D. F., "Volatile Alcohols, Aldehydes, Ketones, and Esters," in Paech & Tracey 2 403-443.
Nicholas, H. J., "Miscellaneous Volatile Plant Products," in Miller 2 381-399.

BIBLIOGRAPHY

1. Schildknecht, H. and Rauch, G. (1961) Z. Naturforsch. 16b 422-429.
2. Liu, T., Oppenheim, A., and Castelfranco, P. (1965) Plant Physiol. 40 1261-1268.
3. Tressl, R., Drawert, F., Heimann, W., and Emberger, R. (1969) Z. Naturforsch. 24b 781-783.
4. Heinz, D. E. and Jennings, W. G. (1966) J. Food Sci. 31 69-80.
5. Spencer, M. D., Pangborn, R. M., and Jennings, W. G. (1978) J. Agric. Food Chem. 26 725-732.
6. Schreier, P., Drawert, F., and Junker, A. (1976) J. Agric. Food Chem. 24 331-336.
7. Moshonas, M. G. and Shaw, P. E. (1973) J. Food Sci. 38 360-361.
8. Azzouz, M. A., Reineccius, G. A., and Moshonas, M. G. (1976) J. Food Sci. 41 324-328.
9. Drawert, F., Tressl, R., Staudt, R. and Köppler, H. (1973) Z. Naturforsch. 28c 488-493.
10. Winter, M. and Enggist, P. (1971) Helv. Chim. Acta 54 1891-1898.
11. Guadagni, D. G., Buttery, R. G., and Venstrom, D. W. (1972) J. Sci. Food Agric. 23 1445-1450.
12. Nursten, H. E. and Williams, A. A. (1969) J. Sci. Food Agric. 20 91-98.
13. Gascó, L., Barrera, R., and de la Cruz, F. (1969) J. Chromatog. Sci. 7 228-238.
14. Lieberman, M. (1979) Ann. Rev. Plant Physiol. 30 533-591.
15. Lieberman, M. (1975) Physiol. Vég. 13 489-499.
16. Siegel, S. M., Renwick, G. and Rosen, L. A. (1962) Science 137 683-684.
17. Fischer, K. and Lüttge, U. (1978) Nature 275 740-741.
18. Heinz, D. E., Sevenants, M. R., and Jennings, W. G. (1966) J. Food Sci. 31 63-68.
19. Jennings, W. G. and Filsoof, M. (1977) J. Agric. Food Biochem. 25 440-445.
20. Schwartz, D. P. and Weihrauch, J. L. (1973) Microchem. J. 18 249-255.
21. Merritt, C., Jr., Robertson, D. H., Cavagnaro, J. F., Graham, R. A., and Nichols, T. L. (1974) J. Agric. Food Chem. 22 750-755.
22. Holley, A. D. and Holley, R. W. (1952) Anal. Chem. 24 216-218.
23. Meigh, D. F. (1952) Nature 169 706-707.
24. Gordon, B. E., Wopat, F., Burnham, H. D., and Jones, L. C. (1951) Anal. Chem. 23 1754-1758.
25. Ronkainen, P. (1967) J. Chromatog. 27 380-383.
26. Roberts, J. D. and Green, C. (1946) J. Am. Chem. Soc. 68 214-216.
27. Thompson, A. R. (1951) Austral. J. Sci. Res. B4 180-186.
28. Tressl, R. and Drawert, F. (1973) J. Agric. Food Chem. 21 560-565.
29. Yu, M.-H., Olson, L. E., and Salunkhe, D. K. (1968) Phytochemistry 7 561-565.
30. Yu, M.-H., Salunkhe, D. K., and Olson, L. E. (1968) Plant and Cell Physiol. 9 633-638.
31. Paillard, N. M. M. (1979) Phytochemistry 18 1165-1171.
32. Yamashita, I., Nemoto, Y., and Yoshikawa, S. (1976) Phytochemistry 15 1633-1637.
33. Galliard, T. and Matthew, J. A. (1977) Phytochemistry 16 339-343.
34. Sessa, D. J. (1979) J. Agric. Food Chem. 27 234-239.
35. Phillips, D. R., Matthew, J. A., Reynolds, J., and Fenwick, G. R. (1979) Phytochemistry 18 401-404.
36. John, W. W. and Curtis, R. W. (1977) Plant Physiol. 59 521-522.
37. Sanders, T. H., Pattee, H. E., and Singleton, J. A. (1975) Lipids 10 568-570.
38. Adams, D. O. and Yang, S. F. (1979) Proc. Nat. Acad. Sci. U. S. 76 170-174.
39. Konze, J. R. and Kende, H. (1979) Planta 146 293-301.
40. Lürssen, K., Naumann, K., and Schröder, R. (1979) Z. Pflanzenphysiol. 92 285-294.
41. Baker, J. E. (1976) Plant Physiol. 58 644-647.
42. Ghooprasert, P. and Spencer, M. (1975) Physiol. Vég. 13 579-589.
43. Jerie, P. H. and Hall, M. A. (1978) Proc. Roy. Soc. London B 200 87-94.
44. Blomstrom, D. C. and Beyer, E. M., Jr. (1979) Plant Physiol. 63 Suppl. 374.
45. Beyer, E. M., Jr. (1975) Plant Physiol. 56 273-278.
46. Bidwell, R. G. S. and Bebee, G. P. (1974) Can. J. Botany 52 1841-1847.

Chapter 8
TERPENOIDS AND STEROIDS

The diverse compounds covered in this chapter are not traditionally grouped together but are usually put under such categories as essential oils, sterols, alkaloids, pigments, cardiac glycosides, etc. Only from a consideration of biosynthetic studies is it evident that they may be reasonably grouped together as compounds whose basic skeletons are all derived from mevalonic acid or a closely related precursor. This biosynthetic unity does not imply any functional unity or, indeed, any detailed unity in chemical properties, which depend more on functional groups than on carbon skeleton.

As the structures of this group of compounds were elucidated, it became apparent that many of them could be regarded as built up of isoprene or iso-pentane units linked together in various ways and with different types of ring closures, degrees of unsaturation, and functional groups.

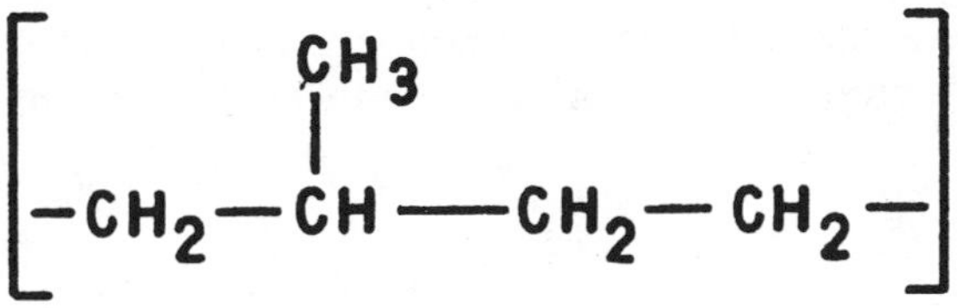

$$\left[-CH_2 - \underset{\underset{CH_3}{|}}{CH} - CH_2 - CH_2 - \right] \qquad \text{iso-pentane unit}$$

The commonest arrangement appeared to be "head-to-tail":

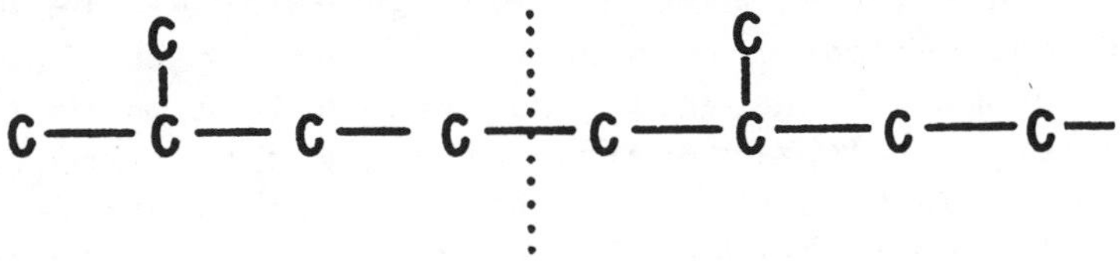

$$C - \underset{\underset{C}{|}}{C} - C - C \; \vdots \; C - \underset{\underset{C}{|}}{C} - C - C -$$

and this head-to-tail rule was regarded as so general that the correctness of proposed structures could be judged by seeing whether they conformed to it. As more compounds have been discovered, both types of possible exceptions have been found to this isoprene rule -- i.e. isoprenoid-type compounds have been found which do not contain even numbers of isoprene units, and compounds have been found where the head-to-tail arrangement is not followed. Individual cases will be discussed below, but they do not destroy the great utility of the isoprene rule as a working hypothesis. However, there is danger in supposing that any molecule which can be shown on paper to contain an isoprene residue is actually formed by reactions similar to those of terpene biosynthesis.

Most compounds discussed in this chapter are considered to have their basic structures built up entirely of isoprenoid units. Other classes of plant constituents occasionally have isoprenoid side chains attached to obviously non-isoprenoid central structures. The placement of such compounds is clearly arbitrary, but some examples may be seen among the flavonoids (calophyllolide, rotenone), aromatics (tocopherols) and porphyrins (Chlorophyll).

The fundamental isoprenoid building pattern is one of the most widespread in natural products. Every living organism apparently contains some compounds built on this basis. All of these may be regarded as evolutionary modifications of a primeval mevalonic acid pathway. The adaptive importance of these different ramifications, however, remains almost completely obscure. There seems merit in the possibility that some of these compounds merely represent ways of disposing of excess acetate. In other cases more specific functions appear reasonable and will be mentioned in the appropriate places. It is a general observation that lower terpenoids are rather restricted to phylogenetically young plant groups while carotenoids and steroids are more widespread.

HEMITERPENOIDS

Isoprene itself is rare in plants but does occur (1). Some other natural five carbon compounds with an isoprene skeleton may have no actual biogenetic relationship to the terpenoids, but are probably derived from leucine. Nevertheless some examples are listed in Table 8-1. The natural occurrence of tiglic and angelic acids has been reviewed by Buckles et al. (2)

MONOTERPENOIDS

The monoterpenoids appear to be built of two isoprene residues and normally have ten carbon atoms, although rare examples are known of compounds which seem constructed on this general principle but have lost one or more carbon atoms. Both cyclic and open-chain compounds are known. In fact almost every possible arrangement of ten carbon atoms seems to occur in nature. Only some of the more common examples can be given here as illustrations. The term "terpenoid" is preferred for reference to all compounds built of isoprene units, regardless of the functional groups present, while "terpene" refers specifically to hydrocarbons. Over one hundred different monoterpenoids have been isolated from plants. They are the major components of many essential oils and as such have great economic importance as flavors, perfumes, and solvents. They are characteristically colorless, water-insoluble, steam distillable liquids having a fragrant odor. Some are optically active. Study of their chemistry is complicated by the difficulty of obtaining pure compounds from the complex mixtures in which they usually occur and by the readiness with which they undergo rearrangement.

The distribution of monoterpenoids in economically important essential oils is surveyed in the treatise of Guenther (see General References). The

TABLE 8-1. SOME HEMITERPENOIDS

Compound	Source
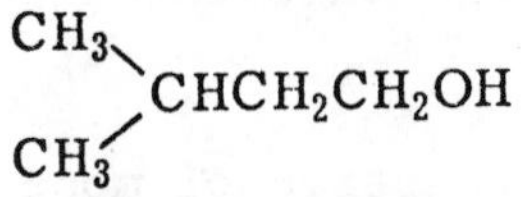 CH_3 $\quad$ $CHCH_2CH_2OH$ $\quad$ CH_3 *iso*-Amyl Alcohol	as an ester in essential oils of *Mentha, Eucalyptus, Ribes,* etc.
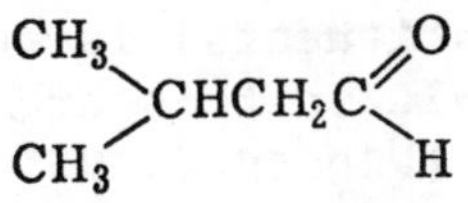 CH_3 $\quad$ $CHCH_2C$ $\overset{O}{\underset{H}{\diagup\diagdown}}$ $\quad$ CH_3 *iso*-Valeraldehyde	in essential oil of *Eucalyptus, Eugenia, Santalum,* etc.
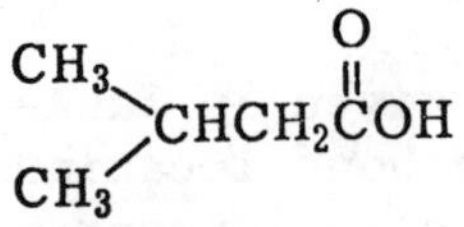 CH_3 $\quad$ $CHCH_2\overset{\overset{O}{\|}}{C}OH$ $\quad$ CH_3 *iso*-Valeric Acid	widespread, e.g. in *Valeriana* spp.
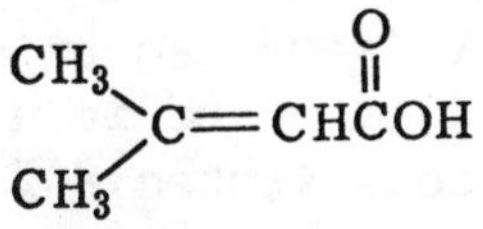 CH_3 $\quad$ $C=CH\overset{\overset{O}{\|}}{C}OH$ $\quad$ CH_3 Senecioic Acid	*Senecio kaempferi* and elsewhere
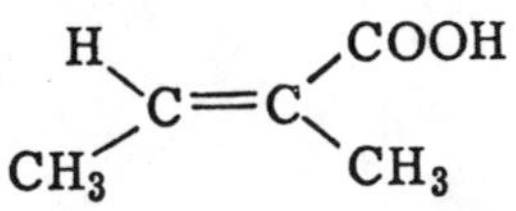 $\overset{H}{\underset{CH_3}{}}C=C\overset{COOH}{\underset{CH_3}{}}$ Tiglic Acid	widespread, e.g. *Geranium* spp.
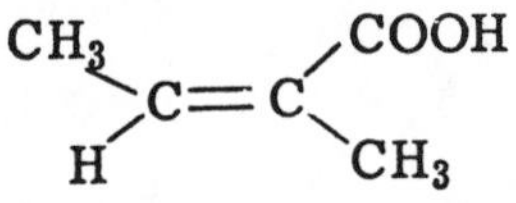 $\overset{CH_3}{\underset{H}{}}C=C\overset{COOH}{\underset{CH_3}{}}$ Angelic Acid	widespread, e.g. *Archangelica officinalis*
$CH - C-COOH$ $\|\| \quad \|\|$ $CH \quad CH$ $\diagdown O \diagup$ β-Furoic Acid	*Phaseolus multiformis*

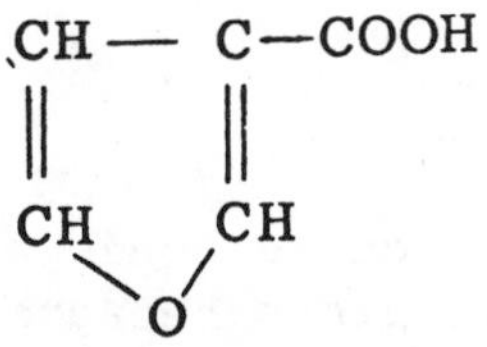

majority of these compounds occur widely and are not characteristic of particular plants or plant groups. It is rare for a single plant to contain only one terpenoid, but one may be predominant. Although the presence of monoterpenes is best documented in the seed plants, there are scattered reports of the occurrence of terpene-containing volatile oils throughout the plant kingdom down to the bryophytes and even fungi.

Most investigators are of the opinion that the function of most lower terpenoids in plants may be described as ecological rather than physiological. Many of them inhibit the growth of competing plants and may also be insecticidal or toxic to higher animals. The possible ecological significance of terpenoids (and other secondary plant constituents) is well described in (3) and (4). The great specificity possible in this area is illustrated by the finding that the Douglas fir beetle (*Dendroctonus pseudotsugae*) is attracted to α-pinene but repelled by β-pinene. Both are present in the host tree but vary in relative concentration from tree to tree (5).

Structures of some open-chain monoterpenoids are given in Table 8-2. They have been chosen to illustrate a variety of double bond locations, functional groups, and deviations from the usual head-to-tail isoprene rule. Terpenoid alcohols frequently are found as esters rather than free alcohols.

It will be noted that opportunity for geometrical isomerism exists in geraniol and geranial. Their isomers, nerol and neral, occur in nature; and a mixture of geranial and neral, known as citral, constitutes 80% of the commercially valuable lemon grass oil.

The great majority of monocylic monoterpenoids have the so-called p-menthane skeleton:

Variations are introduced into this basic structure by double bonds and functional groups. The most important compound of this group because of its widespread occurrence and commercial value is limonene. It is the chief constituent of citrus fruit oils but occurs in many other essential oils as well. A few other monocyclic compounds lacking the p-menthane structure also are known. Some examples are shown in Table 8-3. The sources given are intended only to be typical. Most of the compounds are widely distributed. Asymmetric carbon atoms are pointed out by asterisks, but generally both

TABLE 8-2.   OPEN-CHAIN MONOTERPENOIDS

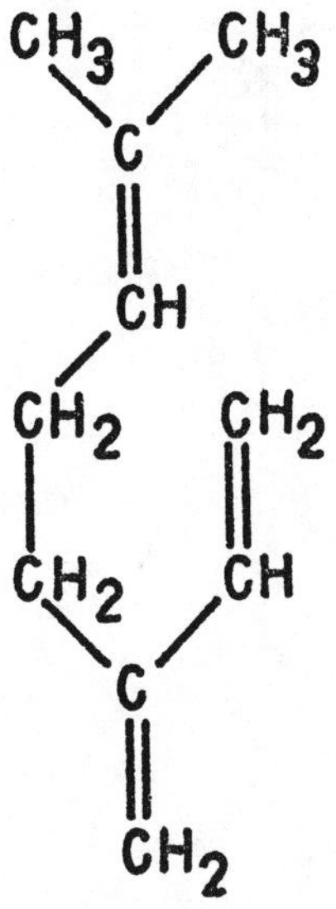

myrcene 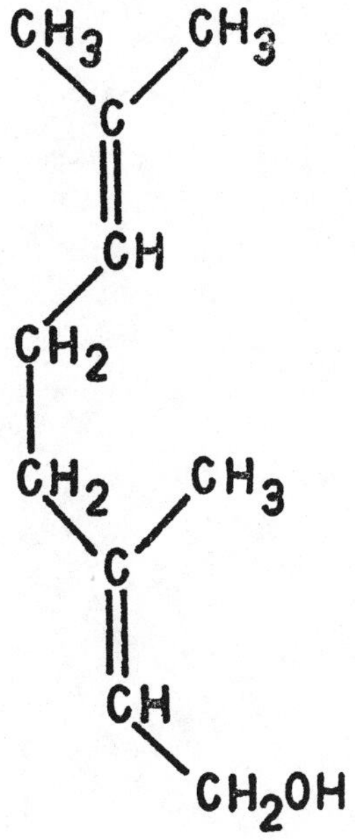   geraniol 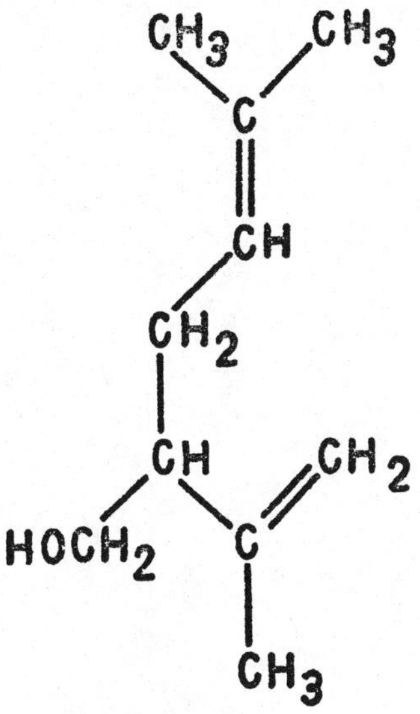   lavandulol

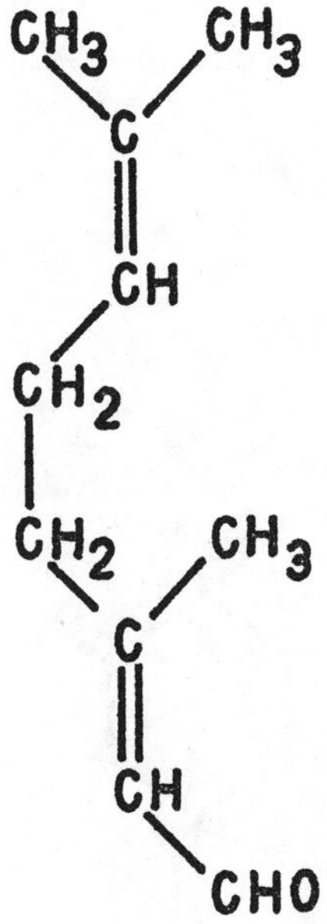

geranial 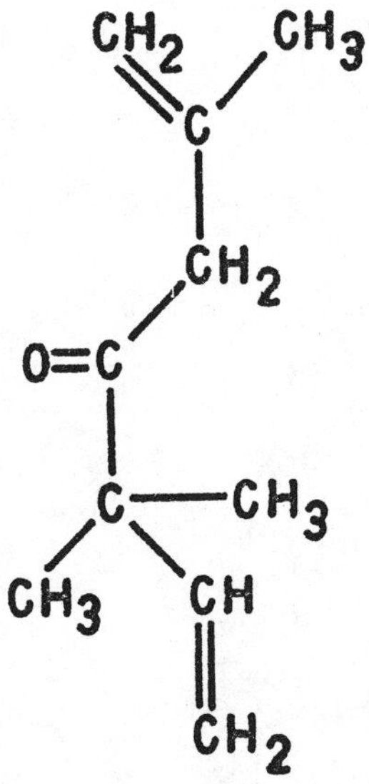   artemisia   perillene
                           ketone

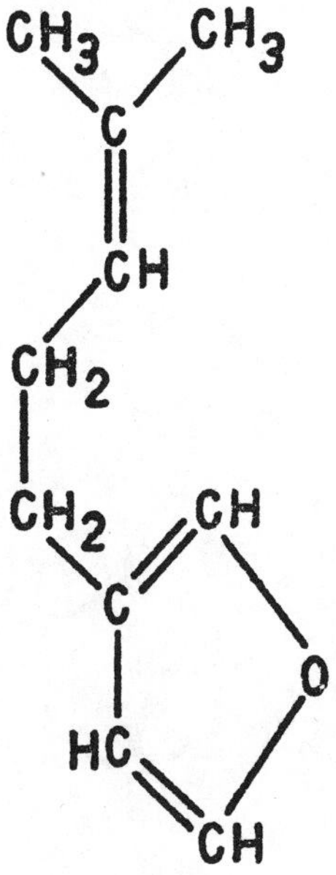

TABLE 8-3.   SOME MONCYCLIC MONOTERPENOIDS,
STRUCTURES AND OCCURRENCE

limonene (*Citrus* spp.)

α-phellandrene (*Eucalyptus* spp.)

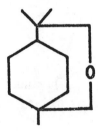

1:8 cineole (*Artemisia maritima*)

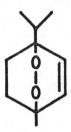

ascaridole *(Chenopodium
ambrosioides)*

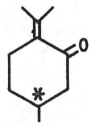

pulegone *(Mentha pulegium)*

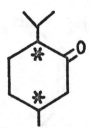

menthone *(Mentha piperita)*

Table 8-3. Continued

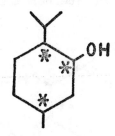

menthol *(Mentha piperita)*

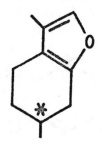

menthofuran *(Mentha piperita)*

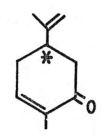

carvone *(Carum carvi)*

cryptone *(Eucalyptus* spp.*)*

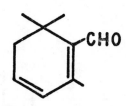

safranal *(Crocus sativus)*

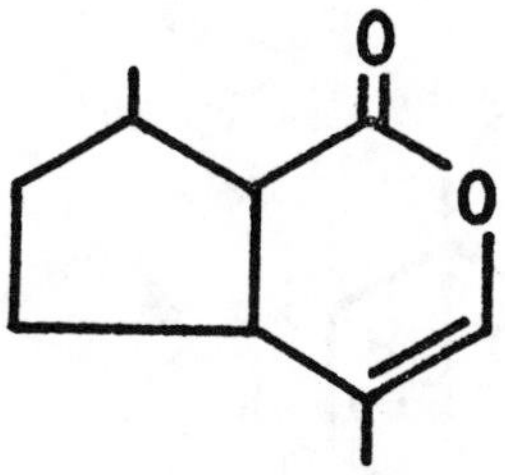

nepetalactone *(Nepeta cataria)*

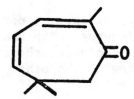

eucarvone *(Asarum sieboldi)*

isomers are known in nature either from two different plants or sometimes both from the same plant. The (+), (−) mixture of limonenes is known commercially as dipentene. The ionones and irone are important perfumery materials which closely resemble the monocyclic monoterpenoids in structure but have additional carbon atoms:

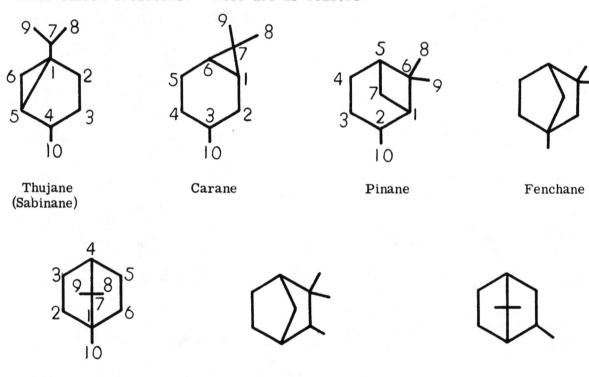

α-ionone *(Boronia megastigma)*   irone *(Iris florentina)*

The bicyclic monoterpenoids are divided into seven classes according to their carbon skeletons. These are as follows:

Thujane
(Sabinane)   Carane   Pinane   Fenchane

Camphane (Bornane)   *iso*-Camphane   *iso*-Bornylane

These forms are easily visualized as derived from the monocyclic compounds by additonal ring closures. The best known of this group (and possibly of all terpenoids) is α-pinene, the chief component of turpentine. The structure of it and of a few of the other more important bicyclic monoterpenoids are given in Table 8-4.

Although usually classed as aromatic compounds, some constituents of essential oils are clearly related to the terpenoids. For example

TABLE 8-4. BICYLIC MONOTERPENOIDS,
STRUCTURE AND OCCURRENCE

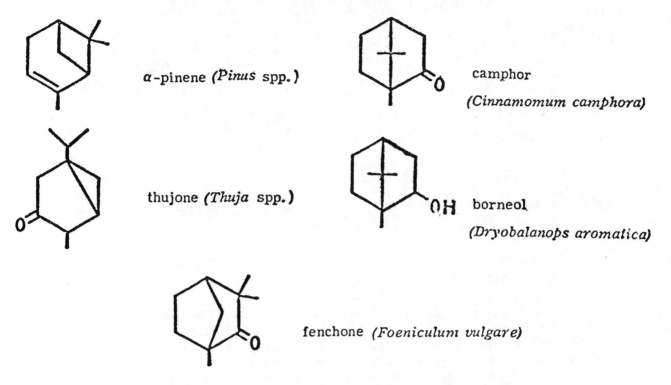

α-pinene *(Pinus* spp.)

camphor

(Cinnamomum camphora)

thujone *(Thuja* spp.)

borneol

(Dryobalanops aromatica)

fenchone *(Foeniculum vulgare)*

p-cymene and thymol found in oil of thyme are respectively:

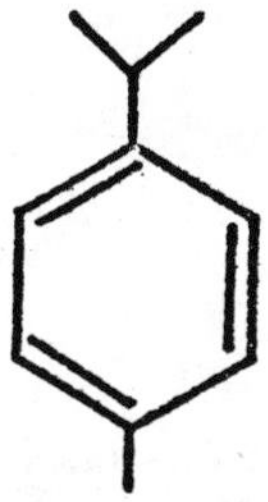

and

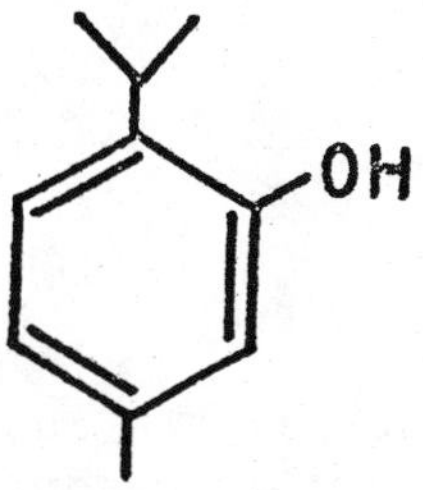

    A group of monoterpenoids with structural similarities is widely distributed in plants and known as the "iridoids." Many are found as glucosides that have physiological effects on mammals and microorganisms. Some are responsible for the darkening observed in grinding certain plants (7, 8). Structures of two examples of this group are shown below. About 80 are known in all (9, 10).

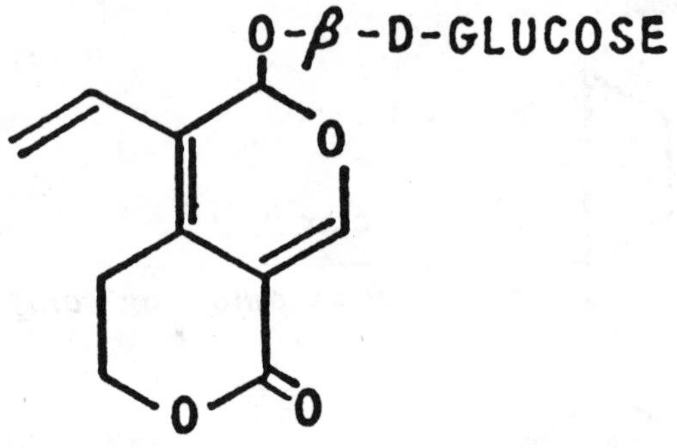

gentiopicroside *(Gentiana lutea)* 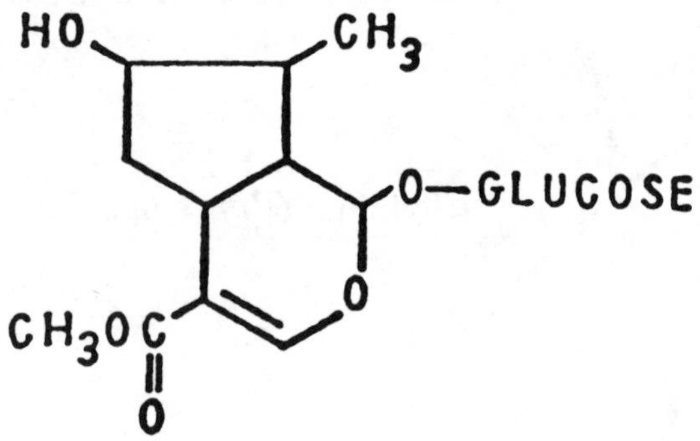   loganin   *(Strychnos nux-vomica)*

SESQUITERPENOIDS

The sesquiterpenoids are C_{15} compounds, usually regarded as derived from three isoprene residues. Like monoterpenoids they are found as constituents of steam-distillable essential oils. The general utility and occasional exceptions to the isoprene rule which were mentioned earlier apply also in this group of compounds. Rücker has recently reviewed the sesquiterpenoids (11).

The most important member of the acyclic sesquiterpenoids is the widely-distributed alcohol farnesol:

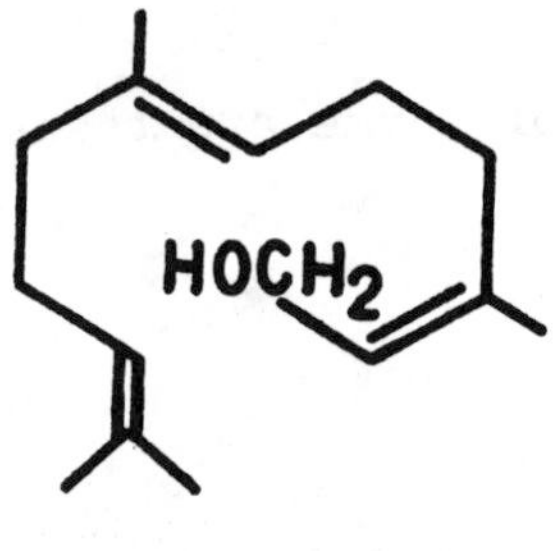

Its pyrophosphate is a key intermediate in terpenoid biosynthesis. Most of the monocyclic sesquiterpenoids have the skeleton shown below with variations in double bond location and functional groups. Some examples of this type are shown in Table 8-5.

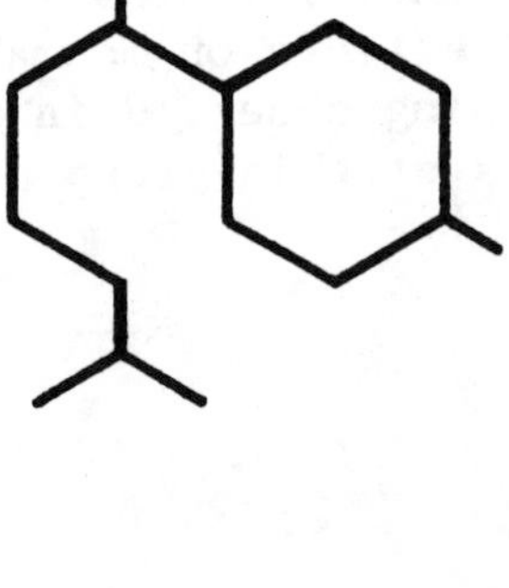

TABLE 8-5.   MONOCYCLIC SESQUITERPENOIDS, STRUCTURES AND OCCURRENCE

γ-bisabolene (widely distributed)

zingiberene *(Zingiber officinale)*

lanceol *(Santalum lanceolatum)*

ar-turmerone *(Curcuma longa)*

perezone *(Trixis pipitzahuac)*

There are some unusual monocyclic structures found among the sesquiterpenoids that cannot be conveniently constructed from isoprene residues.
Presumably rearrangements and oxidation play a part in their formation from
isoprenoid precursors. A few examples are given in Table 8-6.

Most of the bicyclic sesquiterpenoids can be divided into naphthalene
types and azulene types according to which of these two aromatic structures
they give on dehydrogenation. Further subdivision takes into account the
locations of substituent groups on the rings. Low temperature distillation
may be sufficient to convert some azulenogenic terpenoids into azulenes, and
it is generally believed that the azulenes themselves never occur in nature,
although this is open to some question (12, 13).

Naphthalenic:

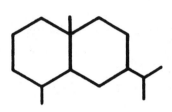

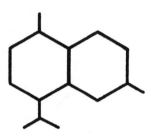

eudalene type   cadalene type

Azulenic:

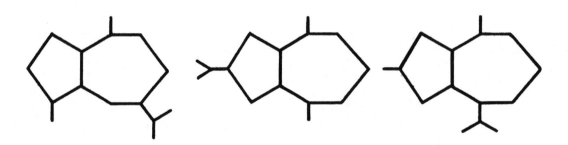

guaiazulene type   vetivazulene type   zierazulene type

Some specific examples are shown in Table 8-7.

Additional examples of bicyclic and tricyclic sesquiterpenoids are
also shown in Table 8-8 to indicate some of the more unusual structures
that are found. One of the most interesting of these is iresin whose
bicyclofarnesol type structure is similar to that of many diterpenoids
but otherwise unknown among the sesquiterpenoids (14).

Physiologically, one of the most interesting of the sesquiterpenoids
is abscisic acid, a hormone which antagonizes the effects of gibberellins
and inhibits bud growth (15). Although the particular isomer shown in
Table 8-6 is regarded as the normal hormone, other isomers occur naturally (16)

TABLE 8-6.   UNUSUAL SESQUITERPENOID STRUCTURES

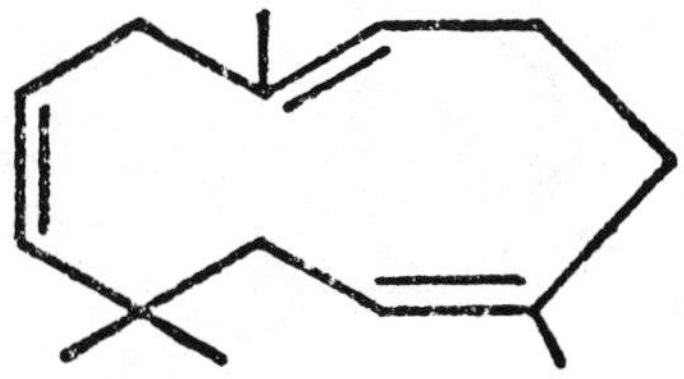

humulene *(Humulus lupulus)*

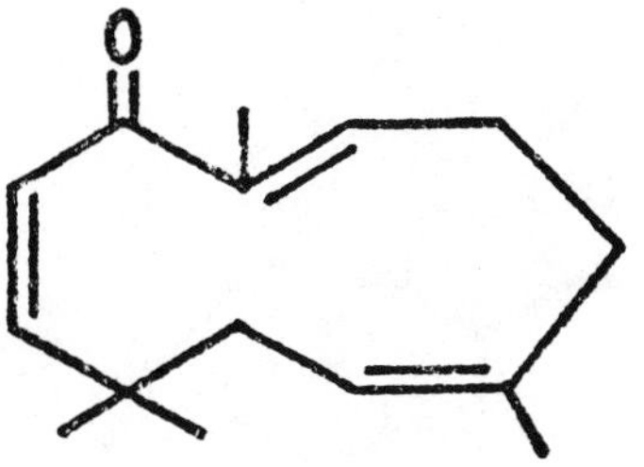

zerumbone *(Zingiber zerumbet)*

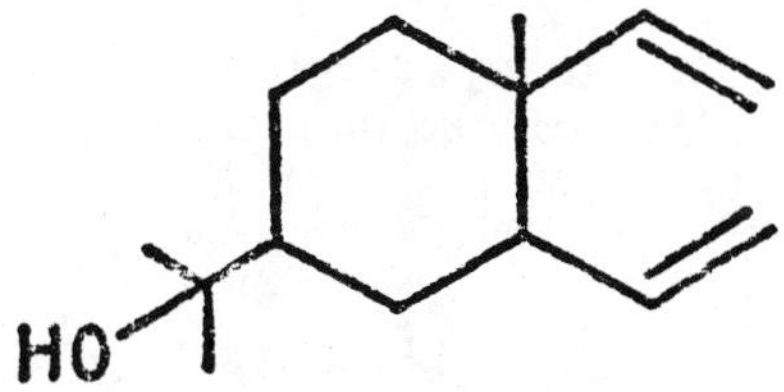

elemol *(Canarium luzonicum)*

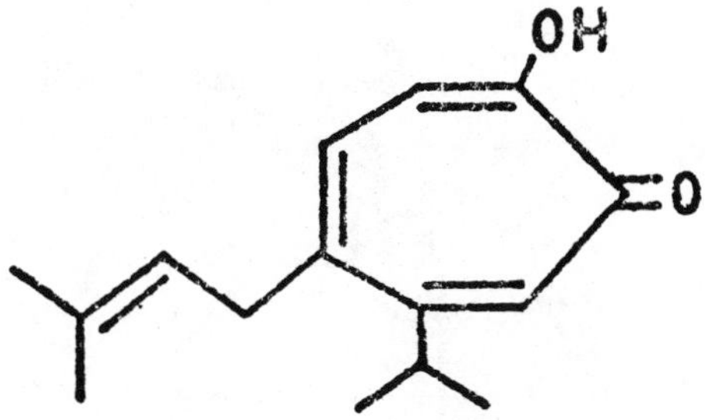

nootkatin *(Cupressus macrocarpa)*

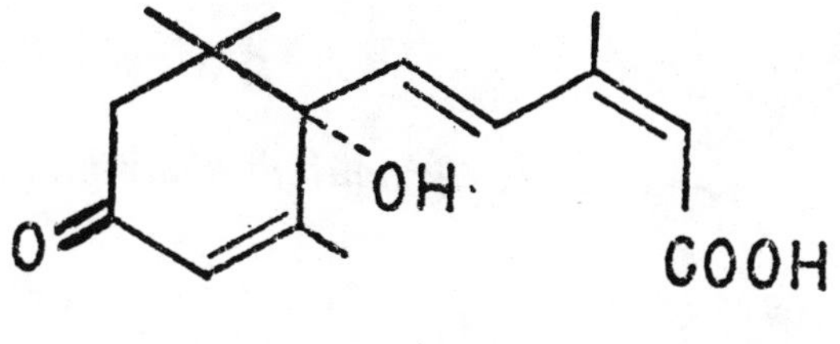

(S)-abscisic acid (widespread)

TABLE 8-7.   BICYCLIC SESQUITERPENOIDS, STRUCTURES AND OCCURRENCE

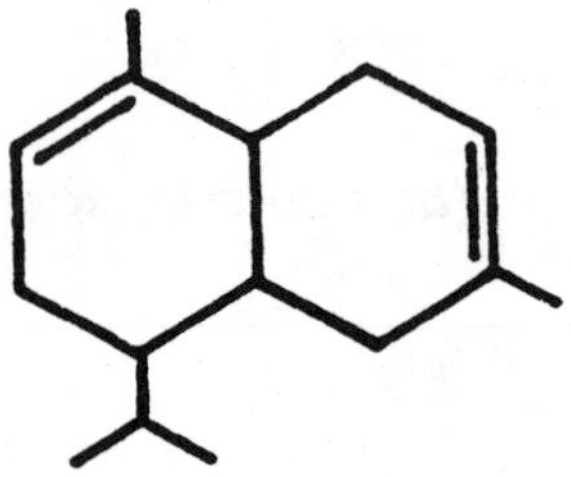

α-cadinene (*Cedrus* spp.)

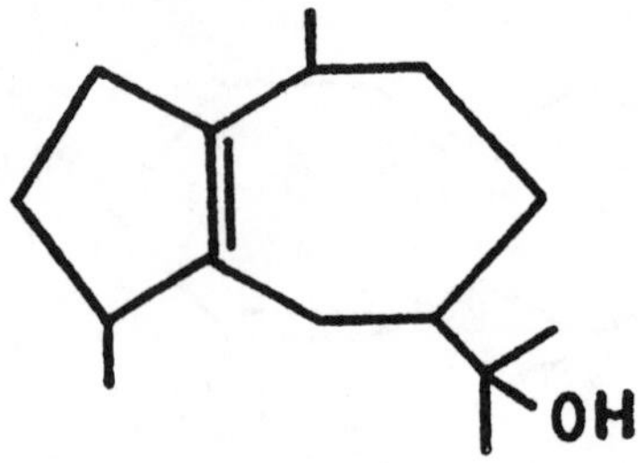

guaiol (*Guaiacum officinale*)

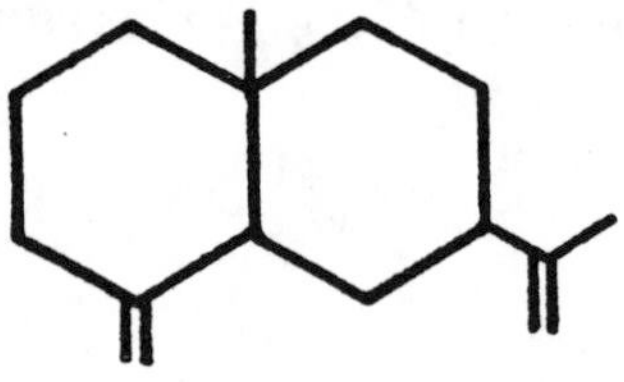

β-selinene (*Apium graveolens*)

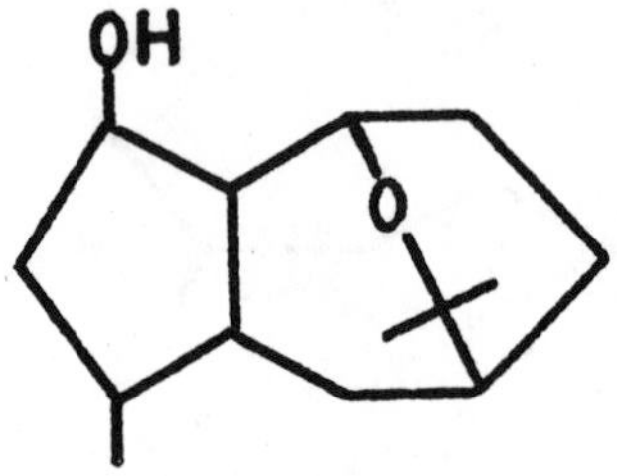

kessyl alcohol (*Valeriana officinalis*)

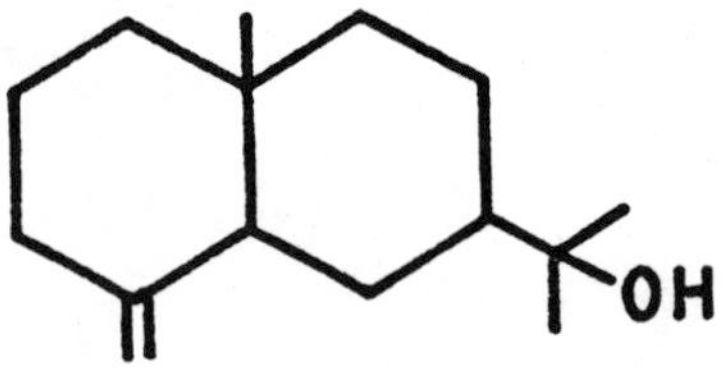

eudesmol (*Eucalyptus piperita*)

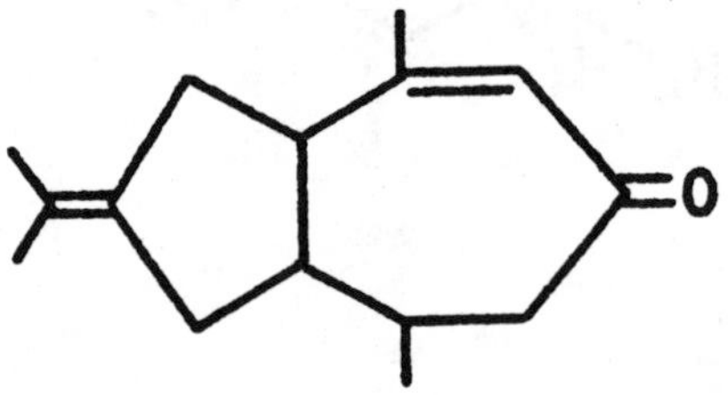

vetivone (*Vetiveria zizanioides*)

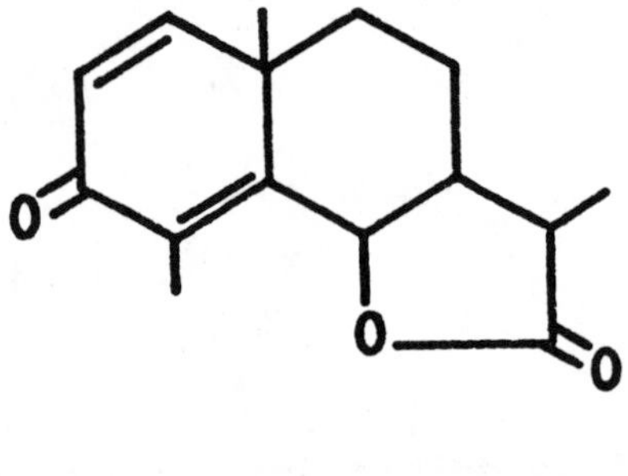

santonin (*Artemisia* spp.)

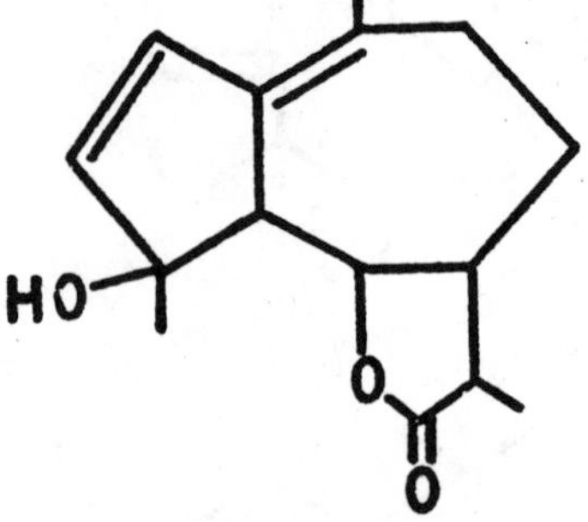

artabsin (*Artemisia absinthium*)

TABLE 8-8.   UNUSUAL SESQUITERPENOID STRUCTURES

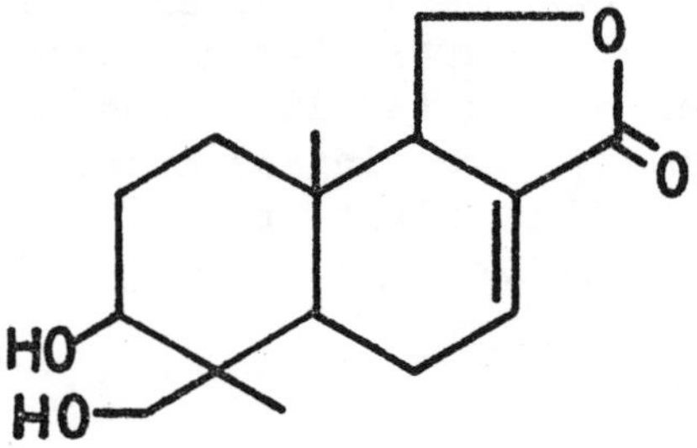

iresin *(Iresine celosiodes)*

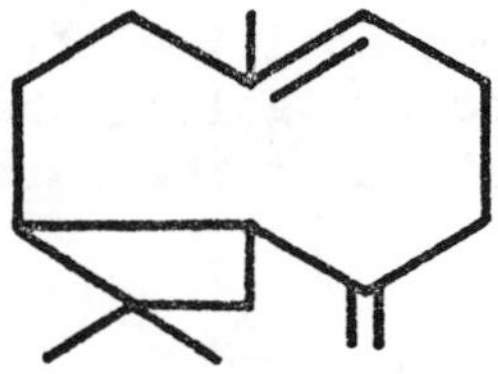

caryophyllene *(Eugenia caryophyllata)*

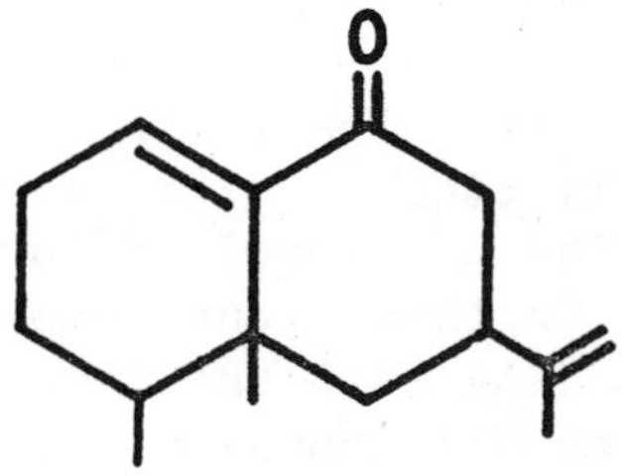

eremophilone *(Eremophilia mitchelli)*

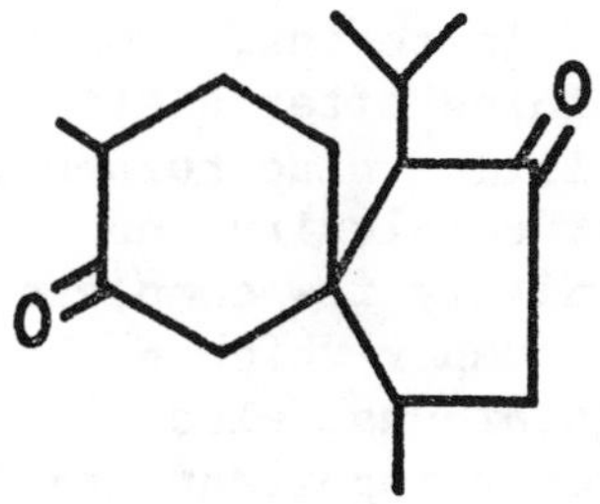

acorone *(Acorus calamus)*

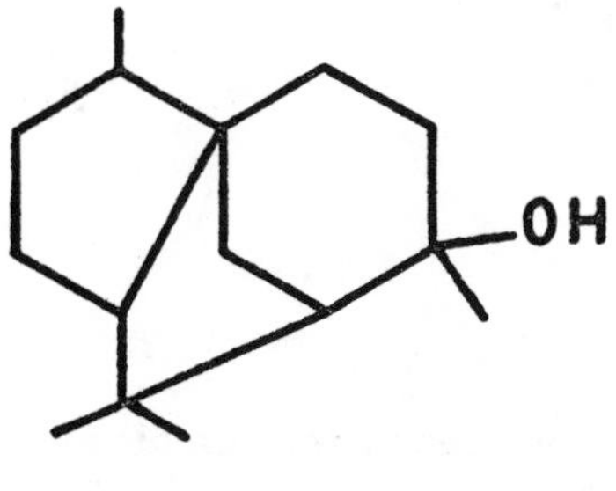

cedrol *(Cedrus* spp.)

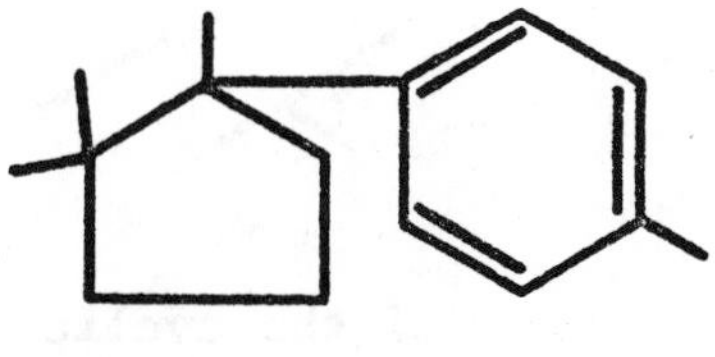

cuparene *(Cupressus* spp.)

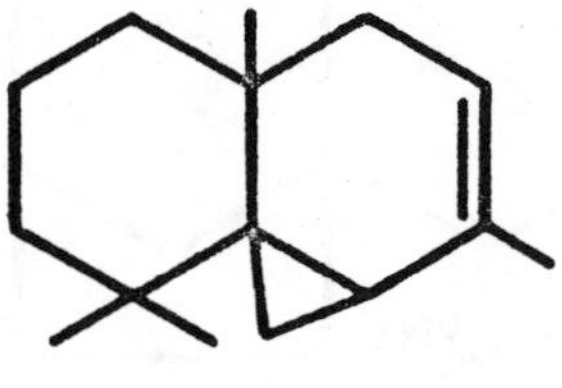

thujopsene *(Thuja* spp.)

and as phototransformation products (17). Structurally related compounds
with similar activity are also known (18, 19). Many other types of sesquiterpenoids are known to inhibit plant growth (20, 21) or to be toxic to
higher and lower animals (22-25). Some human allergens and agents of
contact dermatitis are in this group (26, 27). Among the antifungal phytoalexins there are several sesquiterpenoids -- particularly studied in
sweet and white potatoes and sweet pepper plants (28-30). Some sesquiterpenoids
also have positive effects. Several stimulate rooting of cuttings (31,
32); and strigol is the factor released by host plants that stimulates
germination of the parasitic plant *Striga lutea* (33).

DITERPENOIDS

The diterpenoids are C_{20} compounds which may be formally regarded
(with some exceptions) as derived from four isoprenoid residues. Because
of their high boiling points, they are not usually found in volatile
oils of plants although a few of the lower boiling ones may be. They are
found in resins, gummy exudates, and in the resinous high boiling fractions
remaining after distillation of essential oils. The rosin remaining after
distilling pine turpentine, for instance, is rich in diterpenoids. Their
great complexity and difficulty of separation has resulted in only a
relatively few completely known structures in this group compared to the
vast number which probably occur in nature. As with the lower terpenes,
hydrocarbons, alcohols, ethers and acids are all known in this group.
The only important acyclic member is the alcohol phytol which forms a part
of the chlorophyll molecule.

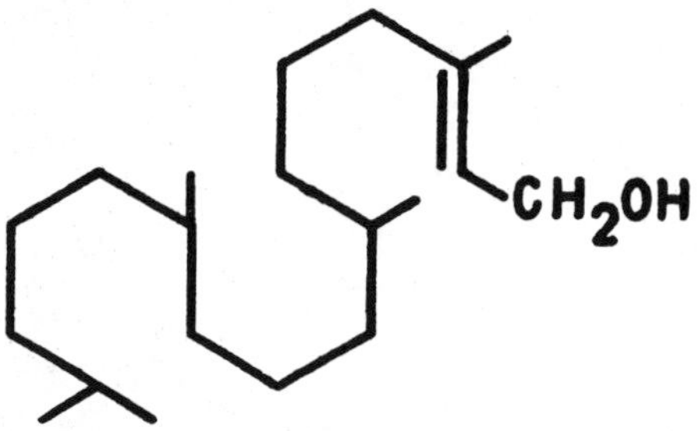

phytol

Many of the cyclic diterpenoids may be regarded as derived from phytol
by ring closures, but others do not show the head-to-tail type of linkage.
Some examples are given in Table 8-9. Diterpenoids have been reviewed by
Hanson (34). The group of diterpenoids includes some compounds of considerable
physiological interest such as the group of plant hormones known as gibberellins. The best-known of these is gibberellin A_3 (gibberellic acid):

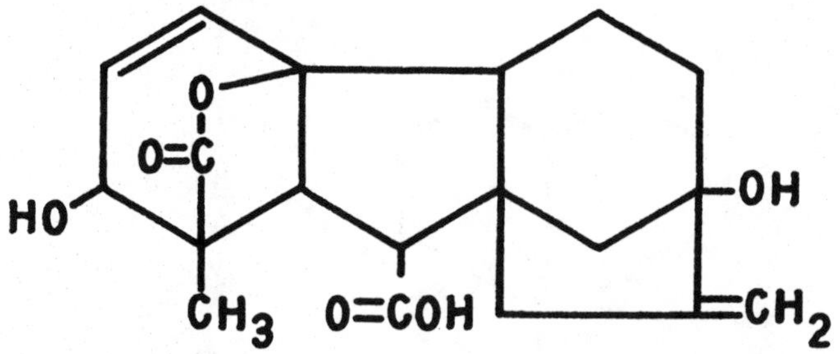

gibberellic acid

TABLE 8-9. CYCLIC DITERPENOIDS, STRUCTURES AND OCCURRENCE

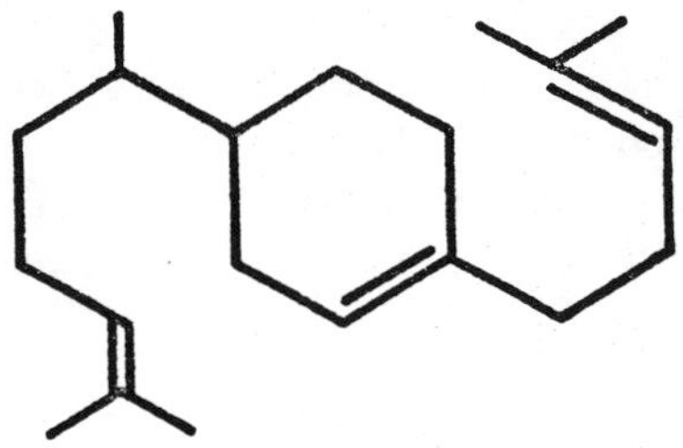

α-camphorene *(Cinnamomum camphora)* 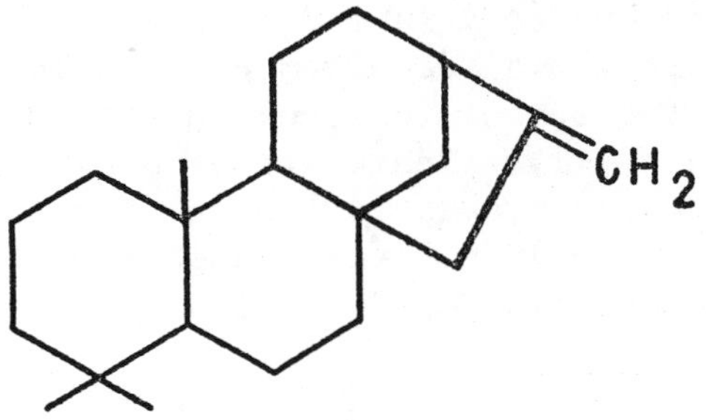   (-)-Kaurene

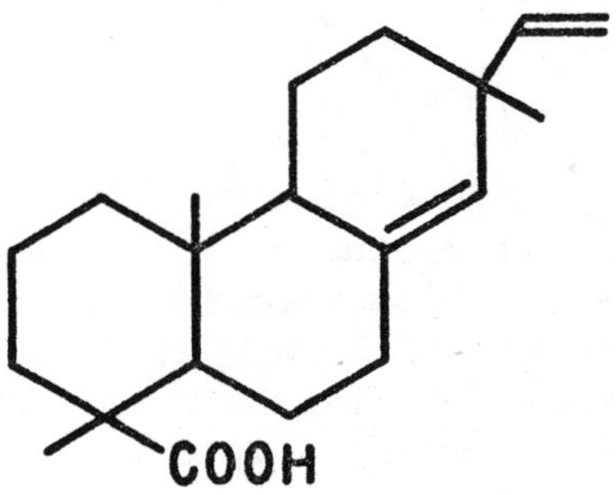

dextro-pimaric acid *(Pinus maritima)* 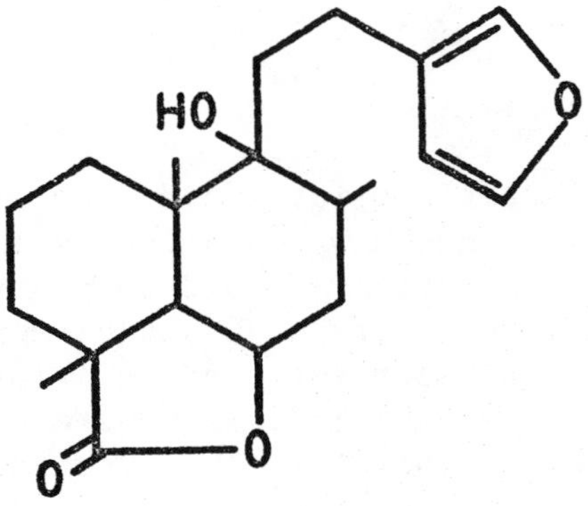   **marrubiin** *(Marrubium vulgare)*

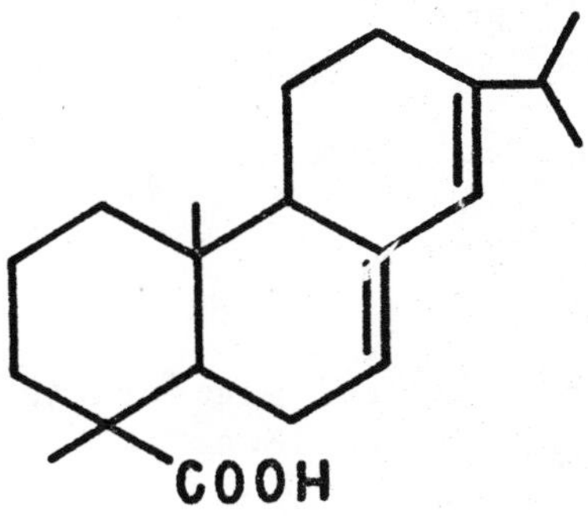

abietic acid *(Pinus palustris)* 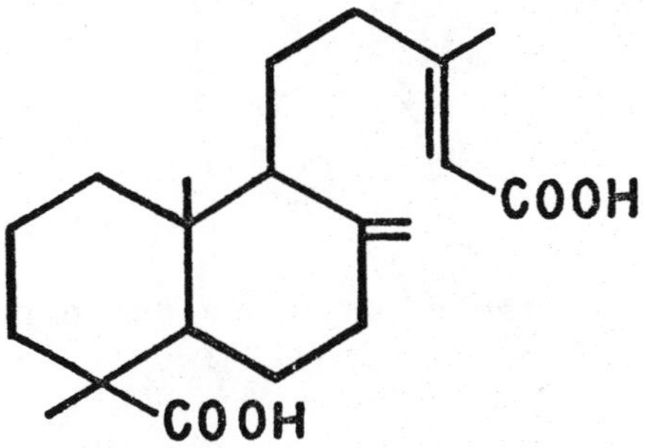   agathic acid *(Agathis alba)*

Over fifty gibberellins are now known, although not all from higher plants
(35, 36).   Several glucosides and esters of gibberellins have also been
isolated (37).   The antheridogens of ferns are based on a structure obviously related to the gibberellins (38).   The insecticide ryanodine of
Ryania speciosa is a diterpenoid (39).   Kaurenoic acid and related compounds
inhibit larval development of several insects (40), and diterpenoids of a
peculiar structure found in the Verbenaceae inhibit feeding of the tobacco
cutworm (41).   There are also natural inhibitors of higher plant growth (42)
and fungal growth (43) among the diterpenoids.   Diterpenoids toxic to higher
animals include the grayanotoxins of Ericaceae (44), atractylate from
Atractylis gummifera (45) and gossypol of cotton (46):

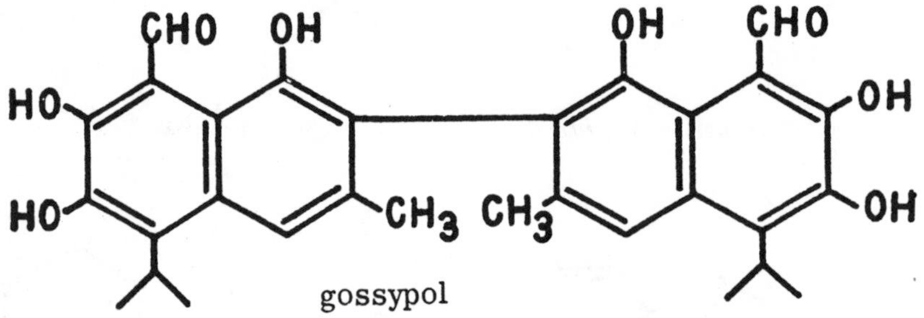

gossypol

The latter two interfere with oxidative phosphorylation (46- 48).   Recently
gossypol has shown promise as a male antifertility drug (49).   Considerable
attention has been paid to a group of complex   diterpenoid esters isolated
from members of the Euphorbiaceae.   These are powerful skin irritants but
also act under various conditions both as tumor promoters and anti-leukemic
substances (50-53).   Many are esters of phorbol, whose structure is given
below, but several other variant structures also occur.

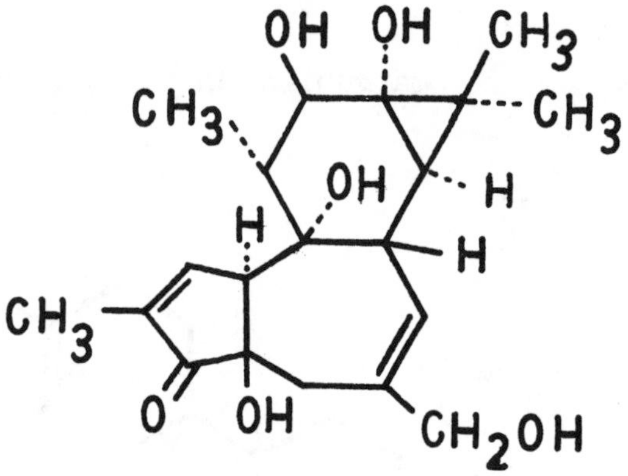

phorbol

A few diterpenoid quinones are responsible for red pigmentation in
certain plants (54).   Two structures of these are as follows:

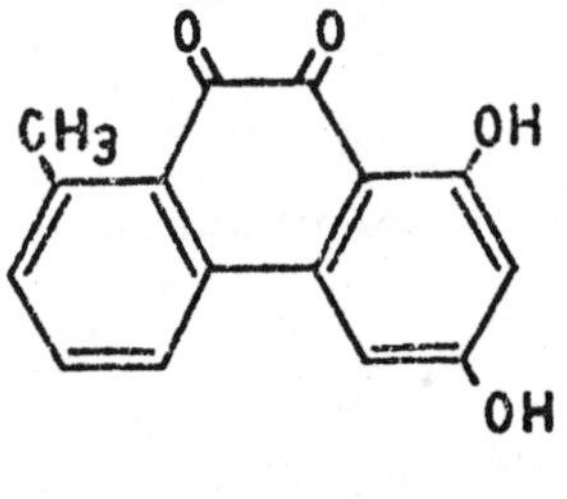

denticulatol (*Rumex chinensis*) 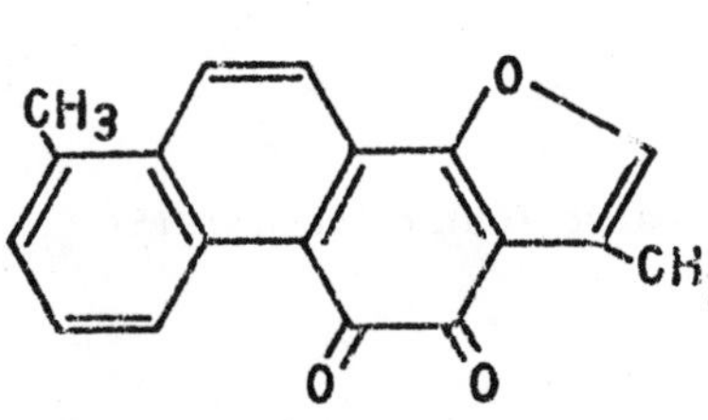   royleanone (*Inula royleana*)

TRITERPENOIDS

Since the C_{25} sesterpenoids are very rare in higher plants (55, 56), there is a great increase in complexity on going from the diterpenoids to the C_{30} triterpenoids. Only a few of them have been highly purified and have had their structures completely determined. Triterpenoids are widely distributed in plant resins, cork, and cutin. The so-called resin acids are triterpenoid acids frequently associated with polysaccharide gums in gum resin. Triterpenoid alcohols occur both free and as glycosides. Many of the glycosides are classed as saponins (q.v.). Triterpenoid hydrocarbons and ketones are also known. There are recent reviews on triterpenoid chemistry and occurrence (57, 58).

The only important acyclic triterpenoid is the hydrocarbon squalene which was first isolated from shark liver oils but is also found in some plant oils (e.g. olive oil). Since it is presumed to be an intermediate in steroid biosynthesis, it must be made at least in small amounts by all organisms which synthesize steroids.

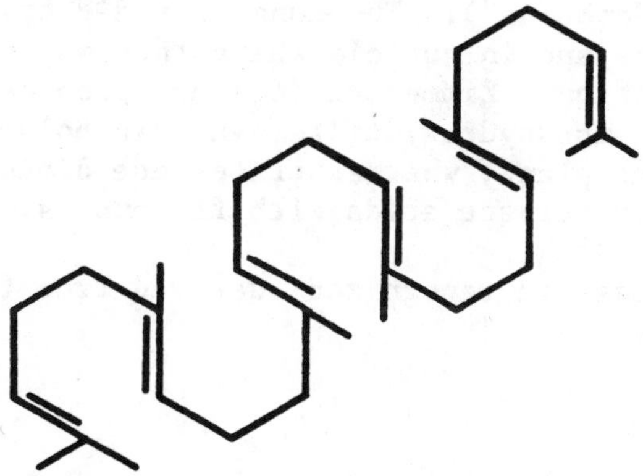

squalene

No triterpenoids so far have been found to have monocyclic or dicyclic structures. Tricyclic ones are rare. Several tetracyclic triterpenoids are known. They are of interest chiefly because of their resemblance and probably biogenetic relationship to the steroids. For a long time some of them were thought to be sterols, and this misconception is reflected in their names. The best known of these compounds is lanosterol which occurs in wool fat, yeast, and some higher plants (e.g. *Euphorbia electa*). It is an intermediate in steroid biosynthesis in animals, but is replaced in plants by cycloartenol (59). Other tetracyclic triterpenoids are the alcohol euphol from *Euphorbia* spp. and the so-called elemi acids of *Canarium commune*:

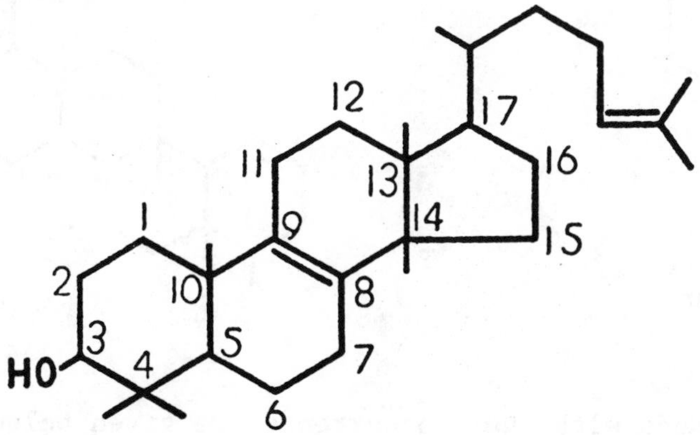

lanosterol

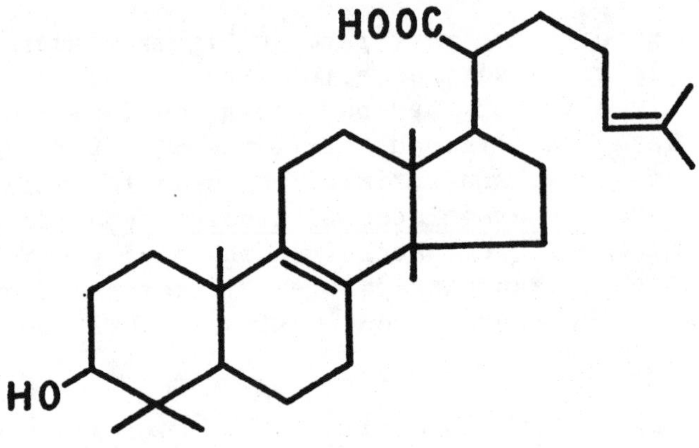

elemadienolic acid

The most important and widely distributed triterpenoids are the pentacyclic compounds. They have been found in plants as primitive as *Sphagnum* (60) but are most common among the seed plants, both free and as glycosides (see also under "Saponins"). The nonglycosidic triterpenoids are frequently found as excretions and in cuticle where they may have a protective or waterproofing function. Zimmerman (61) has proposed the interesting generalization that monohydroxy triterpene alcohols are not accompanied by pigments in the plant, whereas triterpene diols occur along with carotenoids, and triterpene acids with flavonoids.

Four basic ring skeletons are recognized, derived from four hypothetical hydrocarbons.

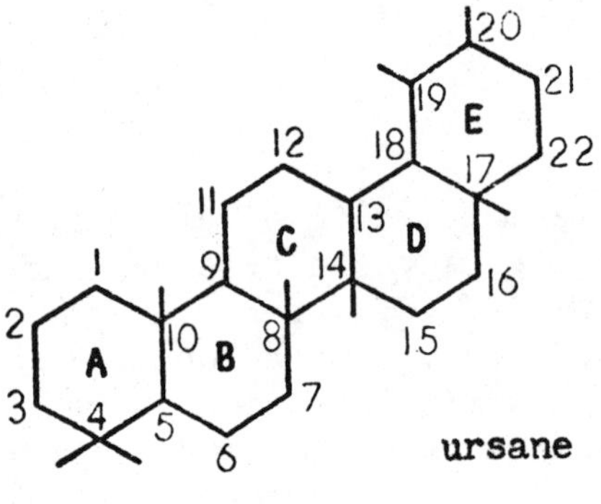

ursane

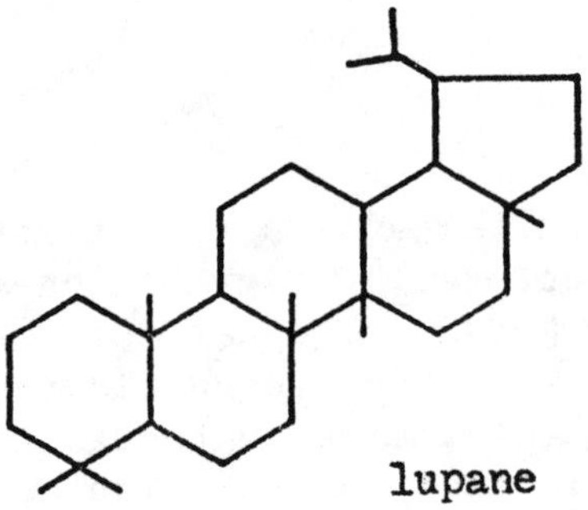

lupane

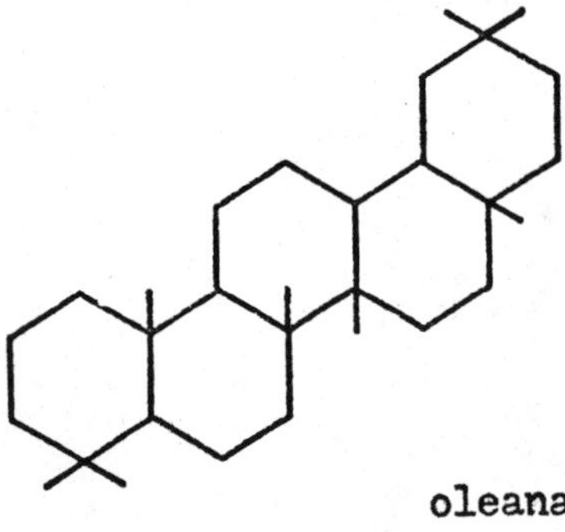

oleanane

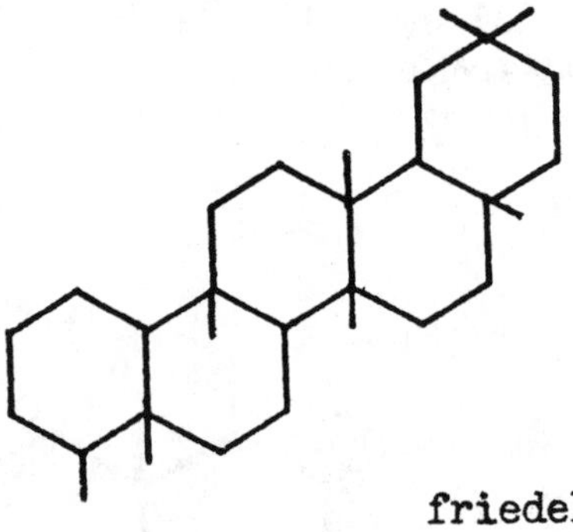

friedelane

Some specific compounds with their occurrence are given below. All known members of this group are oxygenated at C-3 usually as alcohols but some as ketones. They are distinguished from each other by unsaturations, additional hydroxyl groups, and frequently carboxyl groups. Stereochemical differences also play an important role in this group, but their consideration is beyond the scope of this book, and no configurations are indicated in the accompanying formulas. The β-amyrin type structure is most common and occurs in both primitive and advanced plants. Interesting correlations between plant classification and triterpenoid structures are presented by Brieskorn (62). Physiologically some of the most interesting compounds of this group are the gymnenic acids that abolish the ability to taste sweet substances (63). They are various derivatives of Δ12-oleanene.

oleanolic acid (widely distributed, e.g. *Olea europaea*)

β-amyrin (resins, latex and waxes of many plants, e.g. *Canarium commune*)

ursolic acid (in waxy coating of many leaves and fruits, e.g. *Arctostaphylus uvaursi*)

betulin (bark of *Betula alba*)

STEROLS

The fundamental steroid nucleus is the same as that of lanosterol and other tetracyclic triterpenoids, but only two methyl groups are attached to the ring system, at positions 10 and 13. The eight-carbon side chain found in lanosterol is also present in many steroids, especially from animal sources; but most plant steroids have one or two additional carbon atoms. The name "sterol" applies specifically to steroid alcohols; but since practically all plant steroids are alcohols with a hydroxyl group at C-3, they are frequently all called sterols. The steroid numbering system is as follows:

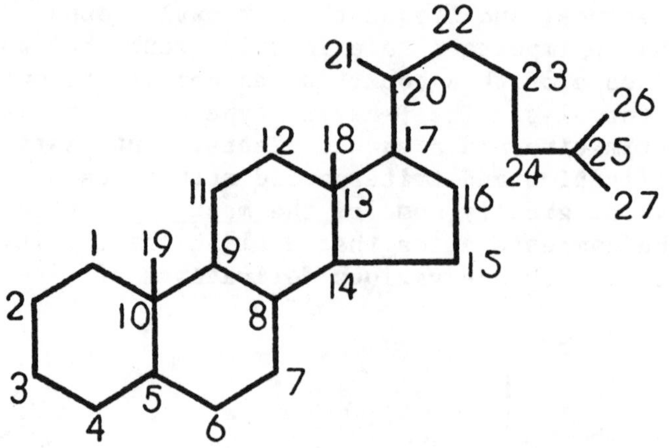

Nomenclature of the steroids is complicated by the necessity of distinguishing between possible stereochemical configurations. In the majority of plant steroids the rings are all joined to one another by *trans* linkages.   The result of this is that the entire ring system is coplanar, and substituent groups extend perpendicularly to the plane of the rings. The methyl group at C-10 is defined as sticking up. Any group *trans* to it is described as α and groups *cis* to it β. Steroids with A/B ring juncture *trans* may therefore be described as 5α, since the hydrogen on C-5 is below the plane. All natural sterols have the C-3 hydroxyl group and the C-17 side chain β. A greater variety of configurations is found in the tetracyclic triterpenoids which closely resemble the steroids in other respects (see above). Other nomenclature rules may be found in the general references.

Classification of sterols is done on the basis of their optical **rotations**. This is not purely arbitrary but reflects important structural differences as summarized in Table 8-10.

TABLE 8-10.

Specific Rotation	Structural Type	Example
greater than -90°	conjugated double bonds in ring B	ergosterol
-70° to -50°	double bonds at 5, 6 and 22, 23	stigmasterol
-45° to -30°	double bond at 5, 6	β-sitosterol
-25° to +10°	double bond at 7, 8 and possibly 22, 23 also	α-spinasterol
+10° to +30°	completely saturated ring system	stigmastanol
+40° to +50°	double bond at 8, 9 and possibly in side chain also	zymosterol
greater than +50°	not a sterol	lanosterol

Sterols of the zymosterol type are known in the fungi but have not been established yet in any higher plants. The stigmasterol type is most characteristic of higher plants, and most higher plant sterols have an

α-24 alkyl group (64). Structures and occurrence of some plant steroids
are shown below. They frequently occur not free but as more complex derivatives (65, 66). The typical "animal" steroid, cholesterol, occurs in
chloroplasts and mitochondria of plants; but it has frequently been overlooked because it is present as esters and glycosides that are not soluble
in the same solvents normally used for free sterols (67, 68). Various
other animal steroids such as cholanic acid (69) and 1, 25-dihydroxyvitamin
D_3 (70, 71) have also been found in plants as well as the insect hormones
ecdysone and ecdysterone (72, 73). The question of whether typical animal
sex hormones occur in plants is still controversial. The presence of estrone
in plants has been reported several times (74) and also strongly denied (75).
The effects of exogenous animal hormones on plants are also controversial
(76-78). Some of these substances, if they do occur in plants, might have
a protective role; but the only good cases for such a function are provided
by two groups of peculiar steroids, the nicandrenones of *Nicandra physaloides*
(79) and the cucurbitacins of Cucurbitaceae (80). A thorough survey of
plant sterol biochemistry is given in (81); and the role of sterols in
plants is reviewed in (82) and (83).

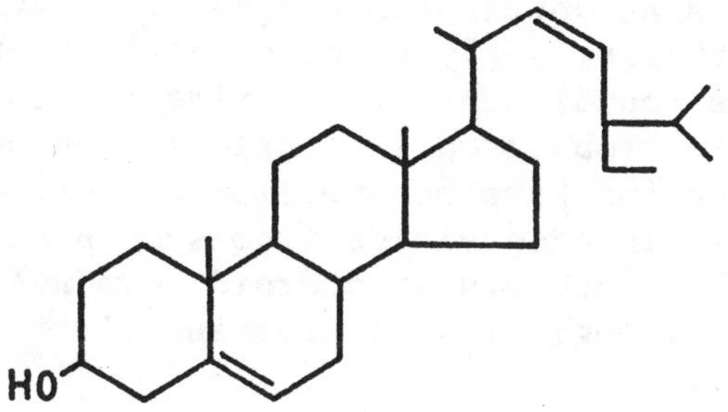

stigmasterol *(Glycine max)*

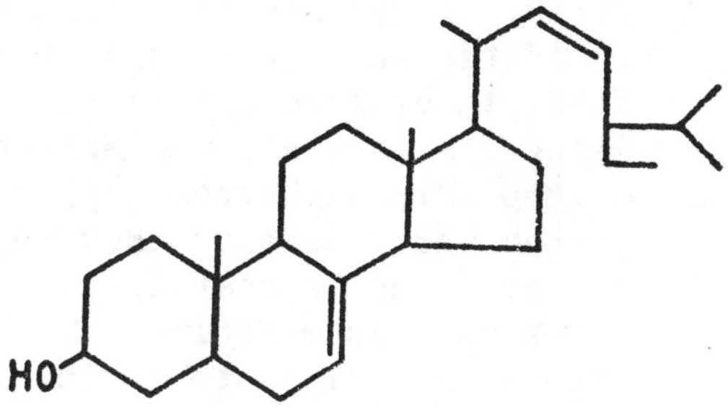

spinasterol *(Spinacia oleracea)*

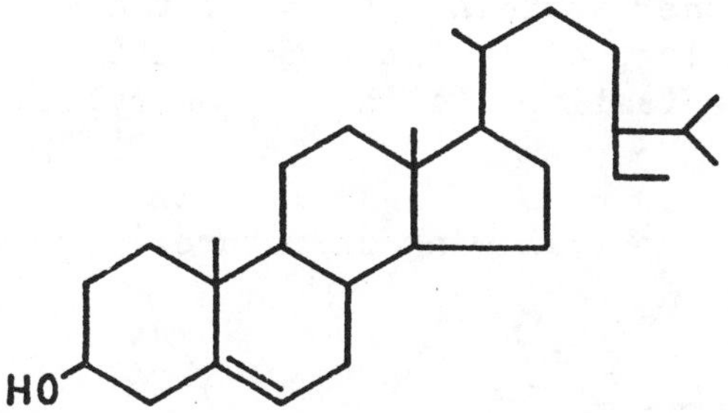

β-sitosterol *(Pinus* spp.)

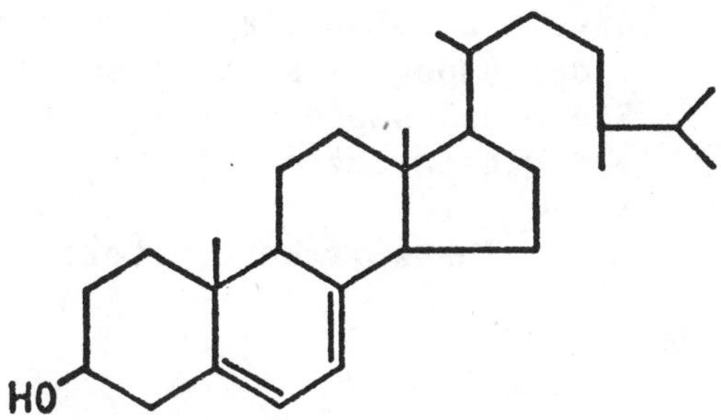

ergosterol *(Triticum sativum)*

STEROLINS AND SAPONINS

As has been mentioned previously, many terpenoid and steroid alcohols
exist in nature not as free alcohols but as glycosides. Names have been
assigned to certain types of these glycosides: "sterolins", "saponins",
"cardiac glycosides", etc. The cardiac glycosides and glycosyl alkaloids
will be considered in later sections.

Sterolins or sterol glycosides are widespread in unrelated plant species. They are found along with free sterols in the unsaponifiable lipid fraction but may be distinguished from free sterols by their much higher melting points and low solubility in such fat solvents as ethyl ether. They are distinguished from saponins (see below) by their insolubility in water and lack of toxicity to animals. The first sterolin to be discovered was ipuranol of *Ipomoea purpurea*. It is a β-sitosterol glycoside. Similar glycosides of the higher plant sterols are also known; but as β-sitosterol is the most widely distributed plant sterol, so its glycosides are the commonest sterolins. The ginsenosides of ginseng root are an interesting group both structurally and because of their physiological activity. They are steroidal glycosides with oxygen substitution at positions 3, 12, and 20 (84, 85).

The saponins were originally named because of their soap-like characteristics. They are powerful surface active agents which cause foaming when shaken with water and in low concentration often produce hemolysis of red blood cells. In very dilute solution they are quite toxic to fish, and plants containing them have been used as fish poisons for hundreds of years. They have also been implicated as a contributing cause of bloat in cattle on some forage crops. Glycyrrhizin, a glycoside of glycyrrhetic acid, is of interest as the chief active constituent of licorice root. Among its many claimed effects the best-corroborated is a stimulating action on the adrenal cortex (86). Certain saponins have become important in recent years because they may be obtained in good yields from some plants and are used as starting material for the synthesis of steroid hormones to be used in medicine. The chemistry, biological activity, and distribution of saponins are reviewed in (87-90).

Two types of saponins are recognized--glycosides of triterpenoid alcohols, and glycosides of a particular steroid structure described as having a spiroketal side chain. Both types are soluble in water and ethanol but insoluble in ether. Their aglycones, called sapogenins, are prepared by acid or enzymatic hydrolysis, and without the sugar residues have the solubility characteristics of other sterols. A few of the steroidal sapogenins are distinguished by having a *cis* A/B ring juncture. Steroidal saponins are most common in the families Liliaceae, Amaryllidaceae and Dioscoraceae.

The spiroketal steroid nucleus has the following structure:

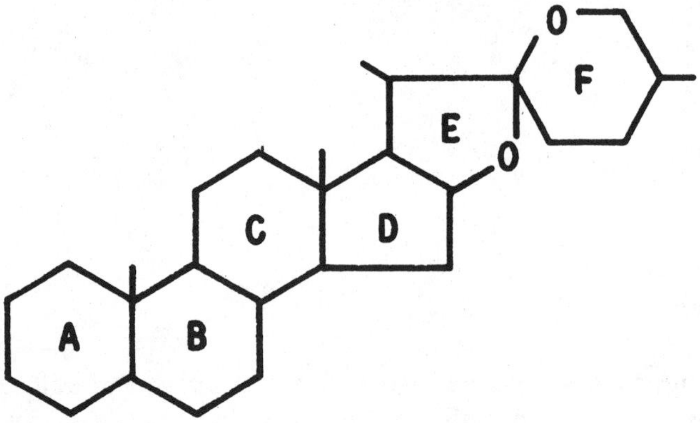

Rings E and F contain the same basic carbon skeleton as common animal steroids but lack the extra carbon atoms found in most plant sterols. It is possible that at least in some instances the spiroketal structure is an artifact formed by ring closure of an open chain precursor.

The triterpenoid saponins may have as their aglycones such compounds as oleanolic acid which also occur uncombined with sugars. In some cases though, the aglycones are known only as sapogenins. Oleanane-type sapogenins are much more common than either ursane or lupane types.

Some sapogenin structures are given in Table 8-11. Glycosylation is generally at C-3. Several different monosaccharides are usually present, as an oligosaccharide. Uronic acids may also be present. For example, digitonin is derived from digitogenin plus an oligosaccharide composed of 1 xylose, 2 glucose, and 2 galactose units. Several different saponins may all have the same sapogenin but different sugars.

CARDIAC GLYCOSIDES

The cardiac glycosides, cardenolides, or heart poisons bear a structural resemblance to the steroid saponins and have the same solubility and foaming characteristics. They are distinguished from other steroid glycosides by an unsaturated lactone ring attached at C-17, a *cis*-juncture of rings C and D, a 14β hydroxy group, and by the peculiar sugars composing them.

The usual basic nucleus is as follows:

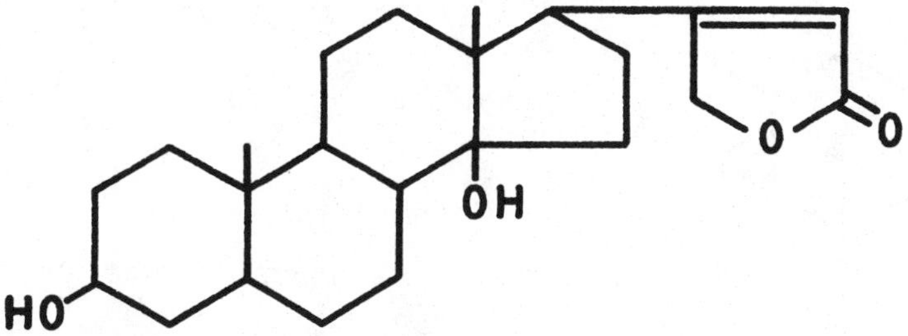

Other substituent groups may be present, for example additional hydroxy groups at C-1, 11, 12, 16, and 19. The sugars are always linked at C-3. Some members have an aldehyde group rather than a methyl group at C-19, and many have a *cis* A/B ring fusion. The so-called scilladienolides of squill and hellebore have a six-membered lactone ring:

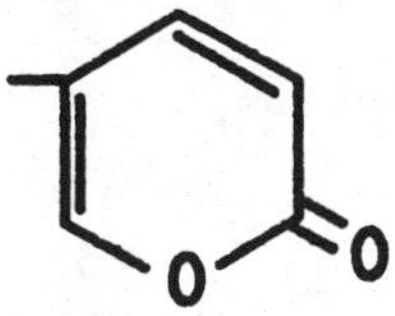

The cardiac glycosides are found in several quite unrelated plant families such as Apocynaceae, Liliaceae, Moraceae, and Ranunculaceae (91).

TABLE 8-11.   SOME SAPOGENINS, STRUCTURES AND OCCURRENCE

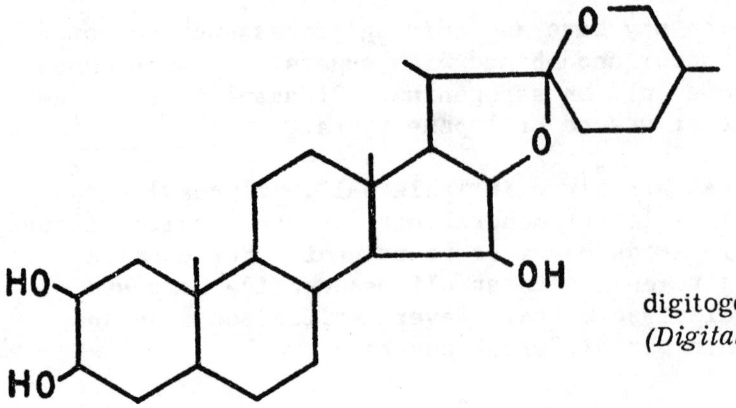

digitogenin
(Digitalis purpurea)

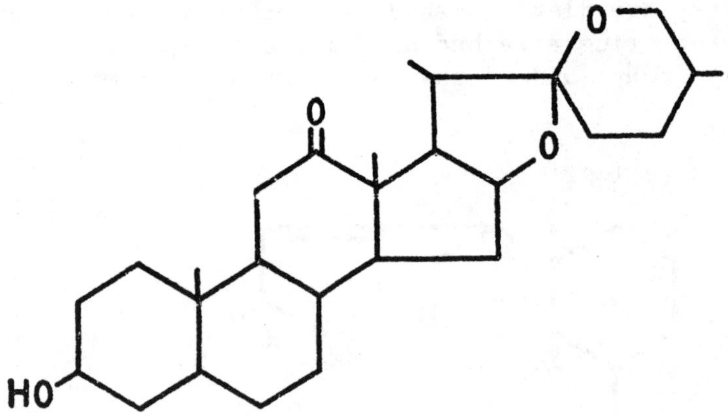

hecogenin (*Agave* spp.)

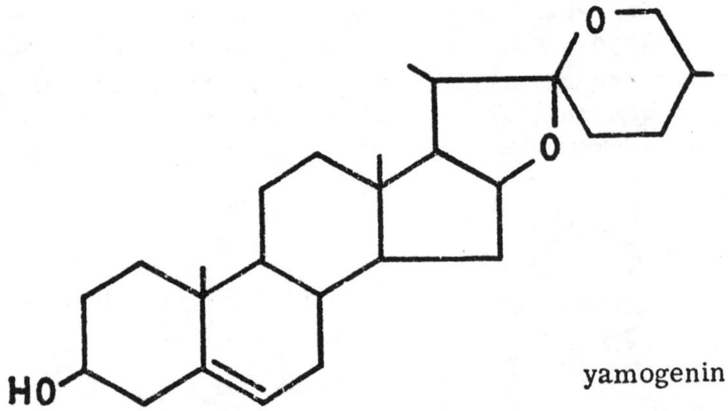

yamogenin *(Dioscorea* spp.)

Table 8-11. Continued

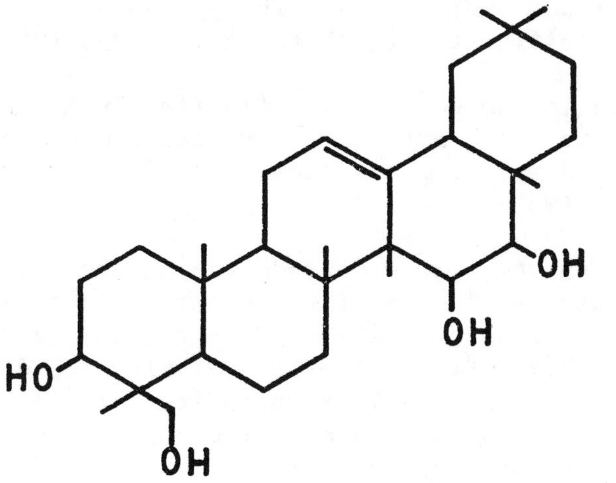

soyasapogenol A (*Soja* spp.)

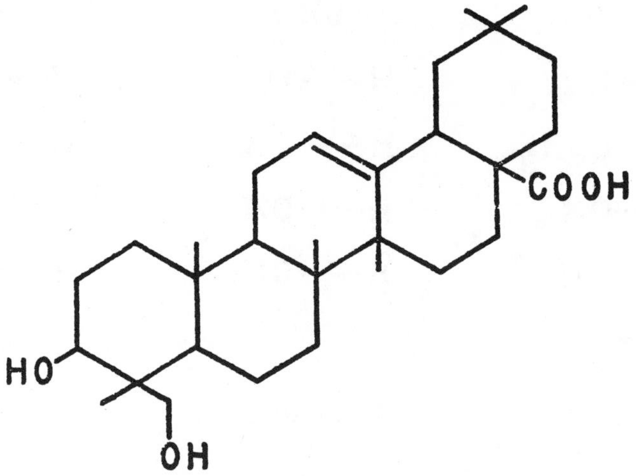

hederagenin *(Hedera helix)*

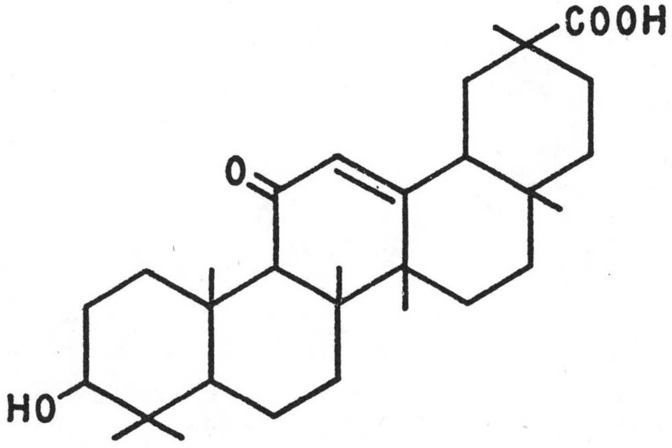

glycyrrhetic acid
(Glycyrrhiza glabra)

Plants containing them have been used since prehistoric times as arrow
and ordeal poisons. The glycosides have a specific cardiotonic effect and
their molecular site of action is a membrane-bound ATPase that regulates
cation transport (92, 93). Possibly by the same kind of mechanism they
also inhibit leaf movements in *Mimosa pudica* (94). The aglycones are also
toxic but do not duplicate the specific effects of the glycosides (95).

The chief commercial source is the genus *Digitalis* (family Scrophul-
ariaceae). Several species of this genus are used, and active material
is extracted from seeds, leaves and roots. This same genus is the source
of the steroid saponin, digitonin (96).

By the usual methods of preparation some degradation occurs, both by
enzymatic and non-enzymatic hydrolysis of some of the sugar residues and
ester groups which may be present. Thus what were originally believed to
be the three active glycosides of *Digitalis* (digitoxin, gitoxin, and digoxin)
are known to be derived from the actual natural products (the digilanides,
A, B, and C) by loss of a glucose residue and an acetyl group. The same
aglycone or genin may be present in different plants but joined with different sugars. Structures of some of the rare sugar components are given
below:

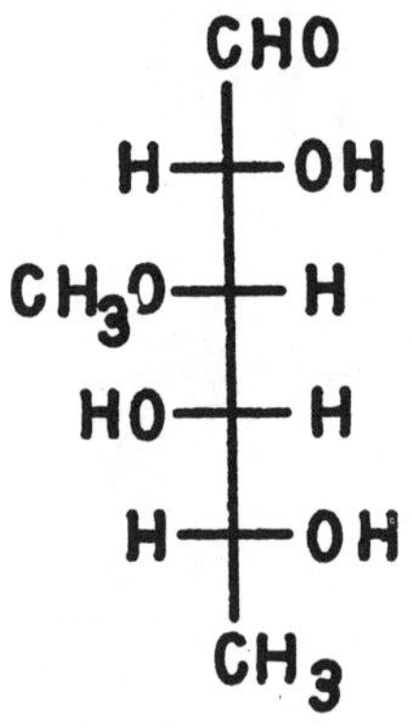

D-digitalose 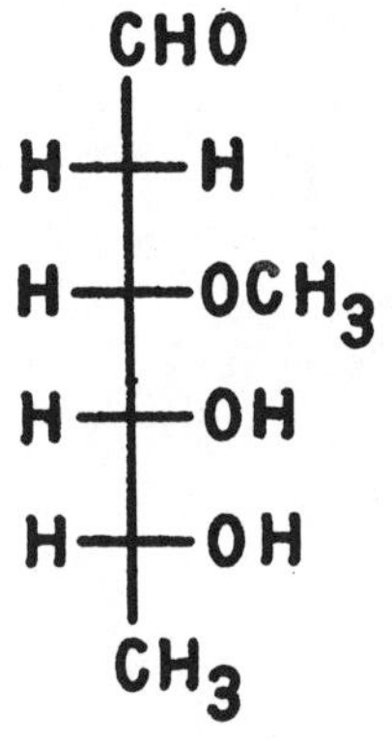   D-cymarose 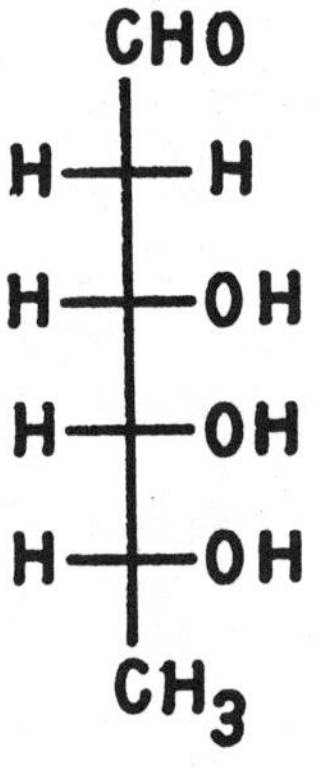   D-digitoxose 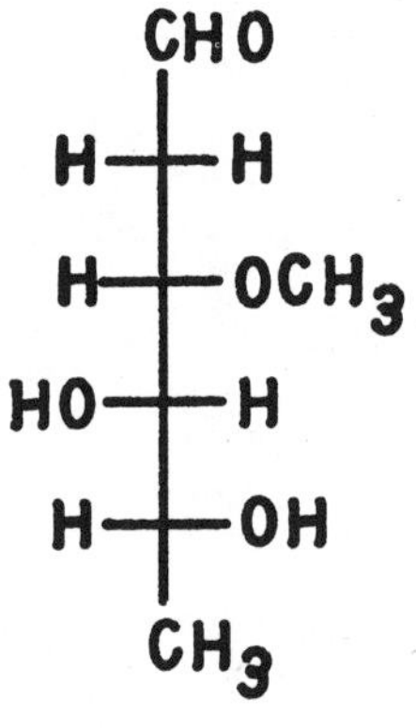   D-sarmentose

The heart poisons of *Calotropis procera* cannot truly be called glycosides
since instead of a sugar residue they have methylreductic acid. This
compound is, however, closely related to the sugars:

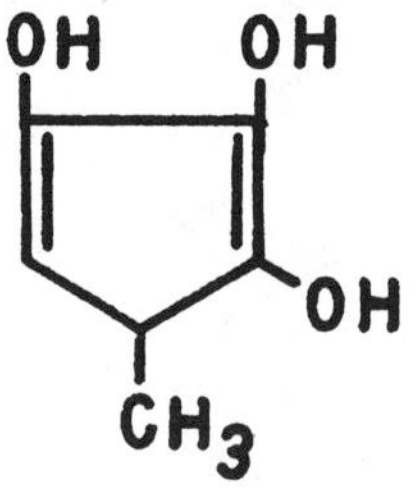

Examples of some cardiac glycosides with their occurrence are given below.
The name of the aglycone follows the name of the glycoside.

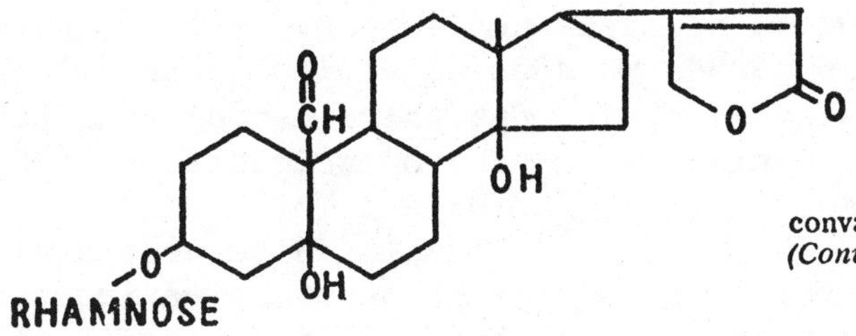

convallatoxin, strophanthidin
(Convallaria majalis)

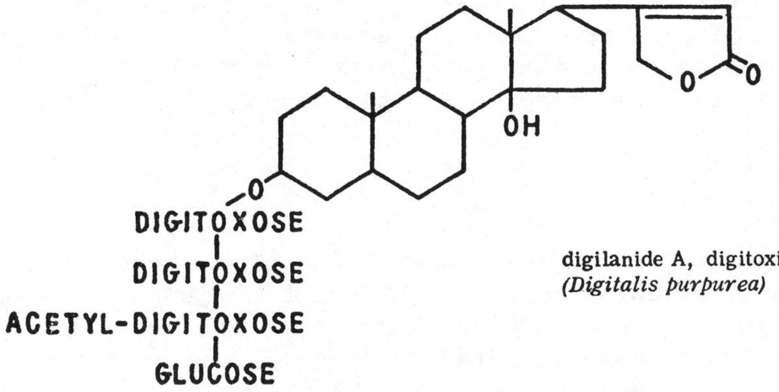

RHAMNOSE

digilanide A, digitoxigenin
(Digitalis purpurea)

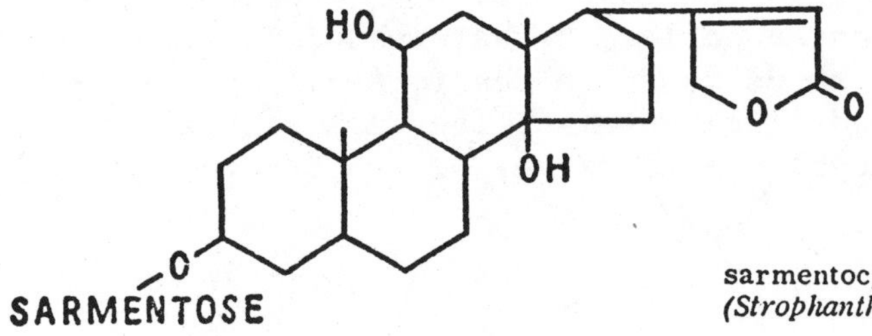

DIGITOXOSE
DIGITOXOSE
ACETYL-DIGITOXOSE
GLUCOSE

sarmentocymarin, sarmentogenin
(Strophanthus spp.)

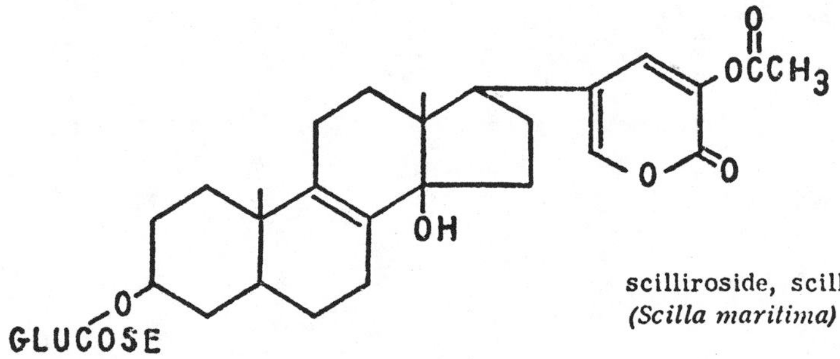

SARMENTOSE

scilliroside, scillirosidin
(Scilla maritima)

GLUCOSE

A seemingly related group of steroid glycosides are the digitanolides which are also found in *Digitalis*. They contain the same kinds of 2, 6-deoxy-hexoses as the cardiac glycosides but the steroid moiety is C_{21} and has no lactone ring. The digitanolides are physiologically inactive. All of the above compounds are reviewed thoroughly in (97).

ALKALOIDS

Nitrogen-containing compounds are included in many of the groups discussed in this chapter. Such compounds possess alkaloidal properties and
are normally classed with the alkaloids although their carbon skeletons
clearly mark them as isoprenoid derivatives. The most important members
of this group are the aconite and steroid alkaloids. The former are reviewed
in (98). the latter are in (99, 100). Several complex diterpenoid alkaloids
with structures similar to aconitine and veatchine occur in various species of
Aconitum, Delphinium, and *Garrya.* The steroid and modified steroid alkaloids
normally occur as C-3 glycosides or esters. A close resemblance of such
structures to the saponins is apparent; in fact solanine has saponin-like
properties and is sometimes described as a nitrogen-containing saponin.
Some examples of terpenoid and steroid alkaloids are shown in Table 8-12.

TETRATERPENOIDS

The most familiar tetraterpenoids are the carotenoids--yellow to red,
fat soluble pigments occurring throughout the plant kingdom and in many
different types of tissues. Over 400 of them are known. Hydrocarbon pigments are called carotenes and oxygenated derivatives are xanthophylls.
Colorless tetraterpenoids are also known (e.g. phytoene, phytofluene) but
have been studied much less than the carotenoids. Structurally the only
difference between colored and colorless tetraterpenoids is the larger
number of conjugated double bonds found in the former. The tetraterpenoids
never contain large condensed ring systems. They are either acyclic,
monocyclic, or bicyclic. Acyclic members may be depicted by the following
skeleton:

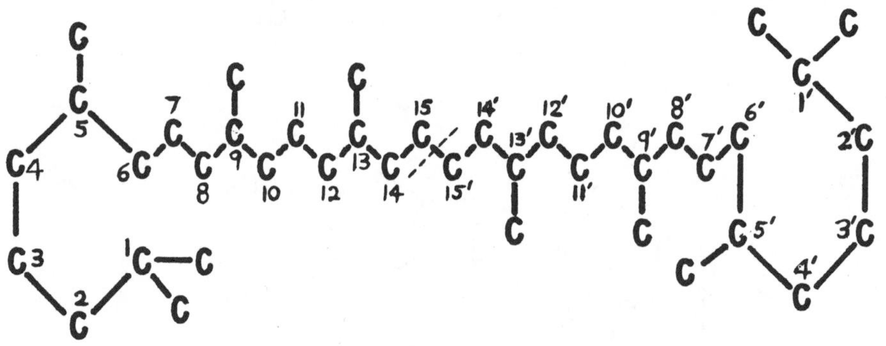

It will be noted that the molecule is symmetrical on each side of the
dotted line and may be viewed as formed by joining two diterpene radicals
of the phytyl type. Variations are introduced by double bonds and functional groups such as hydroxyl and carboxyl. As double bonds are added,
opportunities for *cis-trans* isomerism are introduced; and many of the
problems in carotenoid chemistry arise from difficulty in distinguishing
and separating geometrical isomers of this type. Most native carotenoids
are all *trans*, and an all *trans* configuration is implied unless in the
name of the compound any *cis* double bonds are cited.

TABLE 8-12.   SOME TERPENOID AND STEROID ALKALOIDS

Monoterpenoid:

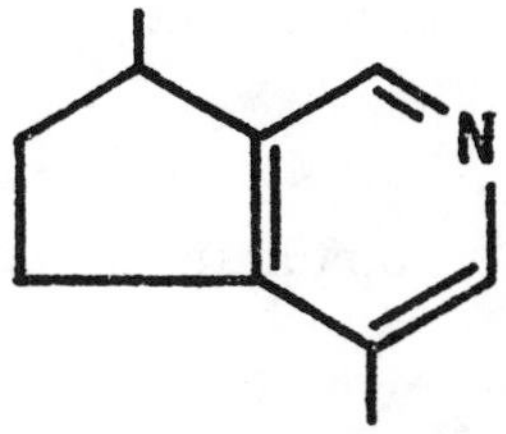

actinidine *(Actinidia polygama)*

Sesquiterpenoid:

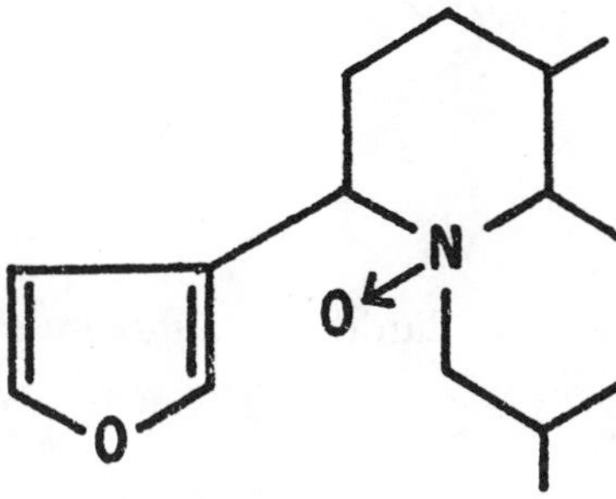

nupharidine *(Nuphar japonicum)*

Diterpenoid:

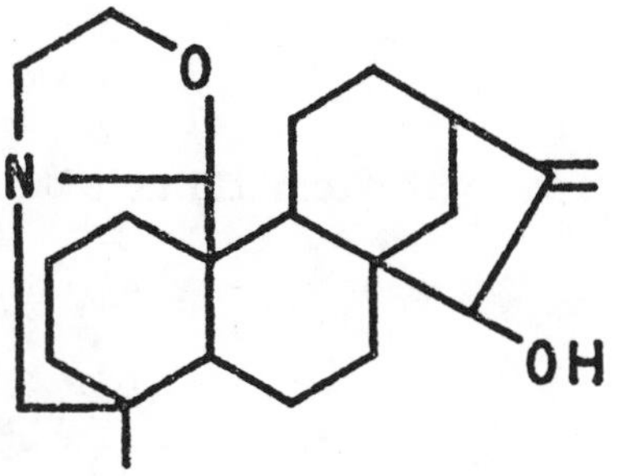

veatchine *(Garrya veatchii)*

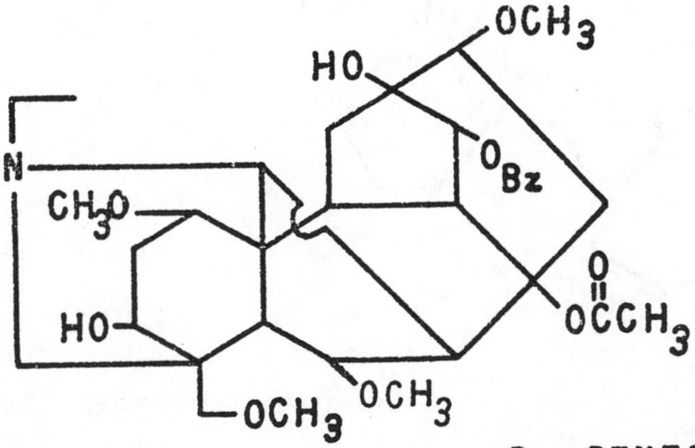

aconitine *(Aconitum spp.)*

Bz = BENZOYL

TABLE 8-12. Continued.

Steroid:

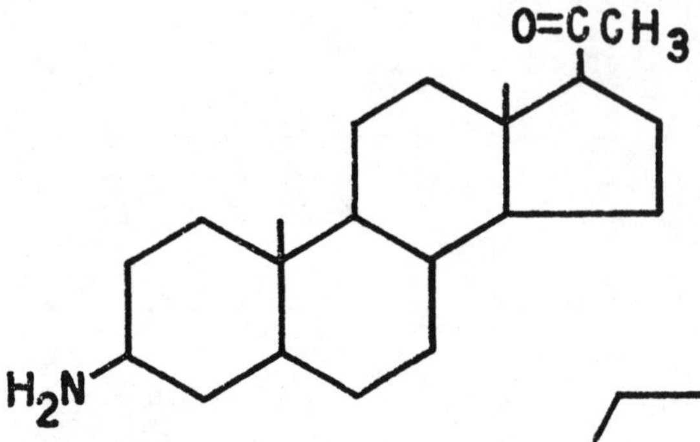

funtumine *(Funtumia latifolia)*

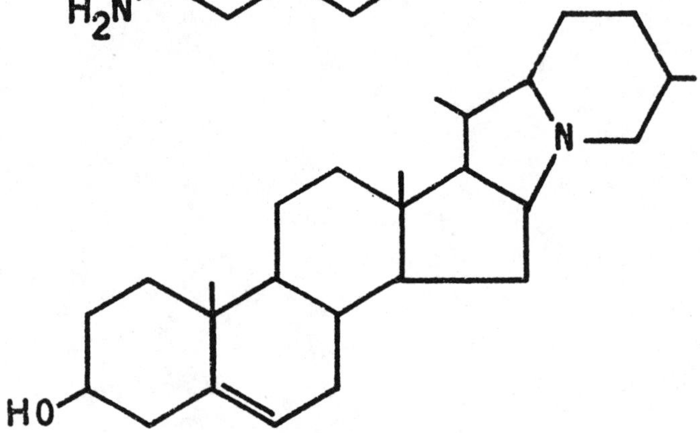

solanidine *(Solanum* spp. *)*

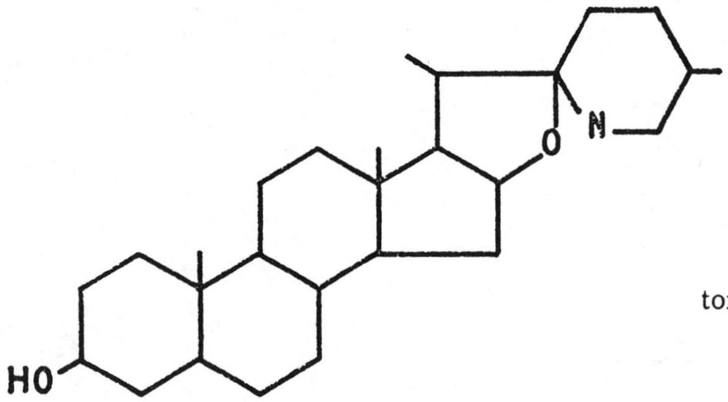

tomatidine *(Solanum* spp. *)*

Modified steroid:

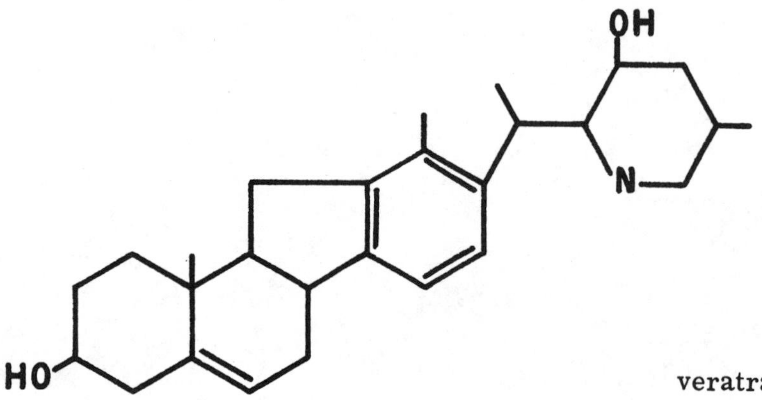

veratramine *(Veratrum* spp. *)*

Cyclization at one or both ends of the carbon chain gives rise to the other two fundamental types of carotenoids--i.e.:

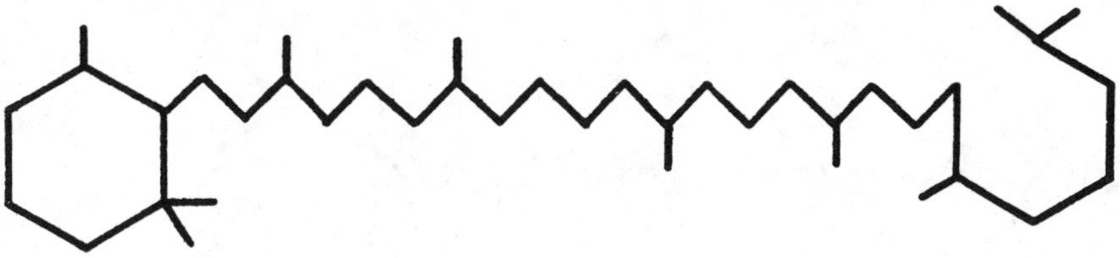

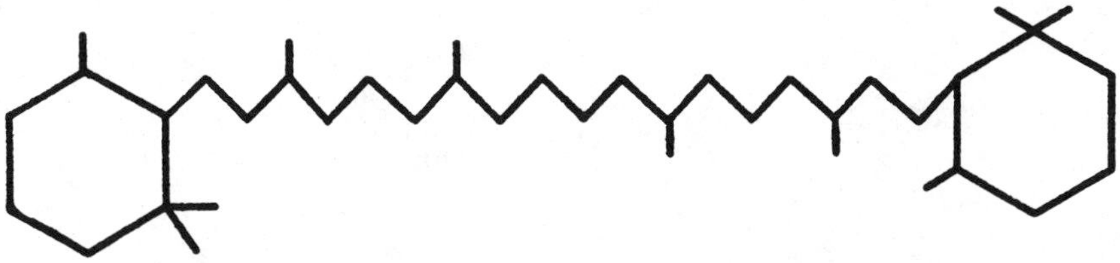

If only one -ionone type ring is present, it is written to the left. Some other compounds (e.g. bixin, crocetin) are known which have fewer than 40 carbon atoms but are classed with the carotenoids because peculiarities in their structure suggest that they have been derived from degradation of carotenoids rather than built up from smaller units. The apo-carotenoids are C_{27} and C_{30} compounds, probably derived from degradation of xanthophylls (101, 102).

No general function can be assigned to the carotenoids. There is some indication that they function as light receptors for phototropism. As flower pigments they may play a role in attracting insects, but most attention has been given to their possible function as leaf chloroplast pigments. To some extent light absorbed by carotenoids can be transferred to chlorophyll or ferredoxin (103) and used in photosynthesis. There is also evidence that the carotenoids protect chlorophyll against photodestruction by short wavelength light--i.e. at a wavelength of about 400 nm where both carotenoids and chlorophylls have strong absorption maxima. Albino plants lack both carotenoids and chlorophyll under normal conditions of growth, but in dim light they are able to accumulate chlorophyll. In normal light the chlorophyll is rapidly destroyed since carotenoids are not present to protect it (104, 105).

The most widespread carotenoid is β-carotene, which may make up as much as 0.1% of dried green leaves. Lutein is the most important leaf xanthophyll and may occur in green leaves at a greater concentration than β-carotene. Most carotenoids have the same central carbon chain as β-carotene and differ only in the portions corresponding to the two rings. Therefore in the formulas of Table 8-13, the complete structure is given only for β-carotene and the straight chain represented by a dotted line unless it differs from that of β-carotene. All-*trans* structures are shown for phytoene and phytofluene although it is likely that the 15-*cis* structures are more important for these two compounds.

BITTER PRINCIPLES

The various bitter substances distributed through the plant kingdom constitute no chemically homogeneous group. It is commonly believed that

TABLE 8-13.   SOME CAROTENOIDS, STRUCTURES AND OCCURRENCE

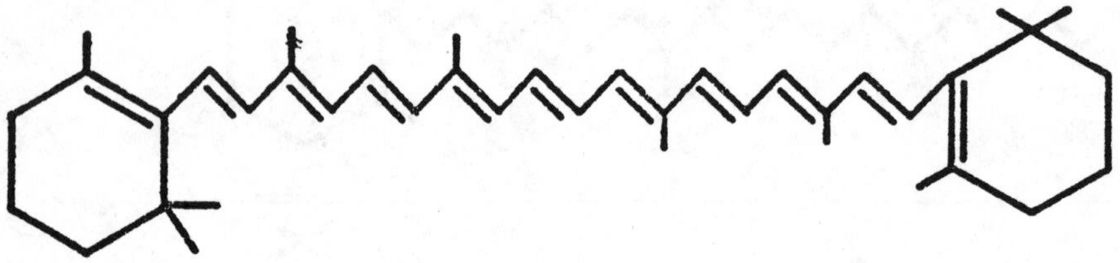

β-carotene

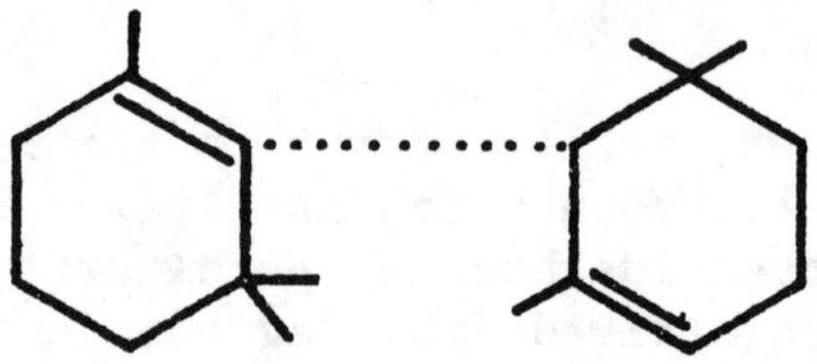

α-carotene (leaf pigment)

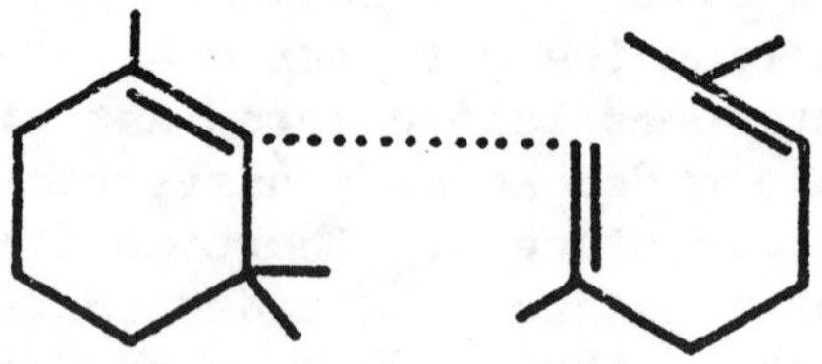

γ-carotene (flower and fruit pigment)

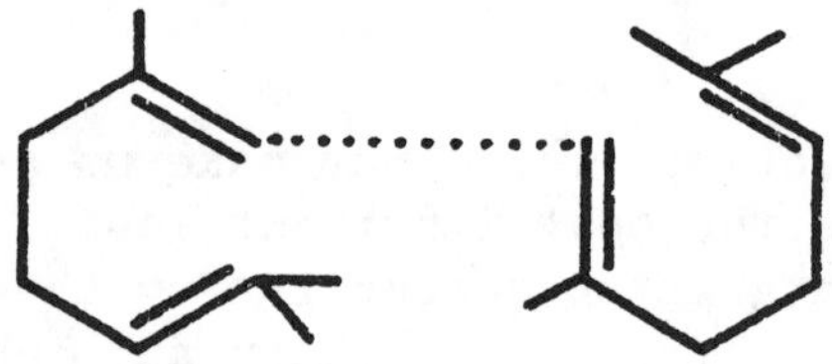

lycopene (fruit pigment)

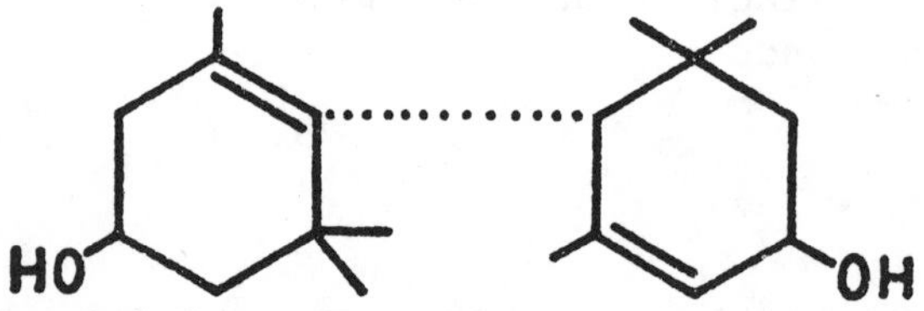

lutein (leaf pigment)

Table 8-13.   Continued

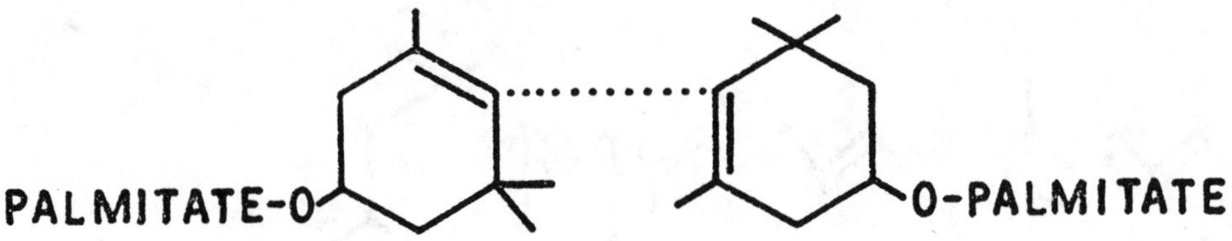

physalien, zeaxanthin palmitate (fruits)

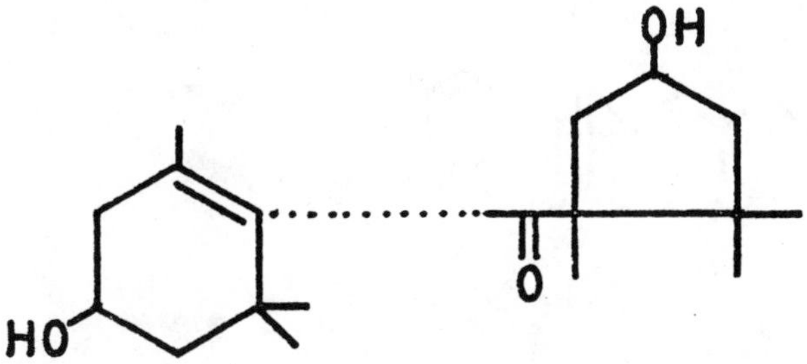

capsanthin *(Capsicum annuum)*

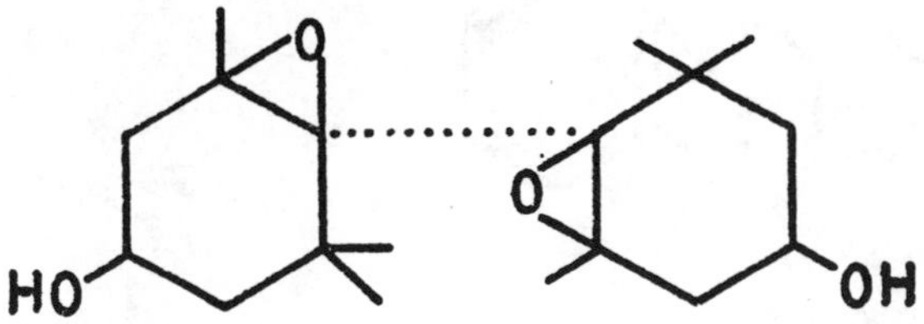

violaxanthin (flowers, fruits, and leaf)

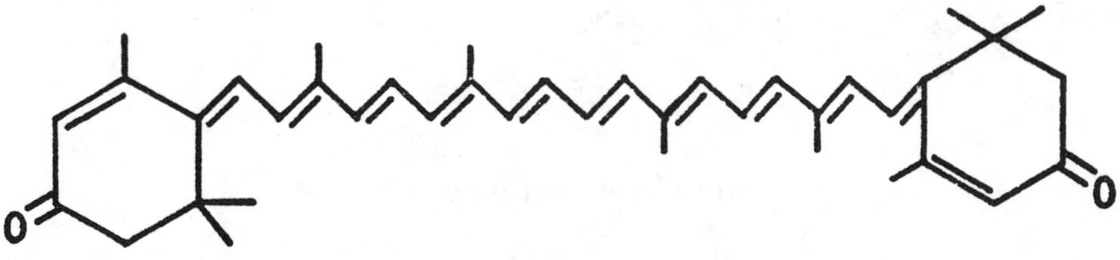

rhodoxanthin (many Gymnosperms, horsetails,
club mosses)

Table 8-13.   *Continued*

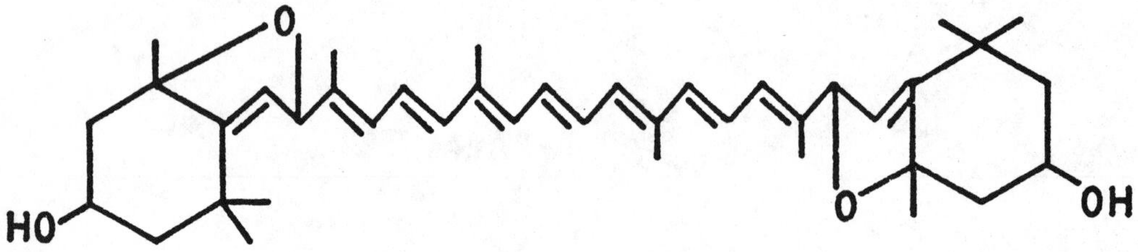

auroxanthin (flowers and fruits)

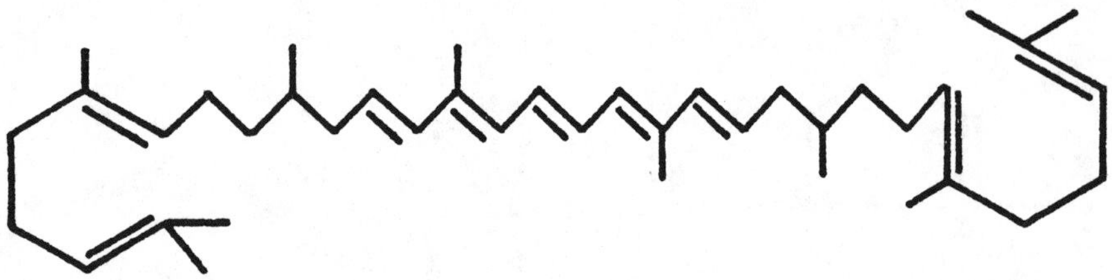

phytofluene (fruits and seeds)

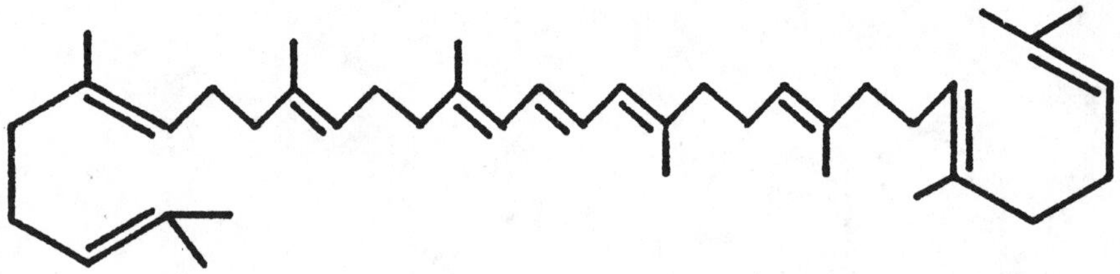

phytoene (leaves fruits, seeds)

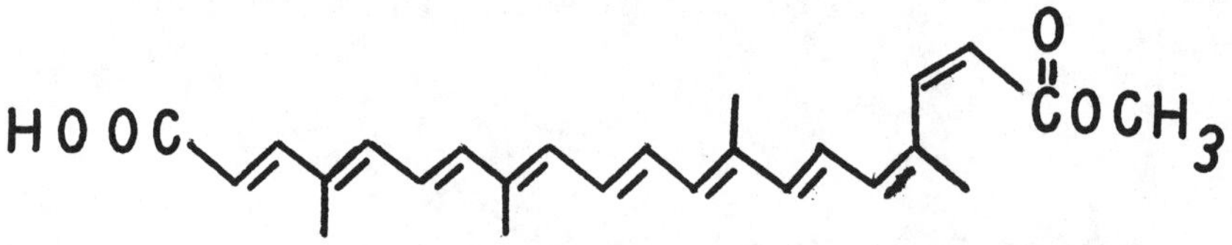

bixin *(Bixa orellana)*

crocetin *(Crocus sativus;* as crocin,
an ester of gentiobiose)

alkaloids are usually the cause of bitterness in plants, but in many cases terpenoids have been found to be responsible. For example, both the saponins and cardiac glycosides are bitter. Bitter principles generally have been reviewed in (106) and (107). Many of the bitter terpenoids contain ketone or lactone groupings, but bitterness does not seem to be ascribable to any particular functional groups (108). Some bitter principles are known to be terpenoids but the complete structures are not known. The cucurbitacins are bitter substances found in the Cucurbitaceae and certain Cruciferae. They are triterpenoid glycosides with the carbon skeleton of lanosterol (109). They attract beetles but repel bees and mites (80, 110). They also have an anti-gibberellin effect (111). The bitterest natural product known is a diterpenoid, amarogentin. Structures and occurrence of some other compounds of this nature are given in Table 8-14.

In contrast to the terpenoid bitter principles, it should be mentioned that the sweetest natural products known are also diterpenoids, stevioside and rebaudoside, found in *Stevia rebaudiana*:

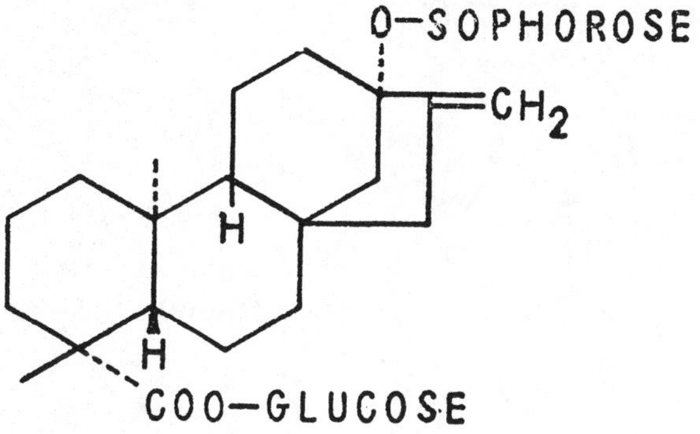

stevioside

TROPONES

The basic tropone nucleus is a seven-membered ring containing a double bond system conjugated with a keto group:

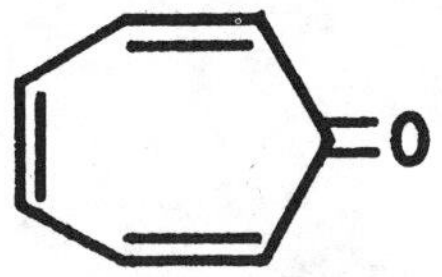

The parent member of the group, tropolone, has in addition a hydroxyl group--hence the name ol - one:

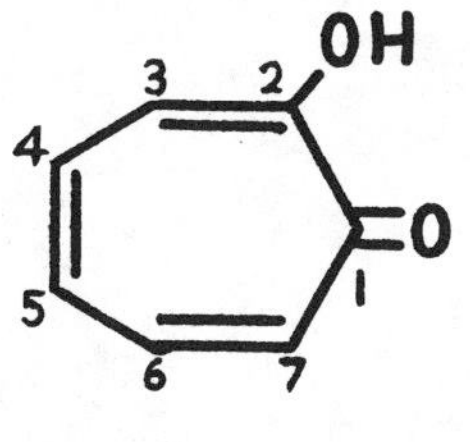

On the basis of biosynthesis there appear to be two classes of tropolones in nature, one derived from terpenoid-like precursors and the other by ring expansion of 6-membered aromatic rings. Since the common tropolones of higher plants resemble the terpenoids, they are included in this chapter. Tropolones derived from aromatic acids seem to be the predominant form in the fungi. In some cases no clear-cut decision regarding precursors is

TABLE 8-14. SOME BITTER PRINCIPLES, STRUCTURE AND OCCURRENCE

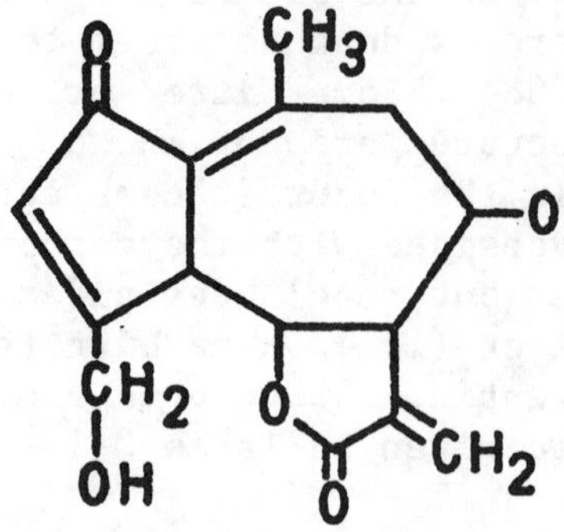

lactucin *(Cichorium intybus)*

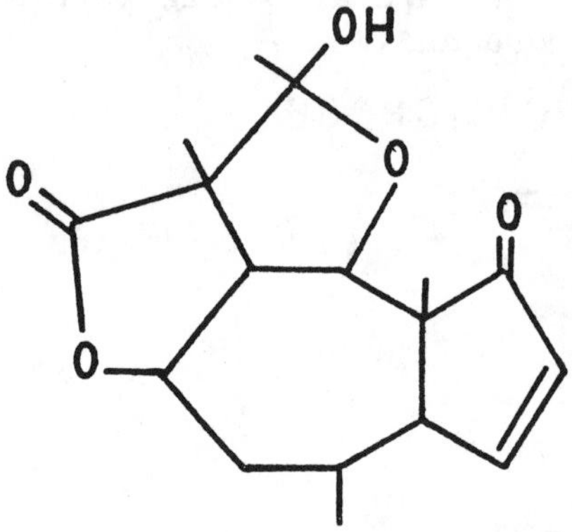

tenulin *(Helenium* spp. *)*

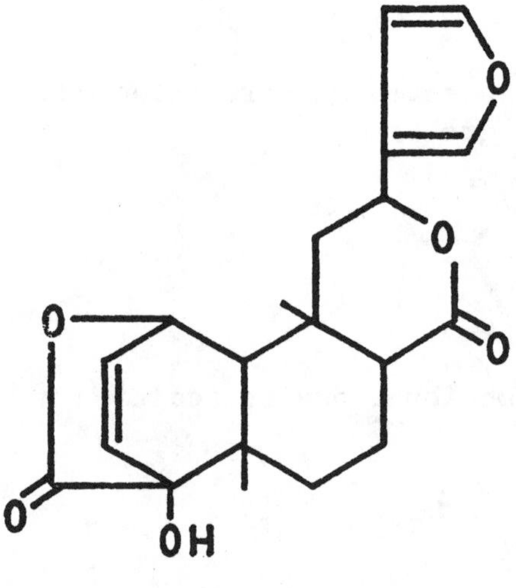

columbin *(Jatrorrhiza palmata)*

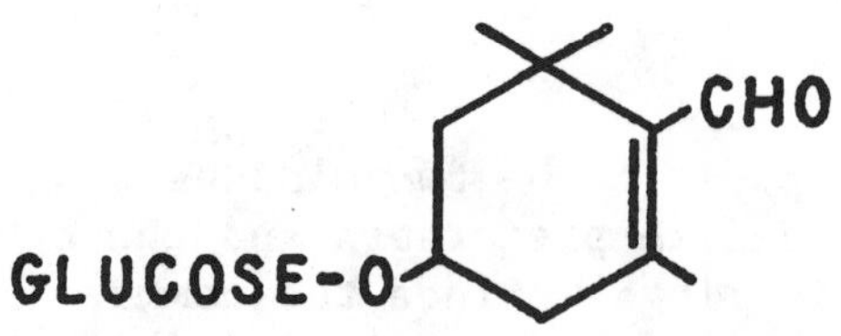

picrocrocin *(Crocus sativus)*

Table 8-14. Continued

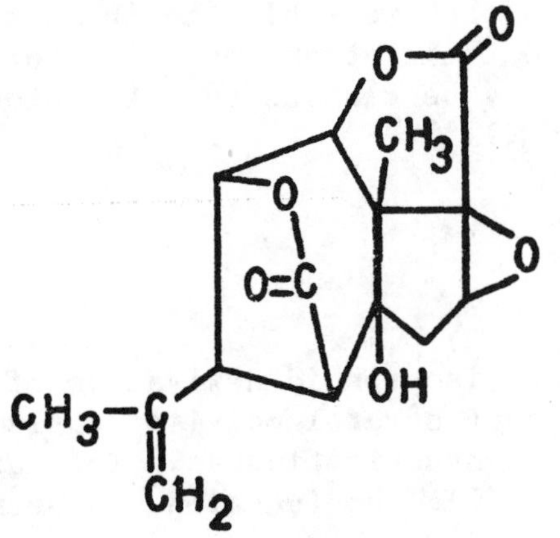

picrotoxinin *(Cocculus indicus)*

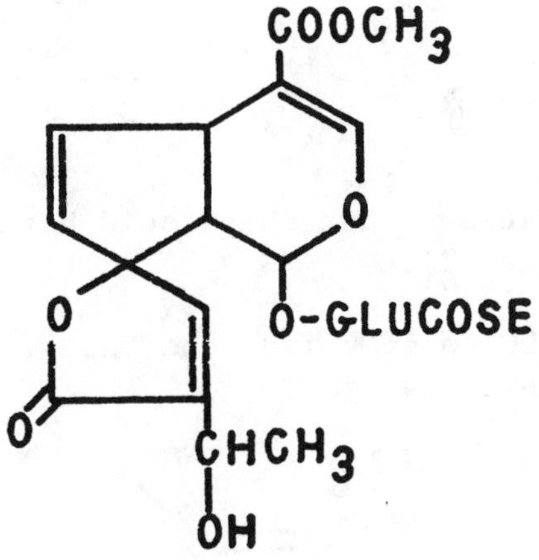

plumieride (*Plumiera* spp.)

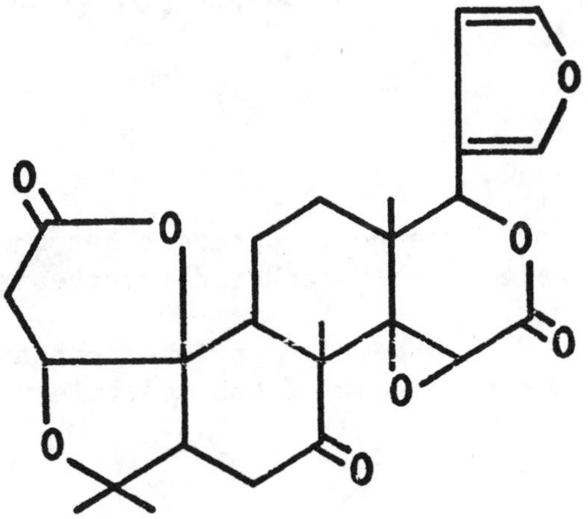

limonin (*Citrus* spp.)

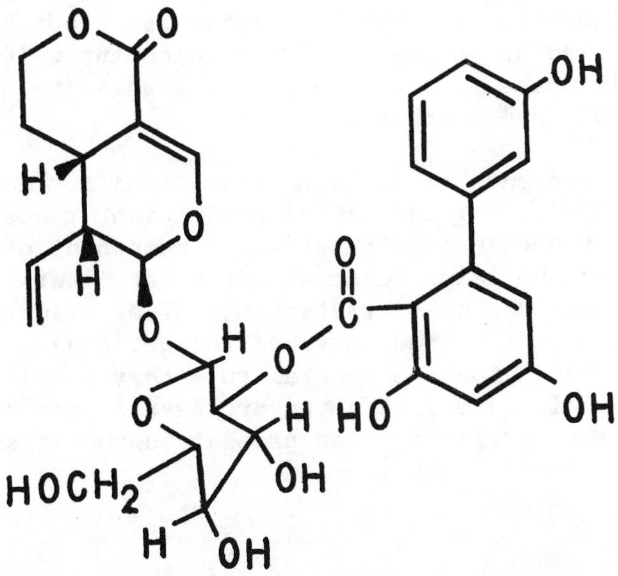

amarogentin (Gentianaceae)

possible at present. Structures of some tropolones have already been given
along with related terpenoids (e.g. nootkatin); and there seems no reason
to set them apart. These compounds are of interest primarily because of
their strong fungicidal action. In this they resemble the phenols, but
their toxicity may also be attributed to their strong capacity for chelation
(112). The alkaloid colchicine (q.v.) may be classed as a tropolone. Tropolones
have been reviewed in (113), (114), and (115).

RUBBER AND OTHER HIGH POLYMERS OF ISOPRENE

Rubber is by far the most important isoprenoid derivative of molecular
weight higher than the tetraterpenoids, but several polyisoprenols (e.g.
solanesol) have been identified in photosynthetic tissues. They are
alcohols ranging from C_{45} to C_{110} (116, 117). No function has been established

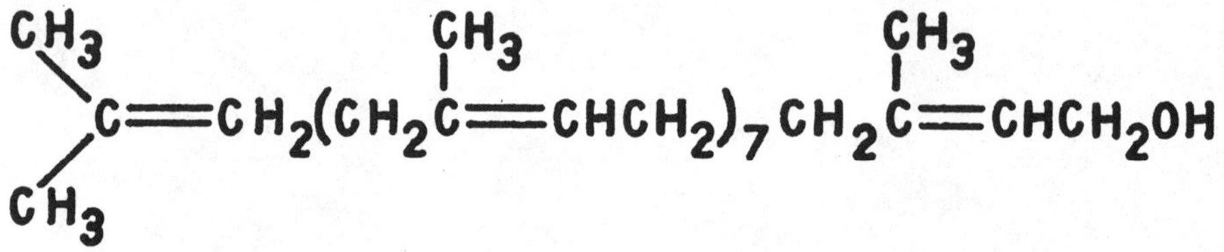

$$\underset{\underset{CH_3}{|}}{\overset{\overset{CH_3}{|}}{C}}=CH_2(CH_2\underset{}{\overset{\overset{CH_3}{|}}{C}}=CHCH_2)_7CH_2\overset{\overset{CH_3}{|}}{C}=CHCH_2OH$$

solanesol

for these polyisoprenols but there are suggestions that they could have a
role in polysaccharide synthesis (118 and Chap. 2).

Rubber is a polymer containing from 3000 to 6000 isoprene units. A
small portion of the molecule may be represented as:

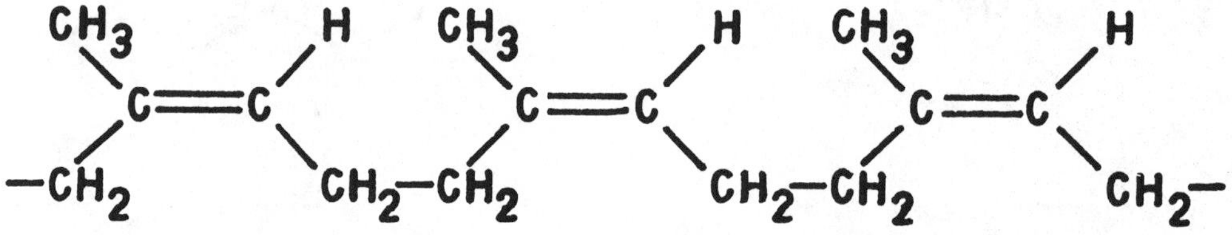

It will be noted that the stereochemistry at all the double bonds is *cis*.
Gutta and balata are also high molecular weight polyisoprenes but have an
all-*trans* structure. Gutta also has a lower average molecular weight than
rubber. Rubber may be distinguished from gutta by its elasticity and in-
complete solubility in aromatic hydrocarbons.

Although only a very few plants (e.g. *Hevea brasiliensis*, *Taraxacum*
spp., guayule) offer possibilities for commercial production, rubber occurs
in many dicotyledons. It is found in some plants as a component of latex
and may be obtained by tapping the latex vessels. In other plants it is
found throughout the tissues and can be extracted only after grinding up
the plant. The plant kingdom has not been surveyed for gutta as extensively
as it has for rubber, but it seems to be a general rule that no plants
have both. The chief commercial sources of gutta are East Indian plants of
the genera *Payena* and *Palaquium*; but it is also present in some grasses (119).

MIXED TERPENOIDS

The mixed terpenoids are a miscellaneous group of compounds which seem to be built predominantly from isoprene residues but which contain additional carbon atoms or lack the required number. In some cases they may come from strictly isoprenoid precursors as the result of extensive rearrangement and/or loss of carbon atoms. The most general category to be placed in this group are the naturally occurring furans, which, as has been seen with the furancoumarins, are derived from isoprenoid units with loss of three carbons. Some of the other compounds in this group are among the most interesting natural products from a physiological point of view.

The pyrethrins are a very valuable group of insecticides found only in the flowers of some members of the genus *Chrysthanthemum* (120). The most important commercial source is *C. cinerariaefolium.* Four substances of very similar structure have been isolated. They are all esters; and while the acid portion of the molecule is clearly an isoprenoid structure, the keto-alcohol part is not derived either from mevalonic acid or acetate (121).

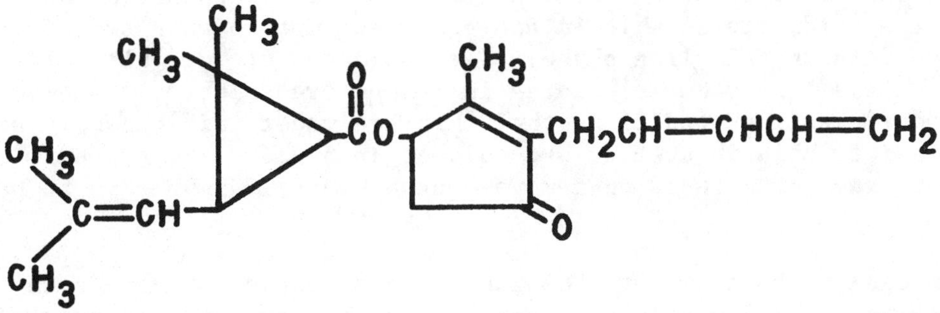

pyrethrin I

The compounds responsible for the physiological action of marihuana (*Cannabis sativa*) contain one ring having a p-menthane type structure and a second ring which does not appear to be related to the terpenoids but comes from acetate (122). The structure of Δ'-tetrahydrocannabinol is given below. These substances are reviewed in (123).

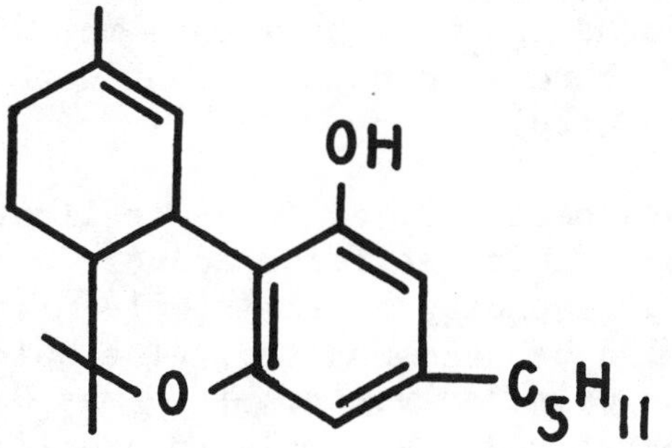

ISOLATION

It is clear from the great variety of structures found among the terpenoids and steroids that no general method of isolation can be applicable to all of them. However, a large number are decidedly non-polar compounds and may, therefore, be separated from polar plant constituents by extraction with such solvents as benzene or ether. Such an extract would also contain other types of lipids, esters, waxes, etc. Most of these may be removed by saponification in alcoholic alkali followed by extraction with ether. Acids and low molecular weight alcohols remain in the alkaline phase while most terpenoids and steroids will go into the ether extract along with high molecular weight alcohols, non-terpenoid hydrocarbons, etc. The use of acetone in extraction can produce condensation artifacts (102).

A few exceptions to this general procedure must be noted. Glycosidic compounds such as the saponins and cardiac glycosides are insoluble in non-polar solvents. They are most conveniently extracted from plants with 70-95% hot ethanol and extraneous lipids and pigments removed from this solution by extraction into benzene or precipitation with lead hydroxide (124). The order of extraction may also be reversed--i.e. lipids extracted first with ether or benzene and then glycosides extracted with hot alcohol. Some of the glycosides will precipitate when a hot alcoholic solution of them is cooled, and this may aid in separations (125). Cholesterol was evidently overlooked in plants for many years because it is found in the water-soluble fraction (126). Acidic terpenoids, when present as the free acid, are soluble in non-polar solvents but on saponification will pass into the alkaline phase. Terpenoid and steroid alkaloids, of course, behave like other alkaloids in being more soluble in non-polar solvents under alkaline conditions than they are under acidic conditions. Rubber is insoluble in acetone but soluble in benzene, so a preliminary acetone extraction is used to remove contaminants if rubber is to be isolated.

Special methods of purification are applicable to various categories of compounds. The low molecular weight terpenes are usually separated by simple distillation or steam distillation. The most likely contaminants are volatile esters which may be removed by saponification. In purification of the carotenoids saponification of contaminants is carried out without heating in order to avoid degradations. The carotenoids may be separated according to their solubilities. The so-called epiphasic ones go preferentially into the petroleum ether layer when shaken with a mixture of this with methanol. Hypophasic carotenoids are those with two or more hydroxy groups. They are preferentially extracted into the methanol layer. Some monohydroxy compounds are found in both layers. A more elaborate exploitation of solubilities can be found in countercurrent separation of carotenoids (127) and gibberellins (128).

Formation of molecular complexes has found application in purifying some compounds of this group. Thiourea forms adducts with many types of branched hydrocarbon chains, depending on their molecular dimensions. Some cyclic compounds may also be accommodated. The thiourea adducts are insoluble in alcohol and non-polar solvents. They may be prepared by mixing alcoholic solutions of thiourea and the sample to precipitate the adduct, or dry material may be triturated with thiourea and a small amount of methanol. When the adduct has formed, uncombined lipids are extracted with benzene, ether, etc. The thiourea adduct is then decomposed with hot water and the desired material extracted into ether. For a general discussion of this technique see (129). Straight-chain aliphatic compounds can be removed from the branched or cyclic terpenoids by converting the former to urea complexes (130).

Complex formation is very common between various members of the steroids. This phenomenon causes difficulties in purification, but may also be put to practical use. In particular, digitonin is frequently used to precipitate sterols from alcoholic solution as insoluble digitonides. The reaction is specific for 3- β-OH sterols (as almost all natural ones are). Free sterols are then regenerated by partitioning the complex between mixtures of hot water and benzene or xylene whereupon the saponin goes to the aqueous and sterol to the organic layer. Another method used for splitting the complex involves boiling it with pyridine, cooling and adding ether to precipitate the saponin and leave sterol in solution. Conversely, this same technique may be applied to purifying many saponins by adding cholesterol to form an insoluble addition complex.

Further purification s usually carried out by column chromatography as a general technique, although special methods may be available for individual examples (e.g. fractional distillation for the low molecular weight terpenoids). Purification of saponins and other glycosides is difficult and not commonly performed. These compounds are usually first hydrolyzed to their aglycones by boiling for several hours with 1-4N HCl, the aglycones extracted with benzene and purified as such (131). Alumina is the most common adsorbent used for chromatography of these compounds, with nonpolar developing solvents such as petroleum ether, benzene, etc. In most cases highly active alumina is undesirable since it may cause degradative reactions. It may be neutralized with acid and a few per cent water added to lower its activity. Column chromatography of steroids is discussed in (132) and (133). Sterols can be converted to colored urethanes to aid visualization of their separation on florisil columns. After separation, the original sterols are quantitatively regenerated (134). Some carotenoids are too sensitive for chromatography on even deactivated alumina, and milder adsorbents such as magnesium oxide and sucrose are recommended for them. Chromatographic purification of carotenoids is extensively discussed by Strain (135). Carotenoids can be separated from steroids by chromatography on Sephadex LH-20 (136). Other common adsorbents such as calcium carbonate and silica gel have been used for some of the terpenoids, cardiac glycosides, etc. Tropolones are isolated by procedures similar to those used for plant phenols, but in addition, advantage can be taken of their property of forming chelate complexes (137). Many procedures have been published for the preparative chromatography of gibberellins, for example partition on silica gel (138), Sephadex G-15 (139), and Sephadex LH-20 (140) or ion exchange on DEAE Sephadex (141). Porous polystyrene beads have been a useful medium for chromatography of both gibberellins and abscisic acid (142).

CHARACTERIZATION

There is no single test which will distinguish terpenoids and steroids as a group from all other plant constituents. The closest approach to this goal is to describe them all as unsaponifiable lipids although such an operational grouping will include a few other types of compounds. There is no simple test to distinguish between the volatile terpenoids and such unsaponifiable aromatic compounds as eugenol or cinnamaldehyde. Classically hydrogenation to known cyclohexane derivatives or pyrolysis of terpenoids to form isoprene have been used to make such a differentiation. Infra-red spectra also indicate whether a compound is aromatic or aliphatic. Characterization of the lower terpenoids usually depends on their functional groups rather than on the carbon skeleton. A standardized procedure for identification of sesquiterpenes using distillation and chromatography on alumina has been developed by Pliva et al. (143). Paper chromatographic identification is based on recognition of functional groups. Because of their volatility and non-polar nature ordinary paper chromatography of the lower terpenoids is difficult, except for such compounds as the iridoid glycosides (144). Carbonyl compounds may be chromatographed as their bisulfite complexes and alcohols as 3, 5-dinitrobenzoates (145). One of the earliest uses of thin layer chromatography was its application to lower terpenoids (146). The best adsorbent layer was found to be silicic acid and the best general purpose solvent 15% ethyl acetate in hexane. Most compounds could be detected by spray reagents specific for functional groups. Unreactive materials were detected by charring with a sulfuric-nitric acid mixture and heat. Thin layer chromatography of lower terpenoids has now become widely used and applied to many plant essential oils (147, 148). Several color reactions have been recommended for the detection of many kinds of terpenoids on TLC plates (149, 150).

Gas chromatography is now probably the method of choice for characterization of volatile terpenoids. References to many published procedures are given in Chapter 7. See also (151) and (152).

The various structural types of the higher terpenoids and the steroids have classically been recognized by the aromatic hydrocarbons formed on dehydrogenation. Dehydrogenation is carried out either catalytically with palladium or by heating with sulfur or selenium at about 300° to form hydrogen sulfide or selenide as the other product. Yields in such reactions are usually very low; but if an identifiable product is obtained, it may be enough to determine the ring structure of the starting material (153).

Paper chromatography of the higher terpenoids and steroids has generally been unsuccessful by normal methods because of the non-polar nature of most of these compounds. Thin layer chromatography and gas chromatography are clearly the methods of choice, and a few references to published procedures are given in Table 8-14. For gas chromatography non-volatile alcohols can be acetylated, other compounds converted to trimethylsilyl derivatives, or methyl esters. High performance liquid chromatography has not yet been used extensively for these compounds, but some applications are tabulated.

TABLE 8-14. LITERATURE REFERENCES TO CHROMATOGRAPHY OF TERPENOIDS AND STEROLS

Type of Compound	Thin Layer	Gas	HPLC
Miscellaneous Terpenoids	154	155, 156	---
Sterols, Triterpenoids	157-159	160, 161	162
Saponins, Sapogenins	163, 164	165	---
Cardiac glycosides	166, 167	---	168, 169
Miscellaneous steroids	170	---	---
Alkaloids	171	173	172
Carotenoids	175-177	156	178-180
Gibberellins	181-183	128, 183, 184	37, 185
Pyrethrins	186	---	---
Cannabinoids	187, 188	189	189
Resin acids	---	190	---
Abscisic acid	---	191, 192	192-194

Many color reactions of the higher terpenoids and steroids have been recorded in the literature, and some of them could probably be adapted for use on chromatograms. One of the best known is the Liebermann-Burchard reaction, giving a blue-green color with most sterols and triterpene alcohols when they are mixed with acetic anhydride and a drop of concentrated sulfuric acid. The mechanism and specificity of this test are discussed by Brieskorn and Hofmann (195) and Cook (196). This, and some of the other common color reactions, cannot be applied to paper strips because of their destructive effect on the paper, but might be used on glass fiber paper or on silica coated glass strips. The well-known Légal reaction for cardiac glycosides is given by many substances containing the grouping CH-CO and is, therefore, of value only for testing substances already shown to be steroids. It is also not given by the scilladienolides. For showing up cardenolides on chromatograms the Kedde reaction with 3, 5-dinitrobenzoic acid is useful (197). Pentacyclic triterpenoids give a violet color when heated with 2, 6-di-tert-butyl-p-cresol in ethanol. Steroids give no color or a yellow-green one (198). Gerlach (199) has reviewed eleven well-known color reactions and recommends the reagent of Brieskorn and Briner (chlorosulfonic acid and Sesolvan NK) for specifically distinguishing between triterpenoids (red color) and steroids (brown color). Several color reactions for detecting steroids and terpenoids on chromatograms have been reviewed by Wachsmuth and Koeckhoven (200). Most saponins are readily recognized by their hemolytic property, and methods to combine this observation with chromatographic behavior have been devised (201). Analytical methods for Δ^5-sapogenins are reviewed in (202). The presence of tannins inhibits hemolysis by saponins in crude mixtures (203) but this should not be a problem in applying the test to chromatograms.

The identification of gas chromatograph fractions by direct coupling to a mass spectrometer is a technique of great general utility that has been powerfully exploited for the analysis of gibberellins (128, 183, 184), abscisic acid (191), cannabinoids (189), and volatile terpenoids (see Chap. 7). Mass spectral data for a number of sapogenins are also available (204).

If pure compounds have been separated by chromatography or other means, determination of absorption spectra is of great value in assigning them to groups. In the ultra-violet and visible region absorption of these compounds is mostly due to the presence of conjugated double bond systems. Compounds with isolated double bonds have no absorption peaks in the visible or ultra-violet spectrum above 200 nm.

Woodward (205) has presented rules for predicting the absorption maximum for a diene system, taking the base value of 217 nm for a conjugated double bond and adding appropriate increments for different structural features. Measurements are generally in close agreement with predicted values. Ultraviolet and infrared spectra of over 200 sesquiterpenes are recorded by Pliva et al. (143). The carotenoids show strong absorption peaks in the visible usually at about 450 nm. Many spectra of individual carotenoids will be found in the appropriate general references and in a review which also tabulates many other analytically useful properties of carotenoids (206). It should be noted that the exact absorption maximum may vary slightly with the solvent used. Ultraviolet and infrared absorption spectra of steroids have been compiled by Dorfman (207) and Dobriner et al. (208) and infra-red spectra for many steroid sapogenins and their derivatives by Jones et al. (209). Diaz et al. (210) have recorded the absorption spectra observed on treating 16 different sapogenins with concentrated sulfuric acid. Bernstein and Lenhard (211) have correlated steroid structures with their spectra in concentrated sulfuric acid. Rubber can be distinguished from gutta by infra-red spectra. Rubber has 42% more absorption than gutta at 12 μ. Characterizations by nuclear magnetic resonance (212) and optical rotatory dispersion (213) have also been used in certain special cases. Optical rotations of all known triterpenoids and steroids have been compiled by Mathieu et al. (214, 215). NMR spectra are particularly useful for the iridoids (216).

Because of their powerful biological activity the gibberellins can be detected in chromatogram eluates by a suitable bioassay (217).

METABOLIC PATHWAYS

There is reasonable agreement regarding the early steps in the biosynthesis of isoprenoid compounds and some scattered evidence regarding the biosynthesis of some of the major categories. These generally acceptable pathways are outlined in Figure 8-1. In addition to articles in the general references there are a number of reviews covering this area of metabolism (218-222). More and more of the reactions are being studied in cell-free enzyme systems (223-225).

It should be noted that much of the work on steroid biosynthesis has been carried out with animal tissues and fungi. Much work on carotenoid biosynthesis has been done using fungi. It is, of course, uncertain how far such results apply to the higher plants; but where evidence is available, it indicates a similarity of pathways in all organisms. Several specific areas will be discussed below.

Unlike the fatty acid biosynthetic pathway malonyl-CoA is not a precursor of the terpenoids, the first two condensation reactions using acetyl-CoA (226). In a few special cases it appears that mevalonic acid is derived preferentially from leucine rather than from acetate (227, 228). The normal head-to-tail condensation of an allylic pyrophosphate with isopentenyl pyrophosphate leading to the building up of polyisoprenoid structures is readily visualized as an ionic reaction (229). The formation of head-to-head and irregular terpenoids is more of a problem; but several reasonable mechanisms have been proposed involving cyclopropane intermediates, condensation of two allylic pyrophosphates, or rearrangements (230-232).

Early in the study of terpene chemistry frequent intra-molecular rearrangements of these compounds were observed. On the basis of such observations it has been assumed that molecular rearrangements can account for many in vivo transformations. The most important general type of rearrangement is the Wagner-Meerwein reaction which occurs in the presence of acids. It may be pictured as resulting from the addition of hydrogen ion to a double bond to form a carbonium ion. Electrons from another part of the molecule are attracted to the positively charged carbon atom and a new bond is formed with elimination of a hydrogen ion or addition of a negative ion. This type of reaction is illustrated for the simple case of

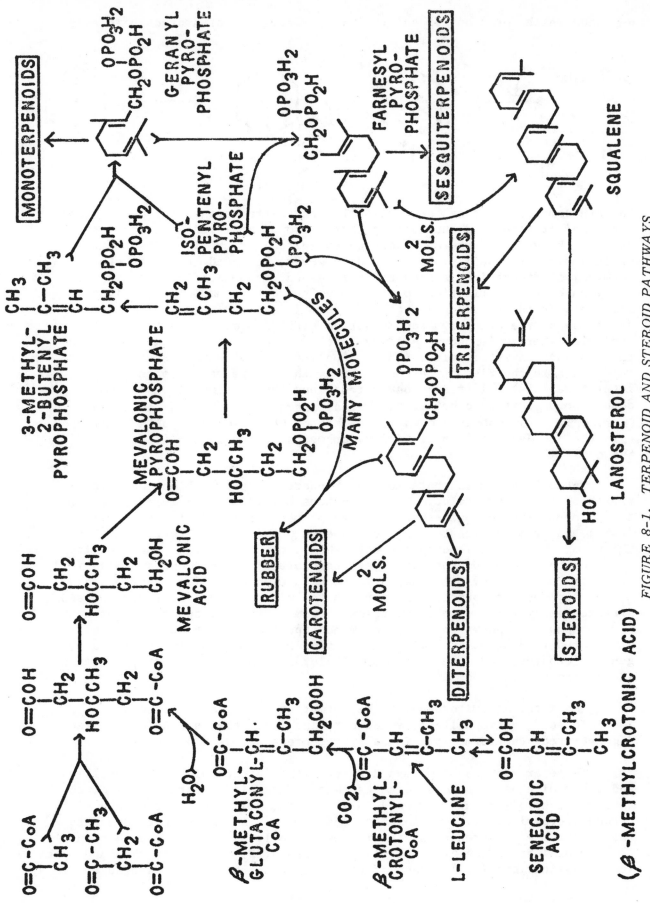

FIGURE 8-1. TERPENOID AND STEROID PATHWAYS

α-pinene which forms bornyl chloride in the presence of hydrochloric acid:

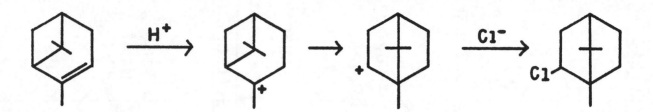

In more complicated cases several different rearrangements may occur before
the final structure is attained so that profound modifications are introduced. The general references may be consulted for critical discussion
of this type of reaction. It should, however, be noted here that stereochemical configuration is frequently retained, and, therefore, it is probably an oversimplification to picture a free carbonium ion as an intermediate. There is evidence that in *Lavandula stoechas* camphor may be
formed by a free carbonium ion mechanism since its optical activity is
variable, whereas fenchone is always pure (+) and therefore cannot go
through such an intermediate (233). Applications of Wagner-Meerwein rearrangements to theories of terpenoid biosynthesis are very common in the
literature (234). In ring-closure reactions the configuration around
double bonds must be considered, but although the carbonium ion derived
from neryl pyrophosphate looks like a better precursor of cyclic monoterpenes
than the one derived from geranyl pyrophosphate, the latter is preferred by
the cyclizing enzyme (235).

Metabolite compartmentation has hindered tracer work on the biosynthesis of lower terpenoids. Thus exogenous mevalonic acid is much better
as a precursor of sesquiterpenoids than of monoterpenoids in peppermint
(236); and from mevalonate, or even labeled CO_2 as a precursor, the C_5
halves of the monoterpenoids are not labeled equally (237). Such results
lead to the conclusion that there are separate sites for mono-and sesquiterpenoid biosynthesis and that a large unlabeled pool of preexistent dimethylallyl pyrophosphate is present in the plants. This pool may be used
preferentially for the monoterpenoids. From geranyl pyrophosphate or neryl
pyrophosphate pathways to the other monoterpenoids are gradually being
elucidated (238-240), including the complex reactions leading to loganin,
gentiopicroside, and other iridoids (241-243), the C_{10} unit of pyrethrins
(244), and skytanthine (245).

Among the sesquiterpenoids the formation of isomeric farnesols,
abscisic acid, caryophyllene, and dendrobine from mevalonic acid has been
demonstrated, the former two in cell-free preparations (246-249).

There are dozens of papers dealing with biosynthesis of gibberellins
and other diterpenoids related to kaurene. Metabolic relationships of the
various gibberellins are reviewed in (35) and (250). An intermediate
between geranylgeranyl pyrophosphate and kaurene is copalyl pyrophosphate
(251). From ent-kaurene a succession of oxidative steps and contraction of
the B-ring lead to the gibberellin ring system (223, 252) that then undergoes
many modifications (253). Many of these reactions have been carried out in

cell-free systems; and it is interesting that a microsomal P450-type system is responsible for several of the oxidations (223), and protein-bound substrates may be involved (254). The feeding of labeled gibberellins to plants has shown that not only do modifications of the parent structure occur but also several conjugated derivatives are made (255, 256). Kaurene is also a precursor of steviol in a sequence that does not involve contraction of the B-ring (257). Biosynthesis of a few other diterpenoids has been studied, including gossypol (258), phytol (259) and beyerene derivatives (260). The enzymology of the various cyclizations is of special interest (261).

The formation of squalene by head-to-head condensation of two molecules of farnesyl pyrophosphate is now known to occur by way of the intermediate presqualene pyrophosphate:

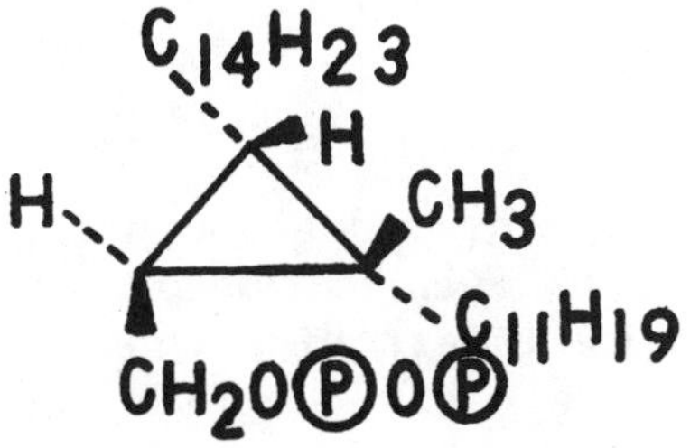

A loss of pyrophosphate, carbonium ion rearrangement, and reduction occur (262). In peppermint squalene biosynthesis is evidently segregated from both mono- and sesquiterpenoid pathways (263). Cyclization of squalene to some cyclic triterpenoids may be simply proton catalyzed (264), but for other cyclic triterpenoids and all the steroids there is intermediate formation of squalene – 2, 3-epoxide (265, 266) or the 2(3), 22(23) diepoxide (267).

Some type of rearrangement must be involved in formation of most of the pentacyclic triterpenoids in which ring E and its substituents cannot be derived by any simple ring closure from a squalene-type compound. Simple rearrangements, however, can account for the conversion of any one of the basic types to the others. Synthesis of a soybean sapogenin has been shown by Arigoni (268) to proceed from mevalonic acid-2-C^{14} with incorporation of label at the circled positions in the carbon skeleton:

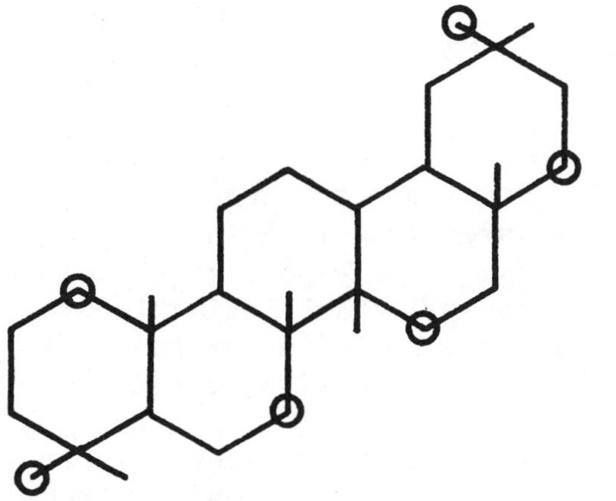

A pentacyclic compound formed from squalene might be expected to have a structure and label distribution as follows:

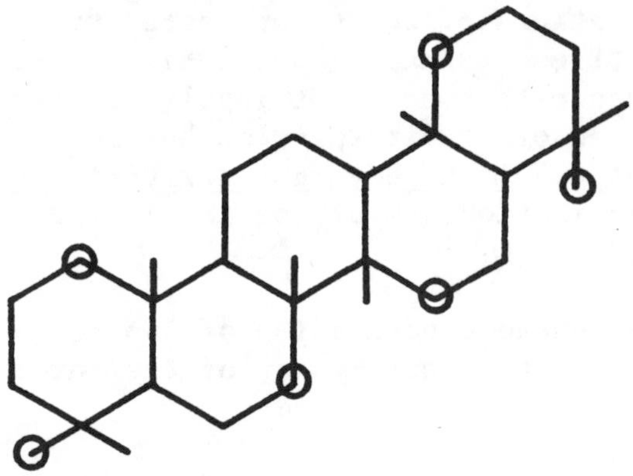

or

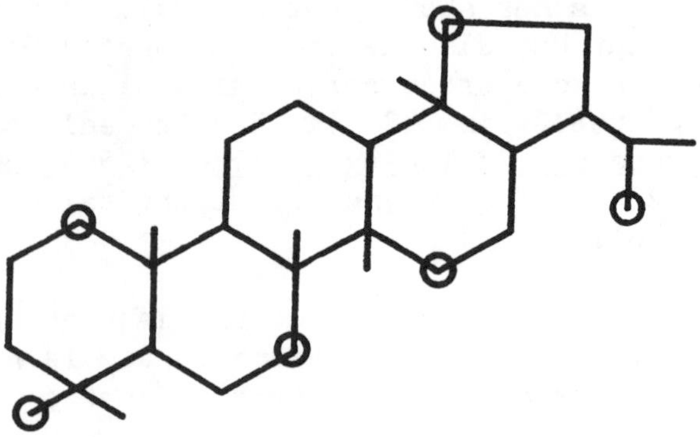

A few natural compounds of the second structure are known, and a possible mechanism of rearrangement has been proposed to account for the more usual structures (269, 270). It is interesting that anatomically more primitive plants seem to have terpenoids derivable from squalene without rearrangement (271).

In spite of the fact that squalene and lanosterol are not commonly found in plants, it is usually taken for granted that they function as intermediates in the biosynthesis of plant sterols just as they do in animals; but in fact the place of lanosterol is more often taken in plants by cycloartenol:

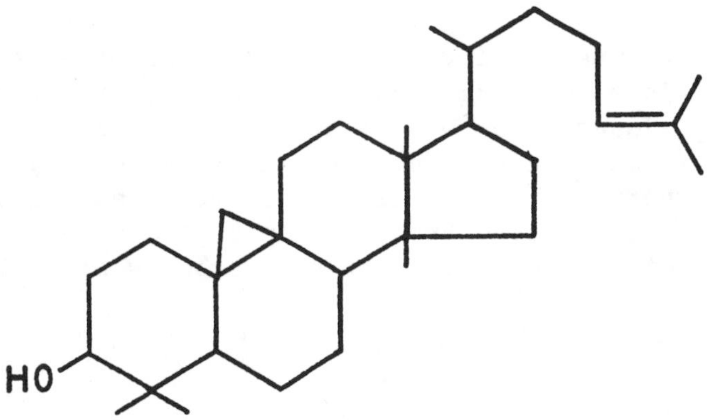

cycloartenol

Cycloartenol is formed in preference to lanosterol, not derived from lanosterol, and is a better precursor than lanosterol for most other plant steroids (219, 222, 272). Traces of lanosterol do occur in plants, and the lanosterol pathway may exist as a primitive vestige (273). Although cycloartenol is convertible to other plant sterols, it may not be the obligatory intermediate for all of them (266, 274).

The C-24 ethyl group found in many plant sterols is derived by successive additions of carbon atoms from the methyl group of methionine. Detailed mechanisms for this process have been proposed (222, 275-277). Further transformations among the various phytosterols have also been

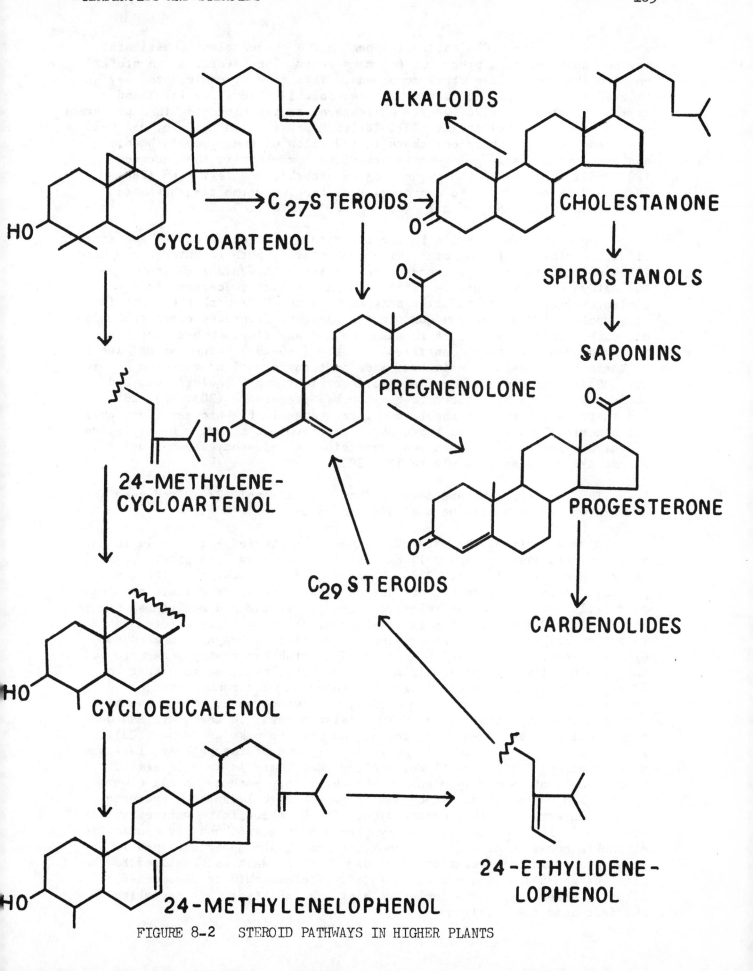

FIGURE 8-2   STEROID PATHWAYS IN HIGHER PLANTS

studied (278, 279). Cholesterol, though not a common plant constituent may be important as a precursor for many other plant steroids, in preference to the common C-24 ethyl compounds. This role of cholesterol may be related to its usual occurrence as water-soluble glycosides (126) and acylated glycosides (126, 280). Cholesterol or its glucoside is a precursor of the saponins of Digitalis (281, 282). Hydroxylation at C-16, and C-26 are steps in the conversion, there is reduction of the 5 double bond, and there is probably a 3-keto intermediate somewhere in the sequence (283-285). Closure of the pyran ring is probably the last step (286, 287). Cholesterol is also a precursor of the insect molting hormones present in *Polypodium vulgare* (288).

There are similarities in the biosynthesis of cardenolides and steroidal saponins. Both can start with cholesterol, both go through a 3-keto intermediate, and both processes occur actively in *Digitalis* spp. The two pathways are reviewed in (289). In the pathway to cardenolides the cholesterol side chain is split between C-21 and C-22 with the formation of pregnenolone. The next compound in the sequence is progesterone that adds a 2-carbon unit from acetate to make the lactone ring. Other possible intermediates have been identified recently (290-292). The unusual sugars of these glycosides are evidently made by transformation of common hexoses (97, 293). For the steroidal alkaloids cycloartenol, cholesterol, and cholestanone have been shown to be possible precursors (283, 294, 295); and there is information about some late stages in the process (296, 297); but practically nothing is known about intermediate steps. The acylation and glycosylation of sterols and terpenoid alkaloids have been studied in enzyme preparations from plants (298-300).

The cucurbitacins are derived from cycloartenol (274), and some interconversions of them have been studied in homogenates (301).

Biosynthesis of the carotenoids has been studied extensively in both higher plants and fungi as well as cell-free extracts from both. Several reviews are available (142, 222). There is little doubt that the general pathways shown in Figure 8-1 are followed, but there are certain problems of detail, for example the relative roles of leucine and acetate as precursors. The chief question is to what extent the various carotenoids are interconvertible rather than arising by parallel pathways from a common C_{40} precursor. The initial C_{40} compound is probably prephytoene pyrophosphate, a homologue of presqualene pyrophosphate, that can go either to 20-cis or 20-trans phytoene (302). Phytoene is most commonly regarded as the precursor of all other carotenoids; but lycopersene, which resembles squalene in being saturated at C-20 is also a possible candidate and would then require a subsequent dehydrogenation step to make phytoene (303). In any case 20-cis-phytoene is an early compound of the pathway, followed soon after by 20-cis phytofluene. After that there is less agreement. Some investigators put lycopene on the obligatory pathway to all other carotenoids while others branch the pathway before lycopene. Lycopene can be converted to other carotenoids. The question is to what extent it normally is in vivo (304). For synthesis of the xanthophylls epoxidation of double bonds is probably an important step. Atmospheric oxygen is incorporated in this reaction (305) and further reactions can lead to the other oxygen-containing compounds (306). Violaxanthin is decomposed by light to several products including a growth inhibitor that resembles abscisic acid (19, 307).

The control of all these terpenoid pathways in plants is a fascinating problem. The control arising from compartmentation has been mentioned earlier. Control by cofactor availability is also a likely possibility (308). The rigorous control of sterol biosynthesis is stressed in (309). The possible roles of sterol esters and glycosides in controlling metabolism by their effects on structure and viscosity are discussed in (82, 83, 310, 311). The induction of furanoterpenoid phytoalexins by fungal infection is an exciting problem of plant pathology (312).

GENERAL REFERENCES

Bean, G. A. (1973) "Phytosterols," Adv. Lipid Res. 11 193-218.

Clayton, E., ed. (1969) Methods in Enzymology 15, Steroids and Terpenoids, Academic Press, N. Y.

Devon, T. K. & Scott, A. I. (1972) Handbook of Naturally Occurring Compounds, 2, Terpenes, Academic Press, N. Y.

Goodwin, T. W., ed. (1976) Chemistry and Biochemistry of Plant Pigments, 2nd ed., 2 Vols., Academic Press, N. Y.

Goodwin, T. W., ed. (1979) Carotenoids-5, Pergamon Press, Oxford.

Gurr, M. I. & James, A. T. (1976) Lipid Biochemistry: An Introduction, Halsted Press, N. Y.

Hanson, J. R., ed. (1978) Terpenoids and Steroids, The Chemical Society, London.

Heftmann, E., ed. (1973) Modern Methods of Steroid Analysis, Academic Press, N. Y.

Heftmann, E. (1970) Steroid Biochemistry, Academic Press, N. Y.

Isler, O., Gutman, H., and Solms, U., eds. (1971) Carotenoids, Birkhäuser, Basel.

Nes, W. R. & McKean, M. L. (1977) Biochemistry of Steroids and Other Isopentenoids, University Park Press, Baltimore

Newman, A. A., ed. (1972) Chemistry of Terpenes and Terpenoids, Academic Press, N. Y.

Runeckles, V. C. & Mabry, T. J., eds. (1973) Terpenoids: Structure, Biogenesis and Distribution, Academic Press, N. Y.

Straub, O. (1976) Key to Carotenoids, Birkhäuser, Basel.

Tevini, M. & Lichtenthaler, H. K., eds. (1977) Lipids and Lipid Polymers in Higher Plants, Springer-Verlag, N. Y.

Yoshioka, H., Mabry, T. J., & Timmerman, B. N. (1973) Sesquiterpene Lactones, Univ. of Tokyo Press, Tokyo, Japan.

Several articles in Miller 2

Several articles in Paech & Tracey 3

BIBLIOGRAPHY

1. Rasmussen, R. A., and Jones, C. A. (1973) Phytochem. 12 15-19.
2. Buckles, R. E., Mock, G. V. and Locatell, L., Jr. (1955) Chem. Revs. 55 659-677.
3. Fraenkel, G. (1959) Science 129 1466-1470.
4. Meinwald, J., Prestwich, G. D., Nakanishi, K., and Kubo, I. (1978) Science 199 1167-1173.
5. Heikkenen, H. J. and Hrutfiord, B. F. (1965) Science 150 1457-1459.
6. Lloyd, D. (1964) Alicyclic Compounds, Elsevier, N. Y.
7. Wieffering, J. H. (1966) Phytochemistry 5 1054-1064.
8. Bobbit, J. M., Rao, K. V. and Kiely, D. E. (1966) Lloydia 29 90-93.
9. Taylor, W. I., ed. (1969) Cyclopentanoid Terpene Derivatives, Marcel Dekker, Inc., N. Y.
10. Plouvier, V. and Favre-Bonvin, J. (1971) Phytochemistry 10 1697-1722.
11. Rücker, G. (1973) Angew. Chem. Intern. Ed. 12 793-806.
12. Nozoe, T. and Ito, S. (1961) Fortschr. Chem. Org. Naturstoffe 19 32-119.
13. Meuche, D. and Huneck, S. (1966) Chem. Ber. 99 2669-2674.
14. Rossmann, M. G. and Lipscomb, W. N. (1958) Tetrahedron 4 275-293.
15. Milborrow, B. V. (1974) Ann. Rev. Plant Physiol. 25 259-307.
16. Cheng, C.-Y. and Schrandolf, H. (1974) Z. Pflanzenphysiol 71 366-369.
17. Milborrow, B. V. (1970) J. Exper. Botany 21 17-29.
18. Stuart, K. L., Roberts, E. V., and Whittle, Y. G. (1976) Phytochemistry 15 332-333.
19. Dörffling, K. (1978) Phil. Trans. Royal Soc. B 284 499-507.
20. Rodriguez, E., Towers, G. H. N., and Mitchell, J. C. (1976) Phytochemistry 15 1573-1580.
21. Asakawa, Y., Toyota, M., Takemoto, T., and Suire, C. (1979) Phytochemistry 18 1007-1009.
22. Knoche, H., Ourisson, G., Perold, G. W., Foussereau, J., and Maleville, J. (1969) Science, 166 239-240.
23. Doskotch, R. W. and Hufford, C. D. (1969) J. Pharm. Sci. 58 186-188.
24. Boyd, M. R. and Wilson, B. J. (1972) J. Agric. Food Chem. 20 429-430.
25. Kubo, I., Lee, Y.-W., Pettei, M., Pilkiewicz, F., and Nakanishi, K. (1976) Chem. Commun. 1013-1014.
26. Inayama, S., Ohkura, T., Kawamata, T., and Yanagita, M. (1974) Chem. Pharm. Bull. 1435-1437.
27. Mitchell, J. C. and Epstein, W. L. (1974) Arch. Dermatol. 110 871-873 (Chem. Abstr. 82 133694).
28. Gross, D. (1979) Biochem. Physiol. Pflanzen 174 327-344.
29. Grisebach, H. and Ebel, J. (1978) Angew. Chem. Intern. Ed. 17 635-647.
30. Alves, L. M., Heisler, E. G., Kissinger, J. C., Patterson, J. M., III, and Kalan, E. B. (1979) Plant Physiol. 63 359-362.
31. Kalsi, P. S., Vij, V. K., Singh, O. S., and Wadia, M. S. (1977) Phytochem. 16 784-786.
32. Kalsi, P. S., Singh, O. S., and Chhabra, B. R. (1978) Phytochemistry 17 576-577.
33. Heather, J. B., Mittal, R. S. D., and Sih, C. J. (1976) J. Am. Chem. Soc. 98 3661-3669.
34. Hanson, J. R. (1972) Progress in Phytochemistry 3 231-285.
35. Hedden, P., MacMillan, J., and Phinney, B. O. (1978) Ann. Rev. Plant Physiol. 29 149-192.
36. Sponsel, V. M., Gaskin, P., and MacMillan, J. (1979) Planta 146 101-105.
37. Yamaguchi, I., Yokota, T., Yoshida, S., and Takahashi, N. (1979) Phytochemistry 18 1699-1702.
38. Zanno, P. R., Endo, M., Nakanishi, K., Näf, U., and Stein, C. (1972) Naturwiss. 59 512.
39. Wassermann, O. (1967) Arzneimittel-Forsch. 17 543-546.
40. Elliger, C. A., Zinkel, D. F. Chan, B. G. and Waiss, A. C., Jr. (1976) Experientia 32 1364-1366.
41. Hosozawa, S., Kato, N., Munakata, K., and Chen, Y.-L. (1974) Agric. Biol. Chem. 38 1045-1048.
42. Springer, J. P., Clardy, J., Cox, R. H., Cutler, H. G., and Cole, R. J. (1975) Tetrahedron Letters 2737-2740.
43. Sitton, D. and West, C. A. (1975) Phytochem. 14 1921-1925.
44. Mancini, S. D. and Edwards, J. M. (1979) J. Nat. Prod. 42 483-488.
45. Santi, R. and Luciani, S., eds. (1978) Atractyloside--Chemistry, Biochemistry, and Toxicology, Piccin Medical Books, Padua.
46. Myers, B. D. and Throneberry, G. O. (1966) Plant Physiol. 41 787-791.
47. Brandolin, G., Lauquin, G. J. M., Lima, M. S., and Vignais, P. V. (1979) Biochim. Biophys. Acta 548 30-37.
48. Lima, M. S. Denslow, N. D. and de Melo, D. F. (1977) Physiol. Plantarum 41 193-196.
49. Peyster, A. D. and Wang, Y. Y. (1979) New England J. Med. 301 275-276.
50. Diamond, L., O'Brien, T. G., and Rovera, G. (1978) Life Sciences 23 1979-1988.
51. Rochette-Egly, C. and Castagna, M. (1979) FEBS Letters 103 38-42.
52. Shoyab, M., DeLarco, J. E., and Todaro, G. J. (1979) Nature 279 387-391.
53. Evans, F. J. and Soper, C. J. (1978) Lloydia 41 193-233.
54. Miyase, T., Rüedi, P., and Eugster, C. H. (1977) Helv. Chim. Acta 60 2770-2779, 2789-2803.

55. Cordell, G. A. (1974) Phytochem. 13 2343-2364.
56. Stipanovic, R. D., Bell, A. A., O'Brien, D. H., and Lukefahr, M. J. (1977) Tetrahedron Letters 567-570.
57. Boar, R. B. and Allen, J. (1973) Phytochemistry 12 2571-2578.
58. Pant, P. and Rastogi, R. P. (1979) Phytochemistry 18 1095-1108.
59. Boar, R. B. and Romer, C. R. (1975) Phytochem. 14 1143-1146.
60. Ives, D. A. J. and O'Neill, A. N. (1958) Can. J. Chem. 36 434-439.
61. Zimmerman, J. (1946) Helv. Chim. Acta 29 1455-1456.
62. Brieskorn, C. H. (1956) Pharmazeut. Zentral. 95 235-247.
63. Stöcklin, W. (1969) J. Agric. Food Chem. 17 704-708.
64. Nes, W. R. and 6 others (1977) Lipids 12 511-527.
65. Kintia, P. K. and Wojciechowski, Z. A. (1974) Phytochem. 13 2235-2238.
66. Aneja, R. and Harries, P. C. (1974) Chem. Phys. Lipids 12 351-362.
67. Knights, B. A. (1971) Lipids 6 215-218.
68. Brandt, R. D. and Benveniste, P. (1972) Biochim. Biophys. Acta 282 85-92.
69. Mandava, N., Anderson, J. D., Dutky, S. R. and Thompson, M. J. (1974) Steroids 23 357-361.
70. Wasserman, R. H., Henion, J. D., Haussler, M. R., and McCain, T. A. (1976) Science 194 853-855.
71. Napoli, J. L., Reeve, L. E., Eisman, J. A., Schnoes, H. K., and DeLuca, H. F. (1977) J. Biol. Chem. 252 2580-2583.
72. Heftmann, E. (1970) Recent Advances in Phytochem. 3 211-227.
73. Hardman, R. and Benjamin, T. V. (1976) Phytochem. 15 1515-1516.
74. Amin, E. S. and Bassiouny, A. R. (1979) Phytochemistry 18 344.
75. van Rompuy, L. L. L. and Zeevart, J. A. D. (1979) Phytochemistry 18 863-865.
76. Jones, T. K. and Roddick, J. G. (1977) New Phytol. 79 493-499.
77. Geuns, J. M. C. (1978) Phytochemistry 17 1-14.
78. Buchala, A. J. and Schmid, A. (1979) Nature 280 230-231.
79. Bates, R. B. and Morehead, S. R. (1973) Chem. Commun. 125-126.
80. Nielsen, J. K., Larsen, L. M. and Sørensen, H. (1977) Phytochem. 16 1519-1522.
81. Grunwald, C. (1975) Ann. Rev. Plant Physiol. 26 209-236.
82. Nes, W. R. (1974) Lipids 9 596-612.
83. Grunwald, C. (1978) Phil. Trans. Royal Soc. B 284 541-558.
84. **Iijima, M. and Higashi, T. (1979) Chem. Pharm. Bull. (Tokyo) 27 2130-2136.**
85. Chen, S. E. and Staba, E. J. (1978) Lloydia 41 361-366.
86. Gibson, M. R. (1978) Lloydia 41 348-354.
87. Tschesche, R. and Wulff, G. (1973) Fortschr. Chem. Org. Naturstoffe. 30 461-606.
88. Takeda, K. (1972) Progress in Phytochemistry 3 287-333.
89. Agarwal, S. K. and Rastogi, R. P. (1974) Phytochem. 13 2623-2645.
90. Kesselmeier, J. and Budzikiewica, H. (1979) Z. Pflanzenphysiol. 91 333-344.
91. Zoz, I. G. and Komissarenko, N. F. (1968) Doklady Akad. Nauk SSSR 178 238-240.
92. Fullerton, D. S., Yoshioka, K., Rohrer, D. C., From, A. H. L., and Ahmed, K. (1979) Science 205 917-919.
93. Heller, M. and Beck, S. (1978) Biochim. Biophys. Acta 514 332-347.
94. Jonas, H. (1976) Z. Pflanzenphysiol. 80 395-406.
95. Gold, H., Kwit, N. T., Shane, S. J., and Dayrit, C. (1969) J. Clin. Pharmacol. 9 148-154.
96. Evans, F. J. and Cowley, P. S. (1972) Phytochemistry 11 2971-2975.
97. Singh, B. and Rastogi, R. P. (1970) Phytochemistry 9 315-331.
98. Wiesner, K. and Valenta, Z. (1958) Fortschr. Chem. Org. Naturstoffe 16 26-89.
99. Wall, M. E. and Davis, K. H., Jr. (1972) in Toxins of Animal and Plant Origin, Vol. 2 ed. by A. deVries and E. Kochva, Gordon and Breach, London. pp. 597-624.
100. Roddick, J. G. (1974) Phytochemistry 13 9-25.
101. Gross, J. and Eckhardt, G. (1978) Phytochemistry 17 1803-1804.
102. Stewart, I. and Wheaton, T. A. (1973) Phytochemistry 12 2947-2951.
103. Lundegårdh, H. (1966) Proc. Nat. Acad. Sci. U. S. 55 1062-1065.
104. Anderson, I. C. and Robertson, D. S. (1960) Plant Physiol. 35 531-534.
105. Foote, C. S., Chang, Y. C., and Denny, R. W. (1970) J. Am. Chem. Soc. 92 5218-5219.
106. Dreyer, D. L. (1968) Fortschr. Chem. Org. Naturstoffe. 26 190-244.
107. Polonsky, J. (1973) Fortschr. Chem. Org. Naturstoffe 30 101-150.
108. Kubota, T. and Kubo, I. (1969) Nature 223 97-99.
109. Lavie, D. and Glotter, E. (1971) Fortschr. Chem. Org. Naturstoffe 29 307-362.
110. daCosta, C. P. and Jones, C. M. (1971) Science 172 1145-1146.
111. Guha, J. and Sen. S. P. (1973) Nature, New Biol. 244 223-224.
112. Belleau, B. and Burba, J. (1961) Biochim. Biophys. Acta 54 195-196.
113. Pauson, P. L. (1955) Chem. Revs. 55 9-136.
114. Erdtman, H. (1955) in Paech and Tracey 3 351-358.
115. Nozoe, T. (1956) Fortschr. Chem. Org. Naturstoffe 13 232-301.
116. Hannus, K. and Pensar, G. (1974) Phytochemistry 13 2563-2566.
117. Hemming, F. W. (1970) Biochem. Soc. Symp. 29 105-117.
118. Hemming, F. W. (1978) Phil. Trans. Royal Soc. B 284 559-568.
119. Buchanan, R. A., Swanson, C. L., Weisleder, D., and Cull, I. M. (1979) Phytochemistry 18 1069-1071.

120. Casida, J. E., ed. (1973) Pyrethrum, Academic Press, N. Y.
121. Crowley, M. P., Inglis, H. S., Snarey, M., and Thain, E. M. (1961) Nature 191 281-282.
122. Shoyama, Y., Yagi, M., Nishioka, I., and Yamauchi, T. (1975) Phytochem. 14 2189-2192.
123. Mechoulam, R., McCallum, N. K., and Burstein, S. (1976) Chem. Revs. 76 75-112.
124. Jonas, H. and Mazzei De Planas, G. (1974) Prep. Biochem. 4 411-434.
125. Heitz, S. (1959) Compt. Rend. 248 283-286.
126. Anding, C., Brandt, R. D., Ourisson, G., Pryce, R. J., and Rohmer, M. (1972) Proc. Royal
     Soc. B 180 115-124.
127. Pfander, H., Haller, F., Bernhard, K. and Thommen, H. (1973) Chimia 27 103-104.
128. Bowen, D. H., Crozier, A., MacMillan, J., and Reid, D. M. (1973) Phytochemistry 12 2935-2941.
129. Kobe, K. A. and Reinhart, L. R. (1959) J. Chem. Educ. 36 300-301.
130. Ives, D. A. J., and O'Neill, A. N. (1958) Can. J. Chem. 36 926-930.
131. Wall, M. E., Krider, M. M., Rothman, E. S., Eddy, C. R. (1952) J. Biol. Chem. 198 533-543.
132. Neher, R., J. Chromatog. 1 122-165., 205-258 (1958)
133. Heftmann, E. (1976) Chromatography of Steroids, Elsevier, Amsterdam.
134. Bergmann, W. and Domsky, I. I. (1960) Ann. N. Y. Acad. Sci. 90 Art. 3, 906-909.
135. Strain, H. H., Sherma, J., and Grandolfo, M. (1967) Anal. Chem. 39 926-932.
136. Suzuki, T. and Hasegawa, K. (1974) Agric. Biol. Chem. 38 871-872.
137. Zavarin, E., Smith, R. M. and Anderson, A. B. (1959) J. Org. Chem. 24 1318-1321.
138. Durley, R. C., Crozier, A., Pharis, R. P., and McLaughlin, G. E. (1972) Phytochemistry 11
     3029-3033.
139. Reynolds, T. (1970) J. Exper. Botany 21 702-711.
140. MacMillan, J. and Wels, C. M. (1973) J. Chromatog. 87 271-276.
141. Gräbner, R., Schneider, G., and Sembdner, G. (1976) J. Chromatog. 121 110-115.
142. Reeve, D. R. and Crozier, A. (1976) Phytochem. 15 791-793.
143. Pliva, J., Horák, M., Herout, V. and Sorm, F. (1960) Die Terpene. Teil 1. Sesquiterpene,
     Akademie Verlag, Berlin.
144. Danielson, T. J., Hawes, E. M., and Bliss, C. A. (1975) J. Chromatog. 103 216-218.
145. Schantz, M. v., Juvonen, S., Oksanen, A., and Hakamaa, I. (1968) J. Chromatog. 38 364-372.
146. Kirchner, J. G., Miller, J. M., and Keller, W. D. (1951) Anal. Chem. 23 420-425.
147. Battaile, J., Dunning, R.L. and Loomis, W. D. (1961) Biochim. Biophys. Acta 51 538-544.
148. Attaway, J. A., Pieringer, A. P., and Barabas, L. J. (1966) Phytochemistry 5 141-151.
149. Kohli, J. C. (1975) J. Chromatog. 105 193-194.
150. ibid. 121 116-117 (1976).
151. von Rudloff, E. (1969) Recent Advances in Phytochemistry 2 127-162.
152. Svendsen, A. B. and Karlsen, J. (1973) Planta Medica 24 266-277.
153. Stahl, E. and Müller, T. K. B. (1974) Z. Anal. Chem. 271 257-264.
154. Attaway, J. A., Barabas, L. J., and Wolford, R. W. (1965) Anal. Chem. 37 1289-1290.
155. Scheffer, J. J. C. and Svendsen, A. B. (1975) J. Chromatog. 115 607-611.
156. Taylor, R. F. and Davies, B. H. (1975) J. Chromatog. 103 327-340.
157. Kasprzyk, Z., Grzelczak, Z. and Pyrek, J. (1965) Bull. Acad. Polon. Sci. Ser. Biol. 13
     661-665.
158. Lindgren, B. C. and Svahn, C. M., (1966) Acta Chem. Scand. 20 1763-1768.
159. Niemann, G. J. and Baas, W. J., (1978) J. Chromatog. Sci. 16 260-26 . 262
160. Nordby, H. E. and Nagy, S. (1973) J. Chromatog. 75 187-193.
161. Homberg, E.(1977) Fette-Seifen-Anstrichsmittel 79 234-241.
162. Hunter, I. R., Walden, M. K., and Heftmann, E. (1978) J. Chromatog. 153 57-61.
163. Bennett, R. D. and Heftmann, E. (1962) J. Chromatog. 9 353-358.
164. Elmunajjed, D. T., Fayez, M. B. E., and Radwan, A. S. (1965) Phytochemistry 4 587-592.
165. Knight, J. C. (1977) J. Chromatog. 133 222-225.
166. Evans, F. J., Flemons, P. A., Duignan, C. F., and Cowley, P. S. (1974) J. Chromatog. 88
     341-346.
167. Züllich, G., Braun, W., and Lisboa, B. P. (1975) J. Chromatog. 103 396-401.
168. Cobb, P. H. (1976) Analyst 101 768-776.
169. Enson, J. M. and Seiber, J. N. (1978) J. Chromatog. 148 521-527.
170. Cohn, G. L. and Pancake, E. (1964) Nature 201 75-76.
171. Cadle, L. S., Stelzig, D. A., Harper, K. L., and Young, R. J. (1978) J. Agric. Food Chem.
     26 1453-1454.
172. Heftmann, E. and Hunter, I. R. (1979) J. Chromatog. 165 283-299.

173. Herb, S. F., Fitzpatrick, T. J., and Osman, S. F. (1975) J. Agric. Food Chem. 23 520-523.
174. Hunter, I. R., Walden, M. K., Wagner, J. R., and Heftmann, E. (1976) 119 223-226.
175. Durand, M. and Laval-Martin, D. (1974) J. Chromatog. 97 92-98.
176. Sherma, J. and Latta, M. (1978) J. Chromatog. 154 73-75.
177. Buckle, K. A. and Rahman, F. M. N. (1979) J. Chromatog. 171 385-391
178. Eskins, K., Scholfield, C. R., and Dutton, H. J. (1977) J. Chromatog. 135 217-220.
179. DeJong, D. W. and Woodlief, W. G. (1978) J. Agric. Food Chem. 26 1281-1288.
180. Fiksdahl, A., Mortensen, J. T., and Liaanen-Jensen, S. (1978) J. Chromatogr. 157 111-117.
181. Jones, K. C. (1970) J. Chromatog. 52 512-516.

182. Cavell, B. D., MacMillan, J., Pryce, R. J., and Sheppard, A. C. (1967) Phytochemistry 6 867-874.
183. Hemphill, D. D., Jr., Baker, L. R. and Sell, H. M. (1972) Planta 103 241-248.
184. Binks, R., MacMillan, J., and Pryce, R. J. (1969) Phytochemistry 8 271-284.
185. Heftmann, E., Saunders, G. A., and Haddon, W. F. (1978) J. Chromatog. 156 71-77.
186. Stahl, E. and Pfeifle, J. (1965) Naturwiss. 52 620.
187. Tewari, S. N., Harpalani, S. P., and Sharma, S. C. (1974) Mikrochim Acta 991-995.
188. Fowler, R., Gilhooley, R. A., and Baker, P. B. (1979) J. Chromatog. 171 509-511.
189. Knaus, E. E., Coutts, R. T., and Kazakoff, C. W. (1976) J. Chromatog. Sci. 14 525-530.
190. Joye, N. M., Jr., Proveaux, A. T., and Lawrence, R. V. (1974) J. Oil Chemists Soc. 51 195-197
191. Andersson, B., Häggstrom, N., and Anderson, K. (1978) J. Chromatog. 157 303-310.
192. Ciha, A. J., Brenner, M. L., and Brun, W. A. (1977) Plant Physiol. 59 821-826.
193. Durlev, R. C., Kannangara, T., and Simpson, G. M. (1978) Can. J. Botany 56 157-161.
194. Cargile, N. L., Borchert, R., and McChesney, J. D. (1979) Anal. Biochem. 97 331-339.
195. Brieskorn, C. H. and Hofmann, H. (1964) Arch. Pharm. 297 577-588.
196. Cook, R. P. (1961) Analyst 86 373-381.
197. Bush, I. E. and Taylor, D. A. H. (1952) Biochem. J. 52 643-648.
198. Brieskorn, C. H. and Mahran, G. H. (1960) Naturwiss. 47 107-108.
199. Gerlach, H. (1958) Planta Med. 6 448-451.
200. Wachsmuth, H. and van Koeckhoven, L. (1960) Anal. Chim. Acta 22 41-49.
201. Segal, R., Milo-Goldzweig, I., Zaitschek, D. V., and Noam, M. (1978) Anal. Biochem. 84 78-84.
202. Sofowora, E. A. and Hardman, R. (1974) Planta Med. 26 385-390.
203. Stahl, E. (1973) Arch. Pharm. 306 693-696.
204. Dawidar, A. M. and Foyez, M. B. E. (1974) J. Pharm. Sci. 63 140-142.
205. Woodward, R. B. (1942) J. Am. Chem. Soc. 64 72-75.
206. Foppen, F. H. (1971) Chromatogr. Rev. 14 133-298.
207. Dorfman, L. (1953) Chem. Revs. 53 47-144.
208. Dobriner, K., Katzenellenbogen, E. R., and Jones, R. N. (1953) Infrared Absorption Spectra of Steroids, Vol. I., Interscience Publishers, N. Y.
209. Jones, R. N., Katzenellenbogen, E., and Dobriner, K. (1953) J. Am. Chem. Soc. 75 158-166.
210. Diaz, G., Zaffaroni, A., Rosenkranz, G., and Djerassi, C. (1952) J. Org. Chem 17 747-750.
211. Bernstein, S. and Lenhard, R. H. (1960) J. Org. Chem. 25 1405-1408.
212. Ponsinet, G. and Ourisson, G. (1965) Phytochemistry 4 799-811.
213. Cornforth, J. W., Milborrow, B. V. and Ryback, G. (1966) Nature 210 627-628.
214. Mathieu, J. P. and Petit, A. (1957) Optical Rotatory Powers, I Steroids Pergamon Press, N. Y.
215. Mathieu, J. P. and Ourisson, G. (1958) Optical Rotatory Powers II Triterpenoids, Pergamon Press, N. Y.
216. Rimpler, H. (1978) Planta Medica 33 213-235.
217. Coombe, B. G., Cohen, D., and Paleg, L. G. (1967) Plant Physiol. 42 105-112, 113-119.
218. Goodwin, T. W. (1971) Biochem. J. 123 293-329.
219. West, C. A., Dudley, M. W., and Dueber, M. T. (1979) Recent Adv. Phytochem. 13 163-198.
220. Cordell, G.A. (1976) Chem. Revs. 76 425-460.
221. Charlwood, B. V. & Banthorpe, D.V. (1978) Prog. Phytochem. 5 65-125.
222. Goodwin, T.W. (1979) Ann. Rev. Plant Physiol. 30 369-397.
223. Hasson, E.P. & West, C.A. (1976) Plant Physiol. 58 473-478; 479-484.
224. Dueber, M. T., Adolf, W., & West, C.A. (1978) Plant Physiol. 62 598-603.
225. Ponlose, A.J. & Croteau, R. (1978) Arch. Biochim. Biophys. 191 400-411.
226. Croteau, R., Hooper, C.L., & Felton, M. (1978) Arch. Biochem. Biophys. 183 182-193.
227. Wickremasinghe, R.L. (1974) Phytochemistry 13 2057-2063.
228. Suga, T., Hirata, T., Shishilori, T., & Tange, K. (1974) Chem. Lett. 1974 189-192. (Chem. Abstr. 81 35547 (1974))
229. Poulter, C. D. & Rilling, H. C. (1978) Accts. Chem. Res. 11 307-313
230. Epstein, W.W. and Poulter, C. D. (1973) Phytochemistry 12 737-747.
231. Poulter, C.D., Muscio, O.J. & Goodfellow, R.J. (1974) Biochemistry 13 1530-1538.
232. Allen, K.G., Banthorpe, D.V., Charlwood, B.V., & Voller, C.M. (1977) Phytochemistry 16 79-83.
233. Granger, R., Passet, J. & Teulade-Arbousset, G. (1973) Compt. Rend. D 276 2839-2842
234. Whalley, W.B. (1962) Tetrahedron 18 43-54.
235. Croteau, R. and Karp, F. (1979) Arch. Biochem. Biophys. 198 512-522, 523-532.
236. Wuu, T.-Y. and Baisted, D.J. (1973) Phytochemistry 12 1291-1297.
237. Allen, K.G., Banthorpe, D.V., Charlwood, B.V., Ekundayo, O., and Mann, J. (1976) Phytochemistry 15 101-107.
238. Shine, W.E. & Loomis, W.D. (1974) Phytochemistry 13 2095-2101.
239. Croteau, R. & Karp, F. (1976) Biochem. Biophys. Res. Commun. 72 440-447.
240. Croteau, R. & Karp, F. (1976) Arch Biochem. Biophys. 176 734-736.
241. Inouye, H., Ueda, S., & Uesato, S. (1977) Phytochemistry 16 1669-1675.
242. Inouye, H., Ueda, S.-I., Uesato, S.-I., & Kobayashe, K. (1978) Chem. Pharm. Bull. 26 3384-3394.
243. Inouye, H. (1978) Planta Medica 33 194-216.
244. Pattenden, G. & Storer, R. (1973) Tetra. Lets. 3473-3476.

245. Gross, D., Berg, W., & Schütte, H.R. (1972) Biochem. Physiol. Pflanzen 163 576-585.
246. Chayet, L., Pont-Lezica, R., George-Nascimento, C., and Cori, O. (1973) Phytochemistry 12 95-101.
247. Milborrow, B.V. (1974) Phytochemistry 13 131-136.
248. Croteau, R. and Loomis, W.D. (1972) Phytochemistry 11 1055-1066.
249. Edwards, O.E., Douglas, J.L., and Mootoo, B., Can. J. Chem. 48 2517-2524 (1970).
250. Bearder, J.R. & Sponsel, V.M. (1977) Biochem. Soc. Trans. 5 569-582.
251. Frost, R.G. & West, C.A. (1977) Plant Physiol. 59 22-29
252. Ropers, H.-J., Graebe, J.E., Gaskin, P., & MacMillan, J. (1978) Biochem. Biophys. Res. Commun. 80 690-697
253. Durley, R.C., Sassa, T., & Pharis, R.P. (1979) Plant Physiol. 64 214-219.
254. Moore, T.C., Barlow, S.A., and Coolbaugh, R.C. (1972) Phytochemistry 11 3225-3233.
255. Stoddart, J. L. and Jones, R. L. (1977) Planta 136 261-269.
256. Yamane, H., Murofushi, N., Osada, H., & Takahashi, N. (1977) Phytochemistry 16 831-835.
257. Hanson, J.R. and White, A.F. (1968) Phytochemistry 7 595-597.
258. Adams, S.R. and Heinstein, P.F. (1973) Phytochemistry 12 2167-2172.
259. Wellburn, A.R., Stone, K.J. and Hemming, F.W. (1966) Biochem. J. 100 23c.
260. Bakker, H.J., Ghisalberti, E.L., and Jefferies, P.R. (1972) Phytochemistry 11 2221-2231.
261. Robinson, D.R. and West, C.A. (1970) Biochemistry 9 70-79, 80-89.
262. Beastall, G.H., Rees, H.H. & Goodwin, T.W. (1972) FEBS Letters 28 243-246.
263. Croteau, R. and Loomis, W.D., Phytochemistry 12 1957-1965 (1973).
264. Barton, D.H.R., Mellows, G. & Widdowson, D.A. (1971) J. Chem. Soc. (c) 110-116.
265. Elder, J.W., Benveniste, P., & Fontenau, P. (1977) Phytochemistry 16 490-492.
266. Reid, W.W., Phytochemistry 7 451-452 (1968).
267. Rowan, M.G. and Dean, P.G.G., Phytochemistry 11 3111-3118 (1972).
268. Arigoni, D. (1958) Experientia 14 153-155.
269. Ruzicka, L. (1953) Experientia 9 357-367.
270. Sliwowski, J.& Kasprzyk, Z. (1974) Phytochemistry 13 1441-1449.
271. Hegnauer, R. (1965) Lloydia 28 267-278.
272. Sliwowski, J. K. and Caspi, E. (1977) J. Am. Chem. Soc. 99 4479-4485.
273. Gibbons, G. F., Goad, L. J., Goodwin, T. W. and Nes, W. R. (1971) J. Biol. Chem. 246 3967-3976.
274. Zander, J. M. and Wigfield, D. C., J. Chem. Soc. (D) 1599-1600 (1970)
275. Goodwin, T. W. (1977) Biochem. Soc. Trans. 5 1252-1255.
276. Largeau, C. L., Goad, L. J., and Goodwin, T. W. (1977) Phytochemistry 16 1925-1930.
277. McKean, M. L. and Nes, W. R. (1977) Phytochemistry 16 683-686.
278. Devys, M., Alcaide, A., and Barbier, M. (1968) Bull. Soc. Chim. Biol. 50 1751-1757.
279. Bennett, R. D. and Heftmann, E. (1969) Steroids 14 403-407.
280. Bush, P. B. and Grunwald, C. (1974) Plant Physiol. 53 131-135.
281. Tschesche, R. and Hulpke, H. (1966) Z. Naturforsch. 21b 494-495.
282. Stohs, S. J., Kaul, B., and Staba, E. J. (1969) Phytochemistry 8 1679-1686.
283. Tschesche, R. and Piestert, G. (1975) Phytochemistry 14 435-438.
284. Tschesche, R. and Leinert, J. (1973) Phytochemistry 12 1619-1620.
285. Heftmann, E. and Weaver, M. L. (1974) Phytochem. 13 1801-1803.
286. Tomita, Y. and Uomori, A. (1974) Phytochemistry 13 729-733.
287. Joly, R. A., Bonner, J., Bennett, R. D., and Heftmann, E. (1969) Phytochemistry 8 1445-1447.
288. deSouza, N. J., Ghisalberti, E. L., Rees, H. H. and Goodwin, T. W. (1970) Phytochemistry 9 1247-1252.
289. Heftmann, E. (1974) Lipids 9 626-639.
290. Stohs, S. J. (1975) Phytochemistry 14 2419-2422.
291. Löffelhardt, W., Kopp, B., and Kubelka, W. (1978) Phytochemistry 17 1581-1584.
292. Kopp, B., Löffelhardt, W., and Kubelka, W. (1978) Z. Naturforsch. 33c 646-650.
293. Franz, G. (1971) Phytochemistry 10 3001-3003.
294. Tschesche, R., Goossens, B., and Töpfer, A. (1976) Phytochemistry 15 1387-1389.
295. Abramson, D., Knapp, F. F., Goad, L. J., and Goodwin, T. W. (1977) Phytochemistry 16 1935-1937.
296. Jadhav, S. J. and Salunkhe, D. K. (1973) J. Food Sci. 38 1099-1100.
297. Kaneko, K., Watanabe, M., Kawakoshi, Y., and Mitsuhashi, H. (1971) Tetra. Letters 4251-4254.
298. Wojciechowski, Z. A. (1975) Phytochemistry 14 1749-1753.
299. Baisted, D. J. (1978) Phytochemistry 17 435-438.
300. Garcia, R. E. and Mudd, J. B. (1978) Plant Physiol. 62 348-353.
301. Schabort, J. C. and Teijema, H. L. (1968) Phytochemistry 7 2107-2110
302. Gregonis, D. E. and Rilling, H. C. (1974) Biochemistry 13 1538-1542.
303. Barnes, F. J., Qureshi, A. A., Semmler, E. J., and Porter, J. W. (1973) J. Biol. Chem. 248 2768-2773.
304. Qureshi, A. A., Andrewes, A. G., Qureshi, N., and Porter, J. W.(1974) Arch. Biochem. Biophys. 162 93-107.
305. Yamamoto, H. Y. and Chichester, C. O. (1965) Biochem. Biophys. Acta 109 303-305.
306. Valadon, L. R. G. and Mummery, R. S. (1977) Z. Pflanzenphysiol 82 407-416.
307. Taylor, H. F. and Burden, R. S. (1970) Phytochemistry 9 2217-2223.
308. Graebe, J. E. (1967) Science 157 73-75.
309. Knights, B. A. (1973) Chem. Brit. 9 106-111.
310. Wojciechowski, Z. A. (1974) Phytochemistry 13 2091-2094.
311. Atallah, A. M. and Nicholas, H. J. (1974) Lipids 9 613-622.
312. Mellon, J. E. and West, C. A. (1979) Plant Physiol. 64 406-410.

Chapter 9
FLAVONOIDS AND
RELATED COMPOUNDS

The flavonoid group may be described as a series of C_6 - C_3 - C_6 compounds. That is, their carbon skeleton consists of two C_6 groups (substituted benzene rings) connected by a three-carbon aliphatic chain.

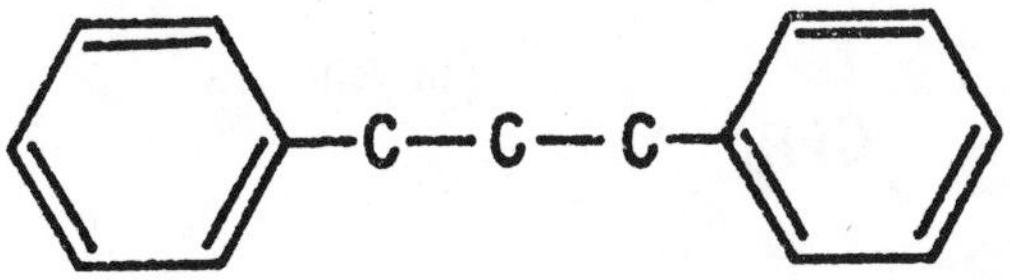

flavonoid skeleton

The different classes within the group are distinguished by additional oxygen-heterocyclic rings and by hydroxyl groups distributed in different patterns. Flavonoids frequently occur as glycosides. The largest group of flavonoids is characterized by containing a pyran ring linking the three-carbon chain with one of the benzene rings. The numbering system for these flavonoid derivatives is given below:

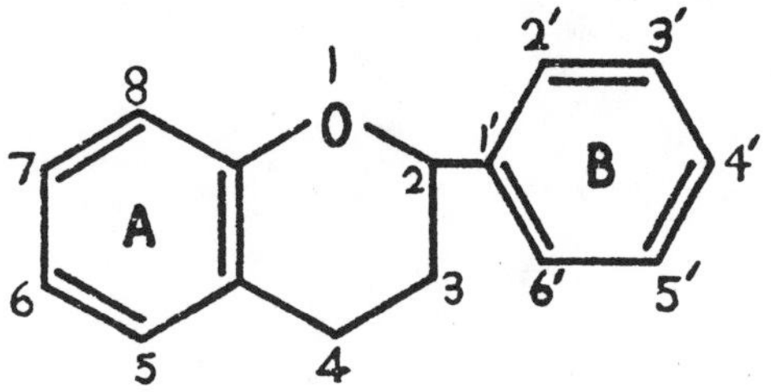

Among the typical flavonoids having the above skeleton the various types are distinguished by the oxidation state of the C_3 chain. Going from most reduced to most oxidized, the structures and their names are as follows (only the key portion of the molecule is shown):

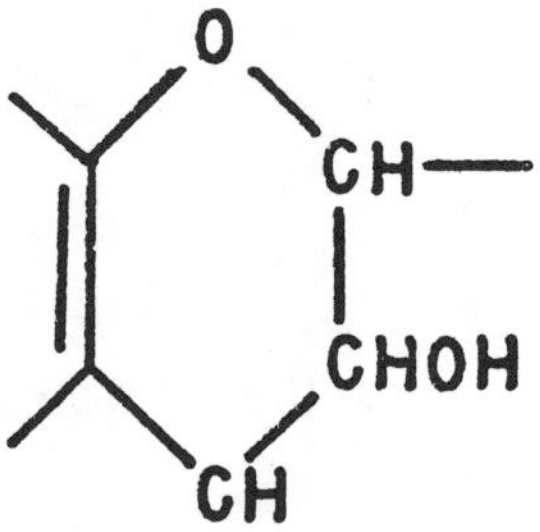

catechins

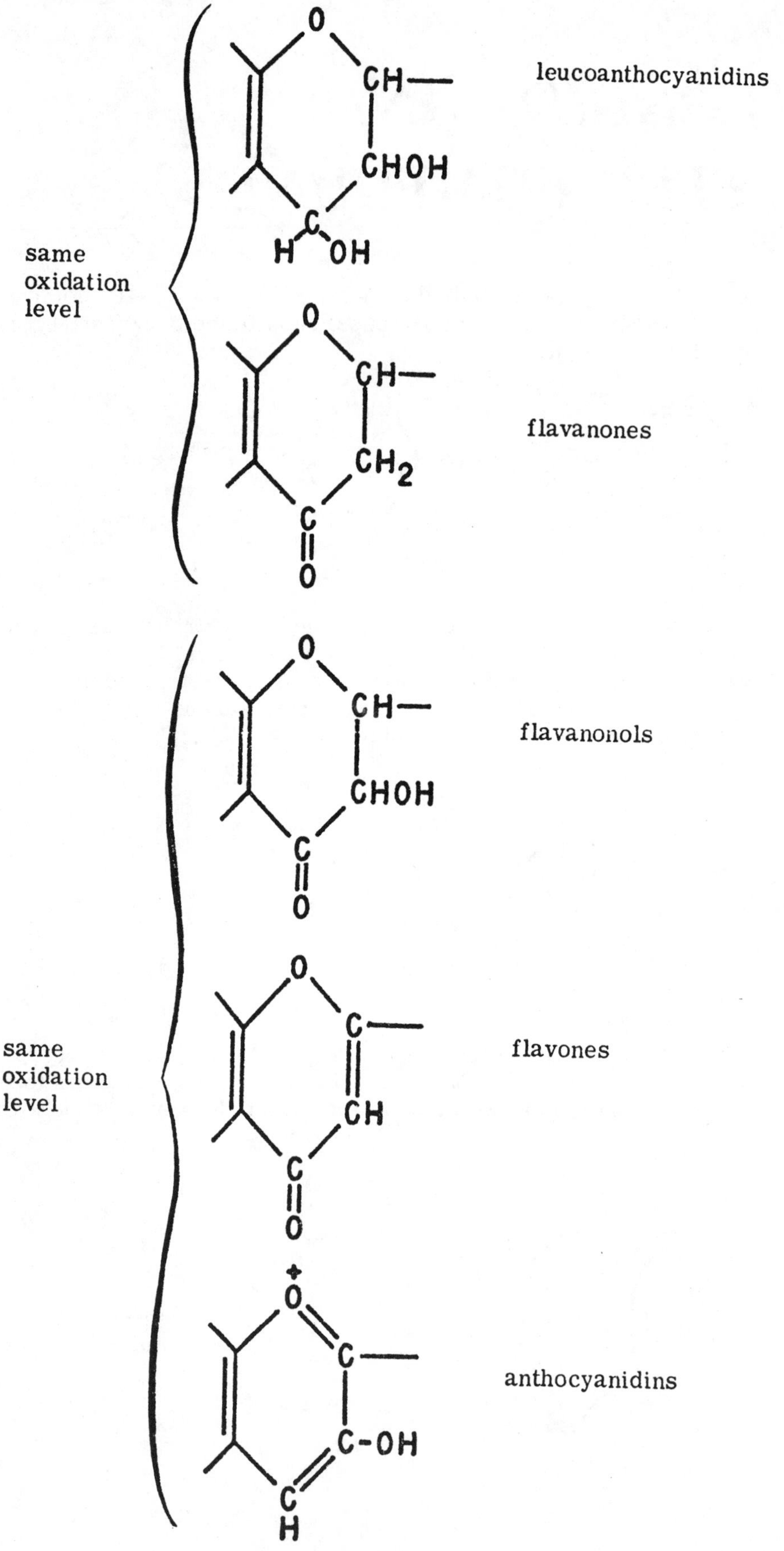

same
oxidation
level

leucoanthocyanidins

flavanones

same
oxidation
level

flavanonols

flavones

anthocyanidins

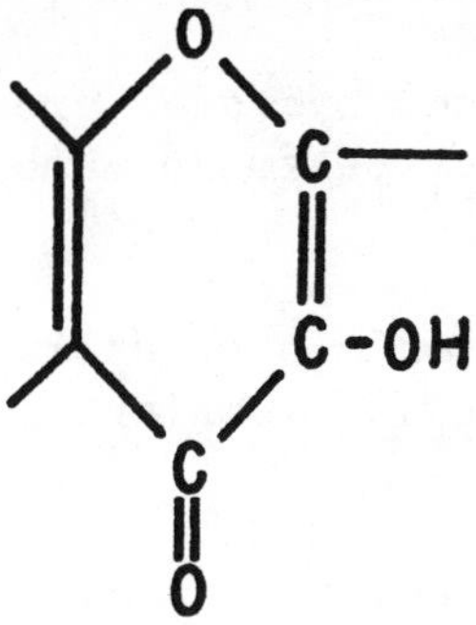

flavonols

Other variations in the $C_6 - C_3 - C_6$ pattern also occur and are denoted as follows:

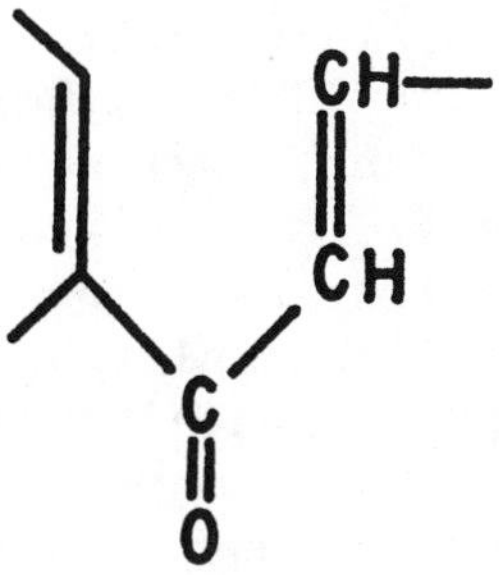

chalcones

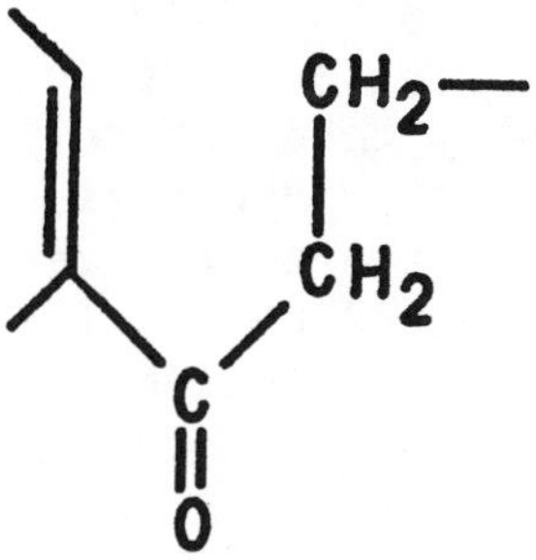

dihydrochalcones

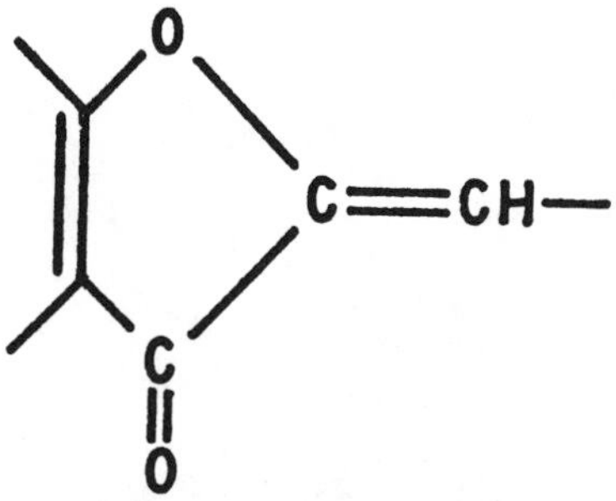

aurones

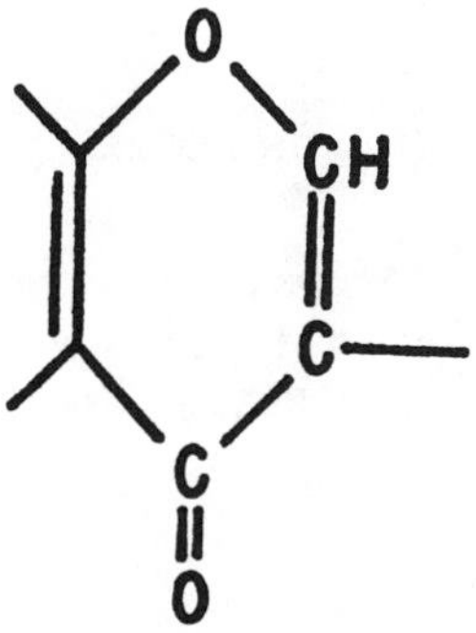

isoflavones

although not indicated by these partial formulas, hydroxyl groups are normally present on the aromatic rings, or they may be found combined as methoxyl groups or glycosides.

In addition to the flavonoids other compounds such as xanthones, condensed tannins, etc. seem to fit into a natural grouping; and they will also be discussed in this chapter.

The flavonoids include many of the most common pigments and occur throughout the entire plant kingdom from the fungi to the angiosperms. About 150 aglycones are known. In higher plants they are found both in vegetative parts and in flowers. As flower pigments they have a well-known role in attracting pollinating birds and insects. Some colorless, but UV absorbing ones are probably also important in orienting insects (1). Many other possible roles for flavonoids are surveyed by Harborne (2). Some possibilities include growth regulation (3, 4), fungicidal action (5, 6) and repellancy or attractiveness to feeding insects (7, 8). Flavonoids can also be powerful inhibitors of oxidative phosphorylation and ATPase (9, 10). For example, 5, 7-dihydroxyisoflavone is as effective as dinitrophenol (11). Quercetin and several other flavonoids are powerful inhibitors of aldose reductases (12). Some flavonoids are abnormal constituents produced only in response to an injury (13, 14). Such protective compounds are known as "phytoalexins" (15). Leucoanthocyanins may also inhibit fungal growth, and their absence as a result of boron deficiency is an interesting correlation (16). Some flavonoids may have significant effects on higher animals. There are persistent reports of an antiscorbutic effect not entirely attributable to ascorbic acid but perhaps partially to a catechin derivative present in citrus fruits (17). Another view is that the antiscorbutic role of flavonoids is to protect ascorbic acid against oxidation (18). A possibly deleterious role of flavonoids is suggested by the finding that quercetin is mutagenic by the Ames Test (19). It is intriguing to find that certain isoflavones act as estrogens for mammals (20), and their structures may be written so as to bear a steric resemblance to those of the steroid hormones, e.g.:

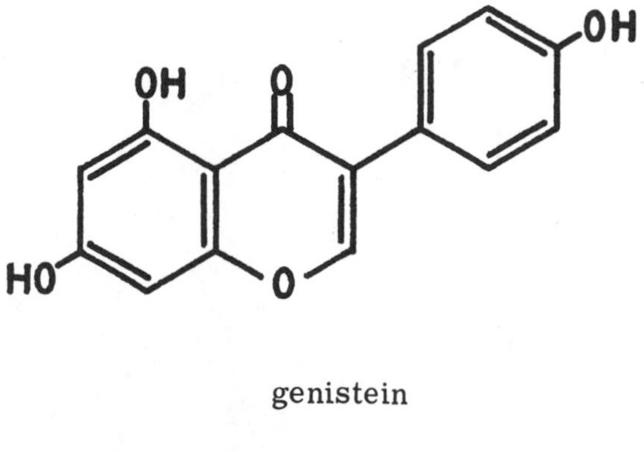

genistein

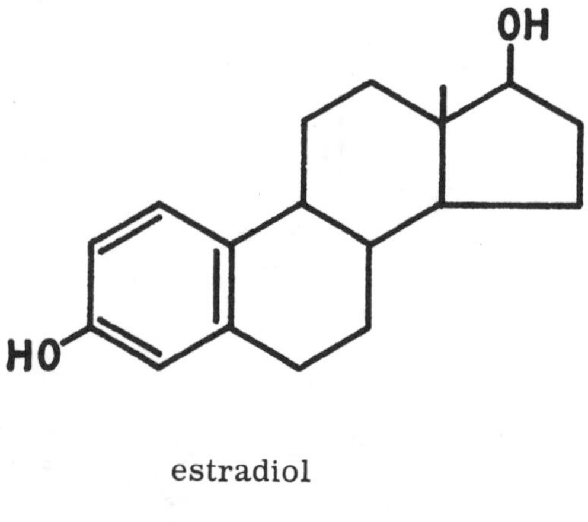

estradiol

Sandalwood contains similar estrogenic isoflavone derivatives, pterocarpin and homopterocarpin (21). Some isoflavones show activity in decreasing serum cholesterol levels (22).

CATECHINS AND PROANTHOCYANIDINS

The catechins and **proanthocyanidins** are two groups which show many similarities. They are all colorless compounds, existing throughout the plant kingdom but especially in the higher woody plants. Proanthocyanidins have been found in ferns and two species of *Equisetum* They are evidently absent from Psilophytes, *Lycopodium* spp. and mosses (23-25). Only three types of catechin are known differing in the number of hydroxyl groups in ring B. They have two asymmetric carbons (starred) and therefore 4 possible isomers:

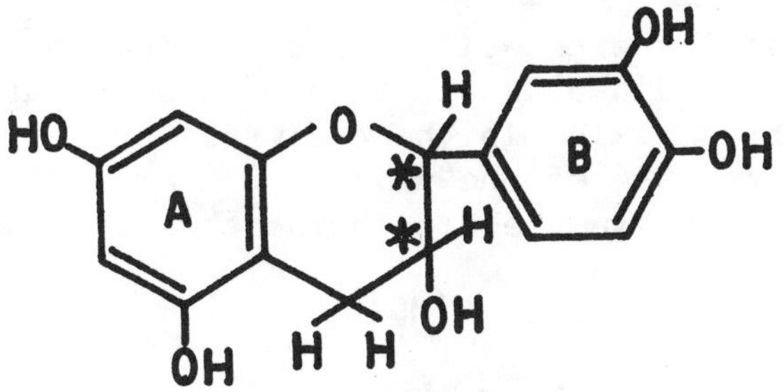

catechin 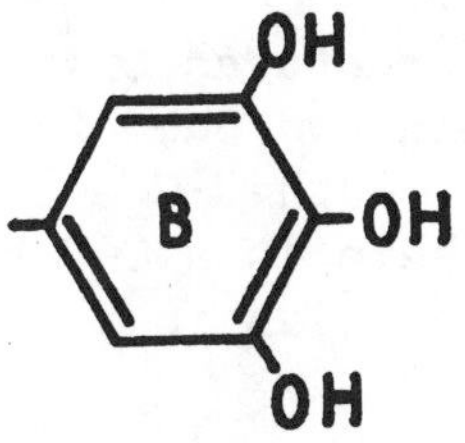   gallocatechin 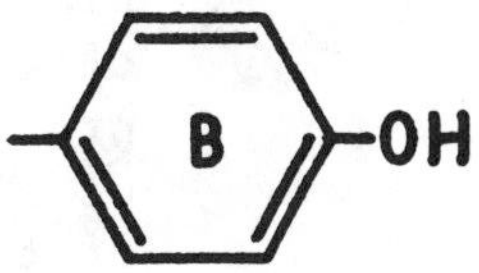   afzelechin

The (+) and (-) catechins have the number 2 and 3 hydrogens <u>trans</u>, whereas they are <u>cis</u> in the epicatechins. Epimerization involves inversion of the 2-aryl group rather than the 3-hydroxy group. One epicatechin glucoside has been found (26), and some catechins may occur as esters of gallic acid.

The proanthocyanidins are subdivided into three classes (27, 28):

1. The classical leucoanthocyanidins are monomeric flavan-3, 4-diols or slight variants of this structure. They rarely exist as gly-cosides but a few are known (29). Some structures follow:

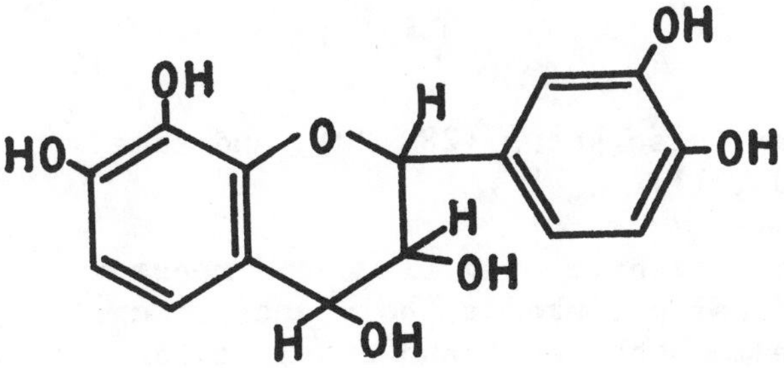

melacacidin
(Australian blackwood)

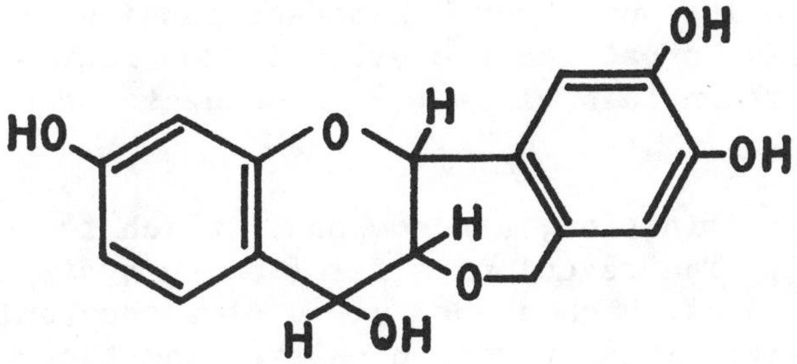

peltogynol
(*Peltogyne porphyrocardia*)

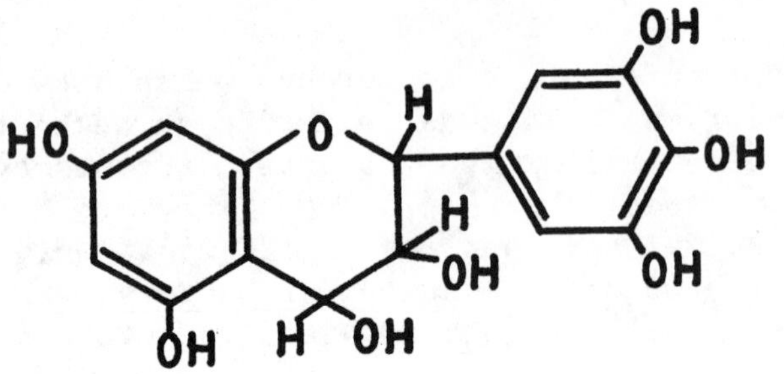

(from *Cleistanthus collinus*)

2. Dimeric structures that on heating with acid give one molecule
    of catechin and one of anthocyanidin plus other complex secondary
    products. Both C-C and C-O bonds exist in these dimers; but
    usually there is a C-C bond from C-4 of one unit to C-6 or C-8
    of the other, as in the following example from horse chestnut (30):

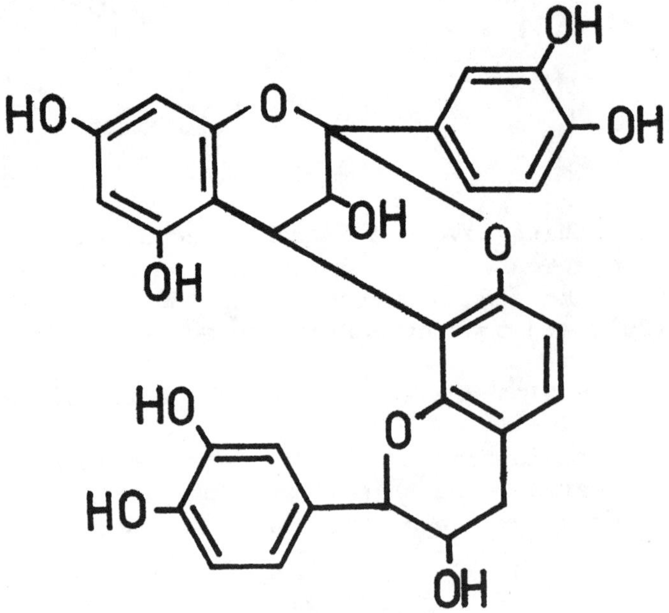

Trimers of this type are also known (28, 30), and some with
esterified gallic acid (31).

3. Polymers, of which some may have only flavonoid monomers; but
    others may be glycosidically linked to polysaccharides. The
    polymers are insoluble in both water and ethyl acetate. The sub-
    stances called "catechol tannins" or "condensed tannins" may be
    identical to this class, or at least overlap it considerably.
    Tannins of grapes   are in this class (32). Condensed tannins are
    reviewed by Roux (33).

The proanthocyanidins, by definition, are compounds which form anthocyanidins on heating with acid. The reaction is far from this simple though.
Many complex products are formed of which a good yield of anthocyanidin
might be 25% (34). An important initial reaction on treating these compounds with acid is condensation between C-2 and C-4 of one unit and C-6 or
C-8 of another (35-37). In this way monomers can form dimers of the type:

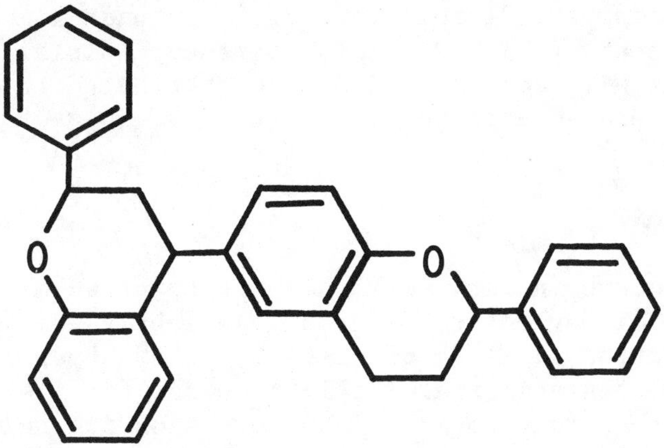

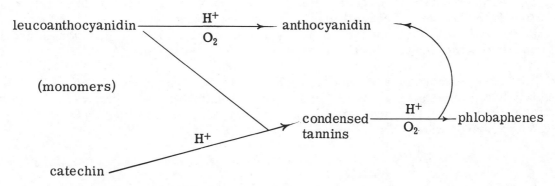

Further treatment with cold acid gives polymers which resemble the naturally occurring condensed tannins (38). Stronger treatment (hot acid, oxygen)
carries the reaction further with formation of some anthocyanidin. The
anthocyanidin-producing reaction can be written for the flavan-3, 4-diols as:

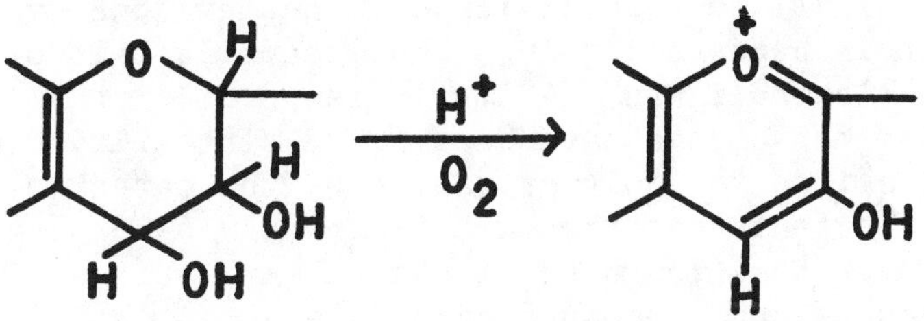

It is oxidative, involving loss of a hydrogen atom as well as dehydration
(39). Under these stronger conditions the dimeric proanthocyanidins give
cyanidin, epicatechin, and other products. Oxidation of the initial colorless polymers gives rise to colored polymers known as "phlobaphenes" or
"tannin reds" whose structures are largely unknown. Catechins form similar,
brown polymers on heating with acid. A summary of these complex reactions
is as follows:

The ill-defined catechutannic acid is a dehydration product of either
catechin or a catechin polymer, probably as follows:

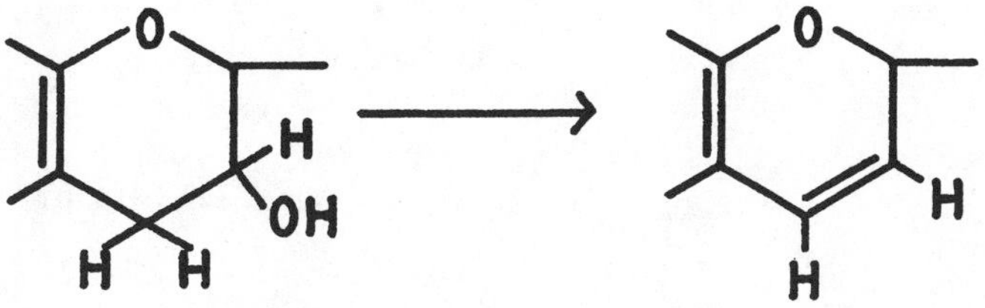

In addition to being artificial products, compounds like the phlobaphenes may exist in nature (40). Red colors present initially in plants
or produced on heating with acid should not be attributed to anthocyanidins
until phlobaphenes have been excluded.

FLAVANONES AND FLAVANONOLS

These compounds occur in very small amounts compared with the other
flavonoids. They are either colorless or only slightly yellow. Because
of their low concentration and lack of color they have been largely neglect-
ed. Glycosides of the flavanones are well-known as, for instance, hesperidin
and naringin from citrus fruit peels. (The corresponding aglycones are
hesperetin and naringenin.) The flavanonols are probably the least known
of the flavonoids, and it is not known whether they normally exist as glycosides. Pacheco (41) has made the most extensive study of these compounds,
but his analytical procedure would have hydrolyzed any glycosidic bonds
if they were present. Only about 8 flavanonols have been isolated. Unlike
the leucoanthocyanins, they are stable to hot hydrochloric acid but are
decomposed by warm alkali to form chalcones. A flavanone type of unit
is probably present in bagasse lignin. The monomeric unit of this lignin
has been called a "flavonolignan" (42). It is peculiar that no condensed
tannins based on the flavanones have been found since flavanones appear to
be structurally as suited for polymerization as the catechins or leucoanthocyanidins.   The fact that they are frequently 5- or 7-glycosides may
hinder condensation at position 6 to give a polymer such as is formed from
the aglyconic catechins and leucoanthocyanidins.

FLAVONES, FLAVONOLS, ISOFLAVONES

The flavones and flavonols are probably the most widely distributed of
all the yellow plant pigments, although the deeper yellow colors of plants
are normally due to carotenoids. Some of the flavones and flavonols are
still economically important, and luteolin was probably the first dye to
be used in Europe. Quercetin is one of the commonest phenolic compounds of
vascular plants, followed closely by kaempferol (43). Isoflavones are much
less important (44). Still rarer are homo-isoflavones (45).

These compounds are usually soluble in hot water and alcohol although
a few highly methylated forms are insoluble in water. They vary in hydroxylation from flavone itself, which occurs as dust on primrose (*Primula* spp.)
flowers, to nobiletin of tangerines (*Citrus nobilis*).

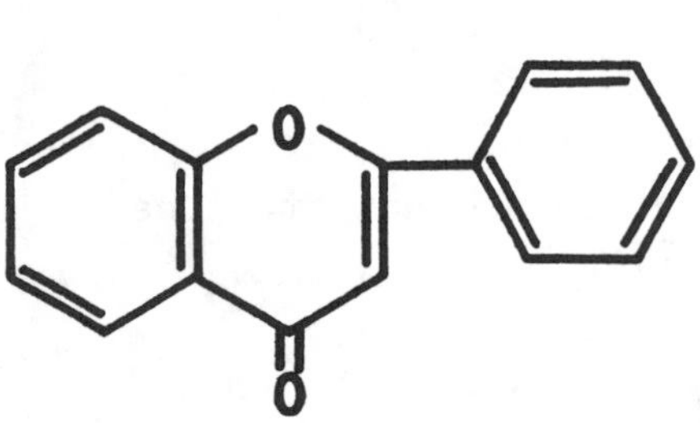

flavone 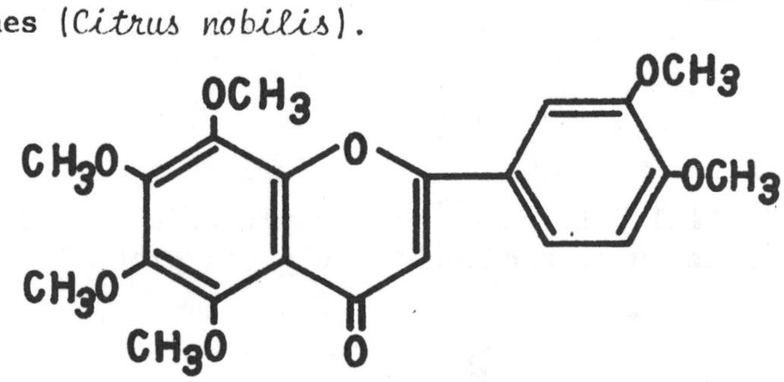   nobiletin

TABLE 9-1. SOME FLAVANONES AND FLAVANONOLS, STRUCTURES AND OCCURRENCE

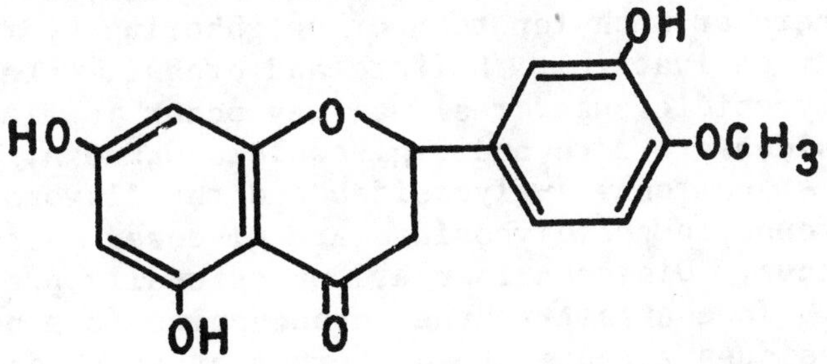

hesperetin (citrus fruits)

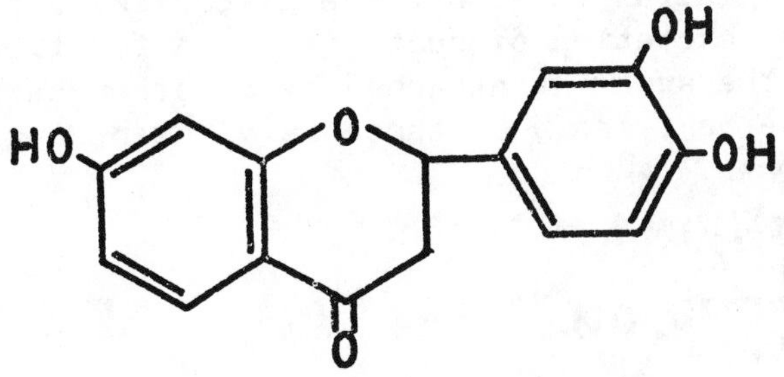

butin (*Butea frondosa*)

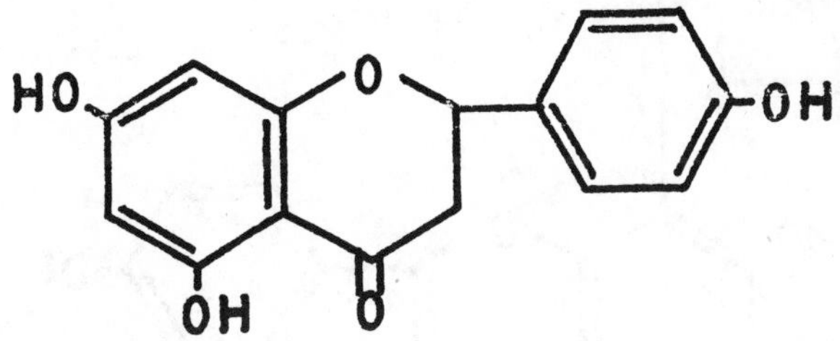

naringenin (citrus fruits)

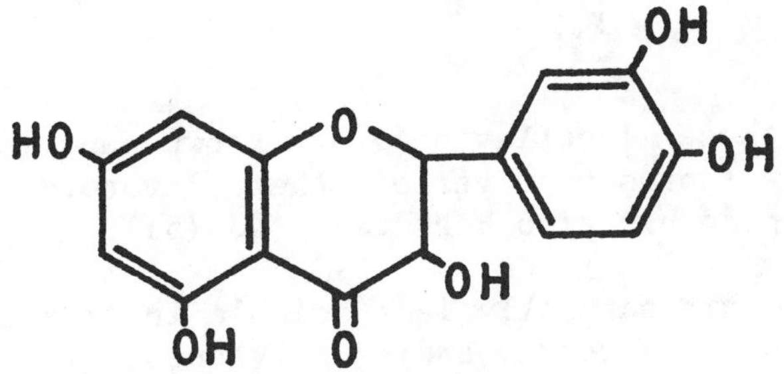

taxifolin (*Pseudotsuga taxifolia*)

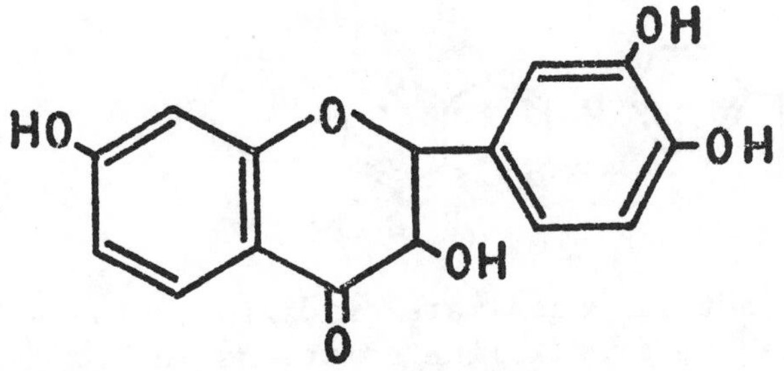

fustin (*Quebracho colorado*)

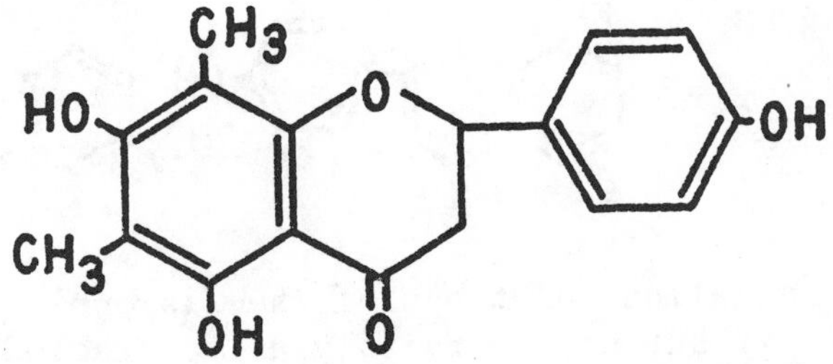

farrerol (*Rhododendron*)

However, the most common derivatives have 5 and/or 7 hydroxylation in ring A and 4' hydroxylation in ring B. Ring B is hydroxylated in positions 3' and 5' only if the 4' position is hydroxylated too. Rarely 2' hydroxylation is found. Additional variation is introduced by methylation of hydroxyl groups to form ethers or methylenation of neighboring hydroxyl groups to form methylenedioxy derivatives. Sulfate and organic esters have also been found (46-48). Glycosidic sugar residues may occur in almost any position, although 4'-glycosides are rare and 6-glycosides unknown. The flavones and isoflavones are most commonly 7-glycosides and the flavonols, 3-glycosides. The usual sugars found in the glycosides are glucose, galactose, and rhamnose although others occur. Disaccharides are occasionally present in the so-called "biosides". In contrast to the anthocyanins (see below) there are never two sugar residues attached to different hydroxyl groups. It has been suggested as a general rule that the glycosides are found within cells and the aglycones as excretion products (49). A few flavone-sugar derivatives are known in which the sugar is attached by a carbon-carbon bond rather than as a glycoside. The best known of these is vitexin, a glucose derivative of apigenin:

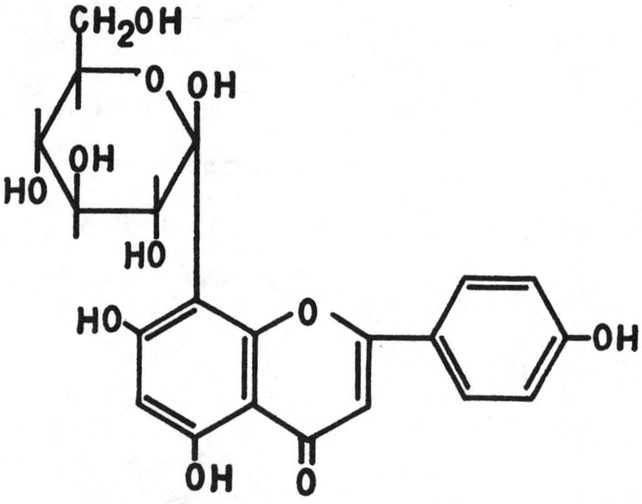

Several others of these glycoflavonols are known, and most are flavones; but there are a few representatives of other flavonoid classes (50). A flavone-polysaccharide has also been reported (51).

The glycosides are naturally less soluble in organic solvents and more soluble in water than the corresponding aglycones. They are also less colored than the aglycones, some being colorless when in neutral or acidic solution. However, they become bright yellow or orange in alkali and may be detected by exposing colorless plant parts to ammonia. This appearance of color is due to salt formation and assumption of a quinoid structure in ring B:

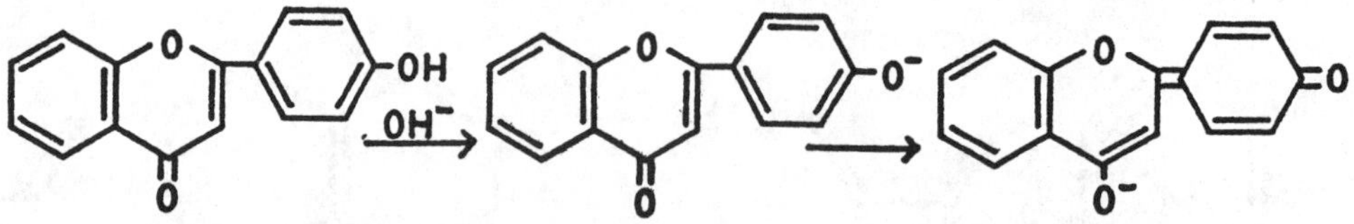

Alkaline solutions of the flavonols (but not flavones) are oxidized in the air but not so rapidly as to preclude the use of alkaline solutions in their preparation. Table 9-2 summarizes the hydroxylation patterns of some well-known flavones, flavonols, and isoflavones. Structures of a few other derivatives are given in Table 9-3 to illustrate some varieties of methylation and glycosidation which are found. Several flavone and flavonol dimers have been isolated especially from Gymnosperms but also from other plants (52-54).

TABLE 9-2. HYDROXYLATION PATTERNS OF SOME FLAVONOIDS

Compounds

Phenolic Hydroxyl Positions	Flavones	Flavonols	Iso-flavones
5, 7	chrysin	galangin	----
5, 7, 4'	apigenin	kaempferol	genistein
5, 7, 3', 4'	luteolin	quercetin	orobol
5, 7, 3', 4', 5'	tricetin	myricetin	----
7, 3', 4'	----	fisetin	----
5, 7, 2', 4'	lotoflavin	morin	----
5, 7, 8, 3', 4'	----	gossypetin	----
7, 4'	----	----	daidzein

ANTHOCYANINS

The anthocyanins are the common red to blue pigments of flower petals, making up as much as 30% of the dry weight in some flowers. They occur also in other parts of higher plants and throughout the plant kingdom except in the fungi. Unlike the other classes of flavonoids, they seem always to occur as glycosides except for traces of the aglycones, anthocyanidins. Hydrolysis may occur during autolysis of plant tissues or during isolation of the pigments so that anthocyanidins are found as artifacts. At the normal pH of vacuoles where they occur the anthocyanins exist as cations. They were originally thought to be oxonium compounds with the positive charge residing on the heterocyclic oxygen. It is probably more accurate to consider the molecule as a whole as possessing a non-localized charge. As the solution becomes more basic, a purple color-base first appears and then a blue colored salt form:

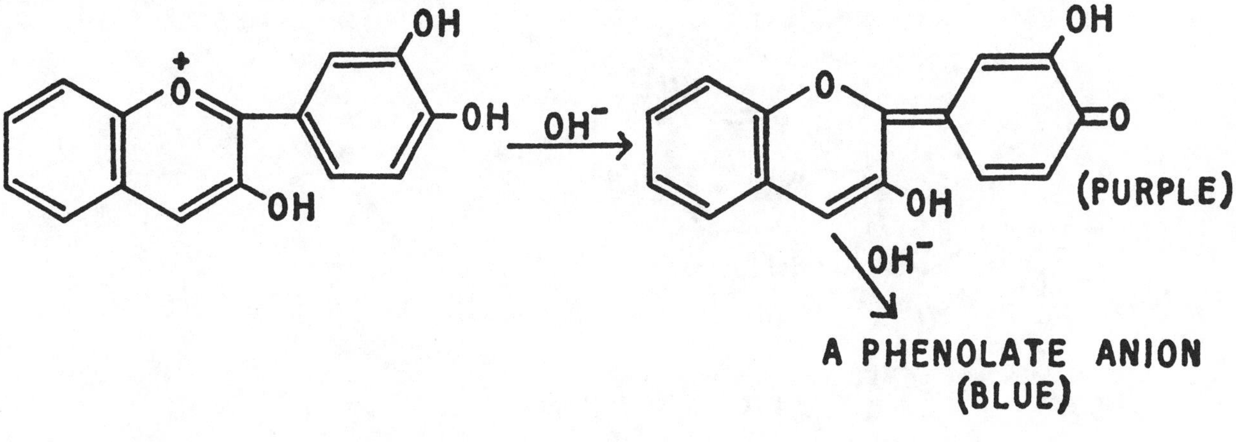

TABLE 9-3. SOME FLAVONES, FLAVONOLS, AND ISO-FLAVONES

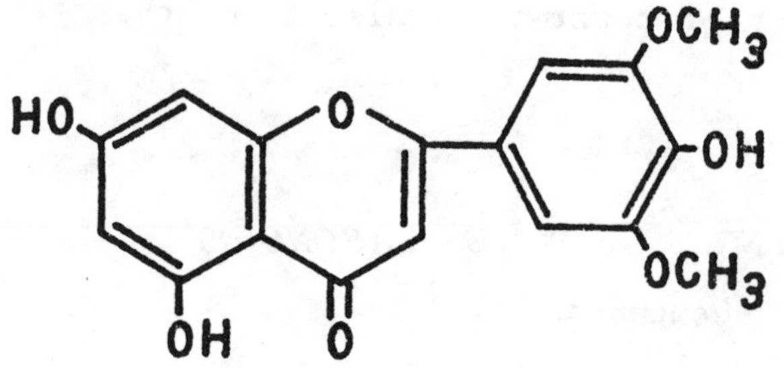

tricin (Khapli wheat)

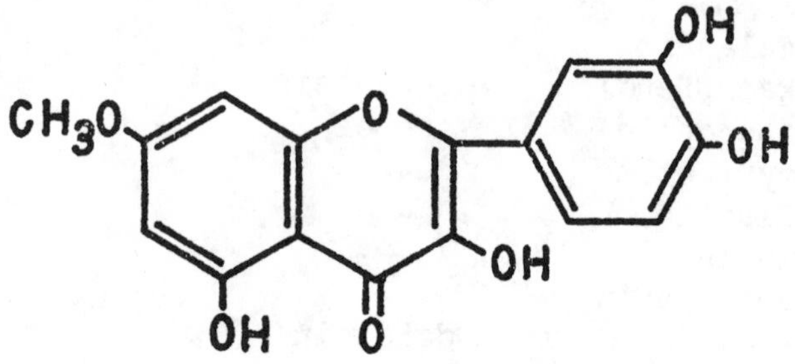

rhamnetin (*Rhamnus* spp.)

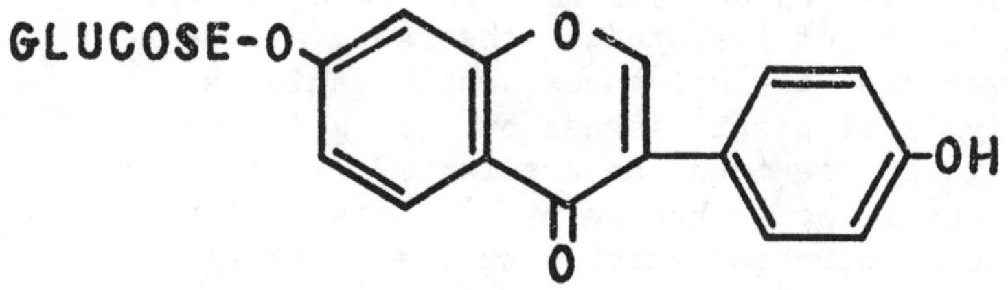

daidzin (Soy beans)

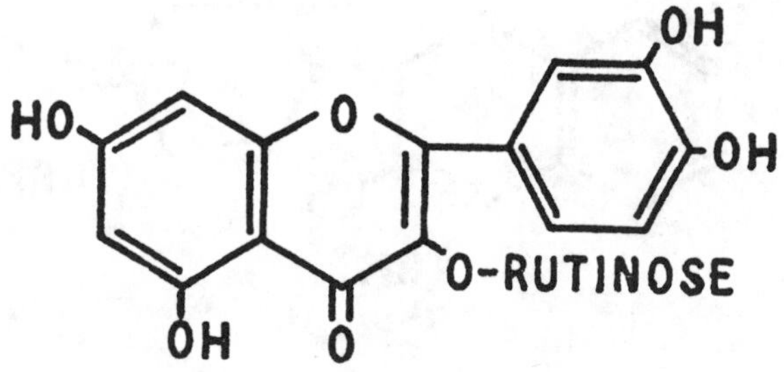

rutin (buckwheat)

Table 9-3. Continued

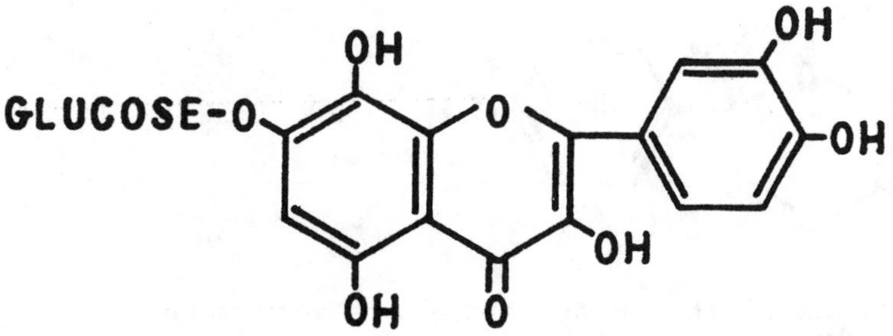

gossypitrin (cotton)

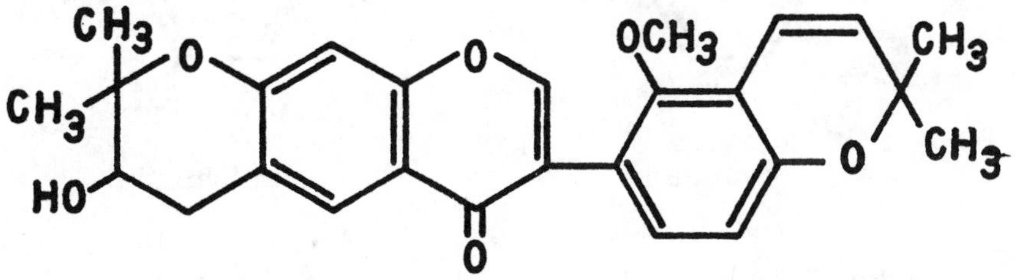

mundulone *(Mundulea sericea)*

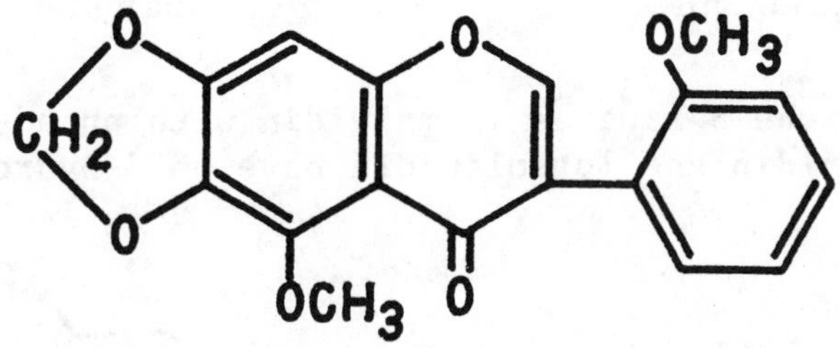

tlatancuayin *(Iresine celosioides)*

In the quinoid form they are rapidly oxidized by air and destroyed. Therefore, they are most safely prepared in slightly acidic solution. Since
they are both glycosides and salts, the anthocyanins are the most water-
woluble of all the flavonoids. On standing or warming in neutral aqueous
solution a colorless isomer ("pseudobase") is formed:

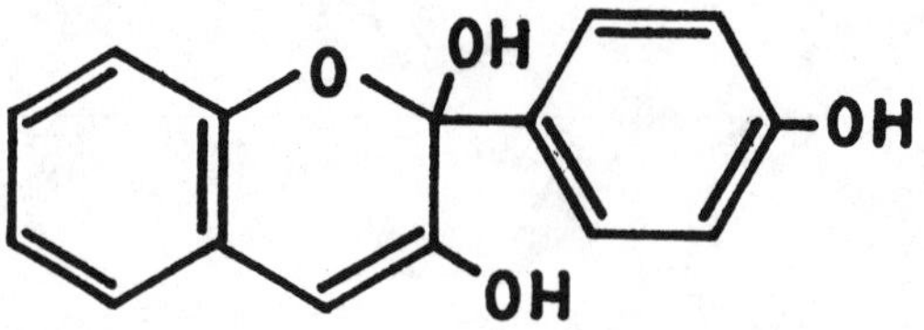

The hydroxylation patterns of the anthocyanins are very much like
those of the flavones. The three basic types of anthocyanins, like the
catechins, depend on the hydroxylation of ring B. All of them have 5, 7-
hydroxyl (or methoxyl) on ring A.

pelargonidin 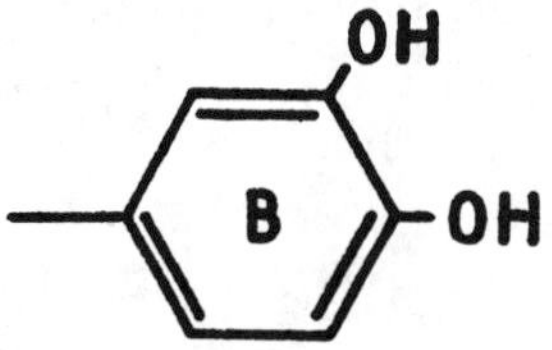   cyanidin 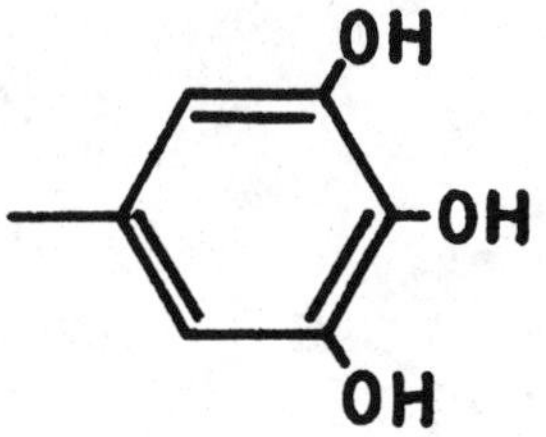   delphinidin

Additional variation is introduced by methylation, giving the structures:

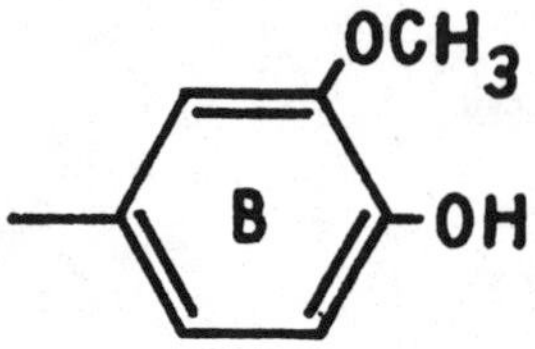

peonidin 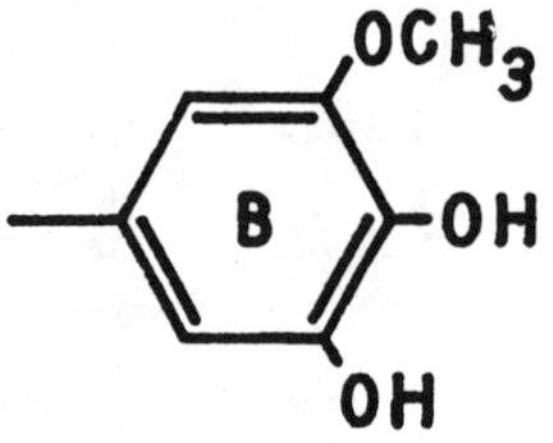   petunidin 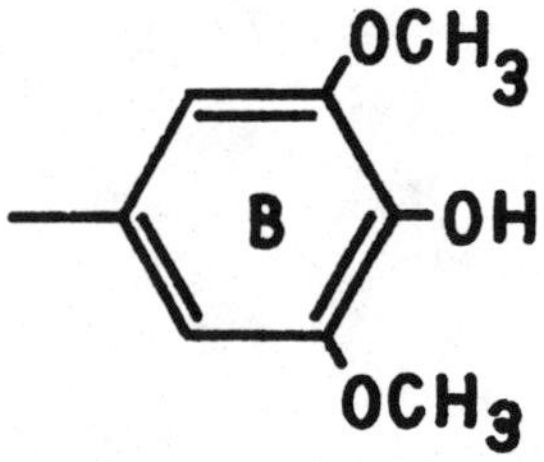   malvidin

Hirsutidin, as mentioned above, has the B ring as in malvidin with an additional 7-methoxyl group. Apigeninidin and luteolinidin have no 3-hydroxyl
group:

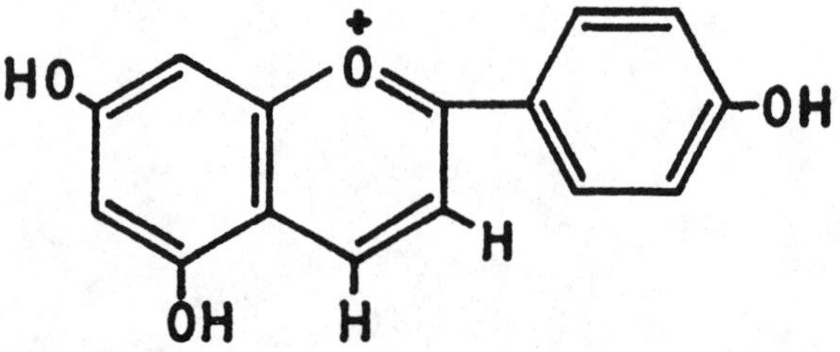

apigeninidin 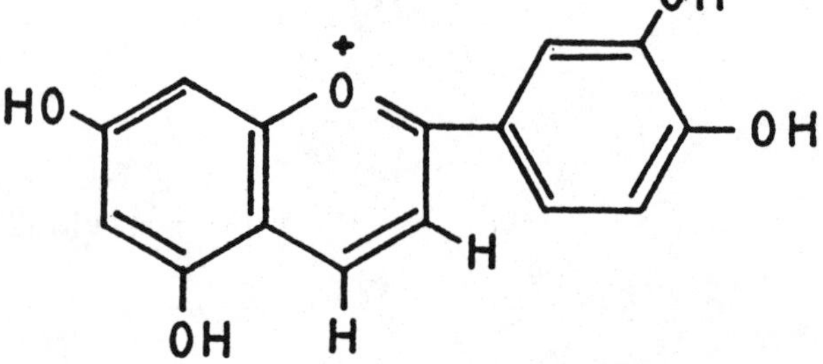   luteolinidin

Methylation is generally restricted to the 3' and 5' hydroxyl groups. Glycosylation is also more restricted in the anthocyanins than in other flavonoids. If only one sugar is attached, it is normally at C-3 (or at C-5 for those compounds lacking oxygen at C-3). If two hydroxyls are glycosylated (which never happens in the flavones), they are almost always at the 3 and 5 positions. These 3, 5-diglycosides are the most common anthocyanins. 3, 7- and 7-glycosides do exist but are rare (55). Even rarer examples are known with sugars at 3' or 4' (56). The sugars which combine seem to be the same ones used in the flavone glycosides. Sometimes acids are present esterifying hydroxyl groups of the sugar.

Some general rules can be given regarding the dependence of color on methylation and glycosylation. Methylation increases the redness, while increase in free hydroxyl groups or addition of a 5-glycosidic group increases the blueness (i.e., a bathochromic shift in absorption maximum and increased intensity). However, the dependency of color on pH and the presence of copigments and metal cations make these rules of little value unless one is dealing with a pure pigment (57, 58).

Table 9-4 lists some well-known anthocyanins with their particular glycosylation and sources. Many, of course, are found in more than one plant. The anthocyanins of ferns and mosses are characteristically glucosides of apigenidin and luteolinidin (2, 59), as their flavones are apigenin and luteolin (60).

TABLE 9-4. SOME WELL-KNOWN ANTHOCYANINS

Anthocyanin	Aglycone	Glycoside	Source
pelargonin	pelargonidin	3, 5-diglucoside	dahlia, pelargonium
cyanin	cyanidin	3, 5-diglucoside	red rose
idaein	cyanidin	3-galactoside	cranberries
violanin	delphinidin	3-rhamnoglucoside	violet
peonin	peonidin	3, 5-diglucoside	red peony
oenin	malvidin	3-glucoside	blue grapes
hirsutin	hirsutidin	3, 5-glucoside	*Primula hirsuta*
gesnerin	apigeninidin	5-glucoside	*Gesneria* spp.

CHALCONES AND DIHYDROCHALCONES

The numbering convention for these compounds differs from that of the flavonoids having a pyran ring:

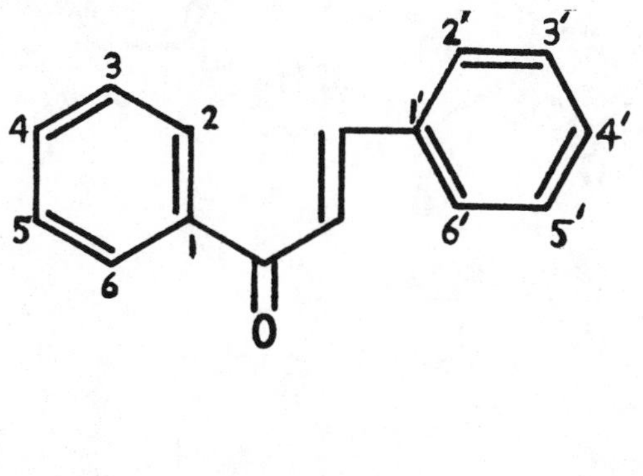

Only a few natural representatives are known, so that far-reaching generalizations about their structure are premature. However, hydroxylation
patterns generally agree with those of the other flavonoids; a hydroxyl
group is always present in position-2, corresponding to the hetero oxygen
atom of the flavanones, etc. The conversion of chalcones to flavanones in
fact occurs readily in acid solution and the reverse reaction in base. This
interconversion is shown for the chalcone butein and the flavanone butin:

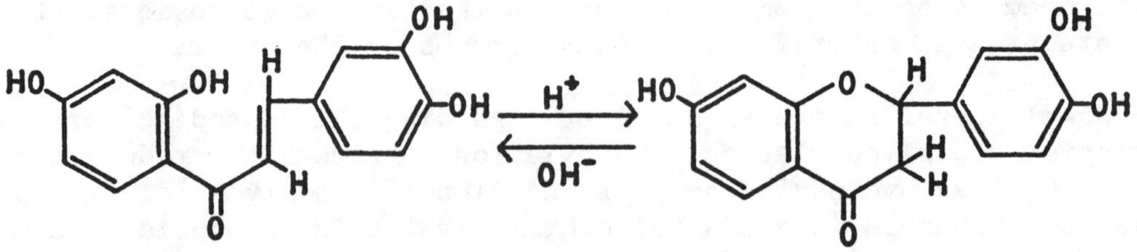

butein   butin

The reaction is easily observable since the chalcones are much more highly
colored than the flavanones, especially in basic solution where they are
orange-red. Because of this reaction acidic hydrolysis of chalcone glycosides yields a flavanone aglycone as an artifact rather than the chalcone.
This is shown for carthamin, a glycosidic pigment of the safflower.

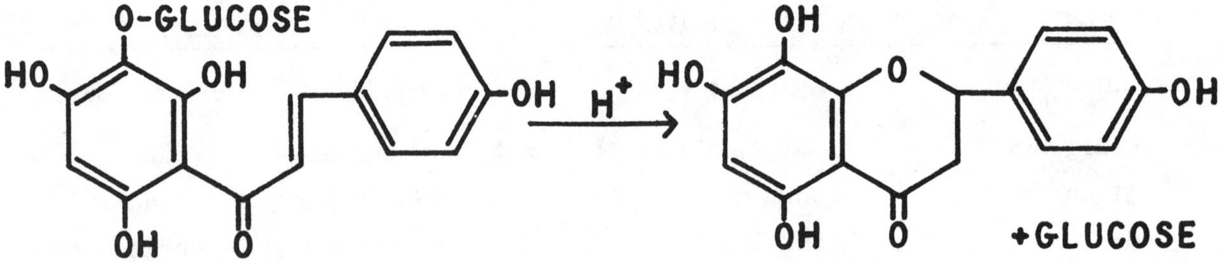

carthamin   carthamidin

Isocarthamidin is also formed by a ring closure involving the 6-hydroxy group.

     One of the most interesting of these rather rare compounds is phlorizin,
a glucoside of the dihydro-chalcone, phloretin, which causes glycosuria in
animals. Phlorizin is also reported to have growth regulatory effects on
apple seedlings and cultures (3, 61). It is limited in its natural occurrence
to the genus *Malus*, but other dihydrochalcones are found in a variety of
plants (62).

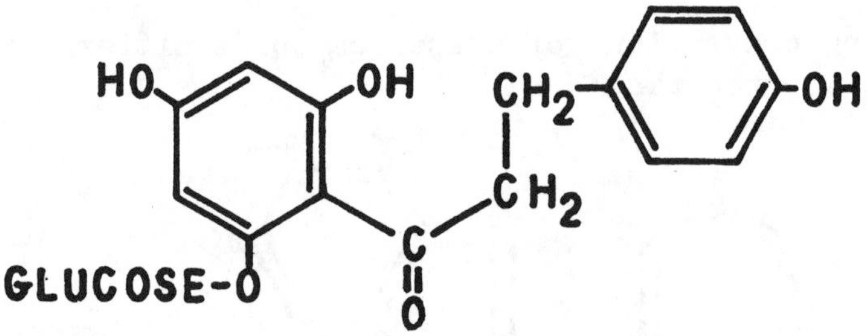

phlorizin

Structures of some other chalcones with their sources are as follows:

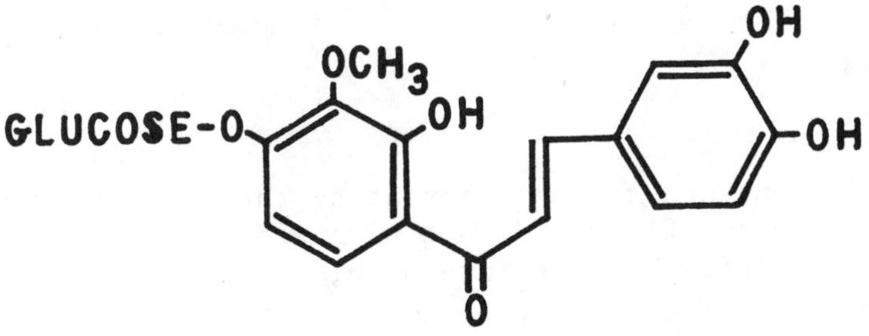

lanceolin
(*Coreopsis* spp.)

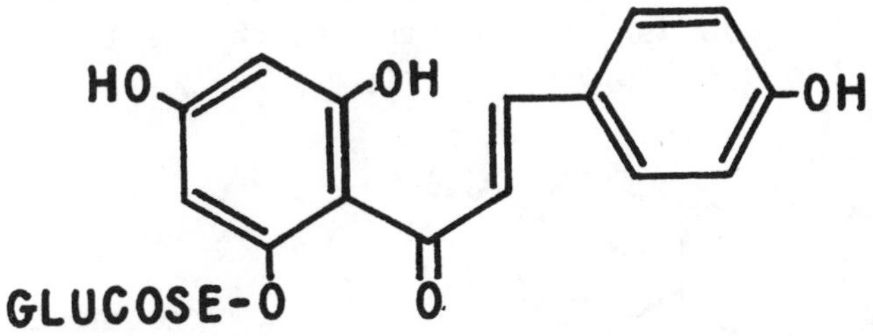

salipurposide
(*Salix purpurea*)

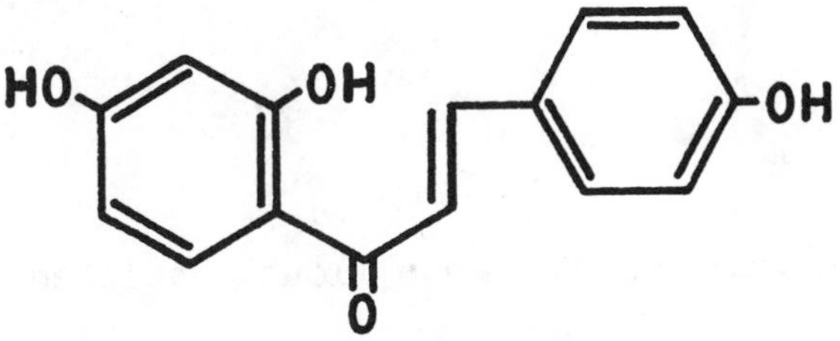

dahlia chalcone
(*Dahlia* spp.)

A rare example of an isodihydrochalcone is angolensin of sandalwood (*Pterocarpus angolensis*):

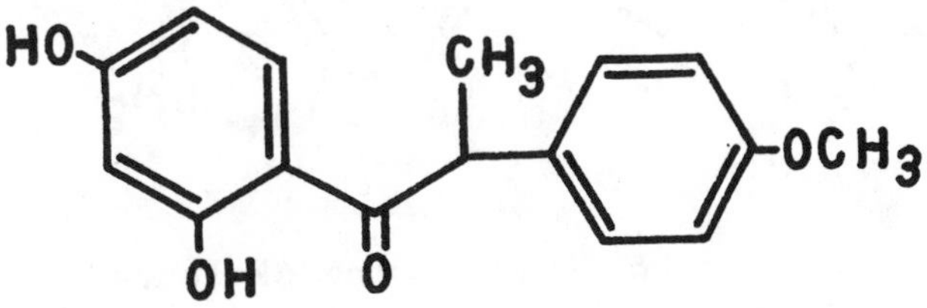

AURONES

The aurone or benzalcoumaranone ring system is numbered in the following way:

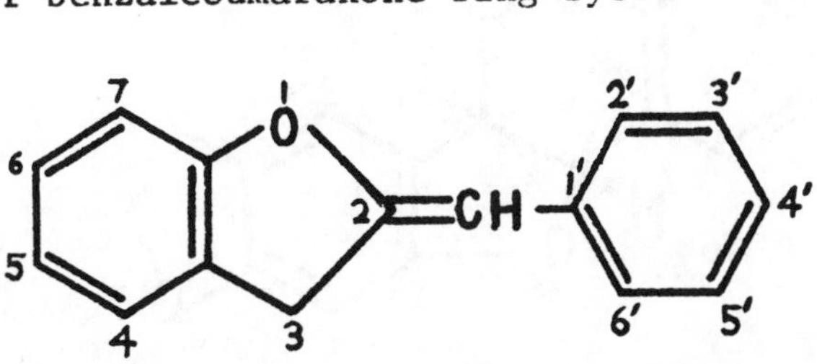

These are golden yellow pigments occurring in certain flowers and bryophytes (63). Only five aglycones are known, but they generally possess the hydroxylation pattern of the other flavonoids as well as being found in the

form of glycosides and methyl ethers.   In alkaline solution they become
rose-red.   Some examples of aurones and their glycosides are shown in
Table 9-5.   (64).

MISCELLANEOUS COMPOUNDS

Several unusual plant constituents appear by their structures to be
biogenetically related to the flavonoids but with additional complexities.
They will be mentioned briefly but fit into no widespread group.

Several compounds may be classed either with the furanocoumarins (see
Chap. 4) or with the flavonoids. Coumestrol is the best-known of this
group known as coumestanes or coumestones:

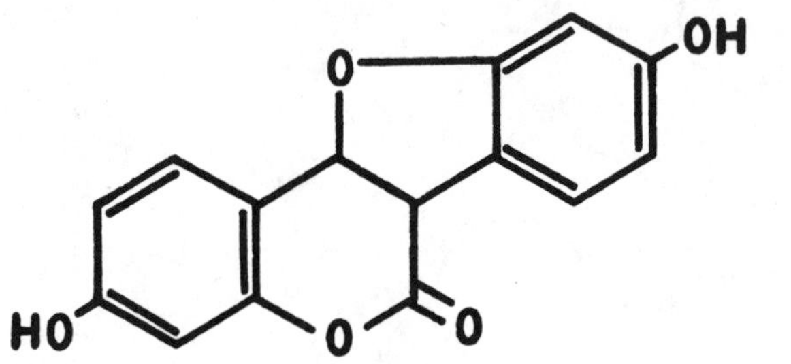

coumestrol
(*Trifolium repens*)

Pachyrrhizin from the yam bean has an obviously related structure:

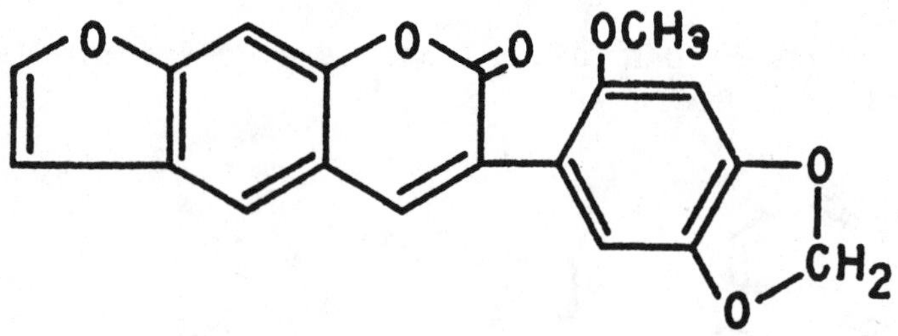

pachyrrhizin

Compounds with the same carbon-oxygen ring skeleton as the coumestones but
lacking the carbonyl group are known as pterocarpanoids after the parent
compound pterocarpin:

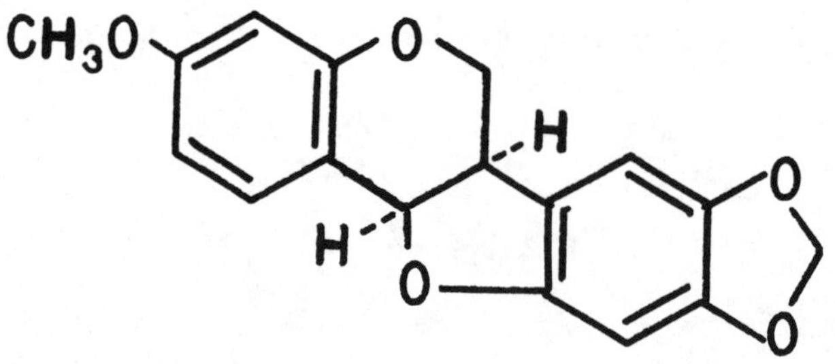

(–)-pterocarpin

TABLE 9-5.   SOME AURONES, STRUCTURES AND OCCURRENCE

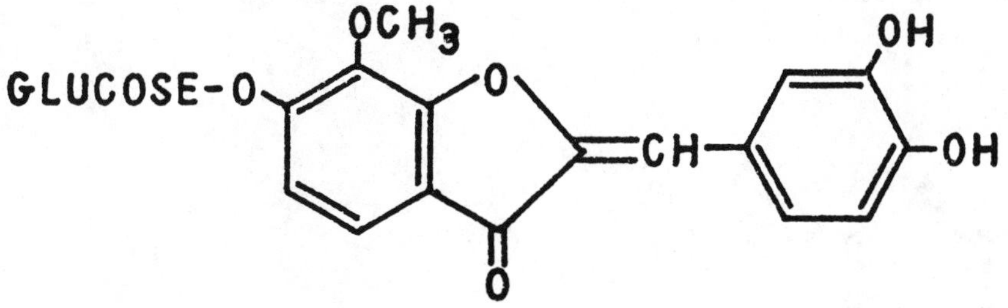

leptosin (*Coreopsis* spp.)

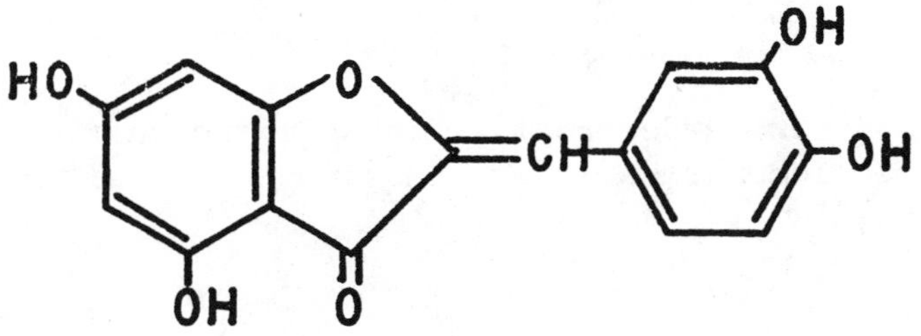

aureusidin (*Antirrhinum majus*)

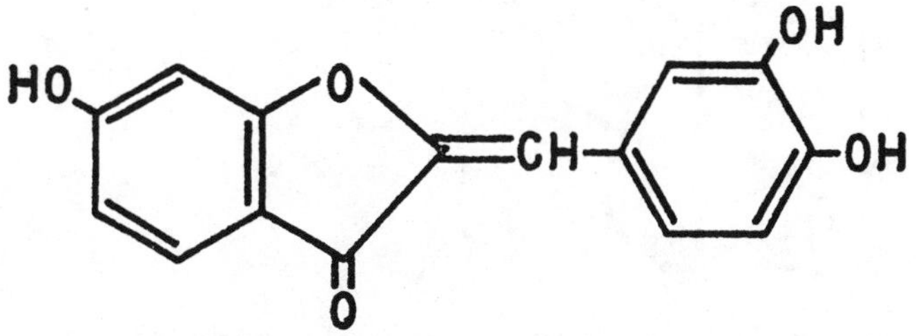

sulphuretin (*Dahlia variabilis*)

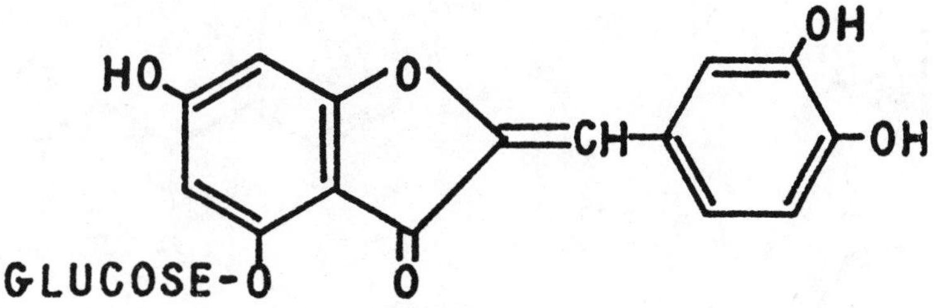

cernoside (*Oxalis cernua*)

There are about twenty pterocarpanoids known, some with interesting fungicidal, allergenic, and estrogenic properties (21, 65, 66). Another important compound of related structure is the insecticide, rotenone, of derris root (67):

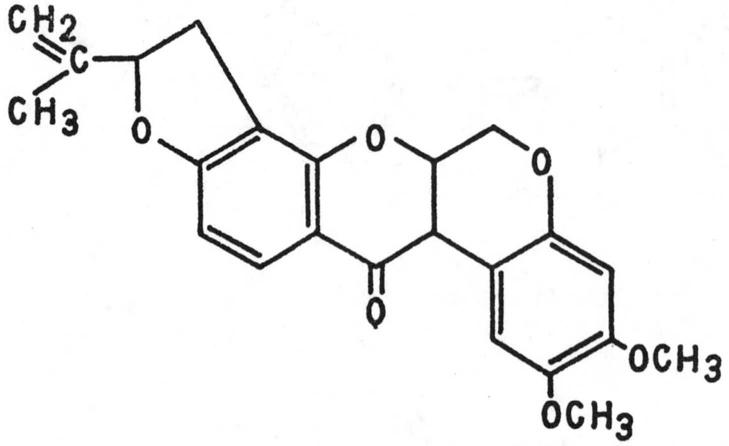

rotenone

The neoflavanoids can be regarded as flavanoids in which ring B is attached to C-4 or as 4-phenylcoumarins (65). An example is calophyllolide from *Calophyllum inophyllum* :

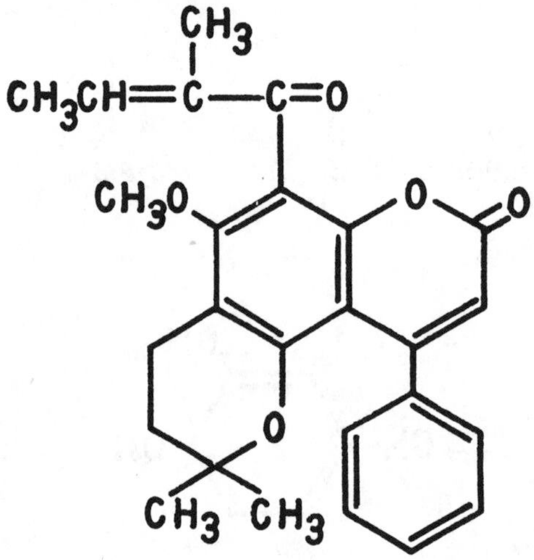

Dalbergin has similar structure lacking the isoprenoid side chains. The dyes of Brazil wood and logwood also appear related to this group but have an extra carbon atom (68).

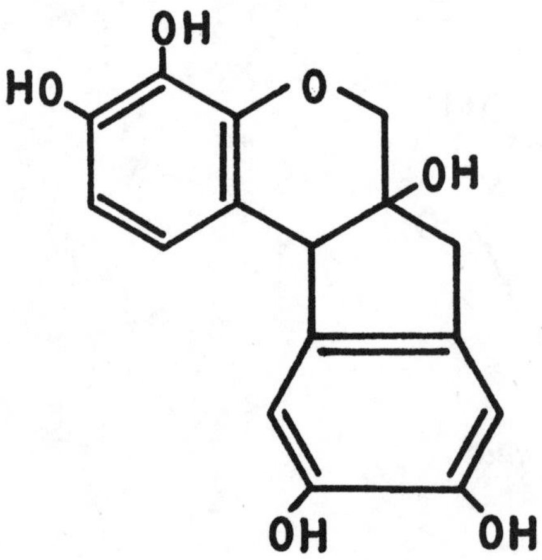

hematoxylin

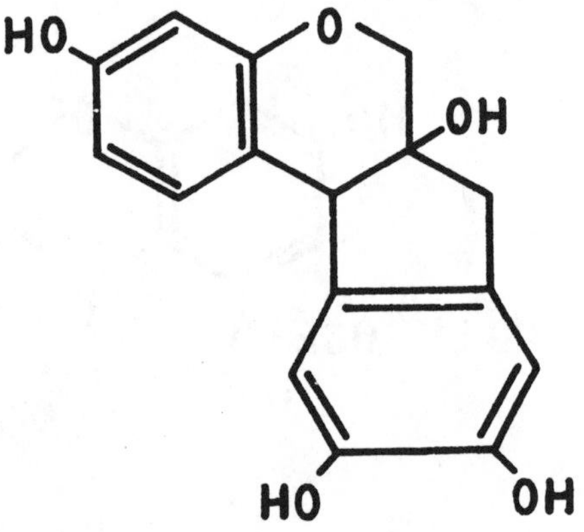

brazilin

Stilbene derivatives have been found in a few unrelated plants. Structurally they represent a C_6-C_2-C_6 group. Their hydroxylation patterns strongly suggest that, like the flavonoids, one ring is formed from acetate and the other from shikimic acid (69). Their chief interest lies in their high toxicity to fungi, fish, insects, and mice. The phytoalexins of grape leaves and some legumes are stilbene derivatives (70-72). They may also act as tannins, and oxidation of them can form condensed products similar to the phlobatannins (73). Some apparently occur as glycosides, but the aglycone structures are given here:

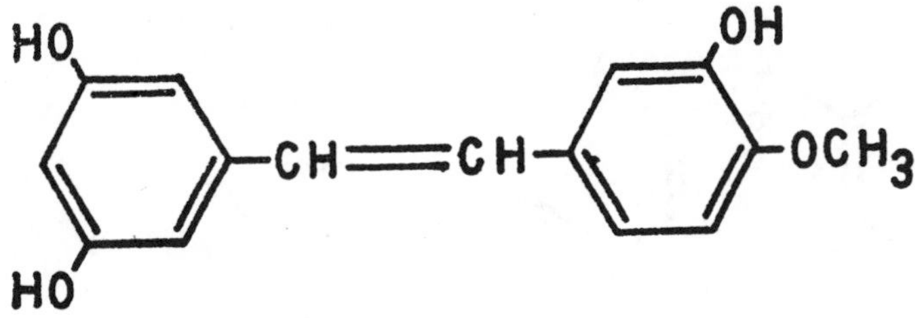

rhapontigenin
(rhubarb)

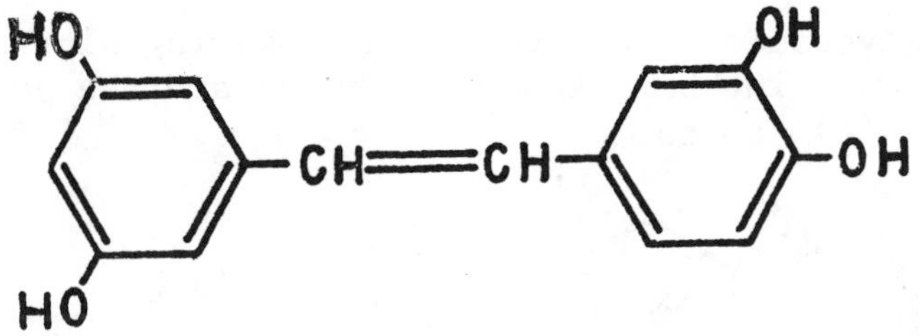

piceatannol (*Picea* spp.)

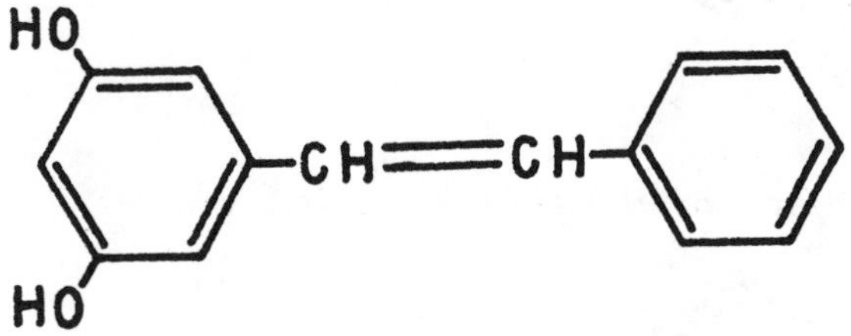

pinosylvin (*Pinus sylvestris*)

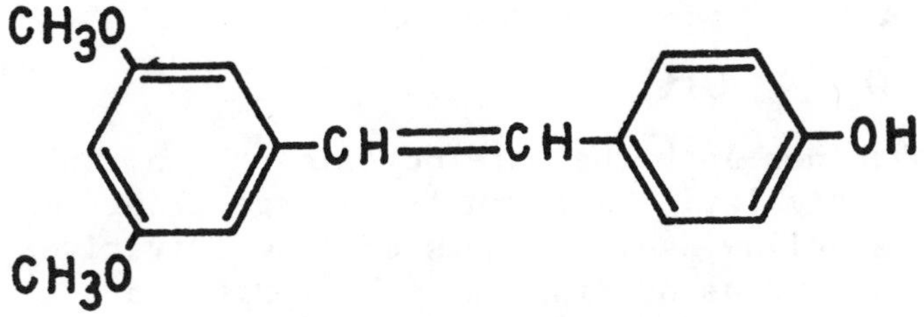

pterostilbene (*Santalum album*)

Dihydrostilbenes are found in liverworts; and one of them, lunularic acid, acts as a growth inhibitor analogous to abscisic acid in higher plants (74-76).

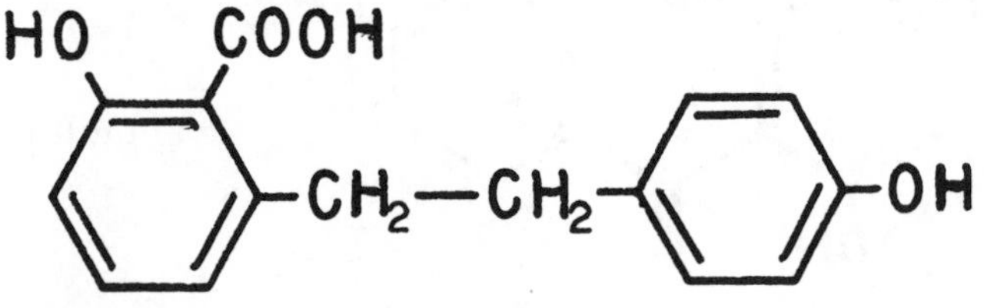

lunularic acid

Similar dihydrostilbenes are growth inhibitors present in yam bulbils (77).
The isocoumarin, phyllodulcin (q.v.), may also be biogenetically related
to the stilbenes.

Benzophenone derivatives have also been found in a few plants. They
may be described as a C_6-C_1-C_6 group, and like the stilbenes are included
in this chapter because the hydroxylation patterns suggest a biogenetic
relationship to the flavonoids. The most important members of this group
are the xanthones which have been used as dyes for hundreds of years.
They have the basic structure and numbering system shown below:

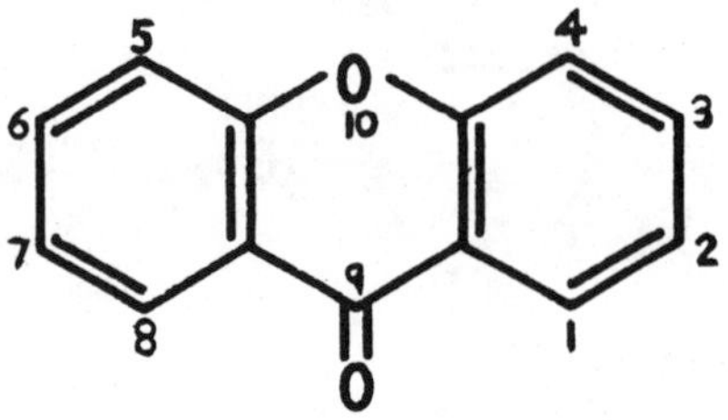

About 80 xanthones and their glycosides are known from flowering plants (78).
They are all hydroxy-derivatives. The best known xanthones are the yellow
pigment gentisin of *Gentiana lutea* roots:

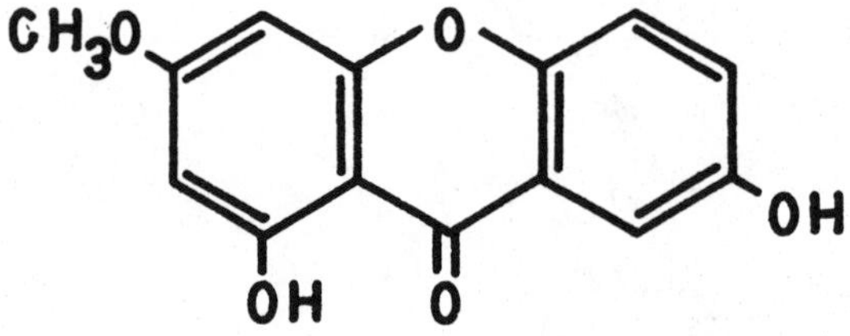

and the C-glucoside mangiferin from roots of *Mangifera indica* :

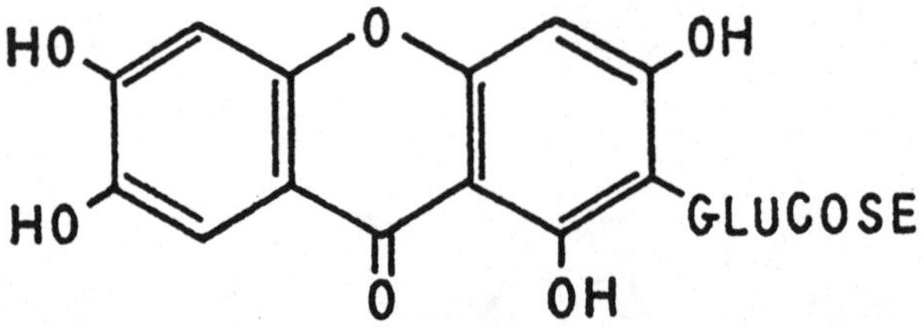

Other naturally occurring benzophenones lack the heterocyclic oxygen ring
of the xanthones but are otherwise similar. Maclurin from osage orange
and fustic wood has been used as a yellow dye. Various cotoin derivatives
of coto bark have been used in medicine as astringents. Hydroxybenzo-
phenone derivatives have been grouped under "condensed tannins."

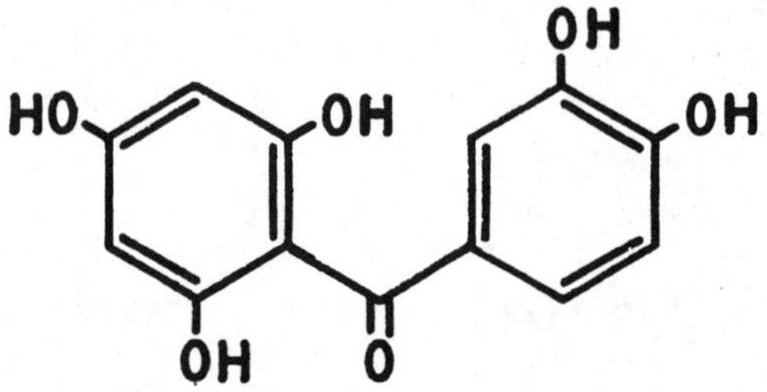

maclurin *(Maclura pomifera)*

cotoin *(Aniba coto)*

ISOLATION

Many compounds of this group are water-soluble, especially in the glycoside forms, and they are, therefore, present in aqueous plant extracts. Even those which are only slightly soluble in water are sufficiently polar to be well extracted by methanol, ethanol or acetone (79), and these are the solvents most frequently used for extraction of the flavonoids. Re-extraction of an aqueous solution with an immiscible but rather polar organic solvent is frequently of value in separating this group from more polar compounds such as carbohydrates. Ethyl acetate is a useful solvent for dealing with catechins and proanthocyanidins in this way (80). Benzene can be used for benzophenones and stilbenes. Amyl alcohol has been extensively used for the anthocyanins. Secondary butyl alcohol is the most polar alcohol to be incompletely miscible with water; and if the aqueous extract is saturated with sodium chloride or magnesium sulfate, it is very successful for removing compounds of this group. Polyphenolic substances such as these are quite sensitive to air oxidation in neutral and basic solution so that it is a good practice to prepare extracts in the presence of a dilute acid (e.g. 0.1 N HCl). However, hot acid or long-standing with acid in the cold may cause hydrolysis of glycosides.

Classically, various precipitating reagents have been used for these compounds. Neutral or basic lead acetate has been particularly recommended. Flavonoids can be freed from the lead precipitate by adding dilute sulfuric acid or hydrogen sulfide leaving the lead as insoluble lead sulfate or sulfide. Other precipitating agents have been picric acid, potassium acetate, barium hydroxide, pyridine, etc. These methods are described in the general references to this chapter.

More recently column chromatography has been used for separation of these compounds although no completely satisfactory system for all of them has been developed. Magnesol and silicic acid partition columns have been used with water-saturated ethyl acetate or ether as developing solvents (81, 82). Alumina is especially useful in separating anthocyanins with only one free hydroxyl group on ring B from those with two or more (83). Forsyth (84) has used a partition column of cellulose powder pulp with amyl alcohol-acetic acid-water as the mobile phase to separate polyphenols of cacao. Garber et al. (85) have used a similar method for anthocyanins. Ion exchange chromatography can be used to separate monomeric flavonoids (86). Affinity chromatography on protein-Sepharose separates polymers (87, 88). Several workers (89-91) recommend the use of polyamide (Nylon) columns for purification of flavonoids. Adsorption on polyvinylpyrrolidone is effective for isolation of anthocyanins either in a batch (92) or column procedure (93). Gel filtration on Sephadex has been used to separate polymeric condensed tannins according to molecular size (94-96), but adsorption phenomena are also important in this process (97), and Sephadex columns are also useful for catechins and proanthocyanidins (98).

CHARACTERIZATION

Classically, many different color reactions and solubility properties were used to characterize the different classes of flavonoid pigments. These are well summarized in the book by Harborne et al. ("General References"). The book of Mabry et al. listed under "General References" gives extensive data on chromatographic and spectral properties but does not include anthocyanins. A summary of a few of the useful tests and properties will be given here.

If interfering pigments are not present, plant tissues (e.g. white flower petals) can be tested for the presence of flavones and flavonols by exposing to ammonia vapor. A yellow coloration indicates the presence of these compounds. Chalcones and aurones turn from yellow to red in this test. If an aqueous pigment extract is made alkaline, various color changes may be observed although the changes in one pigment may mask changes in another:

anthocyanins	purple→blue
flavones, flavonols, xanthones	yellow
flavanones	colorless, becoming orange-red (especially if heated)
chalcones and aurones	immediate red-purple
flavanonols	orange-brown

The reaction with ferric chloride has been widely used to identify phenolic compounds, but it is of little value in distinguishing different classes. Other things being equal, it gives a greenish color with catechol derivatives and a blue color with pyrogallol derivatives; but the "other things" are seldom equal. If a deep blue-black color appears, it is evidence for the presence of a 3, 4, 5-trihydroxy phenol (e.g. gallocatechin) but the formation of a green color does not necessarily indicate the absence of this group nor the presence of a catechol (ortho dihydroxy) group.

Reduction with magnesium and concentrated hydrochloric acid produces red colors with flavonols, flavanones, flavanonols, and xanthones. The red pigments are not anthocyanidins but 4, 4' bis anthocyanidin derivatives (99). Chalcones and aurones give immediate red colors on adding acid rather than a gradual intensification of color as reduction proceeds. Flavones give some color but much less than flavonols. 4-phenylcoumarins give an initial green color which changes to red.

Addition of bromine water has been used to identify catechins and phlobatannins since they give a precipitate while other tannins and other flavonoids do not. At least certain leucoanthocyanidins also give a positive test with bromine water.

Boiling plant parts with 2N HCl has been used to detect catechins and leucoanthocyanidins. The former give a yellow-brown color, the latter a red color. For additional confirmation of anthocyanidins the red color may be extracted with amyl alcohol and further tests for the presence of anthocyanin applied. Pacheco (100) has adapted this method to detect flavanonols. After boiling with acid, he extracted with ether to obtain the flavanonols, which were unaffected. The flavanonols were then reduced to flavan-3, 4-diols (leucoanthocyanidins), converted to anthocyanidins with boiling acid, and the anthocyanidins identified by paper chromatography.

Other color reactions for the flavonoids will be described below under paper chromatography since most of the spray reagents described can be equally well applied to solutions of the compounds.

Although extensive degradations for proof of structure are beyond the scope of this book, it should be mentioned that splitting with base has been a most useful technique for determining hydroxylation patterns of unknown flavonoids. Fusion with potassium hydroxide (or boiling with concentrated solutions) splits flavonoids to form a phenol from ring A and a phenolic acid from ring B. For example, from luteolin there are obtained phloroglucinol and protocatechuic acid:

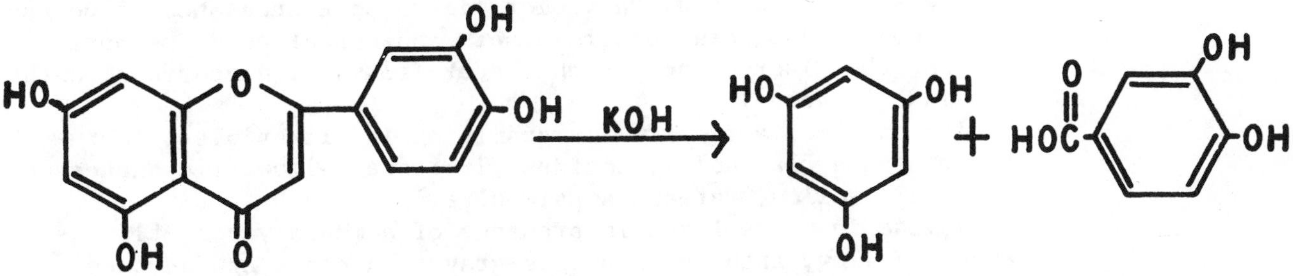

Methyl ethers are also hydrolyzed to phenols by this procedure so that the position of methoxy groups cannot be determined. However, methoxy groups are retained if 10% barium hydroxide in a hydrogen atmosphere is used for the cleavage. A longer reaction time is required for the latter method, but in some cases it is obviously preferable. A reductive cleavage with alkali and sodium amalgam is useful for identifying A and B ring fragments of flavonols but not anthocyanins (101). Split products are identified by paper chromatography (101, 102). Acidic degradation can be used to identify the A-ring of flavonols and permits identification of any attached sugars, which would be destroyed in alkali (103). The position of sugar attachment in glycosides may be determined by methylating all free hydroxyl groups with methyl sulfate, removing the sugar by acid hydrolysis, and locating the position of the now freed hydroxyl group. Paper chromatography can also be applied to identification of the partially methylated aglycone. Chandler and Harper (104) have developed a procedure for identifying the type and location of sugars in flavonoid glycosides. It depends on selective oxidative splitting of the glycoside and identification of the sugar residue that is released. Hydrogen peroxide splits off sugars attached at C-3 whereas permanganate or ozone releases sugars attached to an aromatic system. Hydrolysis by specific enzymes can also give useful information about the structure of flavonoid glycosides (105).

Several of the books listed under "General References" give extensive information on chromatographic procedures for the flavonoids. Although paper chromatography has been very valuable for these compounds and is still a recommended procedure (106), it is being replaced to some extent by thin layer and high performance liquid chromatography. On paper the most popular solvent has been butanol-acetic acid-water (4:1:5) although water is useful for moving glycosides away from aglycones. Basic solvents are likely to cause degradation of flavonoids. Acidic solvents can result in acylation of

sugar moieties giving rise to artifactual spots (107). In organic solvents the
Rf value decreases with hydroxylation of the molecule.

For thin layer chromatography a variety of layers have been used, for
instance cellulose, mixed cellulose and polyvinylpyrrolidone, magnesium
silicate, and silica gel containing lead acetate. Most work has dealt with
anthocyanins, flavones, and flavonols (108-112), but xanthones have also been
studied (113).

Paper electrophoresis has also been applied to anthocyanins (114).

Geissman (115) has outlined a routine procedure for examining chromatograms of flavonoids:

1. Note visible spots (anthocyanins, chalcones, aurones).
2. Examine in long wave ultra-violet light--some substances fluoresce
    (flavonols, chalcones) others absorb and appear as dark spots
    against the fluorescence of the paper (flavonol glycosides, antho-
    cyanins, flavones).
3. Expose to ammonia vapor while examining in ultraviolet light--
    flavones and flavonol glycosides fluoresce yellow, flavonones ap-
    pear pale yellow, catechins pale blue.
4. Reexamine in white light in presence of ammonia vapor--flavones
    appear yellow, anthocyanins blue-gray, chalcones and aurones
    orange-red.

A few other spray reagents are worthy of mention. Diazonium salts react
with all phenols to give colored azo dyes. The diazonium salts that have been
used most frequently are prepared from benzidine, p-nitroaniline, or
sulfanilic acid. Paranitrobenzenediazonium fluoborate is especially convenient since it is a stable compound that can simply be dissolved in water
before use. Compounds other than phenols may react (e.g. histamine), but
not many of them are likely to be encountered in flavonoid preparations.

Flavanones and flavanonols may be detected because they show up as
purple spots when sprayed with 4% Rhodamine B in 0.1N HCl. Flavones and
flavonols do not react (116).

The vanillin-hydrochloric acid reaction is valuable for identifying
phloroglucinol or resorcinol derivatives which do not have a carbonyl group
next to the ring (e.g. catechins and leucoanthocyanidins). This reagent
gives a pink color with such compounds (117).

The phlobaphene reaction of catechins and leucoanthocyanidins is best
applied to paper by spraying with p-toluenesulfonic acid and heating (118).
The former give brown spots, the latter pink. Other flavonoids may also
have their colors intensified by this reagent without heating. Some indole derivatives also give pink colors with this reagent (118).

Hörhammer and Müller (119) have recommended a zirconium oxychloride reagent
to distinguish flavonols from flavones. The 3-glycosides of flavonols do
not react with this reagent and may, therefore, be distinguished by chromato-
gramming before and after hydrolysis and applying this reagent.

High performance liquid chromatography has been applied to the
analysis of flavones (120), anthocyanins (121), xanthones (122), and other
flavonoid derivatives (123).

By combining spectrophotometric methods with chromatography, it is
frequently possible to make a positive identification of a flavonoid aglycone or glycoside in all its structural detail. The amount of material in
a chromatogram spot or column eluate can be enough for spectral measurements
and frequently it is not even necessary to elute the spot. All of the flavonoids have a more or less intense absorption band at about 220-270 nm and
another strong band at a longer wavelength. Additional weaker bands may
also be present. Approximate locations of the long wavelength band for
different flavonoids are as follows:

anthocyanins   500-530 nm

flavones and flavonols   330-375 nm

chalcones and aurones   370-410 nm

flavanones   250-300 nm

leucoanthocyanidins and catechins   ca. 280 nm

iso-flavones   250-290 nm (very weak)

Detailed presentation of spectral curves may be found in several of the
general references and the review of Geissman (115). Infrared spectra (124)
and NMR spectra can also be useful (125-126).

Addition of alkali causes characteristic spectral shifts with most
flavonoids. Sodium acetate and sodium ethylate have been used for this
purpose (127, 128). Flavonols with free hydroxyl groups in positions 3 and
4' are decomposed by alkali, and this can be followed by the decrease in
absorption at the long wavelength band. Sodium acetate causes a shift of
the short wavelength band to shorter wavelengths if a free 7-hydroxyl group
is present. It can also be used to distinguish 8-hydroxy from 6-hydroxy
flavonols (129).

Various methods have been developed for locating hydroxyl groups on
the flavonoids by utilizing reagents which produce spectral shifts with
different hydroxylation patterns. Jurd (130) has presented a method for
detecting ortho dihydroxyl compounds by adding borate which, by complexing
with such groups, produces characteristic shifts in the long wavelength
band. Hörhammer and Hänsel (131) have used boron complexes in a similar
way for analysis of flavones, flavonols and chalcones. Aluminum chloride
has also been applied as a useful complexing agent. Shifts of 20 or more
nm are characteristic of ortho dihydroxyl compounds. Flavanones can be
distinguished from isoflavones by the differences in spectral shifts which
they show with aluminum chloride (132-135). Lead acetate has also been
recommended as superior to aluminum chloride in several respects (136).

Gas chromatography of the flavonoids generally requires their conversion to methylated or trimethylsilyl derivatives (137, 138). Such derivatization also permits mass spectrometry of these compounds (137-140).

METABOLIC PATHWAYS

The primary precursors of the flavonoids proper are known beyond any doubt as a result of many tracer experiments, but many questions remain regarding the detailed pathways followed. Reviews of this area can be found in the general references.

Tracer experiments by several workers have established that the B ring of flavonoids comes from shikimic acid:

The A ring is formed by head-to-tail grouping of three acetate molecules. The aliphatic three-carbon chain is probably added to ring B before ring A is formed to produce a C_6-C_3 compound. More generally, it is presumed that all aromatic rings having <u>ortho</u> hydroxyl groups arise from shikimic acid and all aromatic rings with <u>meta</u> hydroxyl groups arise from acetate. Such C_6-C_3 compounds as phenylalanine, cinnamic acid and ferulic acid are efficient precursors of the C_6(B)-C_3 portion of flavonoids. The accumulation of p-coumaric acid derivatives just before the appearance of anthocyanins also points to p-coumaric acid as a pigment precursor (141, 142). Observations suggesting that shikimic acid may be able to go to flavonoids without the intermediacy of amino acids or cinnamic acids may be the result of cellular compartmentation (143). In tea plants the N-ethyl group of theanine is a better precursor than acetate for ring-A of the catechins (144).

To some degree hydroxylation and O-methylation of cinnamic acids can occur before condensation with the atoms of the A-ring, but other modifications of the B-ring occur late in the pathways (145, 146). The first C_6-C_3-C_6 compound to be formed is probably a flavanone (147-149). The chalcone-flavanone interconversion occurs non-enzymatically but is probably enzymatic <u>in vivo</u> (150, 151). Because of the ready interconversion of chalcones and flavanones it is hard to know whether or not chalcones are always intermediates between flavanones and other classes of flavonoids. Direct dehydrogenation of a flavanone can yield the corresponding flavone (146, 152). Chalcones appear to be direct precursors of aurones (153); and, whether directly or indirectly, can be precursors of other flavonoids (154). The α-hydroxychalcones are probable precursors of peltogynols (155). There is some evidence that flavanonols are precursors of anthocyanidins by way of leucoanthocyanidins (156, 157) and also of catechins and flavonols (158), but there is room for considerable new information in these branches of the pathway.

It is frequently observed that in a given species all of the different flavonoids have the same ring hydroxylation pattern, differing in methylation, glycosylation and the structure of the C_3 portion. Such an observation suggests that there is a common C_{15} intermediate that is converted to the different flavonoids after the ring hydroxylation pattern has been

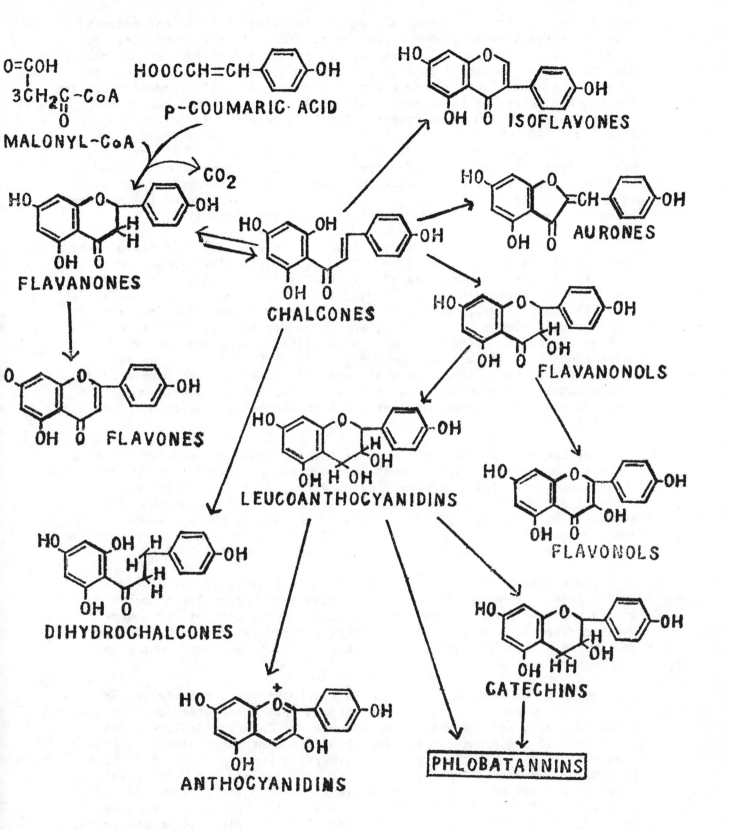

FIGURE 9-1: FLAVONOID PATHWAYS

established. However, it appears that the location of different hydroxyl
groups is actually established at different stages in the synthesis. For
instance, if a 7-hydroxyl is to be present in the end-product (e.g. cyanidin) it must be on ring A in the chalcone (151, 159). The introduction of
a 3'-hydroxyl group into a molecule that already has a 4'-hydroxyl can occur
even at late stages of the pathway (160-162), and once added cannot be
removed (160). This 3'-hydroxylation has been observed in cell-free systems
(146, 163). The more unusual 2'-hydroxyl group is probably added at the
flavanonol level and once added cannot be removed (164). The 3-hydroxyl
characteristic of flavonols and anthocyanidins is also presumably added at
the flavanonol level since flavones are not convertible to flavonols or
anthocyanidins (161, 165). It is likely that at least some of the hydroxylation reactions are catalyzed by a microsomal oxygenase (166).

It is widely accepted that isoflavones are produced from flavones by
migration of the phenyl group from C-2 to C-3. This view has been supported by the experimental work of Grisebach and Doerr (167) who fed car-
boxyl-labelled phenylalanine to *Trifolium pratense* and isolated an isoflavone with label at C-4. Some work has shown that flavanonols or flavonols
cannot be converted to isoflavones, and therefore the aryl migration must
occur at the chalcone (or flavanone) stage (168). Rearrangement of an
enolic tautomer is a suggested mechanism (169, 170). Isoflavones are
actively turned over (171). They are probably precursors of coumestones,
pterocarpanoids, rotenoids, etc. (172-176). The extra carbon atom of the
rotenoids and homoflavonoids is derived from the methyl carbon of methionine
(177, 178).

For the neoflavanoids there is little experimental evidence relating
to their biosynthesis. There could be a second aryl migration from an
isoflavonoid or a direct condensation of a ring A precursor with the β-
carbon of a cinnamic acid derivative (65). The latter is somewhat more
favored (179). The C_5 acyl side chains often seen in these compounds come
from leucine (180) or isoleucine (181). The neoflavanoids are probably precursors of benzophenones and the latter of xanthones (182-183).

The stilbene pinosylvin and the dihydrostilbene lunularic acid are
derived from a cinnamic acid derivative plus three molecules of acetate.
but the carboxyl group of the cinnamic acid becomes part of the second
aromatic ring (184, 185). Dimeric proanthocyanidins seem to be made by
reaction of a catechin with some intermediate that is a precursor of both
catechins and anthocyanidins (186).

Nothing has been said to indicate the point where methylation or
glycosylation occurs. It is usually assumed that these steps are the last
in the sequence, and the genetic experiments of Harborne (187) support
this idea. If one assumes a conversion of leucoanthocyanidins to anthocyanidins, it is indicative that the former are never glycosylated while
the latter always are. Enzymes have also been isolated that catalyze
transfer of sugar units from sugar nucleotides to various flavonoid aglycones (146, 188). It is certainly not ruled out, though, that in some
cases the flavonoid nucleus is transformed from one class to another after
glycosylation occurs (151). Formation of the glycoflavonols, however,
probably involves addition of the glucose at an early stage. It has been
shown experimentally that apigenin is not converted to C-glucosides such

as vitexin but can be converted to its 7-glucoside in *Spirodela polyrhiza*
(161). C-glucosylation may occur at the flavanone level, though, since
naringenin is converted in parallel to apigenin-7-0-glucoside and apigenin-
8-C-glucoside (vitexin) (189). An 8-C-glucoside may also be isomerized to
a 6-C-glucoside (190). The methoxy groups of flavonoids have long been
presumed to come like other methoxy groups from methionine. This route
has been confirmed experimentally (191), and the existence of methyl transferases has been shown (192, 193). In pea flowers the anthocyanins produced at a late stage of development are less methylated than those at
an early stage, presumably because the methylation system loses its ability
to keep up with the rest of the pathway (194). The malonic acid esters
present in sugar moieties of several flavonoids are made from malonyl-CoA
(195). The C-isoprenyl groups that are present as such in some members of
this group (e.g. mundulone) and converted to furan rings in others (e.g.
pachyrrhizin) are transferred from dimethylallyl pyrophosphate. It is
extraordinarily interesting that a transferase for this reaction in the
synthesis of the phytoalexin glyceollin is induced by attack of *Phytophthora
megasperma* on soybeans and that a specific glucan produced by the fungus
is the inducing agent (196).

Biosynthesis of the condensed tannins has not been investigated by
the tracer technique. The consensus is that they are formed by polymerization of catechin or leucoanthocyanidin monomers (197).   Since the exact
structure of the tannins is unknown, different mechanisms for the condensation have been suggested. Freudenberg's condensation (see p. 196) is non-
oxidative. Some such mechanism may be operative in vivo with the 4-carbo-
cation generated from a 3, 4- flavandiol reacting with a nucleophilic
flavan-3-ol (198). Others have proposed an oxidative condensation either
non-enzymatic or catalyzed by a peroxidase or phenol oxidase (199).

Some of the most interesting aspects of flavonoid metabolism are its
control by growth regulators (200) and light (201, 202), its response to
fungal infection (203), and its relation to nucleic acid metabolism (204).

GENERAL REFERENCES

Geissman, T. A., "Anthocyanins, Chalcones, Aurones, Flavones, and Related
    Water-Soluble Plant Pigments," in Paech & Tracey 3 450-498.
Goodwin, T. W., ed. (1976) Chemistry and Biochemistry of Plant Pigments, 2nd
    ed., 2 Vols., Academic Press, N. Y.
Harborne, J. B. (1967) Comparative Biochemistry of the Flavonoids, Academic
    Press, N. Y.
Harborne, J. B., Mabry, T. J., & Mabry, H., eds. (1975) The Flavonoids,
    Chapman & Hall, London.
Mabry, T. J., Markham, K. R., & Thomas, M. B. (1970) The Systematic Identifica-
    tion of Flavonoids, Springer-Verlag, Berlin.
Schmidt, O. T., "Naturliche Gerbstoffe," in Paech & Tracey 3 517-548.

BIBLIOGRAPHY

1. Thompson, W. R., Meinwald, J., Aneshansley, D., and Eisner, T. (1972) Science 177 528-530.
2. Harborne, J. B. (173) in Miller, L. P., ed. Phytochemistry Van Nostrand-Reinhold, N. Y., 2 344-380.
3. Jones, O. P. (1976) Nature 262 392-393.
4. Feucht, W. and Nachit, M. (1977) Physiol. Plantarum 40 230-234.
5. Harborne, J. B., Ingham, J. L., King, L., and Payne, M. (1976) Phytochemistry 15 1485-1487.
6. Van Etten, H. D. (1976) Phytochemistry 15 655-659.
7. Doskotch, R. W., Mikhail, A. A., and Chatterji, S. K. (1973) Phytochemistry 12 1153-1155.
8. Zielske, A. G., Simons, J. N., and Silverstein, R. M. (1972) Phytochemistry 11 393-396.
9. Mirsalikhova, N. M. and Pakudina, Z. P. (1977) Chem. Nat. Compds. 13 37-39.
10. Mukohata, Y., Nakabayashi, S., and Higashida, M. (1978) FEBS Letters 85 215-218.
11. Stenlid, G., (1970) Phytochemistry 9 2251-2256.
12. Varma, S. D., Mikuni, I., and Kinoshita, J. H. (1975) Science 188 1215-1216.
13. Ingham, J. L. and Dewick, P. M. (1979) Phytochemistry 18 1711-1714.
14. Duczek, L. J. and Higgins, V. J. (1976) Can. J. Botany 54 2620-2629.
15. Swain, T. (1977) Ann. Rev. Plant Physiol. 28 479-501.
16. Rajaratnam, J. A., Lowry, J. B., Avadhani, P. N., and Corley, R. H. V. (1971) Science 172 1142-1143.
17. Gazave, J.-M., Roger, C., and Parrot, J.-L. (1974) Compt. Rend (D) 278 525-527.
18. Kühnau, J. (1973) Qualitas Plantarum 23 119-127.
19. Bjeldanes, L. F. and Chang, G. W. (1977) Science 197 577-578.
20. Lyman, R. L., Bickoff, E. M., Booth, A. N., and Livingston, A. L. (1959) Arch. Biochem. Biophys. 80 61-67.
21. Hijwegen, T. (1973) Phytochemistry 12 375-380.
22. Sharma, R. D. (1979) Lipids 14 535-540.
23. Fredga, A. and Bendz, G. (1966) Ann. 691 177-180.
24. Bendz, G., Mårtensson, O. and Nilsson, E. (1966) Acta Chem. Scand. 20 277-278.
25. Cooper-Driver, G. (1977) Science 198 1260-1262.
26. Freudenberg, K. (1956) Sci. Proc. Royal Soc. Dublin 27 153-160.
27. Weinges, K. and 5 others (1969) Arzneimittel-Forsch. 19 328-333.
28. Haslam, E. (1977) Phytochemistry 16 1625-1640.
29. Kumari, D., Mukerji, S. K., and Seshadri, T. R. (1966) Current Sci. 35 223-224.
30. Jacques, D., Haslam, E., Bedford, G. R., and Greatbanks, D. (1974) J. Chem. Soc. Perkin I 2663-2671.
31. Matsuo, T. and Ito, S. (1978) Agric. Biol. Chem. (Japan) 42 1637-1643.
32. Czochanska, Z., Foo, L. Y., and Porter, L. J. (1979) Phytochemistry 18 1819-1822.
33. Roux, D. G. (1972) Phytochemistry 11 1219-1230.
34. Bate-Smith, E. C. and Swain, T. (1953) Chem. and Ind. 1953 377-378.
35. Freudenberg, K. and Weinges, K. (1959) Chem. and Ind. 1959 486-487.
36. Freudenberg, K., Stocker, J. H., and Porter, J. (1957) Chem. Ber. 90 957-962.
37. Jurd, L. and Somers, T. C. (1970) Phytochemistry 9 419-427.
38. Swain, T. (1954) Chem. and Ind. 1954 1144-1145.
39. Bokadia, M. M. (1961) J. Indian Chem. Soc. 38 612-620.
40. Mullick, D. B. (1969) Phytochemistry 8 2205-2211.
41. Pachéco, H. (1957) Bull. soc. chim. biol. 39 971-987.
42. Parthasarathy, M. R., Ranganathan, K. R., and Sharma, D. K. (1979) Phytochemistry 18 506-508.
43. Bate-Smith, E. C. (1956) Sci. Proc. Roy. Dublin Soc. 27 165-176.
44. Wong, E. (1970) Fortschr. Chem. Org. Naturstoffe 28 1-73.
45. Kouno, L., Komori, T., and Kawasaki, T. (1973) Tetra. Lett. 4569-4572.
46. Harborne, J. B. (1977) Prog. Phytochem. 4 189-208.
47. Mues, R., Timmermann, B. N., Ohno, N., and Mabry, T. J. (1979) Phytochemistry 18 1379-1383.
48. Wollenweber, E., Favre-Bonvin, J., and Jay, M. (1978) Z. Naturforsch. 33c 831-835.
49. Charrière, Y. and Tissut, M. (1973) Phytochemistry 12 1443-1450.
50. Alston, R. E. (1968) Recent Adv. Phytochem. 1 305-327.
51. Markham, K. R. (1972) Phytochemistry 11 2047-2053.
52. Locksley, H. D. (1973) Fortschr. Chem. Org. Naturstoffe 30 208-311.
53. Varshney, A. K., Rahman, W., Okigawa, M., and Kawano, N. (1973) Experientia 29 784-786.
54. Lindberg, G., Østerdahl, B.-G., and Nilsson, E. (1974) Chem. Scripta 5 140-144.
55. Tanchev, S. S. and Timberlake, C. F. (1969) Phytochemistry 8 2367-2369.
56. Yoshitama, K. and Abe, K. (1977) Phytochemistry 16 591-593.
57. Asen, S. and Horowitz, R. M. (1974) Phytochemistry 13 1219-1223.
58. Williams, M. and Hrazdina, G. (1978) J. Food. Sci. 44 66-68.
59. Crowden, R. K. and Jarman, S. J. (1974) Phytochemistry 13 1947-1948.
60. Vandekerkhove, O. (1978) Z. Pflanzenphysiol. 86 135-139.
61. Podstolski, A. and Lewak, S. (1970) Phytochemistry 9 289-296.
62. Williams, A. H. (1964) Nature 202 824-825.
63. Markham, K. R. and Porter, L. J. (1978) Phytochemistry 17 159-160.
64. Farkas, L. and Pallos, L. (1967) Fortschr. Chem. Org. Naturstoffe 25 150-174.
65. Ollis, W. D. (1968) Recent Adv. Phytochem. 1 329-378.
66. Ferreira, M. A., Moir, M., and Thomson, R. H. (1974) J. Chem.Soc. Perkin I 1974 2429-2425.
67. Crombie, L. (1963) Fortschr. Chem. Org. Naturstoffe 21 275-325.
68. Robinson, R. (1958) Bull. soc. chim. 1958 125-134.
69. Billek, G. (1964) Fortschr. Chem. Org. Naturstoffe 22 115-152.

70. Preston, M. W., Chamberlain, K., and Skipp, R. A. (1975) Phytochemistry 14 1843-1844.
71. Ingham, J. L. (1976) Phytochemistry 15 1791-1793.
72. Langcake, P., Cornford, C. A., and Pryce, R. J. (1979) Phytochemistry 18 1025-1027.
73. Endres, H. (1959) Qual. Plantarum 5 367-374.
74. Gorham, J. (1978) Phytochemistry 17 99-105.
75. Grotha, R. and Schwabe, W. W. (1978) Biochem. Physiol. Pflanzen 172 167-171.
76. Asakawa, Y., Toyota, M., and Takemoto, T. (1978) Phytochemistry 17 2005-2010.
77. Hashimoto, T. and Tajima, M. (1978) Phytochemistry 17 1179-1184.
78. Hostettmann, K. and Wagner, H. (1977) Phytochemistry 16 821-829.
79. Durkee, A. B. and Jones, J. D. (1969) Phytochemistry 8 909-911.
80. Mathew, A. G., Parpia, H. A. B., and Govindarajan, V. S. (1969) Phytochemistry 8 1543-1547.
81. Ice, C. H. and Wender, S. H. (1952) Anal. Chem. 24 1616-1617.
82. Sondheimer, E. and Karash, C. B. (1956) Nature 178 648-649.
83. Birkofer, L., Kaiser, C., and Donike, M. (1966) J. Chromatog. 22 303-307.
84. Forsyth, W. G. C. (1952) Biochem. J. 51 511-516.
85. Garber, E. D., Redding, W. F., and Chorney, W. (1962) Nature 193 801-802.
86. Levin, H. J. and Harris, L. E. (1958) J. Am. Pharm. Assoc. 47 820-822.
87. Hoff, J. E. and Singleton, K. I. (1977) J. Food Sci. 42 1566-1569.
88. Oh, H. I. and Hoff, J. E. (1979) J. Food Sci. 44 87-89, 96.
89. Chandler, B. V. and Swain, T. (1959) Nature 183 989.
90. Neu, R. (1960) Arch. Pharm. 293 169-174.
91. Strack, D. and Mansell, R. L. (1975) J. Chromatog. 109 325-331.
92. Wrolstad, R. E. and Putnam, T. B. (1969) J. Food Sci. 34 154-155.
93. van Teeling, C. G., Cansfield, P. E. and Gallop, R.A. (1971) J. Chromatog. Sci. 9 505-509.
94. Roux, D. G. and Evelyn, S. R. (1958) J. Chromatog. 1 537-544.
95. Forrest, G. I. and Bendall, D. S. (1969) Biochem. J. 113 757-763.
96. Porter, L. J. and Wilson, R. D. (1972) J. Chromatog. 71 570-572.
97. Bandyukova, V. A. and Zemtsova, G. N. (1970) Chem. Nat. Compounds 6 415-417.
98. McMurrough, I. and McDowell, J. (1978) Anal. Biochem. 91 92-100.
99. Malkin, T. and Nierenstein, M. (1930) J. Am. Chem. Soc. 52 2864-2868.
100. Pacheco, H. (1956) Bull. soc. chim. 1600-1604.
101. Hurst, H. M. and Harborne, J. B. (1967) Phytochemistry 6 1111-1118.
102. Dunlap, W. J. and Wender, S. H. (1960) J. Chromatog. 3 505-507.
103. Niemann, G. J. (1972) J. Chromatog. 74 155-156.
104. Chandler, B. V. and Harper, K. A. (1962) Austral. J. Chem. 15 114-120.
105. Harborne, J. B. (1965) Phytochemistry 4 107-120.
106. Ribéreau-Gayon, P. (1973) Bull. Soc. Chim. 73-78.
107. Timberlake, C. F., Bridle, P., and Tanchev, S. S. (1971) Phytochemistry 10 165-169.
108. Mullick, D. B. (1969) Phytochemistry 8 2003-2008.
109. Larson, R. L. (1969) J. Chromatog. 43 287-290.
110. Pifferi, P. G. (1969) J. Chromatog. 43 530-536.
111. Wildanger, W. and Herrmann, K. (1973) J. Chromatog. 76 433-440.
112. Jay, M., Gonnet, J.-F., Wollenweber, E., and Voirin, B. (1975) Phytochemistry 14 1605-1612.
113. Saleh, N. A. M. (1974) J.Chromatog. 92 467-472.
114. von Elbe, J. H., Bixby, D. G., and Moore, J. D. (1969) J. Food Sci. 34 113-115.
115. Geissman, L. T., in Paech and Tracey 3 450-498.
116. Neu, R. (1959) Arch. Pharm. 292 431-437.
117. Bate-Smith, E. C. (1954) Biochem. J. 58 126-132.
118. Prabhakar, J. V. (1966) Current Science 34 700.
119. Hörhammer, L. and Müller, K. H. (1954) Arch. Pharm. 287 310-313.
120. Strack, D. and Krause, J. (1978) J. Chromatog. 156 359-361.
121. Williams, M., Hrazdina, G., Wilkinson, M. M., Sweeney, J. G., and Iacobucci, G. A. (1978) J. Chromatog. 155 389-398.
122. Hostettmann, K. and McNair, H. M. (1976) J. Chromatog. 116 201-206.
123. Kenyhercz, T. M. and Kissinger, P. T. (1978) Lloydia 41 130-139.
124. Inglett, G. E. (1958) J. Org. Chem. 23 93-94.
125. Holdsworth, D. K. (1973) Phytochemistry 12 2011-2015.
126. Nilsson, E. (1973) Chemica Scripta 4 49-55.
127. Jurd, L. and Horowitz, R. M. (1957) J. Org. Chem. 22 1618-1622.
128. Jurd, L. and Horowitz, R. M. (1961) J. Org. Chem. 26 2561-2566.
129. Harborne, J. B. (1960) Phytochemistry 8 177-183.
130. Jurd, L. (1956) Arch. Biochem. 63 376-381.
131. Hörhammer, L. and Hänsel, R. (1955) Arch. Pharm. 288 315-321.
132. Horowitz, R. M. and Jurd, L. (1961) J. Org. Chem. 26 2446-2449.
133. Markham, K. R. and Mabry, T. J. (1968) Phytochemistry 7 1197-1200.
134. Jurd, L. (1969) Phytochemistry 8 445-462.
135. Porter, L. J. and Markham, K. R. (1970) Phytochemistry 9 1363-1365.
136. Fuleki, T. and Francis, F. J. (1967) Phytochemistry 6 1161-1163.
137. Schmid, R. D. and 6 others (1973) Phytochemistry 12 2765-2772.
138. Bombardelli, E., Bonati, A., Gabetta, B., Martinelli, E. M., and Mustich, G. (1977) J. Chromatog. 139 111-120.
139. Schels, H., Zinsmeister, H. D., and Pfleger, K. (1978) Phytochemistry 17 523-526.

140. Wagner, H. and Seligmann, O. (1973) Tetrahedron 29 3029-3033.
141. Schmidt, H. and Böhme, H. (1960) Biol. Zentr. 79 423-425.
142. Takaishi, K. (1971) Phytochemistry 10 719-722.
143. Steiner, A. M. (1975) Phytochemistry 14 1993-1996.
144. Kito, M., Kokura, M., Izaki, J., and Sasaoka, K. (1968) Phytochemistry 7 599-603.
145. Steiner, A. M. (1970) Z. Pflanzenphysiol. 63 370-383.
146. Grisebach, H. (1972) Phytochemistry 11 862-863.
147. Forkmann, G. (1979) Phytochemistry 18 1973-1975.
148. Sütfeld, R., Kehrel, B., and Wiermann, R. (1978) Z. Naturforsch. 336 841-846.
149. Hrazdina, G. and Creasy, L. L. (1979) Phytochemistry 18 581-584.
150. Boland, M. J. and Wong, E. (1979) Bioorg. Chem. 8 1-8.
151. Raymond, W. R. and Maier, V. P. (1977) Phytochemistry 16 1535-1539.
152. Sutter, A., Poulton, J., and Grisebach, H. (1975) Arch. Biochem. Biophys. 170 547-556.
153. Wong, E. (1967) Phytochemistry 6 1227-1233.
154. Endress, R. (1974) Z. Pflanzenphysiol. 74 179-182.
155. Ferreira, D., van der Merwe, J. P., and Roux, D. G. (1974) J. Chem. Soc. Perkin I 1974 1492-1498.
156. Reddy, A. R. and Reddy, G. M. (1971) Current Science 40 335-337.
157. Kho, K. F. F. (1978) Phytochemistry 17 245-248.
158. Grisebach, H. and Barz, W. (1970) Naturwiss. 56 538-544.
159. Patschke, L., Hess, B., and Grisebach, H. (1964) Z. Naturforsch 19b 1115-1117.
160. Patschke, L. and Grisebach, H. (1968) Phytochemistry 7 235-237.
161. Wallace, J. W., Mabry, T. J., and Alston, R. E. (1969) Phytochemistry 8 93-99.
162. Wallace, J. W. (1975) Phytochemistry 14 1765-1768.
163. Vaughan, P. F. T., Butt, V. S., Grisebach, H., and Schill, L. (1969) Phytochemistry 8 1373-1378.
164. Grambow, H. J. and Grisebach, H. (1971) Phytochemistry 10 789-796.
165. Patschke, L., Barz, W., and Grisebach, H. (1966) Z. Naturforsch. 21b 45-52.
166. Fritsch, H. and Grisebach, H. (1975) Phytochemistry 14 2437-2442.
167. Grisebach, H. and Doerr, N. (1960) Z. Naturforsch 15b 284-286.
168. Barz, W. and Grisebach, H. (1966) Z. Naturforsch. 21b 47-52.
169. Grisebach, H. (1968) Recent Adv. Phytochem. 1 379-406.
170. Grisebach, H. and Zilg, H. (1968) Z. Naturforsch 23b 494-504.
171. Barz, W., Adamek, C., and Berlin, J. (1970) Phytochemistry 9 1735-1744.
172. Berlin, J., Dewick, P. M., Barz, W., and Grisebach, H. (1972) Phytochemistry 11 1689-1693.
173. Crombie, L., Dewick, P. M., and Whiting, D. A. (1973) J. Chem. Soc. Perkin I 1285-1294.
174. Dewick, P. M. (1975) Phytochemistry 14 979-982.
175. Dewick, P. M. and Martin, M. (1979) Phytochemistry 18 591-596, 597-602.
176. Martin, M. and Dewick, P. M. (1979) Phytochemistry 18 1309-1317.
177. Crombie, L., Green, C. L., and Whiting, D. A. (1968) Chem. Commun. 234-235.
178. Dewick, P. M. (1975) Phytochemistry 14 983-988.
179. Kunesch, G. and Polonsky, J. (1967) Chem. Commun. 1967 317-318.
180. Kunesch, G., Hildesheim, R., and Polonsky, J. (1969) Compt. Rend. (D) 265 2143-2145.
181. Kunesch, G. and Polonsky, J. (1969) Phytochemistry 8 1221-1226.
182. Ollis, W. D. and Gottlieb, O. R. (1968) Chem. Commun. 1396-1397.
183. Fujita, M. and Inoue, T. (1977) Tetrahedron Letters 4503-4506.
184. Pryce, R. J. (1972) Phytochemistry 11 1355-1364.
185. Gorham, J. (1977) Phytochemistry 16 915-918.
186. Jacques, D., Opie, C. T., Porter, L. J., and Haslam, E. (1977) J. Chem. Soc. Perkin I 1977 1637-1643.
187. Harborne, J. B. (1960) Biochem. J. 74 262-269.
188. Saleh, N. A. M., Poulton, J. E., and Grisebach, H. (1976) Phytochemistry 15 1865-1868.
189. Wallace, J. W. and Grisebach, H. (1973) Biochim. Biophys. Acta 304 837-841.
190. Wallace, J. W. and Mabry, T. J. (1970) Phytochemistry 9 2133-2135.
191. Ebel, J., Achenbach, H., Barz, W., and Grisebach, H. (1970) Biochim. Biophys. Acta 215 203-205.
192. Poulton, J. E., Hahlbrock, K., and Grisebach, H. (1977) Arch. Biochem. Biophys. 180 543-549.
193. Brunet, G., Saleh, N. A. M., and Ibrahim, R. K. (1978) Z. Naturforsch. 33c 786-788.
194. Statham, C. M., and Crowden, R. K. (1974) Phytochemistry 13 1835-1840.
195. Hahlbrock, K. (1972) FEBS Letters 28 65-68.
196. Zähringer, U., Ebel, J., Mulheirn, L. J., Lyne, R. L., and Grisebach, H. (1979) FEBS Letters 101 90-92.
197. Hillis, W. E. (1958) Nature 182 1371.
198. Botha, J. J., Ferreira, D., and Roux, D. G. (1978) Chem. Commun. 700-702.
199. Hathway, D. E. (1958) Biochem. J. 70 34-42.
200. Heinzmann, U., Seitz, U. (1977) Planta 135 313-318.
201. Tselas, S. K., Georghiou, K. C., and Thanos, C. A. (1979) Plant Sci. Letters 16 81-86.
202. Heller, W. and 6 others (1979) Plant Physiol. 64 371-373.
203. Dixon, R. A. and Lamb, C. J. (1979) Arch. Biochim. Biophys. 586 453-463.
204. Stafford, H. A. (1966) Plant Physiol. 41 953-961.

Chapter 10
AMINO ACIDS

Amino acids, peptides and proteins are among the most important and well-known constituents of living matter. Consequently much of their chemistry and metabolic significance is adequately described in general textbooks of biochemistry. Here some less familiar aspects of them will be pointed out.

WIDELY DISTRIBUTED AMINO ACIDS
AND PROTEIN CONSTITUENTS

Amino acids can be defined as carboxylic acids having at least one amino group. Most naturally occurring ones can be depicted by the general formula $R\ CH(NH_3+)CO_2^-$. These are the so-called alpha amino acids since the amino group is adjacent to the carboxylic acid function. If R is a group other than hydrogen, the compound has an asymmetric carbon atom and can, therefore, occur in an optically active form. The isomers having the L-configuration are the ones most widely distributed in nature. The first amino acid isolated was asparagine. This substance was obtained by Vauquelin and Robiquet in 1806 (1) who succeeded in separating it from asparagus juice by taking advantage of differences in the shape, transparency and flavor of the crystals. Since then chemists have continued their attempts to isolate new amino acids; and new ones are being discovered yearly. It is convenient to divide the amino acids into two major groups; one group is found in all living systems either in the free state or condensed as peptides while the members of the second group apparently occur only in a limited number of organisms and do not serve as protein monomers. Plant saps differ from animal tissue fluids in frequently containing many free amino acids in significant amounts. A balanced proportion of these compounds appears necessary for the health of the plant (2). They may also make an important contribution to the nutrition of insect pollinators (3).

The physical properties of the amino acids are to a very large extent determined by the dipolar ionic structure of these compounds. Thus, they are all white solids. They either have high melting points or decompose on heating. As a group they display much greater solubility in water than in organic solvents. Since they are amphoteric, they form salts with acids or bases. Under appropriate conditions they will migrate in an electric field, i.e. show electrophoretic properties. Each amino acid has one pH value at which there is no net charge on the molecule and at which, therefore, no migration in an electric field will occur. This pH value is called the isoelectric point. It is between pH 5 and 6 for the "neutral" amino acids - the mono carboxylic, mono amino compounds, near pH 3 for the dicarboxylic mono amino acids, and above 7.5 for the basic amino acids. The latter group includes diamino mono carboxylic acids and mono amino mono carboxylic acids with other basic substituents.

The structure and R_f values of the most widely distributed amino acids are listed in Table 10-1. These are also the amino acids commonly found as the monomeric units of proteins. Glycine, alanine, valine, leucine and isoleucine are "neutral" amino acids and differ from each other only with respect to the aliphatic side chain. Of these, glycine is the only one without any asymmetric carbon atom and is, therefore, the only one that cannot occur in an optically active form.

Serine and threonine contain one hydroxyl group adjacent to the amino function. Because of this they are unstable in hot sodium hydroxide solution and react quantitatively with sodium periodate (4). Cysteine, in which a sulfhydryl group replaces the hydroxyl group of serine also gives the above reactions. However, cysteine can be easily distinguished from the oxygen analogue by the red color obtained with nitroprusside reagent. Also cysteine is very easily oxidized aerobically to the disulfide cystine and to cysteic acid. Therefore, the isolation of cystine or cysteic acid is no proof that the compounds existed in that oxidation state in the intact cell. Methionine, another important sulfur-containing amino acid, can also yield spurious oxidation products. In this case, methionine sulfoxide or methionine sulfone are formed. Methionine is known to play an important biological role in transmethylation reactions, and there is ample evidence that the methyl group attached to the sulfur of methionine can be transferred in plants to yield oxygen and nitrogen methylated substances. The actual reactant in these methyl group transfers is S-adenosylmethionine ("active" methionine) formed by reaction of methionine with ATP:

L-methionine + ATP ⟶ S-adenosylmethionine + pyrophosphate + orthophosphate

Proline is a cyclic aliphatic amino acid and differs from the above compounds due to the presence of a secondary amino group. It is quite soluble in 95% ethanol.

Phenylalanine, tyrosine and tryptophan contain aromatic rings and therefore absorb light in the ultraviolet region. In fact, the light absorption of the simple proteins is attributable to the presence of these amino acids. Tyrosine, has abnormally low water solubility, 45 mg. in 100 ml. at 25° C. This property can be taken advantage of in isolation procedures. Tryptophan is readily oxidized in hot acidic solutions and is, therefore, completely destroyed during acid-catalyzed hydrolysis of proteins. It can be recovered from proteins by using either alkaline or enzymatic hydrolysis.

The acidic amino acids, aspartic acid and glutamic acid, as well as their amides asparagine and glutamine, are very widely distributed in higher plants and play a key role in metabolic reactions. Glutamine is quite reactive and is readily decomposed in boiling water to ammonium pyrrolidone carboxylate. Glutamic acid can also be cyclized but requires somewhat more vigorous reaction conditions than glutamine. Due to unfavorable steric factors, asparagine and aspartic acid do not give these reactions. Due to the lability of the primary amide bonds neither glutamine nor asparagine can be recovered from the acid or base catalyzed hydrolyses of proteins.

Aspartic and glutamic acids are important links between carbohydrate and protein metabolism. Both function, in different plants, as storage

TABLE 10-1. WIDELY DISTRIBUTED AMINO ACIDS

A. Neutral Amino Acids

	Name	Structure	Ninhydrin color	R_f values[1]	
				phenol water (pH 5.0-5.5)	n-butanol-acetic acid (9:1) - water
1.	glycine	$CH_2(NH_2)CO_2H$	Red violet	.38	.06
2.	L-alanine	$CH_3CH(NH_2)CO_2H$	Violet	.59	.11
3.	L-serine	$HOCH_2CH(NH_2)CO_2H$	Violet	.36	.05
4.	L-cysteine	$HSCH_2CH(NH_2)CO_2H$	-	-	-
5.	L-cystine	$[-SCH_2CH(NH_2)CO_2H]_2$	-	-	-
6.	L-cysteic acid[2]	$HO_3SCH_2CH(NH_2)CO_2H$	Violet	.07	.01
7.	L-threonine	$CH_3CH(OH)CH(NH_2)CO_2H$	Violet	.49	.09
8.	L-valine	$(CH_3)_2CHCH(NH_2)CO_2H$	Violet	.78	.24
9.	L-methionine	$CH_3S(CH_2)_2CH(NH_2)CO_2H$	-	-	-
10.	L-methionine sulfoxide[3]	$CH_3SO(CH_2)_2CH(NH_2)CO_2H$	Violet	.79	.05
11.	L-methionine sulfone[3]	$CH_3SO_2(CH_2)_2CH(NH_2)CO_2H$	Violet	.60	.27
12.	L-leucine	$(CH_3)_2CHCH_2CH(NH_2)CO_2H$	Violet	.84	.34
13.	L-isoleucine	$CH_3CH_2CH(CH_3)CH(NH_2)CO_2H$	Violet	.84	.36

[1] R_f values are those reported by F. C. Steward, R. M. Zacharius and J. K. Pollard, Suomalaisen Tiedeakat Toimituksia series A 60, 321 (1955). The R_f values have been rounded off to two decimal places here and were determined on Whatman number 1 filter paper.
[2] from cystine or cysteine
[3] from methionine

No.	Amino acid	Structure	Color		
14.	L-proline	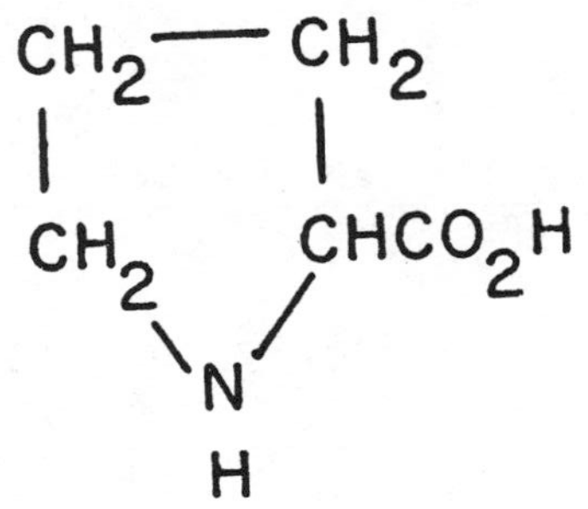	Yellow	.86	.14
15.	L-phenylalanine	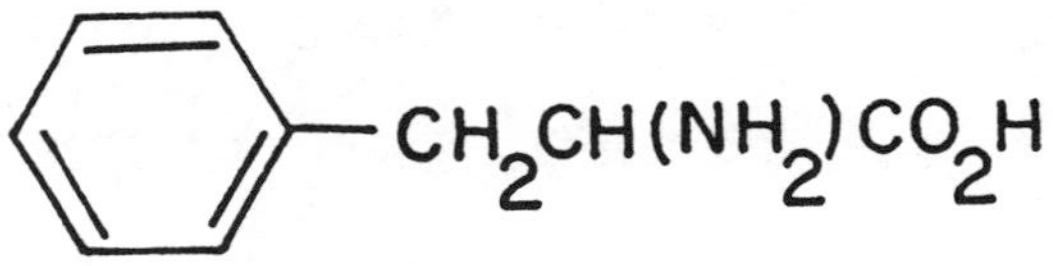 $CH_2CH(NH_2)CO_2H$ (phenyl)	Grey-violet	.84	.28
16.	L-tyrosine	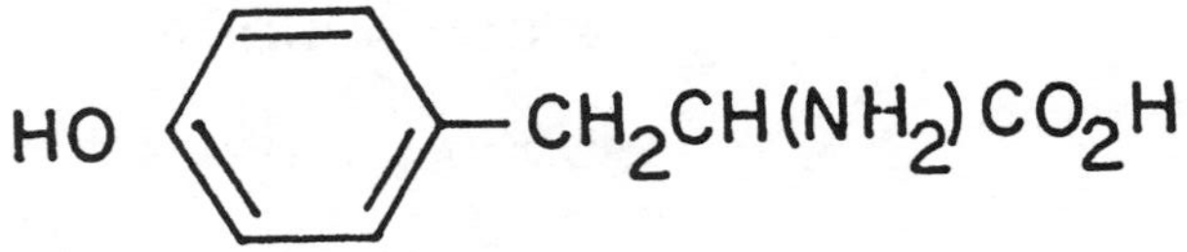 $CH_2CH(NH_2)CO_2H$ (HO-phenyl)	Grey-violet	.67	.16
17.	L-tryptophan	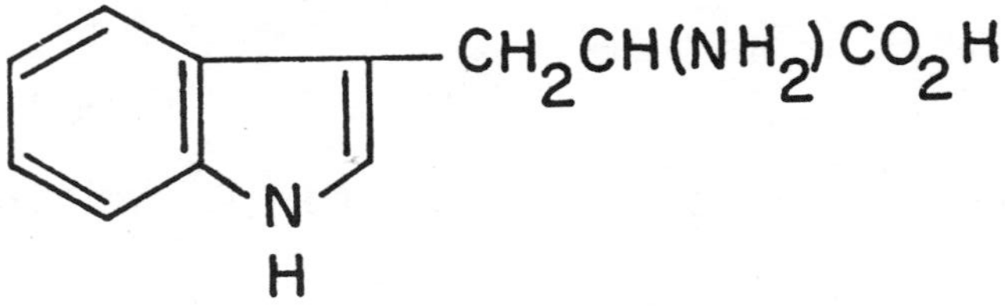 $CH_2CH(NH_2)CO_2H$ (indole)	Grey-violet	.80	.22
18.	L-asparagine	$H_2NOCCH_2CH(NH_2)CO_2H$	Orange-brown	.44	.02
19.	L-glutamine	$H_2NOC(CH_2)CH(NH_2)CO_2H$	Violet	.60	.04

Table 10-1. Continued

B. Acidic Amino Acids

No.	Name	Structure	Color		
20.	L-aspartic acid	$HO_2CCH_2CH(NH_2)CO_2H$	Blue-violet	.18	.03
21.	L-glutamic acid	$HO_2C(CH_2)_2CH(NH_2)CO_2H$	Violet	.31	.05

C. Basic Amino Acids

No.	Name	Structure	Color		
22.	L-arginine[4]	$NH_2C(=NH)NH(CH_2)_3CH(NH_2)CO_2H$	Violet	.56	.03
23.	L-lysine[4]	$NH_2(CH_2)_4CH(NH_2)CO_2H$	Violet	.48	.02
24.	L-histidine	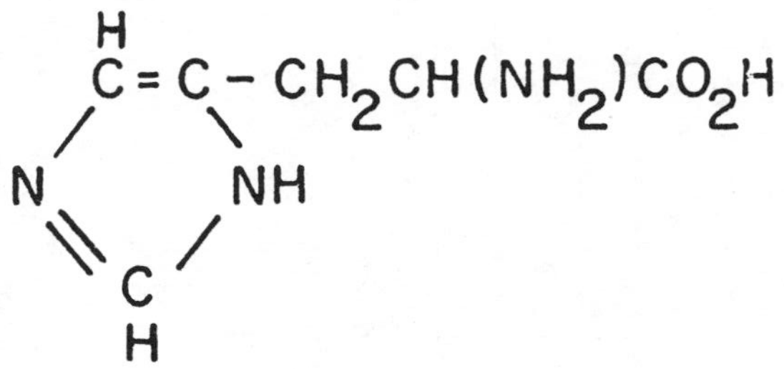 (imidazole structure)	Grey-violet	.64	.03

[4]Chromatographed as the mono hydrochloride

and transport forms of nitrogen (5, 6, 7).

The basic amino acids found in proteins and in the free state in higher plants are histidine, lysine and arginine. Of these, arginine is by far the strongest base having an isoelectric point of 10.76. Although arginine is quite stable in acidic medium, it is readily hydrolyzed to citrulline, $NH_2C(=O)NH(CH_2)_3CH(NH_2)CO_2H$, or ornithine, $NH_2(CH_2)_3CH(NH_2)CO_2H$, in basic solution. Both of these amino acids occur in higher plants. The unusual compound ε-N-trimethyllysine must be included among the protein amino acids since it is one of the components of wheat germ cytochrome C (8). Lysine owes its basic character to the presence of two amino groups in the molecule. Plant proteins are poor sources of this amino acid and since lysine is an essential amino acid for man, a diet containing plant proteins as the sole source of nitrogen will lead to a deficiency syndrome.

Although the isoelectric point of histidine is only 7.6, it is listed with the basic amino acids because it contains an imidazole group. This group is also involved in the formation of colored derivatives when proteins are treated with diazotized amines.

SPECIAL AMINO ACIDS FOUND IN HIGHER PLANTS

Since the introduction of partition chromatography, the isolation techniques available to chemists have gained in sophistication to the point where the number of new amino acids being discovered is increasing at an almost exponential rate. More than two hundred are now known. Therefore, no attempt will be made to list all the new plant amino acids, but it is hoped that the compounds selected for discussion will indicate the scope of the chemical variations being encountered. These compounds are not constituent amino acids of proteins and are found as free amino acids in a variety of higher plants. Comprehensive reviews of these non-protein amino acids have been published (9-11). The processing of huge amounts of plant material has revealed that many of these rare amino acids are, in fact, widely present in plants but in concentrations usually too low to be detected (12). The plants where they appear as significant constituents may be peculiar more in their ability to accumulate or failure to degrade than in their synthetic capacity.

The discovery of amino acids which are widely distributed in higher plants in which the amino group is not in the alpha position is of interest. Their structures are listed in Table 10-2. Of these, γ-aminobutyric acid (GABA) is the most widely distributed compound, and it is a rare event when it is absent from a plant extract. Physiologically it may serve as a temporary nitrogen storage compound (13). It is also a growth factor for crown gall tumors (14).

One recently emerging group of non-protein amino acids comprises the D-enantiomers of some common L-amino acids. D-alanine and D-tryptophan are well established but occur as N-malonyl and N-γ-L-glutamyl derivatives rather than free (15). More recently the natural occurrence of D-forms of glutamic, aspartic, and γ-aminobutyric acids has been reported (16, 17). Many D- amino acids have inhibitory effects on plant growth and metabolism (18 19). Their metabolism is discussed in the last section of this chapter.

TABLE 10-2 NON-ALPHA-AMINO ACIDS

Name	Structure	Ninhydrin color	Rf values	
			phenol water (pH 5.0-5.3)	1-butanol-acetic acid (9:1) water
gamma-aminobutyric acid	$H_2N(CH_2)_3CO_2H$	violet	.75	.15
beta-alanine	$H_2N(CH_2)_2CO_2H$	blue	.65	.09
alpha-methylene-gamma aminobutyric acid	$H_2N(CH_2)_2CHCO_2H$ $\underset{}{\overset{\|}{C}H_2}$			
beta amino isobutyric acid	$H_2NCH_2CH(CH_3)CO_2H$	grey-violet	.76	.20
gamma-amino-alpha-hydroxy-butyric acid	$H_2N(CH_2)_2(OH)CO_2H$			

Among the non-protein aromatic amino acids some are simple derivatives
of phenylalanine (20), and there are some derived from tyrosine and tryptophan. L-dihydroxyphenylalanine (DOPA) is widely distributed and in some
tissues may reach concentrations high enough to be repellant and toxic to
insects and animals (21-22). A plant growth inhibitory substance of *Abrus
precatorius* seeds is N, N-dimethyltryptophan (23). 5-Hydroxytryptophan
is found in a number of plants (24). Somewhat more restricted are several
m-carboxyphenyl-glycines and alanines and N-methylated arginines (25).

Another interesting class contains new heterocyclic and alicyclic
amino acids. Thus in addition to the long familiar histidine, proline and
tryptophan, the compounds listed in Table 10-3 must now be added. It will
be noted that with the finding of azetidine-2-carboxylic acid and pipecolic
acid a homologous series of 4, 5 and 6-membered nitrogen-containing rings
is now established. A cyclopropyl derivative, 1-aminocyclopropane-1-car-
boxylic acid, occurs in pears. Several other cyclopropane amino acids
are found in *Aesculus* spp. and *Blighia sapida* (26, 27). The first discovered of the *Blighia* compounds, hypoglycine A, has the ability to lower
blood glucose levels.

$$H_2C=C \overset{\displaystyle CH_2}{\diagup \diagdown} CH \ CH_2 \ CH(NH_2)CO_2H$$

hypoglycine A

4-Methylene-DL-proline, present in loquat seeds, inhibits plant growth (28).
More complex N-substituted derivatives of azetidine-2-carboxylic acid have
been found in several, unrelated plant families; and it has been suggested
that they have a role in iron chelation (29).

The number of naturally occurring dicarboxylic acids and amides has
also been extended. Representative compounds are listed in Table 10-4.
There is particular interest in γ-methyleneglutamine since evidence
exists that in the peanut this compound plays a major role in nitrogen
transport (30). In most cases, however, the biological function of these
compounds, if any, is still obscure.

New sulfur containing amino acids have also been discovered, Table
10-5. As already mentioned, great caution is required in those cases where
the only difference between the previously known compounds and the newer
ones is in the oxidation state of the sulfur. There is always the possibility that these substances are artifacts which are formed during isolation. S-methylcysteine sulfoxide which has been isolated from cabbage (31)
and from turnip roots appears to be a true plant constituent since
S-methylcysteine cannot be oxidized to the sulfoxide at room temperature
(32). This is contrary to the behavior of methionine which is oxidized
under those conditions. Alliin, which is also a sulfoxide, has been isolated
from garlic (33). (cf. Chap. 15).

Possibly alliin is also closely related biochemically to cyclo-alliin,
isolated from onion bulbs (34), since the latter is the cyclized form of
alliin. Djenkolic acid was first isolated from the urine of natives of

TABLE 10-3 STRUCTURE OF HETEROCYCLIC AMINO ACIDS

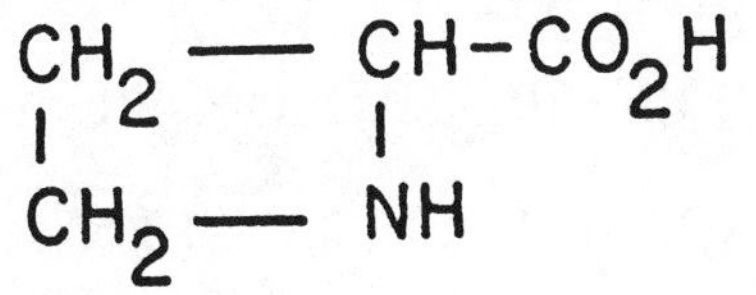

azetidine-2-carboxylic acid

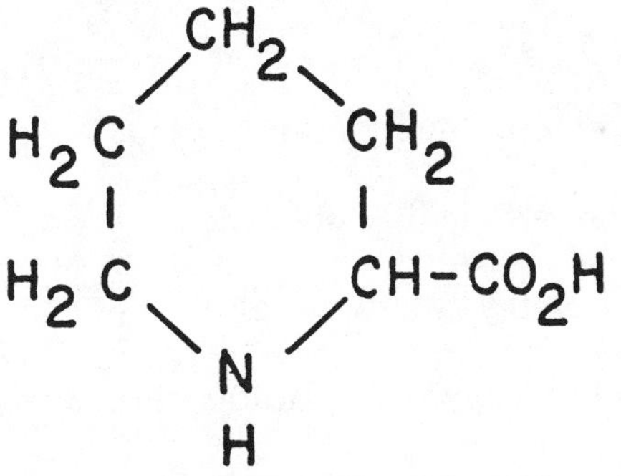

pipecolic acid

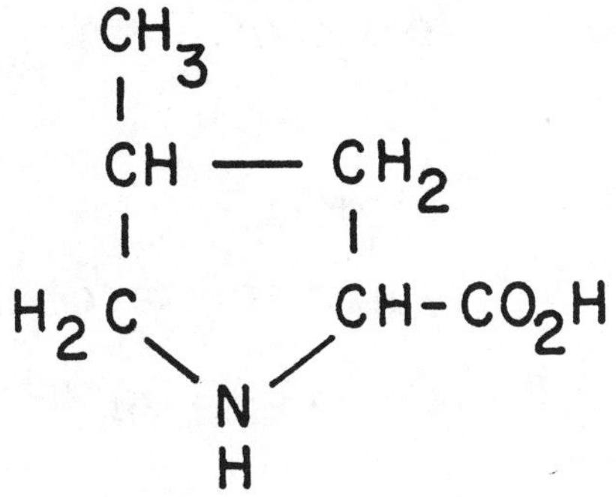

4-methyl proline

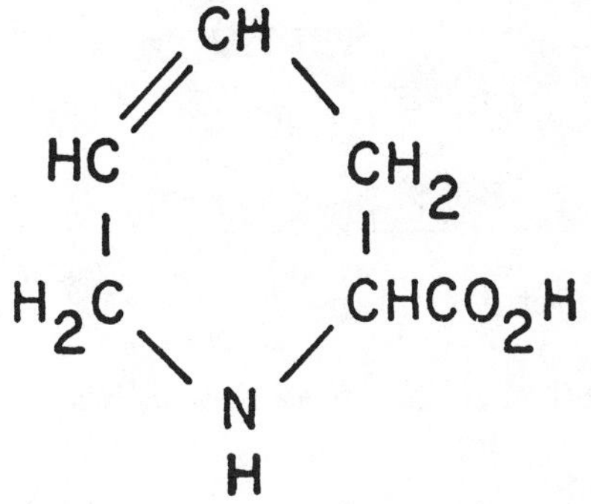

baikiain

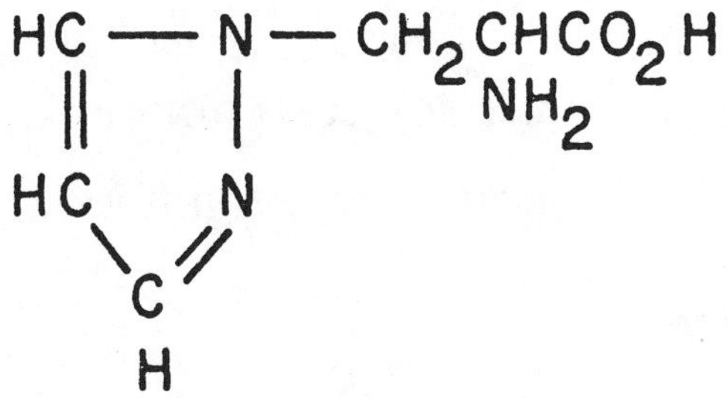

beta pyrazol-1-ylalanine

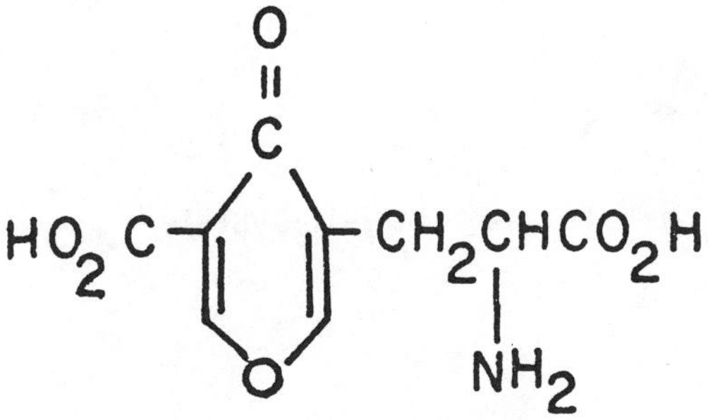

stizolobic acid

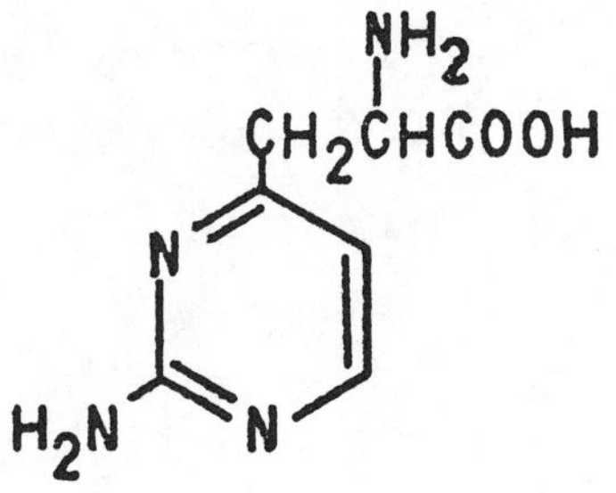

lathyrine

TABLE 10-4. DICARBOXYLIC AMINO ACIDS

Name	Structure
γ-methylene glutamic acid	$HO_2CC(=CH_2)CH_2CH(NH_2)CO_2H$
γ-methylene glutamine	$H_2NOCC(=CH_2)CH_2CH(NH_2)CO_2H$
γ-methyl glutamic acid	$HO_2CCH(CH_3)CH_2CH(NH_2)CO_2H$
γ-glutamyl ethylamide (theanine)	$C_2H_5HNOC(CH_2)_2CH(NH_2)CO_2H$
α-amino adipic acid	$HO_2C(CH_2)_3CH(NH_2)CO_2H$
α-amino pimelic acid	$HO_2C(CH_2)_4CH(NH_2)CO_2H$

TABLE 10-5. SULFUR CONTAINING AMINO ACIDS

Name	Structure
S-methylcysteine	$CH_3SCH_2CH(NH_2)CO_2H$
Methyl methionine sulfonium hydroxide	$[(CH_3)_2S^+(CH_2)_2CH(NH_2)CO_2H]OH^-$
Djenkolic acid	$HO_2CCH(NH_2)CH_2SCH_2SCH_2CH(NH_2)CO_2H$
S-methyl cysteine sulfoxide	$CH_3\overset{O}{\overset{\|}{S}}CH_2CH(NH_2)CO_2H$
Alliin	$H_2C=CHCH_2\overset{O}{\overset{\|}{S}}CH_2CH(NH_2)CO_2H$
S-2-carboxyethyl-L-cysteine	$HO_2CCH_2CH_2SCH_2CH(NH_2)CO_2H$
Cycloalliin	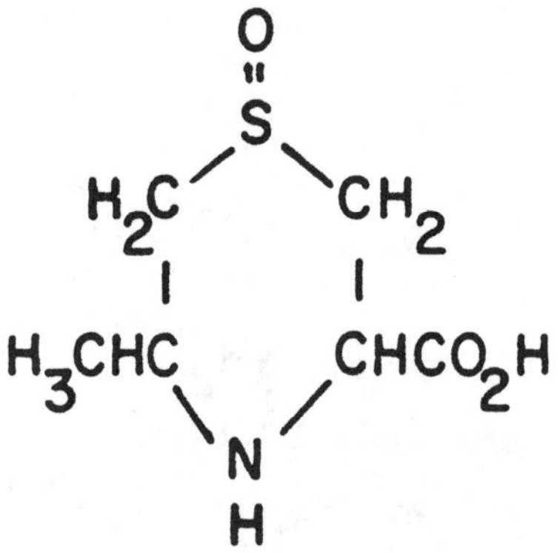

$$\begin{array}{ccc}
 & \overset{O}{\overset{\|}{S}} & \\
H_2C & & CH_2 \\
| & & | \\
H_3CHC & & CHCO_2H \\
 & \underset{H}{N} &
\end{array}$$

Java who had eaten the djenkol bean but was later shown to occur in the bean (35). Inspection of the structural formula (Table 10-5) shows that this compound can be considered to be a thio acetal between cysteine and formaldehyde.

A number of amino acids have been discovered in higher plants in which the presence of a hydroxyl group is the major distinction from the more common compounds, Table 10-6. However, this is not meant to imply that the biosynthesis of these compounds proceeds by oxidation of the parent compounds. Homoserine is an especially prominent member of this group and may function in nitrogen transport (36, 37). O-oxalylhomoserine occurs in *Lathyrus sativus* (38). Another interesting compound which may be considered in this group is canavanine, which, as the structure below indicates,

$$\begin{array}{c} NH \\ \parallel \\ H_2N-C-NOCH_2CH_2CHCO_2H \\ \quad\quad | \quad\quad\quad\quad | \\ \quad\quad H \quad\quad\quad\quad NH_2 \end{array}$$

is a hydroxyguanidine derivative. The similarity of this compound to arginine is sufficient to permit hydrolysis of canavanine by arginase to urea and canaline, $H_2NOCH_2CH_2CH(NH_2)CO_2H$. The latter compound is frequently found together with canavanine in jackbean meal and other leguminous species (39, 40). There is evidence that a canavanine-urea cycle functions in the jackbean plant and that several compounds of this cycle are potent antimetabolites (41). Canavanine, in particular, is toxic to many insects (42, 43).

TABLE 10-6   HYDROXY AMINO ACIDS

1.	homoserine	$HO(CH_2)_2CH(NH_2)CO_2H$
2.	gamma-hydroxy valine	$HOCH_2CH(CH_3)CH(NH_2)CO_2H$
3.	gamma-hydroxy glutamic acid	$HO_2CCH(OH)CH_2CH(NH_2)CO_2H$
4.	beta-gamma-dihydroxy glutamic acid	$HO_2CCH(OH)CH(OH)CH(NH_2)CO_2H$
5.	gamma-methyl-gamma hydroxy-glutamic acid	$\begin{array}{c} CH_3 \\ | \\ HO_2CCCH_2CHCO_2H \\ | \quad\quad | \\ OH \quad NH_2 \end{array}$
6.	5-hydroxy pipecolic acid	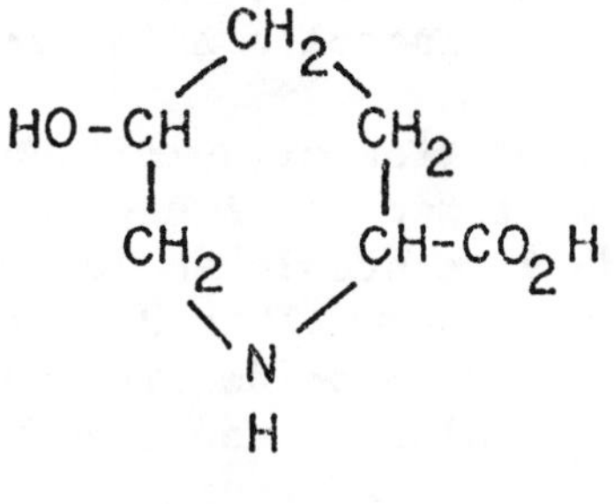

$$\begin{array}{ccc} & CH_2 & \\ HO-CH & & CH_2 \\ & & \\ CH_2 & & CH-CO_2H \\ & N & \\ & H & \end{array}$$

The neurotoxic effects of eating certain species of *Lathyrus* can be attributed to their content of certain peculiar amino acids, the most important of which are 2, 4-diaminobutyric acid, β-oxalyl 2, 3-diaminopropionic acid, β-cyanoalanine, and γ-glutamyl β-cyanoalanine (44, 45). Species of *Lathyrus* which lack 2, 4-diaminobutyric acid may contain instead the C_7 compound homoarginine and its derivatives, γ-hydroxyhomoarginine and lathyrine (46, 47). Some of these same, and related, compounds account for toxic properties of *Vicia*, *Crotolaria*, and *Cycas* species (48-50).

Since the number of plant species examined for various amino acids
is still very small, it is difficult to reach definite conclusions on the
distribution of the amino acids that are not generally found in proteins.
Some are rather widely distributed. Others are of only very limited
distribution. There is considerable speculation about a role for unusual
amino acids in plants. It has been noted above that certain ones are toxic
to insects and other herbivores and could have a protective function.
Several reviews discuss this possibility further (51-54).

ISOLATION

Before the advent of ion exchange and partition chromatography most
amino acids were isolated from specific protein hydrolysates or from the
amino acids present in the tissues of particular plants or animals. Thus
asparagine, the first amino acid to be isolated from nature was obtained
by concentration of asparagus juice (1). Aspartic acid can be prepared
from asparagine by acid hydrolysis. Glutamic acid is obtained from acid
hydrolysates of wheat gluten. Isoleucine was isolated from sugar beet
molasses. Phenylalanine and arginine were isolated from etiolated lupine
seedlings. The other common amino acids can in most cases be conveniently
isolated from animal sources.

The isolation of the newer plant amino acids generally requires more
sophisticated techniques, since these compounds are present in the cell
sap together with a large number of other cell constituents and frequently
occur only in small amounts. Almost every case presents unique problems
that have to be solved on an individual basis. However, ion exchange
processes in one form or another are often extremely useful. As an initial procedure ion exchange can be used for the concentration of amino
acids, the removal of neutral contaminants, and the subdivision of the amino
acids into neutral, acidic, and basic fractions (55). After preliminary
concentration and purification steps have been taken, it may be necessary to
separate the desired amino acids from a number of closely related compounds.
More refined ion exchange procedures can be used for this purpose, paying
close attention to such variables as pH and temperature (56). A classical
example of the application of ion exchange procedures was the isolation of
13.4 g. of L- pipecolic acid from 150 lbs. of green beans (57).

The isolation of γ-aminobutyric acid from potato tubers illustrates
a very elegant method of separating a non-alpha amino acid (58). The alpha
amino acids form stable chelates with divalent cations, whereas the non-
alpha acids do not. This difference can be utilized to effect separation
of non-alpha amino acids from the alpha amino acids by using a column
consisting of alumina and copper carbonate. With this technique the alpha amino acids are retained on the column under conditions which cause
elution of the non-alpha amino acids.

Quantitative amino acid determinations are most conveniently carried
out by column procedure utilizing chromatography with ion exchange resins
(59). Completely automatic recording analyzers are available commercially;
but since commercial instruments are not designed to cope with the great
variety of unusual amino acids that are encountered in plants, some modifications are required (60). Another procedure is the use of volatile

buffers as eluting solvents for ion-exchange columns (61). With these
solvents the amino acids are frequently obtained in a very high state of
purity after evaporation of the solvents. Mention should also be made of
procedures which combine ion exchange resins with filter paper partition
chromatography (62). Thin layer chromatography on 1 mm. layers of cellulose
can be used preparatively for samples as large as 40 mg. (63).

CHARACTERIZATION

At present the best-known method for rapid identification of the amino
acids in a mixture is paper chromatography. Usually two dimensional chromatography is needed for good separations of complex mixtures. The required
apparatus is inexpensive, the manipulations can be learned rapidly, and in
most cases as little as 5-10 micrograms of a given amino acid can be
detected routinely. The R_f values for a large number of naturally occurring
and synthetic amino acids have been compiled (64, 65), and some of these
are presented in Table 10-1. The most popular developing solvents seem to
be 1-butanol/acetic acid/water mixtures and water-saturated phenol. In
spite of the vast literature on paper chromatography of amino acids, there
seem to be more publications recently on thin layer methods (66-70).
Cellulose powder layers are most frequently used, and with two-dimensional
development great resolution is possible. Paper electrophoresis and combined electrophoresis-chromatography have also been used (71).

For detection of spots on paper sheets or thin layer plates a 0.1%
solution of ninhydrin in butanol or ethanol is most commonly used. Spots
appear after standing at room temperature for several hours, or in a few
minutes with heating to 100° after spraying. The chemistry and specificity
of the ninhydrin reaction are discussed in (72). Some improved ninhydrin
reagents have been devised to give a greater range of colors with different
compounds (70 73). Some keto acids also give colors with ninhydrin (74).
A spray based on o-phthalaldehyde can be used for sensitivity greater than
that obtainable with ninhydrin (75).

High pressure liquid chromatography has been found a rapid and
convenient method for analysis of amino acid mixtures either unmodified
or after derivatization. Most of these separations are based on partition
and adsorption phenomena rather than the ion exchange reactions described
above (76-78). Prior derivatization has the advantage that fluorescent
derivatives can be used for convenient detection of peaks in the column
effluent (79). To detect unmodified amino acids the effluent can be
monitored at 200-206 nm (80).

Gas chromatography can be used with the amino acids by first converting
them to volatile derivatives. This is commonly done by making n-butyl
esters of the carboxyl groups and trifluoroacetyl derivatives of the amino
groups (81-83).

The special problem of identifying D-amino acids where quantities do
not permit optical rotation measurements has been met by the use of D-amino
acid oxidase. As little as 5 nmoles of D-amino acid can be detected (84, 85).

REACTIONS WITH AMINO ACID SIDE CHAINS

Specific tests, which in some cases are quantitative, have been developed for several amino acids. These depend on differences in the structure of the side chains for their selectivity and can be applied to peptides and proteins. Thus, the guanidine group of arginine permits the colorimetric determination of this compound by reaction with sodium hypochlorite and alpha naphthol in alkaline solution (86). Histidine and tyrosine are converted to azo dyes by treatment with diazotized sulfanilic acid (87). Tyrosine also gives a positive Millon test, a red precipitate with mercurous nitrate in nitric acid, a reaction which is specific for phenols containing a free ortho position (88). Cysteine, due to the presence of a sulfhydryl group, gives a transient purple violet color with sodium nitroprusside, $Na_2 Fe(CN)_5 (NO)$ in the presence of base (89). Tryptophan yields various colored products on reaction with various aldehydes in the presence of sulfuric acid (90).

METABOLIC PATHWAYS

Striking advances have been made in the elucidation of the biosynthetic pathways of amino acids and proteins. However, because of the ready availability of mutants of microorganisms most of the work has been carried out with these primitive plants. Unfortunately, one has no assurance that these processes are universal, and it is extremely risky to attempt to apply the results obtained with micro-organisms to higher plants. The pathways shown in Figures 10-1 - 10-3 represent a composite derived from many different organisms, and in some cases intermediate steps are omitted in the transformations. Reviews of amino acid biosynthesis and breakdown appear frequently in the literature (5). Some other papers that deal with broad aspects of amino acid interrelationships in plants are (91-93).

NITROGEN FIXATION AND NITRATE REDUCTION

Molybdenum appears to be of prime significance in both the symbiotic and non-symbiotic nitrogen fixations. A great deal of evidence can be cited to support the belief that atmospheric nitrogen is reduced stepwise to the ammonia level, and that it enters the metabolic pools in the form of glutamine and glutamic acid. The exact nature of the intermediates is not known, and they may remain bound to the enzyme until released as ammonia. Cell-free preparations with which nitrogen fixation can be carried out are available and should be of great utility in the determination of the intermediates and enzymes involved in the process (94).

Most species of higher plants possess the ability to reduce nitrate to the ammonia level. The first intermediate in this process is nitrite. The enzyme involved in this process in some organisms is a soluble molybdenum flavoprotein, and the electron donor is NADH (95, 96). The reduction of nitrite to ammonia occurs both in chloroplasts and in roots. The actual reductant in chloroplasts is probably ferredoxin (97). In roots the reductant is unknown (98).

BIOSYNTHESIS OF AMINO ACIDS

The close interrelationship between carbohydrate and amino acid metabolism has been known for a long time. Thus, pyruvic acid, oxalacetic acid and alpha-ketoglutaric acid, compounds arising during the oxidation of glucose, can be converted by transamination or reductive amination reactions to L-alanine, L-aspartic acid and L-glutamic acid, respectively. Glutamic acid and aspartic acid, are in turn, precursors of a large number of other amino acids. The incorporation of nitrogen from ammonia into glutamic acid has two possible routes. The reaction catalyzed by glutamic dehydrogenase has been known the longest, but it appears that in higher plants the major route is a two-step one involving first the formation of glutamine and then reaction of glutamine and α-ketoglutaric acid to yield two molecules of glutamic acid (5, 99-101). Glutamic acid is a close precursor of ornithine (102), proline (103), and γ-aminobutyric acid (104). Ornithine is in turn a precursor of arginine (105, 106). Ornithine can also be converted to proline or back to glutamic acid (107). Proline is also convertible to glutamic acid but not to ornithine (108). Arginine may exist in two pools -- one associated with polyamine metabolism, and one with the urea cycle (109).

Asparagine in most plants is made from aspartic acid by transfer of an amido group from glutamine, rather than directly from ammonia by a reaction analagous to glutamine synthesis (110). In corn roots, however, there is an asparagine synthetase that can use ammonia as well as glutamine (111). In addition, a peculiar pathway to asparagine has been found to be potentially present in many plants. In this pathway hydrogen cyanide reacts with cysteine or serine to form β-cyanoalanine (112, 113). A specific enzyme then hydrolyzes the β-cyanoalanine to asparagine (114). The function of the cyanide pathway remains dubious since few plants with the necessary enzymes contain cyanogenic compounds. The pathway may represent a way of detoxifying hydrogen cyanide produced by soil microorganisms (115). Aspartic acid is also a close precursor of 2,4-diaminobutyric acid (analogous to ornithine from glutamic)(116) of lysine, and of homoserine. In turn homoserine is a precursor of threonine, methionine, and many other compounds. The regulation of pathways leading from aspartic acid to lysine, threonine, and methionine has received much experimental attention. Kinetic properties of several of the enzymes permit delicate feedback control by the end-products (117-121). Most lysine synthesis occurs in chloroplasts and follows a pathway characteristic of prokaryotes, having 2,6-diaminopimelic acid as an intermediate. However, some cytoplasmic lysine synthesis may also occur by a pathway with α-aminoadipic acid as intermediate (122, 123). Lysine is further converted to pipecolic acid in many plants and is a reasonable precursor of homoarginine and lathyrine (124, 125). However, recent evidence suggests that the latter two compounds come, rather, from a preformed pyrimidine (126). The catabolic pathway for lysine leads to acetyl CoA (127). β-alanine, which might reasonably arise from decarboxylation of aspartic acid, evidently comes rather from pyrimidine or polyamine degradation (128, 129).

Serine, which can come from 3-phosphoglycerate, and glycine, which can come from glycolate, are interconvertible by a reaction involving a tetrahydrofolate derivative (130, 131). Thus the question arises whether most serine is made from glycine or most glycine from serine; and it appears that both ways are possible depending on the system studied (132, 133).

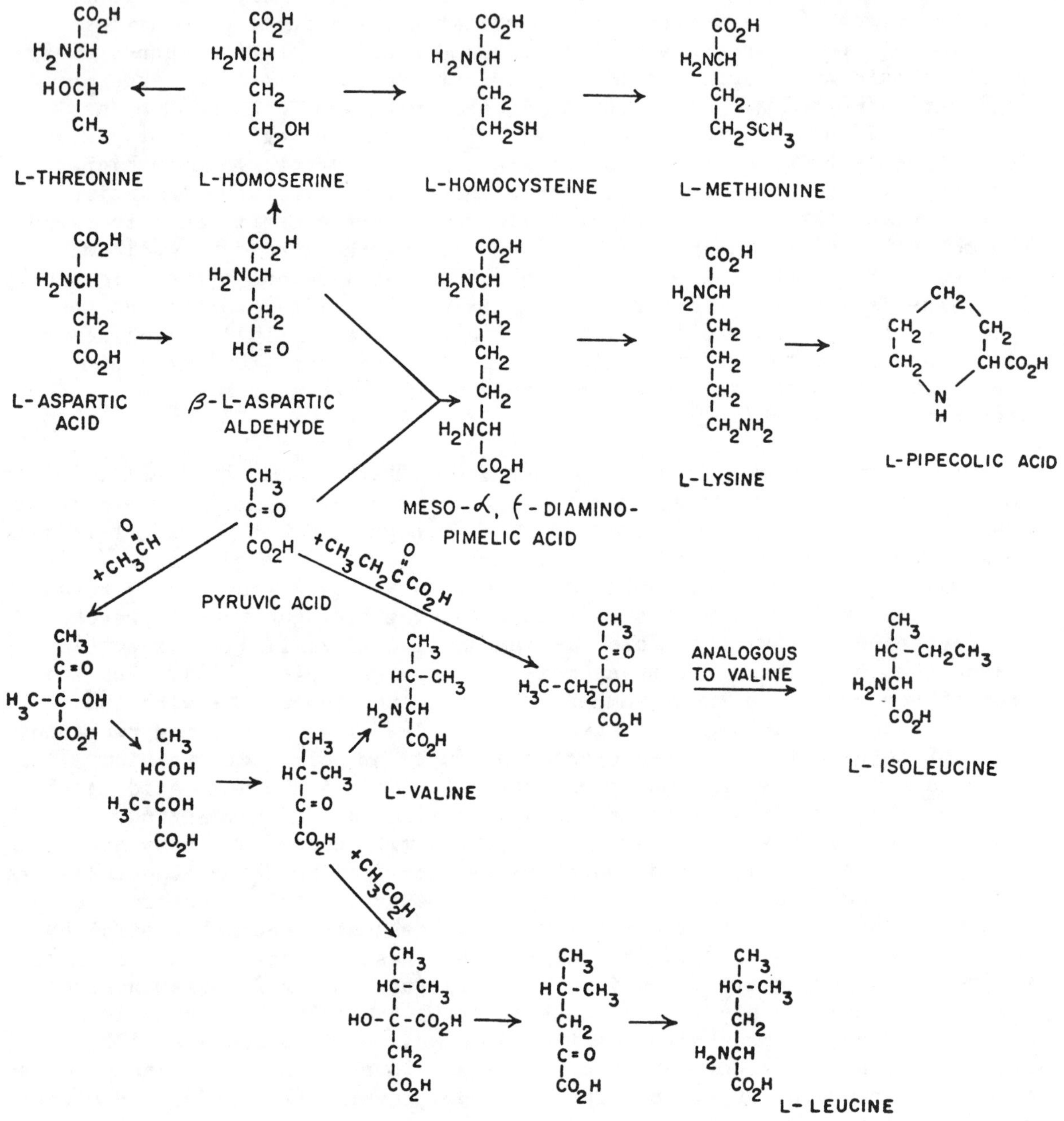

FIGURE 10-1 AMINO ACID PATHWAYS

There are also two pathways from 3-phosphoglycerate to serine -- one using phosphorylated intermediates (134, 135) and one using non-phosphorylated intermediates (136). Serine can also be metabolized to pyruvate (137, 138). Catabolism of glycine yields carbon dioxide from the carboxyl group and a one-carbon unit that can be used for methyl group synthesis as well as for serine synthesis (139). O-Acetylserine appears to be the precursor of many peculiar β-substituted alanines found in plants. A widely distributed transferase of low specificity catalyzes exchange of the acetate unit for many different groups (140-142).

O-acetylserine is also a key precursor of the sulfur amino acids. In this pathway the acetate unit is replaced by sulfhydryl giving cysteine (142, 143). Reaction of cysteine with O-phosphorylhomoserine gives cystathionine, which is split to serine plus homocysteine, and the latter is methylated to make methionine (145, 146). The importance of methionine (as its S-adenosyl derivative) in transmethylation reactions is well-established in plants. It may also be a precursor of azetidine-2-carboxylic acid (147), although another pathway from 2,4-diaminobutyric acid is also indicated (148).

Biosynthesis of the branched chain acids has not been intensively investigated in higher plants, but clearly pyruvic acid is the primary source of their carbon skeletons through a series of complex condensations and rearrangements (149). Leucine appears to be the precursor of γ-methyl- and γ-methylene-glutamic acids (150).

The biosynthesis of proline has already been mentioned. The 4-trans-L-hydroxyproline found in proteins is not made by hydroxylation of free proline but only after incorporation of the proline into a peptide. An enzyme system from carrots catalyzes this hydroxylation (151). Another plant enzyme will hydroxylate free proline to 3-trans-L-hydroxyproline (148). Enzymes of the histidine biosynthetic pathway have been studied in extracts of several plants (152).

Most studies on aromatic amino acid biosynthesis have been carried out with microorganisms, but the pathways shown in Figure 10-3 have been mostly confirmed for higher plants (153). The pathway to chorismic acid is given in Figure 4-1. The m-carboxy substituted aromatic acids such as 3-(3-carboxyphenyl)-alanine are made by an alternate pathway starting at chorismic acid (154). The possibility of direct conversion of phenylalanine to tyrosine remains in doubt, although claims of this reaction have appeared from time to time. Similarly, the natural system responsible for converting tyrosine to dihydroxyphenylalanine remains unknown (155). Many details of the tryptophan synthetase reaction have been studied in higher plants. The responsible enzyme has two subunits, and both are needed for utilization of indole-3-glycerol phosphate; but the B subunit alone catalyzes condensation of indole with serine. The A subunit alone catalyzes a slow cleavage of the phosphate to indole plus glyceraldehyde-3-phosphate (156, 157). All five enzymes for the pathway of chorismic acid to tryptophan have been identified in carrots (156) and wheat (158). Although they are not themselves aromatic, stizolobic acid and stizolobinic acid are made from dihydroxyphenylalanine by a complex sequence of reactions (159).

The deamination of amino acids to unsaturated acids has been most studied with phenylalanine and tyrosine (Chap. 4). However, the same reaction can occur with many other amino acids and is catalyzed by enzymes of peroxisomes or glyoxysomes (160).

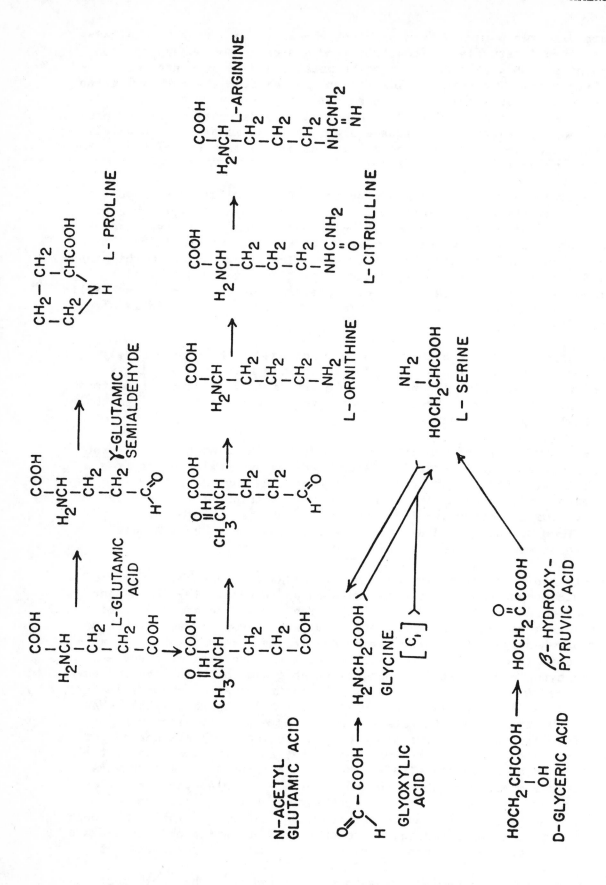

FIGURE 10–2 AMINO ACID PATHWAYS

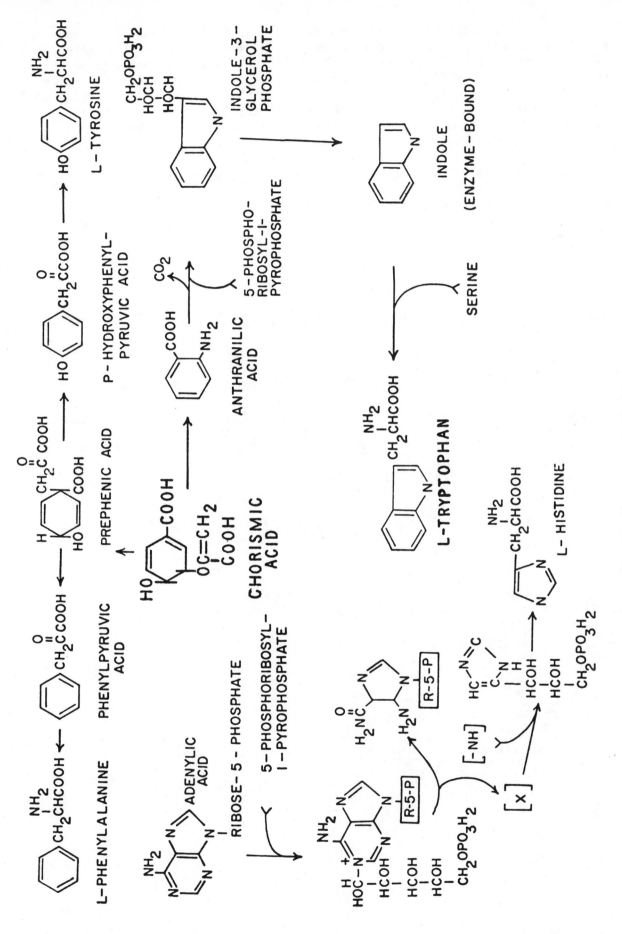

FIGURE 10-3 AMINO ACID PATHWAYS

The special metabolism of D-amino acids in higher plants has been receiving attention. In general, exogenous D-amino acids are converted by plants to N-malonyl derivatives (161-163). This could be regarded as an artifact or detoxification mechanism, but some N-malonyl-D-amino acids seem to occur naturally. There are other possible pathways for D-amino acids. Some transaminases have high specificity for the D-amino acids (164-166) and could mediate conversion to the L-isomers. Some direct interconversion of L and D isomers can occur, presumably by action of a racemase (167-169); and D-isomers can be metabolized ultimately to carbon dioxide (170). Most interesting is the possibility of quite different products from the two isomers as in the case where L-lysine is the preferred precursor of anabasine in *Nicotiana glauca* while D-lysine in the same plant is the precursor of pipecolic acid (171). This finding suggests that many experiments with labeled racemic mixtures may require reexamination.

GENERAL REFERENCES

Beevers, L. (1976) Nitrogen Metabolism in Plants, University Park Press, Baltimore.
Greenstein, J. P. & Winitz, M. (1961) Chemistry of the Amino Acids, 3 Vols., Wiley, N. Y.
Meister, A. (1965) Biochemistry of the Amino Acids, 2nd ed., Academic Press, N. Y.
Niederwieser, A. & Pataki, G. (1971) New Techniques in Amino Acid, Peptide, and Protein Analysis, Ann Arbor Science Publishers, Ann Arbor, Mich.
Sheppard, R. C. (1976) Amino Acids, Peptides, and Proteins 6, Chemical Society, London.
Several articles in Paech & Tracey 4

BIBLIOGRAPHY

1. Vauquelin, L. N. and Robiquet, P. J. (1806) Ann. Chim. (Paris) 57 88-93.
2. Martin, C. and Thimann, K. V. (1972) Plant Physiol. 50 432-437.
3. Baker, H. G. and Baker, I. (1973) Nature 241 543-545.
4. Nicolet, B. H. and Shinn, L. A. (1941) J. Biol. Chem. 139 687-692.
5. Miflin, B. J. and Lea, P. J. (1977) Ann. Rev. Plant Physiol. 28 299-329.
6. Streeter, J. G. (1977) Plant Physiol. 60 235-239.
7. Maxwell, M. A. B. and Bidwell, R. G. S. (1970) Can. J. Bot. 48 923-927.
8. DeLange, R. J., Glazer, A. N. and Smith E. L. (1969) J. Biol. Chem. 244 1385-1388.
9. Fowden, L. (1974) Recent Adv. Phytochem. 8 95-122.
10. Fowden, L., Lea, P. J., and Bell, E. A. (1979) Adv. Enzymol. 50 117-176.
11. Bell, E. A. (1976) FEBS Letters 64 29-35.
12. Fowden, L. Phytochem. 11 2271-2276 (1972).
13. Selman, I. W. and Cooper P. (1978) Ann. Botany 42 627-636.
14. Peters, K. E., Lippincott, J. A., and Studier, M. (1974) Phytochem. 13 2383-2386.
15. Robinson, T. (1976) Life Sciences 19 1097-1102.
16. Ogawa, T., Bando, N., and Sasaoka, K. (1976) Agric. Biol. Chem. (Japan) 40 1661-1662.
17. Ogawa, T., Kimoto, M., and Sasaoka, K. (1977) Agric. Biol. Chem. (Japan) 41 1811-1812.
18. Nicolle, J. and Hedin, L. (1969) Compt. Rend. D 269 2611-1213.
19. Aldag, R. W. and Young, J. L. (1970) Agron. J. 62 184-189.
20. Mothes, K., Schütte, H. R., Müller, P., Ardenne, M. v. and Tümmler, R., (1964) Z. Naturforsch. 19b 1161-1162.

21. Bell, E. A. and Janzen, D. H. (1971) Nature 229 136-137.
22. Rehr, S. S., Janzen, D. H., and Feeny, P. P. (1973) Science 181 81-82.
23. Mandava, N., Anderson, J. D., and Dutky, S. R. (1974) Phytochemistry 13 2853-2856.
24. Fellows, L. E. and Bell, E. A. (1970) Phytochem. 9 2389-2396.
25. Kasai, T., Sano, M., and Sakamura, S. (1976) Agric. Biol. Chem. 40 2449-2453.
26. Fowden, L., MacGibbon, C. M., Mellon, F. A., and Sheppard, R. C. (1972) Phytochem. 11 1105-1110.
27. Bressler, R. (1976) New Eng. J. Med. 295 500-501.
28. Gray, D. O. and Fowden, L. (1972) Phytochem. 11 745-750.
29. Takemoto, T. and 8 Others (1978) Proc. Japan Acad. 54 B 469-473.
30. Fowden, L. (1954) Ann. Botany 18 417-440.
31. Synge, R. L. M. and Wood, J. C. (1955, 1956) Biochem. J. 60 xv, 64 252-259.
32. Morris, C. J. O. R. and Thompson, J. F. (1956) J. Am. Chem. Soc. 78 1605-1608.
33. Stoll, A. and Seebeck, E. (1947) Experientia 3 114-115.
34. Virtanen, A. I. and Matikkala, E. J. (1959) Acta Chem. Scand. 13 623-626.
35. duVigneaud, V. and Patterson, W. I. (1936) J. Biol. Chem. 114 533-538.
36. Goas, G. (1966) Compt. rend. 262 1534-1537.
37. Grant, D. R. and Voelkert, E. (1970) Phytochemistry 9 985-990.
38. Przybylska, J. and Pawełkiewicz, J. (1966) Bull. Acad. Polon. Sci., Ser. Biol. 13 327-329.
39. Rosenthal, G. A. (1970) Plant Physiol. 46 273-276.
40. Rosenthal, G. A. (1972) Plant Physiol. 50 328-331.
41. Rosenthal, G. A., Gulati, D. K. and Sabharwal, P. S. (1976) Plant Physiol. 57 493-496.
42. Rosenthal, G. A. (1978) Life Sciences 23 93-98.
43. Rosenthal, G. A., Janzen, D. H., and Dahlman, D. L. (1977) Science 196 658-660.
44. Ressler, C. (1964) Fed. Proc. 23 1350-1353.
45. Rosmus, J., Trnavský, K., and Deyl, Z. (1966) Biochem. Pharmacol. 15 1405-1410.
46. Bell, E. A. and O'Donovan, J. P. (1966) Phytochemistry 5 1211-1219.
47. Bell, E. A. and Przybylska, J. (1965) Biochem. J. 94 34P.
48. Ressler, C., Nigam, S. N., and Giza, Y.-H. (1969) J. Am. Chem. Soc. 91 2758-2765.
49. Bell, E. A. (1968) Nature 218 197.
50. Vega, A. and Bell, E. A. (1967) Phytochemistry 6 759-762.
51. Janzen, D. H. (1973) Pure Appl. Chem. 34 529-538.
52. Norris, R. D. and Lea, P. J. (1976) Sci. Prog. 63 65-85.
53. Lea, P. J. and Norris, R. D. (1976) Phytochemistry 15 585-595.
54. Evans, C. S. and Bell, E. A. (1979) Phytochemistry 18 1807-1810.
55. Lazarus, W. (1973) J. Chromatog. 87 169-178.
56. Thönes, S., Furch, B. and Tutschek, R. (1978) J. Chromatog. 153 536-538.
57. Grobbelaar, N., Zacharius, R. M., and Steward, F. C. (1954) J. Am. Chem. Soc. 76 2912-2915.
58. Thompson, J. F., Pollard, J. K., and Steward, F. C. (1953) Plant Physiol. 28 401-414.
59. Spackman, D. H., Stein, W. H., and Moore, S. (1958) Anal. Chem. 30 1190-1206.
60. Charlwood, B. V. and Bell, E. A. (1977) J. Chromatog. 135 377-384.
61. Hirs, C. H. W., Moore, S., and Stein, W. H. (1952) J. Biol. Chem. 195 669-683.
62. Tuckerman, M. M. (1958) Anal. Chem. 30 231-233.
63. Spener, F. and Dieckhoff, M. (1973) J. Chromatog. Sci. 11 661-662.
64. Fowden, L. and Steward, F. C. (1957) Ann. Botany 21 53-67.
65. Solberg, Y. J. (1965) Acta Chem. Scand. 19 1269-1270.
66. Pataki, G. (1968) Thin Layer Chromatography in Amino Acid and Peptide Chemistry, Ann Arbor Science Publishers, Ann Arbor, Mich.
67. Ogner, G. (1969) Acta Chem. Scand. 23 2185-2186.
68. Haworth, C. and Heathcote, J. G. (1969) J. Chromatog. 41 380-385.
69. Pillay, D. T. and Mehdi, R. (1970) J. Chromatog. 47 119-123.
70. Krauss, G.-J. and Reinbothe, H. (1970) Biochem. Physiol. Pflanzen. 161 577-592.
71. Gramroth, B. (1968) Acta Chem. Scand. 22 3333-3335.
72. McCaldin, D. J. (1960) Chem. Rev. 60 39-51.
73. Tyihák, E. and Vágujfalvi, D. (1970) J. Chromatog. 40 343-348.
74. Schilling, E. D., Burchill, P. I., Coffman, J. R., and Clayton, R. A. (1961) Biochem. Biophys. Res. Commun. 5 217-220.
75. Davies, H. M. and Miflin, B. J. (1978) J. Chromatog. 153 284-286.
76. Fong, G. W.-K. and Grushka, E. (1977) J. Chromatog. 142 299-309.
77. Kroeff, E. P. and Pietrzyk, D. J. (1978) Anal. Chem. 50 502-511.
78. Lundanes, E. and Greibrokk, T. (1978) J. Chromatogr. 149 241-254.
79. Bayer, E., Grom, E., Kaltenegger, B., and Uhmann, R. (1976) Anal. Chem. 48 1106-1109.
80. Molnar, I. and Horvath, C. (1977) J. Chromatog. 142 623-640.
81. **Iwase, H., Takeuchi, Y., and Murai, A. (1979) Chem. Pharm Bull. (Tokyo) 27 1306-1316.**
82. Adams, R. F. (1974) J. Chromatog. 95 189-212.
83. Husek, P. and Macek, K. (1975) J. Chromatog. 113 139-230.
84. Larson, D. M., Snetsinger, D. C., and Waibel, P. E. (1971) Anal. Biochem. 39 395-401.
85. Aldag, R. W., Young, J. L., and Yamamoto, M. (1971) Phytochemistry 10 267-274.
86. Sakaguchi, S. (1925) J. Biochem. (Japan) 5 25-31, 133-142.
87. Hanke, M. (1926) J. Biol. Chem. 66 475-488.
88. Folin, O. and Ciocalteu, V. (1927) J. Biol. Chem. 73 627-650.

89. Brand, E., Harris, M. M., and Biloon, S. (1930) J. Biol. Chem. 86 315-331.
90. Holm, G. E. and Greenbank, G. R. (1923) J. Am. Chem. Soc. 45 1788-1792.
91. Bauer, A., Urquhart, A. A., and Joy, K. W. (1977) Plant Physiol. 59 915-919.
92. Bauer, A., Joy, K. W., and Urquhart, A. A. (1977) Plant Physiol. 59 920-924.
93. Macnicol, P. K. (1977) Plant Physiol. 60 344-348.
94. Shanmugam, K. T., O'Gara, F., Andersen, K., and Valentine, R. C. (1978) Ann. Rev. Plant Physiol. 29 263-276.
95. Wells, G. N. and Hageman, R. H. (1974) Plant Physiol. 54 136-141.
96. Wallsgrove, R. M., Lea, P. J., and Miflin, B. J. (1979) Plant Physiol. 63 232-236.
97. Neyra, C. A. and Hageman, R. H. (1974) Plant Physiol. 54 480-483.
98. Ida, S., Mori, E., and Morita, Y. (1974) Planta 121 213-224.
99. Chiu, J. Y. and Shargool, P. D. (1979) Plant Physiol. 63 409-415.
100. Nicklisch, A., Geske, W., and Kohl, J.-G. (1976) Biochem. Physiol. Pflanzen 170 85-90.
101. Stewart, G. R. and Rhodes, D. (1977) New Phytol. 79 257-268.
102. McKay, G. and Shargool, P. D. (1977) Plant Sci. Letters 9 184-193.
103. Mazelis, M. and Fowden, L. (1969) Phytochemistry 8 801-809.
104. Streeter, J. G. and Thompson, J. F. (1972) Plant Physiol. 49 572-578, 579-584.
105. Dougall, D. K. and Fulton, M. M. (1967) Plant Physiol. 42 387-390.
106. Kleczkowski, K. and Grabarek-Bralczyk, J. (1969) Acta Biochim. Polon. 15 283-291.
107. Mestichelli, L. J. J., Gupta, R. N., and Spenser, I. D. (1979) J. Biol. Chem. 259 640-647.
108. Rena, A. B. and Splittstoesser, W. E. (1975) Phytochemistry 14 657-661.
109. Schuber, F. and Lambert, C. (1974) Physiol. Végétale 12 571-584.
110. Stulen, I., Israelstam, G. F., and Oaks, A. (1979) Planta 146 237-241.
111. Lea, P. J. and Fowden, L. (1975) Biochem. Physiol. Pflanzen 168 3-14.
112. Lever, M. and Butler, G. W. (1971) J. Exper. Botany 22 285-290.
113. Oaks, A. and Johnson, F. J. (1972) Phytochemistry 11 3465-3471.
114. Castric, P. A., Farnden, K. J. F. and Conn, E. E. (1972) Arch. Biochem. Biophys. 152 62-69.
115. Lever, M. and Butler, G. W. (1971) J. Exper. Botany 22 279-284, 285-290.
116. Nigam, S. N. and Ressler, C. (1966) Biochemistry 5 3426-3431.
117. Thoen, A., Rognes, S. E., and Aarnes, H. (1978) Plant Sci. Letters 13 103-112, 113-119.
118. Aarnes, H. (1978) Planta 140 185-192.
119. Bright, S. W. J., Shewry, P. R., and Miflin, B. J. (1978) Planta 139 119-125.
120. Davies, H. M. and Miflin, B. J. (1978) Plant Physiol. 62 536-541.
121. Matthews, B. F. and Widholm, J. M. (1979) Phytochemistry 18 395-400.
122. Mazelis, M., Whatley, F. R., and Whatley, J. (1977) FEBS Letters 84 236-240.
123. Mazelis, M., Miflin, B. J., and Pratt, H. M. (1976) FEBS Letters 64 197-200.
124. Kleczkowski, K. (1966) Bull. Acad. Polon. Sci., Ser. Sci. Biol. 14 281-283.
125. Hider, R. C. and John, D. I. (1973) Phytochemistry 12 119-124.
126. Brown, E. G. and Al-Baldawi, N. F. (1977) Biochem. J. 164 589-594.
127. Møller, B. L. (1976) Plant Physiol. 57 687-692.
128. Tsai, C. S. and Axelrod, B. (1965) Plant Physiol. 40 39-44.
129. Terano, S. and Suzuki, Y. (1978) Phytochemistry 17 550-551.
130. Keys, A. J. and 5 others (1978) Nature 275 741-743.
131. Woo, K. C. (1979) Plant Physiol. 63 783-787.
132. Carpe, A. I. and Smith, I. K. (1974) Biochim. Biophys. Acta 370 96-101.
133. Platt, S. G., Plaut, Z., and Bassham, J. A. (1977) Plant Physiol. 60 230-234.
134. Cheung, G. P., Rosenblum, I. Y., and Sallach, H. J., Plant Physiol. 43 1813-1820 (1968).
135. Chapman, D. J. and Leech, R. M. (1976) FEBS Letters 68 160-164.
136. Randall, D. D., Tolbert, N. E., and Gremel, D. (1971) Plant Physiol. 48 480-487.
137. Hill, H. M. and Rogers, L. J. (1972) Phytochemistry 11 9-18.
138. Mazelis, M. and Fowden, L. (1972) Phytochemistry 11 619-622.
139. Clandinin, M. T. and Cossins, E. A. (1975) Phytochemistry 14 387-391.
140. **Murakoshi, I., Ikegami, F., Ariki, T., Harada, K., and Haginiwa, J. (1979) Chem. Pharm. Bull. (Tokyo) 27 2484-2487.**
141. Murakoshi, I. and 6 others (1978) Phytochemistry 17 1571-1576.
142. Murakoshi, I., Ikegami, F., Harada, K., and Haginiwa, J. (1978) Chem. Pharm. Bull. 26 1942-1945.
143. Ngo, T. T. and Shargood, P. D. (1974) Can. J. Biochem. 52 435-440.
144. Ascano, A., and Nicholas, D. J. D. (1977) Phytochemistry 16 889-893.
145. Datko, A. H., Mudd, S. H., and Giovanelli, J. (1977) J. Biol. Chem. 252 3436-3445.
146. Hanson, A. D. and Kende, H. (1976) Plant Physiol. 57 528-537.
147. Leete, E. (1975) Phytochemistry 14 1983-1984.
148. Sung, M.-L. and Fowden, L. (1971) Phytochemistry 10 1523-1528.
149. Satyanarayana, T. and Radhakrishnan, A. N. (1965) Biochem. Biophys. Acta 110 380-388.
150. Peterson, P. J. and Fowden, L. (1972) Phytochemistry 11 663-673.
151. Sadava, D. and Chrispeels, M. J. (1971) Biochim. Biophys. Acta 227 278-287.
152. Wiater, A., Krajewska-Grynkiewicz, K. and Kłopotowski, T. (1971) Acta Biochim. Polon. 18 299-307.
153. Rubin, J. L. and Jensen, R. A. (1979) Plant Physiol. 64 727-734.

154. Larsen, P. O., Onderka, D. K., and Floss, H. G. (1975) Biochim. Biophys. Acta 381 397-408.
155. Griffith, T. and Conn, E. E. (1973) Phytochemistry 12 1651-1656.
156. Widholm, J. M. (1973) Biochim. Biophys. Acta 320 217-226.
157. Nagao, R. T. and Moore, T. C. (1972) Arch. Biochem. Biophys. 149 402-413.
158. Singh, M. and Widholm, J. M. (1974) Physiol. Plant. 32 240-246.
159. Saito, K. and Komamine, A. (1976) Europ. J. Biochem. 68 237-243.
160. Ruis, H. and Kindl, H. (1971) Phytochemistry 10 2627-2631.
161. Rosa, N. and Neish, A. C. (1968) Can. J. Biochem. 46 797-806.
162. Ladešić, B. and Keglević, D. (1969) Phytochemistry 8 51-55.
163. Pokorny, M. (1974) Phytochemistry 13 965-971.
164. Durham, J. I., Morgan, P. W., Prescott, J. M., and Lyman, C. M. (1973) Phytochemistry 12 2123-2126.
165. Matheron, M. E. and Moore, T. C. (1973) Plant Physiol. 52 63-67.
166. Ogawa, T., Fukuda, M. and Sasaoka, K. (1973) Biochem. Biophys. Res. Commun. 52 998-1002.
167. Miura, G. A. and Mills, S. E. (1971) Plant Physiol. 47 483-487.
168. Führ, F. and Steffens, W. (1972) Ldw. Forschung 25 226-236.
169. Ogawa, T., Kawasaki, Y., and Sasaoka, K. (1978) Phytochemistry 17 1275-1276.
170. Aldag, R. W. and Young, J. L. (1974) Z. Pflanzenphysiol. 71 83-85.
171. Gilbertson, T. J. (1972) Phytochemistry 11 1737-1739.

Chapter 11

PEPTIDES AND PROTEINS

Peptides and proteins are condensation polymers of amino acids in which the elements of water have been eliminated between an amino and a carboxyl group. If the molecular weight of the compound is below 6000, it is generally classified as a peptide. All available evidence indicates that the amino acids of the proteins have the L-configuration and that amide bonds form only between alpha amino and alpha carboxyl groups of amino acids. Sixteen to twenty different amino acids are usually found on hydrolysis of a given protein. The amino acids in proteins are linked together to form linear polymer chains with cross-links possible between the sulfhydryl groups of cysteine, resulting in disulfide bridges. Greater variations are found with peptides. For example, peptides are known that contain D-amino acids, others have non-amino acid substituents, and some are known in which not all the amide links are between the alpha amino and alpha carboxyl groups.

Since the general properties of peptides and proteins are treated thoroughly in general textbooks of biochemistry and even more comprehensively in some of the general references listed to this chapter, the treatment here will confine itself to the more particular properties of these compounds from higher plants.

PEPTIDES

Most likely the number of pure peptides that have been isolated from higher plants represents only a small portion of the total. Thus, a large number of unidentified, acid labile, ninhydrin-positive substances have been detected by paper chromatography in higher plants. Many of these may turn out to be new peptides (1). There is a review of naturally occurring peptides in animals, plants, and bacteria (2).

Glutathione, γ-L-glutamyl-L-cysteinyl-glycine, was first found in yeast but has now been shown to be very widely distributed and can be detected by paper chromatography in the extracts from many higher plants (3). Many other low molecular weight peptides from plants are γ-glutamyl derivatives of common amino acids such as glycine, cysteine, phenylalanine, etc. (4, 5). γ-Glutamyl-D-alanine is produced abundantly by germinating pea seedlings (6), and D-alanyl-D-alanine is present in *Phalaris tuberosa* (7). Some suggested roles for small peptides are as transport or storage forms of amino acids (8). In germinating barley peptides are absorbed by the embryo faster than free amino acids, and there appears to be a specific membrane transport system for peptides (9, 10). Some of the barley peptides result

from protein hydrolysis, but others appear to be newly synthesized (11).
Several versions of a so-called " γ-glutamyl cycle" have been proposed as
a mechanism for amino acid transport across membranes (12, 13). Some di-
peptides of common amino acids are toxic to cell cultures while others are
stimulatory (14, 15).

Peptides which contain non-amino acid moieties are also known.
Pteroyl-L-glutamic acid, also called folic acid, is an example of this group
and can be detected in the leaves of a large number of green plants (cf. Chap.
15). Another representative of this group of peptides is the "lathyrus
factor", isolated from *Lathyrus odoratus* seeds. (cf. Chap. 15). Pantothenic
acid, an integral part of the coenzyme A molecule (Chap. 12) is a peptide of
pantoic acid and β-alanine. As its name indicates, it is universally
distributed in nature although at very low concentrations. It is a growth
factor for many organisms.

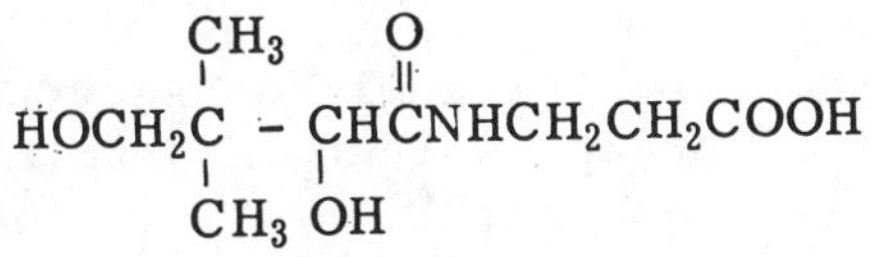

$$\underset{\underset{CH_3}{|}}{\overset{\overset{CH_3}{|}}{HOCH_2C}} - \underset{\underset{OH}{|}}{CH}\overset{\overset{O}{\|}}{C}NHCH_2CH_2COOH$$

pantothenic acid

A bound form of nicotinic acid in wheat is a glycopeptide containing nicotinic acid attached to a glucose unit (16).

The toxins of mistletoe are peptides, those from the European species
(*Viscum album*) being known as viscotoxins and those from the American
mistletoes (*Phoradendron* spp.) known as phoratoxins. They are all similar
with molecular weights of about 5000. Amino acid sequences have been
determined for some of them (17, 18).

A cyclic heptapeptide, evolidine, has been isolated from leaves of
Evodia xanthoxyloides (19); and cyclic peptides could be much more common
than is believed, because they would not be detected by the common ninhydrin
reaction. Some compounds originally classed as alkaloids are now recognized as resembling cyclic peptides in which further modification of the
amino acid residues has occurred. Pandamine and hymenocardine, for example,
fall into this group (20).

PROTEINS

All living systems contain a large number of different proteins.
These may differ in the amino acid composition, in the sequence of the
amino acids, in the non-amino acid constituents, in molecular weight, and
in those factors that determine the conformation of the protein. In order
to elucidate the structure of a given protein it is necessary that the
substance be separated from non-proteinaceous material as well as from
other proteins. This is sometimes a most formidable task and a number of
different criteria have to be used in order to establish the homogeneity
of a given sample.

The complexity and diversity of the proteins has prompted a number of different classification schemes. However, these have been only partially successful. Plant proteins have been classified according to their source, thus one speaks of seed or leaf proteins. These are further subdivided into endosperm and embryo proteins for the seed, and chloroplastic proteins for those found in leaf tissue. Another scheme rests on a subdivision into simple proteins,which on hydrolysis yield only alpha-amino acids, and conjugated proteins, which on hydrolysis yield amino acids plus other stubstances. The major subdivisions of the simple proteins are listed below. It must be recognized, though, that some proteins do not fall clearly into one subdivision. For instance, there may be a continuous range of solubilities between albumins and globulins.

Albumins - proteins that are soluble in water and in dilute salt solutions and are coagulable by heat. An example of an albumin is the leucosin from wheat.

Globulins - proteins that are insoluble in water but soluble in dilute salt solutions. Globulins are very prevalent in vegetable seeds and have been extensively studied in legumes (21,22).

Glutelins - proteins that are insoluble in all neutral solvents but readily soluble in very dilute acids and bases. Examples are the glutenin from wheat and oryzenin of rice.

Prolamines - proteins that are insoluble in water but soluble in 70-80% ethanol. Typical examples are zein from corn, gliadin from wheat, and hordein from barley. The peculiar solubility of these proteins is probably due to their high proline content. Proline itself has unusually high solubility in ethanol.

Histones - basic proteins occurring in association with DNA and characteristically having a high percentage of lysine or arginine. They may play an important role in regulation of nucleic acid function. There is great similarity between histones of different organs on the same plant and even considerable homologies between plant species (23, 24). However, there are noticeable differences between cytoplasmic, chloroplastic, and mitochondrial histones from the same source (24). Extensive comparisons have also been made between plant and animal histones (25, 26).

Acidic Nuclear Proteins - these have been very little investigated, but some believe that they may have a role as regulators of gene action (27).

Seed proteins generally, are discussed in (28, 29). They include many special types with different physiological effects on animals:

Allergens - Low molecular weight (ca. 10,000) proteins with sensitizing effects on certain susceptible individuals are widespread in seeds, particularly fatty seeds. They have been called "proteones" (30). Although they usually contain carbohydrate, the allergenic properties are retained by preparations freed of carbohydrate. The proteones are soluble in water or water containing up to 25% ethanol. They are stable to boiling and have high contents of arginine and glutamic acid. An allergen preparation from castor beans has been fractionated electrophoretically into 7 or 8 similar components (31,

32), which are in fact the albumin storage proteins of the seed (33).
Allergens of ragweed pollen also have relatively low molecular weights
(34). However many other food allergens are glycoproteins with molecular
weights in the range 25,000-40,000 (35).

Hemagglutinins have the property of agglutinating red blood
cells. They may also be mutagenic (36). They are a sub-class of
lectins -- proteins that interact specifically with carbohydrates.
Most are glycoproteins with as much as 50% carbohydrate. All contain
metal ions (Mn and Ca). Their molecular weights are usually over
100,000. The high specificity that some show for agglutinating a
particular blood type depends on differences in reactivity with
different carbohydrates of the cell surface. For example, one from
castor bean seeds reacts with branched-chain galactomannans (37).
Although best-known from seeds, hemagglutinins have been found in
other parts of plants. Surveys have suggested that about 1/3 of all
plants contain them. There have been a variety of suggestions as to
their functions -- for example: protection against bacteria or
insects (38), chemotactic agents for nitrogen-fixing bacteria (39-41),
structural components (42, 43), or membrane transport modulators (44).
Reviews of these substances are (45) and (46).

Enzyme inhibitors are found in several plant seeds -- specifically
protease inhibitors in legumes and α-amylase inhibitors in wheat.
They have molecular weights ranging from 4300 to 10,000. It has been
suggested that they may have a role in regulating endogenous proteases
or in protecting the plant against its enemies (47-49).

Toxic proteins are present in a few seeds. The most intensively studied has been ricin of the castor bean (50). Ricin is a
mixture of three similar glycoproteins. One of these, ricin D has
493 amino acids and 23 sugar units. Its total molecular weight is
55,000 divisible into two subunits (51). Its toxicity is due to an
interaction with the mammalian 60S ribosomal subunit and resulting
inhibition of protein synthesis (52, 53). It is immunologically
related to the much less toxic lectin found in the same seed (54).
Several other plants have toxic proteins that act the same way as
ricin (53, 55-57).

The name given to the conjugated proteins is determined by the nature
of the non-amino acid moieties of the protein. Thus, nucleoproteins contain nucleic acids, glycoproteins are composed partially of carbohydrate,
and chromoproteins are colored due to the presence of porphyrin ring systems,
flavins or other pigmented fragments.

Some toxic glycoproteins have been singled out for special consideration above, but glycoproteins are actually widespread constituents of plants
where they serve as storage proteins and components of membranes and cell
walls. Of the storage glycoproteins vicilin and legumin are present in several legumes. Both have glucosamine, probably linked to asparagine, and
mannose. Legumin also has glucose (21, 22, 58). Chloroplast membranes
have glycoproteins with 90% glucosamine and the rest galactosamine (59). The
cell walls of several plants have glycoproteins rich in hydroxy amino acids
such as hydroxyproline, serine, and threonine. The hydroxyl groups are
evidently in glycosidic linkages with hexoses and arabinose (60-62). The
lability of these linkages is suggested to account for some of the plasticity
of developing cell walls (63).

Lipoproteins and proteolipids of plants are not well characterized except for a group known as thionins that are present in wheat and rye seeds. They are basic proteins of molecular weight about 5000 that are notable for their solubility in methanol/chloroform. They are toxic to some microorganisms and show homologies to viscotoxins in their amino acid sequence (64-67).

Aside from the many plant enzymes that have been purified for study, there are several other plant proteins that will be mentioned because of some special properties. Ferredoxins have been purified from several seed plants (68-70). They are identical to each other, slightly different from the ferredoxin of *Equisetum*, and quite different from bacterial ferredoxin (71). An iron-protein complex, "phytoferritin", is present as crystalline inclusions in plastids of several plants (72). The contractile protein, actin, has been purified from wheat germ (73). Thioredoxin and Ca-modulin, two important regulatory proteins have both been isolated from higher plants (74, 75), as have several heme proteins. The latter group are listed more fully in Chap. 14. Amino acid sequences for cytochrome C's of 14 plants are available (76). A few plant proteins have powerful taste-stimulating properties, some being unusually sweet and some making acids taste sweet. Several of them have been highly purified and characterized (77, 78).

ISOLATION

The isolation of peptides can usually be accomplished by the same techniques as those used for amino acids. Liquid chromatography, for example, has been applied effectively to peptide isolation (79-81) as has ion exchange chromatography (82). Separation of peptides according to molecular size can be accomplished by gel filtration (83), and separation of peptides from alpha amino acids can be accomplished on an adsorbent containing bound copper ions (84). Detection of peptides in column effluents can be accomplished by measuring absorbance at 200-220 nm or by their reaction with fluorescamine (85, 86).

Tremendous variations exist in the degree of difficulty encountered in the purification of proteins. Some can be obtained in a homogeneous, crystalline state by exceedingly simple procedures. For example, extraction of jack bean meal with aqueous acetone, filtration, and storage of the filtrate near 0° yields a precipitate which after several recrystallizations consists of pure urease. On the other hand, cases are known where the most persistent efforts of highly skilled operators have been fruitless. However, no matter what procedure is finally adopted, it is of paramount importance that conditions be employed which do not lead to denaturation of the protein. Generally it is advisable to work at low temperatures and to avoid extreme pH ranges. The choice of initial extraction medium is of great importance in preparation of plant proteins. Alkaline buffers extract more proteins in a soluble form and help neutralize acidic saps, but they obscure any conclusions about localization in specific organelles (87). A frequent problem in the isolation of native proteins (especially enzymes) from plants is brought about by the common occurrence of phenolic compounds which complex with proteins and may inactivate enzymes. Polymeric, oxidized phenols are worse than simple phenols. One approach to this problem is to inhibit the oxidation of simple phenols to the polymeric ones by adding such compounds as 2-mercapoethanol or sodium metabisulfite (88). Another approach is to add materials that preferentially bind the phenols — for example, inert protein, caffeine, polyvinylpyrrolidone. These procedures are reviewed in (89). The addition of polyhydroxy compounds may also be useful to prevent aggregation and precipitation of proteins (90). A recent suggestion is the addition of porous polystyrene, which binds some inhibitory substances that are not adsorbed by polyvinylpyrrolidone (91).

The extraction of proteins from fatty tissues such as oil seeds should follow removal of lipids by extraction with ether and acetone (92). However, thionins may be lost in this way.

To subdivide proteins according to the classical categories successive extractions are made with 70% ethanol, water, 10% sodium chloride, and 0.2% sodium hydroxide. Fractionation of these extracts can be achieved by additional manipulations of pH and ionic strength. Precipitations with ammonium sulfate or organic solvents are frequently employed.

For example, a crystalline globulin fraction has been obtained from squash seeds by extraction of the ground seeds with 10% sodium chloride at 40° (93). When the filtered and centrifuged extract was diluted with four volumes of water and stored at 2° C., crystalline protein precipitated.

Where these relatively simple techniques do not prove satisfactory, the protein chemist can turn to more sophisticated methods. Gel filtration on Sephadex or polyacrylamide gel is a convenient early step (94, 95). Gel filtration on thin layers can also be adapted for preparative separations (96). Ion exchange chromatography of proteins is performed on ion exchange celluloses or Sephadexes. An example is in the purification of ricin (97). Many preparative electrophoresis methods have been described and applied to plant proteins. Acrylamide gel (98, 99), starch gel (95) and Sephadex G-25 (100) are commonly used supports. Isoelectric focusing has been used preparatively for isolating soybean trypsin inhibitor (101). Sucrose gradient centrifugation has also been applied to soybean proteins (99). A special technique for the hemagglutinins is affinity chromatography in which a carbohydrate for which the desired hemagglutinin has a high affinity is covalently bound to the column packing. In this way the hemagglutinin can be very selectively adsorbed from a complex mixture (102-104).

With the simpler organic solids, crystallinity can usually be taken as a safe criterion for homogeneity. Unfortunately, this is not true for proteins since many crystalline preparations can be shown to be heterogeneous according to other tests. The purity of an isolate can be tested by phase solubility studies, electrophoretic separations at different pH values, ultracentrifugation, and chromatography. Only after application of each of these tests has indicated lack of heterogeneity can it be concluded that according to these criteria the isolate is homogeneous.

CHARACTERIZATION

The specific tests for amino acids and peptides are, of course, also given by many proteins. Sometimes it is found that reactive side chains

are more accessible after a protein has been denatured. In addition to
these reactions there are a few that are more or less diagnostic for proteins. The biuret test is given by proteins and other substances that
contain two amide groups either joined directly or through a single atom
of nitrogen or carbon (105). The reagent consists of copper sulfate in
concentrated sodium hydroxide, and a positive test is indicated by a pink
or purple color. The action of many agents in converting soluble proteins
to insoluble products is also useful. General precipitants are heavy metal
ions (mercuric chloride, silver nitrate, lead acetate), "alkaloidal reagents" (picric acid, phosphotungstic acid, tannic acid), and concentrated
salt solutions (ammonium sulfate, sodium chloride, and sodium sulfate).
A reagent especially useful for small peptides depends on substituting
chlorine for hydrogen in the NH group, then testing for this reactive chlorine with a starch-iodine reaction. The method is applicable to any compound with an $N-H$ bond and so will detect peptides or proteins that have
few or no NH_2 groups to react with ninhydrin (106).

In recent years dozens of papers have appeared on the use of acrylamide gel electrophoresis for the characterization of plant proteins.
Some general reviews and improved procedures are (107-111). Some particular applications to plant proteins are (28, 51, 112, 113). Gel electrophoresis can be used not merely to show how many proteins are present
but may be calibrated to permit estimation of molecular weights (114, 115).
Enzyme activities of separated zones can also be determined (116, 117).

The methods used for characterization of proteins are also usable
for smaller peptides, but high performance liquid chromatography has become
an especially useful tool for the analysis of mixtures of small peptides.
Many papers describe the application of HPLC to peptides, but so far none
of these are applications to higher plants (85, 86, 118, 119). In a few
cases the method has also been extended to include proteins with molecular
weights of several hundred thousand (120). Thin layer chromatography
has also been used for peptide analysis (121), and it can be combined with
electrophoresis for greater resolution (122).

Molecular weight determinations are of extreme importance in work
with proteins. Many different methods have been developed. Osmotic pressure measurements can be used, but since they give number average molecular
weights a small percentage of a low molecular weight impurity produces a
rather large error. Light scattering procedures and ultracentrifugation,
methods that yield weight average molecular weights, are used very extensively (123). The use of gel filtration either in thin layer or columns is
the simplest technique now available for estimation of protein molecular
weights. The relationship between rate of migration and molecular weight
has been found linear up to molecular weights of several hundred thousand
(with the exception of glycoproteins). Small mesh size Sephadex G-100 or
G-200 is most often used (124-126). Combination of gel filtration with
density gradient centrifugation permits still more accurate determinations
(125). One of the problems encountered in molecular weight determinations
of proteins is that under different conditions the apparent molecular
weight of a protein may vary greatly. This is due to the ability of proteins to form dissociable aggregates. It is, therefore, necessary to
state the conditions used in the molecular weight determination very precisely and to bear in mind that a given experimental value may not represent

the minimum molecular weight. Many procedures call for the addition of
sodium dodecyl sulfate (SDS) or guanidine hydrochloride to favor complete
dissociation of proteins into subunits. Measurements therefore give minimal
molecular weights.

METABOLIC PATHWAYS

The process of protein biosynthesis has been studied exhaustively
during recent years and is thoroughly described in textbooks of general
biochemistry. No evidence has appeared to suggest that the process in
higher plants differs in any significant way from that in other organisms.
In summary, free amino acids are activated by a reaction with ATP and
specific activating enzymes (aminoacyl-tRNA synthetases) to yield enzyme-
bound aminoacyladenylates. In this complex the amino acid is linked through
its carboxyl group as a mixed anhydride with the 5'-phosphate of AMP:

ATP + amino acid + enzyme ⟶ enzyme-(AMP-amino acid) + PP

The activated amino acid is next transferred to a molecule of transfer
ribonucleic acid (tRNA) specific for it and to which it is bonded by an
ester linkage in equilibrium between the 2' and 3' positions of the terminal
AMP unit of the tRNA:

enzyme-(AMP-amino acid) + tRNA ⟶ tRNA-amino acid + enzyme

By triplet base-pairing the different tRNA molecules each with its amino
acid are lined up along a molecule of messenger RNA and by the enzymatic
machinery of the ribosomes peptide bonds are made successively between
adjoining amino acids, beginning at the one which is to be the N-terminal
end of the protein. Finally the protein is released from the ribosome.
There is a review on t-RNA and the aminoacyl-tRNA synthetases of plants
(126). A book by Cherry (127) describes several techniques useful in
studying protein synthesis by higher plant preparations. As in other
organisms plants have more than one aminoacyl-tRNA synthetase and more
than one tRNA for each amino acid. This multiplicity probably can reflect
a contribution from different tissues of the plant (128). In
cotyledons of soybean plants, the amounts of six different species of
leucyl-tRNA's change relative to each other with the physiological state
of the cotyledon (129, 130). Many organisms have separate protein synthesis
systems in cytoplasm and mitochondria. Green plants in addition have a
ribosomal system in the chloroplasts (131). Cytoplasmic ribosomes are larger
than the chloroplastic ones (80s vs. 70s). Initiation of the polypeptide
chain needs methionine-tRNA in the cytoplasmic system but N-formylmethionine-
tRNA in the chloroplastic system (132).   The chloroplast system is
preferentially inhibited by chloramphenicol and the cytoplasmic system
by cycloheximide (133, 134). Since cycloheximide has several other effects
on plants, it cannot always be assumed that observations following cycloheximide treatment are the consequences of inhibited protein synthesis
(135, 136) For some recent studies on protein synthesis by plant ribosomes see (137, 138).

The toxic effects of some of the unusual free amino acids of plants
can be attributed to their being activated by aminoacyl-tRNA synthetases

that normally activate similar protein amino acids. For example, proline activating enzymes can react with azetidine-2-carboxylic acid, glutamate activating enzymes with γ-substituted glutamic acids. In this way improper proteins can be made or the synthetic machinery sabotaged. As a beautiful adaptation, plants which contain these unusual amino acids have activating enzymes that can discriminate against them (139, 140).

After completion of the polypeptide chain proteins may be modified in various ways (141). Some are glycosylated to make glycoproteins (142, 143), some are phosphorylated (144, 145), and histones in particular are methylated on the free amino groups of lysine (146).

The regulation of protein synthesis is an area of obvious importance and intensive study. Stimulation and retardation of protein synthesis may be influenced at several different points in the overall process. Synthesis of messenger RNA in the nucleus may be inhibited by histones (147) and some hormones (148) or stimulated by other hormones (149). The availability of the mRNA to ribosomes may be controlled (150, 151). In germinating seeds the rate-limiting step for initial protein synthesis is probably the formation of polysomes using mRNA that exists preformed in the dry seed (152-155).

GENERAL REFERENCES

Bogorad, L. & Weil, J. H., eds. (1977) Nucleic Acids and Protein Synthesis in Plants, Plenum, N. Y.
Boulter, D., "Flowering Plant Proteins", in Miller 2 30-60.
Harborne, J. B. & van Sumere, C. F., eds. (1975) The Chemistry and Biochemistry of Plant Proteins, Academic Press, N. Y.
Neurath, H., ed. (1963-1966) The Proteins, 2nd ed., 5 Vols., Academic Press, N. Y.
Niederwieser, A. & Pataki, G., (1971) New Techniques in Amino Acid, Peptide, and Protein Analysis, Ann Arbor Science Publishers, Ann Arbor, Mich.
Norton, G., ed. (1978) Plant Proteins, Butterworths, London.
Pirie, N. W., ed. (1971) Leaf Protein, Blackwell, Oxford.
Pirie, N. W. (1975) "Leaf Protein: A Beneficiary of Tribulation," Nature 253 239-241.
Several articles in Paech & Tracey 4
Advances in Protein Chemistry, Vol. 1, 1946-present.

BIBLIOGRAPHY

1. Carnegie, P. R. (1961) Biochem. J. 78 697-707.
2. Waley, S. G. (1966) Adv. Protein Chem. 21 1-112.
3. Tkachuk, R. and Mellish, V. J. (1977) Can. J. Biochem. 55 295-300.
4. Ito, K. and Fowden, L. (1972) Phytochemistry 11 2541-2545.
5. Kasai, T., Larsen, P. O., and Sørensen, H. (1978) Phytochemistry 17 1911-1915.
6. Fukuda, M., Ogawa, T., and Sasaoka, K. (1973) Biochim. Biophys. Acta 304 363-366.
7. Frahn, J. L. and Illman, R. J. (1975) Phytochemistry 14 1464-1465.
8. Bergmann, L. and Rennenberg, H. (1978) Z. Pflanzenphysiol. 88 175-185.
9. Sopanen, T. (1979) Plant Physiol. 64 570-574.
10. Higgins, C. F. and Payne, J. W. (1978) Planta 142 299-305.

11. Hendry, G. A. F. and Stobart, A. K. (1977) Phytochemistry 16 1339-1346.
12. Samuels, S. (1977) J. Theoret. Biology 64 729-738.
13. Mazelis, M. and Creveling, R. K. (1978) Plant Physiol. 62 798-801.
14. Salonen, M.-L. and Simola, L. K. (1977) Physiol. Plantarum 41 55-58.
15. Simola, L. K. (1978) Physiol. Plantarum 44 315-318.
16. Mason, J. B. and Kodicek, E. (1973) Cereal Chem. 50 637-646,.646-654.
17. Samuelsson, G., Seger, L., and Olson, T. (1968) Acta Chem. Scand. 22 2624-2642.
18. Mellstrand, S. T. and Samuelsson, G. (1973) Europ. J. Biochem. 32 143-147.
19. Studer, R. O. and Lergier, W. (1965) Helv. Chim. Acta 48 460-470.
20. Warnhoff, E. W. (1970) Fortschr. Chem. Org. Naturstoffe 28 162-203.
21. Millerd, A. (1975) Ann. Rev. Plant Physiol. 26 53-72.
22. Derbyshire, E., Wright, D. J., and Boulter, D. (1976) Phytochemistry 15 3-24.
23. Fambrough, D. M. and Bonner, J. (1969) Biochim. Biophys. Acta 175 113-122.
24. Gualerzi, C., Janda, H. G., Passow, H., and Stöffer, G. (1974) J. Biol. Chem. 249 3347-3355.
25. Spiker, S., Key, J. L., and Wakim, B. (1976) Arch. Biochem. Biophys. 176 510-518.
26. Spiker, S. and Isenberg, I. (1977) Biochemistry 16 1819-1826.
27. Sugita, M., Yoshida, K., and Sasaki, K. (1979) Plant Physiol. 64 780-785.
28. Altschul, A. M., Yatsu, L. Y., Ory, R. L., and Engelman, E. M. (1966) Ann. Rev. Plant Physiol. 17 113-136.
29. Inglett, G. E., ed. (1972) Seed Proteins, A Symposium, Avi Publishing Co., Westport, Conn.
30. Spies, J. R., Coulson, E. J., Chambers, D. C., Bernton, H. S., Stevens, H., and Shimp, J. H. (1951) J. Am. Chem. Soc. 73 3995-4001.
31. Spies, J. R. (1967) Ann. Allerg. 25 29-34 (C.A. 66 63801v).
32. Daussant, J., Ory, R. L., and Layton, L. L. (1976) J. Agric. Food Chem. 24 103-107.
33. Youle, R. J. and Huang, A. H. C. (1978) Plant Physiol. 61 1040-1042.
34. Mole, L. E., Goodfriend, L., Lapkoff, C. B., Kehoe, J. M., and Capra, J. D. (1975) Biochemistry 14 1216-1220.
35. Spies, J. R. (1974) J. Agric. Food Chem. 22 30-36.
36. Waxdal, M. J. (1975) Biochemistry 13 3671-3677.
37. Van Wauwe, J. P., Loontiens, F. G., and De Bruyne, C. K. (1973) Biochim. Biophys. Acta 313 94-105.
38. Janzen, D. H., Juster, H. B., and Liener, I. E. (1976) Science 192 795-796.
39. Currier, W. W. and Strobel, G. A. (1977) Science 196 434-436.
40. Marx, J. L. (1977) Science 196 1429-1430, 1478.
41. Bhuvaneswari, T. V. and Bauer, W. D. (1978) Plant Physiol. 62 71-74.
42. Bowles, D. J., Schnarrenberger, C., and Kauss, H. (1976) Biochem. J. 160 375-382.
43. Basha, S. M. M. (1979) Plant Physiol. 63 Suppl. 324.
44. Cuatrecasas, P. and Tell, G. P. E. (1973) Proc. Nat. Acad. Sci. U. S. 70 485-489.
45. Liener, I. E. (1976) Ann. Rev. Plant Physiol. 27 291-319.
46. Rüdiger, H. (1978) Naturwissenschaften 65 239-244.
47. Richardson, M. (1977) Phytochemistry 16 159-169.
48. Buonocore, V., Petrucci, T., and Silano, V. (1977) Phytochemistry 16 811-820.
49. Mosolov, V. V., Loginova, M. D., Fedurkina, N. V., and Benken, I. I. (1976) Plant Sci. Letters 7 77-80.
50. Balint, G. A. (1974) Toxicology 2 77-102.
51. Funatsu, G. and Funatsu, M. (1977) Agric. Biol. Chem. 41 1211-1215.
52. Hedblom, M. L., Cawley, D. B., and Houston, L. L. (1976) Arch. Biochem. Biophys. 177 46-55.
53. Fernandez-Puentes, C., Carrasco, L., and Vazquez, D. (1976) Biochemistry 15 4364-4369.
54. Saltvedt, E. (1976) Biochim. Biophys. Acta 451 536-548.
55. Olsnes, S., Refsnes, K., Christensen, T. B., and Pihl, A. (1975) Biochim. Biophys. Acta 405 1-10.
56. Sperti, S., Montanaro, L., Mattioli, A., Testoni, G., and Stirpe, F. (1976) Biochem. J. 156 7-13.
57. Gasperi-Campani, A. and 6 others (1978) Biochem. J. 174 491-496.
58. Basha, S. M. M. and Beevers, L. (1976) Plant Physiol. 57 93-97.
59. Izumi, K. (1971) Phytochemistry 10 1777-1778.
60. Sadava, D., Walker, F., and Chrispeels, M. J. (1973) Developmental Biol. 30 42-48.
61. Cho, Y. P. and Chrispeels, M. J. (1976) Phytochemistry 15 165-169.
62. Akiyama, Y. and Kato, K. (1977) Agric. Biol. Chem. 41 79-81.
63. Lamport, D. T. A. and Miller, D. H. (1971) Plant Physiol. 48 454-456.
64. Mak, A. S. and Jones, B. L. (1976) Can. J. Biochem. 54 835-842.
65. Hase, T., Matsubara, H., and Yoshizumi, H. (1978) J. Biochem. (Japan) 83 1671-1678.
66. Hernández-Lucas, C., Carbonero, P., and García-Olmedo, F. (1978) J. Agric. Food Chem. 26 794-796.
67. Salcedo, G., Prada, J., and Aragoncillo, C. (1979) Phytochemistry 18 725-727.
68. Huisman, J. G., Stapel, S., and Muijsers, A. O. (1978) FEBS Letters 85 198-202.
69. Thauer, R., Schirrmacher, H., Schymanski, W., and Schönheit, P. (1978) Z. Naturforsch. 33c 495-497.
70. Shin, M., Yokoyama, Z., Abe, A., and Fukasawa, H. (1979) J. Biochem. (Japan) 85 1075-1081.

71. Aggarwal, S. J., Rao, K. K., and Matsubara, H. (1971) J. Biochem. (Japan) 69 601-603.
72. Crichton, R. R., Ponce-Ortiz, Y., Koch, M. H. J., Parfait, R., and Stuhrmann, H. B. (1978) Biochem. J. 171 349-356.
73. Ilker, R. A., Breidenbach, R. W., and Murphy, T. M., (1979) Phytochemistry 18 1781-1783.
74. Wolosiuk, R. A., Crawford, N. A., Yee, B. C., and Buchanan, B. B. (1979) J. Biol. Chem. 253 1627-1632.
75. Charbonneau, H. and Cormier, M. J. (1979) Biochem. Biophys. Res. Commun. 90 1039-1047.
76. Boulter, D. and Ramshaw, J. A. M. (1972) Phytochemistry 11 553-561.
77. Iyengar, R. B. and 7 others (1979) Europ. J. Biochem. 96 193-204.
78. Giroux, E. L. and Henkin, R. I. (1974) J. Agric. Food Chem. 22 595-601.
79. Gabriel, T. F., Michalewsky, J., and Meienhofer, J. (1976) J. Chromatog. 129 287-293.
80. Bennett, H. F. J., Hudson, A. M., McMartin, C., and Purdon, G. E. (1977) Biochem. J. 168 9-13.
81. Hancock, W. S., Bishop, C. A., Prestidge, R. L., Harding, D. R. K., and Hearn, M. T. W. (1978) J. Chromatog. 153 391-398.
82. James, L. B. (1979) J. Chromatog. 172 481-483.
83. Carnegie, P. R. (1965) Nature 206 1128-1130.
84. Rothenbühler, E., Waibel, R., and Solms, J. (1979) Anal. Biochem. 97 367-375.
85. Hancock, W. S., Bishop, C. A., and Hearn, M. T. W. (1976) FEBS Letters 72 139-146.
86. Mendez, E. and Gavilanes, J. G. (1976) Anal. Biochem. 72 473-479.
87. Brandon, P. C. (1969) Plant Physiol. 44 461-462.
88. Kelley, W. A. and Adams, R. P. (1977) Phytochemistry 16 513-516.
89. Loomis, W. D. (1974) Methods Enzymol. 31 528-544.
90. Heitefuss, R., Buchanan-Davidson, D. J., and Stahmann, M. A. (1959) Arch. Biochem. Biophys. 85 200-208.
91. Loomis, W. D., Lile, J. D., Sandstrom, R. P., and Burbott, A. J. (1979) Phytochemistry 18 1049-1054.
92. Ioffe, K. G., Rakhimov, A. R., Asatov, I. A., and Lamm, G. Y. (1968) Biokhimiya 33 652-657.
93. Fuerst, C. R., McCalla, A. G., and Colvin, J. R. (1954) Arch. Biochem. Biophys. 49 207-221.
94. Fawcett, J. S. and Morris, C. J. O. R. (1966) Separation Sci. 1 9-26.
95. Moureaux, T. and Sallantin, M. (1967) Compt. rend. 264D 1619-1623.
96. Maier, C. L., Jr. (1968) J. Chromatog. 32 577-579.
97. Hara, K., Ishiguro, M., Funatsu, G., and Funatsu, M. (1974) Agric. Biol. Chem. 38 65-70.
98. McLeester, R. C., Hall, T. C., Sun, S. M., and Bliss, F. A. (1973) Phytochemistry 12 85-93.
99. Hill, J. E. and Breidenbach, R. W. (1974) Plant Physiol. 53 742-746.
100. Whitehead, J. S., Kay, E., Lew, J. Y., and Shannon, L. M. (1971) Anal. Biochem. 40 287-291.
101. Catsimpoolas, N., Ekenstam, C., and Meyer, E. W. (1969) Biochim. Biophys. Acta 175 76-81.
102. Kortt, A. A. (1979) Biochim. Biophys. Acta 577 371-382.
103. Bessler, W. and Goldstein, I. J. (1973) FEBS Letters 34 58-62.
104. Nicolson, G. L., Blaustein, J., and Etzler, M. E. (1974) Biochemistry 13 196-204.
105. Kurzer, F. (1956) Chem. Revs. 56 95-197.
106. Mazur, R. H., Ellis, B. W., and Cammarata, P. S. (1962) J. Biol. Chem. 237 1619-1621.
107. Righetti, P. G. and Drysdale, J. W. (1974) J. Chromatog. 98 271-321.
108. Chrambach, A. and Rodbard, D. (1971) Science 172 440-451.
109. Van Welzen, H. and Zuidweg, M. H. J. (1974) Anal. Biochem. 59 306-315.
110. Rosemblatt, M. S., Margolies, M. N., Cannon, L. E., and Haber, E. (1975) Anal. Biochem. 65 321-330.
111. Storring, P. L. and Tiplady, R. J. (1978) Biochem. J. 171 79-82.
112. McMullan, E. E. and Ebell, L. F. (1970) Phytochemistry 9 2281-2285.
113. Basha, S. M. M. (1979) Plant Physiol. 63 301-306.
114. Lambin, P. and Fine, J. M. (1979) Anal. Biochem. 98 160-168.
115. Manwell, C. (1977) Biochem. J. 165 487-495.
116. Shaw, R. and Prasad, R. (1970) Biochem. Genetics 4 297-320.
117. Frenkel, C. and Hess, C. E. (1974) Can. J. Botany 52 1411-1414.
118. Hansen, J. J., Greibrokk, T., Currie, B. L., Johansson, K. N.-G., and Folkers, K. (1977) J. Chromatog. 135 155-164.
119. Mönch, W. and Dehnen, W. (1977) J. Chromatog. 140 260-262.
120. Rubinstein, M. (1979) Anal. Biochem. 98 1-7.
121. Schiltz, E., Schackerz, K. D., and Gracy, R. W. (1977) Anal. Biochem. 79 33-41.
122. Fujiki, H. and Zurek, G. (1977) J. Chromatog. 140 129-130.
123. Atassi, M. Z. and Gandhi, S. K. (1965) Naturwiss. 52 259.
124. Grover, A. K. and Kapoor, M. (1973) Anal. Biochem. 51 163-172.
125. McGuinness, E. T. (1973) J. Chem. Educ. 50 826-830.
126. Hung, C.-H., Strickland, D. K., and Hudson, B. G. (1977) Anal. Biochem. 80 91-100.
127. Cherry, J. (1973) Molecular Biology of Plants, Columbia Univ. Press, N. Y.
128. Augustyniak, H. and Pawelkiewicz, J. (1978) Phytochemistry 17 15-18.
129. Shridhar, V. and Pillay, D. T. N. (1976) Phytochemistry 15 1809-1812.
130. Lester, B. R., Morris, R. O., and Cherry, J. H. (1979) Plant Physiol. 63 87-92.

131. Doherty, A. and Gray, J. C. (1979) Europ. J. Biochem. 98 87-92.
132. Guillemant, P., Burkard, G., and Weil, J. H. (1972) Phytochemistry 11 2217-2219.
133. Billington, R. W. and Heyes, J. K. (1970) Nature 227 858-860.
134. Reger, B. J., Smillie, R. M., and Fuller, R. C. (1972) 50 19-23.
135. ap Rees, T. and Bryant, J. A. (1971) Phytochemistry 10 1183-1190.
136. McMahon, D. (1975) Plant Physiol. 55 815-821.
137. Rattanapannone, N., Speirs, J., and Grierson, D. (1978) Phytochemistry 17 1485-1486.
138. Evans, I. M. and 5 others (1979) Planta 144 455-462.
139. Norris, R. D. and Fowden, L. (1972) Phytochemistry 11 2921-2935.
140. Lea, P. J. and Fowden, L. (1972) Phytochemistry 11 2129-2138.
141. Uy, R. and Wold, F. (1977) Science 198 890-896.
142. Karr, A. L., Jr. (1972) Plant Physiol. 50 275-282.
143. Ericson, M.C. and Delmer, D. P. (1978) Plant Physiol. 61 819-823.
144. Greengard, P. (1978) Science 199 146-152.
145. Murray, M. G., Guilfoyle, T. J., and Key, J. L. (1978) Plant Physiol. 61 1023-1030.
146. Patterson, B. D. and Davies, D. D. (1969) Biochem. Biophys. Res. Commun. 34 791-794.
147. Srivastava, B. I. S. (1971) Physiol. Plantarum 24 27-33.
148. Wareing, P. F. (1978) Phil. Trans. Royal Soc. B 284 483-498.
149. Wasilewska, L. D. and Kleczkowski, K. (1976) Europ. J. Biochem. 66 405-412.
150. Beevers, L. and Poulson, R. (1972) Plant Physiol. 49 476-481.
151. Chin, T. Y., Poulson, R., and Beevers, L. (1972) Plant Physiol. 49 482-489.
152. Dzięgielewski, T., Kędzierski, W., and Pawełkiewicz, J. (1979) Biochim. Biophys. Acta 564 37-42.
153. Cuming, A. C. and Lane, B. G. (1978) Can. J. Biochem. 56 365-369.
154. Roberts, L. M. and Lord, J. M. (1979) Plant Physiol. 64 630-634.
155. Bewley, J. D. and Larsen, K. M. (1979) Phytochemistry 18 1617-1619.

Chapter 12
NUCLEIC ACIDS AND DERIVATIVES

Toward the end of the nineteenth century nucleic acid was established as the universal component of cell nuclei and recognized to be a complex high-molecular weight material which could be hydrolyzed to yield a sugar, several nitrogen bases, and inorganic phosphate. Later developments seemed to show that nucleic acid from animal cells was characterized by having D-2-deoxyribose as its sugar constituent, while plant nucleic acid had D-ribose. However, by the 1930's it became clear that plants and animals each have both types of nucleic acid but that the deoxyribonucleic acid is found predominantly in the nucleus, and ribonucleic acid in the cytoplasm. The earlier supposition resulted from the fact that the animal cells used had been ones with a prominent nucleus and little cytoplasm, while the reverse was true of the plant cells. It was early recognized that each type of nucleic acid contains four different nitrogen bases, two purines and two pyrimidines. The purines adenine and guanine and the pyrimidine cytosine are common to both types of nucleic acid, whereas, deoxyribonucleic acid (DNA) has thymine as its second pyridine base, and ribonucleic acid (RNA) has uracil. There have been reports of the occurrence of other nitrogen bases in nucleic acid from some sources. The structures will be discussed in more detail in a later section.

Partial hydrolysis of nucleic acids yields varied sized fragments known as polynucleotides if they contain several nitrogen bases combined with sugar and phosphate, mononucleotides if they have only one nitrogen base plus sugar and phosphate, or nucleosides when they have merely a nitrogen base bound to sugar by a glycosidic bond. Smaller molecules of these different types also occur as such in nature as well as being derived from breakdown of nucleic acid. Some nucleotides of great physiological importance contain nitrogen bases which are not found in the nucleic acids. They are, nevertheless, included in this chapter.

Very little of our present knowledge of nucleic acids and related compounds has been derived from observations on the higher plants. Animal tissues and microorganisms have been most frequently used as experimental material, and possibly some generalizations derived from them may not be applicable to higher plants. An attempt will be made to indicate which facts are certainly known for higher plants and which are derived from observations on other types of organisms.

FREE PURINES AND PYRIMIDINES

The parent substances purine and pyrimidine have the structures and ring numbering shown on the following page.

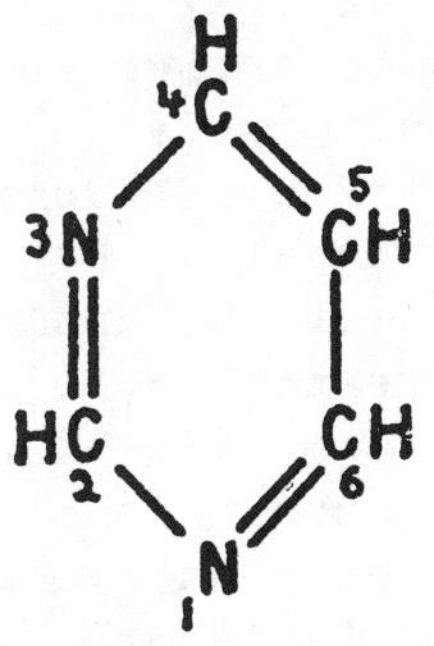

pyrimidine 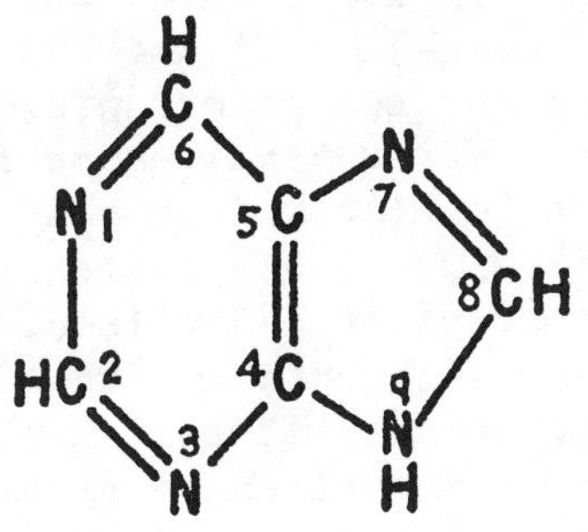   purine

Neither of them occurs free in nature, although a nucleoside of purine occurs in *Clitocybe nebularis* (1).

The two purines and the pyrimidine found in all nucleic acids are as follows:

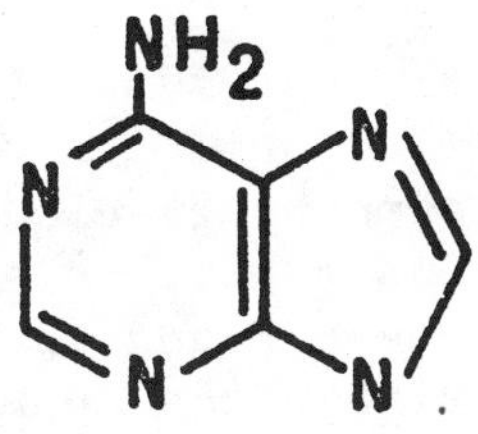

adenine 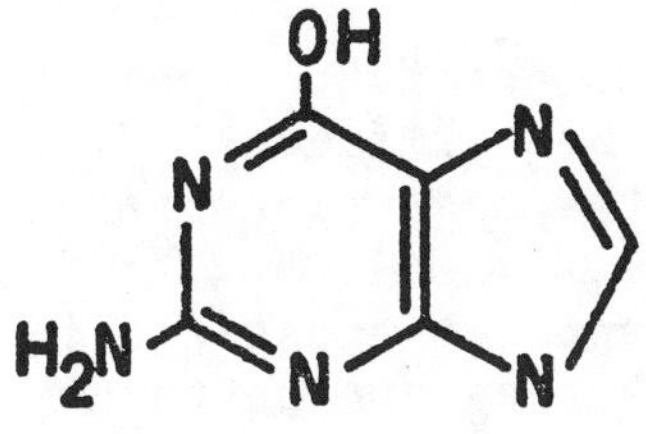   guanine 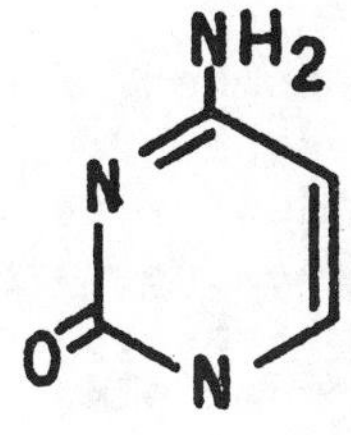   cytosine

Thymine and uracil found respectively in deoxyribonucleic acid and ribonucleic acid are:

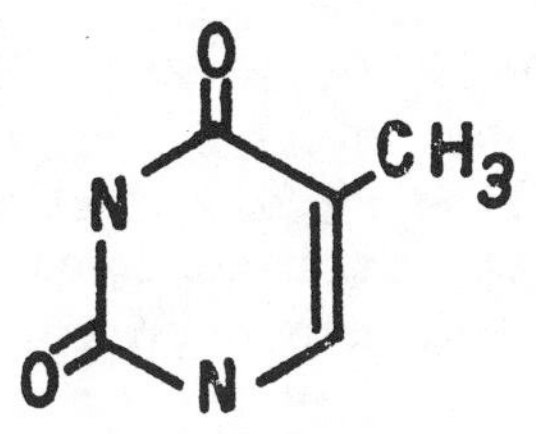

thymine 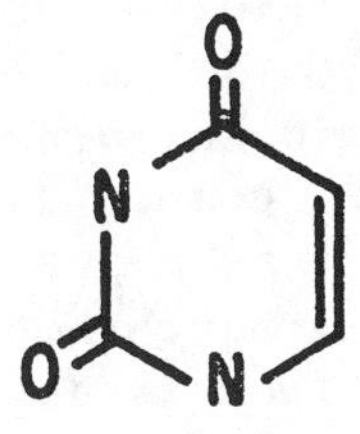   uracil

Although structures are shown with fixed double bonds, it should be recognized that in many cases their reactivities can be understood better if they are regarded as resonance hybrids. Tautomerization also may play an important role. Thus, uracil may be represented by three different contributing structures:

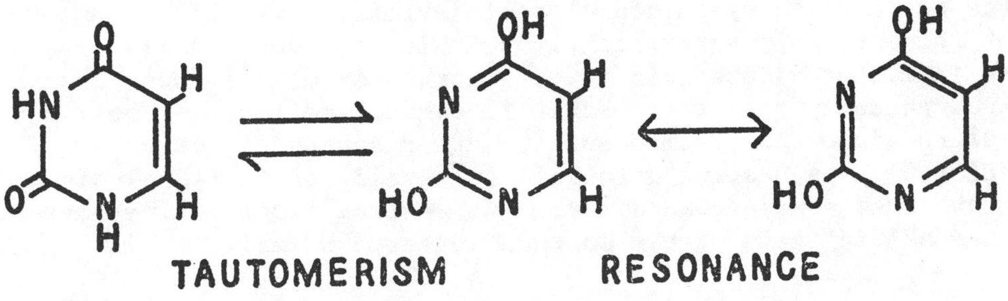

TAUTOMERISM   RESONANCE

Deoxyribonucleic acid from wheat germ and the leaves of several plants
contains in addition to the expected bases, 5-methyl-cytosine (2). Methylation of bases in DNA and RNA is known to be a widely occurring process and
accounts for the appearance of methylated bases on hydrolysis (3). Quite
a variety of unusual 6-substituted purine bases are found in hydrolysates
of low molecular weight RNA from plants. Careful degradation has shown
that the unusual bases are located next to the 3'-end of the anticodon in
certain transfer RNA molecules. One of them is _cis_-zeatin (4, 5). Others
have 6-substituents and in addition a 2-methylthio group (6). Many adenine
derivatives substituted on the 6-nitrogen show pronounced morphological
effects when applied to plants artificially and are known as cytokinins.
Some of them are probably natural growth regulators. Their precise mechanism
of action is unclear because of complex interrelationships with auxins,
gibberellins, light, and abscisic acid (7, 8). It is probable that the
activity of cytokinins is unrelated to the presence of similar residues in
tRNA. While free zeatin has the _trans_ configuration, zeatin derived from
hydrolysis of tRNA is _cis_ (9). Less well-known are the cytokinesins, substituted hypoxanthines present in crown gall tumors. It is thought by some
that they may mediate the actions of cytokinins (10).

A number of other bases are found free in plants, but some of them
that have been reported may be artifactual decomposition products of nucleic
acid. Adenine is probably the most widespread, followed by guanine. Free
thymine has been found in _Equisetum palustre_ (11). Other purines and pyrimidines which are not components of nucleic acid have been found to occur
free in some plants although they are certainly not widespread in the plant
kingdom. As nitrogen-containing compounds they are often classed with the
alkaloids, but biosynthetically they are presumably closely related to
other purines and pyrimidines. Structures of some of these compounds are
given in Table 12-1 with selected natural sources.

Although uric acid is usually regarded as an end product of purine
metabolism in animals, it has been found in several different plants. In
many animals uric acid is further broken down to allantoin and then allantoic acid. These two compounds are also widely distributed in plants.
They seem to function as major nitrogen storage compounds in some trees and
legumes (12 13). Although not purines, the structural relationship of
these two to the purines is obvious.

allantoin   allantoic acid

The free purines and pyrimidines are colorless, crystalline compounds.
Many of them are only very slightly soluble in water but all are readily
soluble in either dilute acid (e.g. guanine) or alkali (e.g. uric acid).
They are generally rather insoluble in organic solvents. Their characteristic ultra-violet absorption spectra are discussed below under "Characterization." Long heating with acid or alkali (as in hydrolysis procedures) may cause some decomposition, but generally the purines and pyrimidines are sufficiently stable so that losses are small.

TABLE 12-1 SOME NATURALLY OCCURRING PURINES

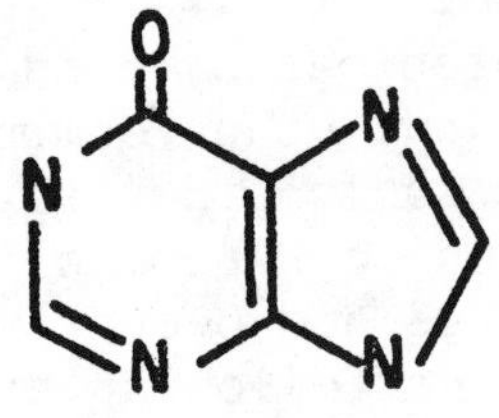

hypoxanthine *(Lupinus luteus)*

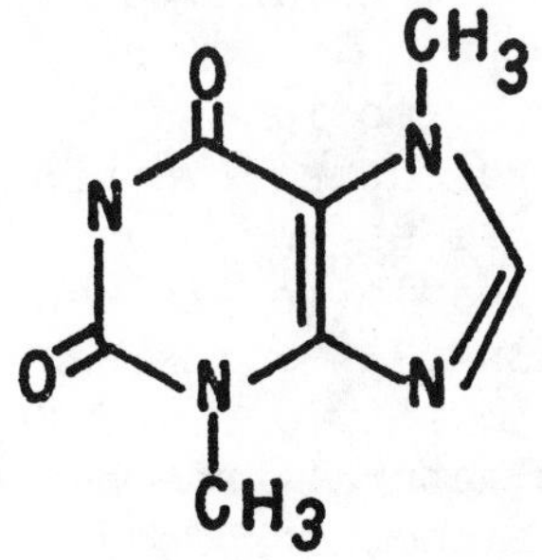

theobromine *(Theobroma cacao)*

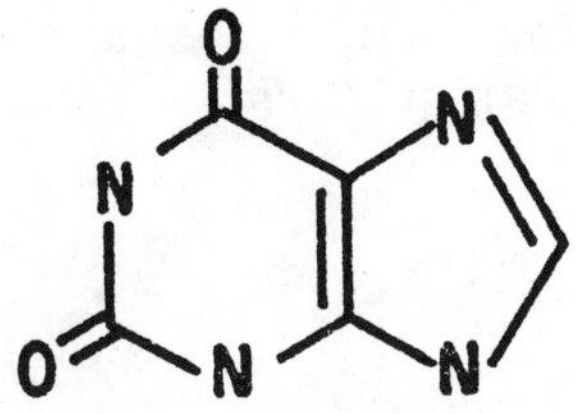

xanthine *(Coffea* spp.*)*

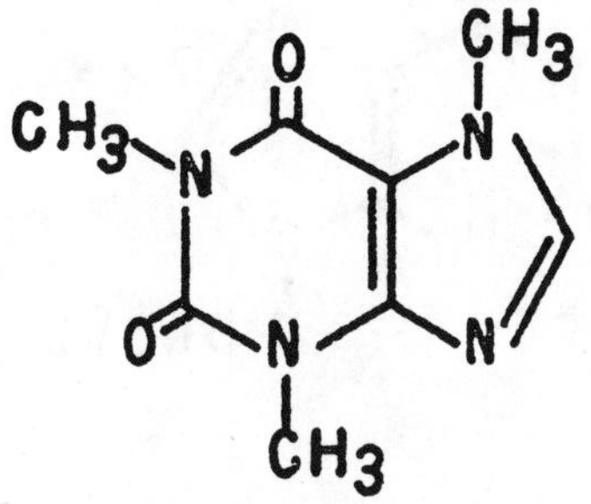

caffeine *(Coffea* spp.*)*

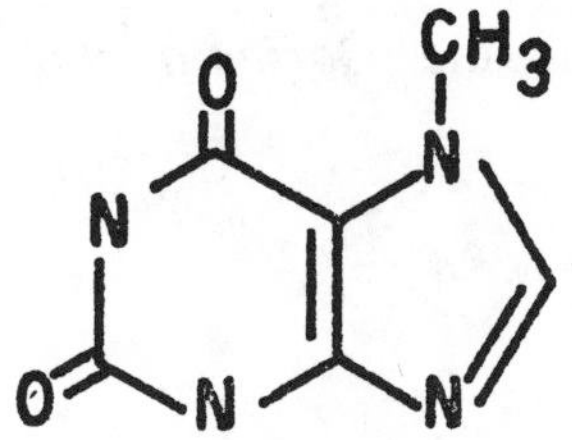

heteroxanthin *(Beta vulgaris)*

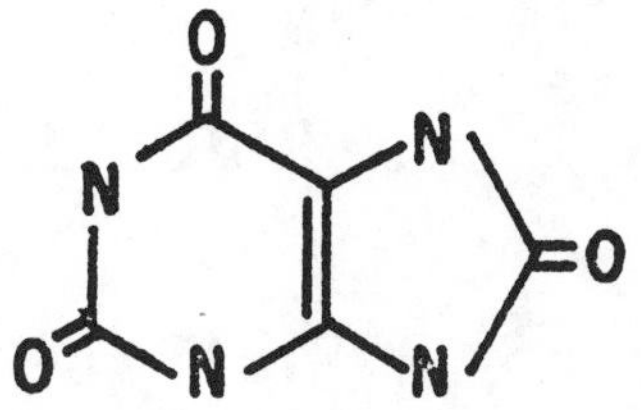

uric acid *(Melilotus officinalis)*

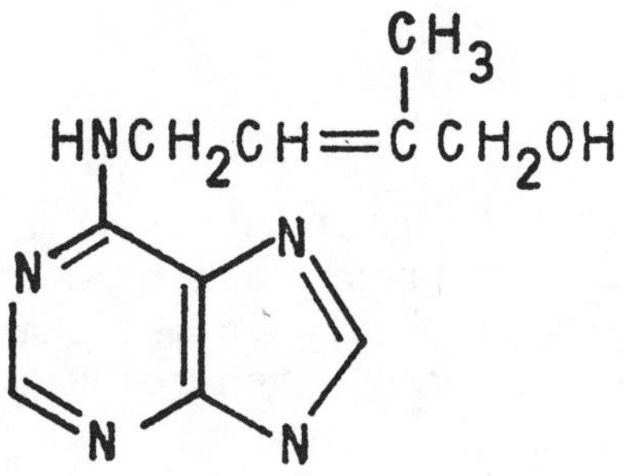

zeatin *(Zea mays)*

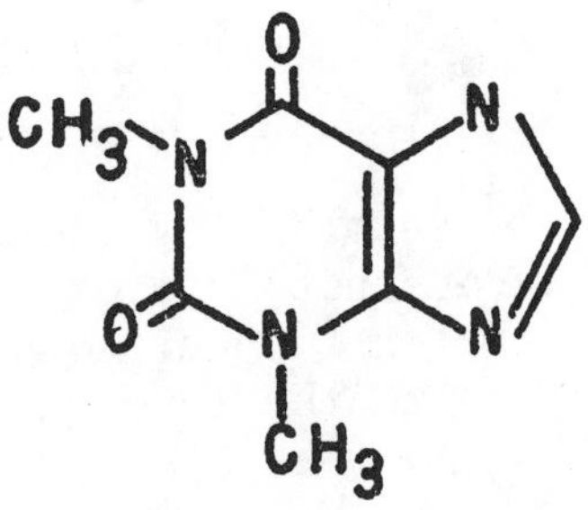

theophylline *(Camellia sinensis)*

NUCLEOSIDES

The nucleosides have a sugar molecule bound by a β-glycosidic bond to position-1 of the pyrimidines or position-9 of the purines. Deoxyribonucleosides occur only as break-down products of DNA or of nucleotides, but a few ribonucleosides apparently occur as such in plants --- e.g. adenosine and guanosine (vernine). Some of the nitrogen bases found in specific nucleosides are never found as components of any other compound. The vitamin, riboflavin, is usually included with the nucleosides although, strictly speaking, it contains a ribityl moiety related to D-ribitol rather than a ribosyl moiety derived from D-ribose. Structures and occurrence of some of the natural free nucleosides are given in the following pages. A review on the chemistry and natural occurrence of pyrimidine nucleosides has appeared (14).

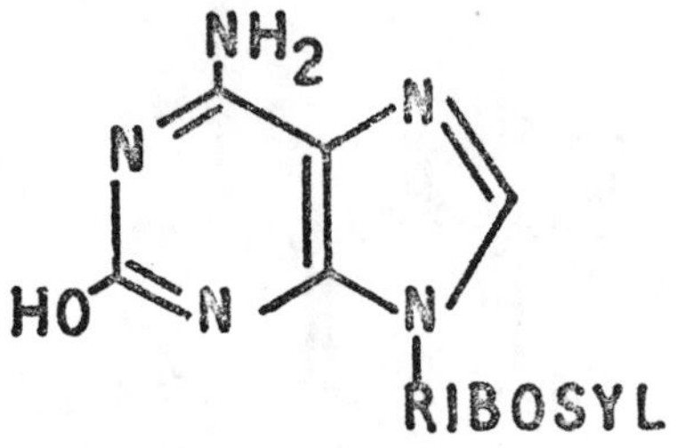

crotonoside, riboside of isoguanine (*Croton tiglium*)

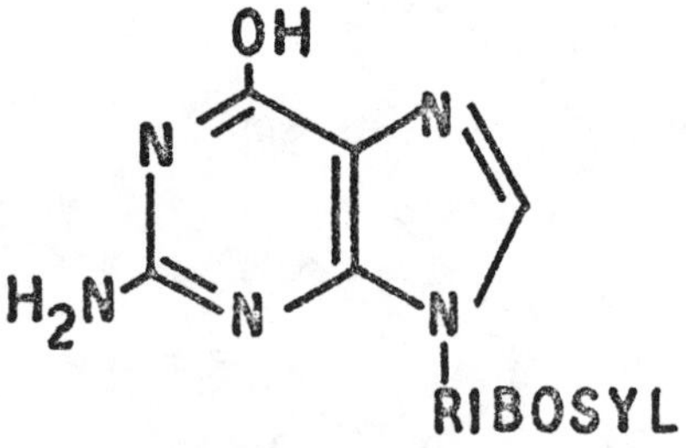

guanosine (*Coffea arabica*)

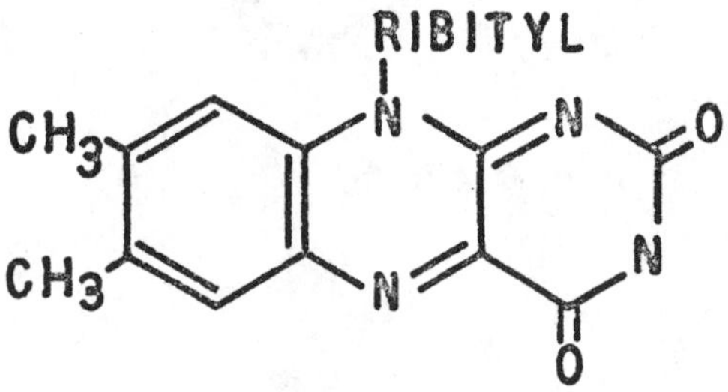

riboflavin

Two unusual pyrimidine glucosides occur in vetch (*Vicia* spp.), peas, and beets. They are not nucleosides since the glucosyl group is linked through oxygen rather than nitrogen. However, in chemical properties they bear a resemblance to the true nucleosides. Structures are given below:

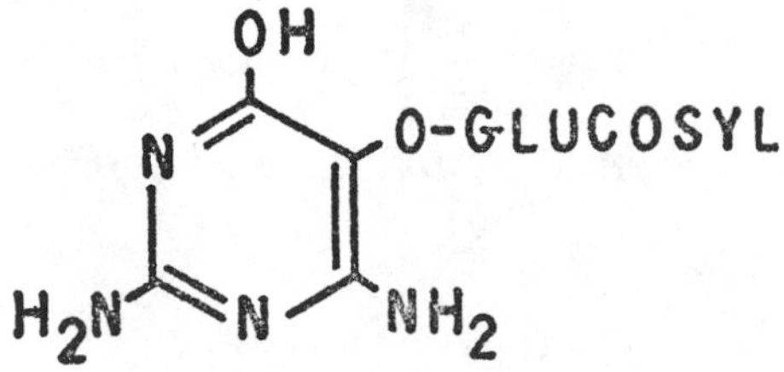

vicin, glucoside of divicin

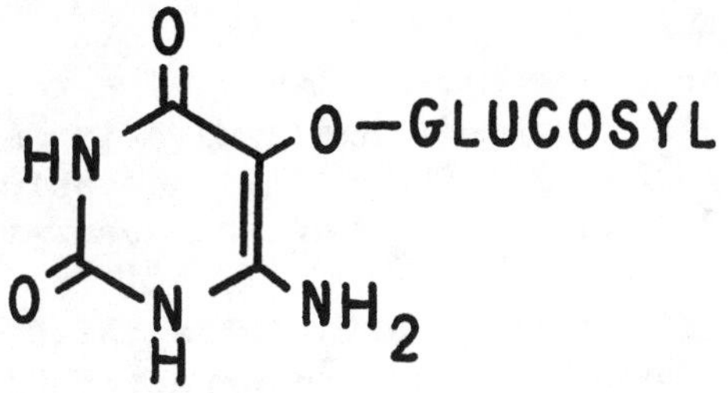

convicin, glucoside of
5-hydroxy-6-aminouracil

The nucleosides are colorless, crystalline compounds, generally more soluble in water than are the free nitrogen bases. Pyrimidine nucleosides are more soluble in water than purine nucleosides. Purine nucleosides are readily hydrolyzed to base and sugar by boiling with dilute acid, while pyrimidine nucleosides are considerably more resistant to hydrolysis so that autoclaving with strong acid is required, and some decomposition may occur (e.g. deamination of cytosine to form uracil).

NUCLEOTIDES

The nucleotides, aside from their function as components of nucleic acid, constitute one of the most physiologically interesting groups of natural products. Many of the important coenzymes for dehydrogenation and group transfer reactions are nucleotides. The mononucleotides have one or more phosphoric acid groups esterified to the sugar portion of a nucleoside. The dinucleotides may be regarded as having two nucleoside units joined through a pyrophosphate bridge which esterfies their sugar units. Additional phosphate groups may also be present. Nucleotides containing adenine appear to be the most common in nature. Muscle adenylic acid is the 5'-phosphate, while 2' and 3' phosphates have been isolated from hydrolyzed nucleic acid of both fungi and higher plants. These last two compounds have not been reported to occur in a free form in higher plants. Mono-, di-, and triphosphates of adenosine, guanosine, cytidine, and uridine have all been found in plants (15,16). Deoxyribonucleotides are present in concentrations distinctly less than concentrations of the ribonucleotides (17).

By far the most important adenine mononucleotide is adenosine-5'-triphosphate (ATP):

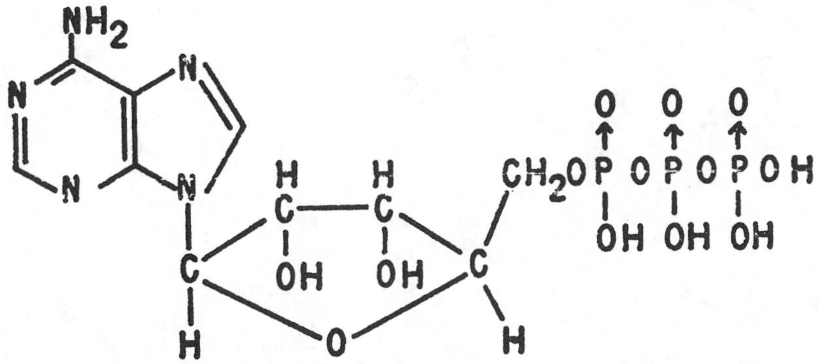

ATP

It has been isolated from animals, fungi and higher plants where it serves as a coenzyme for many phosphokinases and may be regarded as an energy storage compound since hydrolysis of the third phosphate group releases energy which can be used to drive endergonic reactions. The role of ATP in activating amino acids for protein synthesis and activating methionine for transmethylation is discussed in Chaps. 10 and 11. Adenosine-5'nucleotides are also found as subunits of some other important coenzymes.

In animal tissues a compound of great importance is the so-called "second messenger," cyclic 3', 5'-adenosine monophosphate (cAMP). There is still controversy about the possible presence and function of cAMP in higher plants. Some claims for its presence are certainly based on faulty assays, and even the best ones suggest much less than 1 nmole per gram of fresh tissue (18-20). Cyclic AMP does have effects on plant metabolism, but the specificity and significance of most of them are doubtful (21).

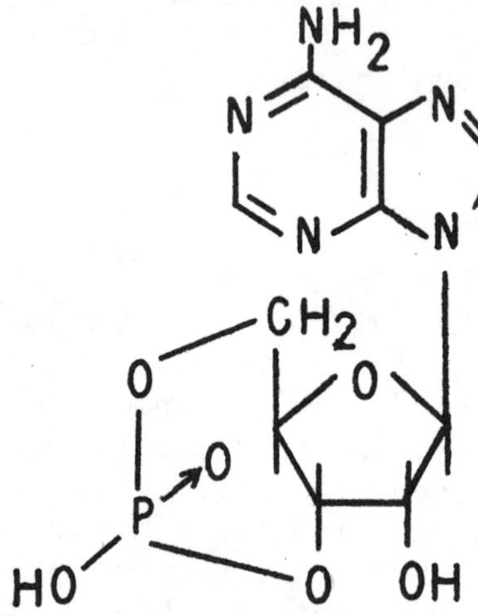

3',5'-cyclic AMP

Diphosphopyridine nucleotide (DPN) or nicotinamide adenine dinucleotide (NAD), triphosphopyridine nucleotide (TPN) or nicotinamide adenine dinucleotide phosphate (NADP), riboflavin phosphate (flavin mononucleotide, FMN), and flavin-adenine dinucleotide (FAD) serve as hydrogen carriers in oxidation-reduction reactions. Their complete structures are given in Table 12-2. In the first two coenzymes the pyridine ring is involved in the reversible reduction, and in the flavin coenzymes the isoalloxazine ring functions, as follows:

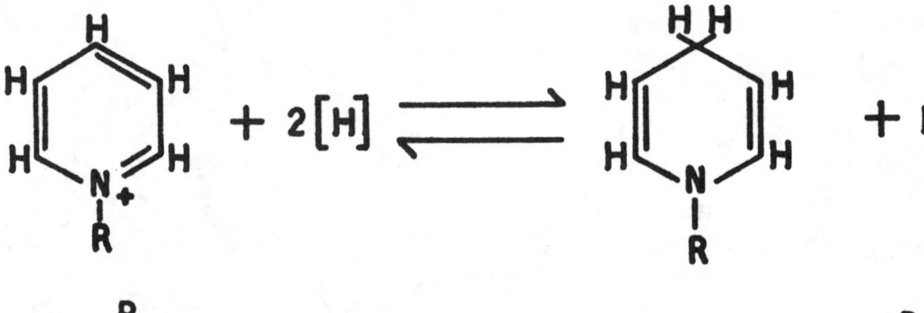

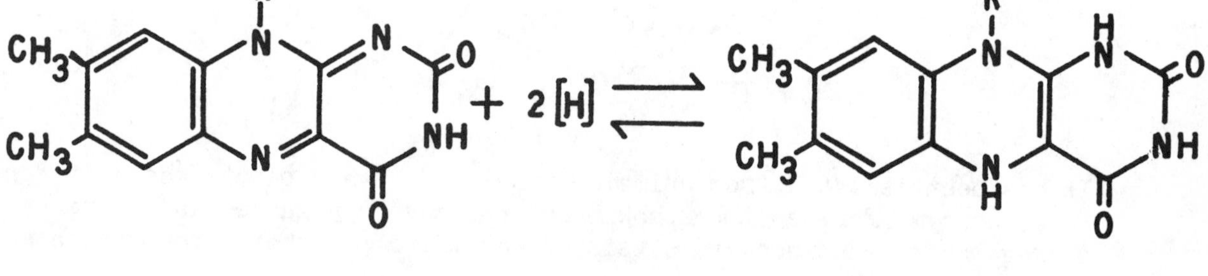

TABLE 12-2 NUCLEOTIDE STRUCTURES

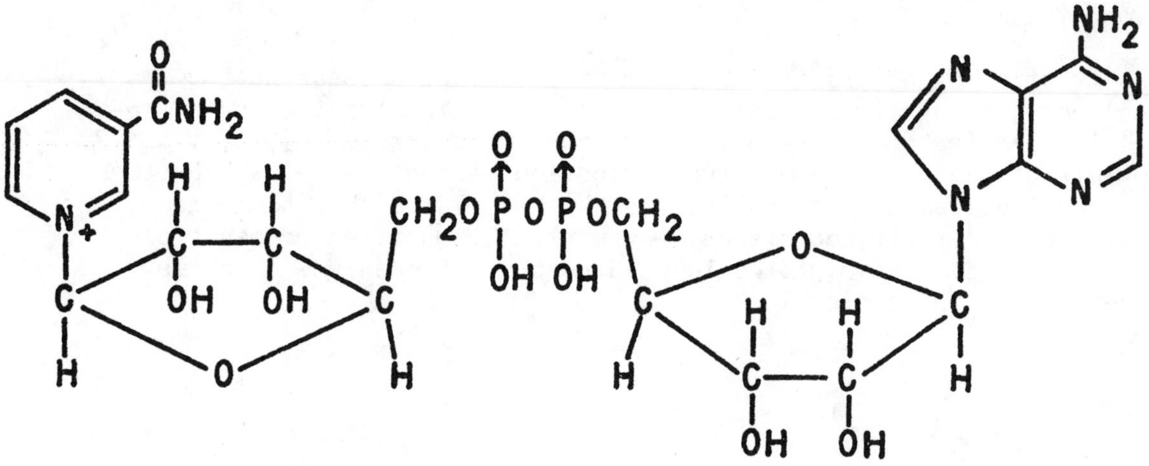

nicotinamide adenine dinucleotide

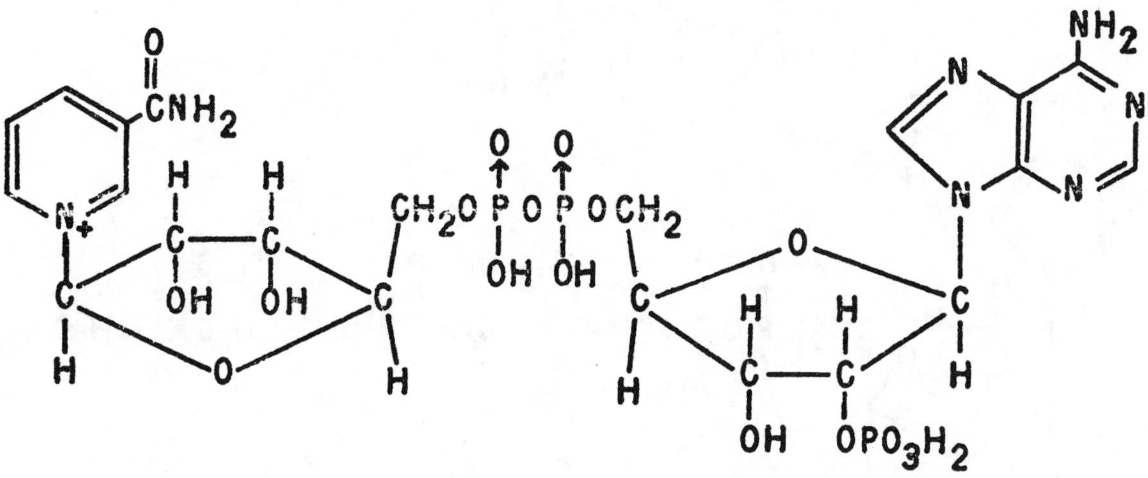

nicotinamide adenine dinucleotide phosphate

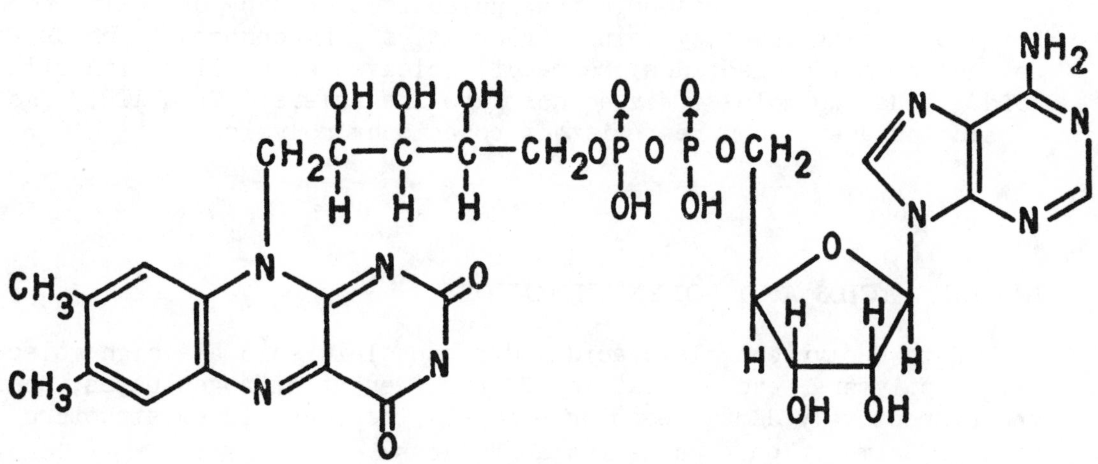

flavin adenine dinucleotide

Some plant tissues, e.g. tobacco leaves, have a higher concentration of NADP than of NAD---the reverse of the situation in animal tissues (22). Very little free riboflavin is extractable from tissues. It is largely in the coenzyme form, and this is rather tightly bound to proteins known as flavoproteins.

The functioning of uridine triphosphate (UTP) as a coenzyme for transfer of glycosyl groups is discussed in Chapter 2. The functioning of coenzyme A in transfer of acyl groups is discussed in Chapters 3, 5, 6 and 7. The complete structures of these two nucleotides are given below. Neither one has been isolated in high purity from higher plants, but there is ample evidence for their occurrence, and partially purified preparations have been obtained. The pantothenic acid portion of coenzyme A is discussed separately in Chapter 10.

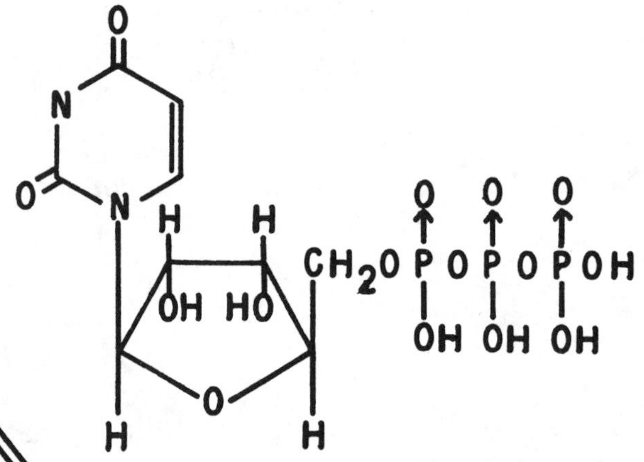

UTP

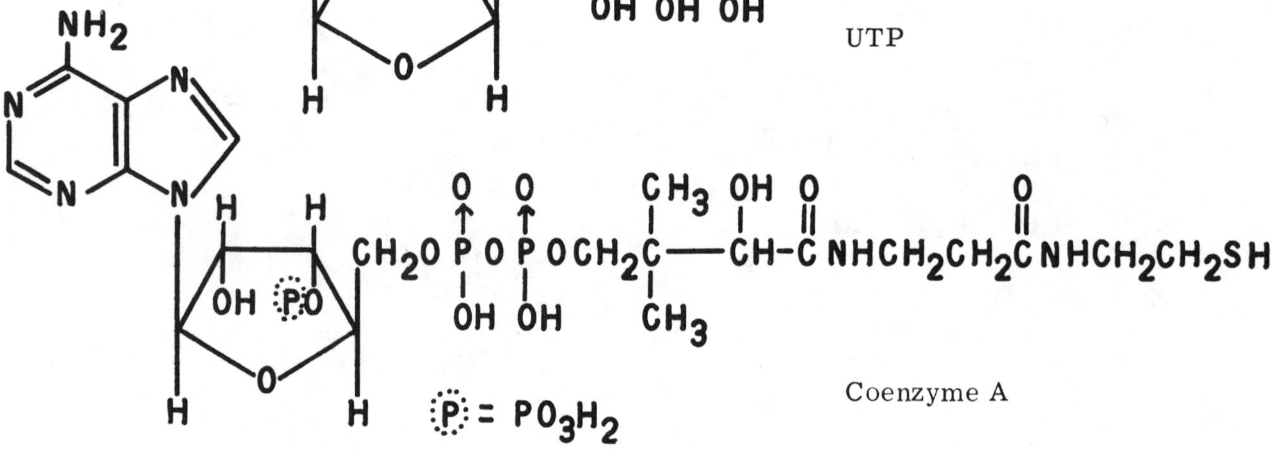

Coenzyme A

$\dot{P} = PO_3H_2$

The nucleotides resemble the nucleosides in many of their properties but are distinguished by being strong acids. Pyrophosphate bonds found in several of the nucleotides are readily cleaved by boiling with dilute acid. Thus two moles of orthophosphate are released from ATP. The monophosphates are much more resistant to acid hydrolysis.

NUCLEIC ACIDS AND POLYNUCLEOTIDES

Both deoxyribonucleic acid and ribonucleic acid are high molecular weight polymers, each containing four different nitrogen bases, phosphate, and respectively deoxyribose or ribose. The generalized structure of both of them may be represented as follows:

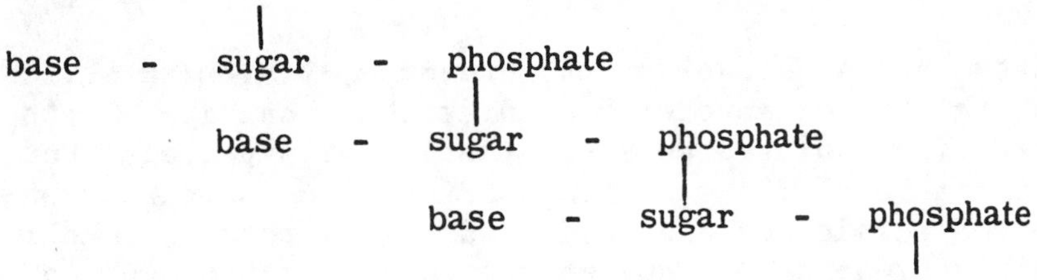

base   -   sugar   -   phosphate

     base   -   sugar   -   phosphate

          base   -   sugar   -   phosphate

Phosphate is present as a diester between C-3' of one nucleotide and C-5' of the next. The detailed structure for a segment containing adenine and cytosine would be:

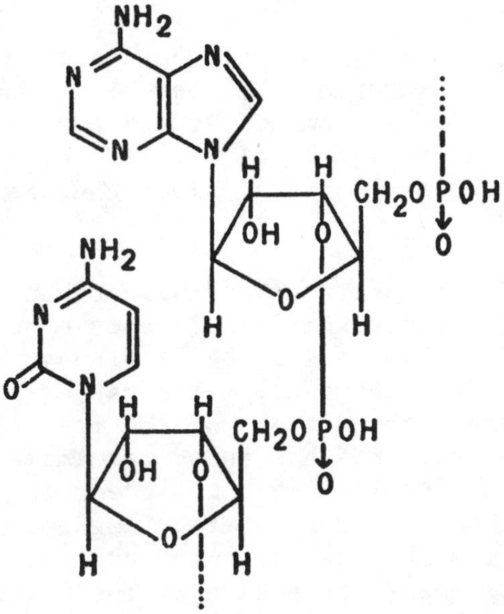

    Deoxyribonucleic acid (DNA) contains the bases adenine, guanine, cytosine and thymine. Some plant DNA has been found to contain, in addition, 5-methylcytosine. DNA prepared from various sources has been found to have molecular weights ranging from somewhat less than a million to several million. There is no reason to believe that all the DNA even in a single nucleus is homogeneous, and a wide range of molecular weights may be present. The accepted macromolecular structure of DNA represents it as a two stranded helix with each strand consisting of a chain of poly-nucleotides and the strands bound together by hydrogen bonds. Adenine of one chain is always paired with thymine of the other, and guanine with cyto-sine. The hydrogen bonding of the latter pair may be represented as:

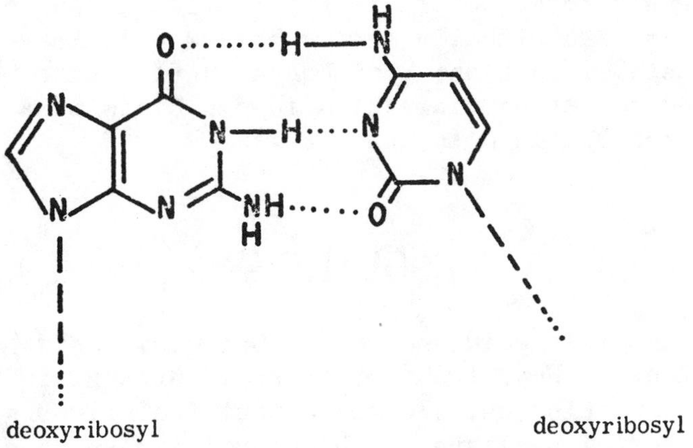

GUANINE   CYTOSINE

The geometry of the helix allows for the presence of a third strand, and it is possible that in the cell protein occupies this position. Both DNA and RNA can be readily isolated as a combination with protein, but the biological significance of these nucleoproteins is not clear. Non-specific binding between the acidic nucleic acids and basic proteins readily occurs so that the protein present in a nucleoprotein preparation may not be the same protein originally combined with the nucleic acid in the cell. As would be predicted for a long-chain, polar polymer, DNA forms very viscous solutions in water. So-called "satellite DNA's" are derived from mitochondria and chloroplasts. They differ in base ratios from the nuclear DNA of the same cell, and only nuclear DNA has 5-methylcytosine (23, 24). In mature green leaves chloroplast DNA can be as much as 12% of the total DNA (25). Mitochondrial DNA from pea leaves has a circular conformation and a molecular weight of about 7×10^7 (26). It is striking that flowering segments of tobacco stem may have ten times the DNA concentration of non-flowering segments (27).

Ribonucleic acid, in addition to having ribose rather than deoxyribose and uracil rather than thymine, differs in some other properties from DNA. It generally is found to have a somewhat lower average molecular weight, ranging around one hundred thousand. This use of an overall average is, however, misleading since three types of RNA may be clearly distinguished (cf. Chapter 11). Transfer RNA has an average molecular weight of about 30,000. The complete nucleotide sequences are known for some higher plant tRNA's. A phenylalanine-tRNA from wheat or legumes has 76 nucleotides with only 16 differences from the phenylalanine-tRNA of yeast (28). Messenger RNA constitutes a very small percentage of the total RNA. In addition to its high molecular weight it is characterized by being rapidly labeled in pulse feeding experiments, hybridizing with homologous DNA, and containing sequences of polyadenine resistant to ribonuclease (29-32). The lifetimes of different mRNA molecules are different. That for nitrate reductase of corn roots has a half-life of only about 20 min. (33). Others may be hours or days. Dormant seeds evidently can retain active mRNA for months or years and on taking up water use it to make active polysomes (34). Plant cytoplasmic ribosomes contain about 50% RNA in three classes according to their sedimentation rates of 28s, 18s, and 5s (35). Chloroplast rRNA is 23s, 16s, 5s, and possibly 4.5s (36, 37). A species of RNA present in nuclei is known as heterodisperse nuclear RNA (hnRNA). Its function is still obscure, but it is present in plants as well as animals (38). Knowledge of RNA secondary structure is still slight. An RNA-polyphosphate complex which is metabolically active has been isolated from wheat leaves (39). The possible functioning of RNA as a flowering hormone (40) is presumably related to its participation in synthesis of a particular protein by the mechanisms outlined in Chapter 11.

ISOLATION

Both ribonucleic acid and deoxyribonucleic acid have been prepared from higher plants. However, the latter is present in very low concentration in most plant tissues, and successful isolations generally require as starting material a tissue in which nuclei make up a large proportion of the cells. Pollen, root tips, and wheat germ have been used for this purpose (41). Many plant tissues contain reasonable amounts of RNA (e.g. 0.01% per weight of leaves), and it may be prepared fairly readily.

Thorough homogenization of the tissue is the first essential for extraction of either type of nucleic acid. Older methods of preparing nucleic acid depended on extraction with alkali but yielded a product which had suffered some degradation. Current methods use extraction with phenol or neutral salt solutions and undoubtedly yield a less degraded product, but in the absence of any absolute standard it cannot be claimed that the isolated nucleic acid is obtained in its unchanged, native state. Isolation of nucleoprotein is even more open to question. Products can readily be prepared which contain nucleic acid more or less bound to protein, but in the absence of any standards they may be regarded as anything from the intact nucleoprotein as it exists in the cell to nucleic acid contaminated with extraneous protein. The phenolic compounds present in many plants interfere with extraction of nucleic acids and nucleotides. Several methods have been devised to remove phenolics by adsorption or to prevent their binding to nucleic acid (42-44).

The four types of non-dialyzable, water-soluble substances likely to be encountered in tissue extracts are polysaccharides, proteins, ribonucleic acids, and deoxyribonucleic acid. The rationale for separating the nucleic acids is generally based on denaturing and coagulating proteins with acid (trichloracetic or perchloric) or by surface denaturation brought about by shaking or homogenization in the presence of detergents or chloroform-alcohol mixtures. Nucleic acids may then be freed of polysaccharides by making the solution weakly acidic to precipitate the nucleic acid or basic to dissolve the nucleic acid and leave polysaccharides as an insoluble residue. Dialysis removes any small molecules.

DNA is separated from RNA by the choice of original extraction medium. DNA is more tightly bound to cell structure than is RNA. The latter is solubilized by homogenization with dilute (e.g. 0.1 M NaCl). After removal of this supernatant solution, DNA may be extracted with 1-3 M NaCl and reprecipitated by diluting to 0.1 M NaCl. Nuclear DNA is more difficult to solubilize than chloroplast DNA (45). The chief drawback to this extraction procedure is the presence of enzymes which may degrade the nucleic acids. Enzymes may be inactivated by first dropping the tissue into boiling ethanol, which does not dissolve nucleic acid, or by the use of nuclease inhibitors such as diethylpyrocarbonate (46) or sodium dodecyl sulfate plus magnesium ion (47). Tissues containing much lipid or fat-soluble pigment should also be defatted before extraction. It must always be kept in mind that techniques developed for animal tissues may have to be modified for use with plants. Some recent publications describing methods for isolation of higher plant RNA and DNA are respectively (42, 47-49) and (43, 45, 49). The special problems of extraction from woody tissue are dealt with in (50). Separation of nucleic acids into different fractions has made use of countercurrent distribution, chromatography on ion exchange celluloses, and chromatography on MAK (methylated albumin-kieselguhr). MAK chromatography has been applied to purification of both DNA and RNA fractions from a variety of plant materials.(50-52). Gel filtration (43, 49, 53-55) and ion exchange chromatography (56) have also been useful in the purification of nucleic acids. Preparative electrophoresis has been used for plant DNA (57); and an elegant procedure for isolating RNA that contains long stretches of polyadenylate is affinity chromatography on poly-U-Sepharose (54, 58).

Isolation of nucleotides from plants has been greatly aided by ion exchange chromatography. Initial extraction of the tissue is usually

carried out with 10% trichloracetic or perchloric acid so that proteins and
nucleic acids are left with the residue. Further steps often depend on
precipitating phosphates as barium salts. Careful control of pH is important at this stage since barium salts of nucleotides tend to be more soluble than the barium salt of phytic acid, a common constituent of seedlings.
Thus at pH 4 barium phytate is insoluble and the barium salt of ATP remains
in solution (59). Further separation and purification of the various nucleotides is most conveniently performed by chromatography over anion exchange resin such as Dowex 1 or ion exchange cellulose (16, 44, 60). Ion
exchange high performance liquid chromatography can be used for both mono-
and polynucleotides (61). The special problems of purifying and determining
ATP in plant tissues are dealt with in (62).

Nucleosides and free nitrogen bases are also extracted with dilute
acid from plant tissues. It is hard to make any generalizations concerning
methods of purifying them. A few techniques can be mentioned, but there
are wide differences in solubility and reactivity so that the general references should be consulted for details. The free bases and their nucleosides are often precipitated as complex mercury salts and then regenerated
by removing mercury with hydrogen sulfide. Ion exchange chromatography may
be carried out using either anion or cation exchangers since at very high
pH values most of the bases act as weak anions. Column partition chromatography was successful in resolving 18 nucleosides derived from hydrolysis
of yeast tRNA (63). The methylated xanthines which occur in such commercially important plants as coffee and cocoa may be extracted with such
organic solvents as ethanol, chloroform or trichloroethylene and chromatographed on silicic acid (64) or Sephadex G-10 (65). Tannins, which tend to
complex with them, may be removed by adsorption on magnesium oxide. Since
some of these compounds may be classified as alkaloids, methods discussed
in Chapter 13 may be consulted.

Because of the special interest in cytokinins several chromatographic
methods have been devised for their isolation. Light and drying are especially to be avoided (66-69).

CHARACTERIZATION

The discussion of characterization for most plant constituents has
been directed toward deciding whether or not they are present in a given
tissue. No such question arises for the nucleic acids. One analytical
problem may be to characterize the distribution of molecular weights in a
sample. Density gradient centrifugation and gel electrophoresis are used
for this purpose (24, 35, 37, 45, 55). An approximate determination of the
base composition of DNA can be made by measuring the melting temperature of
a double-stranded sample. This measurement is unaffected by the presence
of 5-methyl-cytosine, but the buoyant density is (70).

For determination of the bases present in a nucleic acid sample acid
hydrolysis followed by paper chromatography is quite satisfactory. If it
is desired to separate larger quantities of the bases for additonal characterization, ion exchange chromatography may be applied to the hydrolysate.
RNA is hydrolyzed with normal hydrochloric acid for one hour at 100° C.

This yields free purines (adenine and guanine), but the pyrimidine-sugar bond is more resistant so that cytidylic and uridylic acids are formed rather than the free bases. DNA is hydrolyzed with 72% perchloric acid at 100° for 2 hours and yields free bases for both purines and pyrimidines.

For characterization of the mixture of hydrolysis products from nucleic acid by paper chromatography a spot of acidic hydrolysis mixture is applied directly to paper and run in a solvent composed of 170 ml. iso propyl alcohol, 41 ml. concentrated hydrochloric acid, and water to make 250 ml. (71). After drying the paper, spots may be detected by the fact that they absorb ultra-violet light and therefore appear as dark spots against background fluorescence when a U.V. lamp (250-265 nm) is held behind the paper. Guanine fluoresces in ultra-violet if the paper is strongly acidic. Other nitrogen bases do not. Photographic methods have been developed to provide a permanent record (72). Spray reagents have also been developed with varying specificities. The method of Wade and Morgan (73) detects phosphate esters (i.e. nucleotides) by spraying the paper with ferric chloride followed by salicylsulfonic acid. Wood's method (74) detects most purines and cytosine but not uracil, thymine or cytidylic acid. Methods for distinguishing between pyrimidines and purines (75) and methods specific for adenine derivatives have been described (76, 77). Paper chromatography and ion exchange chromatography of oligonucleotides are reviewed by Cramer (78).

Thin layer chromatography is claimed to offer many advantages over paper chromatography for separation of nucleotides, nucleosides, purines, and pyrimidines. The method is much faster than chromatography on paper, and better resolution is attained (79-82). Thin layer chromatography on silica gel has been applied to xanthine derivatives (83). Gas chromatography of bases, nucleosides, and nucleotides is possible if they are converted to their trimethylsilyl derivatives (67, 84, 85). For better identification the gas chromatograph can be interfaced with a mass spectrometer (86). High performance liquid chromatography has proved itself to be extremely useful for the analysis of cytokinins in plant extracts (87, 88). Separated fractions can be further identified by bioassay (89).

Identification of free bases, nucleosides or nucleotides in plant extracts is basically the same problem as identifying them in nucleic acid hydrolysates. Some preliminary purification is probably necessary before applying unknowns to paper. Precipitation or ion exchange methods as described under "Isolation" can be used for this purpose. The reader is referred to papers of Rowan (90, 91) and Cherry and Hageman (92) for methods suitable for detection of free nucleotides in plant extracts.

Detailed characterization of many nucleic acid derivatives has rested heavily on the action of specific enzymes on purified materials. Thus an enzyme has been prepared from germinating barley (Hordeum spp.) or rye grass (Lolium spp.) which specifically hydrolyzes nucleotide 3'-phosphates (93). Application of this and other enzymes to structure determinations may be found in the general references.

Absorption spectra are also useful for identification of purified compounds. All purine and pyrimidine derivatives show strong absorption at about 260 nm, but shifts in absorption occur with changes in pH. These shifts are characteristic for specific purines and pyrimidines since they

depend on the ionizable groups present. In many cases enough material can
be extracted from a paper chromatogram to permit its identification by
measuring spectra at different pH values. Further discussion and presentation of spectra may be found in the general references as well as references (94, 95). NAD (DPN), NADP (TPN), and riboflavin derivatives have
spectral properties useful in characterizing them. The first two have
identical spectra with a peak at about 260 nm; but more important is the
appearance of a peak at 340 nm upon reduction with sodium dithionite or
with appropriate enzymes and substrates. Riboflavin derivatives show a
strong yellow-green fluorescence when illuminated with light of about 445 nm.

Qualitative and quantitative analysis for the nucleotides which function as cofactors in enzyme systems may be carried out by setting up the
enzyme system without the required cofactor, adding unknown material, and
measuring enzyme activity.

METABOLIC PATHWAYS

The biosynthetic pathways leading to formation of nucleic acid derivatives have been well clarified in bacteria and avian liver. Observations
with higher plants are less complete but indicate that by and large the
same pathways are followed with possible differences in detail. Examples
of studies on plants are given in references (96–98). In the accompanying
figures where CO_2, NH_3, and formate are shown as reactants, it is probable
that they actually participate as derivatives. These may be, respectively,
carboxylated biotin, glutamine, and N^{10}-formyltetrahydrofolic acid.

In addition to compounds directly related to the nucleic acids, compounds of similar structure have been considered in this chapter since they
are probably synthesized along somewhat similar pathways. Riboflavin,
for instance, at least in the microorganism *Eremothecium ashbyii* seems
to be synthesized from various purines (99). Guanine is the best precursor.
The cytokinins might be degradation products of nucleic acids that have
N–6–substituted purines (100). It has been shown that isopentenylation
can be performed on macromolecules rather than nucleotides or smaller
units (100). It now seems more likely, though, that the cytokinin residues
present in tRNA are not the usual precursors of free cytokinins (101, 102).
Similarly, the methylated xanthines do not appear to be derived from
methylated nucleic acids but from a pool of free nucleotides (103–105).
Normal degradation of nucleic acids leads to nucleotides, nucleosides, and
free bases (106). Oxidative enzymes that can degrade purines successively
to xanthine, uric acid, allantoin, allantoic acid, and glyoxylic acid have
been shown to occur in plants (107–109). The pathway of pyrimidine degradation is more obscure.

The most important generalization which has emerged from studies of
the biosynthetic sequence is that transformations of the nitrogen bases
are always carried out not on the free bases but on nucleotide derivatives.
There is no information on the synthesis of deoxyribonucleotides in higher
plants. In other organisms that have been studied they are made by a reduction of ribonucleotides.

The nucleic acids are formed by condensation of nucleotides. DNA
is synthesized from nucleotide triphosphates by an enzyme obtained from

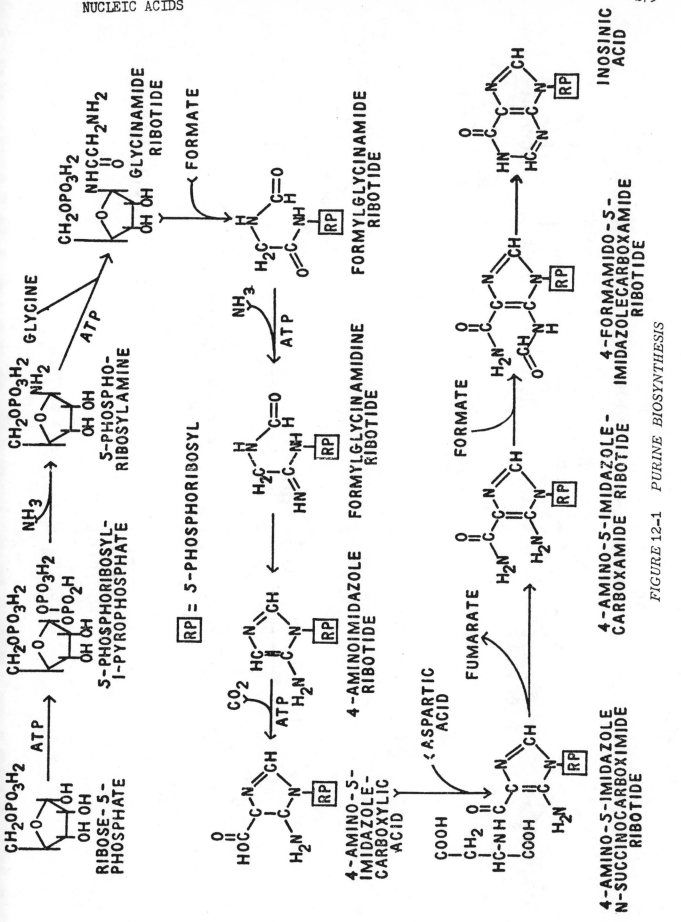

FIGURE 12-1   PURINE BIOSYNTHESIS

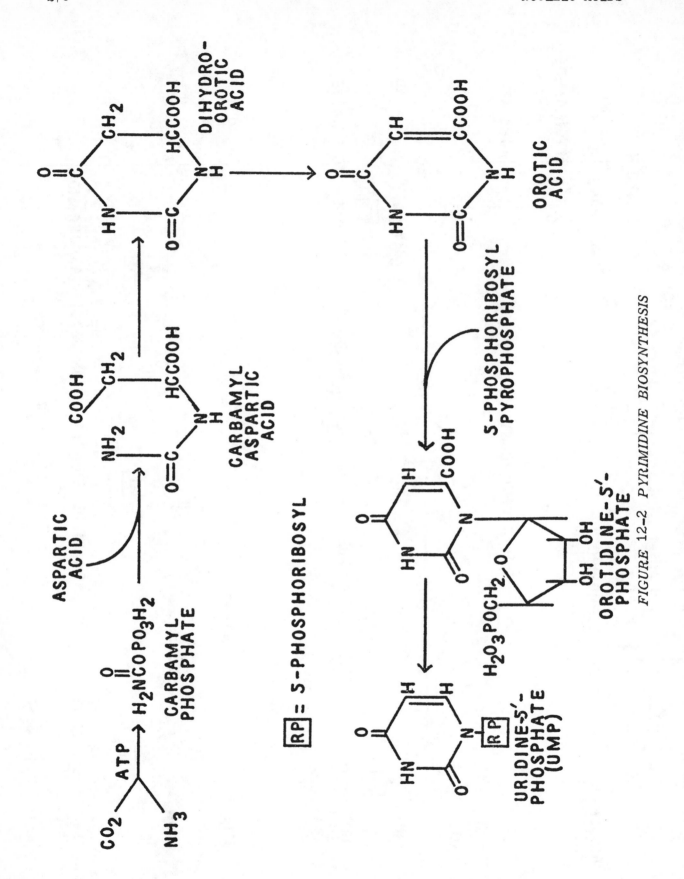

FIGURE 12-2 PYRIMIDINE BIOSYNTHESIS

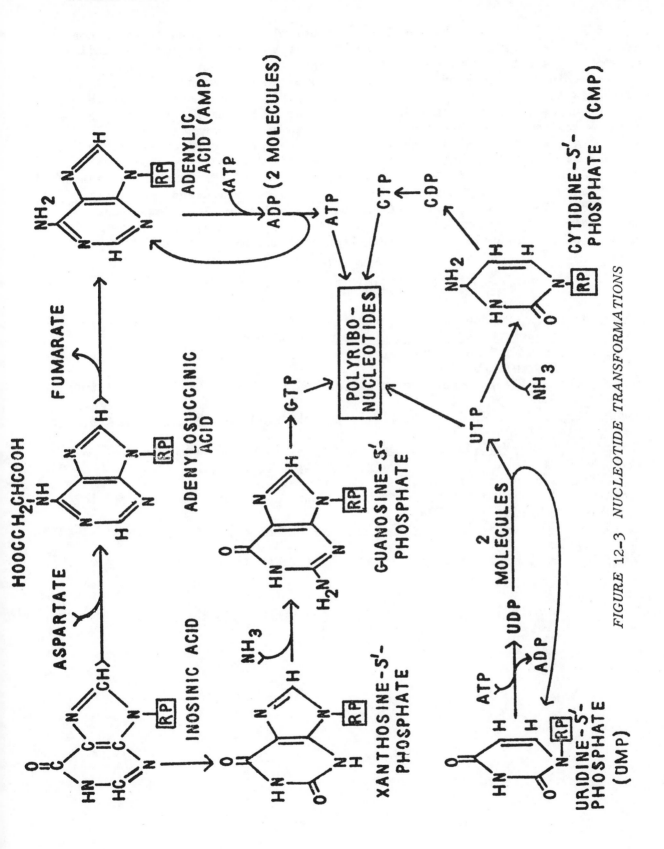

FIGURE 12–3 NUCLEOTIDE TRANSFORMATIONS

Escherichia coli. The other product is inorganic pyrophosphate, and a small amount of DNA "primer" must be present to initiate the reaction. A similar enzyme is present in mung beans (110). There is still doubt, though, whether this DNA polymerase reaction provides the true mechanism of DNA synthesis *in vivo*. RNA polymerase has been purified from several plants. Active enzyme is present in dry seeds, and one of the earliest events in germination is the synthesis of mRNA catalyzed by this enzyme (111). The RNA polymerase of seeds is present in nucleoli of endosperm cells and is classed as a type I polymerase (112). Type II and type III polymerases are also present in plants (113-115). After formation of RNA further processing of it may occur, involving partial cleavage, polyadenylation and methylation (3, 116-118). The sequence of these various steps during plant development has received much recent attention (34, 38, 117, 119-121), as has the regulation of ribonucleic acid metabolism by plant hormones (122, 123).

GENERAL REFERENCES

Adams, R. L. P., Burdon, R. H., Campbell, A. M., & Smellie, R. M. S. (1977) The Biochemistry of the Nucleic Acids, Academic Press, N. Y.

Amrhein, N. (1977) "The Current Status of Cyclic AMP in Plants," Ann. Rev. Plant Physiol. 28 123-132.

Becker, W. M. (1979) "Genome Organization and Expression in Plants," Nature 280 719-720.

Bogorad, L. & Weil, J. H., eds. (1977) Nucleic Acids and Protein Synthesis in Plants, Plenum, N. Y.

Cherry, J. (1973) Molecular Biology of Plants, Columbia Univ. Press, N. Y.

Hall, T. C. & Davis, F. W. (1979) Nucleic Acids in Plants, 2 Vols., CRC Press, West Palm Beach, Florida.

Markham, R., "Nucleic Acids, Their Components, and Related Compounds," in Paech & Tracey 4 246-304.

Smith, H., ed. (1977) The Molecular Biology of Plant Cells, Univ. Calif. Press, Berkeley.

Wang, D., "Purines and Pyrimidines and Their Derivatives," in Miller 2 61-117.

BIBLIOGRAPHY

1. Löfgren, N., Lüning, B., and Hedstrom, H. (1954) Acta Chem. Scand. 8 670-680.
2. Thomas, A. J. and Sherratt, H. S. A. (1956) Biochem. J. 62 1-4.
3. Cecchini, J.-P. and Miassod, R. (1979) Europ. J. Biochem. 98 203-214.
4. Letham, D. S. (1973) Phytochemistry 12 2445-2455.
5. Einset, J. W., Swaminathan, S. and Skoog, F. (1976) Plant Physiol. 58 140-142.
6. Burrows, W. J. (1978) Planta 138 53-57.
7. Horgan, R. (1978) Phil. Trans. Royal Soc. (B) 284 439-447.
8. Laloue, M. (1978) Phil. Trans. Royal Soc. B 284 449-456.
9. Kaminek, M. (1974) J. Theoret. Biol. 489-492.
10. Wood, H. N., Rennekamp, M. E., Bowen, D. V., Field, F. H. and Braun, A. C. (1974) Proc. Nat. Acad. Sci. U.S. 71 4140-4143.
11. Karrer, P. and Eugster, C. H. (1949) Helv. Chim. Acta 32 957-960.
12. Bollard, E. G. (1956) Nature 178 1189-1190.
13. Herridge, D. F., Atkins, C. A., Pate, J. S. and Rainbird, R. M. (1978) Plant Physiol. 62 495-498.
14. Fox, J. J. and Wempen, I. (1959) Adv. Carbohyd. Chem. 14 283-380.
15. Elnaghy, M. A. and Nordin, P. (1966) Arch. Biochem. Biophys. 113 72-76.
16. Isherwood, F. A. and Selvendran, R. R. (1970) Phytochemistry 9 2265-2269.
17. Nygaard, P. (1972) Physiol. Plantarum 26 29-33.
18. Hintermann, R. and Parish, R. W. (1979) Planta 146 459-461.
19. Ashton, A. R. and Polya, G. M. (1978) Plant Physiol. 61 718-722.
20. Brown, E. G., Al-Najafi, T. and Newton, R. P. (1979) Phytochemistry 18 9-14.
21. Wiedmaier, J. and Kull, U. (1978) Biochem. Physiol. Pflanzen. 172 421-437.
22. Rhodes, M. J. C. and Wooltorton, L. S. C. (1968) Phytochemistry 7 337-353.
23. Baxter, R. and Kirk, J. T. O. (1969) Nature 222 272-273.
24. Douglass, S. A., Criddle, R. S. and Breidenbach, R. W. (1973) Plant Physiol. 51 902-906.
25. Lamppa, G. K. and Bendich, A. J. (1979) Plant Physiol. 64 126-130.
26. Kolodner, R. and Tewari, K. K. (1972) Proc. Nat. Acad. Sci. U. S., 69 1830-1834.
27. Wardell, W. L. and Skoog, F. (1973) Plant Physiol. 52 215-220.
28. Dudock, B. S., Katz, G., Taylor, E. K. and Holley, R. W. (1969) Proc. Nat. Acad. Sci. U. S., 62 941-945.
29. Delseny, M., Aspart, L., Balat, H. and Guitton, Y. (1974) Compt. Rend. D 278 1225-1228.
30. Aspart, L., Cooke, R. and Delseny, M. (1979) Biochim. Biophys. Acta 564 43-54.
31. Wheeler, A. M. and Hartley, M. R. (1975) Nature 257 66-67.
32. Bowden-Bonnett, L. and Lord, J. M. (1979) Plant Physiol. 63 769-773.
33. Oaks, A., Wallace, W. and Stevens, D. (1972) Plant Physiol. 50 649-654.
34. Payne, P. I. (1976) Biol. Rev. 51 329-363.
35. Shih, D. S., Adams, R. E., and Barnett, L. B. (1973) Phytochemistry 12 263-269.
36. Loening, U. E. (1968) J. Molec. Biol. 38 355-365.
37. Whitfield, P. R., Leaver, C. J., Bottomley, W., and Atchison, B. A. Biochem. J. 178 1103-1112 (1978).
38. Van de Walle, C. and Deltour, R. (1974) FEBS Letters 49 87-91.
39. Wang, D. and Mancini, D. (1966) Biochim. Biophys. Acta. 129 231-239.
40. Gulich, L. (1960) Planta 54 374-393.
41. Chang, C. W. and Kivilaan, A. (1964) Phytochemistry 3 693-699.
42. Newbury, H. J. and Possingham, J. V. (1977) Plant Physiol. 60 543-547.
43. Stein, D. B. and Thompson, W. F. (1978) Plant Sci. Letters 11 323-328.
44. Nieman, R. H., Pap, D. L. and Clark, R. A. (1978) J. Chromatog. 161 137-146.
45. Pascoe, M. J. and Ingle, J. (1978) Plant Physiol. 62 975-977.
46. McIntosh, L. and Cattolico, R. A. (1978) Anal. Biochem. 91 600-612.
47. Bourque, D. P., Hagiladi, A. and Naylor, A. W. (1973) Biochem. Biophys. Res. Commun. 51 993-999.
48. Pillay, D. T. N. (1974) Z. Pflanzenphysiol. 73 172-177.
49. Laulhere, J.-P. and Rozier, C. (1976) Plant Sci. Letters 6 237-242.
50. Gusta, L. V. and Weiser, C. J. (1971) Phytochemistry 10 1733-1743 (1971).
51. Nitta, T. (1977) Biochem. Physiol. Pflanzen 171 333-348.
52. Chandra, G. R. and Abdul-Baki, A. (1977) Plant Cell Physiol. 18 271-275.
53. Lurquin, P. F., Tshitenge, G., Delaunoit, G. and Ledoux, L. (1975) Anal. Biochem. 65 1-10.
54. Grotha, R. (1976) Biochem. Physiol. Pflanzen 170 273-277.
55. El-Gewely, M. R. and Tyson, H. (1974) Anal. Biochem. 62 341-348.
56. Romani, R. J., Sproule, B. V., Mettler, I. J., and Tuskes, S. E. (1975) Phytochemistry 14 2563-2567.
57. Durante, M., Giorgi, L. and Parenti, R. (1974) Anal. Biochem. 60 626-630.
58. Trapy, G. and Esnault, R. (1978) Phytochemistry 17 1859-1861.
59. Albaum, H. G. and Ogur, M. (1947) Arch. Biochem. Biophys. 15 158-160.
60. Rajcsanyi, P. M., Csillag, M. and Kriskovics, E. (1974) Separ. Purif. Methods 3 167-205.
61. Edelson, E. H., Lawless, J. G., Wehr, C. T. and Abbott, S. R. (1979) J. Chromatog. 179 409-419.
62. Sofrova, D. and Leblova, S. (1970) Photosynthetica 4 162-184.
63. Hall, R. H. (1965) Biochemistry 4 661-670.

64. Shingler, A. J. and Carlton, J. K. (1959) Anal. Chem. 31 1679-1680.
65. Sweetman, L. and Nyhan, W. L. (1968) J. Chromatog. 32 662-675.
66. Thomas, T. H., Carroll, J. E., Isenberg, F. M. R., Pendergrass, A. and Howell, L. (1975) J. Chromatog. 103 211-215.
67. Hahn, H. (1975) Physiol. Plant. 34 204-207.
68. Vreman, H. J. and Corse, J. (1975) Physiol. Plantarum 35 333-336.
69. Sachs, R. M., Ryugo, K. and Messerschmidt, O. (1976) Plant Physiol. 57 98-100.
70. Kemp, J. D. and Sutton, D. W. (1976) Biochim. Biophys. Acta 425 148-156.
71. Venner, H. (1960) Z. Physiol. Chem. 322 122-134.
72. Markham, R. and Smith, J. D. (1951) Biochem. J. 49 401-407.
73. Wade, H. E. and Morgan, D. M. (1953) Nature 171 529-530.
74. Wood, T. (1955) Nature 176 175-176.
75. Letham, D. S. (1965) J. Chromatog. 20 184-186.
76. Gerlach, E. and Döring, H.-J. (1955) Naturwiss. 42 344.
77. Tyihak, E. (1964) J. Chromatog. 14 125-126.
78. Cramer, F. (1961) Z. Anal. Chem. 181 545-549.
79. Harris, A. B. and Warburton, R. (1966) Nature 212 1359-1360.
80. Drach, J. C. and Novack, J. M. (1973) Anal. Biochem. 52 633-636.
81. Pačes, V. and Kamínek, M. (1978) J. Chromatog. 153 291-294.
82. Tomashefski, J. F., Jr., Barrios, R. J. and Sudilovsky, O. (1974) Anal. Biochem. 60 589-595.
83. Heftmann, E. and Schwimmer, S. (1971) J. Chromatog. 59 214-215.
84. Hattox, S. E. and McCloskey, J. A. (1974) Anal. Chem. 46 1378-1383.
85. Muni, I. A. and Altshuler, C. H. (1974) American Laboratory, May 19-28.
86. Young, H. (1977) Anal. Biochem. 79 226-233.
87. Kannagara, T., Durley, R. C. and Simpson, G. M. (1978) Physiol. Plantarum 44 295-299.
88. Horgan, R. and Kramers, M. R. (1979) J. Chromatog. 173 263-270.
89. Thomas, T. H., Carroll, J. E., Isenberg, F. M. R., Pendergrass, A., and Howell, L. (1975) Plant Physiol. 56 410-414.
90. Rowan, K. S. (1957) J. Exptl. Botany 8 256-271.
91. Rowan, K. S. (1959) Biochim. Biophys. Acta 34 270-271.
92. Cherry, J. H. and Hageman, R. H. (1960) Plant Physiol. 35 343-352.
93. Wilson, C. M. (1975) Ann. Rev. Plant Physiol. 26 187-208.
94. Cohn, W. E. (1955) Methods Enzymol. 3 724-743.
95. Felsenfeld, G. (1968) Methods Enzymol. 12 247-253.
96. Lovatt, C. J. and Albert, L. S. (1979) Plant Physiol. 64 562-569.
97. Guranowski, A. and Barankiewicz, J. (1979) FEBS Letters 104 95-98.
98. Vandiver, V. V., Jr. and Fites, R. C. (1979) Plant Physiol. 64 668-670.
99. Plaut, G. W. E., Smith, C. M. and Alworth, W. L. (1974) Ann. Rev. Biochem. 43 899-922.
100. Chen, C.-M. and Hall, R. H. (1969) Phytochemistry 8 1687-1695.
101. Beutelmann, P. (1973) Planta 112 181-190.
102. Armstrong, D. J., Murai, N., Tatler, B. J. and Skoog, F. (1976) Plant Physiol. 57 15-22.
103. Suzuki, T. and Takahashi, E. (1976) Biochem. J. 160 171-179.
104. Baumann, T. W., Dupont-Looser, E., and Wanner, H. (1978) Phytochemistry 17 2075-2076.
105. Roberts, M. F. and Waller, G. R. (1979) Phytochemistry 18 451-455.
106. Silver, A. V. and Gilmore, V. (1969) Phytochemistry 8 2295-2299.
107. Nirmala, J. and Sastry, K. S. (1975) Phytochemistry 14 1971-1973.
108. Tajima, S. and Yamamoto, Y. (1975) Plant Cell Physiol. 16 271-282.
109. Thomas, R. J., Feller, U. and Erismann, K. H. (1979) Plant Physiol. 63 Suppl. 275.
110. Schwimmer, S. (1966) Phytochemistry 5 791-794.
111. Rejman, E. and Buchowicz, J. (1973) Phytochemistry 12 271-276.
112. Guilfoyle, T. J., Lin, C.-Y., Chen, Y.-M. and Key, J. L. (1976) Biochim. Biophys. Acta 418 344-357.
113. Glicklich, D., Jendrisak, J. J. and Becker, W. M. (1974) Plant Physiol 54 356-359.
114. Rizzo, P. J., Cherry, J. H., Pedersen, K. and Dunham, V. L. (1974) Plant Physiol. 54 349-355.
115. Guilfoyle, T. J. (1976) Plant Physiol. 58 453-458.
116. Van de Walle, C., Bernier, G., Deltour, R. and Bronchart, R. (1976) Plant Physiol. 57 632-639.
117. Melanson, D. L. and Ingle, J. (1978) Plant Physiol. 62 761-765.
118. Abeels, M. J. F. (1977) Biochem. Soc. Trans. 5 957-958.
119. Ahmed, Z. U. and Kamra, O. P. (1975) FEBS Letters 51 277-280.
120. Spiegel, S. and Marcus, A. (1975) Nature 256 228-230.
121. Payne, P. I. (1977) Phytochemistry 16 431-434.
122. Jacobsen, J. V. (1977) Ann. Rev. Plant Physiol. 28 537-564.
123. Wielgat, B. and Kahl, G. (1979) Plant Physiol. 64 863-866, 867-871.

Chapter 13
ALKALOIDS

    The alkaloids do not represent a chemically homogeneous group, so that any generalizations about them are subject to many exceptions. They all contain nitrogen, frequently in a heterocyclic ring, and many but not all, are basic as their name indicates. Simple, aliphatic amines are not included here although the distinction is not sharp -- ephedrine and mescaline are often placed with the alkaloids although their nitrogens are aliphatic:

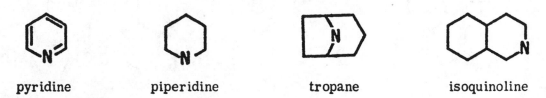

mescaline   ephedrine

Classification of alkaloids is done on the basis of the ring system present, e.g.

pyridine   piperidine   tropane   isoquinoline

    The purines and pyrimidines are conveniently considered separately because of their biochemical relation to the nucleic acids. The purines, caffeine and theobromine, are frequently placed with the alkaloids though; and the distinction appears to be a physiological rather than a chemical one. Some alkaloid structures with their ring-numbering systems are given in Figure 13-1.

    The alkaloids as a group are distinguished from most other plant components by their basic (cationic) nature. Therefore, they normally exist in plants as the salts of various organic acids and are frequently handled in the laboratory as salts of hydrochloric or sulfuric acid. These salts, and frequently the free alkaloids, are colorless crystalline compounds. A few alkaloids are liquids, and colored ones are even more rare (berberine and serpentine are yellow). Alkaloids are frequently optically active; and normally only one of the optical isomers is found naturally, although in a few cases racemic mixtures are known.

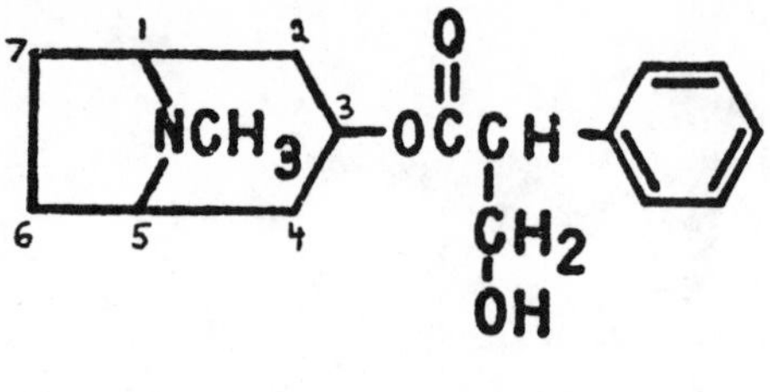

atropine (DL-hyoscyamine)

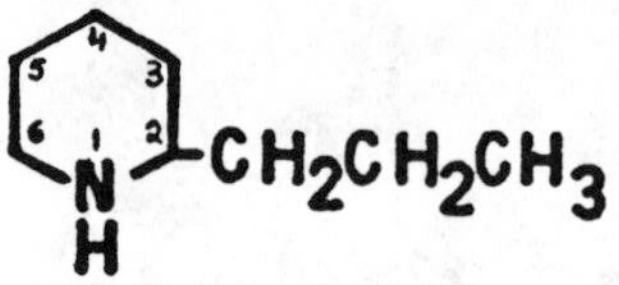

coniine

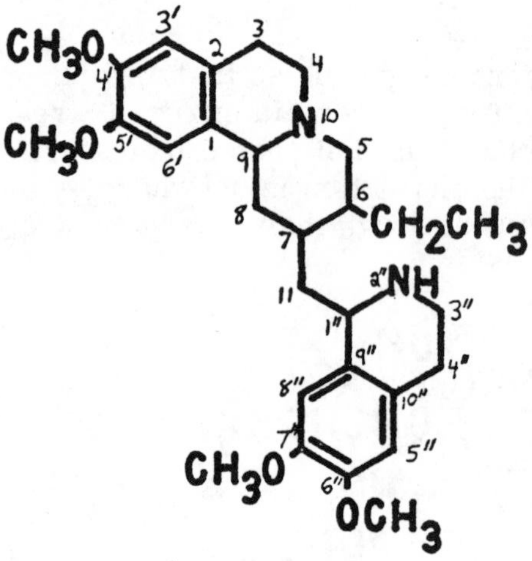

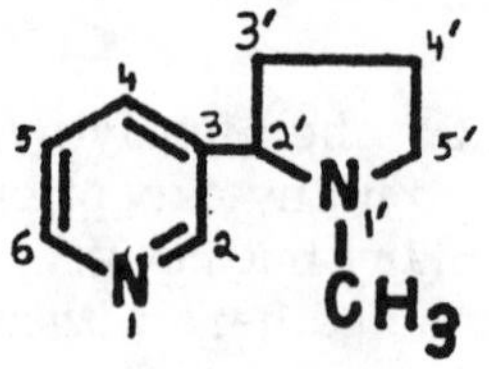

nicotine

emetine

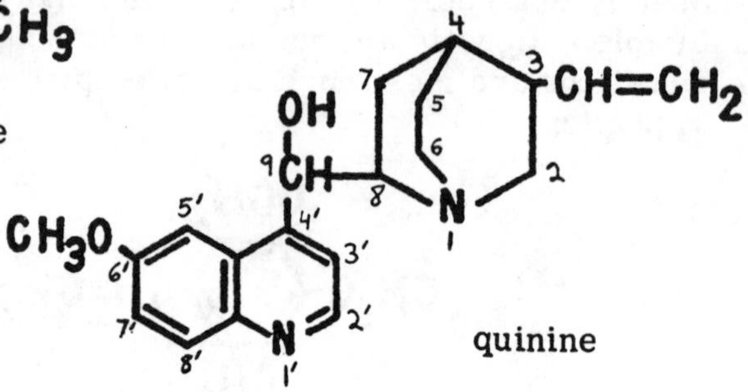

quinine

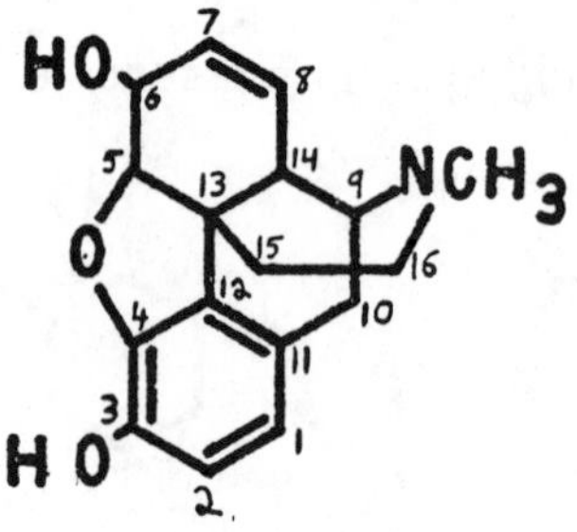

morphine

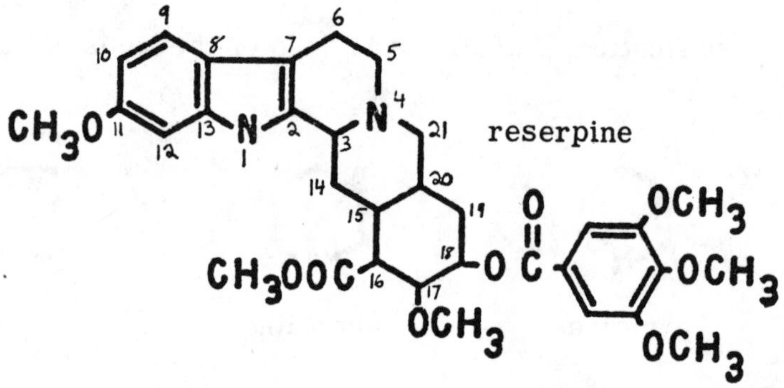

reserpine

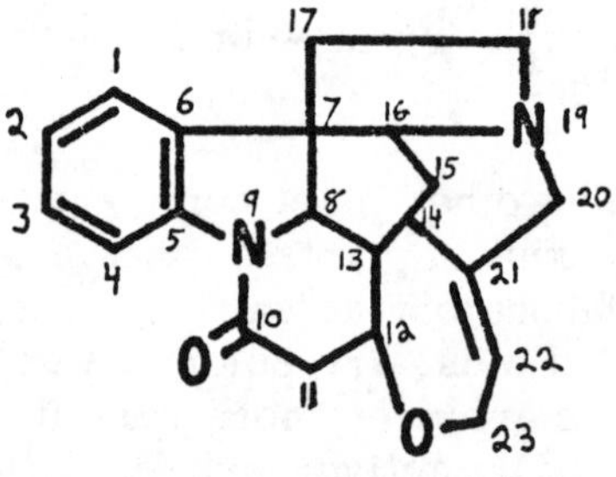

strychnine

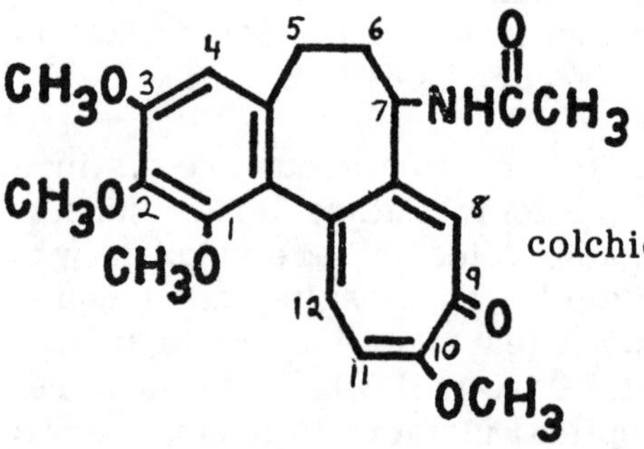

colchicine

FIGURE 13-1 STRUCTURES AND NUMBERING
FOR SOME WELL-KNOWN ALKALOIDS

The alkaloids have been known for many years and have been of interest mostly because of their physiological effects on man and their use in pharmacy, but the function of alkaloids in plants is almost completely obscure. Some suggestions regarding possible roles follow:

1. One of the earliest suggestions was that alkaloids function as nitrogen waste products like urea and uric acid in animals.
2. Some alkaloids may serve as nitrogen storage reservoirs although many seem to accumulate and are not farther metabolized even in severe nitrogen starvation.
3. In some cases alkaloids may protect the plant against attack by parasites or herbivores. Although evidence favoring this function has been brought forward in some instances (1-3), it is probably an overworked and anthropocentric concept.
4. Alkaloids may serve as growth regulators since structures of some of them resemble structures of known growth regulators. Maisuryan (4) has shown that lupine alkaloids may act as germination inhibitors. A growth stimulator from rice and an inhibitor from corn have related quinoline structures (5).
5. It was originally suggested by Liebig that the alkaloids being mostly basic might serve in the plant to replace mineral bases in maintaining ionic balance. In line with this suggestion is the observation of Dawson (6) that feeding nicotine to tobacco root cultures increased their uptake of nitrate. Laroze and Alves da Silva (7) favor the view that alkaloids function by exchanging with soil cations, and they have found alkaloids to be excreted by the roots of several alkaloid plants.

Further discussion of the possible functions of alkaloids may be found in some of the general references and (8-10).

Alkaloids are widely distributed throughout the plant kingdom. Various estimates put the percentage of alkaloid-containing plant species somewhere in the range of 15-30% (11, 12). The number is arbitrary because of variation in the sensitivity of detection methods, and as a rule of thumb an alkaloidal plant can be defined as one that has more than 0.05% alkaloid by dry weight. By processing prodigious amounts of material it has been found that the "non-alkaloidal" common cabbage contains 0.0004% narcotine (12). Another kind of arbitrariness arises from the fact that even well established alkaloidal plants may not contain alkaloids in all tissues or at all stages of development (9). There does not appear to be any facile generalization to be made about alkaloid distribution. There is some tendency for higher plants to have more than lower plants, but alkaloids are well known in the club mosses and horsetails, not to mention certain fungi (ergot). Alkaloids (except for some simple indoles) are not known in the Bryophytes. It has been suggested (13) that the formation of volatile terpenes somehow competes with the formation of alkaloids so that plants having one lack the other. A special illustration of this principle is shown by the work of Tallent and Horning (14) who found that species of pine which have alkaloids also have straight-chain, aliphatic hydrocarbons rather than terpenes in their turpentines.

ISOLATION

The single, most important chemical property of the alkaloids is their basicity. Purification and characterization methods generally rely on this property, and special approaches must be developed for those few alkaloids (e.g. rutaecarpine, colchicine, ricinine) which are not basic.

Alkaloids are normally obtained by extracting the plant material with an acidic, aqueous solvent which dissolves the alkaloids as their salts, or the plant material may be made alkaline with sodium carbonate, etc. and the free bases extracted into organic solvents such as chloroform, ether, etc. A continuous extraction and concentration apparatus especially useful for heat-labile alkaloids has been described (15). Several artifactual alkaloids arising from the use of reactive solvents have been described (16-19). Such well-used reagents as chloroform, acetone, ammonia, and methylene chloride may have to be avoided in certain cases. Some volatile alkaloids such as nicotine may be purified by steam distillation from an alkaline solution. An acidic aqueous solution containing alkaloids may be made basic and the alkaloids extracted with an organic solvent so that neutral and acidic water-soluble compounds are left behind. Another useful way of removing alkaloids from acidic solution is by adsorption on Lloyd's reagent (20). They can then be eluted with dilute base. Many alkaloids can be separated by precipitating them with Mayer's reagent (potassium mercuric iodide) (21) or Reinecke salt (22); and the precipitates can then be resolved into their components by ion exchange chromatography (21-23). For detailed methods of alkaloid isolation the articles of Cromwell (24), Manske (25), Sangster (26), Graf (27), and Hultin (28) may be consulted. The most general and convenient method of separation now available for separation of mixtures is column chromatography either using ion exchange resins (29) or adsorbents such as aluminum oxide or silica gel. High molecular weight impurities that interfere with chromatography can be removed by preliminary ultrafiltration (30). Paper chromatography (see below) is useful for preliminary determination of the number of components to be separated and something of their nature. A procedure for isolation and identification of alkaloids from milligram quantities of plant material uses a combination of column chromatography on alumina and paper chromatography (31). A method that divides alkaloids according to basicity and polarity uses successive extractions from buffer of gradually increasing pH (32).

CHARACTERIZATION

Qualitative evidence for the presence of alkaloids and a rough characterization may be obtained by application of the various "alkaloidal reagents". Rapid screening procedures are available to test plants for the presence of alkaloids (33, 34), and the localization of alkaloids within plant tissues may be determined by specific staining reactions (35).

Mayer's reagent (potassium tetraiodomercurate) is most commonly used for detection of alkaloids since it gives a precipitate with nearly all of them (36). As it also precipitates other plant components, a preliminary purification is advisable before applying the test. Other

reagents such as Wagner's reagent (iodine in potassium iodide), 5% silico-
tungstic acid, 5% tannic acid, Dragendorff's reagent (potassium tetra-
iodobismuthate), and saturated picric acid are also frequently used. Some
alkaloids contain specific functional groups which may be determined by
special reagents. For example, morphine is phenolic so that phenol reagents
can be used to distinguish it. Systematic application of such reagents can
be used for classification of alkaloids, and procedures have been given by
Fulton (37) for dividing the alkaloids into large groups on the basis of
orderly use of reagents.

If a more complete characterization of alkaloids is desired, the techniques of paper or thin layer chromatography and spectrophotometry can be
used to provide the most information with the least effort. Macek et al.
(38) have proposed a classification scheme based on paper chromatographic
behavior. By using several different solvents and reagents, an alkaloid
may be placed into one of 6 major categories. The application of special
reagents and comparison with knowns can then be used for a more nearly complete identification. Another paper chromatographic classification based
on polarity is described by Waldi (39). It is impossible here to describe
the very many systems that have been used for paper chromatography of alkaloids. General books on chromatography give good coverage of them. Neutral
solvent mixtures are suitable only for neutral alkaloids that show no
tendency to become protonated or for quaternary alkaloids that are positively
charged at all pH values. For most alkaloids either basic or acidic solvents
are used to insure that the molecules are either all unprotonated or all
protonated. With weakly basic alkaloids solvents buffered at pH values in
between the pKa values of the alkaloids to be separated have given good
results (40, 41). The most used detection reagent for spraying chromatograms
is Dragendorff's Reagent, which exists in several variations (42). It
does, however, react with some non-alkaloids although the sensitivity is
about ten-fold greater for alkaloids (43). Some recently developed reagents
for alkaloid detection are fluorescamine (44) and 7,7,8,8- tetracyanoquinone-
dimethane (45). Their advantage is that they react differently with different types of structure. Phenolic alkaloids can be detected by special
phenol reagents (46, 47).

Thin layer chromatography is also a rapid technique which can be applied to alkaloid separations. Waldi et al. (48) have devised a routine
procedure for alkaloid identification using silica gel G as the adsorbent
with 8 different solvent systems. Other thin layer procedures have been
devised using silica gel and other adsorbents (28, 49-53). Worthy of special notice is the use of $MgO-CaCl_2$ since this support is completely
soluble in acid allowing elution and spectral determination of spots (54). The
same detection reagents can be used for thin layer plates as for paper
chromatograms.

High speed liquid chromatography is a relatively new development that
has been applied to analysis of some alkaloids (55-57). In spite of the
low volatility of many alkaloids it has been possible to use gas chromatography for some of them either directly or as trimethylsilyl derivatives
(58-60). Coupling of the output of the gas chromatograph to a mass spectrometer further increases the power of this method (58, 61, 62). Solid
probe mass spectrometry can be used directly on plant material to show the
presence of particular alkaloids and even to localize alkaloids to within
1 mm^3 of tissue (63-66).

Electrophoresis of alkaloids on paper sheets or thin layers has been useful for certain alkaloids. It is often faster and more reproducible than paper chromatography (67, 68).

An elegant technique recently available for the detection of minute amounts of specific alkaloids is radioimmunoassay. Once the appropriate antibodies are on hand, less than 1 nanogram of alkaloid can be assayed (69).

If a pure alkaloid can be obtained, determination of its absorption spectrum can provide a valuable means of identification. Elution of a spot from a chromatogram may provide enough material for this purpose. Ultraviolet absorption spectra for a great many alkaloids have been brought together and discussed (70-74). Infra red spectra are given by Levi et al. (75) and by Marion et al. (76). A veritable encyclopedia of spectral data and physical constants of alkaloids is now available (77).

METABOLIC PATHWAYS

The schemes of alkaloid biosynthesis shown in the accompanying diagrams are largely based on the proposals made by Sir Robert Robinson in 1917 (78). These ideas have since been elaborated both by him and others (cf. (79, 80). They constitute a comprehensive and reasonable picture of alkaloid biosynthesis that was based primarily on analogy with reactions of organic chemistry and by considerations of structural similarity rather than direct, biochemical evidence. Nevertheless, a vast number of tracer experiments beginning in about 1954 have confirmed most of the suggestions in a general sense, going on from there to fill in many details of intermediates and reaction mechanisms. The assumptions of Robinson's scheme of biosynthesis may be summarized as follows:

1. The basic skeletons of alkaloids are derived from common amino acids and other small biological molecules.
2. A few simple types of reactions suffice to form complex structures from these starting materials. For example the aldol condensation:

$$\text{\\C}=\text{O} + \text{H}\overset{|}{\text{C}}-\text{X} \rightarrow -\overset{|}{\text{C}}-\overset{\overset{\text{OH}}{|}}{\text{C}}-$$

the carbinolamine condensation:

$$\text{\\N}-\overset{|}{\text{C}}-\text{OH} + \text{H}-\overset{|}{\text{C}}-\text{X} \rightarrow \text{\\N}-\overset{|}{\text{C}}-\overset{|}{\text{C}} + \text{H}_2\text{O}$$

as well as simple dehydrations, oxidations, and decarboxylations. (X represents an "activating" group such as carbonyl.)

The Robinson proposals are not tied to specific compounds or to specific sequences of intermediates. Rather, the pyrrolidine ring may be thought of as derived from any one of a group of related compounds (i.e. ornithine, glutamic acid, succinic acid) which have structural similarities and which are now known to be biochemically interrelated as well. The first specific intermediate that is irrevocably committed to forming an alkaloid rather than some other compound remains unknown in most cases. In fact, it would

seem that the crucial problem in alkaloid biosynthesis is the identification
of the point in the pathways of metabolism where an intermediate is formed
whose subsequent transformations are directed solely toward an alkaloid
with no links to other classes of compounds.

In addition to general reviews of alkaloid biosynthesis listed under
"General References" several reviews dealing with particular groups of
alkaloids are listed below. Mothes has described the methodology for
studying alkaloid biosynthesis (81, 82).

Alkaloid Group	Reference
piperidines	83
benzylisoquinolines	84
morphinans	85-87
tropanes	88
phenethylamines, isoquinolines	89
pyridines	90
acridines, quinolines	91
indoles	92

In Figs. 13-2 and 13-3 pathways to alkaloids are summarized in a
very general way with only carbon skeletons indicated. Names in parentheses
are specific alkaloids having the accompanying skeleton. Other names
refer to classes of alkaloids. One generalization that can be made concerning alkaloid precursors concerns the methyl groups found in many alkaloids,
both as N-methyl and O-methyl groups. Tracer experiments have, almost
without exception, shown that, as might be expected, these are derived
from the methyl group of methionine (93, 94). Enzyme systems from various
plants have been shown to catalyze the transfer of methyl groups from
S-adenosylmethionine to form gramine, hordenine, trigonelline, and several
opium alkaloids (95-97). Byerrum et al. (98) have found, however, that
glycine-2-^{14}C was at least as good a donor for the methyl group of nicotine.
Formate does not appear to be an efficient precursor in this system although
it apparently works well as a methyl donor for ephedrine formation (99).
Choline and betaine have also been found to act as methyl donors in some
cases.

The participation of C_3 and C_4 compounds at various points in the
scheme is evident, and these participants are most likely interrelated--
for example, as acetone and acetoacetic acid. These compounds, although
readily derived from plant components by well-known enzymatic reactions,
are found, if at all, in very small amounts. Some intermediate with a C_4
chain is probably made by addition of acetoacetate or successive additions
of two acetate units to some precursor of the heterocyclic ring. Decarboxylation at some later stage produces a C_3 unit (100-103).

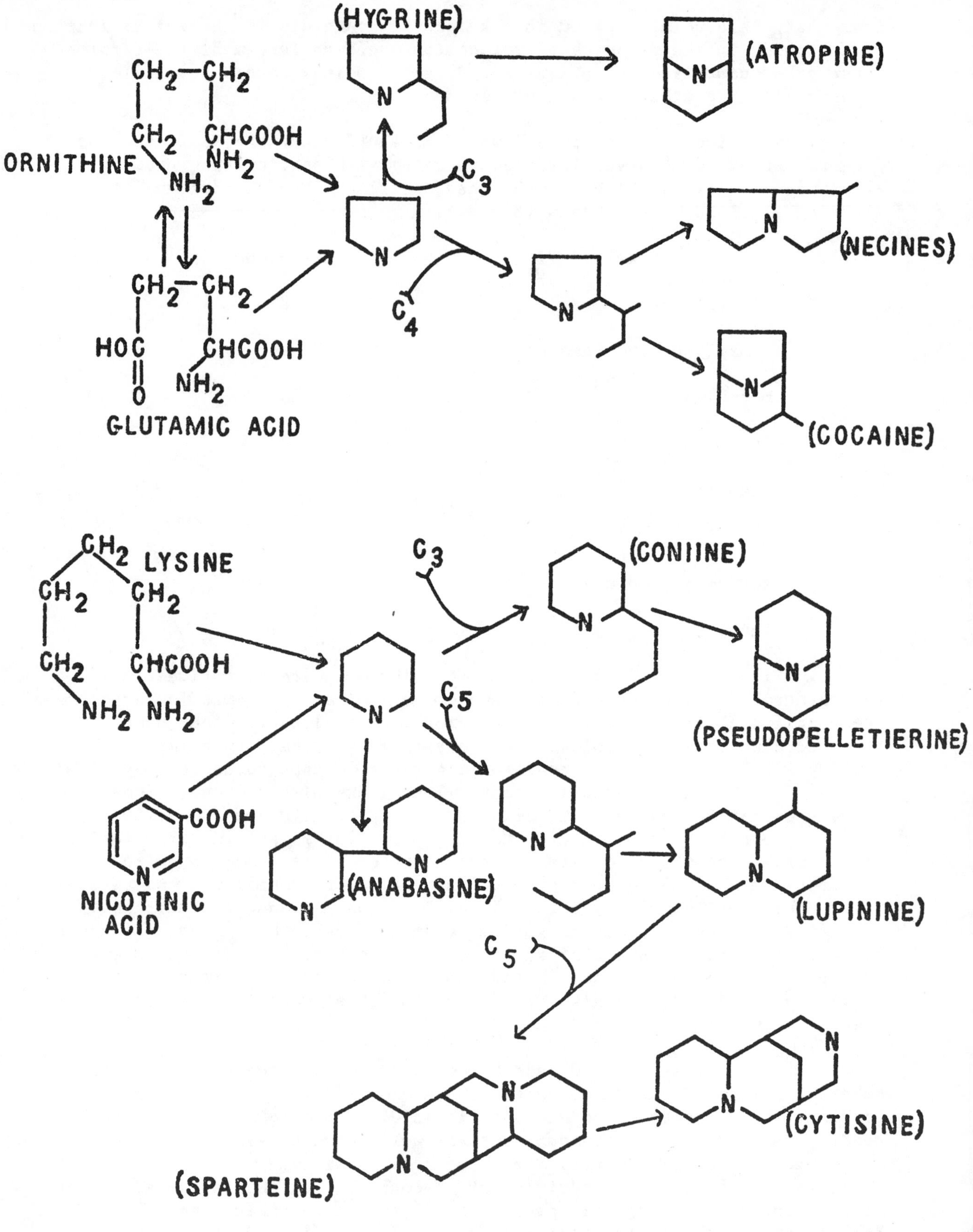

FIGURE 13-2   PATHWAYS OF ALKALOID BIOSYNTHESIS

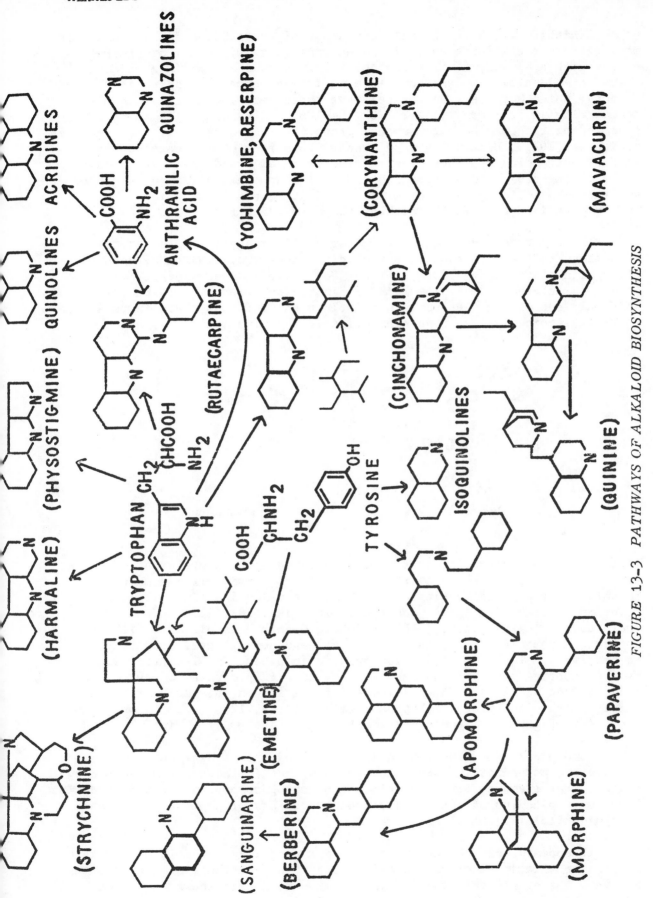

FIGURE 13-3 PATHWAYS OF ALKALOID BIOSYNTHESIS

Ornithine is the amino acid precursor of pyrrolidine rings present in many different alkaloids as an isolated ring (e.g. nicotine) or one condensed with a C_3 unit (e.g. atropine). For some alkaloids (e.g. nicotine) there is evidently a symmetrical intermediate such as putrescine in the pathway; but others (e.g. atropine) have their pyrrolidine rings labeled asymmetrically from ornithine-2-^{14}C (104-106). Alkaloids with an N-methyl-pyrrolidine ring may have the methyl group introduced as early as N^5-methyl-ornithine (107). Diamine oxidase preparations from plants catalyze conversion of putrescine or N-methylputrescine to an aminoaldehyde that spontaneously ring-closes to a pyrroline ring. The same aminoaldehyde could be generated by action of a transaminase, and it is not clear which enzyme may be more important in the pathway to pyrrolidine rings (108-110).

The precursors of 6-membered heterocyclic rings are more diverse. By analogy to the formation of pyrrolidine rings from ornithine, some piperidine rings are derived from lysine. For example, anabasine of *Nicotiana glauca* is labeled from lysine-2-^{14}C as indicated below. It is to be noted that only one of the α-carbon atoms is labeled, and thus there is no symmetrical intermediate such as cadaverine in this instance (111).

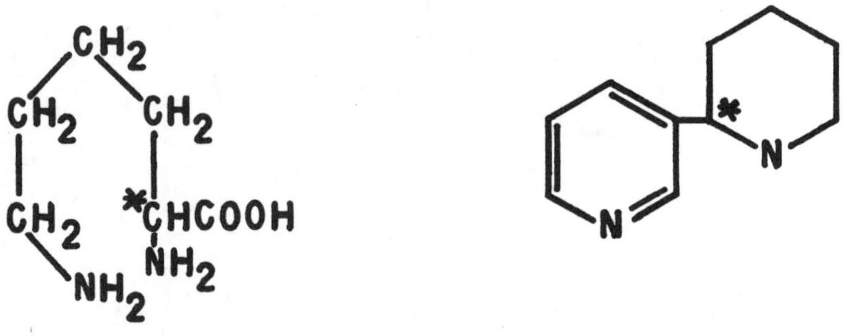

lysine   anabasine

In other cases, though, cadaverine is indicated to be a precursor of piperidine rings (112). Whatever the intermediates, lysine is a good precursor of the piperidine rings in such alkaloids as lobeline (113), N-methylisopelletierine (114), and the lupine alkaloids (115). Such intermediates as Δ^1-piperideine (116) or 2-keto-6-aminohexanoic acid (117) are suggested intermediates in the symmetrical and non-symmetrical pathways respectively. The role of diamine oxidase in producing Δ^1-piperideine from cadaverine would be analogous to its role in producing Δ^1-pyrroline from putrescine (118). There is some information on interconversions occurring within the group of lupine alkaloids (119, 120). The C_5 units indicated in Figure 13-2 come from additional molecules of lysine.

Some piperidine alkaloids are not derived from lysine but are, rather, polyacetate compounds in which nitrogen has been introduced from an unknown source. For example, octanoic acid and other C_8 compounds presumably derived from four molecules of acetate are good precursors of coniine and related alkaloids (121-123).

It appears that the aromatic-type pyridine ring found in many alkaloids and in the vitamin nicotinic acid is not derived via the lysine-cadaverine pathway. Nicotinic acid and/or nicotinamide have been shown to be good precursors of the pyridine ring in such alkaloids as nicotine (124), and ricinine (125). However, the pyridine ring is, of course, already present in nicotinic acid; and how it is originally formed remains unknown. There is some indication that C-2, C-3 and the carboxyl group may be derived from a C_4 compound such as succinate whereas C-4, C-5, and C-6 may come from a C_3 precursor such as dihydroxyacetone phosphate (126, 127). There is convincing evidence that in higher plants nicotinic acid is not made by the pathway:

tryptophan→kynurenine→3-hydroxyanthranilic acid→nicotinic acid

even though this pathway has been well-established in fungi (128). Quinolinic acid and pyridine nucleotide intermediates are probably found in the pathway from nicotinic acid to the pyridine alkaloids (129, 130).

Many alkaloids are derived from the aromatic amino acids phenylalanine and tyrosine. The simplest are phenethylamines such as mescaline that are sometimes called "protoalkaloids". They come from tyrosine by decarboxylation to tyramine followed by a series of hydroxylations and methylations (131-132). A 3, 4-dimethoxy-5-hydroxyphenethylamine of this sequence condenses with pyruvic acid to form the isoquinoline alkaloids that occur together with the phenethylamines (133-135). Other isoquinoline alkaloids may be regarded as modified dimers of tyrosine in which the two monomers that condense are closely related respectively to dopamine and dihydroxyphenylpyruvic acid. The resulting benzylisoquinoline structure is found in such alkaloids as papaverine and laudanosoline. Further ring closures and rearrangements yield many other ring systems. These pathways have been intensively studied but cannot be discussed here. Oxidative phenol coupling reactions are very important in producing the different ring skeletons. Some recent reports in this area are (136-139).

Indole alkaloids are the most varied and complex group known. They include some valuable drugs such as reserpine and vincristine. There is no question about the place of tryptophan as a precursor of the indole alkaloids and at a very early stage in the pathway tryptamine (or a hydroxytryptamine) probably condenses with a C_{10} terpenoid unit closely related to secologanin. Following this, many complex ring closures and rearrangements lead to the various alkaloid structures. Some papers dealing with these pathways are (92, 140-143).

Several important quinoline alkaloids, including quinine, are actually closely related biosynthetically to the indole alkaloids. One of the rearrangement pathways mentioned above leads to formation of the quinuclidine and quinoline rings characteristic of the cinchona alkaloids (144). Other quinoline alkaloids are derived by a totally different pathway starting with anthranilic acid (145-148).

GENERAL REFERENCES

Cromwell, B. T., "The Alkaloids," in Paech & Tracey 4 367-516.

Glasby, J. S. (1975-1977) Encyclopedia of the Alkaloids, 3 Vols., Plenum Press, N. Y.

Grundon, M. F. (1978) The Alkaloids, 8, Chemical Society, London.

Manske, R. H. F. et al. eds. (1951-1979) The Alkaloids, 17 Vols., Academic Press, N. Y.

Mothes, K. & Schütte, H. R. (1969) Biosynthese der Alkaloide, VEB Deutscher Verlag der Wissenschaften, Berlin.

Pelletier, S. W., ed. (1970) Chemistry of the Alkaloids, Van Nostrand Reinhold, N. Y.

Raffauf, R. F. (1970) A Handbook of Alkaloids and Alkaloid-Containing Plants, Wiley-Interscience, N. Y.

Robinson, T. (1968) The Biochemistry of Alkaloids, Springer-Verlag, Berlin.

Swan, G. A. (1967) An Introduction to the Alkaloids, Wiley, N. Y.

Waller, G. R. & Nowacki, E. K. (1978) Alkaloid Biology and Metabolism in Plants, Plenum Press, N. Y.

Willaman, J. J. & Sshubert, B. G. (1961) Alkaloid-Bearing Plants and Their Contained Alkaloids, Tech. Bull. No. 1234, U. S. Dept. Agric., Washington, D. C.

Willaman, J. J. & Li, H.-L. (1970) "Alkaloid-Bearing Plants and Their Contained Alkaloids, 1967-1968", Lloydia 33 No. 3A

BIBLIOGRAPHY

1. Levinson, H. Z. (1976) Experientia 32 403-413.
2. Levin, D. A. and York, B. M., Jr. (1978) Biochem. Systematics Ecol. 6 61-76.
3. Robinson, T. (1979) in G. Rosenthal and D. H. Janzen, eds., Herbivores: Their Interaction with Secondary Plant Metabolism, Academic Press, N. Y. pp. 413-448.
4. Maisuryan, N. A. (1956) Doklady Akad. Nauk. Armyan. S.S.R. 22 91-95 (Chem. Abstr. 50 10863),
5. Matsushima, H., Fukumi, H., and Arima, K. (1973) Agric. Biol. Chem. 37 1865-1871.
6. Dawson, R. F. (1946) Plant Physiol. 21 115-130.
7. Laroze, A. and Alves da Silva, J. (1952) Anais. fac. farm. Porto. 12 85-105 (C.A. 48 233).
8. Mothes, K. (1969) Experientia 25 225-239.
9. Robinson, T. (1974) Science 184 430-435.
10. Mothes, K. (1960) in R. H. G. Manske and H. L. Holmes, eds., The Alkaloids 6, Academic Press, N. Y. pp. 1-29.
11. Smolenski, S. J., Silinis, H., and Farnsworth, N. R. (1975) Lloydia 38 411-441.
12. Hegnauer, R. (1963) in T. Swain, ed., Chemical Plant Taxonomy, Academic Press, N. Y. pp. 389-427.
13. Treibs, W. (1955) Perfum. Essent. Oil Rec. 46 222-225.
14. Tallent, W. H., Stromberg, V. L., and Horning, E. C. (1955) J. Am. Chem. Soc. 77 6361-6364.
15. Deagen, J. T. and Deinzer, M. L. (1977) Lloydia 40 395-397.
16. Householder, D. E. and Camp, B. J. (1965) J. Pharm. Sci. 54 1676-1677.
17. Roberts, M. F., Cromwell, B. T., and Webster, D. E. (1967) Phytochemistry 6 711-717.
18. Schröder, P. and Luckner, M. (1968) Arch. Pharm. 301 39-46.
19. Phillipson, J. D. and Bisset, N. G. (1972) Phytochemistry 11 2547-2553.
20. Lloyd, J. V. (1916) J. Am. Pharm. Assoc. 5 381-390.
21. Jordan, W. and Scheuer, P. J. (1965) J. Chromatog. 10 175-176.
22. Kum-Tatt, L. (1960) Nature 188 65-66.
23. Ghosal, S., Banerjee, P. K., and Banerjee, S. K. (1970) Phytochemistry 9 429-433.
24. Cromwell, B. T. (1955) in Paech and Tracey 4 367-516.
25. Manske, R. H. F. (1951) in R. H. F. Manske and H. L. Holmes, eds., The Alkaloids 1, Academic Press, N. Y., pp. 1-14.
26. Sangster, A. W. (1960) J. Chem. Educ. 37 454-459, 518-525.
27. Graf, E. (1966) Arch. Pharm., Mitt. Deutsch. Pharm. Ges. 36 213-228, 237-257.
28. Hultin, E. (1966) Acta Chem. Scand. 20 1588-1592.
29. Berggren, A., Björling, C. O., and Willmann-Johnson, B. (1958) Acta Chem. Scand. 12 1521-1527.

30. Lyon, R. L., Fong, H. H. S., Farnsworth, N. R., and Svoboda, G. H. (1973) J. Pharm. Sci. _62_ 218-221.
31. Clarke, E. G. C. and Hawkins, A. E. (1961) Forensic Sci. Soc. J. _1_ 120-122 (Chem. Abstr. _56_ 5046).
32. Aripov, K. N. (1977) Chem. Nat. Compds. _13_ 624-634.
33. Hultin, E. and Torssell, K. (1965) Phytochemistry _4_ 425-433.
34. Smolenski, S. J., Silinis, H., and Farnsworth, N. R. (1972) Lloydia _35_ 1-34.
35. White, H. A. and Spencer, M. (1964) Can. J. Botany _42_ 1481-1483.
36. Szász, G. and Buda, L. (1971) Z. Anal. Chem. _253_ 361-363.
37. Fulton, C. C. (1939) Am. J. Pharm. _111_ 184-192 (Chem. Abstr. _33_ 7486).
38. Macek, K., Hacaperkova, J., and Kakac, B. (1956) Pharmazie _11_ 533-538.
39. Waldi, D. (1959) Arch. Pharm. _292_ 206-220.
40. Bräuniger, H. (1954) Pharmazie _9_ 643-654.
41. Bonnichsen, R., Maehly, A. C., and Nordlander, S. (1957) Acta Chem. Scand. _11_ 1280-1282.
42. Raffauf, R. F. (1962) Econ. Botany _16_ 171-172.
43. Anderson, L. A., Doggett, N. S., and Ross, M. S. F. (1977) Planta Medica _32_ 125-129.
44. Ranieri, R. L. and McLaughlin, J. L. (1975) J. Chromatog. _111_ 234-237.
45. Rücker, G. and Taha, A. (1977) J. Chromatog. _132_ 165-167.
46. Chrastil, J. (1975) J. Chromatog. _115_ 273-275.
47. Guha, K. P., Mukherjee, B., and Mukherjee, R. (1979) Lloydia _42_ 1-84.
48. Waldi, D., Schnackerz, K., and Munter, F. (1961) J. Chromatog. _6_ 61-73.
49. Rama Rao, N. V. and Tandon, S. N. (1978) J. Chromatog. Sci. _16_ 158-161.
50. Baiulescu, G. E. and Constantinescu, T. (1975) Anal. Chem. _47_ 2156-2160.
51. Verpoorte, R. and Svendsen, A. B. (1976) J. Chromatog. _124_ 152-156.
52. Lepri, L., Desideri, P. G., and Lepori, M. (1976) J. Chromatog. _123_ 175-184.
53. Wijesekera, R. O. B., Rajapakse, L. S., and Chelvarajan, D. W. (1976) J. Chromatog. _121_ 388-389.
54. Ragazzi, E. and Veronese, G. (1965) Mikrochim. Ichnoanal. Acta _1965_ 966-975.
55. Hostettmann, K., Pettei, M., Kubo, I., and Nakanishi, K. (1977) Helv. Chim. Acta _60_ 670-672.
56. Wu, C. Y. and Wittick, J. J. (1977) Anal. Chem. _49_ 359-363.
57. Qualls, C. W., Jr. and Segall, H. J. (1978) J. Chromatog. _150_ 202-206.
58. Cho, Y. D. and Martin, R. O. (1971) Anal. Biochem. _44_ 49-57.
59. Weeks, W. W., Davis, D. L., and Bush, L. P. (1969) J. Chromatog. _43_ 506-509.
60. Liebisch, H.-W., Bernasch, H., and Schütte, H. R. (1973) Z. Chem. _13_ 469-470.
61. Grove, M. D., Spencer, G. F., Wakeman, M. V., and Tookey, H. L. (1976) J. Agric. Food Chem. _24_ 896-897.
62. Deinzer, M., Thomson, P., Griffin, D., and Dickinson, E. (1978) Biomed. Mass Spectrom. _5_ 175-179.
63. Weber, J. M. and Ma, T. S. (1976) Microchim. Acta _1976_ I 217-225.
64. Holmstedt, D., Jäätmaa, E., Leander, K., and Plowman, T. (1977) Phytochemistry _16_ 1753-1755.
65. Kondrat, R. W., Cooks, R. G., and McLaughlin, J. L. (1978) Science _199_ 978-980.
66. Youssefi, M., Cooks, R. G., and McLaughlin, J. L. (1979) J. Am. Chem. Soc. _101_ 3400-3402.
67. Calderwood, J. M. and Fish, F. (1969) J. Pharm. Pharmacol. _21_ Suppl. 126S-128S.
68. Wan, A. S. C. (1971) J. Chromatog. _60_ 371-376.
69. Arens, H., Stöckigt, J., Weiler, E. W., and Zenk, M. H. (1978) Planta Medica _34_ 37-46.
70. Elvidge, W. F. (1940) Quart. J. Pharm. Pharmacol. _13_ 219-236.
71. Oestreicher, P. M., Farmilo, C. G., and Levi, L. (1954) United Nations Bull. Narcotics _6_ 42-70.
72. Sangster, A. W. and Stuart, K. L. (1965) Chem. Revs. _65_ 69-130.
73. Shamma, M., Hillman, M. J., and Jones, C. D. (1969) Chem. Rev. _69_ 779-784.
74. Hruban, L., Šantavý, F., and Hegerová, S. (1970) Collec. Czech. _35_ 3420-3444.
75. Levi, L., Hubley, C. E., Hinge, R. A. (1954) Bull. Narcotics U. N. Dept. Soc. Affairs _6_ No. 3/4 42-84.
76. Marion, L., Ramsay, D. A., and Jones, R. N. (1951) J. Am. Chem. Soc. _73_ 305-308.
77. Holubek, J. and Strouf, O., eds., (1965-1973) _Spectral Data and Physical Constants of Alkaloids_, 8 Vols., Heydon, London.
78. Robinson, R. (1917) J. Chem. Soc. _111_ 876-899.
79. Robinson, R. (1955) _The Structural Relations of Natural Products_, Oxford.
80. Woodward, R. B. (1956) Angew. Chem. _68_ 13-20.
81. Mothes, K. (1959) Pharmazie _14_ 121-132.
82. Mothes, K. (1959) Pharmazie _14_ 177-190.
83. Gupta, R. N. (1968) Lloydia _31_ 318-326.
84. Spenser, I. D. (1966) Lloydia _29_ 71-89.
85. Kirby, G. W., (1967) Science _155_ 170-173.
86. Blaschke, G. (1969) Arch. Pharm., Mitt. _39_ 225-234.
87. Stuart, K. L. (1971) Chem.Rev. _71_ 47-72.
88. **Leete, E. (1979) Planta Med. _36_ 97-112.**
89. Paul, A. G. (1973) Lloydia _36_ 36-45.
90. Gross, D. (1970) Fortschr. Chem. Org. Naturstoffe _28_ 109-161.
91. Gröger, D. (1969) Lloydia 32 221-246.
92. Cordell, G. A. (1974) Lloydia _37_ 219-298.

93. Roberts, M. F. (1974) Phytochemistry 13 1841-1845.
94. Gupta, R. N. and Spenser, I. D. (1963) Biochem. Biophys. Res. Commun. 13 115.-120.
95. Mack, J. P. G. and Slaytor, M. (1979) Phytochemistry 18 1921-1925.
96. Joshi, J. G. and Handler, P. (1960) J. Biol. Chem. 235 2981-2983.
97. Antoun, M. D. and Roberts, M. F. (1975) Planta Medica 28 6-11.
98. Byerrum, R. U., Hamill, R. L., and Ball, C. D. (1954) J. Biol. Chem. 210 645-650.
99. Shibata, S., Imaseki, I., and Yamazaki, M. (1957) Pharm. Bull. (Tokyo) 5 594-597 (Chem. Abstr. 52 8286).
100. Tuppy, H. and Faltaous, M. S. (1960) Monatsh. 91 167-175.
101. Gupta, R. N. and Spenser, I. D. (1969) Phytochemistry 8 1937-1944.
102. Leete, E. (1969) J. Am. Chem. Soc. 91 1697-1700.
103. Baralle, F. E. and Gros, E. G. (1969) Phytochemistry 8 849-851.
104. Leete, E. (1976) J. Org. Chem. 41 3438-3441.
105. Nakane, M. and Hutchinson, C. R. (1978) J. Org. Chem. 43 3922-3931.
106. Leete, E. (1964) Tetra. Lett. 1619-1622.
107. Ahmad, A. and Leete, E. (1970) Phytochemistry 9 2345-2347.
108. Smith, T. A. (1975) Phytochemistry 14 865-890.
109. Mizusaki, S., Tanabe, Y., Noguchi, M., and Tamaki, E. (1972) Phytochemistry 11 2757-2762.
110. Wink, M. and Hartmann, T. (1979) FEBS Letters 101 343-346.
111. Leete, E. (1956) J. Am. Chem. Soc. 78 3520-3523.
112. Kushmuradov, Y. K., Aslanov, K. A., Schütte, H. R., and Kuchkarov, S. (1977) Chem. Nat. Compds. 13 244-247.
113. O'Donovan, D. G., Long, D. J., Forde, E., and Geary, P. (1975) J. Chem. Soc. Perkin I 415-419.
114. Keogh, M. F. and O'Donovan, D. G. (1970) J. Chem. Soc. (C) 1970 1792-1997.
115. Leistner, E. and Spenser, I. D. (1979) Polish J. Chem. 53 49-56.
116. Golebiewski, W. M. and Spenser, I. D. (1976) J. Am. Chem. Soc. 98 6726-6728.
117. Gupta, R. N. and Spenser, I. D. (1968) Chem. Commun. 85-86.
118. Mothes, K., Schütte, H. R., Simon, H., and Weygand, F. (1959) Z. Naturforsch. 14b 49-51.
119. Cho, Y. D. and Martin, R. O. (1971) Can. J. Biochem. 49 971-977.
120. Kushmuradov, Y. K., Schütte, H. R., Aslanov, K. A., and Kuchkarov, S. (1977) Chem. Nat. Compds. 13 210-212.
121. Leete, E., Lechleiter, J. C., and Carver, R. A. (1975) Tetra. Lett. 3779-3782.
122. Roberts, M. F. (1977) Phytochemistry 16 1381-1386.
123. Roberts, M. F. (1978) Phytochemistry 17 107-112.
124. Leete, E. (1977) Bioorg. Chem. 6 273-286.
125. Waller, G. R. and Henderson, L. M. (1961) J. Biol. Chem. 236 1186-1191.
126. Wicks, R. D., Sakakibara, S., Gholson, R. K., and Scott, T. A. (1977) Biochim. Biophys. Acta 500 213-216.
127. Nasu, S., Sakakibara, S., and Gholson, R. K. (1978) Lloydia 41 646.
128. Desaty, D. and Vining, L. C. (1967) Can. J. Biochem. 45 1953-1959.
129. Saunders, J. W. and Bush, L. (1978) Lloydia 41 646.
130. Neuhann, H., Leienbach, K.-W., and Barz, W. (1979) Phytochemistry 18 61-64.
131. Hosoi, K. (1974) Plant Cell Physiol. 15 429-440.
132. Basmadjian, G. P., Hussain, S. F., and Paul, A. G. (1978) Lloydia 41 375-382.
133. Khanna, K. L., Takido, M., Rosenberg, H., and Paul, A. G. (1970) Phytochemistry 9 1811-1815.
134. Bruhn, J. G., Svensson, U., and Agurell, S. (1970) Acta Chem. Scand. 24 3775-3777.
135. Riggin, R. M., McCarthy, M. J., and Kissinger, P. T. (1976) J. Agric. Food Chem. 24 189-191.
136. Battersby, A. R., Staunton, J., Wiltshire, H. R., Francis, R. J., and Southgate, R. (1975) J. Chem. Soc. Perkin I 1147-1156.
137. Hodges, C. C., Horn, J. S., and Rapoport, H. (1977) Phytochemistry 16 1939-1942.
138. Bhakuni, D. S., Singh, A. N., Tewari, S., and Kapil, R. S. (1977) J. Chem. Soc. Perkin I 1662-1666.
139. Furuya, T., Nakano, M., and Yoshikawa, T. (1978) Phytochemistry 17 891-893.
140. Hutchinson, C. R., Heckendorf, A. H., Straughn, J. L., Daddona, P. E., and Cane, D. E. (1979) J. Am. Chem. Soc. 101 3358-3369.
141. Stöckigt, J. (1979) Phytochemistry 18 965-971.
142. Lee, S. L., Hirata, T., and Scott, A. I. (1979) Tetra. Lett. 691-694.
143. Baxter, R. L., Dorschel, C. A., Lee, S.-L., and Scott, A. I. (1979) Chem. Commun. 257-259.
144. Battersby, A. R. and Parry, R. J. (1971) J. Chem. Soc. (D) 1971 30-31; 31-32.
145. Waiblinger, K., Johne, S., and Gröger, D. (1972) Phytochemistry 11 2263-2265.
146. Steck, W., Gamborg, O. L., and Bailey, B. K. (1973) Lloydia 36 93-95.
147. Grundon, M. F., Harrison, D. M., and Sypropoulos, C. G. (1974) J. Chem. Soc. Perkin I 1974 2181-2184.
148. Collins, J. F., Donnelly, W. J., Grundon, M. F., and James, K. J. (1974) J. Chem. Soc. Perkin I 1974 2177-2181.

Chapter 14
PORPHYRINS

The porphyrin ring system is widely distributed in nature, occurring throughout the plant and animal kingdoms. Porphyrins serve as part of the oxygen transport and storage systems of vertebrates, in the respiratory chains of most cells, and as prosthetic groups of certain enzymes in plants and animals. A different modification of the porphyrin nucleus serves as a basis for the chlorophyll and related pigments of green plants.

The parent nucleus of the natural porphyrins is the simplest cyclic tetrapyrrole, porphin (here shown with the ring-numbering used for all porphyrins):

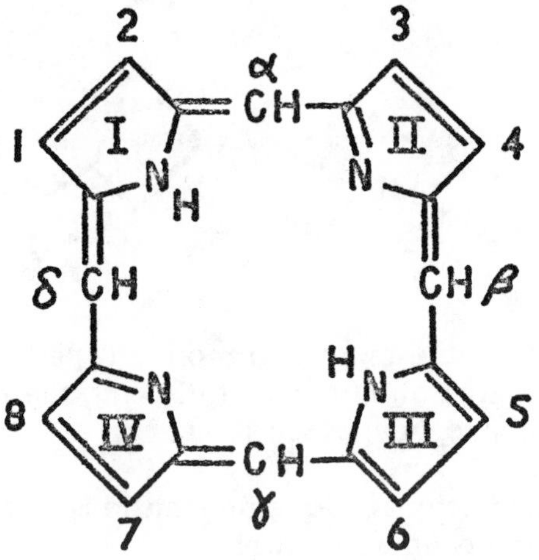

Although fixed double bond positions are shown, it is more likely that the entire molecule is a resonance hybrid of several possible double bond arrangements. The two central hydrogen atoms may also be shared among the four nitrogens. These considerations also apply to the more complex porphyrins, although certain combinations of substituent groups may stabilize one resonance form more than another.

All of the natural porphyrins carry alkyl substituents in the available positions of the pyrrole rings. The variety and arrangement of substituents is quite limited so that important generalizations may be drawn concerning them. The reasons for these regularities in porphyrin structure become apparent on considering the pathways of biosynthesis. The groups which occur may be divided into two categories:

a. $-CH_3$, $-C\overset{O}{\underset{H}{\big\Vert}}$ and $-CH_2COOH$

b. $-CH_2CH_3$, $-CH=CH_2$ and $-CH_2CH_2COOH$

A given pyrrole ring always has one type a and one type b substituent, never two of the same type.   Four basic types of porphyrins would then appear to be possible:

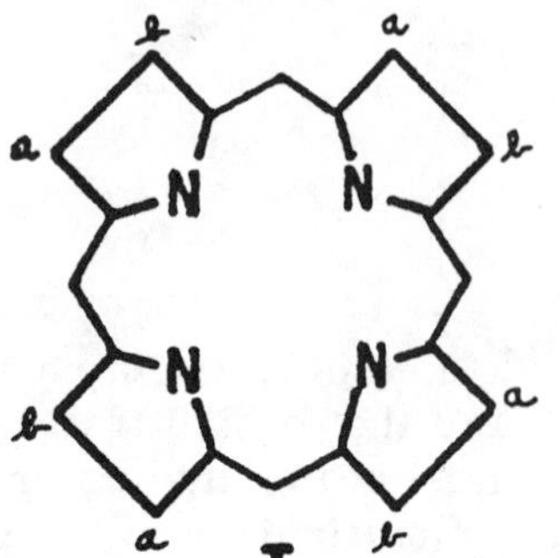

Fortunately type III porphyrins are by far the most common.   Type I occurs rarely and the other two types never in nature.   A Roman numeral following the name of a porphyrin refers it to one of these types (e. g. "coprophorphyrin III").

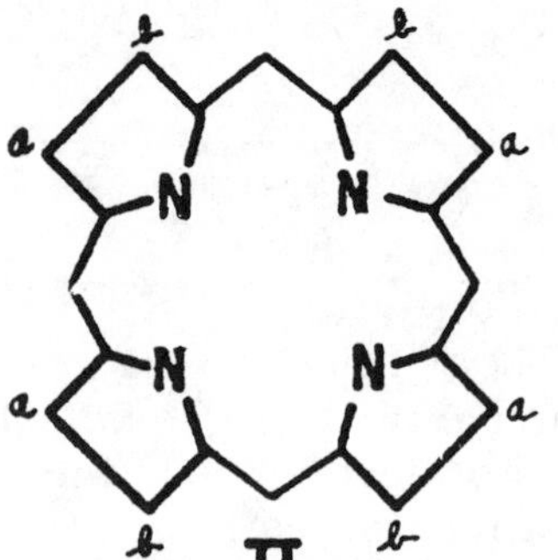

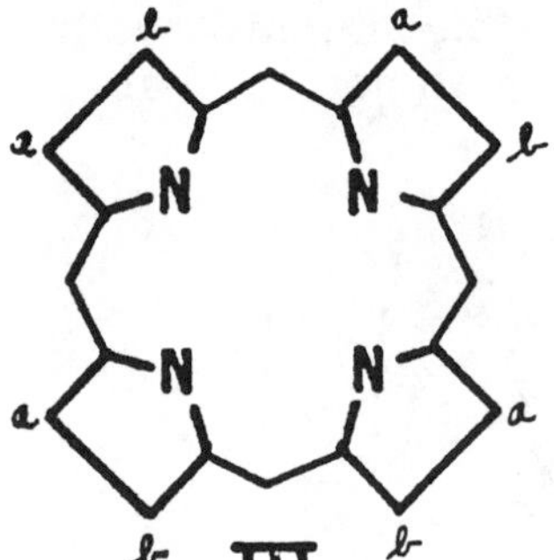

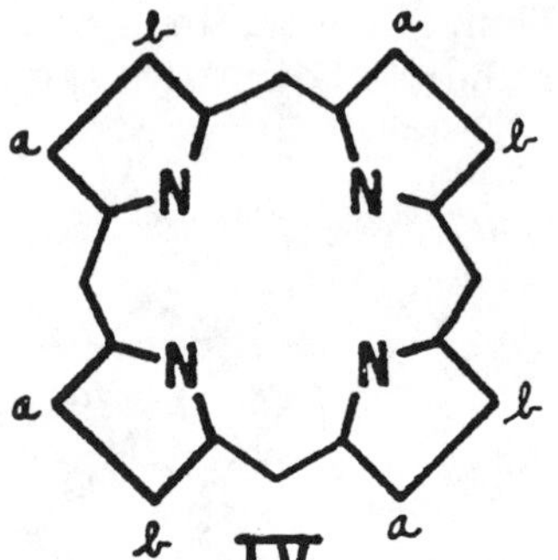

Chlorophyll derivatives have an additional 5-membered ring derived from a propionic acid side-chain on position 6.   It is numbered as shown:

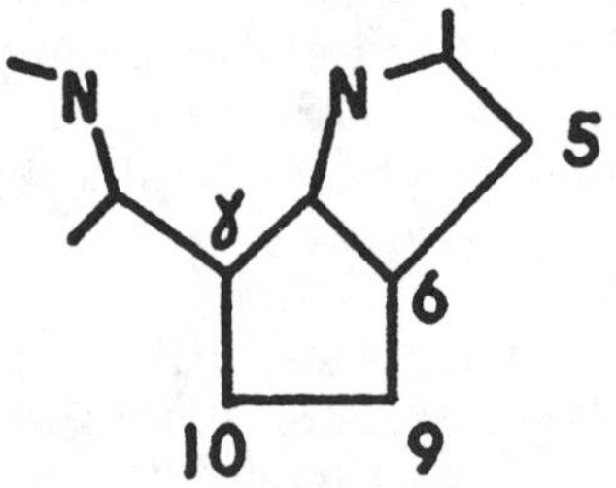

The functional forms of natural porphyrins all seem to have a metal bound as a chelate complex in the center of the molecule replacing the two hydrogens otherwise present. Naturally-occurring porphyrins which do not contain a metal are precursors or degradation products of the functional compounds.   Significant amounts of them are found only under abnormal circumstances.

In plants we are most concerned with iron-containing hematin pigments and magnesium-containing chlorophyll pigments.   These are biogenetically closely related, but experimentally they are approached in quite different ways.   The hematin pigments are tightly bound to protein, difficult to purify and present in plants in very small concentrations.   Chlorophyll, conversely, is easily extractable in large quantities and more conveniently purified. Probably in its functional form it is bound loosely to protein, and chlorophyll-protein complexes have been isolated from leaves by special techniques (1-3). Non-polar solvents such as benzene are unable to split chlorophyll from its complex, but only slightly polar ones such as acetone readily extract the pigment. Since hematin compounds can be isolated only in special cases, they must be studied and identified by indirect techniques in crude homogenates or in situ. The study of chlorophyll derivatives, on the contrary, usually begins with their purification. The quantitative difference in these two pigment types becomes apparent when one considers that on a dry weight basis a green leaf may have about 1% chlorophyll pigments, whereas, total hematin in the richest tissues is practically never more than 0.1% and usually about 0.001%.

Vitamin B_{12} has a porphyrin-like structure. It has been reported to occur in turnip greens but may actually be synthesized by associated microorganisms (4). However, its presence has seemingly been demonstrated in some aseptically grown plants (5, 6); and some plant enzymes are stimulated by added coenzyme B_{12} (7, 8).

Phytochrome, the pigment responsible for controlling many of the light-growth responses of plants, is a biliprotein whose prosthetic group is a linear tetrapyrrole of unknown structure (9-12). Its active form (P_{730}) is made by exposure to red light and absorbs most strongly light of about 730 nm which converts it to the inactive red-absorbing form (P_{660}). Conversion to P_{660} also occurs slowly in darkness. The chromophore separated from the protein does not show these spectral changes. Phytochrome is present in seed plants, ferns, mosses, and some green algae.

HEME AND RELATED COMPOUNDS

The hematin (or iron porphyrin) pigments have been well-known in animal tissues for many years (e.g. hemoglobin), but they are equally widespread and important in plants. Hemoglobin itself occurs in the root nodules of legumes but is produced only in the presence of the bacterial partner (13). The enzymes catalase and peroxidase occur throughout the plant kingdom and have iron porphyrin prosthetic groups. However, the predominant hematin compounds are the cytochrome respiratory pigments which in all aerobic tissues transport electrons along the chain (or slight variants of it) (14):

cytochrome b_{557} ⟶ cytochrome b_{560} ⟶ cytochrome c_{549} ⟶ cytochrome $\dot{c}_{547}$ ⟶
cytochrome a_{557} ⟶ cytochrome a_3 (cytochrome oxidase) ⟶ O_2

Other cytochromes are known in plants. Of these cytochrome f, b_3, and b_6 are peculiar to chloroplasts and presumably are involved in photosynthetic electron transport (15, 16). (Cytochrome f is also known as b_{553}, cytochrome b_3 as b_{559}, and cytochrome b_6 as b_{564}). Plant mitochondria contain at least three B-type cytochromes. Whether all of these function successively in the major electron transport pathway or some in bypasses is still uncertain (14, 17, 18). Small letters are used to refer to individual cytochrome molecules, whereas capital letters refer to a group of cytochromes with a particular type of structure (19). The heme pigment known as P-450 that has been well characterized in animal microsomes also occurs in plant microsomes along with cytochrome b_5 and other less definite entities that may be degradation products of the native cytochromes (20). The best-established role for microsomal P-450 in plants is in the 4-hydroxylation of cinnamic acid (21). Another B-type cytochrome is present in nitrate reductase (22).

The most common porphyrin structure among the hematin pigments is protoporphyrin IX. (Here the Roman numeral refers to the particular side-chain arrangement among all the isomers having the same groups as substituents.) Its structure is shown in Figure 14-3, p. 306. As the ferrous chelate complex this is the pigment known specifically as "heme." Peroxidase, catalase, hemoglobin, oxyhemoglobin, methemoglobin, and the B-cytochromes all contain the same porphyrin as a ferrous or ferric complex. Four of iron's six coordinate valences are utilized in this complex; the other two are directed as summarized in Table 14-1. Cytochromes c and f apparently differ in structure from the B type in having their vinyl side-chains condensed with sulfhydryl groups of the protein as well as bound through iron to the protein:

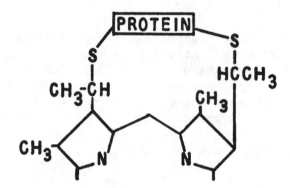

TABLE 14-1. NOMENCLATURE OF SOME IRON PROTOPORPHYRIN DERIVATIVES

Compound	Iron Oxidation Number	Coordination Positions 5	and 6
heme	2	water	water
hematin	3	water	OH^-
hemin	3	water	Cl^-
hemochromogen	2	nitrogen base	nitrogen base
peroxidase	3	water or CN^-	protein
catalase	3	water	protein
hemoglobin	2	water	protein
oxyhemoglobin	2	oxygen	protein
methemoglobin	3	water or OH^-	protein
B cytochromes	2 or 3	protein	protein

The structure of the porphyrin associated with A cytochromes has a formyl side chain at C-8 and a large terpenoid side chain at C-2 (23). Siroheme, present in nitrite reductase, is an iron-containing tetrahydroporphyrin with 8 carboxylate side-chains (24).

Other porphyrins related structurally to this group are occasionally found and probably represent precursors. Hence their structures are given in the section on biosynthesis.

CHLOROPHYLL AND RELATED COMPOUNDS

Chlorophylls a and b are the only green pigments of all plants higher than the algae. The ratio of chlorophyll a to b is usually about 3:1, and there is no ready interconversion between them. There is evidently some segregation of the two chlorophylls in chloroplasts since fragments can be obtained with different ratios of chlorophyll a to chlorophyll b ranging from 2 to 6 (25). The structure is given for chlorophyll a. Chlorophyll b has a formyl group instead of methyl at position 3:

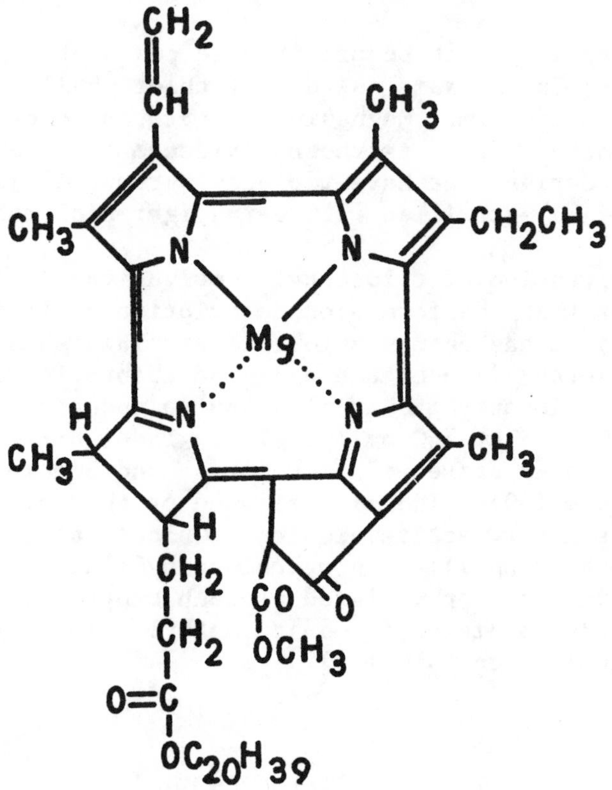

Note particularly that ring IV has been partially reduced in comparison with the hematin porphyrins. The C_{20} alcohol esterified to one of the carboxyl groups is phytol, a diterpene. The various chlorophyll derivatives which occur naturally or as artifacts in working with chlorophyll involve removal of the magnesium and hydrolysis of one or both ester groups. A summary of such derivatives is given in Table 14-2. An additional compound in this group is

TABLE 14-2. NOMENCLATURE OF CHLOROPHYLL DERIVATIVES

NAME	STRUCTURE
chlorin	a dihydroporphyrin
rhodin	a dihydroporphyrin with carbonyl adjacent to a pyrrole ring
phorbin	dihydroporphyrin with additional carbocyclic ring
phorbide	an ester of phorbin
pheophorbide	methyl ester of phorbin
phytin	phytyl ester of phorbin
pheophytin	methyl and phytyl ester of phorbin
phyllin	a magnesium derivative of any of the above
chlorophyllin	magnesium derivative of phytin
chlorophyllide	magnesium derivative of pheophorbide

protochlorophyll, which occurs in seed coats of the Cucurbitaceae (26).
Its structure is the same as that of chlorophyll a except that ring IV is
in the unreduced form. Magnesium-free protopheophytin may also occur in
some seed coats. There is recent evidence that several naturally-occurring
chlorophyll derivatives have two vinyl groups (27) and that a very small
fraction may be esterified with geranylgeraniol rather than phytol (28).

The situation of chlorophyll derivatives in living chloroplasts is
more complex than the foregoing description would indicate. By careful
spectroscopy it has been possible to distinguish as many as six different
forms of chlorophyll a on the basis of absorption maxima ranging from 663
to 700 nm. Chlorophyll b in vivo has an absorption maximum at 650 nm
with a small band at 640 nm (25, 29). These different forms probably depend
on differences in degree of aggregation and binding to other lipid or protein molecules (30). The significance of them all to the process of photosynthesis is a very active problem. Chloroplasts of etiolated plants contain proto-chlorophyll and protochlorophyllide, which is the unreduced form of
chlorophyllide (or dephytylated protochlorophyll). Chlorophyllide is bound
in lipoprotein complexes (31-33). Methyl chlorophyllide a is also present,
but its role is uncertain (34).

ISOLATION

The metal-free porphyrins may be extracted at a pH of 2-5 using ether
or ether-acetic acid mixtures. The highly carboxylated uroporphyrins, however, are insoluble in ether and can be adsorbed on talc or calcium phosphate gel after ether extraction to remove any other porphyrins (cf. Sveinsson et al., (35).

There are no generally applicable procedures for the preparation of
hematin compounds from plants. Since all of them are firmly bound to protein,
the procedures used are those of protein chemistry rather than porphyrin

chemistry. A method suitable for preparing a given cytochrome from one
organism may be entirely unsuited for preparing the same cytochrome from
another organism, or for preparing a different cytochrome from the same
organism. A few specific papers in this field may be cited as guides and
are listed below.

COMPONENT	SOURCE	REFERENCE
Cytochrome B's	mung beans	36
	spinach	37, 38
Cytochrome c	many plants	39, 40
Cytochrome f	parsley	41
	barley	42
	spinach	43
Peroxidase	horse radish	44
Catalase	spinach	45
Hemoglobin	soybean nodules	46

This situation is somewhat better with regard to the chlorophyll pigments. Here the problem is not so much one of obtaining a goodly quantity
of pigment as in being assured that the pigment obtained is not an artifact,
since degradation easily occurs during the purification procedure (47, 48).
Acetone is most commonly used to extract the pigments from either fresh or
dried leaves (80% acetone is used for dried leaves). Ethanol is effective,
but the enzyme chlorophyllase present in fresh leaves catalyzes the reaction:

$$\text{ethanol} + \text{chlorophyll} \longrightarrow \text{phytol} + \text{ethyl chlorophyllide}$$

so that unless chlorophyllase is inactivated or extraction is carried out
for a very short time, the chlorophyll will be contaminated. Another pit-
fall in the initial extraction is the ready removal of magnesium from chlorophyll in acidic solution. Many plant extracts contain enough organic
acids to bring about this degradation to pheophytin. It can be avoided by
grinding with acetone in the presence of a weak base such as 1% magnesium
carbonate or dimethylaniline. Other precautions may sometimes be taken
such as grinding in the cold and/or in the dark.

Some separation of the pigments in the acetone extract may be achieved
by solvent partition methods. By adding 1/7 volume of dioxane to an 80%
acetone solution chlorophylls can be precipitated leaving carotenoids in
solution (49). Column chromatography is generally the method of choice for
pigment purification. Water and petroleium ether are added to the acetone
extract and the petroleium ether layer which now contains the pigments is
washed with water to remove acetone and dried with anhydrous sodium sulfate
before chromatography. The most valuable adsorbent is powdered sucrose.
Stronger adsorbents, such as magnesium oxide, which are useful for carotenes,
may cause subtle, isomeric changes in the delicate chlorophyll pigments.
Anderson and Calvin (50) have found that the purest chlorophyll can be

obtained by chromatographing first on powdered polyethylene and then on
sucrose. Phytylated chlorophyll derivatives can be separated from non-
phytylated ones by gel filtration (51). Several procedures permit a clean
separation of chlorophyll a from chlorophyll b (52-55). Preparation of
chlorophyll-protein complexes is described in (1-3) and of protochlorophyllide-
protein complexes in (32, 52). More detailed purification procedures and
tests for impurities are given in the review of Smith and Benitez (53) and
the book by Vernon and Seely (54).

Several methods have been published for the isolation of phytochrome
from plants (55, 56).

CHARACTERIZATION

The observation of absorption spectra is probably the one most important technique for characterization of both hematin and chlorophyll derivatives, although it does not permit distinction between closely related compounds. All porphyrins have four absorption bands in the visible region between 500-700 nm. The heights of these peaks relative to each other vary
with the particular structure. Stronger than any of these bands is the so-
called Soret band in the near ultra violet at about 400-450 nm. Application of a low dispersion, direct vision spectroscope to intact plant tissues
has yielded many important results and is still the most useful method for
studying plant cytochromes. Details of the procedures are well described
by Hartree (57). Because of the low concentration of hematin compounds in
most plant tissues, rather thick sections must be used to observe light absorption; a powerful light source is required, and the tissues may be in-
filtrated with glycerol or pyridine to increase transparency. Since the
bands of reduced cytochromes are most distinct and informative, oxygen must
be excluded or a reducing agent such as sodium dithionite (hydrosulfite)
added. Under these conditions a spectrum like that of Figure 14-1 may be
observed in, for example, an onion bulb:

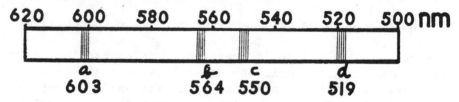

FIGURE 14-1.

The bands labelled a, b, and c represent the so-called α-bands of cytochromes
a, b, and c. Band d represents the combined β-bands of cytochromes b and
c. If bands are not observable in the intact tissue because other pigments
interfere (e.g. chlorophyll in leaves) or because the hematin compounds are
too dilute, modified approaches may be possible (58). Interfering pigments
can be removed by solvent extraction and/or a particulate preparation from
the homogenized tissue used for observation as in the procedure of Bhagvat
and Hill (59). Faint bands may be intensified by observation at the temperature of liquid air. This intensification, which may be as much as 20-fold,
depends on the microcrystalline structure of the frozen medium rather than
any change in the pigments themselves. A sensitive method for determining
total hematin involves treatment of the material with pyridine (20%) and
sodium dithionite (1%) in alkaline solution (0.1N NaOH). This results in

denaturation of associated proteins and formation of hemochromogens from any iron porphyrins which may be present. In these derivatives the 5 and 6 coordination positions of ferrous porphyrin are occupied by pyridine, and a strong absorption band at 556 nm results for protoporphyrin hemochromogen, at 551 nm for the hemochromogen from cytochrome c, and 585 nm for the hemochromogen of the A cytochromes.

The absorption spectra of chlorophyll derivatives may be observed in intact tissues using the direct vision spectroscope, but more frequently purified preparations are studied spectrophotometrically. The exact positions of absorption maxima may vary slightly with the solvent used. Figure 14-2 gives the spectra for chlorophylls a and b. The sharp band at about 660 nm is characteristic of dihydroporphyrins. It is also seen in pheophytin,

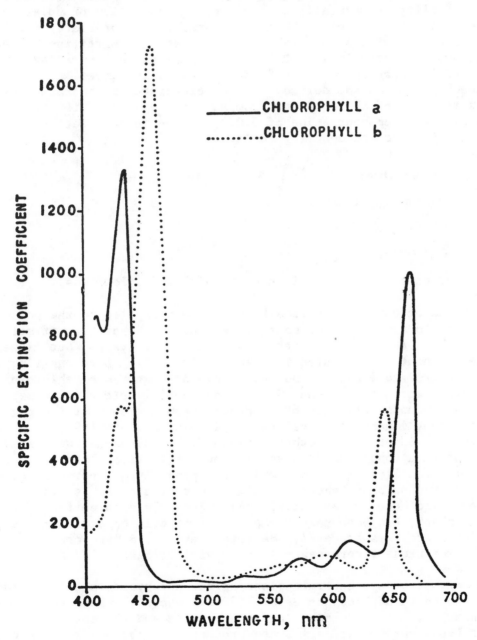

FIGURE 14-2: ABSORPTION SPECTRA OF CHLOROPHYLLS

but the addition of chelated magnesium makes it even more intense. The absorption spectroscopy of chlorophyll and other porphyrins has been reviewed (60). The application of spectrophotometry to quantitative measurement of chlorophyll is described in (53, 61, 62).

Fluorescence spectra of porphyrins have also been extensively studied and are important in characterization. However, among natural products only the metal-free porphyrins and chlorophylls fluoresce. The iron porphyrins do not. Fluorescence spectrum curves for a variety of compounds are presented by French et al. (63).

The second most important property in characterizing porphyrins has been their solubility behavior especially with regard to dilute hydrochloric acid. This solubility is naturally related to the proportion of polar and non-polar groups in the molecule. Phytol-containing compounds are much less soluble than compounds with free carboxyl groups, so that partition between ether and various concentrations of HCl has been useful in separating porphyrins from mixtures. Quantitatively a "hydrochloric acid number" can be assigned to each porphyrin and defined as the percentage concentration of HCl which will extract 2/3 of the compound from an equal volume of its ether solution (usually at a concentration of 0.02%). Some representative HCl-numbers are given in the accompanying table.

COMPOUND	HCl NUMBER
Coproporphyrin III	0.09
Protoporphyrin IX	2.0
Pheophytin a	29.0

A larger compilation of values is given by Granick and Gilder (64).

Paper chromatographic procedures have not been applied to the porphyrins as extensively as to some other classes of compounds. Separation of metal-free porphyrins has been achieved with a lutidine-water system, but closely related isomers cannot be separated in this way (65, 66). By converting porphyrins to their methyl esters and using solvent mixtures of chloroform, kerosene, propanol and dioxane, Chu, Green and Chu (67) were able to separate closely allied compounds (cf. also 68). Paper chromatography of the pigments related to chlorophyll has been developed by several workers (69, 70). Non-polar solvents such as petroleum ether, toluene, chlorobenzene, with sometimes a trace of an alcohol added, have been most effective. Thin layer chromatography on layers of cellulose gives similar but probably sharper separations than can be achieved on paper sheets. Thin layers of starch, sucrose, and silica gel have also been successful (71-74). Recently high performance liquid chromatography has been used for analysis of chloroplast pigments (75, 76). Spots on the chromatograms are easily detected, even at minute concentrations, because of their intense fluorescence in ultraviolet light.

Preliminary structure determinations on the porphyrins should be facilitated by the procedure of Nicolaus et al. (77-79) whereby small quantities of porphyrin can be oxidized with alkaline permanganate and the split products identified on paper chromatograms. These products are pyrrole acids and can be detected by spraying with diazotized sulfanilic acid. The acids obtained indicate what side-chains are present but not, of course, the order of the pyrrole rings around the porphyrin nucleus.

METABOLIC PATHWAYS

The accompanying chart shows the probable course of biosynthesis for both the hematin and chlorophyll pigments in higher plants.

Most of the reactions of the porphyrin pathway have now been characterized in higher plants and many studied in cell-free systems. 5-Aminolevulinic acid may be made in plants by some variant of the reaction shown in Figure 14-3. Much data now exist to show that a major pathway to 5-aminolevulinic acid does not start with glycine and succinyl-CoA but with glutamate that is converted, successively, to glutamic-1-semialdehyde and 4, 5-dioxovaleric acid. Transamination of the latter gives 5-aminolevulinic acid (80-83). Other evidence makes it appear that the pathway from glutamate is most important in the light, when photorespiration is active, and the one from glycine in other circumstances (84, 85). The conversion of 5-aminolevulinic acid to porphobilinogen and the conversion of porphobilinogen to uroporphyrinogen I have both been observed in somewhat purified enzyme systems from plants (86, 87). The condensation of the four pyrrole units making up the porphyrin ring evidently occurs by successive additions of single units rather than dimerization of a first-formed dipyrrylmethane (88, 89). There are several mechanisms proposed to explain why type III porphyrins are made in preference to type I (90, 91). A single pool of 5-aminolevulinic acid appears to serve as the precursor of both the chlorophylls and the hemes (92). Enzyme preparations from plants grown in the dark can catalyze the formation of protochlorophyllide and its phytyl ester, protochlorophyll from 5-aminolevulinic acid. Magnesium protoporphyrin monomethyl ester is the branch-point intermediate for synthesis of both these products (93-95). Just as in the intact plants light is required for chlorophyll formation, so homogenates must be prepared from light-grown plants for them to be capable of chlorophyll synthesis from 5-aminolevulinic acid (96). Although both protochlorophyllide and protochlorophyll are phototransformable (97) (i.e. capable of being reduced at positions 7-8), current opinion favors the view that the predominant pathway is transformation of protochlorophyllide to chlorophyllide, followed by esterification of the latter. In normal plants in the light there is no accumulation of proto pigments, so various observations made with long-etiolated plants should be regarded as pathological (97). With this reservation, it can be said that there are several different protein-bound forms of protochlorophyllide in etiolated plants and the only one that is phototransformable to chlorophyllide has an absorption maximum at 647-650 nm (31-33, 98). Forms absorbing at shorter wavelengths are present but non-transformable in older etiolated plants. In young etiolated plants or normal green plants, though, short wavelength forms can be transformed (99). After the fast photoreduction step a slower esterification occurs, not directly with phytol but with geranylgeraniol. Successive dehydrogenation steps then lead to the phytyl ester (100, 101). Other slow reactions involving aggregation and binding to proteins occur leading to all the different spectrally distinguishable forms of chlorophyll a _in vivo_ (25, 29, 30, 102, 103). While leaf homogenates (104) thylakoid preparations (105), and etiolated leaves (106) can convert exogenous chlorophyll a to chlorophyll b, it appears that in whole plants only one type of chlorophyll a is a precursor of chlorophyll b. This convertible form of chlorophyll a is probably one of the earliest to appear (107, 108), and the system is dependent on phytochrome activation (109). Many intricate control mechanisms related to chlorophyll

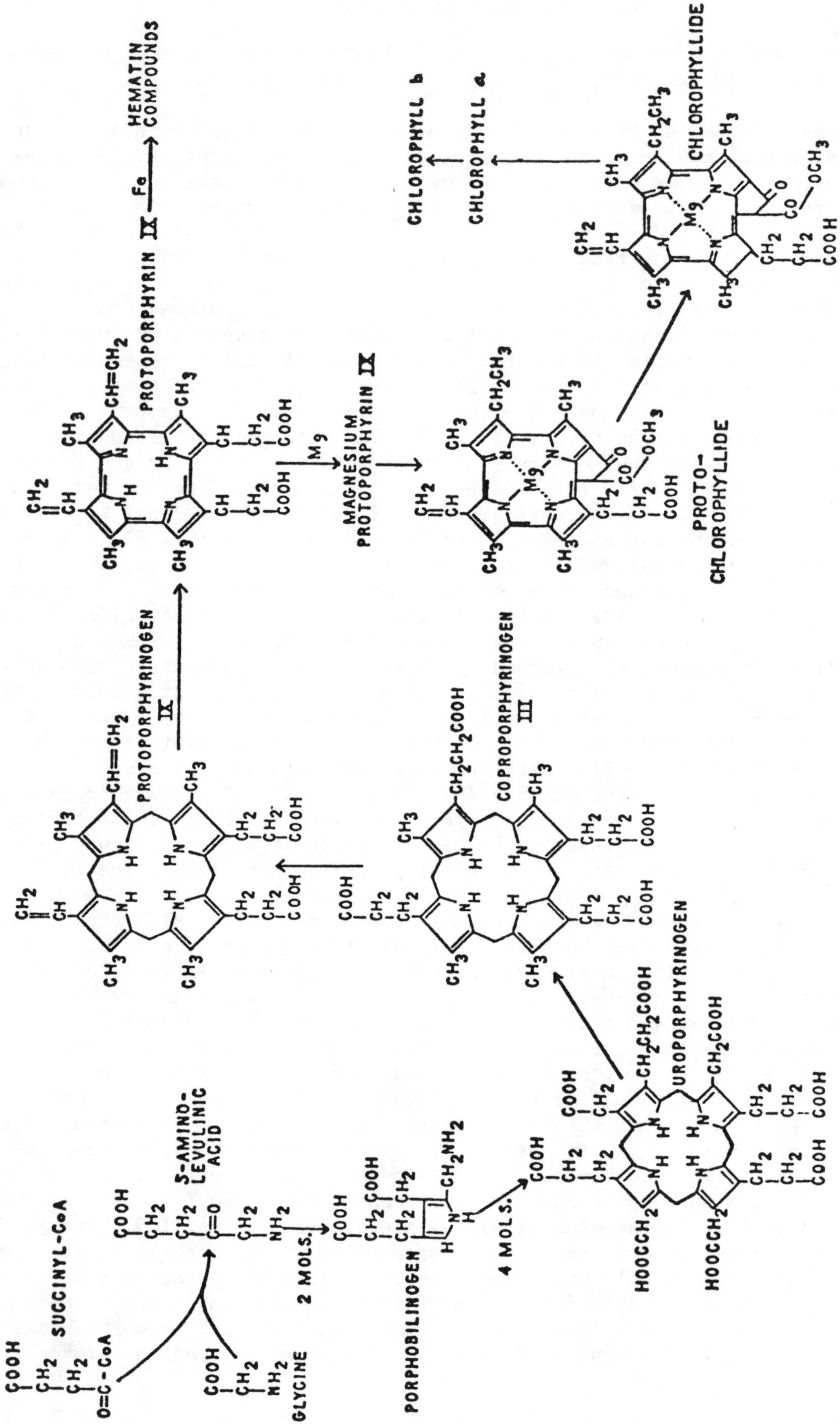

FIGURE 14-3 PATHWAYS OF PORPHYRIN BIOSYNTHESIS

biosynthesis are reviewed in (110). There is no comparable information for the heme pigments of plants.

The linear tetrapyrroles including phytochrome are probably made from porphyrins but the actual porphyrin precursor and all details of the pathway are unknown (111). Breakdown of chlorophyll in senescent leaves gives mostly unknown products, but one of these has phytol attached to some fragment of ring IV (112).

GENERAL REFERENCES

Goodwin, T. W., ed. (1966, 1967) Biochemistry of Chloroplasts, 2 Vols., Academic Press, N. Y.

Goodwin, T. W., ed. (1976) Chemistry and Biochemistry of Plant Pigments, 2nd ed., 2 Vols., Academic Press, N. Y.

Granick, S. & Gilder, H. (1947) "Distribution, Structure, and Properties of Tetrapyrroles," Adv. Enzymol. 7 305-368.

Hartree, E. F., "Haematin Compounds," in Paech & Tracey 4 197-245.

Jones, O. T. G., "Chlorophyll," in Miller 1 75-111.

Marks, G. S. (1969) Heme and Chlorophyll, Van Nostrand, London.

Smith, J. H. C. & Benitez, A., "Chlorophylls," in Paech & Tracey 4 142-196.

Vernon, L. P. & Seely, G. R., ed. (1966) The Chlorophylls, Academic Press, N. Y.

BIBLIOGRAPHY

1. Thornber, J. P., Markwell, J. P., and Reinman, S. (1979) Photochem. Photobiol. 29 1205-1216.
2. Henriques, F. and Park, R. B. (1978) Plant Physiol. 62 856-860.
3. Anderson, J. M., Waldron, J. C. and Thorne, S. W. (1978) FEBS Letters 92 227-233.
4. Gray, L. F. and Daniel, L. J. (1959) J. Nutrition 67 623-634.
5. Fries, L. (1962) Physiol. Plantarum 15 566-571.
6. Blondeau, R. (1971) Compt. rend. 272 2781-2784.
7. Poston, J. N. (1977) Science 195 301-302.
8. Poston, J. M. (1978) Phytochemistry 17 401-402.
9. Kendrick, R. E. and Frankland, B. (1976) Phytochrome and Plant Growth, Arnold, London.
10. Smith, H. (1975) Phytochrome and Photomorphogenesis, McGraw-Hill, N. Y.
11. Schopfer, P. (1977) Ann. Rev. Plant Physiol. 28 223-252.
12. Marmé, D. (1977) Ann. Rev. Plant Physiol. 28 173-198.
13. Lehtovaara, P. and Ellfolk, N. (1974) FEBS Letters 43 239-240.
14. Palmer, J. M. (1976) Ann. Rev. Plant Physiol. 27 133-157.
15. Cramer, W. A. and Whitmarsh, J. (1977) Ann. Rev. Plant Physiol. 28 133-172.
16. Butler, W. L. (1978) FEBS Letters 95 19-25.
17. Storey, B. T. (1974) Plant Physiol. 53 840-845.
18. Passam, H. C., Berden, J. A. and Slater, E. C. (1973) Biochim. Biophys. Acta 325 54-61.
19. Thompson, R. H. S. (1962) Science 137 405-408.
20. Rich, P. R. and Bendall, D. S. (1975) Europ. J. Biochem. 55 333-341.
21. Potts, J. R. M., Weklych, R., and Conn, E. E. (1974) J. Biol. Chem. 249 5019-5026.
22. Notton, B. A., Fido, R. J., and Hewitt, E. J. (1977) Plant Sci. Letters 8 165-170.
23. Lemberg, R. (1965) Revs. Pure Appl. Chem. 15 125-136.
24. Hucklesby, D. P., James, D. M., Banwell, M. J., and Hewitt, E. J. (1976) Phytochemistry 15 599-603.
25. French, C. S., Brown, J. S., and Lawrence, M. C. (1972) Plant Physiol. 49 421-429.
26. Jones, O. T. G. (1966) Biochem. J. 101 153-160.
27. Belanger, F. C. and Rebeiz, C. A. (1979) Plant Physiol. 63 Suppl. 536.
28. Wellburn, A. R. (1976) Biochem. Physiol. Pflanzen 169 265-271.
29. Seely, G. R. (1973) J. Theor. Biol. 40 189-199.
30. Kreutz, W. (1968) Z. Naturforsch. 23b 520-527.
31. Dujardin, E. and Sironval, C. (1970) Photosynthetics 4 129-138.
32. Murray, A. E. and Klein, A. O. (1971) Plant Physiol. 48 383-388.
33. Gassman, M. L. (1973) Plant Physiol. 52 590-594.
34. Hines, G. D. and Ellsworth, R. K. (1969) Plant Physiol. 44 1742-1744.
35. Sveinsson, S. L., Rimington, C. and Barnes, H. D. (1949) Scand. J. Clin. Lab. Invest. 1 2-11.
36. Kasinsky, H. E., Shichi, H. and Hackett, D. P. (1966) Plant Physiol. 41 739-748.

37. Duffy, J. J., Katoh, S. and San Pietro, A. (1966) Biochim. Biophys Acta 121 201-203.
38. Stuart, A. L. and Wasserman, A. R. (1973) Biochim. Biophys. Acta, 314 284-297.
39. Richardson, M., Richardson, D., Ramshaw, J.A.M., Thompson, E. W. and Boulter, D. (1971) J. Biochem. (Japan) 69 811-813.
40. Brown, R. H. and Boulter, D. (1973) Biochem. J. 133 251-254.
41. Davenport, H. E. and Hill, R. (1952) Proc. Royal Soc. (B) 139 327-345.
42. Forti, G., Bertole, M. L. and Zanetti, G. (1965) Biochim. Biophys. Acta 109 33-40.
43. Singh, J. and Wasserman, A. R. (1971) J. Biol. Chem. 246 3532-3541.
44. Kenten, R. H. and Mann, P. J. G. (1954) Biochem. J. 57 347-348.
45. Galston, A. W., Bonnichsen, R. K., and Arnon, D. I. (1951) Acta Chem. Scand. 5 781-790.
46. Sternberg, H. and Virtanen, A. I. (1952) Acta Chem. Scand. 6 1342-1352.
47. Hynninen, P. H. (1973) Acta Chem. Scand. 27 1487-1495.
48. Hynninen, P. H. and Assandri, S. (1973) Acta Chem. Scand. 27 1478-1486.
49. Iriyama, K., Ogura, N. and Takamiya, A. (1974) J. Biochem. 76 901-904.
50. Anderson, A. F. H. and Calvin, M. (1962) Nature 194 285-286.
51. Schenk, J. and Dässler, H.-G. (1969) Pharmazie 23 419.
52. Iriyama, K. and Yoshiura, M. (1979) J. Chromatog. 177 154-156.
53. Hynninen, P. H. (1977) Acta Chem. Scand. B 31 829-835.
54. Sato, N. and Murata, N. (1978) Biochim. Biophys. Acta 501 103-111.
55. Iriyama, K., Yoshiura, M., and Shiraki, M. (1979) Chem. Commun. 406-407.
56. Smith, H. and Elliott, J. (1975) Plant Sci. Letters 5 1-6.
57. Hartree, E. F. (1955) in Paech and Tracey 4 197-245.
58. Lundegårdh, H. (1962) Physiol. Plantarum 15 390-398.
59. Bhagvat, K. and Hill, R. (1951) New Phytol. 50 112-120.
60. Goedheer, J. C. (1966) in L. P. Vernon and G. R. Seeley, eds. The Chlorophylls, Academic Press, N. Y. pp. 147-184.
61. Jeffrey, S. W. and Humphrey, G. F. (1975) Biochem. Physiol. Pflanzen 167 191-194.
62. Porra, R. J. and Grimme, L. H. (1974) Anal. Biochem. 57 255-267.
63. French, C. S., Smith, J. H. C., Virgin, H. I. and Airth, R. L. (1956) Plant Physiol. 31 369-374.
64. Granick, S. and Gilder, H. (1947) Adv. Enzymol. 7 305-368.
65. Nicholas, R. E. H. (1951) Biochem. J. 48 309-313.
66. Kehl, R. and Stich, W. (1952) Z. Physiol. Chem. 290 151-154.
67. Chu, T. C., Green, A. A., and Chu, E. J. (1951) J. Biol. Chem. 190 643-646.
68. Falk, J. E. and Benson, A. (1953) Biochem. J. 55 101-104.
69. Strain, H. H., Sherma, J., Benton, F. S., and Katz. J. J. (1965) Biochem. Biophys. Acta 109 1-15. 16-22, 23-32.
70. Holden, M. (1962) Biochim. Biophys. Acta 56 378-379.
71. Sherma, J. and Lippstone, G. S. (1969) J. Chromatog. 41 220-227.
72. Ellsworth, R. K. and Nowak, C. A. (1972) Anal. Biochem. 51 656-662.
73. Sievers, G. and Hynninen, P. H. (1977) J. Chromatog. 134 359-364.
74. Petrović, S. M., Kolarov, L. A. and Perišić-Janjić, N. U. (1979) J. Chromatog. 171 522-526.
75. Shoaf, W. T. (1978) J. Chromatog. 152 247-249.
76. Braumann, T. and Grimme, L. H. (1979) J. Chromatog. 170 264-268.
77. Nicolaus, R. A., Mangoni, L. and Caglioti, L. (1956) Ann. Chim. (Rome) 46 793-865.
78. Nicolaus, R. A., Mangoni, L. and Nicoletti, R. (1957) Ann. Chim. (Rome) 47 178-188.
79. Mangoni, L. and Nicolaus, R. A. (1959) Ann. Chim. (Rome) 49 531-537.
80. Beale, S. I. (1978) Ann. Rev. Plant Physiol. 29 95-120.
81. Harel, E., Meller, E. and Rosenberg, M. (1978) Phytochemistry 17 1277-1280.
82. Castelfranco, P. A., Weinstein, J. D., Schwarcz, S., Pardo, A. D. and Wezelman, B. E. (1979) Arch. Biochem. Biophys. 192 592-598.
83. Meller, E., Harel, E. and Kannangara, C. G. (1979) Plant Physiol. 63 Suppl. 548.
84. Hendry, G. A. F. and Stobart, A. K. (1977) Phytochemistry 16 1567-1570.
85. Hendry, G. A. F. and Stobart, A. K. (1978) Phytochemistry 17 671-674.
86. Stobart, A. K. and Thomas, D. R. (1968) Phytochemistry 7 1313-1316.
87. Rebeiz, C. A. and Castelfranco, P. A. (1973) Ann. Rev. Plant Physiol. 24 129-172.
88. Battersby, A. R. (1978) Experientia 34 1-13.
89. Battersby, A. R., Fookes, C. J. R., Matcham, G. W. J. and McDonald, E. (1979) Chem. Commun. 539-541.
90. Scott, A. I., Hu, K. S., Kajiwara, M. and Takahashi, T. (1976) J. Am. Chem. Soc. 98 1589-1591.
91. Battersby, A. R. and McDonald, E. (1979) Accts. Chem. Res. 12 14-22.
92. Castelfranco, P. A. and Jones, O. T. G. (1975) Plant Physiol. 55 485-490.
93. Ellsworth, R. K. and Hervish, P. V. (1975) Photosynthetica 9 125-139.
94. Mattheis, J. R. and Rebeiz, C. A. (1977) J. Biol. Chem. 252 8347-8349.
95. Shien, J., Miller, G. W. and Psenak, M. (1974) Biochem. Physiol. Pflanzen 165 100-103.
96. Rebeiz, C. A. and Castelfranco, P. A. (1971) Plant Physiol. 47 33-37.
97. Lancer, H. A., Cohen, C. E. and Schiff, J. A. (1976) Plant Physiol. 57 369-374.
98. Horton, P. and Leech, R. M. (1975) Plant Physiol. 56 113-120.
99. Cohen, C. E. and Rebeiz, C. A. (1978) Plant Physiol. 61 824-829.
100. Schoch, S., Lempert, U. and Rüdiger, W. (1977) Z. Pflanzenphysiol. 83 427-436.
101. Schoch, S. (1978) Z. Naturforsch. 33c 712-714.
102. Mathis, P. and Sauer, K. (1973) Plant Physiol. 51 115-119.
103. Láng, F. and Sárvári, E. (1974) Photosynthetica 8 9-17.

104. Shlyk, A. A., Vlasenok, L. I., Akhramovich, N. I., Vrubel, S. V. and Akulovich, E. M. (1975)
      Doklady Akad. Nauk SSSR 221 1234-1236.
105. Aronoff, S. and Kwok, E. (1977) Can. J. Biochem. 55 1091-1095.
106. Rudoi, A. B. and Vezitsky, A. Y. (1976) Biokhimiya 41 91-97.
107. Argyroudi-Akoyunoglou, J. H. and Akoyunoglou, G. (1970) Plant Physiol. 46 247-249.
108. Shlyk, A. A., Rudoĭ, A. B. and Vezitskiĭ, A. Y. (1970) Photosynthetica 4 68-77.
109. Oelze-Karow, H. and Mohr, H. (1978) Photochem. Photobiol. 27 189-193.
110. Harel, E. (1978) Prog. Phytochemistry 5 127-180.
111. Barrett, J. (1967) Nature 215 733-735.
112. Park, Y., Morris, M. M. and Mackinney, G. (1973) J. Agric. Food Chem. 21 279-281.

Chapter 15
MISCELLANEOUS NITROGEN
AND SULFUR COMPOUNDS

The compounds treated in this chapter have a wide diversity of chemical and functional characteristics. Their biogenetic interrelationships are also for the most part obscure. However, in the absence of metabolic evidence, it seems likely that many of the simpler nitrogen and sulfur compounds found in plants are derived by common types of reaction schemes from the amino acids. By extension, plausible pathways can be suggested leading from the amino acids to more complex compounds of this group. The plausibility of such pathways has justified the organization of this chapter; but as direct evidence becomes available, considerable revision may be necessary. Because of the diversity of compounds covered, each section of this chapter is independent of the others as regards characterization, isolation, and metabolic pathways.

AMINES

It is not generally realized how widespread simple amines are in higher plants although they are well-known as metabolic products of microorganisms. A survey of 220 species of flowering plants and mosses by Kamienski (1) revealed amines in a large number of them. Most widespread was isopentyl amine:

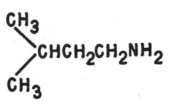

This occurred in 75 of the species examined. Twenty-five species had methylamine and 19 trimethylamine. Strangely, only one had dimethylamine. The chemistry of simple amines is described in general textbooks of organic chemistry and will not be discussed in any detail here. The amines of plants are reviewed by Smith (2) and polyamines by Cohen (3). There is no sharp dividing line between amines and alkaloids. This ambiguity becomes particularly evident with the more complex amines such as histamine which might be called an alkaloid except that it was first found in animals and does not occur at a high concentration in plants. Several distinctions have been made to separate simple amines from alkaloids, but none is completely satisfactory--e.g.:

1. Alkaloids must have nitrogen in a heterocyclic ring.
2. Alkaloids are more soluble in organic solvents like chloroform, while simple amines are more soluble in water.

The distinction made here, based on biogenesis, is that a simple amine has its complete carbon skeleton (except for N-methyl groups) derived from a single precursor, normally an amino acid. In the formation of alkaloids carbon--carbon and carbon-nitrogen condensations occur both inter- and intra-molecularly. Thus, by decarboxylation, methylamine is derived from glycine, ethylamine from alanine, ethanolamine from serine, putrescine from ornithine, etc. (4-7). Although methylamine might be made by decarboxylation of glycine, its actual precursor in plants is obscure (8). The N-methyl groups found in secondary and tertiary amines, or quaternary ammonium compounds like choline, are derived from methionine and/or formate. Although putrescine is most obviously related to ornithine, it probably more often comes from arginine _via_ agmatine inasmuch as arginine is a common amino acid and ornithine is rare (9-11). Another kind of route to amines is the transamination of aldehydes (12). Serinol (2-amino-1, 3-propandiol) of sugar cane is made by transamination of dihydroxyacetone phosphate followed by hydrolysis (13). Amines are degraded by the action of amine oxidases. Both monamine and polyamine oxidases are known (14, 15). Methylamine is converted to methylamine oxide and also enters the C_1 pool (8). Various hydroxylated phenethylamines are derived from tyramine (16).

Of great pharmacological interest are the so-called pressor amines which have a powerful effect on increasing the blood pressure of animals. Many of these compounds are decarboxylation products of aromatic amino acids. On the contrary, histamine, the decarboxylation product of histidine, acts as a depressor. In some cases the presence of amines may account for the toxicity or pharmacodynamic effects of certain plants (17). Tyramine is the most widely occurring of the phenolic amines (18). The irritant effects of stinging nettles (*Urtica* spp.) are due to their content of histamine, serotonin, and acetyl choline (19). Ephedrine is the active ingredient of the ancient Chinese drug plant ma-huang (*Ephedra* spp.). Tracer experiments have confirmed its origin from phenylalanine (20). Norepinephrine, synephrine, and octopamine are three other pharmacologically active phenolic amines found in plants (16, 21-23). The active principles of red pepper, capsaicins, are amides of vanillylamine (24). There are many other naturally-occurring amides in which the amine moiety comes from such amines as putrescine, agmatine, tyramine, etc.: and the acyl group comes from aromatic acids such as caffeic, p-coumaric, ferulic, etc. (25-27).

Some amine structures are given in Table 15-1, which shows the amino acid from which each is derived. The common names of corresponding N-methyl and quaternary ammonium compounds (betaines) are given in the third column only if these are known as higher plant constituents. Indole amines derived from tryptophan are discussed in a later section.

No generalization can be expected to describe the function of all amines in plants, and for most of them even suggestions are lacking. Methylated compounds may serve as reservoirs for methylation reactions. Choline has been the most widely investigated of these compounds. It is a part of many phospholipids (q.v.; its phosphoryl derivative may function as an important phosphate carrier in plant sap (28):

$$(CH_3)_3 \overset{+}{N}CH_2CH_2O \overset{\displaystyle O}{\underset{\displaystyle OH}{\overset{\uparrow}{\underset{|}{P}}}} O^-$$

TABLE 15-1 SOME NATURALLY OCCURRING AMINES

AMINO ACID	AMINE	N-METHYL DERIVATIVES
glycine	CH_3NH_2 methylamine	$(CH_3)_4N^+$ tetramine
serine	$HOCH_2CH_2NH_2$ ethanolamine (colamine)	$(CH_3)_3N^+CH_2CH_2OH$ choline
ornithine	$H_2N(CH_2)_4NH_2$ putrescine	-------
lysine	$H_2N(CH_2)_5NH_2$ cadaverine	-------
valine	 isobutylamine	-------
phenylalanine	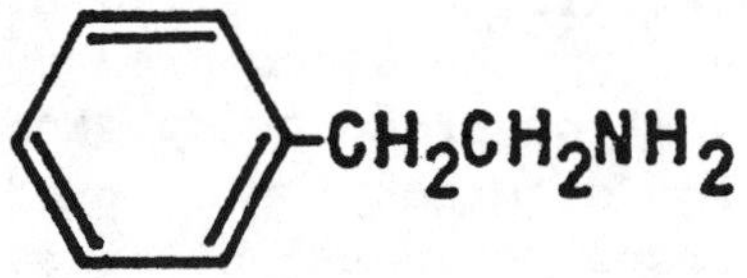 β-phenylethylamine	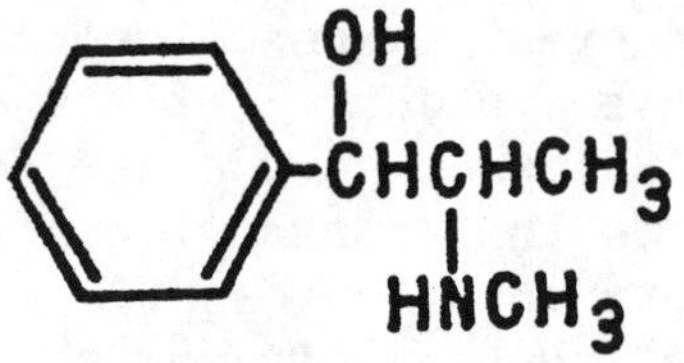 ephedrine
tyrosine	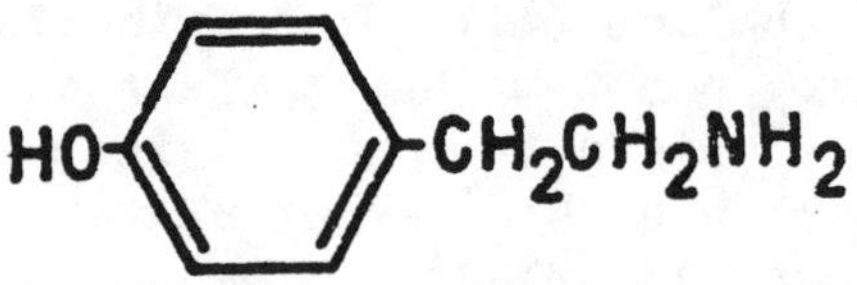 tyramine	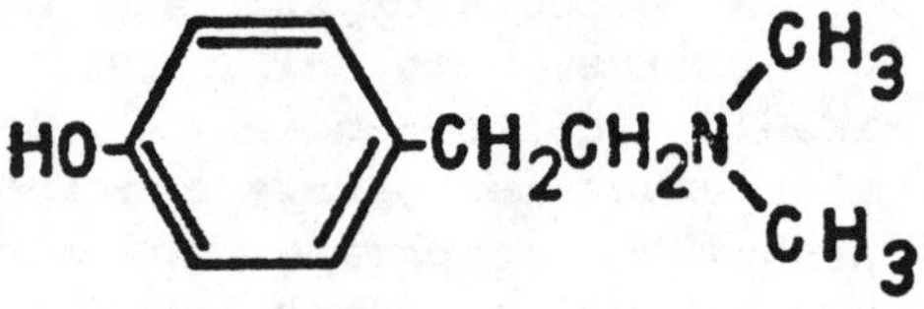 hordenine 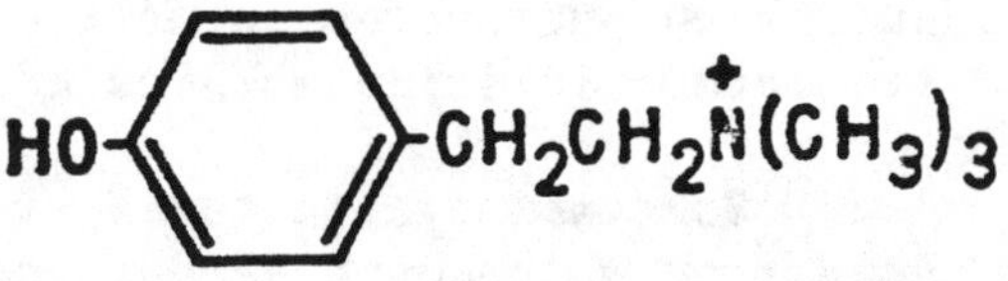 candicine
histidine	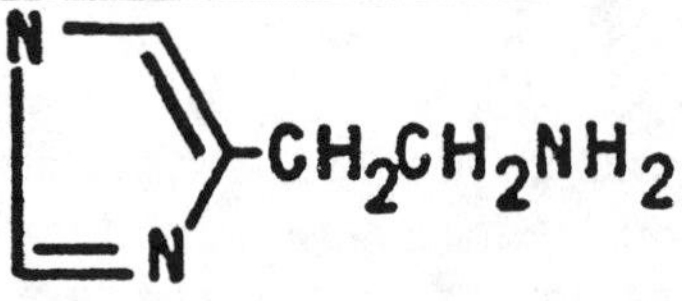 histamine	-------
leucine	 isopentylamine	-------

AMINO ACID	AMINE	N-METHYL DERIVATIVES
pipecolic acid	piperidine	-------
arginine	$H_2N-(CH_2)_4$ $NHCNH_2$ ‖ NH agmatine	-------

After oxidation to glycinebetaine, choline can sometimes serve as a methyl donor (e.g. in nicotine synthesis). Choline sulfate may function as a sulfur transporting agent and reservoir (29). Acetyl choline has some hormone-like actions in plants (30). Betaines may protect against micro-organisms (31). In halophytes they have been suggested to have a role in osmotic regulation (32). Putrescine and other polyamines have both stimulatory and inhibitory effects depending on the particular plant tissue studied (33, 34). They increase under a deficiency of potassium, perhaps as a mechanism to counteract lowering of pH (9, 35). In the last few years there has been a burst of interest in putrescine, spermine, and other polyamines because of their involvement in ribosomal protein synthesis. They can replace magnesium as a necessary factor for the charging of tRNA with some amino acids, but their role may be more specific than just pro-viding a cation (36, 37); and there is considerable speculation about a role for them in cellular differentiation and development (38-40). Amines apparently account for the repulsiveness to man and attractiveness to insects of aroids (41). Some other ecological involvements are that serinol activates toxin production by *Helminthosporium sacchari* (13), while certain other amine derivatives are said to confer some resistance to fungal and viral infections (17, 25, 27, 42).

Isolation of the simple amines from plants takes advantage of their basic nature. Thus, they may be separated on cation exchange resins. The more volatile ones may be separated from plant materials by steam distill-lation from an alkaline mixture (after preliminary removal of volatile neutral and acidic compounds) (42). One danger to be recognized is that many plants contain amine oxidases which must be promptly inactivated if amines are to be preserved when cellular structure is broken down. Non-volatile amines can be isolated by first removing proteins from the plant extract with heat, trichloracetic acid, etc. and then precipitating the amines with various reagents. A reagent useful for precipitating amines from protein-free solutions is phosphotungstic acid in 5% H_2SO_4. Ammonium and potassium ions should be removed since they are also precipitated by this reagent. Several techniques are available for fractionating the phos-photungstate precipitate and recovering free amines from it. Dragendorff's reagent ($KBiI_4$) and Reinecke's salt ($NH_4Cr(NH_3)_2 (SCN)_4H_2O$) have been exten-sively used to precipitate the quaternary ammonium bases (43, 44). Ion exchange chromatography is useful for separating all types of amines (45-47). Electrophoresis has been used for quaternary ammonium compounds (48).

Several simple tests are available for characterization of amines, in particular for determining whether an unknown compound is a primary, secondary,

or tertiary amine or a quaternary ammonium base. Some of these tests may
be effectively applied to paper chromatograms so that separation and at
least a partial identification can be made at once. Methods have been
developed for determination of volatile amines in plants (42, 49). Paper
chromatography is carried out with a butanol-acetic acid-water solvent.
Primary amines are detected with ninhydrin, secondary amines with nitroprusside, and tertiary amines with phosphomolybdic acid. Secondary and
tertiary amines may also be detected with iodine vapor. Tertiary amines
and quaternary ammonium compounds can be detected with potassium tetra-
iodobismuthate (Dragendorff's reagent). A preliminary separation of the
amines by distillation, precipitation, etc. is necessary before paper
chromatography since the detection reagents are not specific---i.e. ninhydrin reacts with amino acids, nitroprusside with sulfhydryl compounds, and
alkaloids with Dragendorff's reagent. Other special reagents may be applied
for detection of certain amines, such as diazotized sulfanilic acid (Pauli's
reagent) for tyramine, histamine, etc. Blau (50) has identified amines
in biological materials by concentrating them on ion exchange resin and
then chromatographing on paper. High performance liquid chromatography
has been applied to the analysis of certain amines (51). Many other specific
reactions will be found in the general references.

ISOBUTYLAMIDES

Brief mention needs to be given to a group of isobutylamine derivatives which are combined by an amide linkage with various unsaturated
fatty acids. Analogous compounds involving other aliphatic amines are not
known to be naturally occurring, and the isobutylamides are of particular
interest because of their insecticidal properties. Several plants which
have been used as insecticides since ancient times owe their effectiveness
to the presence of isobutylamides. Pellitory (*Anacyclus pyrethrum*) is
probably the best known of these plants. Its roots yield the insecticide
pellitorine which has been shown to be a mixture of several different isobutylamides. The most abundant is an amide of 2, 4-decadienoic acid:

$$CH_3\text{--}CHCH_2NHCCH\text{==}CHCH\text{==}CH(CH_2)_4CH_3$$

Other isobutylamides of unsaturated acids (some acetylenic) from C_{10} to C_{18}
are found in the same plant and also in a few others. In most cases mixtures seem to be present and it is difficult to separate them, so that it
is not always possible to decide which component is the active ingredient
of a natural isobutylamide insecticide. Characterization of the isobutylamides depends on acidic hydrolysis and identification of the fatty acid
and isobutylamine. A discussion of these compounds may be found in a review of naturally occurring insecticides (52).

THIOLS AND SULFIDES

The simple alkyl thiols (mercaptans) and sulfides have much in common
with the amines discussed in the previous section. They are both volatile,

with an offensive odor; and biogenetically they are probably both derived from amino acids. The basic structures of the sulfur compounds to be discussed in this section are as follows:

RSH   thiols (mercaptans)

RSR'   sulfides

RSSR'   disulfides

RS_xR' polysulfides

$$\overset{O}{\overset{\uparrow}{R\overset{}{S}R'}}$$ sulfoxides

$(CH_3)_2\overset{+}{S}R$ methylsulfonium compounds

Examples of all of these types occur in higher plants, and many more probably remain to be discovered. Various examples of these sulfur compounds are the characteristic flavor ingredients of such plants as onion, garlic, and asparagus (53). The volatile constituents of onions and garlic have been extensively characterized (53 -55). As a general rule onions have propyl and 1-propenyl derivatives, whereas garlic has allyl derivatives as their most characteristic contributors to flavor. Asparagus contains 2, 2'-dithioisobutyric acid, its cyclic disulfide (asparagusic acid), and related compounds which are interesting for influencing plant growth (56, 57). Several well-known components of the processed plants are actually artifacts that appear on heating or crushing (58).

The simple mercaptans are readily soluble in aqueous alkali and form insoluble mercaptides with many heavy metal cations. The name mercaptan was originally given to them because of the readiness with which they form mercury salts. Mercaptans are readily oxidized in the air to disulfides, so that it may be advisable to maintain a nitrogen atmosphere while working with them.

The dialkyl sulfides are less volatile than the mercaptans and have a less unpleasant odor. Several tropical fruits such as pineapple and passion fruit contain them (59). With mercuric salts they form coordination complexes rather than true salts.

A large number of sulfur compounds is now known from roots of the family Compositae. They include thioketones, sulfides, cyclic sulfides, and cyclic disulfides -- even some that contain covalently linked chlorine (60). All are obviously related to the polyacetylene compounds found in the same family, and radiotracer experiments have confirmed that the polyacetylenes are precursors of the sulfur compounds (61-63). Some examples are as follows:

α-terthienyl

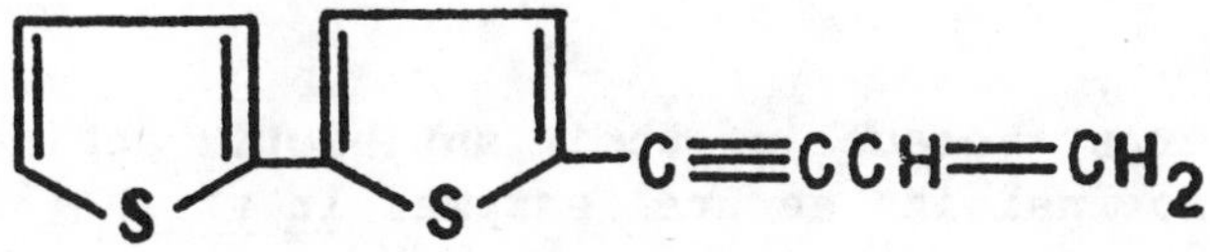

5-(3-buten-1-ynyl)-2, 2'-bithienyl

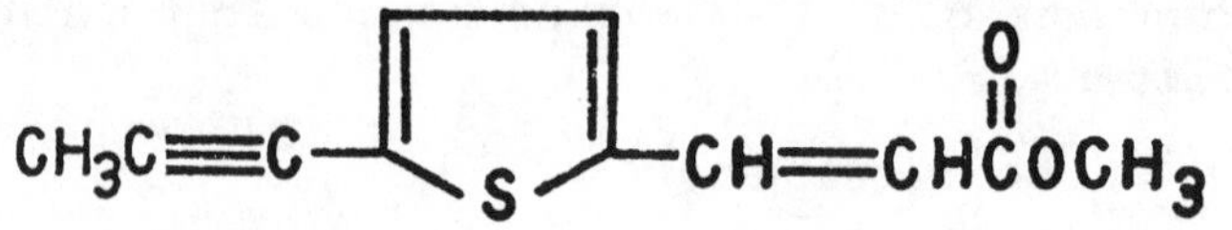

$$CH_3C \equiv C - \underset{S}{\boxed{}} - CH = CHCOCH_3$$

methyl
3-[5-(1-propynyl)-thienyl-2]-
acrylate

Disulfides and polysulfides are less volatile than the sulfides but have a more offensive odor. They react slowly with mercuric chloride. The S—S bond is split and mercaptide-like derivatives are formed. Polysulfides tend to lose sulfur and form disulfides when they are distilled. Although di- and polysulfides are found in essential oils of garlic, asafetida and onion, they probably arise through secondary transformations brought about by plant enzymes and the heat of distillation. Nevertheless, in some plants they may be truly native constituents (64). Alliin, the native constituent of garlic, is broken down enzymatically to allicin when the plant is crushed(65):

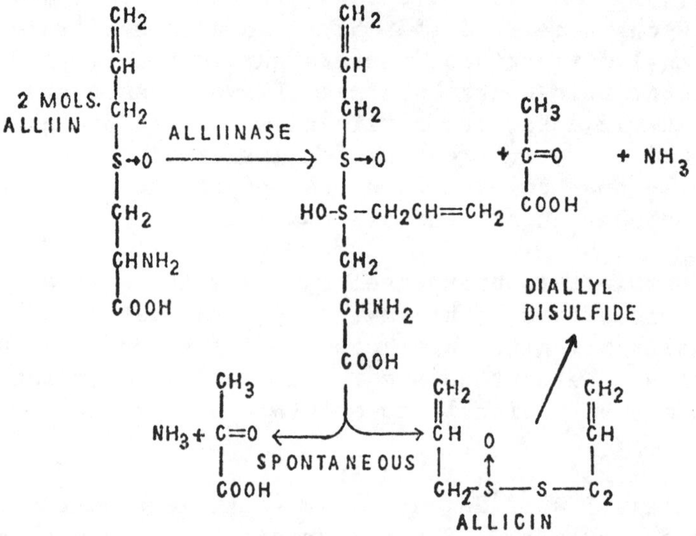

Upon distillation the sulfoxide, allicin, forms diallyl-disulfide, diallyltrisulfide and allyl propyl disulfide which are constituents of commercial garlic oil. In onions the isomer of allicin, 1-propenyl-L-cysteine sulfoxide, is a precursor of an analogous sequence of reactions (53, 66); and some such series probably accounts for the presence of disulfides in other similar oils.

Alliin was the first natural sulfoxide to be discovered, but a few others have since been found. Some sulfoxide amino acids are included in Chapter 10. Other natural sulfoxides are also isothiocyanates and will be mentioned with this group of compounds. Further oxidation of a sulfoxide yields a sulfone (RSO_2R'). Only a few natural sulfones are known, and they are regarded as secondary products derived from sulfoxides. A sulfonic acid, sulfoacetic acid, has been found in *Erythrina* spp. (67), and another sulfonic acid is present as the sulfolipid of chloroplasts (cf. Chap. 5).

The sulfoxides are of interest because of their antibiotic action. Allicin is bacteriocidal and also inhibits several enzymes in vitro (68).

In onion S-methyl- and S-n-propylcysteine-sulfoxides occur. When the onion is crushed, these are enzymatically converted to thiosulfinates which have an even stronger anti-microbial action (69, 70):

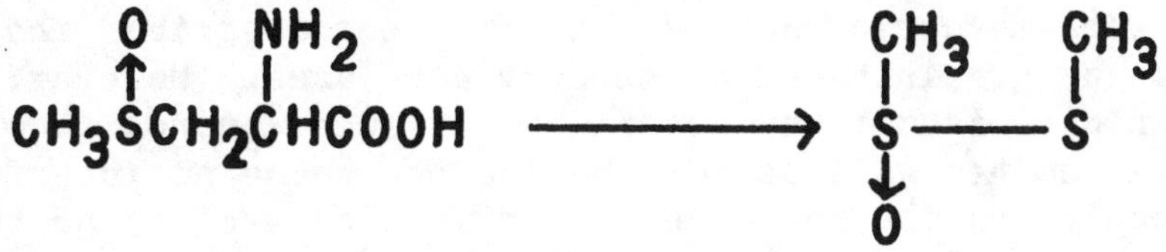

$$CH_3\overset{\overset{O}{\uparrow}}{S}CH_2\overset{\overset{NH_2}{|}}{C}HCOOH \longrightarrow CH_3-\overset{\overset{CH_3}{|}}{\underset{\underset{O}{\downarrow}}{S}}-\overset{\overset{CH_3}{|}}{S}-CH_3$$

This reaction is clearly analogous to the formation of allicin shown previously. The most powerful lachrymator among the onion compounds is *cis* propanethiol-S-oxide (71):

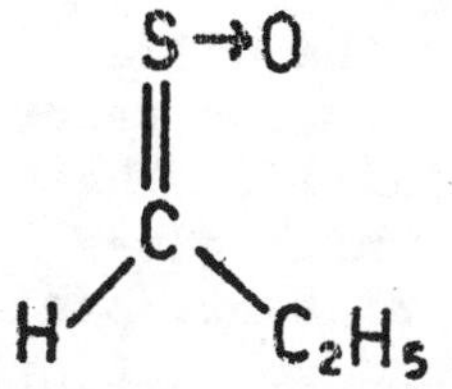

$$\overset{S\rightarrow O}{\underset{H\diagup\overset{||}{C}\diagdown C_2H_5}{}}$$

The thetins are sulfonium salts analogous to the quaternary nitrogen bases. Like the quaternary nitrogen compounds they may be precipitated as Reineckates, picrates, etc. Dimethyl-ᵧ-propiothetin:

$$(CH_3)_2\overset{+}{S}CH_2CH_2COOH$$

was the first sulfonium compound to be found in plants. It is rather common in algae, but has not been reported in higher plants, although similar compounds have been identified in *Equisetum* spp., ferns, and some halophytes (32, 72, 73). On treatment with cold alkali or with an enzyme present in some marine algae dimethyl-β-propiothetin decomposes as follows:

$$(CH_3)_2\overset{+}{S}CH_2CH_2COOH \rightarrow (CH_3)_2S + CH_2 = CHCOOH + H^+$$

Where dimethyl sulfide is found as a natural product, it may result from a similar reaction. Methylmethioninesulfonium salts have been detected in a variety of plants. They release dimethyl sulfide on treatment with boiling alkali.

The simple thiols and sulfides are generally isolated by taking advantage of the insoluble salts or complexes which they form with certain metal ions, primarily mercuric. Insoluble mercaptides are formed by reacting thiols with mercuric chloride or cyanide. Sulfides form insoluble coordination complexes with mercuric chloride but not with mercuric cyanide. This difference in reactivity may be used to separate mercaptans from sulfides. The original compounds are regenerated by treating the insoluble precipitates with acid. As noted before, disulfides are split by mercuric salts; so that they may not be isolated in their original form by this method. However, it must be recalled that simple disulfides are probably artifacts rather than true natural products, and their precursors (i.e. amino acid sulfoxides) may be isolated by the methods used for other amino acids. The sulfonium compounds are distinguished from other sulfur compounds by their positive charge, and may therefore be separated on cation exchange resins or precipitated by complex anions such as Reineckates, chloroplatinates, phosphotungstates, etc. The original compound is then regenerated by treatment of the precipitate with acid. No procedures can be discussed in general terms for isolating the more unusual sulfur compounds since each one represents a special case.

Characterization of the simple sulfur compounds has relied heavily on the reactions with mercuric salts which have been described above. Basic amines may also be precipitated as mercury complexes. However, by distilling from an acidic mixture and passing volatile compounds into a solution of mercuric salt amines will be left behind and cause no interference. Under these conditions the appearance of a precipitate may be taken as evidence for simple sulfur compounds. It should also be noted that in many cases odor alone may be sufficient evidence for distinguishing between amines and volatile sulfur compounds.

For distinguishing among the different classes of sulfur compounds specific modifications of the mercury reaction have been developed. Other special reagents are also available. The best known of these is alkaline sodium nitroprusside solution which gives a purple color with sulfhydryl compounds. If disulfides are present, preliminary treatment with potassium cyanide splits the S-S bond so that nitroprusside is able to react. Amines also react with nitroprusside in the presence of carbonyl compounds such as acetone or acetaldehyde. The presence of methyl sulfonium compounds is indicated by the evolution of dimethyl sulfide on treating with alkali. Some sulfonium compounds require boiling with sodium hydroxide solution; others release dimethyl sulfide in the cold.

The non-volatile sulfur compounds have been characterized by paper chromatography (74-76). The volatile ones are well suited to gas chromatography and mass spectrometry (55, 77, 78).

A few suggestions have been made regarding the biosynthetic pathways of simple sulfur compounds, and in the case of asparagus some tracer experiments have been done to support the general impression that amino acids are probable precursors (79). In some cases sulfur compounds may be artifacts resulting from the reaction of reactive compounds with sulfur (80).

GLUCOSINOLATES (MUSTARD OIL GLYCOSIDES)

The mustard oils have been known for many years and are economically important as the flavor constituents of such condiments as mustard, horseradish, and water cress. For the most part they are colorless liquids with a sharp, irritating odor and the ability to raise blisters on the skin. Before 1900 it was understood that the mustard oils are actually secondary products arising from breakdown of glucosides when cellular structure is disrupted. It seems probable that a single general structure can be written for all glucosides of this group. Upon hydrolysis, however, the aglycones undergo rearrangement. In some cases the rearrangements are so extensive that the final product bears no apparent resemblance to the aglycone as it exists in the glucoside.

The general structure of all the parent glucosides is:

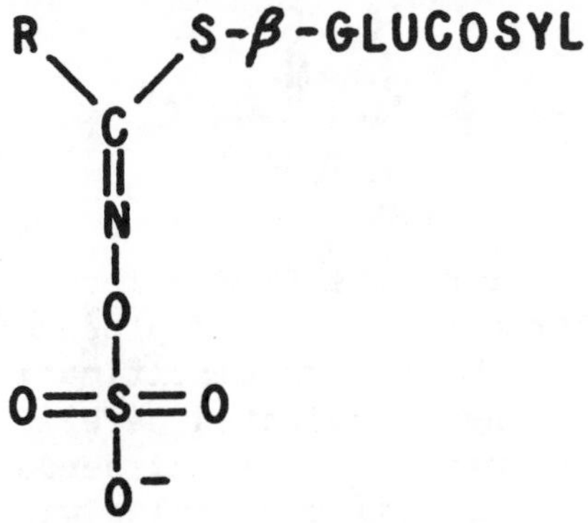

$$R-\underset{\underset{\underset{O^-}{|}}{\underset{\overset{||}{O=S=O}}{\underset{|}{O}}}}{\overset{|}{\underset{||}{\underset{N}{C}}}}-S\text{-}\beta\text{-GLUCOSYL}$$

R may be a simple alkyl group or may be complex. As shown, the glucosides
are anions which normally are found as potassium salts but may also occur
as salts of organic nitrogen bases. The salts are colorless, water-soluble
compounds which can be crystallized with difficulty. The glucosides are
split by the action of an enzyme or enzyme complex known as myrosinase or
thioglucosidase (81), which is present in all plants containing these glucosides. Simple hydrolysis would be expected to yield a hydroxamic acid,
glucose, and inorganic sulfate. In fact, the hydroxamic acid usually
undergoes an immediate Lossen rearrangement to form an iso-thiocyanate:

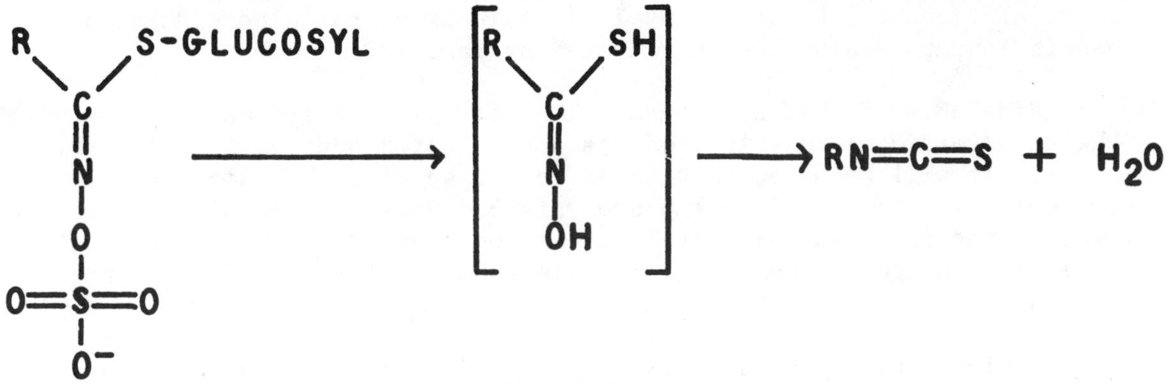

$$R-\underset{\underset{\underset{O^-}{|}}{\underset{\overset{||}{O=S=O}}{\underset{|}{O}}}}{\overset{|}{\underset{||}{\underset{N}{C}}}}-S\text{-GLUCOSYL} \longrightarrow \left[R-\underset{\underset{OH}{|}}{\overset{|}{\underset{||}{\underset{N}{C}}}}-SH \right] \longrightarrow RN=C=S + H_2O$$

There are other alternate enzymatic processes which frequently occur to
some extent. In some plants the R group migrates to sulfur rather than to
nitrogen so that thiocyanates rather than iso-thiocyanates are formed (82).
Both types of reaction can go on simultaneously. In other plants nitriles,
amines, and epithio derivatives appear. Presumably these all come from
a common intermediate decomposing in various ways; but the mix of products
varies from species to species (83-85).

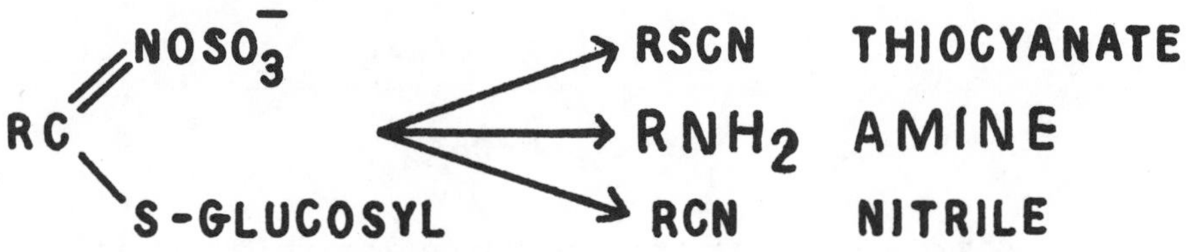

$$RC\overset{\displaystyle NOSO_3^-}{\underset{\displaystyle S\text{-GLUCOSYL}}{\Big\langle}} \quad\begin{array}{l} \longrightarrow RSCN \quad \text{THIOCYANATE} \\ \longrightarrow RNH_2 \quad \text{AMINE} \\ \longrightarrow RCN \quad \text{NITRILE} \end{array}$$

If an iso-thiocyanate is produced, it may undergo further non-enzymatic
reaction with sufficiently active hydroxyl groups which may be present.

This is a well-known reaction of all <u>iso</u>-thiocyanates and results in an N. substituted thiourethane:

$$RNCS + R'OH \longrightarrow \underset{\underset{R}{\overset{|}{N}}}{\overset{H}{\underset{|}{N}}}-\overset{\overset{S}{\parallel}}{C}-OR' \longleftrightarrow RN\overset{SH}{=}\overset{|}{C}-OR'$$

Usually R'OH is actually part of the RNCS molecule so that the reaction is intramolecular, and a heterocyclic ring is produced, or polymers may form. These complex reactions need much more clarification at the single-step, enzymatic level. They have been indicated here in order to show that different types of compound may all arise as secondary products from a single glucoside precursor. Specific examples will be given below.

The mustard oil glucosides are widespread among the Cruciferae but are occasionally found in other plant families as well. About fifty different ones are presently known, and most plants which have them have more than one. There is good reason to believe that they function to protect plants against some parasites (86). It is, of course, the aglycones formed enzymatically upon cellular disintegration which are the active compounds in this respect. Virtanen (87) describes the mustard oils as the most active antibiotics found in hgiher plants. Goitrin (see below for structure) which occurs in *Brassica* spp. is also of economic interest since it acts as a goitrogenic or antithyroid compound toward animals (88). Some possible interrelationships between benzyl glucosinolate, thioglucosidase, and papain in papaya have been considered by Tang (89).

In Table 15-2 some mustard oil glucosides are listed together with their enzymatic hydrolysis products and selected species in which they occur. It will be noted that in different species the same glucoside (e.g. sinigrin) may form different hydrolysis products. It should also be mentioned that although the hydrolysis products are usually called "mustard oils" and thought of as being volatile and odoriferous, some are non-volatile solids.

Only a few of the original glucosides have been isolated and purified. Most work has been done with the hydrolysis products, which are more easily obtained. In order to obtain the unchanged glucosides from plants it is necessary to inactivate the thioglucosidase by heating to 100° C. Glucosides may be extracted with boiling water, ethanol, methanol etc. If lipids are also present, as in some seeds, they should first be removed with fat solvents. Crude glucoside solutions are concentrated, chromatographed on alumina or anion exchange resin and crystallized from alcohol-water. Addition of silver nitrate to the glycosides cleaves off the glucose with precipitation of a silver salt:

$$R-C\overset{\diagup NOSO_3Ag}{\diagdown SAg}$$

This can be converted to the corresponding <u>iso</u> thiocyanate by shaking with aqueous sodium thiosulfate. Volatile mustard oils are prepared by macerating plant parts in water for several hours to permit enzymatic hydrolysis to occur, then steam distilling or extracting with ether to obtain the volatile oil. Further purification can be achieved by fractional distil-

TABLE 15–2   MUSTARD OILS AND THEIR GLYCOSIDES

Glucoside	Hydrolysis Product	Plant Source
not known	HSCN, thiocyanic acid (or its salts)	onion, *Allium cepa*
$CH_2{=}CHCH_2C{\overset{NOSO_3}{\underset{S-GLUCOSE}{}}}$ sinigrin	$CH_2{=}CHCH_2NCS$ allyl *iso*-thiocyanate	Black mustard, *Brassica nigra*
sinigrin	$CH_2{=}CHCH_2SCN$ allyl thiocyanate	Penny cress, *Thlaspi arvense*
glucoraphenin	$CH_3\overset{O}{\overset{\uparrow}{S}}CH{=}CHCH_2CH_2NCS$ sulforaphene	Radish, *Raphanus sativus*

Table 15-2 Continued

Glucoside	Hydrolysis Product	Plant Source
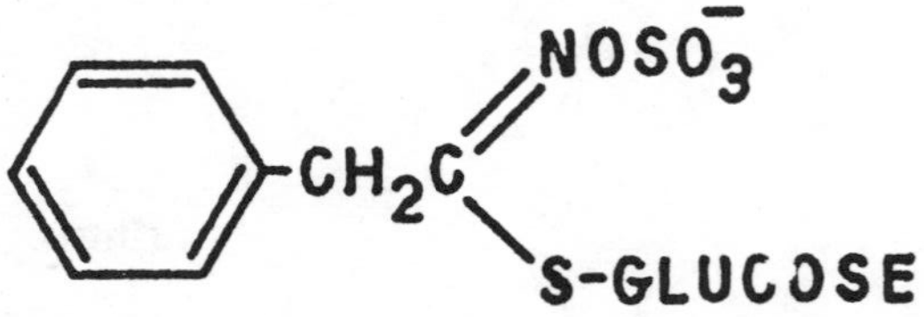 CH_2C =$NOSO_3^-$, S-GLUCOSE glucotropaeolin	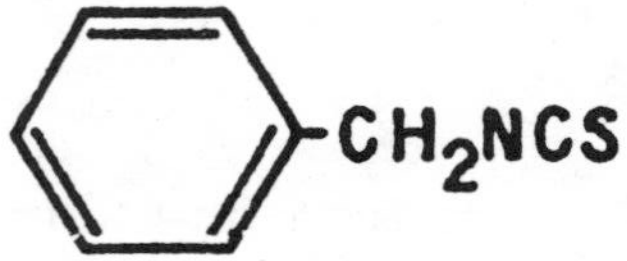 CH_2NCS benzyl *iso*-thiocyanate	Nasturtium, *Tropaeolum majus*
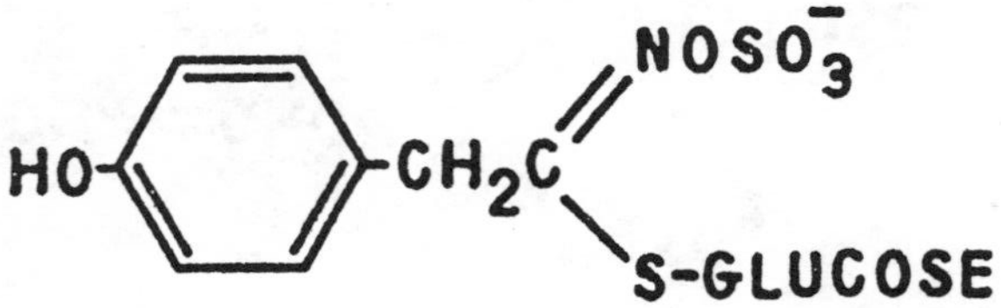 CH_2C =$NOSO_3^-$, S-GLUCOSE, HO sinalbin	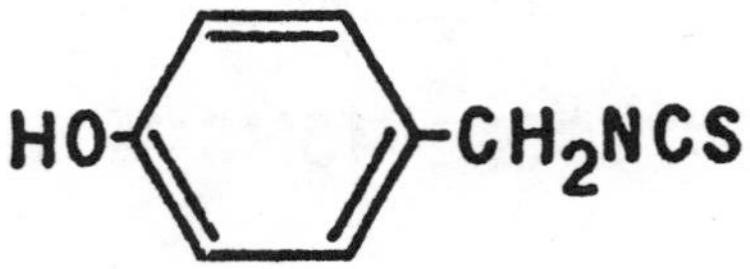 CH_2NCS, HO p-hydroxybenzyl *iso*-thiocyanate	White mustard, *Sinapis alba*
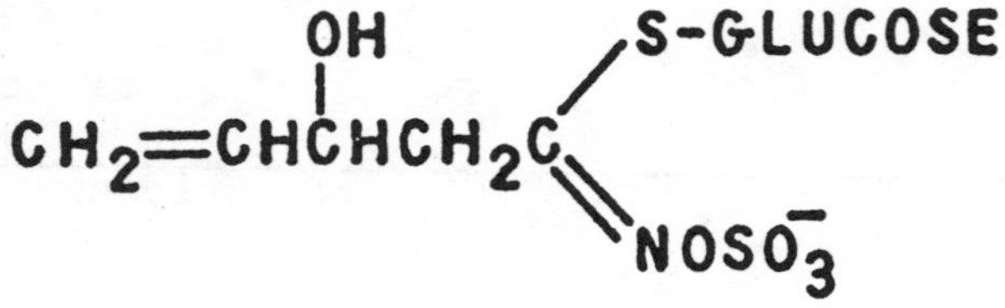 CH_2=CHCHCH$_2$C, OH, S-GLUCOSE, =$NOSO_3^-$ progoitrin, glucoapiferin	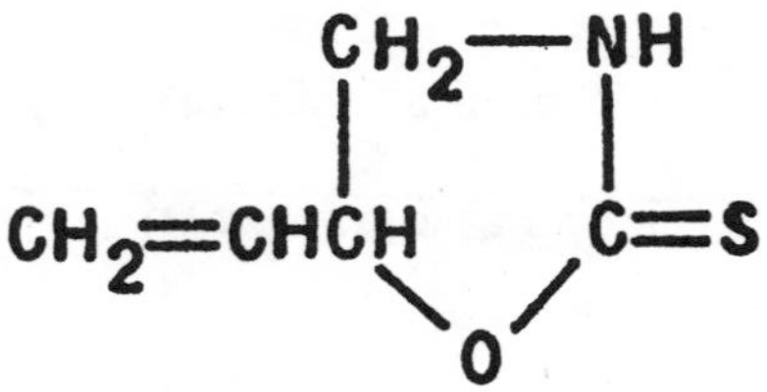 CH_2—NH, CH$_2$=CHCH—O, C=S goitrin, (-)-5-vinyl-2-oxazolidinethione	*Brassica* spp.

lation or column chromatography. Non-volatile hydrolysis products such as goitrin have been purified by extraction with water and ether (90).

Several simple spot reactions have been developed for characterization of the mustard oils and their glucosides. For the volatile mustard oils their sharp odor and biting taste are distinctive enough to indicate their presence. Paper chromatography has been of great assistance in the characterization of these compounds. The glucosides have been extensively chromatographed by Schultz and coworkers (91, 92) using a butanol-acetic acid-water solvent. Thin layer chromatography has also been used (93). The glucosides are recognized by spraying with 0.02M silver nitrate, drying at 100° C. and spraying with 0.02M potassium dichromate. Glucosides appear as yellow spots against a red background of silver chromate. By converting the glucosinolates to trimethylsilyl ethers they can be made volatile enough for analysis by gas chromatography (94). Paper chromatography of the mustard oils is usually carried out using the corresponding thiourea derivatives prepared by allowing the iso-thiocyanate to react with concentrated ammonia in ethanol:

$$RNCS + NH_3 \rightarrow R-NH\overset{\overset{\displaystyle S}{\|}}{C}NH_2$$

These substituted thioureas also make nicely crystalline derivatives for other characterization procedures. The thioureas are chromatographed in solvents such as water-saturated chloroform or butanol-ethanol-water. One of the most used sprays is Grote's reagent--a mixture of sodium nitroprusside, hydroxylamine and bromine which gives blue spots with thiourea derivatives. This method was developed by Kjaer and Rubinstein (95) and has been used in a large number of studies on the mustard oils (96). Similar surveys have been carried out by Delaveau (97) using ammoniacal silver nitrate to detect free iso-thiocyanates. Gas phase chromatography is also useful for volatile members of this group (98). Spectroscopic evidence is valuable in some cases. The mustard oils show an absorption peak at about 250 nm. On reaction with ammonia to form a thiourea this changes to about 243 nm. Compounds such as goitrin (oxazolidinethiones) also show the 243 nm peak.

It is evident that the alkyl groups of many of the mustard oil glycosides resemble the carbon chains of amino acids minus their carboxyl groups. Radiotracer experiments have shown that amino acids are indeed precursors of the glucosinolates. Phenylalanine and tyrosine go to glucotropaeolin and sinalbin by way of their N-hydroxy derivatives and oximes. For other glucosinolates the amino acid precursors are not common protein amino acids but must first be synthesized themselves. For instance several come from methionine by a chain-lengthening process in which acetate contributes the extra carbons. The immediate sources for the two sulfur atoms are unknown, but thioglucose is not a precursor. These pathways are described in the review of Ettlinger and Kjaer (General References), and some more recent findings are (99-101).

NITRILES

The nitriles or organic cyanides are widely distributed throughout the plant kingdom, although certain types appear to be taxonomically restricted. Naturally occurring cyano compounds are reviewed in (102, 103). The largest single group of natural nitriles is made up of the cyanogenic glycosides whose general structure is as follows:

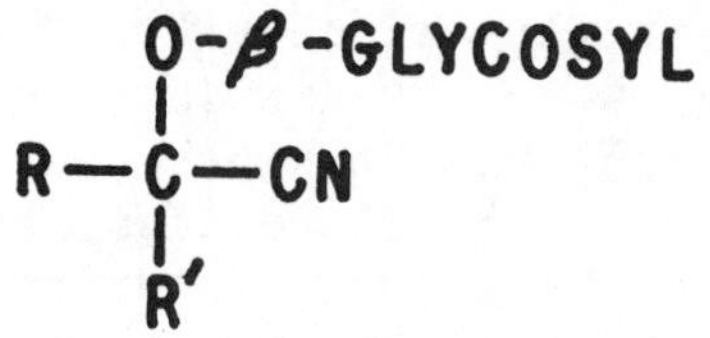

$$R-\underset{\underset{R'}{|}}{\overset{\overset{O-\beta\text{-GLYCOSYL}}{|}}{C}}-CN$$

In some cases R' is hydrogen rather than an alkyl group, and some variant structures are known that do not fit this general form exactly and that release nitriles (organic cyanides) rather than hydrogen cyanide on hydrolysis (104--106). These compounds possess the general characteristics of other glycosides as colorless compounds soluble in water and to some extent in alcohol but insoluble in fat solvents. They are common in seeds of the Rosaceae but occur throughout the plant kingdom, including some ferns and fungi. Only a few different aglycones are known, but there are about two dozen different glycosides since the same aglycone may be found with several different sugar components. Cyanogenic glycosides are reviewed in (107). Like the mustard oil glucosides the cyanogenic glycosides on enzymatic hydrolysis do not normally yield the aglycone as such, but a second reaction occurs to form hydrogen cyanide:

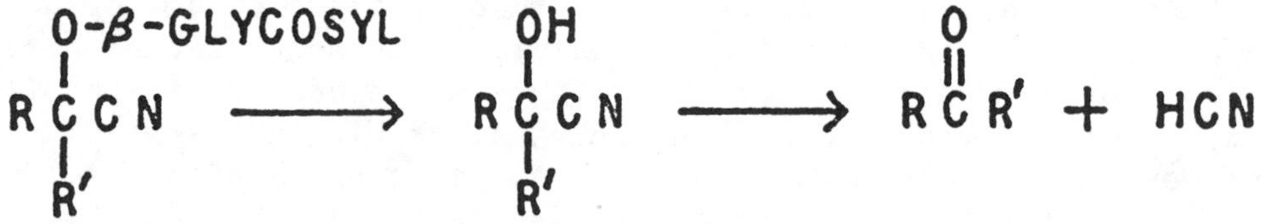

$$R\underset{\underset{R'}{|}}{\overset{\overset{O-\beta\text{-GLYCOSYL}}{|}}{C}}CN \longrightarrow R\underset{\underset{R'}{|}}{\overset{\overset{OH}{|}}{C}}CN \longrightarrow R\overset{\overset{O}{||}}{C}R' + HCN$$

These two reactions are catalyzed by two separate enzymes, β–glycosidase and oxynitrilase. The cyanide poisoning of livestock from eating such leaves as wild cherry is a practical problem of some importance, but hydrocyanic acid as such does not exist in plants. It is evolved according to the reaction outlined above when the plants are injured (108). Table 15-3 lists the structures of some cyanogenic glycosides along with the carbonyl compounds which are formed from them by the two-stage hydrolysis process.

In addition to the cyanogenic glycosides of the structure shown above, it has been noted in the previous section of this chapter that nitriles sometimes arise from hydrolysis of typical mustard oil glucosides. Thus, small amounts of nitriles may be present in some impure mustard oils. For example, enzymatic hydrolysis of glucotropaeolin may produce benzyl cyanide as well as benzyl *iso*-thiocyanate:

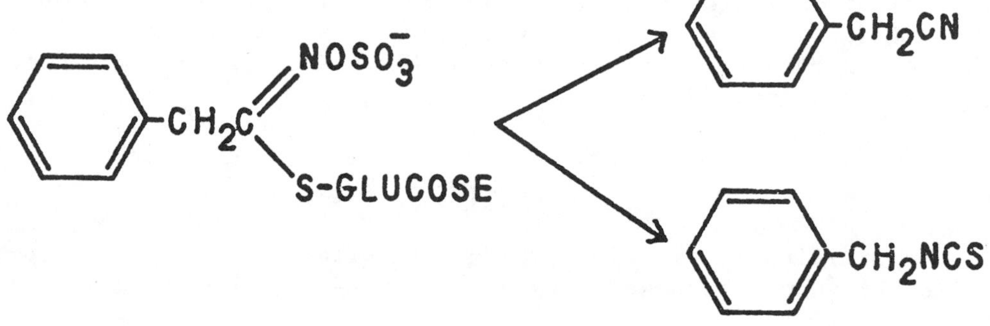

TABLE 15-3 SOME CYANOGENIC GLYCOSIDES, THEIR HYDROLYSIS PRODUCTS AND OCCURRENCE

Glycoside	Carbonyl Compound	Selected Plant Source
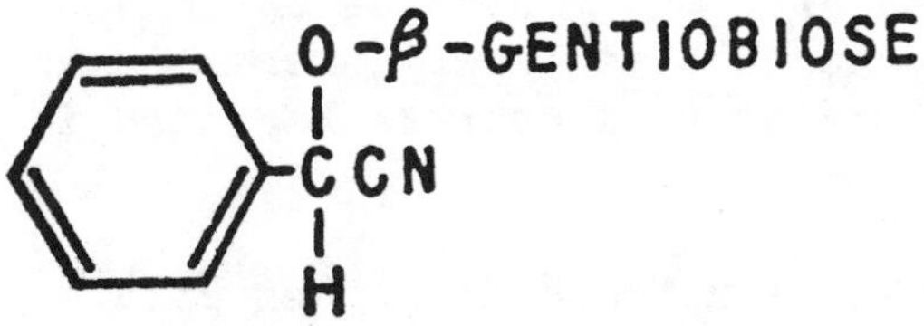 amygdalin (O-β-GENTIOBIOSE)	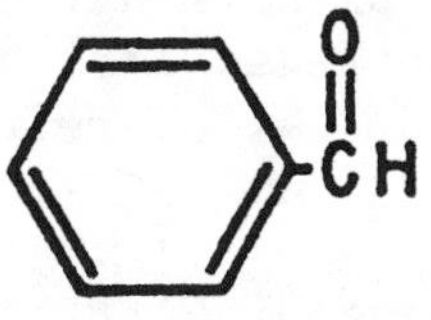 benzaldehyde	*Amygdalus nana*
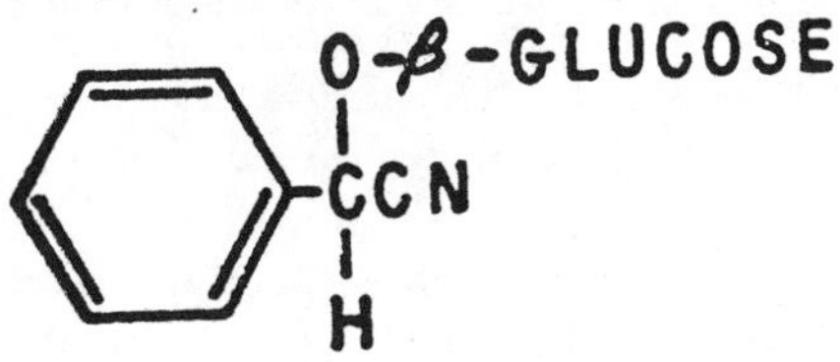 prunasin (O-β-GLUCOSE)	benzaldehyde	*Prunus* spp.
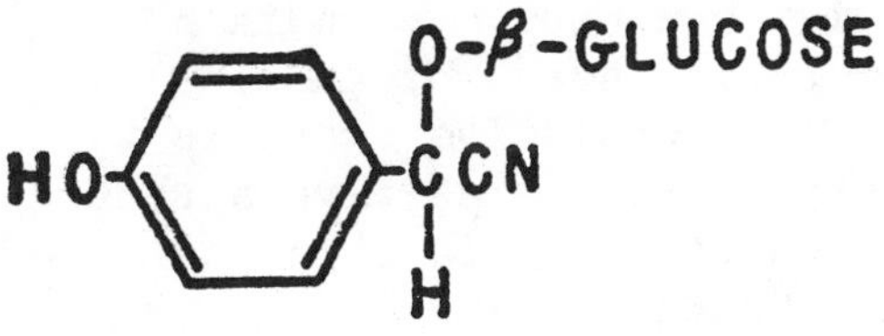 dhurrin (O-β-GLUCOSE)	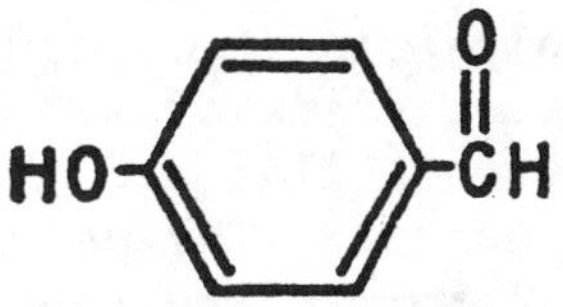 p-hydroxybenzaldhyde	*Sorghum vulgare*
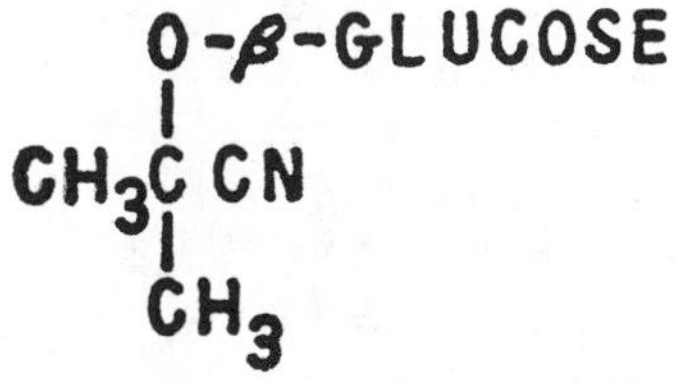 linamarin (O-β-GLUCOSE)	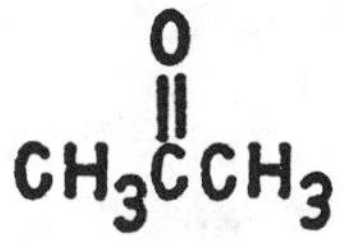 acetone	*Linum* spp.
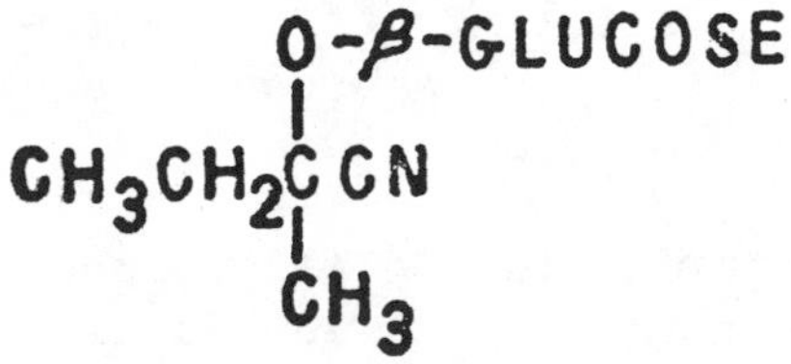 lotaustralin (O-β-GLUCOSE)	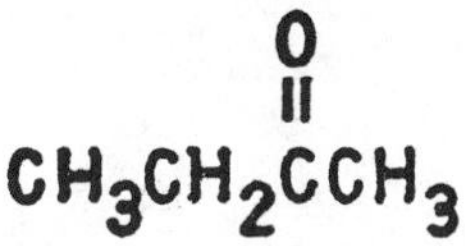 methylethyl ketone	*Lotus* spp.

When a nitrile is formed by such a reaction, the sulfur atom appears as elemental sulfur--the only example of the occurrence of this free element in higher plants. Presumably as the result of analogous reactions allyl cyanide occurs along with allyl *iso*-thiocyanate in black mustard oil and the nitrile corresponding to sulforaphene in radish oil. These nitriles are stable, volatile compounds and do not release hydrogen cyanide. To some extent they may be artifacts formed from unhydrolyzed glucoside during steam distillation, but there is also evidence that at least in some cases they are true natural products. Careful study of this obscure reaction is needed.

A few other miscellaneous nitriles have been found in higher plants. Consumption of seeds of the sweet pea (*Lathyrus odoratus*) by animals causes a disease known as odoratism which is characterized by changes in bone and connective tissue structure. The causative agent is γ-glutamyl-β-aminopropionitrile (109):

$$\underset{\substack{| \\ H}}{\overset{\substack{NH_2 \\ |}}{HOOCCHCH_2CH_2}}\overset{O}{\underset{H}{\overset{||}{C}}}NCH_2CH_2CN$$

Another chronic human disease known as lathyrism has been common in parts of India and Spain. Although it is caused by eating seeds of *Lathyrus sativus* or contaminating seeds of *Vicia* spp., the causative agent is not γ-glutamyl-β-aminopropionitrile; and the chief symptom is paralysis caused by irreversible nerve damage. The poisonous constituents in this case are diaminobutyric acid and related compounds (cf. Chapter 10).

Isolation of the cyanogenic glycosides follows the general lines described for other glycosides based on their solubility in water and lower alcohols and lack of solubility in most fat solvents. They also show some solubility in ethyl acetate, and this property may be used to separate them from other carbohydrates. For isolation of unhydrolyzed glycosides it is necessary to inactivate the hydrolytic enzymes with boiling water or alcohol and to neutralize plant acids with calcium carbonate. There is little interest in isolating the hydrolysis products except where they are needed to establish the structure of the original glycoside. The sugars may be obtained by methods outlined in Chapter 2 and the carbonyl compounds by distillation. The nitriles which occur along with mustard oils may be separated by adding ammonia sufficient to form a nonvolatile thiourea derivative with the iso-thiocyanate and then distilling off the volatile, unreacted nitrile. During the distillation if water is present, some of the nitrile may be hydrolyzed to the corresponding acid.

There is no general method for rapid characterization of all compounds having a nitrile group. The presence of cyanogenic glycosides in plants is indicated by the evolution of HCN when the tissues are broken. This gas is easily detected by putting the crushed plant part in a sealed tube with a piece of filter paper which has been dipped in alkaline picric acid solution. The yellow dye turns red when HCN comes in contact with it. Similar color reactions will be found in the general references. A few plants contain cyanogenic glycosides but not the enzymes to hydrolyze them. In these cases

HCN is evolved only if the required enzymes are added. A method for detecting cyanogenic glycosides on chromatograms depends on enzymatic hydrolysis
followed by a spray reagent to detect cyanide ion (110). Other nitriles
which do not evolve hydrogen cyanide are customarily identified by hydrolyzing them to the corresponding acids and identifying these acids by
methods described in Chapters 3 and 4.

As with the glucosinolates amino acids are precursors of the cyanogenic glycosides. The sequence probably proceeds through modification of
the α-amino group successively to N-hydroxy and oxime, followed by loss
of carbon dioxide and water to yield the nitrile with one less carbon.
The α-carbon of the nitrile is then hydroxylated and the resulting cyanogenic aglycone converted to the glucoside by transfer from UDP-glucose (111).
Although reversal of the oxynitrilase reaction is not part of this normal
pathway, oxynitrilase does catalyze the condensation of hydrogen cyanide with
aldehydes (112). Dhurrin undergoes active turnover in sorghum shoots (113),
and the cyanide released from cyanogenic glucosides can be reutilized in
the synthesis of asparagine (114). In contrast, the linamarin present in
wild lima bean seeds persists unmetabolized during nearly a month of seedling
growth (115). It is interesting that both mustard oil glucosides and cyanogenic glucosides are synthesized from an oxime derivative of an amino acid,
and that no plant contains both types of compound. They may represent
alternative approaches to the same function. Little is known about the
biosynthesis of other types of nitriles except that leucine is a precursor
of the cyanolipids found in *Koelreuteria paniculata* (116). An enzyme,
nitrilase, found in barley but not widely occurring in plants catalyzes a
one-step conversion of nitriles to the corresponding acids (117).

INDOLE DERIVATIVES

Plants contain a large number of compounds based on the indole ring
system:

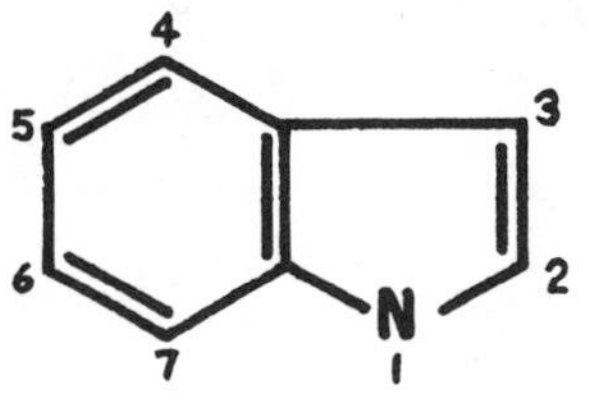

These include the amino acid tryptophan and many alkaloids. Besides these,
there are several other indole compounds which do not fit into any large
category but are too important to be ignored. Indole is partly responsible
for the odor of jasmine flowers. A review of indole derivatives found in
plants has been presented by Stowe (118) and a table summarizing indole
compounds found in plants to date is given in (119).

Of most interest in plant physiology are the compounds closely related
to indole-3-acetic acid, the most important natural auxin. Other natural
indole derivatives whose structures are given below have auxin activity
similar to that of indole-3-acetic acid, but it is generally believed that
they are active only after being enzymatically converted to indole-3-acetic
acid.

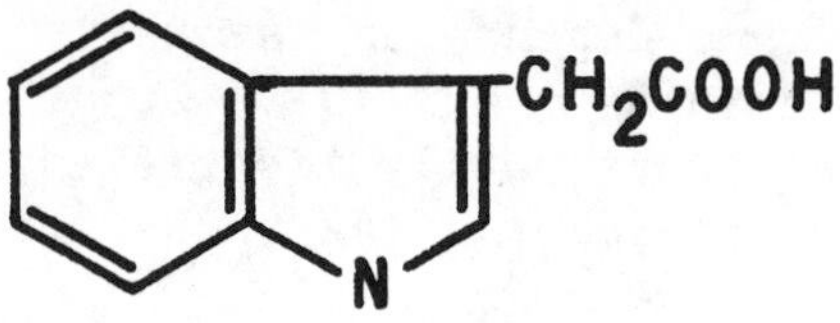

indole-3-acetic acid 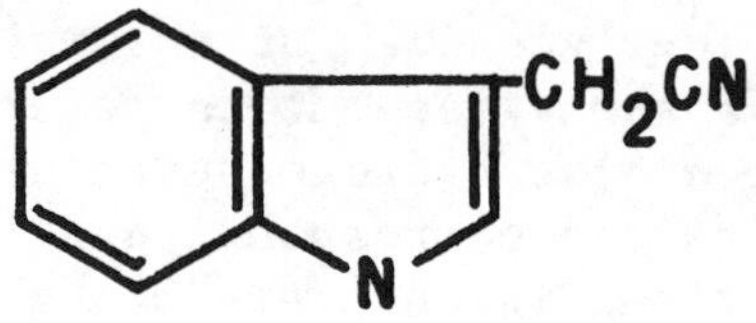   indole-3-acetonitrile

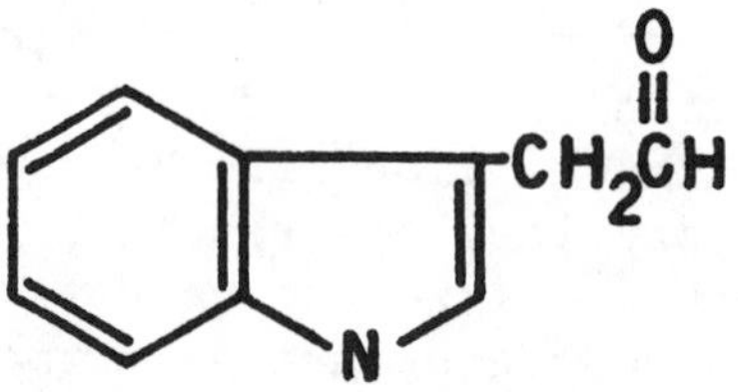

indole-3-acetaldehyde

4-Chloroindole-3-acetic acid and its methyl ester have been identified in immature pea and vetch seeds (120). More complex derivatives such as indole-3-acetylaspartic acid (121) and esters of indole-3-acetic acid with glucose or myo-inositol have also been found (122, 123). It has been estimated that most of the indoleacetic acid in plants is bound to polymeric materials such as polysaccharide, protein, or glycoprotein (124-126).

Whereas the indole auxins are of great interest in plant physiology, other indole compounds found in plants show striking physiological effects on animals. These are tryptamine and derivatives of it such as 5-hydroxy-tryptamine (serotonin).

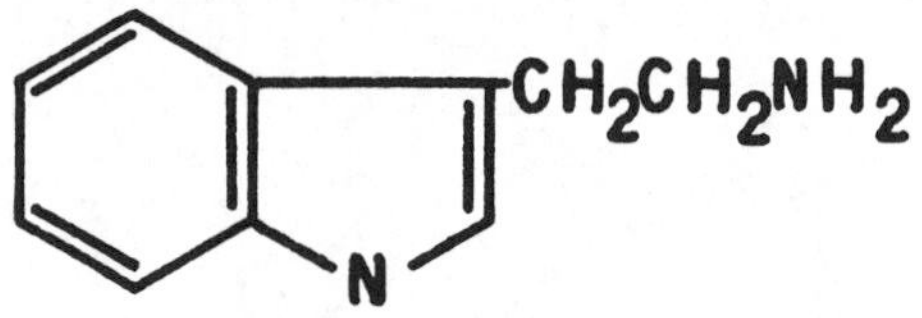

tryptamine 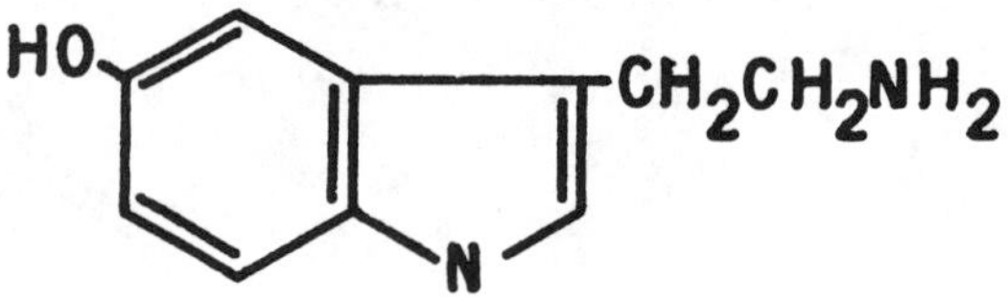   serotonin

Both of these compounds are widely distributed in plants, although usually in small amounts (119, 127). Tryptamine acts as a pressor amine (q.v.), whereas serotonin, in addition to having effects on blood pressure, also produces effects on the central nervous system. Methylated derivatives of serotonin are responsible for the psychic effects produced by certain hallucinogenic mushrooms.

Ascorbigen is an indole derivative of ascorbic acid which has been isolated from *Brassica* spp. but is probably an artifact of isolation (128). It is equal to ascorbic acid in nutritional value but does not react in the usual chemical tests for ascorbic acid. The precursor of the indole moiety of ascorbigen is the mustard oil glucoside, glucobrassicin which is hydro-lyzed by the action of thioglucosidase to form glucose, $SO_4^=$, SCN- and 3-hydroxymethylindole. The last compound immediately reacts with ascorbic acid to form ascorbigen. Under acidic conditions thioglucosidase acts on glucobrassicin to form indole-3-acetonitrile and other products active as auxins, but it is doubtful that these are made in vivo (129). Plants of the family Cruciferae have other compounds structurally related to glucobrassicin (130).

The indole compounds described above are all rather unstable and usually occur in plants in very low concentrations, so that isolation represents a formidable problem. Column chromatography of them has been done using both anion and cation exchangers (131, 132) as well as neutral polystyrene (133). Paper chromatography has been widely used for indole compounds (119, 134), but thin layer chromatography is probably better since its speed gives less opportunity for decomposition to occur (119, 132). Thin layer electrophoresis has also been used (135). Spots can be detected by their fluorescence or by reaction with various reagents such as Salkowski reagent (0.001M ferric chloride in 5% perchloric acid), Ehrlich's reagent (dimethylaminobenzaldehyde in 12N hydrochloric acid), or 2, 4, 7-trinitro-9-fluorenone (136). Spots can be characterized further by measurement of their ultraviolet absorption spectra (137, 138) or fluorescent spectra (139). Infrared spectroscopy and bioassays have also been used (119).

Gas chromatography is a very fast and sensitive method for analysis of indoles after some initial purification (123, 140, 141). Mass spectrometry is also valuable for the identification of separated compounds (123, 142).

The biosynthesis of all these indole compounds probably begins with tryptophan. Decarboxylation of the amino acid leads to tryptamine and various derivatives of it (143). Tryptamine can be a precursor of indole-3-acetic acid (144), but it is more likely that for most plants indolepyruvic acid and indoleacetaldehyde are in the normal pathway (145). There may very well be differences from species to species (122). The 5-hydroxy group of serotonin may be introduced before or after decarboxylation of tryptophan (146). The pathway to glucobrassicin goes through the same types of intermediates as used for other glucosinolates - i.e. N-hydroxyl-tryptophan and indolyl-3-acetaldoxime (147). Indoleacetonitrile may arise from breakdown of glucobrassicin. The oxidative degradation of indole-acetic acid is catalyzed by many peroxidases at varying rates, and whether any one should be called a specific indoleacetic acid oxidase is doubtful (148-150). Several products of the oxidation are known of which a major one is 3-methyleneoxindole (145, 151, 152).

The dye indigo is no longer of any commercial importance, but is interesting as an unusual natural indole compound. Indigo, however, does not occur as such in plants. Leaves of certain species of the genus *Indigofera* contain a glucoside, indican, which is first hydrolyzed to the aglycone indoxyl by crushing the plant in water so that β-glucosidases can act. When air is passed through alkaline solutions of indoxyl, it is oxidized to the blue dye indigotin. These reactions are as follows:

indican   indoxyl   indigotin

Natural indigo contains some other dyes as well as indigotin. The European woad plant (*Isatis tinctoria*) was at one time an important source of blue dye. This blue dye is also indigo but produced from a different precursor, an ester rather than a glucoside of indoxyl (153).

Another pigment (or class of pigments) based on the indole nucleus is melanin. This pigment is responsible for dark hair and skin color in animals. However, its existence in plants is dubious. The probable structure of melanin is indicated below. It is a polymer based on indole-5, 6-quinone.

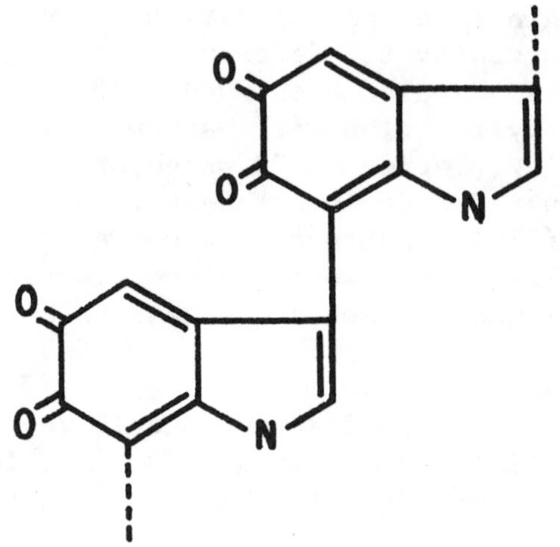

Such compounds may be formed by the action of oxidizing enzymes on tyrosine or dihydroxyphenylalanine (154). The term melanin should be restricted to compounds of this type and not used for any dark pigment. Careful investigation of dark pigments of higher plants will be needed to decide whether true melanins are present. Many dark plant pigments are known to be free of nitrogen and formed by oxidation of such phenolic compounds as chlorogenic acid (see Chap. 4). However, leaves of some composites contain a dark red pigment named intybin which seems to be an indolequinone derivative (155). The red pigments of beets (*Beta vulgaris*) and several other plants (especially in the Chenopodiaceae) were thought for many years to be related to the anthocyanins although they contain nitrogen. It has now been established that they are in fact indole derivatives. The name "betacyanins" has been proposed for them and "betaxanthins" for the related yellow pigments, the group as a whole being known as betalains (156, 157). Betanin, the most thoroughly studied of these compounds, is a glucoside which yields the aglycone betanidin on hydrolysis. The structure of betanidin is as follows:

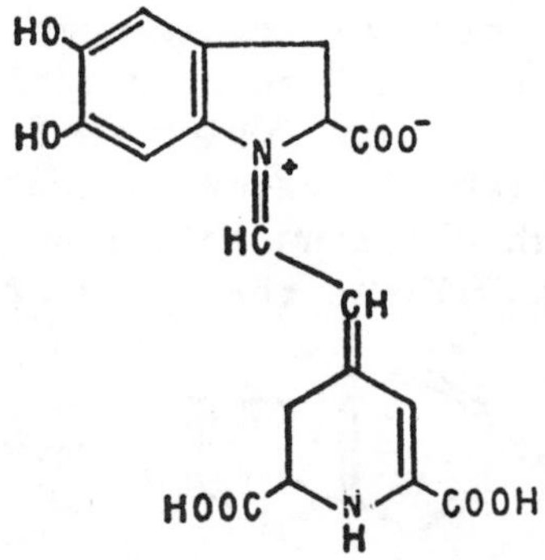

A routine method for separation of betacyanins on polyamide columns has been applied to a survey of their occurrence in plants (158). Other chromatographic procedures are available for purification and analysis of these compounds (159-161). The dihydropyridine part (betalamic acid), common to all betalains, is derived from dihydroxyphenylalanine (162, 163). The indole portion, present in betacyanins, is derived from a second molecule of dihydroxyphenylalanine (164). The betaxanthins have groups derived from other amino acids instead of the indole. Betalains are powerful inhibitors of indoleacetic acid oxidase (165).

SOME VITAMINS

Several important vitamins are nitrogen and/or sulfur compounds which do not fit conveniently under any larger structural category. Some of these will be mentioned briefly here; but since each one is a special case and we are concerned with discussing general categories of compounds, the general references should be consulted for methods of isolation and characterization. For thin layer chromatography and high performance liquid chromatography of the B-vitamins see (166) and (167).

Thiamine or vitamin B_1 probably occurs to some extent in all plants, if not in all cells. Thiamine pyrophosphate (cocarboxylase) is the form in which this vitamin serves as a coenzyme in the decarboxylation of pyruvic acid to acetate, acetyl-coenzyme-A, or other products and in the transketolase reaction. Thiamine biosynthesis has not been investigated in higher plants. In microorganisms the thiazole ring is derived from alanine, glycine, and methionine (168, 169). Many aspects of thiamine chemistry and physiology are presented in a symposium publication (170).

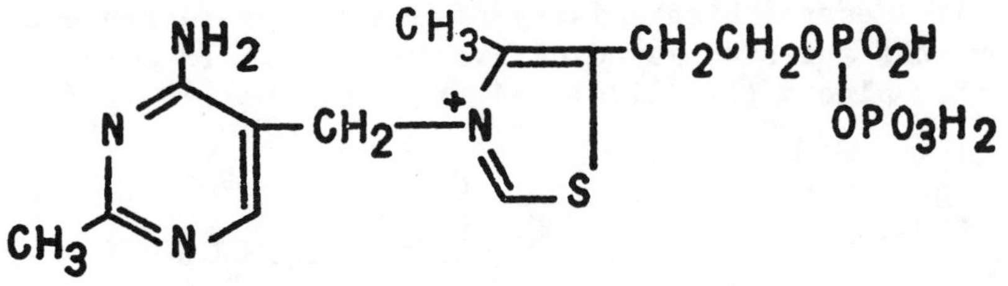

thiamine pyrophosphate

Lipoic acid or 6, 8-thioctic acid has a rather simple structure. It exists in a reduced dithiol form which is readily oxidized to a disulfide.

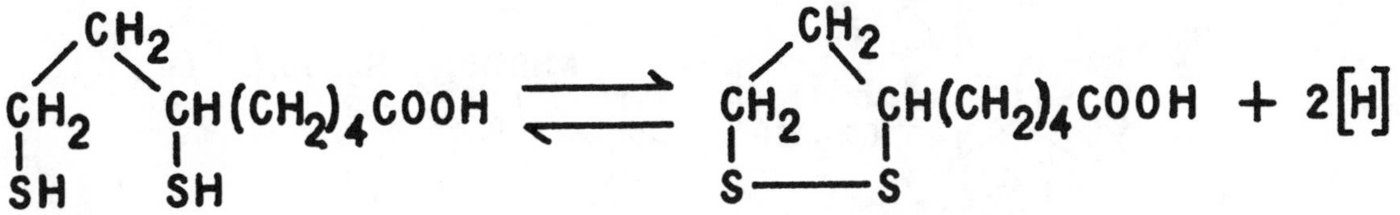

This vitamin functions along with thiamine pyrophosphate as a coenzyme in decarboxylation and acyl group transfer.

Biotin functions as a carrier of carbon dioxide in several carboxylation reactions such as the formation of malonyl-CoA from acetyl-CoA, oxalacetate from pyruvate, and β-methylglutaconyl-CoA from senecioyl-CoA (171). The enzymes catalyzing these reactions contain biotin as a prosthetic group attached by a peptide bond between its carboxyl group and the ε-amino group of a lysine residue.

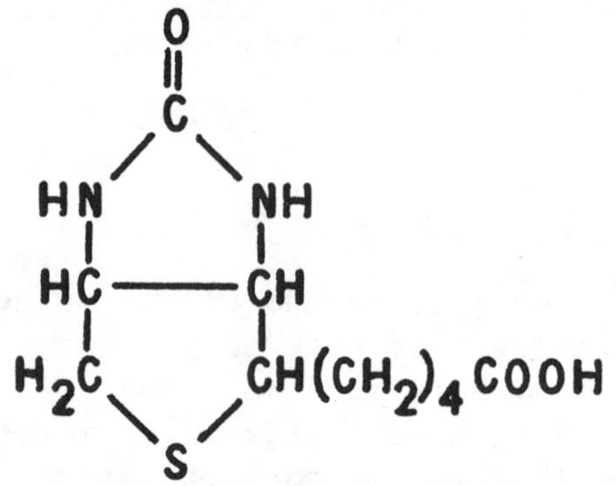

biotin

Folic acid is only one of a series of related compounds which are found widely distributed in nature. It can be regarded as made up of a pteridine nucleus, a molecule of p-aminobenzoic acid, and one or more molecules of glutamic acid. The exact coenzyme form of folic acid may vary from reaction to reaction, but in all cases the coenzymes are tetrahydro derivatives to which one-carbon units may be attached at position 5 or 10. N^5, N^{10}-anhydroformyltetrahydrofolic acid is active in one step of purine biosynthesis, N^{10}-formyltetrahydrofolic acid at another step. N^5-formyltetrahydrofolic acid (folinic acid, leucovorin, citrovorum factor) has been given much prominence since it was the first formylated folic acid to be discovered, but it must be converted to one of the other derivatives before serving as a coenzyme. The general biochemistry of pteridines is reviewed in (172). Several formylated and conjugated derivatives of folic acid have been identified in higher plants (173, 174) and their metabolism studied (175, 176).

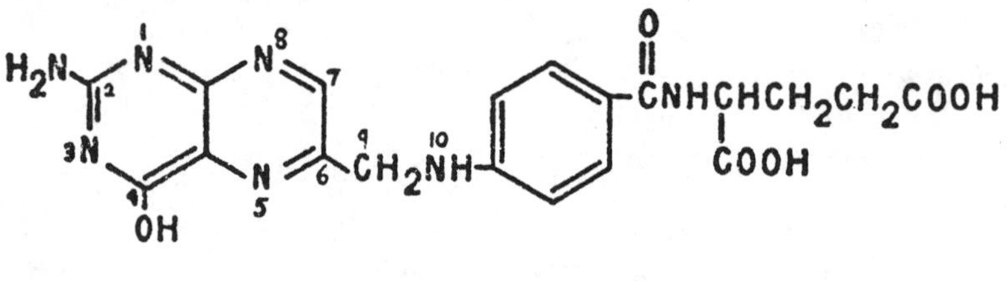

folic acid

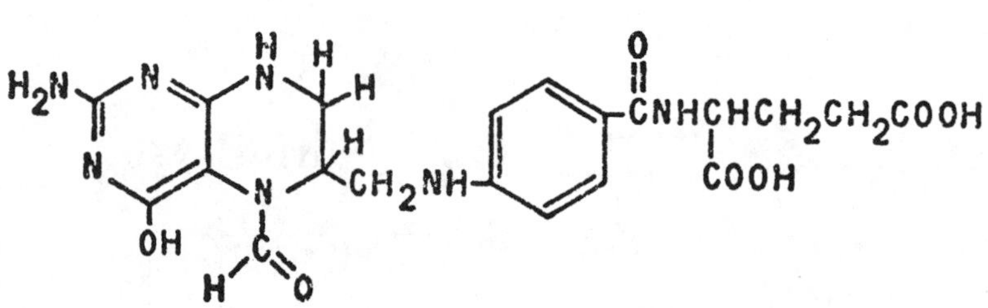

folinic acid

The active form of folic acid functions as a coenzyme in one carbon metabolism involving formate, such as in the interconversion of glycine and serine and in the synthesis of methyl groups. Transformations of folic acid and one-carbon units have been investigated in extracts of several plants (173). Reduced pteridines related to folic acid have also been shown to have a role as cofactors in hydroxylation of aromatic rings (see Chap. 4) and suggested to have some role in the electron transport system of photosynthesis (174). Several chromatographic methods are available for analysis of folic acid derivatives (178-180).

Pyridoxine is one member of the B_6 group of vitamins, all of which are converted to the active coenzyme pyridoxal phosphate:

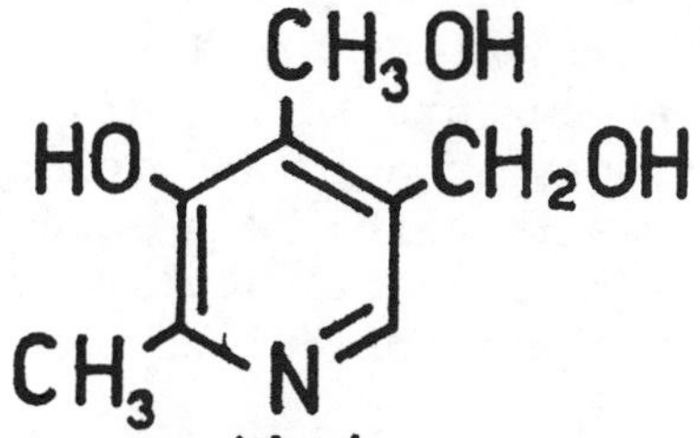

pyridoxine

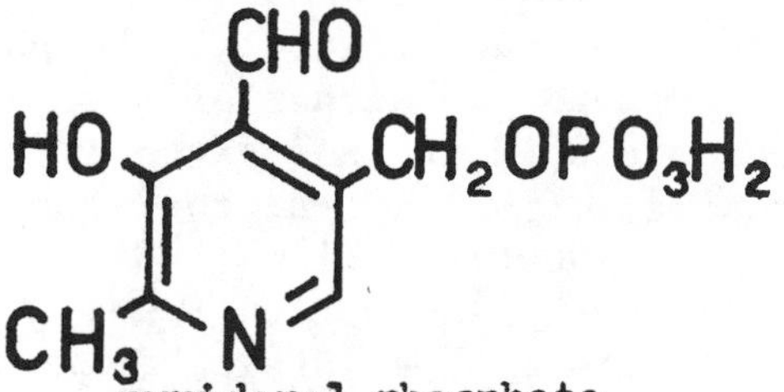

pyridoxal phosphate

Tracer experiments using microorganisms have suggested two different pathways to pyridoxine (181, 182). Chromatographic procedures for the analysis of the vitamin B_6 group are (183) and (184).

NITRO COMPOUNDS

Only a few nitro compounds have been isolated from higher plants, but their very rarity contributes to their interest. Naturally occurring nitro compounds are reviewed by Pailer (185). β-nitropropionic acid (hiptagenic acid) and several glucose esters of it occur in a variety of unrelated plants such as the violet (*Viola odorata*) creeping indigo (*Indigofera endecaphylla*) and the fungus *Aspergillus flavus* (186-188).

A fragrant constituent of several plants has been identified as 1-nitro-2-phenylethane (189, 190). 5-methyl-3-nitrogentisic acid is present in roots of *Primula acaulis* (191). Aristolochic acid and several compounds of related structure are present in *Aristolochia* spp. and some other plants (192, 193).

β-nitropropionic acid

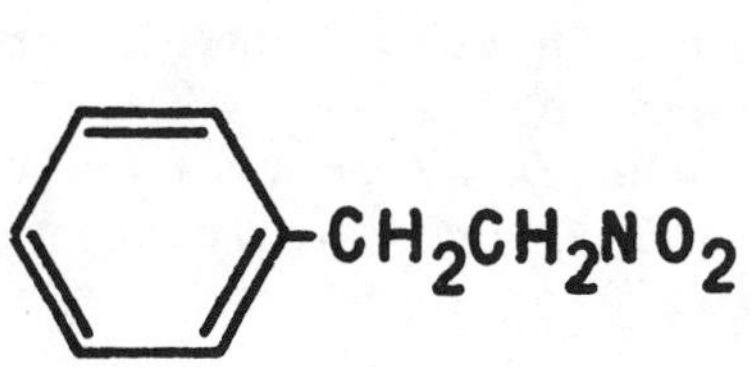

1-nitro-2-phenylethane

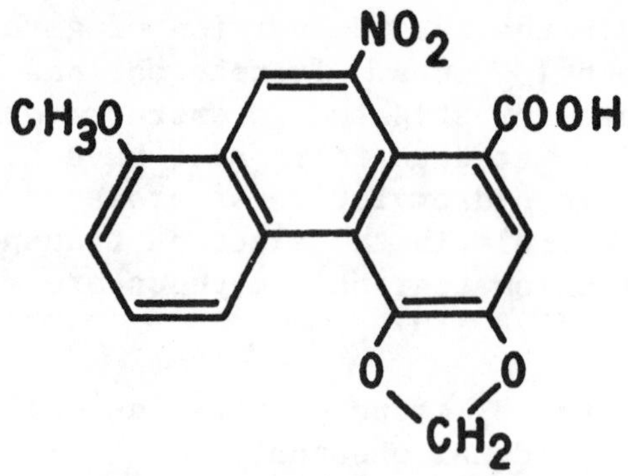

aristolochic acid

Little is known regarding the physiological function or biosynthesis of these compounds in higher plants. The best precursors found for nitropropionic acid in *Indigofera spicata* were malonic acid and malonyl monohydroxamate (194). 1-nitro-2-phenylethane was found to be a good precursor of glucotropaeolin (190). The alkaloids of *Aristolochia* are based on the aporphine nucleus, which has almost the identical carbon-nitrogen structure as aristolochic acid:

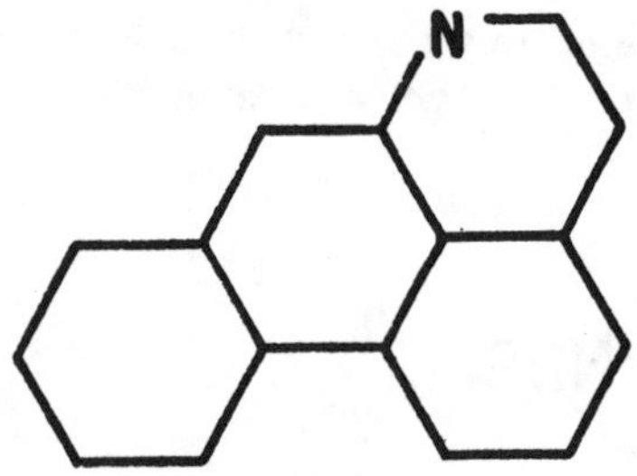

aporphine nucleus

Aporphine alkaloids are presumed to be formed from two molecules of tyrosine, and aristolochic acid is evidently made by oxidation of such an alkaloid (195). Peroxidase catalyzes the oxidation of amines to nitroso compounds (196) which might be oxidized further to nitro derivatives.

Since these compounds are so specialized, the original papers should be consulted for details of isolation and identification. One thin layer chromatographic procedure is generally applicable to aliphatic nitro compounds (197).

HYDROXYLAMINE DERIVATIVES

Hydroxylamine itself has not been isolated from higher plants although it is a postulated intermediate in nitrate reduction (Chapter 10) and possibly in formation of the mustard oil glycosides (q.v.). A small group of compounds so far restricted to such grasses as maize (*Zea mays*) rye (*Lolium* spp.), and wheat (*Triticum* spp.) can be regarded as complex hydroxamates which occur as glucosides (198, 199). Upon hydrolysis the aglycones tend to rearrange forming oxazoles (200):

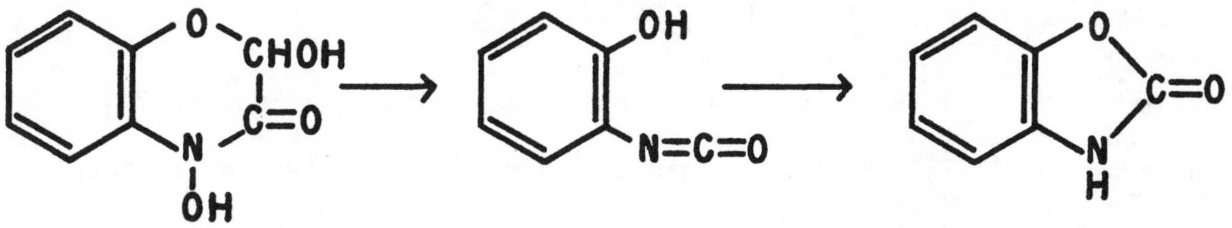

The glycosides have been purified from several plants by fractionation on Sephadex (201). Anthranilic acid is a precursor of them (202). The benzoxazinones can be separated by gas chromatography and identified by their mass spectra (200). The sideramines of microorganisms are derived from hydroxyl-amino acids and are involved in iron binding (203). Similar compounds evidently participate in the transport of iron in higher plants (204, 205), but it is not yet clear that the higher plant compounds are also hydroxylamine derivatives.

UREA AND RELATED COMPOUNDS

In the older literature urea was often reported to be present in higher plants, but the analytical methods used were not beyond reproach, and many workers questioned such reports. More recently it has been found that the ornithine cycle functions in plants (Chapter 10), and the occurrence of free urea in some plant tissues has been well-established. Urea may also arise from purine breakdown via allantoin and allantoic acid (Chapter 12). Guanidine and galegine derive from the guanidino group of arginine (206, 207). Agmatine is made by decarboxylation of arginine and may be further metabolized to N-carbamylputrescine (208). Other compounds which can be regarded as related to urea have also been isolated from plants. Some structures are given below with their occurrence. The whole area of urea, ureide and guanidine metabolism in plants has been reviewed (209).

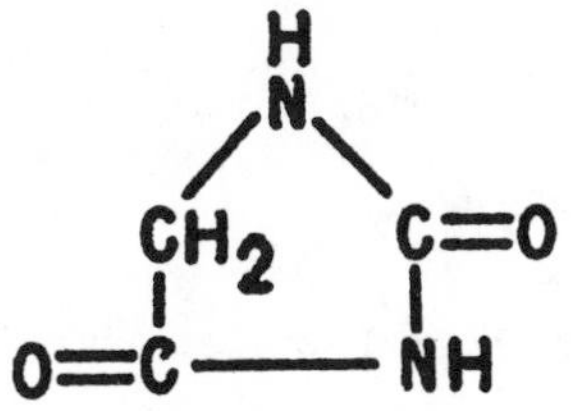

hydantoin
(*Beta vulgaris*)

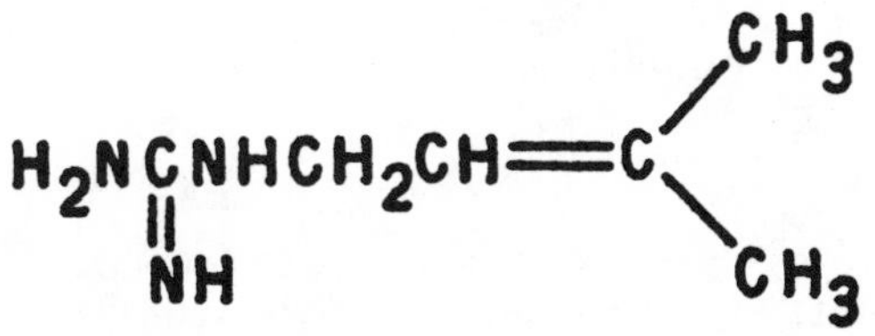

galegine
(*Galego officinalis*)

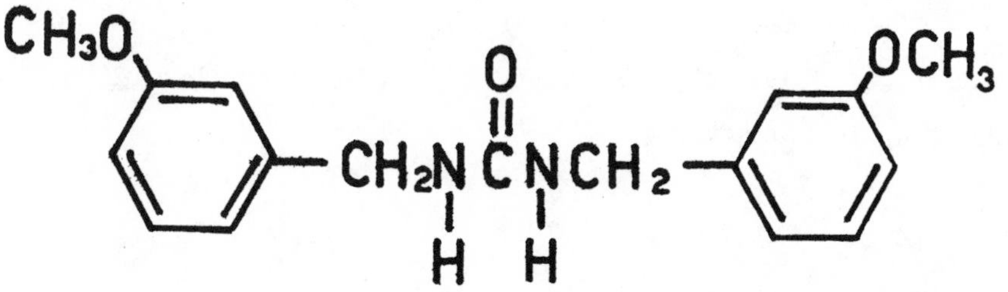

salvadourea
(*Salvadora persica*)

GENERAL REFERENCES

Ettlinger, M. G. & Kjaer, A. (1968) "Sulfur Compounds in Plants", Recent Adv. Phytochem. 1 59-144.
Mahadevan, S. (1973) "Role of Oximes in Nitrogen Metabolism in Plants", Ann. Rev. Plant Physiol. 24 69-88.
Richmond, D. V., "Sulfur Compounds", in Miller 3 41-73.
Robinson, F. A., "Vitamins", in Miller 3 195-220.
Several articles in Paech & Tracey 4.

BIBLIOGRAPHY

1. von Kamienski, E. S. (1957) Planta 50 315-330.
2. Smith, T. A. (1971) Biol. Rev. 46 201-241.
3. Cohen, S. S. (1971) Introduction to the Polyamines, Prentice-Hall, Englewood Cliffs, N. J.
4. Richardson, M. (1966) Phytochemistry 5 23-30.
5. Smith, T. A. (1979) Phytochemistry 18 1447-1452.
6. Tocher, R. D. and Tocher, C. S. (1972) Phytochemistry 11 1661-1667.
7. Takeo, T. (1974) Phytochemistry 13 1401-1406.
8. Suzuki, T. (1973) Biochem. J. 132 753-763.
9. Smith, T. A. (1970) Ann. N. Y. Acad. Sci., 171 988-1001.
10. Le Rudulier, D. and Goas, G. (1974) Compt. Rend. (D) 279 161-163.
11. Suresh, M. R., Ramakrishna, S., and Adiga, P. R. (1978) Phytochemistry 17 57-63.
12. Unger, W. and Hartmann, T. (1976) Z. Pflanzenphysiol. 77 255-267.
13. Babczinski, P., Matern, U., and Strobel, G. A. (1978) Plant Physiol. 61 46-49.
14. Percival, F. W. and Purves, W. K. (1974) Plant Physiol. 54 601-607.
15. Smith, T. A. (1974) Phytochemistry 13 1075-1081.
16. Keller, W. J. (1978) Lloydia 41 37-42.
17. Smith, T. A. (1977) Phytochemistry 16 9-18.
18. Wheaton, T. A. and Stewart, I. (1970) Lloydia 33 244-254.
19. Barlow, R. B. and Dixon, R. O. D. (1973) Biochem. J. 132 15-18.
20. Yamasaki, K., Sankawa, U., and Shibata, S. (1969) Tetra. Lett. 1969 4099-4102.
21. Wheaton, T. A. and Stewart, I. (1969) Phytochemistry 8 85-92.
22. Hardwick, B.C. and Axelrod, B. C. (1969) Plant Physiol. 44 1745-1746.
23. Axelrod, J. and Saavedra, J. M. (1977) Nature 265 501-504.
24. Iwai, K., Suzuki, T., Lee, K.-R., Kobashi, M., and Oka, S. (1977) Agric. Biol. Chem. 41 1877-1882.
25. Smith, T. A. and Best, G. R. (1978) Phytochemistry 17 1093-1098.
26. Yoshihara, T., Takamatsu, S., and Sakamura, S. (1978) Agric. Biol. Chem. (Japan) 42 623-627.
27. Martin-Tanguy, J., Cabanne, F., Perdrizet, E., and Martin, C. (1978) Phytochemistry 17 1927-1928.
28. Martin, B. and Tolbert, N. E. (1979) Plant Physiol. 63 Suppl. 641.
29. Nissen, P. and Benson, A. A. (1961) Science 134 1759.
30. Verbeek, M. and Vendrig, J. C. (1977) Z. Pflanzenphysiol. 83 335-340.
31. Sokolova, V. E., Zvyagintseva, Y. U., and Pel'ts, M. L. (1967) Doklady Akad Nauk. S. S. S R 173 1455-1458.
32. Larher, F., Hamelin, J., and Stewart, G. R. (1977) Phytochemistry 16 2019-2020.
33. Linskens, H. F., Kochuyt, A. S. L., and So, A. (1968) Planta 82 111-122.
34. Cohen, A. S., Popovic, R. B., and Zalik, S. (1979) Plant Physiol. 64 717-720.
35. Smith, T. A. (1965) Phytochemistry 4 599-607.
36. Cohen, A. S. and Zalik, S. (1978) Phytochemistry 17 113-118.
37. Niveleau, A. and Quash, G. A. (1979) FEBS Letters 99 20-24.
38. Cabanne, F., Martin-Tanguy, J., and Martin, C. (1977) Physiol. Vég. 15 429-443.
39. Montague, M. J., Koppenbrink, J. W., and Jaworski, E. G. (1978) Plant Physiol. 62 430-433.
40. Anguillesi, M. C., Floris, C., Grilli, I., and Meletti, P. (1978) Biochem. Physiol. Pflanzen 173 340-346.
41. Smith, B. N. and Meeuse, B. J. D. (1966) Plant Physiol. 41 343-347.
42. Cabanne, F. and 6 others (1976) Compt. Rend. D 282 1959-1962.
43. Christianson, D. D., Wall, J. S., Dimler, R. J., and Senti, F. R. (1960) Anal. Chem. 32 874-878.
44. Kum-Tatt, L. (1961) Anal. Chim. Acta 24 397-409.

45. Jandera, P. and Churáček, J. (1974) J. Chromatog. 98 1-54.
46. Wang, L. C. and Selke, E. (1973) Plant Physiol. 51 432-435.
47. Sharpe, S. and Gray, D. O. (1976) J. Chromatog. 120 473-476.
48. Bayzer, H. (1966) J. Chromatog. 24 372-375.
49. Anderson, J. N. and Martin, R. O. (1973) Phytochemistry 12 443-446.
50. Blau, K. (1961) Biochem. J. 80 193-200.
51. Kenyhercz, T. M. and Kissinger, P. T. (1978) J. Food Sci. 43 1354.
52. Jacobson, M. (1971) in M. Jacobson, ed., Naturally Occurring Insecticides, Marcel Dekker, N. Y. pp. 137-176.
53. Johnson, A. E., Nursten, N. E., and Williams, A. A. (1971) Chem. and Indust. 556-565, 1212-1224.
54. Galetto, W. G. and Hoffman, P. G. (1976) J. Agric. Food Chem. 24 852-854.
55. Whitaker, J. R. (1976) Adv. Food Res. 22 73-133.
56. Yanagawa, H., Kato, T., and Kitahara, Y. (1973) Tetra. Lett. 1973 1073-1075.
57. Kuhule, J. A., Corse, J., and Chan, B. G. (1975) Biochem. Physiol. Pflanzen 167 553-556.
58. Wallbank, B. E. and Wheatley, G. A. (1976) Phytochemistry 15 763-766.
59. Winter, M., Furrer, A., Willhalm, B., and Thommen, W. (1976) Helv. Chim. Acta 59 1613-1620.
60. Bohlmann, F. and Abraham, W.-R. (1979) Phytochemistry 18 839-842.
61. Schulte, K. H., Rücker, G., Meinders, W., and Herrmann, W. (1966) Phytochemistry 5 949-953
62. Bohlmann, F. and Burkhardt, T. (1968) Chem. Ber. 101 861-863.
63. Bohlmann, F. and Hopf, P.-D. (1973) Chem. Ber. 106 3772-3774.
64. Apparao, M., Kjaer, A., Madsen, J. Ø., and Venkata Rao, E. (1978) Phytochemistry 17 1660-1661.
65. Tobkin, H. E., Jr. and Mazelis, M. (1979) Arch. Biochem. Biophys. 193 150-157.
66. Schwimmer, S. (1968) Phytochemistry 7 401-404.
67. Folkers, K., Koniuszy, F., and Shavel, J. (1944) J. Am. Chem. Soc. 66 1083-1087.
68. Wills, E. D. (1956) Biochem. J. 63 514-520.
69. Freeman, G. G. and Whenham, R. J. (1976) Phytochemistry 15 187-190.
70. Virtanen, A. I. and Matikkala, E. J. (1959) Acta Chem. Scand. 13 1898-1900.
71. Block, E., Penn, R. E., Revelle, L. K., and Bazzi, A. A. (1979) Proc. Am. Chem. Soc. April 1979, 408.
72. Challenger, F., Bywood, R., Thomas, P., and Hayward, B. J. (1957) Arch. Biochem. Biophys. 69 514-523.
73. Larher, F. and Hamelin, J. (1979) Phytochemistry 18 1396-1397.
74. Karush, F., Klinman, N. R., and Marks, R. (1964) Anal. Biochem. 9 100-114.
75. Stephan, R. and Erdman, J. G. (1964) Nature 203 749.
76. Glaser, C. B., Maeda, H., and Meienhofer, J. (1970) J. Chromatog. 50 151-154.
77. Brodnitz, M. H., Pascale, J. V., and van Derslice, L. (1971) J. Agric. Food Chem. 19 273-275.
78. Nishimura, H., Koike, S., and Mizutani, J. (1973) Agric. Biol. Chem. 37 1219-1220.
79. Tressl, R., Holzer, M., and Apetz, M. (1977) J. Agric. Food Biochem. 25 455-459.
80. Sharpe, F. R. and Peppard, T. L. (1977) Chem. & Ind. 664-665.
81. Pihakaski, S. and Pihakaski, K. (1978) J. Exper. Botany 29 1363-1369.
82. Saarivirta, M. (1973) Planta Medica 24 112-119.
83. Cole, R. A. (1976) Phytochemistry 15 759-762.
84. Dalgaard, L., Nawaz, R., and Sørensen, H. (1977) Phytochemistry 16 931-932.
85. West, L. G., Badenhop, A. F., and McLaughlin, J. L. (1977) J. Agric. Food Chem. 25 1234-1238.
86. Blau, P. A., Feeny, P., Contardo, L., and Robson, D. S. (1978) Science 200 1296-1298.
87. Virtanen, A. I. (1958) Angew. Chem. 70 544-552.
88. Altamura, M. R., Long, L., and Hasselstrom, T. (1959) J. Biol. Chem. 234 1847-1849.
89. Tang, C.-S. (1973) Phytochemistry 12 769-773.
90. Olsen, O. and Sørensen, H. (1979) Phytochemistry 18 1547-1552.
91. Schultz, O.-E. and Gmelin, R. (1952) Z. Naturforsch. 7b 500-506.
92. Schultz, O.-E. and Wagner, W. (1956) Z. Naturforsch. 11b 73-78.
93. Matsuo, M. (1970) J. Chromatog. 40 323-324.
94. Thies, W. (1976) Fette-Seifen-Anstrichmittel 78 231-234.
95. Kjaer, A. and Rubinstein, K. (1953) Acta Chem. Scand. 7 528-536.
96. Rodman, J. E. (1978) Phytochem. Bull. 11 6-31.
97. Delaveau, P. (1957) Bull. soc. botan. France 104 148-152.
98. Daxenbichler, M. E., Van Etten, C. H., and Williams, P. H. (1979) J. Agric. Food Chem. 27 34-37.
99. Underhill, E. W. and Kirkland, D. F. (1972) Phytochemistry 11 1973-1979.
100. Chisholm, M. D. (1973) Phytochemistry 12 605-608.
101. Löffelhardt, W. and Kindl, H. (1975) Z. Naturforsch. 30c 233-239.
102. Seigler, D. S. (1975) Phytochemistry 14 9-29.
103. Seigler, D. S. (1977) Prog. Phytochem. 4 83-120.
104. Sosa, A., Winternitz, F., Wylde, R., and Pavia, A. A. (1977) Phytochemistry 16 707-709.
105. Gondwe, A. T. D., Seigler, D. S., and Dunn, J. E. (1978) Phytochemistry 17 271-274.
106. Booth, A. N., Elliger, C. A., and Waiss, A. C., Jr. (1974) Life Sciences 15 1115-1120.
107. Eyjólfsson, R. (1970) Fortschr. Chem. Org. Naturstoffe 28 74-108.

108. Kojima, M., Poulton, J. E., Thayer, S. S., and Conn, E. E. (1979) Plant Physiol. _63_ 1022-1028.
109. Strong, F. M. (1956) Nutrition Rev. _14_ 65-67.
110. Bennett, W. D. and Tapper, B. A. (1968) J. Chromatog. _34_ 428-429.
111. Conn, E. E. (1979) Naturwissenschaften _66_ 28-34.
112. Gerstner, E. and Pfeil, E. (1972) Z. Physiol. Chem. _353_ 271-286.
113. Bough, W. A. and Gander, J. E. (1971) Phytochemistry _10_ 67-77.
114. Nartey, F. (1969) Physiol. Plantarum. _22_ 1085-1096.
115. Clegg, D. O., Conn, E. E., and Janzen, D. H. (1979) Nature _278_ 343-344.
116. Seigler, D. S. and Butterfield, C. S. (1976) Phytochemistry _15_ 842-844.
117. Thimann, K. V. and Mahadevan, S. (1964) Arch. Biochem. Biophys. _105_ 133-141.
118. Stowe, B. B. (1959) Fortschr. Chem. Org. Naturstoffe _17_ 248-297.
119. Schneider, E. A., Gibson, R. A., and Wightman, F. (1972) J. Exper. Botany _23_ 152-170.
120. Hofinger, H. and Böttger, M. (1979) Phytochemistry _18_ 653-654.
121. Feung, C.-S., Hamilton, R. H., and Mumma, R. O. (1976) Plant Physiol. _58_ 666-669.
122. Shantz, E. M. (1966) **Ann.** Rev. Plant Physiol. _17_ 409-438.
123. Ueda, M., Ehmann, A., and Bandurski, R. S. (1970) Plant Physiol. _46_ 715-719.
124. Percival, F. W. and Bandurski, R. S. (1976) Plant Physiol. _58_ 60-67.
125. Bandurski, R. S. and Schulze, A. (1977) Plant Physiol. _60_ 211-213.
126. Zimmermann, H. (1978) Z. Pflanzenphysiol. _89_ 115-118.
127. Smith, T. A. (1977) Phytochemistry _16_ 171-175.
128. Kiss, G. and Neukom, H. (1966) Helv. Chim. Acta _49_ 989-992.
129. Schraudolf, H. and Weber, H. (1969) Planta _88_ 136-143.
130. Elliott, M. C. and Stowe, B. B. (1971) Plant Physiol. _47_ 366-372.
131. Raj, R. K. and Hutzinger, O. (1970) Anal. Biochem. _33_ 43-46, **471-474.**

132. Woodruffe, P., Anthony, A., and Street, H. E. (1970) New Phytol. _69_ 51-63.
133. Frahn, J. L. and Illman, R. J. (1973) J. Chromatog. _87_ 187-191.
134. Seoane, E., Carnicer, A., and Vieitez, E. (1965) Microchem. J. _9_ 432-439.
135. Johri, R. N. (1970) J. Chromatog. _50_ 340-344.
136. Hutzinger, O. (1969) J. Chromatog. _40_ 117-124.
137. Méndez, J. (1970) Microchem. J. _15_ 1-5.
138. Mollan, R. C., Harmey, M. A., and Donnelly, D. M. X. (1973) Phytochemistry _12_ 447-450.
139. MacNeil, J. D., Häusler, M., Frei, R. W., and Hutzinger, O. (1972) Anal. Biochem. _45_ 100-106.
140. **Dedio, W. and Zalik, S. (1966) Anal. Biochem. _16_ 36-52.**
141. Bittner, S. and Even-Chen, Z. (1975) Phytochemistry _14_ 2455-2457.
142. Jamieson, W. D. and Hutzinger, O. (1970) Phytochemistry _9_ 2029-2036.
143. Baxter, C. and Slaytor, M. (1972) Phytochem. _11_ 2763-2766, 2767-2773.
144. Magnus, V., Iskrić, S., and Kveder, S. (1973) Planta _110_ 57-62.
145. Schneider, E. A. and Wightman, F. (1974) Ann. Rev. Plant Physiol. _25_ 487-513.
146. Fellows, L. E. and Bell, E. A. (1971) Phytochemistry _10_ 2083-2091.
147. Mahadevan, S. and Stowe, B. B. (1972) Plant Physiol. _50_ 43-50.
148. Mazza, G., Ricard, J., and Bouchet, M. (1970) Compt. rend. (D) _270_ 2492-2494.
149. Hoyle, M. C. (1972) Plant Physiol. _50_ 15-18.
150. Bryant, S. D. and Lane, F. E. (1979) Plant Physiol. _63_ 696-699.
151. Be Miller, J. N. and Colilla, W. (1972) Phytochemistry _11_ 3393-3402.
152. Hager, A. and Schmidt, R. (1968) Planta _83_ 372-386.
153. Epstein, E., Nabors, M. W. and Stowe, B. B. (1967) Nature _216_ 547-549.
154. Swan, G. A. (1974) Fortschr. Chem. Org. Naturstoffe _31_ 521-582.
155. Winter, E. (1960) Planta _54_ 326-332.
156. Mabry, T. J. and Dreiding, A. S. (1968) Recent Advan. Phytochem. _1_ 145-160.
157. Köhler, K.-H. (1973) Pharmazie _28_ 18-24.
158. Piattelli, M. and Minale, L. (1964) Phytochemistry _3_ 547-557.
159. Adams, J. P. and van Elbe. J. H. (1977) J. Food Sci. _42_ 410-414.
160. Colomas, J. (1977) Z. Pflanzenphysiol. _85_ 227-232.
161. Vincent, K.R. and Scholz, R. G. (1978) J. Agric. Food Chem. _26_ 812-816.
162. Chang, C., Kimler, L., and Mabry, T. J. (1974) Phytochemistry _13_ 2771-2775.
163. Wyler, H. and Meuer, U. (1979) Helv. Chim. Acta. _62_ 1330-1339.
164. Sciuto, S., Oriente, G., Piattelli, M., Impellizzeri, G., and Amico, V. (1974) Phytochemistry _13_ 947-951.
165. Stenlid, G. (1976) Phytochemistry _15_ 661-663.
166. Petrović, S. E., Belia, B. E., and Vakajlović, D. B. (1968) Anal. Chem. _40_ 1007-1008.
167. Toma, R. B. and Tabekhia, M. M. (1979) J. Food Sci. _44_ 263-265.
168. White, R. L. and Spenser, I. D. (1979) J. Am. Chem. Soc. _101_ 5102-5104.
169. White, R. L. and Spenser, I. D. (1979) Biochem. J. _179_ 315-325.
170. Wuest, H. M., ed. (1962) Ann. N. Y. Acad. Sci. _98_ 385-614.
171. Knappe, J. (1970) Ann. Rev. Biochem. _39_ 757-776.
172. Rembold, H. and Gyure, W. L. (1972) Angew. Chem. _84_ 1088-1099.
173. Batra, K. K., Wagner, J. R., and Stokstad, E. L. R. (1977) Can. J. Biochem. _55_ 865-868.

174. Blondeau, R. (1973) Planta 114 95-100.
175. Ikeda, K. and Iwai, K. (1970) Plant and Cell Physiol. 11 639-656.
176. Cossins, E. A., Roos, A. J., Chan, P. Y., and Sengupta, U. K. (1972) Phytochemistry 11 2481-2488.
177. Fuller, R. C. and Nugent, N. A. (1969) Proc. Nat. Acad. Sci. U. S. 63 1311-1318.
178. Reif, V. D., Reamer, J. T., and Grady, L. T. (1977) J. Pharm. Sci. 66 1112-1116.
179. Rao, K. N. and Noronha, J. M. (1978) Anal. Biochem. 88 128-137.
180. Frost, S. and Bagnara, J. T. (1978) J. Chromatog. 153 279-283.
181. Hill, R. E., Miura, I., and Spenser, I. D. (1977) J. Am. Chem. Soc. 99 4179-4181.
182. Pflug, W. and Lingens, F. (1978) Z. Physiol. Chem. 359 559-570.
183. Håkanson, R. (1964) J. Chromatog. 13 263-265.
184. Williams, A. K. (1974) J.Agric. Food Chem. 22 107-109.
185. Pailer, M. (1960) Fortschr. Chem. Org. Naturstoffe 18 55-82.
186. Harlow, M. C., Stermitz, F. R., and Thomas, R. D. (1975) Phytochemistry 14 1421-1423.
187. Majak, W. and Bose, R. J. (1976) Phytochemistry 15 415-417.
188. Moyer, B. G., Pfeffer, P. E., Moniot, J. L., Shamma, M., and Gustine, D. L. (1977) Phytochemistry 16 375-377.
189. Gottlieb, O. R. and Taveira, M. (1960) Perfumery Essent. Oil Record 51 69-70.
190. Matsuo, M., Kirkland, D. F., and Underhill, E. W. (1972) Phytochemistry 11 697-701.
191. Goris, A. and 5 others(1971) Phytochemistry 10 679-682.
192. Kupchan, S. M. and Merianos, J. J. (1968) J. Org. Chem. 33 3735-3738.
193. Doskotch, R. W. and Vanevenhoven, P. W. (1967) Lloydia 30 141-143.
194. Candlish, E., La Croix, L. J., and Unrau, A. M. (1969) Biochemistry 8 182-186.
195. Schütte, H. R., Orban, U. and Mothes, K. (1967) Europ. J. Biochem. 1 70-72.
196. Böttcher, G. and Kiese, M. (1960) Naturwiss. 47 157.
197. Majak, W. and Bose, R. J. (1974) Phytochemistry 13 1005-1010.
198. Tipton, C. L., Klun, J. A., Husted, R. R., and Pierson, M. D. (1967) Biochemistry 6 2866-2870.
199. Gahagan, H. E. and Mumma, R. O. (1966) Chem. and Ind. 1966 1967-1968.
200. Woodward, M. D., Corcuera, L. J., Schnoes, H. K., Helgeson, J. P., and Upper, C. D. (1979) Plant Physiol. 63 9-13.
201. Hofman, J. and Hofmanová, O. (1969) Europ. J. Biochem. 8 109-112.
202. Tipton, C. L., Wang, M.-O., Tsao, F. H.-C., Lin Tu, C. C., and Husted, R. R. (1973) Phytochemistry 12 347-352.
203. Keller-Schierlein, W., Prelog, V., and Zähner, H. (1964) Fortschr. Chem. Org. Naturstoffe 22 279-322.
204. Page, E. R. (1966) Biochem. J. 100 34 P.
205. Schmid, W. E. and Gerloff, G. C. (1961) Plant Physiol. 36 226-231.
206. Reuter, G. and Barthel, A. (1967) Pharmazie 22 261.
207. Maretzki, A., Thom, M., and Nickell, L. G. (1969) Phytochemistry 8 811-818.
208. Smith, T. A. (1969) Phytochemistry 8 2111-2117.
209. Reinbothe, H. and Mothes, K. (1962) Ann. Rev. Plant Physiol. 13 129-150.

INDEX

Names of persons are indexed only where they are associated with specific reactions or procedures. Plants should be looked up under both English and Latin names; the Latin names are indexed to genus but not species. Iso- compounds are all indexed under this prefix. The most important page numbers are underlined.